Green Building:
Project Planning & Cost Estimating

A Practical Guide for Constructing Sustainable Buildings

- *Cost Data for Green Materials, Components & Systems*
- *Special Project Requirements*
- *Financial Analysis & Incentives*

Green Building:
Project Planning & Cost Estimating

A Practical Guide for Constructing Sustainable Buildings

- *Cost Data for Green Materials, Components & Systems*
- *Special Project Requirements*
- *Financial Analysis & Incentives*

RSMeans

Copyright 2002
Construction Publishers & Consultants
Construction Plaza
63 Smiths Lane
Kingston, MA 02364-0800
(781) 422-5000

The editors for this book were Andrea Keenan and Danielle Georges. The managing editor was Mary Greene. The production manager was Michael Kokernak. The production coordinator was Marion Schofield. Composition was supervised by Paula Reale-Camelio. The electronic publishing specialist was Jonathan Forgit. The proofreader was Robin Richardson. The book and cover were designed by Norman R. Forgit. The cover photographs were taken by Barney Taxel (Living Machine, Oberlin College, Adam Joseph Lewis Center for Environmental Studies) and Oberlin College (courtesy of Oberlin College).

Printed in the United States of America

10 9 8 7 6 5 4 3

Library of Congress Catalog Number pending

ISBN 0-87629-659-2

 Reed Construction Data

Table of Contents

Acknowledgments

The preparation of this book involved a team of experts, support from industry organizations, and input from a number of individuals. The primary and contributing authors and reviewers are listed in the "About the Contributors" section following these acknowledgments. Others who provided guidance and assistance during various stages of the book's development are listed below.

We would like to particularly thank: *Design Cost Data* and David Castelli, Vice President, for allowing permission to reprint case studies that originally appeared in the magazine; *Building Design & Construction*, for allowing us to reprint excerpts from case studies published in the magazine, and Larry Flynn, Senior Editor, for his assistance; Ed Howard, Manager, Services for Builders & Architects, and Mark MaGrann, President/CEO of MaGrann Associates (Mount Laurel, New Jersey), for providing the residential case study; and Scott Wargo, Director of Media Relations at Oberlin College for his assistance in obtaining information on and photographs of the Adam Joseph Lewis Center for Environmental Studies at Oberlin College.

We are grateful to the following standards organizations for allowing us to reprint their logos: the Building Research Establishment, the Climate Neutral Network, the Forest Stewardship Council, the Global Ecolabeling Network, GreenSpec, Green Seal, the National Association of Home Builders, Natural Resources Canada, Natural Step, TerraChoice Environmental Services, Inc., the U.S. Environmental Protection Agency, and the U.S. Green Building Council.

— *Mary Greene, Editor*

About the Contributors

Arthur Adler PE, CEM, author of Chapter 11, "Commissioning the Green Building," is a senior mechanical engineer for Shooshanian Engineering in Boston, Massachusetts. He has more than 20 years of experience in operating, analyzing, and optimizing HVAC systems for commercial, high tech, industrial, and institutional clients. Mr. Adler's responsibilities include developing function test procedures for mechanical/electrical systems, oversight of functional performance testing, and supervising and directing integrated systems tests. Mr. Adler has extensive knowledge of sustainable building design and construction practices, and is an accredited professional with the U.S. Green Building Council's Leadership in Energy and Environmental Design (LEED) Green Building Rating System.

John Albrecht, USGBC, a reviewer of Part 5, "Green Building Cost Data" is a registered architect in Illinois and Minnesota, where he has been practicing since 1977. He is a member of AIA, NCARB, and the Chicago chapter of the U.S. Green Building Council, and has been the LEED and green architect for several public projects for the city of Chicago's Department of General Services. Mr. Albrecht has worked as an architect for the city of Chicago for 21 years, following his work for Skidmore, Owings, and Merrill, and other private architectural firms.

The **American Wind Energy Association** (AWEA) provided the text for Chapter 5, "Wind Power." AWEA is a national trade association that represents wind power plant developers, wind turbine manufacturers, utilities, consultants, insurers, financiers, researchers, and others involved in the wind industry. In addition, AWEA represents hundreds of wind energy advocates from around the world. The association provides up-to-date information on wind energy projects operating worldwide; new projects in various stages of development; companies working in the wind energy field; technology development; and policy developments related to wind and other renewable energy development.

James Armstrong, CPE, CEM, author of Chapter 3, "Efficient Use of Energy & Other Resources," and co-author of Chapter 6, "Health, Comfort & Productivity," has served as project engineer and facilities manager for a variety of prominent institutions, specializing in facilities commissioning, energy studies, operations, and energy systems. He currently works as Program Manager of Energy Efficiency Services for NSTAR Electric and Gas Corporation. His past experience includes applications engineering for Trigen: Boston Energy Corporation; energy engineering for Shooshanian Engineering; and facilities maintenance supervision and management for the Massachusetts Institute of Technology, Massachusetts General Hospital, the Museum of Science in Boston, and Colby Sawyer College in New Hampshire, as well as for a number of large school districts in Massachusetts, Connecticut, New Jersey, and New York.

Robert Bastoni, co-editor of Part 5, "Green Building Cost Data," has been a Contributing Editor at R.S. Means for the last three years. He has more than 15 years of experience in the construction trades and has also worked as a housing inspector in Massachusetts.

Hillary Brown, AIA, author of the Foreword and reviewer of the manuscript, is Principal of New Civic Works, which consults with the public and non-profit sectors on green building programs. She was the founder and former Director of New York City's Office of Sustainable Design, the city's first dedicated initiative in energy- and resource-efficient public facilities, developing policy, demonstration projects, education, and outreach. Her office produced the *City of New York's High Performance Building Guidelines,* which involved collaboration among public, private, nongovernmental, and academic sectors. Ms. Brown teaches sustainable design at Columbia University School of Architecture, Planning, and Preservation.

John Chiang, PE, a co-editor of Part V, "Green Building Cost Data," is an Electrical Engineer at R.S. Means, and Senior Editor of the publications *Means Electrical Cost Data, Means Electrical Change Order Cost Data,* and *Means Building Construction Cost Data, Metric Version.* He has worked on such consulting projects as the Xerox plant expansion, Maine Medical Center, court facilities, and nursing homes. Mr. Chiang also assists with the provision of cost estimates at different construction stages for owners, engineers, and contractors. He is a registered professional engineer and a member of the National Society of Professional Engineers and the Institute of Electrical and Electronics Engineers.

Seiglinde K. Fuller, Ph.D, author of Chapter 13, "Economic Analysis & Green Buildings," is an economist with the Office of Applied Economics of the National Institute of Standards and Technology, a non-regulatory federal agency within the U.S. Commerce Department's Technology Administration. Her areas of expertise include benefit-cost analysis, economic impact studies, and the pricing of publicly supplied goods and services. As project leader of the NIST/DOE collaborative effort to promote the use of economic analysis for energy and water conservation and renewable energy projects, she has been involved in developing techniques, workshops, instructional materials, and computer software for calculating the life-cycle costs and benefits of such projects in accordance with federal legislation.

Mark Kalin, FAIA, FCSI, author of Chapter 10, "Specifying Green Building Products," is a registered architect, certified construction specifier, and author of the original *GreenSpec,* and Kalin Associates' Master Specifications. Kalin Associates Inc. is one of the nation's leading independent specifications firms, specializing in preparation of technical specifications and bidding documents for construction projects, and of guide specifications for building product manufacturers. Kalin Associates' related services include specifications for LEED projects, development of master specifications for agencies and design firms, computer automation of technical documents, and specification coordination for large projects.

Alexis Karolides, author of Chapter 1, "Green Building Approaches," and Chapter 2, "Introduction to Green Building Materials & Systems," is a registered architect and principal with the Rocky Mountain Institute (RMI) in Snowmass, Colorado. Her projects at RMI have included a prototype energy-efficient supermarket for Stop & Shop, a green renovation of a historic building at Hickam Air Force Base, campus-wide energy planning and building retrofit strategies for Berea College, a Hines residential development, the greening of the California State Capitol, and a monastery in Tibet. She is a frequent speaker at national and international conferences and has provided educational seminars and design workshops for communities, businesses, and institutions, including Shell; Perrier; Sherwin Williams; the cities of Milwaukee, Pittsburgh, and Cincinnati; and the Departments of Environmental Protection and Urban Planning in Tianjin, China.

Magda Lelek, PE, CEM, co-author of Chapter 14, "Compliance, Energy Modeling, & Decision-Making Tools," is a principal with Andelman and Lelek Engineering, Inc. She specializes in building energy modeling, energy efficiency studies, design of energy-efficient HVAC systems, and facilities planning and sustainable building development as related to mechanical systems. Ms. Lelek has worked on commercial and institutional projects and is a member of the American Society of

Heating, Refrigerating, and Air Conditioning Engineers, the Association of Energy Engineers, and The International Building Performance Simulation Association. She is also a certified LEED professional.

Barbara Lippiatt, author of Chapter 12, "Evaluating Products Over Their Life Cycle," is an economist with the Office of Applied Economics of the National Institute of Standards and Technology, a non-regulatory federal agency within the U.S. Commerce Department's Technology Administration. Her major interest is in developing economic decision methods and tools primarily for efficiently designing and managing buildings. She has applied these decision tools to a wide variety of building problems. Two of her software publications, BEES and ALARM, have been on the National Technical Information Service's bestseller list—one is being distributed by the Environmental Protection Agency, the U.S. Department of Energy, and the U.S. Green Building Council, and another by the National Fire Protection Association.

Joseph Macaluso, CCC, author of Chapter 8, "Economic Incentives & Funding Sources" and Chapter 9, "Standards & Guidelines," co-author of Chapter 14, "Compliance, Energy Modeling, & Decision-Making Tools," and one of the book's primary editors, is a Certified Cost Consultant and a member of the Association for the Advancement of Cost Engineering International, where he is currently chair of the Government and Public Works Special Interest Group. He works as a construction cost estimator for Empire State Development in New York, a state agency that provides funding for various development projects throughout the state. Over the past 19 years he has prepared and reviewed construction cost estimates and schedules for major public works projects. Mr. Macaluso has also negotiated change orders and worked as a manager in contract administration, specializing in contractor qualification. He has worked for the NYC Transit Authority, NYC Health and Hospitals Corporation, and NYC School Construction Authority, and has taught cost estimating at Long Island University and LaGuardia Community College.

Andy Walker, Ph.D, PE, author of Chapter 4, "Solar Energy Systems" and Chapter 7, "Assembling the Project Team," co-author of Chapter 6, "Health, Comfort, & Productivity," and manuscript reviewer, is a senior engineer with the National Renewable Energy Laboratory (NREL) and is Task Leader for Design Assistance in the Federal Energy Management Program (FEMP). FEMP Design Assistance includes modeling, monitoring, analysis, and alternative financing assistance to support energy conservation and renewable energy projects in federal buildings. Mr. Walker's NREL experience includes serving as Technology Manager for the FEMP Program (1997, 1998) and Task Leader for the Residential Homebuilder Program (Building America), and the Exemplary Buildings Program (1993-1997).

Phillip R. Waier, PE, co-editor of Part 5, "Green Building Cost Data," is a Principal Engineer at R.S. Means, and Contributing Senior Editor of the annually updated publications, *Means Facilities Maintenance & Repair Cost Data* and *Means Building Construction Cost Data*. Mr. Waier manages the activities of editors, cost researchers, and consultants for public and private agencies and firms throughout the United States. He has spent 30 years in the construction industry, serving as President and Chief Engineer for a mechanical contracting firm, Project Manager for numerous industrial construction projects, and Structural Engineer for major foreign and domestic construction projects. Mr. Waier is a registered professional engineer and a member of the Association for Facilities Engineering (AFE), Associated Builders and Contractors (ABC), and Associated General Contractors (AGC).

Foreword

Across the country today, there is growing public awareness of how conventional approaches to real estate development and building construction contribute to long-term environmental degradation, health concerns, and even climate change. While the "smart growth" movement is responding by tackling urban sprawl and promoting urban- and transit-based development patterns, the green building movement is reconsidering the way we build by redefining best practices for design and construction. Green building experts are showing smart building owners and developers how to convert the liabilities of material, water and energy waste, and pollution emissions—all true costs not showing up on any balance sheets—into economic opportunities by realizing environmentally sound, healthier, *and* cost-effective projects.

This total quality management approach to building is variously called "green," "sustainable," or simply "high-performance." Whatever the term, the value-added features and objectives are the same. From the project outset, owners, developers, architects, engineers, and the construction team proactively commit to maximizing operational energy savings, providing optimally healthy interiors, and limiting the detrimental impacts of their construction on the environment. The collective successes of these projects point up shortcomings in a "business-as-usual" approach to facility design, construction, and operation.

The benefits of healthier, energy- and resource-efficient building practices are becoming better known through corporate and institutional leadership, legislative initiatives, and increasingly through forward-looking public works programs. Federal, state, county, and municipal governments have begun to incorporate energy- and resource-efficient principles into courthouses, libraries, post offices, schools, and many other civic building types—all of which demonstrate the economic, environmental, and social benefits of improved building performance. With billions of square feet of space under their direct control, government agencies are becoming major consumers of green design and construction-related services. This purchasing power is expanding markets for green building products and clean energy technologies.

Many municipal and state agency early adopters have published detailed green building guidelines. Others are promulgating green building tax credit programs as incentives. As an intermediate strategy in accelerating improved building practices, these policy instruments are like training wheels: they educate participants in the benefits of sustainable design and coach them through the new processes involved in a more integrated approach to development. *(Note: See the Resources section of this book for a listing of municipalities and states that are involved in these initiatives.)*

In the commercial sector, similar leadership has been demonstrated across a wide range of building types. In speculative ventures we can celebrate the ground-breaking 3 and 4 Times Square developments. Exemplary corporate facilities include the Gap's San Bruno, California headquarters; Genzyme Corporation's new Cambridge, Massachusetts corporate headquarters; a corporate campus project for Sabre, Inc. in Southlake, Texas; and most recently, a commitment by Goldman Sachs to green their 1.5 million square foot new facility in New Jersey. As the nation's corporate community continues to shape financial futures across the world, it can convey how the economic opportunities of global capitalism come joined with environmental responsibilities. By greening headquarters and other real estate, corporate governance signals the importance of being energy independent and natural resource self-sufficient. It demonstrates concern for natural and human, as well as financial capital. And above all, it shows stockholders and employees that forward-looking environmental performance is a good proxy for good fiscal management.

The academic and institutional sectors have also led the way. Through pilot projects, universities and advocacy organizations complement their own environmental literacy initiatives: from Oberlin College's Lewis Center for Environmental Studies and Northland College's Environmental Living and Learning Center in Wisconsin, to the National Audubon Society's exemplary renovation, and the Natural Resource Defense Council's New York, San Francisco, and Washington, D.C. offices. Residential projects that stress improved quality of life include the City of Austin's Green Builder Program, Battery Park City's high-rise, high-end green apartment complex in lower Manhattan, and many other single- and multi-family projects.

With the release by the U.S. Green Building Council of its *Leadership in Energy and Environmental Design* or LEED™ rating system in March 2000, the green building movement has truly taken off. Currently, a large number of programs rely on the Council's LEED rating system as the defining standard for green building performance. Many cities, counties, and state agencies have either recommended or adopted LEED outright for their capital project's performance. Large government programs have capitalized on the flexible architecture of LEED and sought to adapt it to their regional needs or have made certain allowable modifications to address regional or jurisdictional concerns.

The publication of *Green Building: Project Planning & Estimating* is a major jump forward. It has been prepared to enable the spread of these best practices into the mainstream of the construction industry and across all the building sectors. R.S. Means has responded to the growing call for green building resources, tools, services, and especially cost data to support the demand for affordable and cost-effective green technology. The assembly of such information in one location is an enormous gift to the industry.

Now the basic trick for each of us is getting started. As the real estate industry becomes motivated through the perception that green is a source of competitive advantage, it will readily climb the learning curve of new materials, means, and methods. It will engage energy, resource, and health concerns as a catalyst to creating fundamentally better buildings. But ultimately it is the concept of *performance*—that these buildings just work better and feel better—that will forever change the way that building owners and developers approach their work. Higher targets for environmental performance will provide private enterprise the latitude to innovate and deliver. Eventually, public demand will move high performance over the top of the curve and into conventional practice.

In the meantime, strong stewardship by a creative owner or developer is required to overcome what often appears to be industry indifference, but is better characterized simply as inertia. Leadership in the different sectors that comprise the industry, collaborating on improved standards, incentives, and rewards will go a long way towards inventing a future in which high performance building design—the blueprint for long-term sustainable development—is practiced universally.

Hillary Brown, AIA
Principal, New Civic Works; Founding Director, Office of Sustainable Design; and former Assistant Commissioner, NYC Department of Design and Construction

Introduction

Green, or sustainable, building design and construction are increasingly recognized as the clear answer to health, economic, and environmental challenges. A large and growing number of government and private entities are requiring sustainable practices in their projects. As a result, owners, architects, engineers, contractors, estimators, and facility managers are having to quickly educate themselves in the methods, materials, and costs of green building components and systems.

This book is intended as a resource for anyone who seeks to incorporate green features into structures that they are conceiving, designing, specifying, estimating, constructing, or maintaining. There are many (and widespread) excellent resources, including Web sites, periodicals, and publications that offer valuable information on various aspects of green building. (Many are listed in a lengthy Resources section at the back of this book.) The mission of this book is to provide, in one publication, an understanding of green building approaches, materials, project management, and estimating requirements—along with useful cost data on materials and systems that can be difficult to find and price.

Part 1 includes Chapters 1 and 2, which provide an overview of green practices and materials. The author explains the various approaches used to achieve sustainable construction, as well as the multiple criteria for evaluating products and materials. Chapters 3, 4, and 5 delve into proven methods for conserving resources, including energy and water, and implementing renewable resource technologies, such as solar and wind power. Chapter 6 reviews health and comfort considerations in the indoor environment, including ways to achieve a high quality of air, thermal comfort, acoustics, light, and water, which not only promote better health and image, but also productivity.

Part 2 highlights special considerations in the way green building projects are managed. Chapter 7 deals with the interaction of project team members. Chapter 8 presents some specific economic incentives and funding sources for green building, and Chapter 9 showcases the established standards by which buildings are measured for sustainability. Guidance for specifying green products is given in Chapter 10, and commissioning the building in Chapter 11.

Part 3 demonstrates methods for evaluating green versus conventional products and systems from economic (Chapter 12) and environmental (Chapter 13) viewpoints. Chapter 14 is a review of the available software to make this process easier.

The case studies in Part 4 demonstrate how eight very different buildings successfully implemented sustainable design and construction practices. Project goals, special challenges, materials, and systems are outlined, along with cost breakdowns.

Part 5 contains cost data for green building materials and systems. It consists of information on how the data was collected and is presented, unit price line items (organized by applicable MasterFormat divisions), and assemblies costs, along with reference tables, crew descriptions, and location factors that can be used to obtain material, labor, and installation costs in any of more than 900 specific locations in the United States and Canada.

The Resources section of the book is a comprehensive overview of the many additional green building informational sources available, including professional associations, government and research organizations, building rating systems and code agencies, state and municipal initiatives, publications, and Web sites. These resources can also be accessed directly through the book's dedicated Web site: http://www.rsmeans.com/supplement/green.html

The construction industry consumes a major share of resources and produces a lion's share of waste. Its products are the places in which we live and work, and its materials and methods can either enhance or detract from our health, comfort, and productivity, as well as the health of the environment. Choosing green improves not only the quality of our lives in the built environment, but our fiscal health through savings generated by high-performance buildings. The first step in reaping these benefits is gaining an understanding of how to get started on the road to green projects—with information on what is available, how to choose, how to manage these projects, and how much they will cost.

Part 1 Green Building Concepts

Chapter

1 Green Building Approaches

Alexis Karolides, AIA

A common assumption in recent years is that the built environment will necessarily degrade the natural environment. But for most of earth's history, structures built for shelter have typically enhanced bio-diversity and benefited the surrounding community. Beaver dams, for instance, create pools where wetlands form, supporting a vast array of diverse life not possible in the original stream. Why should an office building be any different?

Green building is a way of enhancing the environment. Done right, it benefits human well-being, community, environmental health, and life-cycle cost. This means tailoring a building and its site to the local climate, site conditions, culture, and community in order to reduce resource consumption, augment resource supply, and enhance the quality and diversity of life. More of a building philosophy than a building style, there is no characteristic "look" of a green building. While natural and resource-efficient features can be highlighted in a building, they can also be invisible within any architectural design aesthetic.

Green building is part of the larger concept of "sustainable development," characterized by Sara Parkin of the British environmental initiative, Forum for the Future, as "a process that enables all people to realize their potential and improve their quality of life in ways that protect and enhance the Earth's life support systems." As the World Commission on Environment and Development (the Brundtland Commission) phrased it, "Humanity has the ability to make development sustainable—to ensure that it meets the needs of the present without compromising the ability of future generations to meet their own needs."

Green building is not an assemblage of "environmental" components, nor a piecemeal modification of an already-designed, standard building. These incremental approaches add to the building's cost and produce marginal resource savings, at best. True green building is a holistic approach to programming, planning, designing, and constructing (or renovating) buildings and sites. It involves analyzing such interconnected issues as site and climate considerations, building orientation and form, lighting and thermal comfort, systems and materials, and optimizing all these aspects in an integrated design.

To capture the multiple benefits of synergistic design elements, the "whole system" design process must occur early in the building's conception and must involve interdisciplinary teamwork. In the conventional, linear development process, key people are often left out of decision-making or brought in too late to make a full contribution. Thorough collaboration, on the other hand, can reduce and sometimes eliminate both capital and operating costs, while at the same time meeting environmental and social goals. In addition, the process can anticipate and avoid technical difficulties that would have resulted in added expense to the project. Collaboration can also produce a "big picture" vision that goes beyond the original problem, permitting one solution to be leveraged to create many more solutions—often at no additional cost.

It is precisely the integrated approach described above and the multiple benefits thereby achieved that allow many green buildings to cost no more than standard buildings, even though some of their components may cost more. Green design elements may each serve several functions and allow other building components to be downsized. For example, better windows and insulation can allow for smaller heating systems; photovoltaic panels can double as shade for parking or can replace a building's spandrel glazing.

The U.S. Green Building Council's LEED™ (Leadership in Energy and Environmental Design) rating system for commercial, institutional, and high-rise residential buildings is an instrument used to evaluate environmental performance from a "whole building" perspective over a building's life cycle, providing a definitive standard for what constitutes a green building. It should be used not just to "rate" a building, but as a tool to facilitate greening the building early in the design process. The council has asserted that a LEED silver-rated building should not cost more than a conventional building. (LEED Platinum does typically cost more, however, because it may involve cutting-edge technologies and levels of performance that are far above and beyond standard construction.) Many cities also have local green building guidelines or rating systems that are similarly useful and are sometimes associated with incentives (such as rebates and reduced fees or taxes). Some cities *require* that LEED or their local green building guidelines be followed (typically for government buildings). *(See Chapter 9 for more on the LEED rating system, and Chapter 8 for financial incentives.)*

Many players in the real estate market are realizing that green development is good business. Developers, builders, and buyers are discovering that green enhances not only health and quality of life, but also the pocketbook.

Potential Benefits of Green Building

- Reduced capital cost
- Reduced operating costs
- Marketing benefits (free press and product differentiation)
- Valuation premiums and enhanced absorption rates
- In some cities, streamlined approvals by building and zoning departments
- Reduced liability risk
- Health and productivity gains
- Attracting and retaining employees
- Staying ahead of regulations
- New business opportunities
- Satisfaction from doing the right thing

Resource Efficiency

Buildings use 40% of the total U.S. energy (including two-thirds of the country's electricity) and 16% of the total U.S. water. They are responsible for 40% of all material flows and produce 15-40% of the waste in landfills, depending on the region.[1] Clearly, large-scale improvements in resource productivity in buildings would have a profound effect on national resource consumption. According to *Natural Capitalism*, a book by Paul Hawken, Amory Lovins, and Hunter Lovins, *radical* improvements in resource efficiency are readily possible—today's off-the-shelf technologies can make existing buildings three to four times more resource-efficient, and new buildings up to ten times more efficient.[2]

Reducing energy use in buildings saves resources and money while reducing pollution and CO_2 in the atmosphere. It also leverages even greater savings at power plants. For instance, for the average 33%-efficient coal-fired power plant, saving a unit of electricity in a building saves three units of fuel at the power plant,[3] and that is before transmission losses are factored in. Take a typical industrial pumping system for instance. Insert 100 units of fuel at the power plant to produce 30 units of electricity; 9% of this is lost in transmission to the end user, 10% of the remainder is lost in the industrial motors, 2% in the drivetrain, 25% in the pumps, 33% in the throttle, and 20% in pipes. Of the original 100 units of fuel, the final energy output is a mere 9.5 units of energy.[4]

As Amory Lovins has said, "It's cheaper to save fuel than to burn it." But full financial benefits will *only* be realized by using an integrated, resource-efficient approach (high performance windows *will* increase first costs unless the reduction in heating and/or cooling load is factored into the sizing of the mechanical system). Just as important as what goes into a green building is what can be left out. Green building design eliminates waste and redundancy wherever possible.

One of the key ways of reducing resource consumption and cost is to evaluate first whether a new building needs to be built. Renovating an existing building can save money, time, and resources, and can often enable a company (or a family, if it is a residential building) to be located in a part of town with existing infrastructure and public transportation, enhancing convenience and reducing sprawl. Next, if a new building is required, it should be sized only as large as it really needs to be. Smaller buildings require fewer building materials, less land, and less operational energy. The American cultural assumption is that we should buy (or lease) as much square footage as we can afford. In the residential sector for instance, the average new house size has steadily increased over the last few decades, while families have gotten smaller. Yet smaller houses and commercial buildings allow the budget to be spent on quality, not "empty" quantity.

Energy

The easiest and least expensive way to solve the "energy problem" is not to augment energy supply, but to reduce the amount of energy needed. In buildings, great opportunity lies in simple design solutions that intelligently respond to location and climate. For instance, for most North American sites, simply facing the long side of a building within 15 degrees of true south (and using proper shading to block summer, but not winter sun) can save up to 40% of the energy consumption of the same building turned 90 degrees. *(See Chapter 4 for more on solar heat gain.)*

> *"Each year in the U.S. about $13 billion worth of energy—in the form of heated or cooled air—or $150 per household escapes through holes and cracks in residential buildings."*
> —American Council for an Energy-Efficient Economy

Attention to making the building envelope (exterior walls, roof, and windows) as efficient as possible for the climate can also dramatically reduce loads, especially in "skin-dominated" buildings (residences and other small buildings). For this type of building, optimal sealing, insulation, and radiant barriers, combined with heat-recovery ventilation, can reduce heat losses to less than half that of a building that simply meets code.[5]

Heat travels in and out of buildings in three ways: radiation, convection, and conduction, all of which must be addressed to reduce unwanted heat transfer effectively.

Radiation is the transfer of heat from a warmer body to a cooler one (regardless of position). The way to stop radiation heat transfer is by using reflective surfaces. A reflective roof, for instance, can reduce solar heat gain through the roof by up to 40%. Radiant barriers in attics or crawl spaces can also be used to reflect heat away from or back into occupied spaces of a building. Using light pavement surfaces (or better yet, reducing pavement as much as possible) will lower ambient air

Resource Efficiency: Key Points

- Reduce transportation energy use (and commute time—a valuable human resource) by siting the building within proximity of and convenient to the population who will use it. Brownfield/infill sites, for instance, are usually within an urban core and already connected to public transportation systems.

- Orient the building to optimize solar gain (in the northern hemisphere, this means maximizing southern exposure) and provide shading where appropriate with calculated overhangs or other shading devices. Take advantage of prevailing summer breezes, provide winter wind protection, and orient roofs to accept photovoltaics and solar water panels. Also, take advantage of local vegetation (such as shade trees) and topography (consider building into a hillside or a berm to mitigate temperature extremes). On an urban site, map shadow patterns from adjacent buildings to optimize solar gain on the proposed building.

- Optimize building envelope by specifying high-performance insulation, window glazing, roof materials, and foundation, as appropriate for the local climate. (Specifications in Houston will be very different from those in Anchorage.)

- Use durable, salvaged, recycled, and recyclable materials.

- Use renewable materials that are harvested in a manner that preserves the resource for the long term—such as certified wood from sustainably managed forests.

- Use local, low-tech, indigenous materials and methods to avoid the high energy and resource consumption associated with transportation and to support the local economy and cultural tradition.

temperature around a building, thus reducing the building's "cooling load." High-performance window glazing often includes a thin film or films to reflect infrared light (heat) either out of a building (in a hot climate) or back into a building (in a cold climate). Passive solar design in cold climates usually involves allowing the sun's radiation to enter a building and be absorbed into thermal mass for re-release later.

Convection is the transfer of heat in a fluid or gas, such as in air. Green buildings achieve natural ventilation by using convective forces such as wind, and differences in humidity and temperature. Typically, we experience convection as unwanted heat loss. It is what we experience when we feel a cold draft next to a leaky window or when a door is opened and cold air rushes in. Methods of preventing convective heat transfer include sealing gaps around windows, doors, electrical outlets, and other openings in the building envelope; providing air-lock entrances; and using heat recovery ventilators, which transfer 50-70% of the heat from exhaust air to intake air in cold climates, and vice versa in hot ones. They are an excellent way to ensure adequate ventilation in a tightly sealed house, without losing energy efficiency.

Conduction is the transfer of heat across a solid substance. Every material has a specific conductivity (U-value) and resistance (the inverse of the U-value, called the R-value). Insulation is made of materials with particularly high resistance to conductive heat transfer (high R-values). In climates with significant indoor/outdoor temperature differentials, it is important to insulate the entire building envelope—roof, walls, and foundation. While a moderate amount of insulation can help keep buildings in hot climates cool, buildings in very cold climates need much more insulation because of the greater indoor/outdoor temperature differentials (over 100 degrees Fahrenheit in some climates).

Windows

Much of a building's heat transfer occurs through its windows. Therefore, one of the most critical ways to reduce all three types of building heat loss (or gain) is by selecting the appropriate, high-performance window for the given conditions. Important window properties include solar heat gain coefficient (SHGC), heat loss coefficient (U-value), and visible transmittance. The appropriate combination of these properties will depend on the climate, solar orientation, and building application. Ultra-high-performance windows combine multiple glazing layers, low-emissivity coatings, argon or krypton gas fill, good edge seals, insulated frames, and airtight construction. Because metal is a particularly good conductor, metal window frames need a "thermal break" (an insulating material inserted to block the conductive heat transfer across the metal) to achieve high performance. High-performance windows have multiple benefits besides saving energy. These include:

- Enhancing radiant comfort near the windows (thereby allowing that perimeter space to be used and sometimes enabling perimeter zone heating/cooling to be eliminated).
- Allowing the HVAC (heating, ventilating, and air conditioning) system to be downsized (thereby reducing first costs).
- Reducing fading from ultraviolet light.
- Reducing noise transfer from outside.
- Reducing condensation (and therefore extending the life of the window).
- Improving daylighting.

Heat Load

Besides entering through the building envelope, heat can also be generated inside the building by lights, equipment, and people. Especially in large, "load-dominated" buildings, many of which tend today to be air-conditioned year-round, installing efficient lighting and appliances (which give off less heat) will significantly reduce the building's cooling load. Using daylight as much as possible will reduce cooling loads even more, because daylight contains the least amount of heat per lumen of light. (Incandescent lights are the worst—and thus the least "efficient;" they are basically small heaters that happen to produce a bit of light.)

Integrated Design

Integrated design makes use of the site's natural resources, technological efficiency, and synergies between systems. Once the building envelope is efficiently designed to reduce heat flow, natural heating and cooling methods can be used to greatly downsize, or even eliminate, fossil-fuel-based mechanical heating and cooling systems. Techniques include daylighting, solar heating, natural ventilation and cooling, efficient and right-sized HVAC systems, and utilization of waste heat.

Daylighting

Daylighting provides important occupant benefits, including better visual acuity, a connection to nature, and documented enhancements to productivity and well-being; it also reduces operational energy costs when electric lights are turned off or dimmed while daylight is ample. This points out the importance of integrating all the mechanical systems—daylighting, lighting, and HVAC. It is also important to design systems to modulate with varying loads. *(See Chapter 6 for more on daylighting.)*

Solar Heating

Many methods of solar heating are available. They include passive solar (direct, indirect, and isolated gain), solar water heating, and solar ventilation air preheating. **Direct solar gain** occurs when sunlight strikes a high-mass wall or floor within a room; **indirect gain** is achieved by installing glazing a few inches in front of a south-facing high-mass wall; and **isolated gain** involves an attached sunspace, such as a greenhouse. There are also multiple techniques for natural ventilation and cooling. For example, in hot, dry climates, thermal chimneys and evaporative cooling are effective (and have been used for thousands of years in the Middle East). A thermal chimney uses solar energy to heat air, which rises and is exhausted out the top of the chimney, causing a natural convection loop as cooler air is drawn into the building (sometimes through a cool underground duct) to replace the exhausted hot air. Evaporative cooling draws heat from the air to vaporize water, making the resultant air cooler, but more humid.

Earth sheltering, earth coupling, and nighttime thermal mass cooling can also be used in appropriate climates. **Earth sheltering** and **earth coupling** take advantage of the vast thermal mass of the ground, which remains a constant temperature at a certain depth below grade (the depth depending on the climate). (Earth sheltering can also protect the building from inclement weather, such as strong wind.) In a climate with a large diurnal temperature swing, thermal mass cooling works by running cool nighttime air across a large indoor building mass, such as a slab; the cool thermal mass then absorbs heat during the day. Finally, in a humid climate, lowering humidity and providing airflow can enable people to be comfortable at temperatures up to nine degrees warmer than they otherwise would be.[6]

According to the National Renewable Energy Lab, "Each day more solar energy falls to the earth than the total amount of energy the planet's 5.9 billion people would consume in 27 years." Solar energy is the only energy income the earth receives. (Wind, tidal, and biomass energy are all derived from solar energy.) Of course, the less energy we need after applying all the energy-efficiency measures, the less it will cost to supply the remaining energy demand with renewable sources.

When energy loads are as small as practical, appropriate renewable energy sources should be evaluated. These include wind, biomass from waste materials, ethanol from crop residues, passive heating and cooling, and photovoltaics. Clean, distributed energy production methods include fuel cells and microturbines. If a building is more than a quarter-mile from a power line, it may be less expensive to provide "off-grid" power than to connect to the grid.[7] *(See Chapter 4 for more on solar heating.)*

Third-Party Commissioning

When the building is completed, third-party building commissioning—independent assessment of systems to ensure that their installation and operation meets design specifications and is as efficient as possible—can save as much as 40% of a building's utility bills for heating, cooling, and ventilation, according to Lawrence Berkeley National Laboratory.[8] Ongoing, regularly-scheduled maintenance and inspection are also critical to ensure proper, planned performance and efficiency of the building and its mechanical systems. *(See Chapter 11 for more on commissioning.)*

Enhanced Security

An important benefit of widespread construction of energy-efficient buildings (and building-efficiency retrofits) is the reduction of dependence on foreign fossil fuels, a trend that could greatly enhance U.S. security, while creating a more trade-balanced, resource-abundant world. With centralized power plants being potential targets of terrorist attacks, *distributed* power generation further enhances security.

Demolition/ Construction Practices

With any site development it is important to protect adjoining agricultural areas, rivers, and trees, and to be especially vigilant about erosion control. Rather than degrading the surrounding environment, development can actually enhance it.

Demolition and construction should be carefully planned to reduce or eliminate waste. Typically, demolition and construction debris account for 15–20% (in some places, up to 40%) of municipal solid waste that goes to landfills, while estimates are that potentially 90% of this "waste" could be reusable or recyclable.[9]

Ideally, planning for waste reduction begins not when a building is about to be demolished, but with initial building design. Buildings can be designed for flexibility to accomodate changing uses over time, for ease of alteration, and for deconstructability, should the building no longer be suited for any use. Planning for deconstruction involves using durable materials and designing building assemblies so that materials can be easily separated when removed. For example, rather than adhering rigid foam roof insulation to the roof surface, installing a sheathing layer in between allows the insulation to be reused.

Reusing and recycling construction and demolition waste is the "environmentally friendly" thing to do, and could also result in cost savings while promoting local entrepreneurial activities. A waste reduction plan, clearly outlined in the specifications for the project, would require the following:

- Specification of waste-reducing construction practices.
- Vigilance about reducing hazardous waste, beginning by substituting non-toxic materials for toxic ones, where possible.
- Reuse of construction waste (or demolition) material on the construction site (for instance, concrete can be ground up to use for road aggregate).
- Salvage of construction and demolition waste for resale or donation.
- Return of unused construction material to vendors for credit.
- Delivery of waste materials to recycling sites for remanufacture into new products.

It is critical to note that reusing, salvaging, and/or recycling materials requires additional up-front planning. The contractor must have staging/storage locations and must allot additional time for sorting materials, finding buyers or recycling centers, and delivering the materials to various locations.

Recycling

"Americans produce an estimated 154 million tons of garbage—roughly 1,200 pounds per person—every year. At least 50% of this trash could be, but currently isn't, recycled," according to Alice Outwater.[10] Recycling doesn't stop at the job site. The building should be designed to foster convenient recycling of consumer goods throughout the life of the building. This usually entails easily accessible recycling bins or chutes, space for extra dumpsters or trash barrels at the loading dock, and a recycling-oriented maintenance plan.

Environmental Sensitivity

Learning from the Locals

Every region of the world has a traditional building culture or a "vernacular" architecture. Because people in the past could not rely on providing comfort with the use of large quantities of resources extracted and transported over long distances, they had to make do with local resources and climatically efficient designs. Thus structures in the hot, dry U.S. Southwest made use of high-thermal-mass adobe with water-cooled courtyards. New England homes used an efficient, compact "saltbox" design. In the South, "dogtrot" homes with high ceilings provided relief from the hot, humid climate.

But how did the first settlers decide how to build? It could be that they—and we—have a lot to learn from other types of locals. According to their descendants, the original Mexican settlers of the San Luis Valley of Colorado, wondered how thick to make the walls of their adobe homes in the new climate. To answer the question, they measured the depth of the burrows of the local ground squirrels and built to those exact specifications.

Looking to nature for *design solutions* makes a lot of sense. Over the course of 3.8 billion years of evolution, poorly adapted or inefficient design solutions became extinct—those that are still with us can give us clues as to how our own buildings and site solutions can be better adapted. For instance, human-engineered drainage systems use concrete storm drains to remove water as fast as possible from where it falls, often channeling it to municipal sewage systems where it is mixed with sewage. As more and more of a city gets covered with impermeable surfaces, these combined stormwater/sewage systems cannot handle the load of big storms and can overflow into streets and erode streams. By contrast, a solution modeled on natural drainage would have surface swales, check dams, depressions, temporal wetland areas, and ecologically appropriate plants to absorb water over a large area, closer to where it falls. Clustering the development to allow for open areas where natural drainage can occur provides natural beauty and an effective stormwater solution, reduces the strain on the sewage treatment plant, provides habitat for other species, and costs less to build.

In Stuttgart, Germany, the natural ecology is considered so important that if you remove a patch of it to site a building, you must replace it on top of your building with a living "green" roof. As is true with so many green building solutions, a roof covered in native grasses provides multiple benefits—it helps solve the stormwater runoff problem, increases roof insulation value, greatly extends roof life (due to blocked ultraviolet radiation), lowers ambient air temperature (by reducing radiation from the roof), improves air quality (by producing O_2, absorbing CO_2, and filtering the air), increases wildlife habitat, adds beauty, and can provide pleasant, usable outdoor space, even in a crowded city.

Site Selection & Development

How can development leave a place better than the way it was found? A key tenet of green development is to promote health and diversity for humans and the natural environment that supports us. One approach is to restore degraded land to enhance long-term proliferation of life. Responsible site development also involves attention to human culture and community, as well as to the needs of other species in a diverse ecosystem.

Renovating existing buildings should be considered before looking for new building sites. This reduces construction costs, while salvaging an existing resource. Sometimes it keeps a building from being demolished, which is critical, because a building's biggest energy use is typically associated with its construction. This approach may even preserve cultural heritage by keeping a historic building in use and maintained.

If no suitable existing building can be found, "brownfield" or infill sites should be evaluated next. **Brownfield** sites are abandoned industrial sites that often require remediation prior to new construction. If hazardous wastes are present, the use of the site should be carefully considered, even though remediation will be performed. **Infill** simply means building on a vacant site within an established urban area, rather than on the outskirts.

All three of these options—building renovation, brownfield, and infill development—preserve farmland and ecologically valuable natural areas and limit "urban sprawl." These options also tend to have lower infrastructure costs, because transportation and utilities such as sewage, electricity, and gas are usually already in place. Finally, these sites are usually located close to existing schools, businesses, entertainment, and retail, enhancing convenience and potentially reducing automobile use.

When choosing a new building site, important considerations include the availability of a sufficient, rechargeable water source and access to renewable energy sources (such as solar, wind, geothermal, or biomass). Developing land that is ecologically sensitive (including wetlands or rare habitats), prime for farming, culturally/archeologically critical, or vulnerable to wildfire or floods should be avoided.

Where should a building be sited? "Buildings must always be built on those parts of the land that are in the worst condition, not the best."[11] Open space should not be the "leftover" area. After preserving (and sometimes restoring) the most ecologically valuable land in its natural state, additional open spaces for outdoor activities should be as carefully planned as are the spaces within buildings.

Green development includes regional planning that gives priority to people, not to automobile circulation. People who are too old, too young, or financially or physically unable to drive are accommodated by the design of a green development. Such developments include public transit (preferably pollution-free), parks, pedestrian and bike trails, an unsegregated mix of housing types (from low- to high-income, all in the same neighborhood), and a balance of housing, business, and retail in close proximity. Other goals of a green development are to limit sprawl (with urban growth boundaries, for instance) and to provide distributed electricity generation systems (those located close to the user, such as fuel-cells, photovoltaic arrays, wind microturbines, biomass, and geothermal).

Water/Landscape

A myriad of problems can result from impervious surfaces: urban heat islands (asphalt-laden cities are several degrees hotter than surrounding areas), altered stream flows (lower lows and higher highs; increased flooding), and polluted waters (from unfiltered road- and parking-surface runoff). Fortunately, cities are starting to see the economic and social value of preserving and restoring natural capital. Shade trees can reduce ambient air temperature by 15 degrees. Natural drainage can be far less expensive up-front, and far less costly in avoided flooding, pollution, and stream damage in the long run. There are many options for reducing stormwater runoff from a site, including reinforced grass paving, porous asphalt, rainwater-collection cisterns, infiltration islands in parking lots, swales, dry wells, and planted stormwater retention areas.

One type of landscape often overlooked in development is edible plantings. Gardens, orchards, or crops can and should be incorporated into both residential and commercial projects. These plantings can serve all the functions of non-edible landscaping (e.g., cooling and stormwater absorption) and produce food as well. The Village Homes community in Davis, CA, for instance, has a revenue-producing almond orchard, as well as a wide variety of fruit trees interspersed along pedestrian paths.

Although turf grass serves to facilitate many functions such as play and picnic areas, it need not be planted ubiquitously in areas that are not going to be used for those functions. The turf grass that is planted on lawns and corporate campuses is typically a non-native, monoculture crop that requires constant human input (mowing, watering, fertilizing, and dousing with pesticides and herbicides). These inputs are neither cheap nor environmentally sound. By contrast, native landscape is perfectly adapted to thrive in the local environment and therefore needs no irrigation or fertilizer, is ecologically diverse enough to resist pests, and provides free stormwater management. When landscape architect Jim Patchett replaced turf grass with native prairie on the Lyle, Illinois campus of AT&T, multiple problems were solved, while maintenance costs dropped from $2,000 to $500 per acre.

Sewage Treatment

The average U.S. effluent production is about 100 gallons per capita per day, which creates a tremendous sewage burden. Most cities run sewage through primary and secondary treatment plants that use both mechanical and chemical processes, which typically remove about 90-95% of the solids in the wastewater. Tertiary treatment can remove 99% of solids, but is rarely done because costs are considered too high for the marginal benefit. This means that in most cities, up to 10% of everything that is flushed down the toilet escapes the treatment plant and ends up in the waterways.[12]

The first goal for more sustainable sewage systems is to reduce the amount of effluent that needs to be treated in the first place with water-efficient (or waterless) plumbing fixtures. Waterless urinals not only reduce water consumption, they are also more sanitary and odor-free than standard urinals, because bacteria prefer wet surfaces. Composting toilets detoxify human waste without water (and produce usable fertilizer), but they do require a lifestyle adjustment.

After sewage is minimized, the most ecologically sound methods of treating it should be evaluated. Biological sewage treatment systems detoxify the waste from standard toilets and can treat sewage to tertiary levels. They can take several forms, including constructed wetlands, greenhouse systems, and algal turf scrubber systems. Whether the wastewater is being purified by microorganisms and plants in a wetland, or by bacteria, plants, invertebrates, fish, and sunlight in a series of tanks in a greenhouse, the idea is to use natural processes to purify the water. This significantly reduces chemical use, energy use, and operational costs. Unlike conventional systems, these alternative systems also provide an amenity—they are appealing, typically odor-free "tourist attractions," from which plants can often be harvested for sale to nurseries.

Designing For People: Health & Productivity

Building Design & Materials

The recent exposure that "Sick Building Syndrome" has been given in the news media has raised awareness around the issue of how buildings affect the people occupying them. This is significant, because the average American spends 90% of his or her time indoors. Sick Building Syndrome has been attributed to tighter buildings and poor air quality caused by off-gassing of volatile organic compounds (VOCs) from modern finish materials (such as paints, adhesives, carpets, and vinyl); poorly vented combustion appliances; equipment and chemicals (such as copiers and lab or cleaning compounds); tobacco smoke; soil gases (such as radon, pesticides, and industrial site contaminants); molds and microbial organisms; and intake of outdoor air contaminated with pollen, pollution, or building exhaust.

Air quality should be protected by ensuring adequate ventilation and locating air intakes away from dumpsters, exhaust vents, loading docks, and driveways. Carbon dioxide monitors can be installed to ensure adequate (but not excessive) ventilation, thereby optimizing both air quality and energy efficiency. Heat recovery ventilators can capture heat from the

Sick Building Syndrome

High-risk people: Elderly, children, and people with allergies, asthma, compromised immune systems, or contact lenses.

Symptoms: Headache; fatigue; congestion; shortness of breath; coughing; sneezing; eye, nose, throat, and skin irritation; dizziness; and nausea.

Multiplicative effects: Combining chemicals, poor temperature and lighting, ergonomic stressors, and job stress.

exhausted air (or pre-cool the incoming air, depending on the climate). Most important, however, is to ensure the best possible air quality in the first place, when the building is constructed. Properly vent radon, use non-toxic building materials, and design wall, roof, and foundation assemblies to avoid mold growth by keeping rain and condensation out of them in the first place and providing a way for it to dry out if it does get in. *(See Chapter 6 for more on indoor air quality.)*

Maintenance

Protecting the indoor environment does not stop when building construction is completed. Air quality must be ensured through routinely scheduled maintenance and housekeeping. If roof or plumbing leaks are undetected or neglected, hazardous molds can develop. Also important is *how* a building is maintained and with what type of housekeeping products. A building can be carefully designed with non-toxic finishes, only to have the off-gassing fumes from noxious cleaning products absorbed into soft finish materials. Some systems are easier to maintain than others. For instance, it is harder for microbes to grow on metal air ducts as compared to those lined with fiberboard insulation, and the metal ducts are also easier to clean. Regularly changing air filters and maintaining carpets and other finishes is critical. Occupants and custodial staff should be educated so they understand how to protect a building's healthfulness and performance, as well as its appearance. Human exposure to harmful chemicals should be minimized, and procedures should be established to address potential accidents with hazardous chemicals.

A More Natural Indoor Environment

Despite the difficulty of pinpointing the cause of health problems, there is currently little doubt that poor indoor environmental quality plays a role in many common maladies such as headaches, eyestrain, fatigue, and even more serious illnesses such as asthma and chemical sensitivity.

If poor lighting, stale air, harsh acoustics, and lack of connection to nature can compromise people's health at work or at home, what effect does improving these conditions have? Several studies of green office, school,

Factors that Enhance Productivity and Health

- Quality lighting, including high levels of daylighting
- Increased individual control of workplace, including lighting
- Heating and cooling
- Improved acoustics
- Improved indoor air quality
- Views to nature

and hospital buildings have shown that factors such as high levels of daylighting, views to nature, individual control of workplace environment, and improved acoustics are strongly related to improved productivity, including higher test scores at school, lower absenteeism, and lower stress levels.[13] Researchers in a field called "Biophilia" are studying the correlation between building ecology (specifically more "natural" environments that feature views to nature, daylight, and fresh air) and good health. Their theory is that human evolution predisposed us to thrive in the natural environment, and thus connecting to it at work or at home positively impacts our performance and well-being. There may be other benefits as well. For instance, NASA research has shown that significant quantities of plants can purify many toxins from the air.[14]

Quality Lighting

Daylighting

Quality lighting starts with well-designed daylighting, which is more than just providing windows. In order to avoid glare (the difference in luminance ratio between a window and its adjoining spaces), daylight must be introduced—or reflected—deep into the building, and direct beam light (such as that from standard skylights) should be diffused or reflected onto a ceiling. These goals can be accomplished using light monitors, clerestories, light shelves, advanced skylight systems, atria, courtyards, and transom glass atop partitions. Light-colored finishes greatly enhance the ambient brightness of the room. *(See Chapter 6 for more on daylighting.)*

Indoor Electric Lighting

With daylighting and electric lighting designed as an integrated system, the amount of electric lighting needed during most of the day can be minimized. For instance, if linear fluorescent fixtures are run parallel to window walls, those close to the window can be dimmed with automatic dimming controls when daylight is ample. Rather than dropping a set number of footcandles of light into a volume of space, quality lighting is the careful art of directing light onto surfaces where it is specifically needed—primarily on walls and ceilings (not on floors). Fixtures that provide mainly indirect, but also some direct light will create an even, glare-free ambiance, to which task lighting can be added to accommodate specific activities and individual preferences. Accent lighting can be added to create sparkle and to draw people into or through a space.

Outdoor Lighting

Glaring outdoor light should be avoided in new installations and replaced in existing ones. Bright, glaring light can be intrusive and dangerous (elderly people often take minutes to adapt back to lower light levels), and it imparts light pollution to night skies. This is a serious issue, not only for astronomers, but also for natural systems such as the nesting and migration of birds. Hooded fixtures are a good choice to protect nighttime darkness. White light provides the best peripheral vision. Yellow light, as provided by low- and high-pressure sodium lamps, accommodates no peripheral vision at all.

Individual Environmental Control

Operable windows, furniture with adjustable ergonomic features, dimmable lighting, and available task lighting are all examples of provisions for individual environmental control. Adjustable thermostats, or even better, underfloor air distribution with an airflow diffuser for each occupant, can provide individuals with temperature control. Such provisions allow people to maximize their personal comfort and provide psychological benefit as well. Even people who rarely open their windows appreciate being able to do so.

Green Building Hurdles

If green building has so many advantages, why isn't everyone doing it? There are currently several impediments to the universal practice of green building. First, it is a relatively new field, with the knowledge base still growing among design and construction professionals. Second, developers and builders try to keep things as simple as possible because "experimentation" adds time to a project, and time means money. Moreover, tried and true methods avoid liability risk, because lawsuits are often based on deviation from standard practice.

Market expectation also plays a role in a Catch-22 fashion. Developers build what is selling on the market, while people buy what is available on the market. Without a large sample of green buildings to choose from, there is little room for market demand to drive construction of green buildings. Developers and builders who take the risk to build green are typically well-rewarded, but if no one in the area has tried it yet, there may be few who are bold enough to be the first.

Misguided incentives cause yet another problem. Usually design decisions are made by developers and their hired design teams, but most of the financial and other benefits of a green building accrue to end users—owners or tenants who typically have no input in the design. Other less quantifiable benefits accrue to the community and society at large. Although there is growing evidence that green buildings provide lower operational costs and better quality environments, the mainstream market hasn't recognized this yet. Only when this happens will mainstream developers have the full incentive to build green, knowing that they will enjoy premium rents, lower turnover, fewer liability risks, and a better reputation.

Conclusion

Termites live in inhospitable climates of Africa, Australia, and the Amazon by building air circulation passages in the walls of their structures that can cool the inside by as much as 20° Fahrenheit. These termite mounds are as hard as concrete, but constructed out of locally collected soil, wood fiber, and the termites' own saliva.

We don't have to live in termite mounds to benefit from the ingenuity of their design. Nature's innovations—structures made and operated with local materials, current solar income, and no toxicity—should be the role models for our own built environment. We need to stop asking the question, "how can we do less harm?" and ask instead how we can *enhance* the human experience in the built environment, while enhancing the natural environment at the same time. Toxic building materials, energy-inefficient building systems and methods, and reliance on non-renewable energy sources are short-term, ultimately detrimental solutions. We need to start relying on solutions that are well adapted for life on earth in the long run.

Green building is a turn in the right direction. Many new buildings produce more energy than they consume, use local, non-toxic, low-energy materials, and enhance occupant experience while benefiting the surrounding community. And green buildings make good, long-term economic sense. When systems are properly integrated, overall first costs may be lower for green buildings than for standard buildings, while operational costs are almost always lower for green buildings. Even more important, studies have shown that in green buildings, workers are more productive and take fewer sick days, students learn faster and are absent less often, and hospital patients heal faster and need less medication.[15] Green buildings are fundamentally better buildings; it's time for them to become the norm, not the exception.

1   Roodman, D., and Lenssen, N., 1995: "A Building Revolution: How Ecology and Health Concerns Are Transforming Construction." *Worldwatch Paper #124.* Worldwatch Institute, Washington, DC.

2   Hawken, Lovins & Lovins. *Natural Capitalism: Creating the Next Industrial Revolution.* Little Brown & Company, 1999.

3   Barnett, Dianna Lopez and William D. Browning. *A Primer on Sustainable Building*, Rocky Mountain Institute, 1995.

4   E SOURCE, Inc., *Drivepower Technology Atlas*, Chapter 1. 1993.

5   Barnett, Dianna Lopez and William D. Browning. *A Primer on Sustainable Building.* Rocky Mountain Institute, 1995.

6   Barnett, Dianna Lopez and William D. Browning. *A Primer on Sustainable Building.* Rocky Mountain Institute, 1995.

7   RMI literature.

8   Lawrence Berkeley National Laboratory literature.

9   Triangle J. Council of Governments. *WasteSpec: Model Specifications for Construction Waste.* 1996-2002.

10 Barnett, Dianna Lopez and William D. Browning. *A Primer on Sustainable Building.* Rocky Mountain Institute, 1995.

11 Alexander, Christopher, et al. *A Pattern Language.* Oxford University Press, 1977.

12 Alice Outwater. *Water: A Natural History*, Chapter 11. Basic Books, 1996.

13 Romm, Joseph J. and William D. Browning. *Greening the Building and the Bottom Line: Increasing Productivity through Energy Efficient Design.* 1994; Heshong Mahone Group. *Daylighting in Schools: An Investigation into the Relationship Between Daylighting and Human Performance.* 1999; Ovitt, Margaret A. *Stress Reduction of ICU Nurses and Views of Nature.* 1996.

14 Wolverton, Bill, **http://www.wolvertonenvironmental.com**

15 Romm, Joseph J. and William D. Browning, *Greening the Building and the Bottom Line: Increasing Productivity through Energy Efficient Design,* 1994; Heshong Mahone Group, *Daylighting in Schools: An Investigation into the Relationship Between Daylighting and Human Performance,* 1999; Ovitt, Margaret A., *Stress Reduction of ICU Nurses and Views of Nature,* 1996; Ulrich, R.S. 1984. "View Through a Window May Influence Recovery from Surgery." *Science* 224: 420-421.

Chapter 2 Introduction to Green Building Materials & Systems

Alexis Karolides, AIA

Since cave dwellers first placed brush or animal skins in front of the cave opening, humans have used building materials for shelter. In fact, most animal species alter their immediate environments by building dwellings with collected or self-manufactured materials. Nothing could be more natural. So what is it about *our* current manufacture and use of materials that raises concern?

Animals' dwellings made from nontoxic, energy-efficient materials allow them to survive. The materials are recycled back into the environment after their useful life as a dwelling. Human use of materials, until recent history, followed these same principles. Things began to change with the advent of metals, but it was the industrial revolution that really accelerated the change. Suddenly we had an industrial production system dependent on the most intense energy source yet known, the stored energy of millions of years of photosynthesis buried beneath the earth's crust as fossil fuels. We learned to manufacture all imaginable materials from steel to plastic, and we could transport them across the world. The seemingly endless abundance of fossil fuels, and the vastness of the surrounding environment to absorb the toxic by-products of burning them, seemed to negate the evolutionary rules followed by all other animal species: local supply, low energy, non-toxicity, and recyclability.

But here the problems begin. First of all, using a stored resource is like dipping into a savings account, and the United States' savings account of fossil fuel reserves, once seemingly endless, is dwindling. Second, the earth's ability to assimilate the toxic and slow-to-degrade by-products and end-products of human manufacturing is no longer guaranteed—all of the earth's major life support systems are either stressed or in decline.

Finally, many of our own products are making us sick—they are made with chemicals that our bodies have not evolved enough to handle. To make matters worse, we have made our buildings increasingly airtight, and we are spending on average 90% of our time indoors.

The use of our "natural resource savings account" to construct and operate buildings is by no means trivial. The construction and operation of U.S. buildings uses 40% of the country's energy, 16% of its fresh water, and three billion tons of raw materials per year, which is 40% of total global use. Moreover, building industry "by-products" include air and water pollution, as well as the solid waste that comprises 15-40% of U.S. landfills.

Equally significant is the concern that many contemporary building materials contribute to indoor air quality problems. For weeks or months after installation, standard products such as paints and adhesives off-gas VOCs (volatile organic compounds) that are harmful to humans.

Indoor air quality problems do not stop with material composition; material assembly can also be a culprit. In hot humid climates, for instance, vapor impermeable vinyl wall covering can encourage mold formation when humid air condenses on the back of the wall covering. Certain mold spores, when inhaled, can be toxic and even deadly to humans.

So what can be done, given the myriad of products to choose from and the complex construction decisions to be made? One place to start is from the perspective of improving the indoor environmental quality for building occupants. Reducing exposure to toxic substances such as VOCs, lead, mercury and harmful molds and microbes, can help protect occupant health. Methods to achieve this goal include specifying low-VOC substitues for conventional products (including paints, adhesives, and millwork); detailing interior finishes to minimize porous surfaces that can accumulate mold (for example, if tile is used, seal the grout); carefully designing building assemblies to avoid water entry; and, in some cases, avoiding microbial growth by eliminating certain finishes altogether (such as ceiling tile or carpet).

As important as indoor environmental quality is consideration of the larger environment. One way to address this goal is to favor products that reduce waste or environmental degradation. For instance, if carpet is to be used, modular carpeting (carpet tile) is recommended because only those tiles in the wear pattern need frequent replacement. Recyclable carpet further enhances waste reduction and raw materials savings. Another example of a material specification choice that fosters environmental health is wood that is certified to have been from a sustainably-managed forest.

Purchasing local products reduces transportation and its associated energy consumption and pollution, supports the local economy and culture, and maintains regional identity by promoting the use of indigenous/traditional materials.

A more technical way of evaluating a material is to consider its **embodied energy,** or the energy needed to produce a building product. It does not take into consideration transportation, durability, reuse, and recycling, only the production of a material. Estimated embodied energy of some common materials (in MJ/kg) are:

- Baled straw = 0.24
- Kiln-dried hardwood = 2.0
- Cement = 7.8
- Float glass = 15.9
- Fiberglass = 30.3
- Virgin steel = 32.0
- Recycled steel = 10.1
- Expanded polystyrene plastic (EPS) = 117
- Virgin aluminum = 191
- Recycled aluminum = 8.1[1]

The high embodied energy associated with producing plastic and aluminum makes it all the more important to recycle these products—recycling saves most of the energy for certain plastics, and 95% of the energy for aluminum. Life-cycle assessment, a very involved process, takes a much larger perspective on the comparative impact of material use. It considers the material's embodied energy as well as its durability, efficiency, reusability/recyclability, and overall environmental impact (both in its extraction and its use). Ultimately, each material is part of an entire building, and the goal is to maximize the longevity, environmental sensitivity, and human benefit provided by the whole. *(See Chapter 12 for more on the environmental life cycle.)*

In short, "green" building materials are those that:

- Are healthy for the interior environment—do not produce indoor air quality problems due to the release of VOCs or harmful fibers and do not cause health problems for the factory workers who manufacture the product.
- Are healthy for the natural environment—do not cause environmental degradation, depletion of scarce resources, hazardous by-products, excessive processing waste, or health problems for the people who extract the resources used in the product.

- Help minimize building energy use—by preventing heat gain or loss, reducing electricity consumption, and simplifying maintenance.
- Have low-embodied energy—avoid products that result from energy-intensive manufacturing processes. Materials with a high amount of recycled content fit the bill as long as they don't require energy-intensive remanufacture.
- Are durable, reusable, recyclable, and/or biodegradable. Consider how long the material will last before it needs replacing and what will happen to it after its useful life in the building. Avoid a material that will eventually become a hazardous waste problem.
- Are locally obtained—do not require excessive transportation from resource collection and product manufacture to installation.

Green Material Alternatives by CSI Division

Division 01 – General Requirements

The general requirements should include on-site sorting of materials to facilitate their reuse on the construction site, salvaging for resale or donation, or recycling into other products. While demolition and construction debris consumes on average 15-20% up to a staggering 40% of U.S. landfill capacity, estimates are that potentially 90% of this "waste" could be reusable or recyclable[2]. Because reusing, salvaging, and/or recycling materials requires additional up-front planning, the contractor must have staging/storage locations and must allot additional time for sorting materials, finding buyers or recycling centers, and delivering the materials to various locations.

Division 02 – Site Construction

Sitework/Landscaping

Avoid paving where possible in favor of native vegetation. If paving is necessary, use porous pavement when constructing new paved areas or replacing existing ones. Porous paving products include reinforced grass paving and gravel (for low-traffic areas), block interspersed with gravel, and porous asphalt (which is similar to standard asphalt, but missing the fine aggregate).

Ponds/Reservoirs

Whereas retention and detention ponds serve the single purpose of managing storm water, constructed wetlands can manage storm water while providing multiple human and environmental benefits. When designed according to natural models, wetlands become a diverse ecosystem of plants and animals that filter polluted runoff and provide habitat (that may be threatened elsewhere by development). Unlike engineered ponds with steep concrete sides and barbed-wire fences, constructed wetlands are shallow, vegetated site amenities. Like natural ponds, they do not need fences.

Erosion and Sedimentation Control

Controlling erosion is essential to protecting air and water quality and avoiding loss of topsoil. An erosion plan should ensure that topsoil is stockpiled, that soil is not carried away by storm water runoff or wind, and that particulate matter from construction activities does not cause sedimentation of receiving waterways. Unless local standards are stricter, the management practices outlined in the Environmental Protection Agency's *Storm Water Management for Construction Activities* should be followed.[3]

Rainwater Catchment Systems

Capturing rainwater for irrigation greatly reduces the use of treated water, and the collected rainwater—oxygenated, non-mineralized and non-chlorinated—is much better for plants. Rainwater can also be used for household applications, including drinking water. In fact, people in many regions of the world, including some parts of the United States, have traditionally relied on harvested rainwater for their water supply. Typically a building's roof and gutters double as its rainwater collection device. For potable water collection, it is critical to ensure that the roofing will not leach lead, copper, asbestos, or other hazards. Today's steel roofing is claimed to be the safest option as long as the coating does not contain heavy metals. (Old metal roofs with toxic coatings and lead fastening systems should never be used to collect drinking water.) Cisterns for rainwater storage can be made out of metal, concrete, or plastic.

Water treatment requirements depend on whether the water will be for potable (or non potable) domestic use, or just for irrigation. The first step in water treatment is to remove large debris with gutter screens and roof washers. Sediment can be allowed to settle within the tank or can be removed with cartridge filters. If disinfection is needed, chemical options include chlorine and iodine. While chlorine's dependability, availability, and low price have made it the most common disinfectant, it poses taste and health concerns. Although it can be filtered out at the tap with activated charcoal, there are still larger environmental issues with the widespread use of chlorine. Ultraviolet light, a good, non-chemical option, can be used to kill most microbial organisms once the water has been filtered of particulates. A more expensive chemical-free disinfection system is ozonation (ozone is a form of oxygen produced by passing air through a strong electric field), which kills microorganisms and oxidizes organic matter into CO_2 and water.[4]

Efficient Irrigation Systems: Drip irrigation systems are more efficient than sprinklers because less water evaporates before reaching the plant. The best irrigation timers include buried moisture sensors that ensure that just the right amount of water is delivered to the plant's root zone. Systems programmed to water deeply every several days, rather than shallowly every day or two, use less water and promote healthier plant growth.

Pest Control: Using the least toxic integrated pest management approach to protect from insects, rodents, and other pests will benefit building occupant health as well as the environment. Tightly detailing building penetrations and joints to avoid cracks and moisture leakage is the first step. Termites have traditionally been kept at bay by highly toxic chemicals. Chlordane, the most common insecticide until recently, was taken off the market due to health and environmental problems. Substitute chemicals, though less toxic than chlordane, are not problem-free. One nontoxic solution is to install a sand barrier that termites cannot easily penetrate around the foundation.

Boric acid is relatively non-toxic and used to retard many types of household pests. Added to cellulose insulation, it serves the triple function of retarding fire, inhibiting mold, and deterring insects and rodents.

Division 03 – Concrete

Concrete is a strong, durable material with high heat storage capacity that can be used to moderate building temperature swings. Because traditional concrete is one of the most inert building materials, it is also a good product from an indoor air quality standpoint, even for chemically sensitive people. (This is not completely true for high-tech concretes that contain chemical agents for workability and air-entraining.)

Concrete does, however, have some environmental drawbacks. It can cause water pollution if washout water from equipment at concrete plants finds its way to local waterways. The pH of washout water is so high, it is toxic to aquatic life. Another concern is the production of cement, the binding agent used in concrete. Cement production accounts for approximately 0.6% of total U.S. energy use (because it represents only about .06% of the gross national product), it is ten times as energy-intensive as the economy in general.[5] Cement production is also one of the major contributors to greenhouse gases in the atmosphere, because most of its production energy is provided by coal-fired power plants, and because the chemical process of making cement also releases CO_2. In fact, for every ton of cement, 1.25 tons of CO_2 are released into the atmosphere. Worldwide, cement production accounts for over 8% of the total CO_2 emissions caused by human activity.[6] Fortunately, depending on the application, modern developments in concrete production can reduce environmental impacts. Up to 70% of the cement content used in traditional concrete can be replaced with **fly ash,** a waste product from coal-fired power plants or **blast furnace slag,** a waste product from steel production. Replacing a high percentage of the cement reduces energy consumption, reduces solid waste, and makes the concrete stronger. Because power plants are common in most cities, fly ash can usually be obtained locally. Another waste product that can be used in concrete production is hazardous waste that is typically disposed of by incineration. Burning it in cement kilns captures its waste heat and avoids the need to consume another fuel in the kilns.

To minimize the environmental problems with concrete, the following measures should be taken.

- Reduce concrete waste by recycling crushed concrete for fill material or road base, or grinding it up for aggregate. (Currently only 5% of concrete is recycled. By weight, it represents up to 67% of construction and demolition waste.[7])

- Carefully estimate the amount of concrete required to avoid ordering excess amounts that become waste.

- Consider less material-intensive alternatives to poured-in-place concrete, such as insulation-form walls and autoclaved cellular concrete block. Precast concrete is factory-made to order, and this controlled production also reduces concrete waste.

- Use insulated shallow foundations in northern climates; consider pier-and-beam foundations instead of slabs on grade.

- Protect aquatic ecosystems by washing forms and equipment where runoff will not contaminate waterways.

- Use the maximum amount of fly ash appropriate to the construction application.

Division 04 – Masonry

Masonry, including brick, block, and stone, is a low-embodied-energy material. It is possible to use locally obtained masonry because its components are common in most regions. This is important to avoid energy- and pollution-intensive transportation and to support the local economy. Masonry is resistant to deterioration from moisture and insects, and is well-suited for warm climates where less insulation is required. Adobe is an especially environmentally friendly masonry product, using less than 1/6th the production energy of concrete block. Unlike standard brick, adobe does not require oven-curing. It is made from clay, sand, and water, then cured in the sun and assembled with mud-based mortar. (Traditionally, straw was sometimes added to avoid cracking, but the correct 20% clay/80% sand ratio can prevent cracking.[8])

Division 05 – Metals

Metals have become such a common element in so many building applications, from nails to plumbing fixtures, that it would be hard to imagine building without them. Metals are strong, durable, and generally do not cause indoor air quality problems (airborne dust from lead paint is a notable exception). Sometimes metals are just one of several viable material choices. However, in this case it is instructive to compare the options.

Structural framing is one such example. The debate over which is the "greener" framing material, steel or wood, has no unanimous resolution. While wood is a renewable resource, steel is highly recyclable and its raw materials are plentiful. Both industries have caused serious environmental problems. Clear-cutting forests has caused habitat destruction and siltation of streams (and pesticide-laden, monoculture plantation forests are not much of an improvement). Strip mining for the iron and limestone used in steel has caused severe erosion, ecosystem destruction, and leaching from tailings piles into water systems. Fortunately, both the wood and steel industries are making environmental and efficiency improvements.

The choice of wood or steel should depend on the particular application, because each material has certain advantages and disadvantages. Wood, for instance, is a natural insulator, whereas steel is a conductor (it is 400 times more conductive than wood). The "thermal bridging" that occurs at exterior walls where steel studs span from the inside out can halve the overall R-value[9] of a wall with cavity insulation (as compared to the R-value of the same wall framed with wood). This presents a major energy-efficiency problem for steel-framed exterior walls. Providing a layer of continuous exterior insulation, while it does not completely solve the thermal bridging problem, can significantly increase the overall R-value of the steel-stud wall.[10]

Steel offers the advantage of resistance to insects and water rot, whereas wood that may be exposed to ground moisture or insects needs to be treated with preservatives. Although borate preservatives are relatively non-toxic, arsenic-based preservatives and most pesticides used to deter termites are not. For health reasons, it would be more environmentally sound to use steel than to use wood treated with highly toxic chemicals. In addition to being toxic for building users and factory workers who make preserved wood products, the preservatives also render the wood non-biodegradable. After its useful life it may have to be disposed of as hazardous waste. Steel, on the other hand, is readily recyclable—it is easily separated at the demolition site using a magnet, and steel scrap has a ready market. The overall recycled content of U.S.

steel (on average for all steel products) is 46%, but this doesn't account for the steel scrap that is exported (11% of the total manufactured steel) rather than re-manufactured in the U.S.[11]

If the particular application makes it possible to use non-treated wood (or wood treated with borates), and the wood is obtained from a certified, well-managed forest (such forests are rare, but are increasing), then wood is probably the more environmentally sound option, because the overall process for manufacturing lumber uses much less energy and creates less pollution and environmental degradation than mining and processing steel.[12]

The mining and manufacture of other metals presents environmental concerns similar to those associated with steel and often much more severe. For instance, the embodied energy of copper is about twice that of steel, while aluminum has as much as seven times the embodied energy of steel.[13]

Like steel, other metals used in building are highly recyclable. Although remanufacturing metals uses significant energy, it is much less than the energy and environmental impacts of starting with the virgin resource. Because metals are highly durable and could be recycled indefinitely, their environmental impact (extraction from the earth and the fact that they are non-renewable resources) is significantly reduced.

Finally, metals offer clear advantages for certain applications. For example, if water collected from a roof surface is to be used for drinking, a steel roof will not leach petro-chemicals into the water, as an asphalt-based roof might. Although stone or clay tile roofing could also be used, their greater weight would require more structural support than the lighter steel.

Division 06 – Wood and Plastics
Wood

Certified wood should be used for any wood application for which it is available. Certified wood comes from well-managed forests that replenish, rather than deplete, old growth timber. Certified wood suppliers for specific wood products (in a particular region), can be found by using the interactive Web site: **http://www.certifiedwood.org** and clicking on "Certification Resource Center."

Structural Support Members

Years ago, the dwindling supply of old growth timber spurred the wood industry to manufacture structural products that can be made with smaller diameter, lower quality logs, and even low-strength, fast-growing tree species. Engineered wood products include glu-lam beams and prefabricated wood trusses and joists. These products enhance quality control while reducing pressure on remaining old-growth forests. They can make use of up to 80% of each log as compared to solid-sawn lumber, which only uses about 50%.[14] Glu-lam beams are composed of wood boards glued together to create high-strength beams with depths ranging from five inches to four feet or more (depths and spans are limited only by shipping concerns). Trusses are more structurally efficient than solid beams (because forces are aligned along components of the truss); therefore, they achieve high strength with smaller dimensional components. Similarly, prefabricated I-joists are more structurally efficient than solid joists, thus they require less wood. One downside to engineered wood products is the adhesives that are used in their manufacture. Although off-gassing is minimal once the products have cured, while curing, the adhesives can be highly toxic to factory workers unless proper protective measures are taken.

Sheathing

Composite sheathing products that are made with recycled wood fiber or that use sawmill waste or small-dimensional lumber help to conserve old growth forests. For applications that do not require high strength, sheathing products are currently available that are made of recycled wood fiber (up to 100%), are themselves recyclable (up to 99%), use a relatively nontoxic bonding agent and are manufactured using less energy than oriented strandboard (OSB) or plywood. To reduce air infiltration with any sheathing product, joints and edges must be sealed with air-barrier tape.

Decking/Outdoor Wood Applications

Avoid wood that is pressure-treated with CCA (chromated copper arsenate). These chemicals are highly toxic, both in production and transport, and the CCA-treated wood cannot be disposed of without potential issues of toxic runoff (or toxic smoke if the wood is burned). Using naturally rot-resistant woods (redwood and cedar) is also problematic, because these woods generally come from old-growth forests that are being destroyed. Better alternatives are to use wood treated with less toxic preservatives, such as ACQ (for wood exposed to weather) or borate (for wood not exposed to weather, but requiring pest-resistance), or to use lumber. Substitutes made of pressed wood fiber and/or recycled plastic composites.

Architectural Woodwork

Use of reclaimed timbers, where available, helps preserve old growth forests while making use of, rather than discarding, a valuable existing resource.

Cabinetry

To reduce VOCs and thereby improve air quality, fiberboards that contain formaldehyde-free glues should be specified. Some products are additionally ecologically friendly because they are made out of agricultural waste products such as wheat straw. If standard particleboard or fiberboard is used, the next best option is to be sure that the millwork is completely wrapped in laminate (including the edges) to reduce the off-gassing of VOCs.

Materials Made from Recycled Plastics

This type of recycling is more accurately termed **down-cycling** when, for instance, plastic soda containers are made into park benches rather than reused or remade into soda containers. Nevertheless, this approach is far preferable to the alternative—disposing of plastic in a landfill right away. Even though most down-cycled products cannot be recycled themselves, they keep the plastic out of the landfill much longer, buying time for engineers to develop better waste-elimination technologies. Examples of products available with 100% recycled content include:

- Wheel stops and speed bumps
- Park furnishings and trash receptacles
- Shelves and shower seats
- Drain pipes
- Toilet compartments
- Plastic signage
- Loading dock bumpers

Division 07 – Thermal and Moisture Protection
Insulation

Figure 2.1 shows the maximum R-values and features of common types of insulation.

The following are considerations when choosing an insulation material.

- Does the insulation retard airflow? (Spray foams and rigid insulations with sealed joints do; loose-fill, batt, and cellulose products do not). Even if no perceptible gaps in the insulation are present, air under pressure will travel through products that are not airflow retarders. If gaps are present, the issue becomes even more critical. Even small gaps in fiberglass insulation have been found to decrease its effectiveness by up to almost 50%.[15]
- Which type of insulation will provide the best R-value within a reasonable thickness for the particular application?
- Does the insulation pose potential health risks to installers or manufacturers, and if so, can proper precautions be used to prevent these risks?

Maximum R-Values and Features of Common Types of Insulation[i]

- **Cellulose:** R=3.7/in.

  Typically made from 80% post-consumer recycled paper, with added borates for fire- and pest-resistance, cellulose can be installed as loose-fill or wet spray. One major advantage is its very low embodied energy (1/8th that of fiberglass, 1/25th that of polyisocyanurate, and 1/32nd that of EPS)[ii] and high-recycled content. Its fibers and chemicals could be potential irritants if not installed with proper protection and sealed from the occupied space.

- **Cotton:** R=3.7/in.

  Made from textile scrap (mostly cotton, but including some polyester), cotton insulation (in the form of batts and loose-fill) makes use of an industrial "waste" product. It poses no known health risks to installers or to occupants, although the conventional cotton industry's extremely high pesticide use has high environmental impact.

- **Icynene:** R=4.3/in.

  Icynene made of isocyanurate (derived from fossil fuels) with a CO_2 blowing agent that does not contribute to ozone depletion the way CFC- and HCFC-blowing agents do. One of its main advantages is that it provides both insulating and air sealing benefits. It is considered safe for indoor air quality.

- **Air Krete:** R=3.9/in.

  Made with magnesium oxide from seawater and foamed using compressed air rather than CFCs or HCFCs, air krete is inorganic foam, making it non combustible and inert with very low VOC off-gassing. It is an ideal insulation for people with severe chemical sensitivities.

- **Fiberglass:** R=2.2-4.0/in.

  Fiberglass comes in batts, loose-fill, and rigid boards. It is made from glass, including at least 20% recycled content. The main disadvantages of standard fiberglass products are that they are made with phenol formaldehyde binder, requiring pollution control measures at the plant. Glass fibers are claimed by some to be carcinogenic if inhaled (installing fiberglass with proper protection, and sealing it from the occupied space greatly reduces this risk). Newly developed formaldehyde-free fiberglass batts are considered to be better for indoor air quality and eliminate the need for factory pollution control equipment. In addition, since the fibers are stronger and springier, they are less likely to be released into the air and the batts can be compressed so that four times as much product can be shipped per truck, reducing environmental impacts from transportation. Unfortunately, formaldehyde-free fiberglass products have had difficulty gaining market share. As with many new or "alternative" building products, even though the product may be better in all respects, contractors tend to use what they are familiar with, and stores stock what contractors demand. Even if the alternative product does not cost more, construction costs are nevertheless driven upward, if a product has to be special ordered, slowing down the job and necessitating the purchase of "extra" product for good measure.

- **Mineral Wool:** R=3.7/in.

  Mineral wool is made from natural rock or steel slag, a post-industrial "waste" product. Like fiberglass, it uses phenol formaldehyde binders

Figure 2.1

Maximum R-Values and Features of Common Types of Insulation

and poses the same health consideration, both from the formaldehyde and from potential inhalation of the fibers.

- **Perlite:** R=3.3/in.

  This loose-fill product is made from volcanic rock and is not associated with pollution in its manufacture. Besides nuisance dust, it is considered safe for indoor air quality.

- **Polyurethane:** R=6.8/in.

  This is a sprayed-in foam product made from fossil fuels and an HCFC–blowing agent, implicated in ozone depletion and global warming. Impacts to indoor air quality may be a concern for people with chemical sensitivities. Like icynene, polyurethane foam provides air-sealing benefits.

- **Extruded Polystyrene (XPS):** R=5.0/in.

  XPS rigid boards are made from fossil fuels and an HCFC–blowing agent, implicated in ozone depletion and global warming. Like sprayed foams, rigid foam boards are air flow retarders (as long as their joints are sealed). Impacts to indoor air quality may be a concern for people with chemical sensitivities.

- **Polyisocyanurate:** R=7.5/in.

  Polyisocyanurate is a foil-faced rigid board made from fossil fuels and an HCFC–blowing agent, implicated in ozone depletion and global warming. Like other rigid boards, polyisocyanurate provides air sealing benefits. Impacts to indoor air quality may be a concern for people with chemical sensitivities.

- **Phenolic:** R=8.0/in.

  Phenolic is also a foil-faced rigid board made from fossil fuels and an HCFC–blowing agent, implicated in ozone depletion and global warming. Like other rigid boards, it provides air sealing benefits. Impacts to indoor air quality may be a concern for people with chemical sensitivities.

- **Expanded Polystyrene (EPS):** R=4.17/in.

  As with the other common rigid foam products, EPS is made from fossil fuels. It is, however, the only one that uses pentane as a blowing agent, instead of ozone–depleting HCFCs. (Pentane does, however, contribute to smog.) Like other rigid foams, EPS provides air-sealing benefits. Impacts to indoor air quality may be a concern for people with chemical sensitivities.

[i] Wilson, Alex. *Environmental Building News*, Vol. 4 No. 1 January/February, 1995.

[ii] Franklin Associates, Ltd., "Comparative Energy Evaluation of Plastic Products and Their Alternatives for the Building and Construction and Transportation Industries," prepared for The Society of the Plastics Industry, 1991; and Alex Wilson, *Environmental Building News*, Vol. 4 No. 1 January/February, 1995.

Figure 2.1 (cont.)

- Does the insulation contain ozone-depleting chemicals?
- Does the insulation have the potential to release gaseous pollutants into the building interior?
- In a retrofit situation, what type of insulation is most practical? For instance, it may be possible to retrofit a conventionally framed structure by blowing insulation into the voids between studs (using holes drilled at the top and bottom of a wall and then resealing them). For a masonry building, however, unless there is a cavity between wall wythes, insulation must be added on either the inside or outside of the walls, which might impose space constraints or other considerations.

It should be noted that providing adequate insulation levels, even given the disadvantages of particular insulation products, is better than providing minimal insulation or none at all. The energy saved by the insulation will occur year after year, reducing the amount of heating and cooling required in the building and the burning of fossil fuels typically associated with that heating and cooling. Therefore, if space constraints are the most critical issue, the high insulation value per inch of polyisocyanurate rigid foam (4" provides R-30) may outweigh the fact that isocyanurate is produced with ozone-depleting HCFC-141-b. If space is not as critical, expanded polystyrene (EPS) is preferable over other rigid foam products, because it does not contain ozone-depleting blowing agents.

If chemical sensitivity is the most critical issue, the structure should be designed to accommodate adequate amounts of a product that does not off-gas harmful pollutants. Alternative building materials that provide high insulation value without toxicity (such as straw bale construction) may also be a good choice for chemically sensitive people. *(See the "Alternative Materials" section later in this chapter.)*

Another general consideration is the reduction of insulation waste. Trimmings from insulation batts can be recycled into loose-fill insulation. Rigid foam roofing insulation can be salvaged during roofing retrofits if during the original installation a sheathing layer is installed between the insulation and the roof surface.

For roof insulation, loose-fill, batts, or blown insulation can be added on top of the attic floor or, if the attic is to be used for storage, batt insulation can be stapled to the rafters. In addition, a radiant barrier, which reflects radiant heat back (either into or out of a building, depending on the climate) can be attached to the underside of the rafters (or the underside of the batts), with the shiny side facing down into the attic. It can also be attached on top of the ceiling joists (shiny side facing up into the attic). The radiant barrier must be adjacent to an air gap to work; otherwise heat will travel through the radiant barrier via conduction.

Foundation slabs should be insulated to the climatically appropriate degree by installing rigid insulation underneath them before the concrete is poured. (Short of jack-hammering up the slab, slabs are impossible to insulate after construction.) Pier and beam foundations can be insulated by filling the floor cavities over the crawl space with batt or rigid insulation. Thermal protection can also be achieved by installing a radiant barrier in the floor joist air space above an unheated basement or crawl space.

The R-value of a radiant barrier will vary greatly depending on its location (attic or basement) and whether it is the heating or cooling season. During the heating season, the radiant barrier will be effective in the floor joist air space above an unheated basement because the warm air above the basement will tend to stratify, eliminating convection and making radiation the prime mode of heat transfer. By contrast, in the attic space, during the heating season, convection will carry heat right past a radiant barrier. In the cooling season, however, a radiant barrier located in the attic will reflect the heat of a hot roof out of the cooler attic.

Moisture Protection

Uncontrolled moisture transport is a serious issue. When moisture condenses or is trapped within a wall, roof or floor assembly, it can cause structural damage as well as mold and mildew, a major cause of indoor air quality problems. Moisture can enter a building envelope in three ways—rain transport from outside, diffusion of water vapor through the envelope materials, and transport of water vapor in air that leaks through cracks in the envelope. Rain transport must be controlled with proper drainage planes in the wall assemblies. A properly located vapor diffusion retarder will help retard diffusion through a building envelope assembly. Much more significant than vapor diffusion, however, is the amount of moisture that can be carried through currents of air escaping through cracks and voids; thus the importance of sealing these cracks. As warmer air rises, it causes high pressure at the top of a building and low pressure at the bottom, resulting in what is called the **stack effect**. At these points of greater pressure differential (namely the attic and basement), it is especially crucial to seal air leaks and use airflow retarders.

Water build-up can be avoided by controlling air pressure, ventilation, and humidity, and through building envelope design (notably the placement of insulation, vapor diffusion retarders, and airflow retarders). To avoid condensation within the building envelope, a vapor diffusion retarder should be on the side of the envelope that is typically warmer and more humid. Warm, moist air travels from inside to outside in cold climates (and in mixed climates, during the winter), but from outside to inside in warm climates (and in mixed climates, during the summer). Consequently, there is no one "correct" location for a vapor diffusion retarder for all climates and seasons. No matter how well detailed the building design or renovation is, moisture will still find its way into the envelope assembly. It is therefore critical that the assembly allow for drying to either the exterior or interior. The designer should evaluate the potential for condensation in each unique building envelope assembly over the annual outdoor temperature range and build forgiveness (drying potential) into the system.[16]

Vapor Diffusion Retarders

Vapor diffusion retarders are materials with low permeability to water vapor (low "perm" rates). Materials that are considered to be "impermeable" include polyethylene, rubber membranes, glass, aluminum foil (commonly used as facing on insulation and sheathings), sheet metal, oil based paints, and bitumen-impregnated kraft paper. Materials that are generally considered to be "semi-permeable" and can sometimes be used as vapor diffusion retarders depending on the specific design conditions include plywood, oriented strandboard (OSB), unfaced EPS and XPS, heavy asphalt-impregnated building paper, and most latex paints.[17].

Airflow Retarders

Airflow retarders are continuous materials that are able to resist differences in air pressure caused by mechanical systems, the stack effect, and wind. Materials that are effective at retarding airflow include gypsum board, sheathing materials, rigid insulation, and sprayed foam insulation (assuming all joints, cracks, and penetrations have been properly sealed).

Waterproofing and Dampproofing

If a structure is to be durable, nothing is more important than preventing water entry—from rain above ground and hydrostatic pressure below ground. The rainier the climate, the more rain control is needed. Gravity, wind pressure, momentum, surface tension, and capillary action can all cause rain to penetrate into a building surface. Each has been traditionally prevented by the following design techniques:

- Providing ample roof overhangs can help keep rain off the building surface to begin with.
- Avoiding straight-through openings in walls can prevent rain entry by momentum.

- Providing kerfs or drip edges can interrupt rain entry via surface tension.
- Providing flashings can direct gravity-flow rainwater back toward the building exterior.
- Providing a pressure-equalized or pressure moderated space in the air cavity behind the exterior wall face can prevent water entry via air pressure.[18]

Under the most severe rain exposures, providing a pressure equalized (vented) space behind the exterior cladding, combined with a "drainage plane" behind that, can prevent all these modes of water entry. For low-precipitation areas, an adequate approach (with a long track record) is to provide a face-sealed exterior wall of high mass masonry or concrete, which allows rain to be stored in the wall assembly mass for later drying. The least forgiving system is a face-sealed approach with no rain-storage mass, such as **external insulation finish systems** (EIFS). These systems should be used only in the driest climates.

Asphalt-impregnated felt (or "tarpaper") has been traditionally used as a drainage plane, but water-resistant sheathings, such as rigid insulation or foil-faced structural sheathing, can also serve the purpose. Window, door, and roof/wall intersections must be carefully detailed to ensure drainage plane continuity. Because the drainage plane is toward the outside of the wall assembly, impacts to indoor air quality from the tarpaper or rigid board are typically only an issue for chemically sensitive people.

Hydrostatic pressure can drive water through basement walls unless they are properly detailed. Proper detailing involves sloping the ground away from the foundation and capping it with water-shedding clay, using free-draining granular backfill (such as sand) next to the foundation wall or installing a drainage board (such as rigid fiberglass), and providing perforated sub-grade perimeter footing drains (to drain water so it does not build up around the foundation wall). The drains must be piped to daylight or a sump pump.

Foundations also require dampproofing to resist absorption of water through a foundation wall by capillary action. (Dampproofing is not designed to resist hydrostatic pressure and should not be confused with waterproofing.) Low-VOC dampproofing coatings that will not leach into the groundwater are the environmentally preferable option.

Foundation Ventilation Systems

To keep moisture vapor, as well as radon, methane, and pesticide gases, out of foundations, the pressure next to them must be controlled. This is accomplished by creating negative pressure in the gravel drainage pad under the slab (or in the crawl space) with a ventilation system piped to daylight through the roof. Soil gases are removed by passive stack action or by exhaust fans.

Since no waterproofing system will avoid all moisture entry, and since concrete starts out wet to begin with, concrete slabs must be allowed to dry. With a polyethylene vapor diffusion retarder under the slab to keep ground moisture out, slabs can only dry into the building. Installing vapor-retardant flooring (such as carpet and vinyl) over a slab in a manner that does not permit drying, especially if the concrete has not had sufficient curing time to dry out, can lead to buckled flooring, as well as mold, mildew, and associated indoor air quality problems—which can be quite serious. Installing vapor-retardant finishes (or insulations) on interior basement walls that have dampproofing on their exterior surfaces can create similar problematic scenarios. It is possible to allow slabs to dry to the outside by installing vapor permeable (or semi-permeable) rigid insulation under them, in lieu of a polyethylene vapor diffusion retarder. The insulation causes the slab to be warmer than the ground and as long as there is no major vapor diffusion retarder, moisture will flow from warm to cold, even if the ground is saturated. Drying to the outside also works for foundation walls when dampproofing is replaced by rigid fiberglass or mineral wool insulation (which are vapor-permeable, but also provide drainage and a capillary break).

Unless the floor assembly over a crawl space is constructed like any other exterior envelope assembly (with insulating sheathing and vapor diffusion retarders), crawl spaces should not be vented with exterior air, but should be treated like basements (enclosed, heated during the winter, and cooled during the summer). Otherwise, venting crawl spaces with warm, humid summer air will cause condensation (and potential mold), because the crawl space surfaces will be cooler than the outside air. As mentioned above, crawl spaces should be kept under negative pressure, with soil gases exhausted to the outside.

Roofing

Durability is critical in a roofing system, because failure can cause serious building damage and because frequent re-roofing is highly resource-intensive. For single-ply membrane roofs or built-up asphalt roofs, it is preferable to separate the rigid insulation from the roofing membrane so that when the roof needs to be replaced, the insulation can be reused. Use of a polystyrene insulation that will not be damaged by wetting/drying is also preferable. If water is to be harvested off the roof, a roofing material should be used that does not leach heavy metals or petrochemicals into the rainwater. If renewable energy is a priority, the marginal costs of upgrading to PV-integrated roofing panels or PV shingles (when installing a new roof or replacing an old one) should be considered, because this will be less expensive than providing a roof plus stand-alone PV panels. Finally, environmental impacts of the roofing choice should be considered, including pollutants released from some types of roofing, such as hot-melt asphalt built up roofing.

Reflective Coatings

Even in mild climates, the sun beating down on a roof all day can cause it to reach extreme temperatures and drive considerable heat into a building via conduction. Ways of reducing heat gain through a roof include:

- Adding insulation underneath it.
- Installing a radiant barrier.
- Installing a reflective roof (or painting an existing roof with a reflective coating).

A reflective roof prevents the building from getting hot, reduces heat island effects, and prolongs the life of the roof. Multiple studies of buildings in hot climates (including California, Texas, and Florida) have documented 10–50% energy savings when roofs were retrofitted with reflective coatings.[19] Reflective coatings can be applied to any roof surface and can reflect about 82% of total sunlight. Non-petroleum, water-based reflective coatings are the best environmental choice.

Living "Green" Roof

Living green roofs provide UV-protection for the roof membrane—extending the life of the roof up to 100% and potentially longer, while providing environmental cooling (reduced heat island effect), habitat, added insulation, storm water management, natural beauty (excellent for habitable roofs or roofs visible from above), not to mention cleaner air. Providing a green roof is easier to do for new construction than for retrofits, because the latter can be complicated by structural issues.

Siding

Vinyl siding is a relatively maintenance-free product, but like other vinyl products, it is made with polyvinyl chloride (PVC), which has been linked to cancer, birth defects, and groundwater contamination. Alternative options that avoid these health and environmental problems include wood, plaster, and fiber-cement. Aluminum is a durable and low-maintenance option, but it has very high embodied energy and there are environmental concerns associated with mining its raw materials.

Division 08 – Doors and Windows

Windows

The goal when selecting windows is to specify a product that will provide the climatically appropriate insulating value, while also letting in a high percentage of visible light for daylighting, and providing the appropriate solar heat gain coefficient (SHGC). Due to advances in glazing, there are many options and manufacturers to choose from, and it is possible to "tune" the glazing carefully for the particular orientation and desired conditions.

The following are several key terms that apply to windows.

Daylight Transmittance: The percentage of visible light that a glazing transmits.

Solar Heat Gain Coefficient (SHGC): The percentage of solar energy either directly transmitted or absorbed and re-radiated into the building. SHGC ranges from 0.0 to 1.0; the lower the number, the lower the solar heat gain. *(Note: SHGC has replaced the older term SC (Shading Coefficient), SHGC=0.87 × SC).*

U-Value: Measures the heat loss or gain due to the differences between indoor and outdoor air temperatures (BTU/hr/S.F.). U=1/R. The lower the U-value, the better the insulating performance.

R-Value: Measures the insulation effectiveness of the window (R=1/U). The higher the R-value, the better the insulating performance.

Low-Emissivity (low-E) Coatings: Applied coatings that allow short wave energy (visible light) to be transmitted through glass, but reflect long wave infrared radiation (heat). The lower the emissivity, the lower the resultant U-value.

In the most extreme climates (very cold), the best windows provide low-emissivity, high visible transmittance, insulating gas fill (argon or krypton), good edge seals, insulated frames (with thermal breaks if frames are metal), and airtight construction. Several window manufacturers use low-E coatings applied not to the glass as with regular low-E windows, but to a suspended plastic film in between double panes of glass. Triple-pane windows are also an option, although weight and window depth may be a serious consideration. Newer materials on the market include innovative gels that can be inserted between glazing layers to turn a window from clear to white when it is exposed to a certain heat or sunlight threshold or to an electric current. These gels could be used in skylights to provide full daylighting on cloudy days, while avoiding glare and overheating on hot sunny days. (In their light-blocking white form, they still transmit 10% of incident solar energy—potentially enough for glare-free daylighting.) Another innovative product that could become revolutionary for window technology is a silica gel, which allows over 70% visible light transmission but blocks heat transfer. (Its R-value is three to four times that of common insulation products such as rigid foam and fiberglass.[20])

Frames are available in wood (clad or unclad), metal (which need to be thermally-broken to prevent conduction through the frame), fiberglass, and vinyl. Although vinyl is a low-maintenance option, it is made from PVC, making it a less healthy option than other types of window frames.

As with many products, it is worthwhile to ask window manufacturers whether their products contain recycled materials. Even if the manufacturer does not use recycled content, knowing that customers are requesting it helps to move the marketplace in this direction.

Doors

Glass (or partially glazed) doors should be designed with all the same considerations as windows. In addition, door frames should be carefully detailed, with door sweeps and weatherproofing, to prevent air infiltration. Non-glazed doors should also be insulated, preferably with non-ozone depleting EPS. In cold climates, airlock entryways can save considerable energy.

Division 09 - Finishes

Interior Wall Systems

Particularly green interior wall systems, if available, are those made from agricultural "waste", such as straw. Some products use 100% agricultural waste product, avoid toxic binders, are fire-resistant (with a fire rating from one- to two-hours), and do not require structural studs.

If gypsum board is to be used, recycled content product should be specified if locally available, and gypsum board scrap should be separated on the job site to allow pieces to be recycled. What cannot be recycled back into gypsum board product can be ground up to be used for soil amendment (provided it is free of toxic paints or wall coverings).

Acoustical Panels

When selecting acoustical panels, considerations should include durability and flexibility, low or no toxicity in the panel fabric, and recycled context in both panel and fabric.

Ceiling

Acoustical ceiling tiles are often recyclable. At least one ceiling tile company has a recycling program that will take old tiles, even from other manufacturers. Specifying ceiling tile with recycled content is critical to foster this reuse of resources.

Paints, Coatings, and Adhesives

Most paints, coatings, and adhesives for finishes such as flooring and wall covering off-gas VOCs, formaldehyde, or other toxic chemicals that affect installers as well as building occupants. Therefore, it is critical to specify low- or zero-VOC products, which are readily available today. Off-gassed VOCs can be re-absorbed into soft surfaces, such as fabrics. Because most VOCs are emitted during the application and curing process, this problem can be greatly reduced by providing good ventilation and ensuring a minimum of exposed soft surfaces during installation.

Wall Coverings

Low- or zero-VOC paint is preferable to wall covering applied with toxic adhesive. The best wall coverings from environmental and air-quality standpoints are non-toxic textiles adhered with low-VOC adhesives. Vinyl wall covering poses the environmental concerns associated with chlorine compounds and the health concerns associated with off-gassing. When vinyl decomposes (a process that is accelerated when it gets hot), it off-gasses toxic fumes.

Floor Finish

Solvent-based floor finishes can cause indoor air quality problems, especially during and immediately following installation. Alternatives exist, such as water-based urethane finishes for wood floors.

Carpet

Each year in the United States, landfills acquire millions of tons of carpet that may take 20,000 years to decompose. To stop this needless waste and environmental degradation, it is important to select carpet that has high-recycled content and is itself recyclable. Carpet that can be recycled back into carpet is preferable to carpet that can be, at best, "down-cycled" into other plastic products. By specifying carpet tile instead of broadloom, 100% of the carpet does not have to be removed when only 20% of it (the part in the traffic pattern) shows wear. Finally, low toxicity is another important consideration in carpet selection.

Carpet underlayment should also have recycled content, be non-toxic (formaldehyde-free), and provide both insulation value (commonly R-12) and sound barrier properties.

Resilient Flooring

Like other vinyl products, vinyl flooring is not the most environmentally sound choice. Several other types of resilient flooring can be used instead, including cork, natural linoleum, recycled-content rubber, or chlorine-free polymer resin tile.

Ceramic Tile

Several manufacturers offer products with up to 70% recycled content. Adding recycled glass in ceramic tile makes use of a post-consumer product, and can also add interesting textures and colors to the tile.

Wood Flooring

As with all wood applications, certified wood should be specified if available, and locally or regionally grown and processed products are preferable to those that require significant transportation. Endangered species of tropical woods should absolutely be avoided. Bamboo is becoming a popular flooring option. Not actually a wood, but rather a grass, bamboo is exceptionally strong (it can be used for structural applications) and rapidly renewable (shoots are mature and ready to harvest in three years). Unfortunately the type of bamboo used in the building industry is not native to the United States and is currently imported from Asia.

Division 10 – Specialties
Toilet Compartments
If plastic toilet partitions are to be used in a project, 100% recycled-content products, available from multiple manufacturers, should be specified.

Access Flooring
Access flooring allows for both wiring and air distribution to be provided in the same plenum, eliminating the need for overhead ductwork and cable trays. This can reduce overall floor-to-floor height, enables very convenient data system upgrades and office moves (since wiring is available under any floor tile), and allows for all the energy efficiency benefits of underfloor air distribution. *(See the "Displacement Ventilation" section later in this chapter.)*

Fireplaces & Stoves
Although wood is a renewable resource, burning it can cause considerable air pollution and can compromise indoor air quality, especially if fireplaces and stoves are not properly vented. Furthermore, fireplaces can actually impart an overall heating penalty by drawing heat from the fire and the building up the chimney. A typical masonry fireplace has a heating efficiency of –10 to 10%, Radiant wood-burning stoves burn cleaner and achieve higher efficiency—typically 50–70%. Fireplace efficiency can be improved by installing a fireplace insert—basically a wood burning stove that fits into the fireplace.[21]

Pellet stoves (which burn compressed sawdust or agricultural waste) have higher combustion efficiency and lower particulate emissions than standard wood burning stoves, but overall efficiency (which factors in both combustion efficiency and heat delivery to the occupied space) is similar or only slightly better than EPA-certified wood stoves, about 65-80%.[22]

Masonry stoves can achieve overall efficiency of 70-90%, due to the fact that flue gases travel along circuitous routes through high-mass masonry chambers, which absorb the heat and radiate it into the occupied space.[23]

Sun Control Devices

Sun control devices, such as exterior light shelves, louvers, and fins, can shade interior spaces from glare, while also reducing unwanted heat gain. Interior light shelves can enhance daylighting by bouncing light deeper into a building, thereby evening out the luminance ratios of the spaces immediately adjoining and more distant from the window.

Walk-Off Matts

Much of the dust and dirt in a typical building comes from people's shoes. The simple provision of a walk-off matt in the building entryway can improve indoor air quality by greatly reducing dust and dirt.

Division 11 – Equipment
Efficient Equipment

Appliances are available today that use dramatically less electricity and water than standard older models, yet offer improved performance.

When replacing washing machines, replace with horizontal-axis models (available from various major manufacturers). Compared to top-loading models, horizontal axis washing machines use 60% less energy and 40% less water and detergent. They spin faster to remove more moisture from a load of laundry, do not cause as much wear on the clothes because they spin rather than agitate, and wash more effectively. Clotheslines dry for free without polluting, but if a line is not available, the next best option is an efficient dryer with a moisture sensor to prevent excessive drying, while saving energy.

The American Council for an Energy Efficient Economy has current listings of efficient refrigerator models. A revolutionary technology that has been incorporated into high-efficiency refrigerators is vacuum insulation (thermos bottles operate on the same principle), which can achieve a center-of-panel insulating value of R-75. The insulation is made without ozone-depleting foams, and its high insulating efficiency means that refrigerator walls can be thinner, allowing for more usable space.

Select the most energy-efficient office equipment available, including copiers, fax machines, and printers. For major office equipment, consider leasing rather than purchasing to encourage manufacturers to provide durable, upgradeable, recyclable machines, and to ensure that the most efficient models are provided as leases expire.

Note that Energy Star™ machines (such as copiers and cathode ray tube [CRT] computer monitors) must be set in Energy Star™ mode in order to conserve energy when not in use. Flat screen LCD monitors and laptops outperform CRT monitors optically, and also use less energy, reduce harmful electro-magnetic fields, and save desk space.

Division 12 – Furnishings

Furniture selection should be considered part of the whole building design. Green furnishings are those that provide adjustable ergonomic comfort and are made without toxic, off-gassing fabric dyes and adhesives or unsustainably harvested woods (such as those from clear-cut rainforests). Selecting light-colored finishes reduces the lighting level required, and specifying unupholstered materials in cooling climates and upholstered furniture in heating climates reduces energy use (because people feel more comfortable with less required air conditioning or heating). Durability and reusability are other important features. Finally, renovating or remanufacturing furniture can reduce its embodied energy.

Division 13 – Special Construction

Solar Energy Systems

Except for the manufacture of solar energy equipment, collecting and using solar energy results in none of the greenhouse or acid gas emissions associated with the combustion of fossil fuels. Moreover, sunlight is a widespread resource, and the amount of it that reaches the earth is many times greater than worldwide energy demand. Only *cost* and public perception limit the increased use of solar energy systems.

Solar energy can be actively collected for both thermal energy and electricity. Active thermal solar energy systems include those that collect and distribute solar-heated air or water for immediate use or storage. (As distinguished from passive approaches, active systems contain moving parts such as fans, pumps, or motors.) Solar electric systems collect current solar income—as opposed to solar income stored millions of years ago in the form of fossil fuels—and turn it into electricity. *(See Chapter 4 and the Appendix for more on solar energy.)*

Solar Water Heaters

After reducing water-heating loads with efficient plumbing fixtures, solar water heaters can be used to heat water for domestic, commercial, and industrial purposes. Even if a backup system is required, using the available sun to heat water will save money over the long run, while reducing environmental impact. There are several different types of reliable, freeze-protected systems on the market.

Photovoltaic (PV) Systems[24]

The original and most common semi-conducting material used in PV cells is single crystal silicon. These cells have proven their durability and longevity in space applications and are also generally the most efficient type of PV cells, converting up to 23% of incoming solar energy into electricity. The main disadvantage of single crystal silicon cells is their production costs; growing large crystals of silicon and then cutting them into thin (0.1-0.3 mm) wafers is slow and expensive.

Alternative PV cells include poly-crystalline silicon cells, a variety of "thin film" PV cells, and concentrating collectors. Although poly-crystalline silicon cells are less expensive to manufacture than single crystal silicon (because they do not require the growth of large crystals), they are also less efficient (15-17%). "Thin films" (0.001-0.002 mm thick) of "amorphous" or uncrystallized silicon are inexpensive compared to crystal silicon and may be easily deposited on materials such as glass and metal, making them the mass-produced PV material of choice for the electronics industry and for a variety of other applications. The advantage of amorphous silicon cells for building applications is that they can be deposited on roofing tiles or spandrel glass panels. Achieving the double function of building envelope and electricity production in one product can enhance overall building cost-efficiency. The disadvantage of amorphous silicon cells is that they are not very efficient (12% in the lab, 7% for commercial cells), and they degrade with time, losing up to 50% of their efficiency with exposure to sunlight.

Thin film PV cells made from other materials have been developed in an attempt to overcome the inefficiency and degradation of amorphous silicon thin films, while retaining low production costs. Gallium arsenide (GaAs), copper indium diselenide ($CuInSe_2$), cadmium telluride (CdTe) and titanium dioxide (TiO_2) have all been used as thin film PV cells, with various efficiencies and production costs. Titanium dioxide thin films, just recently developed, have interesting potential because they are transparent and can be used as windows.

In yet another effort to improve the efficiency and reduce the cost of photovoltaics, scientists have developed collectors that concentrate light from a large area onto a small PV cell. Special silicon cells were designed to withstand the increased light levels. Efficiencies as high as 30% have been achieved, and concentrating lenses and reflectors are much less expensive to produce than PV cells. The disadvantage is that only direct sunlight, not light scattered by clouds or reflected off surfaces, can be concentrated; thus concentrating collectors only achieve optimal efficiency in areas that receive a great deal of direct sunlight such as deserts. *(See Chapter 4 and the Appendix for more on photovoltaics.)*

Wind Turbines

Small wind turbines are commercially available for individual building applications. They can either provide off-grid power or they can augment the power supply of a grid-connected building. In many locations, combining wind turbines with a photovoltaic system can ensure a more stable power supply than would be provided by either technology alone. *(See Chapter 5 for more on wind systems.)*

Division 14 – Conveying Systems

Elevators

As with all motorized equipment, selecting the most efficient model possible will reduce energy use for the life of the elevator. Durability is essential—broken elevators are frustrating, and manufacturing new ones is highly resource- and energy-consumptive. As with office equipment, consider leasing rather than purchasing elevators. This gives manufacturers a major incentive to make their product durable and easily maintainable.

Division 15 – Mechanical

Plumbing Fixtures

"When the well is dry, we know the worth of water."
— Benjamin Franklin, 1790.

Humans cannot live without water, but the Western World's practice of using exorbitant amounts of drinking-quality water to transport sewage is not a sustainable practice. This is becoming increasingly evident as the population grows, and water becomes more scarce in the dry regions of the United States. Plumbing fixtures that use low water or no water are available from various manufacturers. They include composting toilets, waterless urinals, low-flow toilets (various models using 1.6 gallons per flush or less, including standard gravity-flush and pressure-assist models), low-flow showerheads (various models using less than 2.5 gallons per minute), low-flow faucets (using less than 2.5 gallons per minute), metered faucets (to ensure that faucets in public bathrooms will not be left on), and shut-off valves for kitchen faucets and showerheads that enable the temperature setting to be "saved" while the water is temporarily shut off.

Gray Water Systems

Treating gray water like black water is not the most efficient strategy. Once-through gray water from sinks and washing machines can often be reused directly for toilet flushing or for subsurface irrigation (depending on regional codes). Gray water can also be used on (non-edible) plantings after treatment with a commercial filter or site-built sand filter.

For showers or other hot-water fixtures, gray water waste heat recovery systems can capture the heat from showers (or other fixtures) as it goes down the drain and transfer that heat to incoming water.

These systems are especially effective in high-use shower areas, such as in locker rooms.

Cogeneration

This technology produces both heat and electricity and makes use of them in the building or campus system. Because the heat associated with standard electricity production is often wasted (simply exhausted into the atmosphere), cogeneration is a much more efficient process. In fact, cogeneration raises fuel utilization efficiency to more than 90% (compared to typicaly 35% efficiency for plants generating electricity alone) and reduces fossil fuel use by over half.

Displacement Ventilation

Instead of mixing high-velocity air from overhead ducts to "dilute" the stale air in a room, a displacement ventilation system supplies fresh, cool air from a pressurized floor plenum (similar to the access floors used for computer rooms) or from low, wall-mounted diffusers. The fresh air displaces the warmer, stale air, which is removed via a ceiling plenum. Displacement systems move more higher-temperature air at a lower velocity and lower pressure drop than conventional systems, thereby reducing required fan power. Low-velocity air is quieter and less drafty. Also, displacing rather than diluting the air affords better pollutant removal. Pollutants and heat from copy machines and other equipment, lights, and people tend to be drawn straight up in a "plume" rather than being mixed laterally in the conditioned air. Furthermore, the warmer supply air means the chillers are more efficient. The underfloor plenum can also be used for wiring, providing superior convenience.

Materials required for underfloor air distribution typically include an access floor system (usually covered with carpet tiles or resilient floor tiles) so that sections of floor can easily be removed to access the floor plenum.

Natural Ventilation

In conventional building operation, a considerable amount of energy is used circulation air for ventilation. By contract, using natural forces to move air can result in effective ventilation without the energy input. Examples include providing cross-ventilation to make use of wind, building chimneys to induce stack ventilation, and using water-evaporation systems in hot dry climates to induce cooling and air movement.

Division 16 – Electrical
Lighting

First and foremost, lighting should be designed effectively and efficiently, avoiding glare and providing light where it is needed (primarily on wall and ceiling surfaces) rather than simply assigning a set number of footcandles of light to a space. Specifying highly reflective (light-colored) interior surfaces is important to evenly distribute light and enhance occupant well being. Ambient overhead lighting should be minimal. For most applications, a direct-indirect lighting fixture will provide the most appealing and efficient ambient light source. It should be dimmable to integrate with daylighting and to afford user-flexibility. *(See Chapter 3 for more on lighting efficiencies and Chapter 6 for daylighting.)*

Task lighting provides for flexibility, and accent lighting enhances visual interest. Automatic lighting controls can greatly reduce lighting energy consumption. They include occupancy sensors that turn lights off when a room is not in use (especially appropriate for infrequently used rooms) and photosensitive dimmers that dim lights when daylight is ample. Finally, lights should be easily maintainable.

Today's fluorescent lighting is efficient, has excellent color rendition and is appropriate for most applications. The latest fluorescent technology includes T-8 and T-5 lamps with dimmable electronic ballasts. Compared to the older T-10 and T-12 lamps, the newer lamps contain less mercury and significantly improve energy efficiency. Compact fluorescent lights (CFLs) should be used instead of inefficient incandescent lamps. CFLs come in pleasant color spectrums, use 75% less energy than incandescent lights, and last ten times as long. Electronic ballasts (rather than magnetic ballasts) should be used in all linear and compact fluorescent luminaires. LED (light emitting diode) technology provides light with even less energy than fluorescent lights. Currently common in exit signs and other niche applications, LED technology is being developed for broader use.

Disposal of fluorescent, mercury vapor, metal halide, neon, and high-pressure sodium lamps is a critical issue, as they all contain mercury, direct exposure to which is toxic. Magnetic ballasts for fluorescent lights made before the late 1970s also contain highly toxic PCBs (polychlorinated biphenyls). All lamps containing mercury should be recycled with a qualified lamp recycling company and protected from breakage during transport. If lamps do break, they should be collected (with proper protection) and stored in a sealed container. Expired PCB ballasts should be stored in sealed containers and disposed of with extreme caution and scrupulous labeling, using a PCB disposal company that is registered with the Environmental Protection Agency.[25]

Exterior Lighting: The luminous Milky Way that spans majestically across the night sky is never seen by 75% of American children, due to nighttime light pollution.[26] Recent research has also shown harmful physiological effects that result from interrupting sleep by viewing light.[27] Minimizing **light pollution** and **light trespass** will help protect dark skies for humans and nocturnal animals alike. This can be done by eliminating unshielded floodlighting and providing "cut-off" luminaires.

Full cut-off (FCO) luminaires considerably reduce wasteful upward lighting by directing all light down toward the intended area of illumination. (None is allowed above the horizontal plane.) Replacing defective, non-functioning, or non cut-off luminaires with FCO luminaires allows for substantial lowering in the wattage of the new fixture, thereby realizing a cost and energy savings. Cut-off luminaires also enhance safety for both pedestrians and drivers by eliminating glaring light.

Uniform light distribution is important for comfort, safety, and energy efficiency. Light levels need not be high. In fact, studies have shown that about three footcandles is all that is needed for security purposes.[28] Much brighter light (often 100 footcandles or more), which has become prevalent at all-night gas stations and other stores, is actually dangerous, because drivers (especially the elderly) can take two to five minutes to readjust their vision.

Exterior lighting controlled by motion detectors can enhance safety while reducing energy use. Some schools have reduced both energy use and vandalism by keeping the campus dark after hours. Police are informed that light seen on campus should be treated with suspicion. The security director at one San Antonio school, where vandalism dropped 75% with the dark campus approach, suggested that vandalism loses its appeal when people cannot see what they are doing.[29]

High-pressure sodium lamps (the characteristic yellow parking lot lights) should be avoided, as they reduce peripheral vision. White light sources, such as metal halide and fluorescent, improve visibility with less light.

Plug Loads

Plug loads are the electric loads drawn by all the equipment that is plugged into outlets. Computers, printers, and faxes do not draw energy at one constant rate. Energy use spikes when equipment is turned on and then falls to a much lower operating level. Rating labels on the equipment are for start-up loads (maximum energy draw) and should be used to size the wires and devices in the electrical system. Adding up the nameplate ratings of various pieces of equipment in an office and dividing by the area will typically result in the determination of a "connected" load of 3-4 watts per square foot. This connected load is not, however, the same as the average operating, or "as-used," load, which is likely to be less than 1 watt per square foot. A study of U.S. office buildings found that the measured average as-used plug load was 0.78 watts per square foot. This as-used load, rather than the connected load, should be used to calculate the sizing of mechanical systems, which must compensate for the actual heat generated by the equipment, not the amount of heat that would be generated if the equipment remained in start-up mode. The resultant downsizing of the mechanical system can have a significant impact on the first cost of the facility.[30]

Alternative Materials

A chapter on green building materials would not be complete without discussion of non-conventional building materials. Several natural, low-tech building techniques—including straw bale, adobe, rammed earth, and cob—have a long history of use around the world, but are just beginning to regain popularity in the U.S., mainly among do-it-yourself homebuilders. Although these building techniques are labor-intensive and unfamiliar to the conventional contractor, they provide many environmental and health advantages. Typically they are associated with very low-embodied energy, no harmful off-gassing of pollutants, locally sourced materials, and good energy performance in appropriate climatic regions.

Straw Bale

Straw is a very low-embodied-energy by-product of the farming industry. While it would be a bad idea to remove all the straw from the field, since some of it needs to be tilled into the soil to provide aeration and organic matter, current agricultural practices produce an excess of straw, much of which is typically burned as "waste," creating air pollution. Use of straw for straw bale construction not only makes use of this "waste" product, it also provides good insulation, fire-resistance (because the tight packing in bale walls eliminates the necessary oxygen for burning), and even protection from most termites. (Only one species will eat straw.) The primary concern with straw bale construction is protection from moisture, but this has been successfully addressed with big overhangs, high foundations with a capillary break next to the straw, and proper interior and exterior plaster detailing.

Adobe

Earthen, sun-cured brick is another relatively labor-intensive, but low-embodied-energy material with a long history of use in hot, dry climates. Adobe lacks the insulating properties of straw, but provides instead a large thermal heat sink that soaks up excess heat during the hot day and re-releases it during the cool night, thereby moderating the building's internal temperature.

Other Earthen Materials

Rammed earth—earth formed into thick, durable monolithic walls, and **cob**—earth and straw molded by hand into sculptural walls, work in hot, dry climates along the same principles as adobe. Any of these materials can be (and are) used in other climates, but may require supplemental insulation or additional heating or cooling.

A myriad of alternative factory-made materials (such as autoclaved cellular concrete, structural stressed skin panels, and fiber-concrete block) are also available. They combine the ease and familiarity of conventional, modular construction techniques (a big plus for buildings that are to be built by conventional contractors) with benefits that often include better energy efficiency, lower toxicity, use of waste products, and lower embodied energy than their conventional counterparts.

Conclusion   Choosing green building materials is not a cut-and-dried process. There is a myriad of considerations—sometimes conflicting with each other—including indoor environmental quality, energy use, embodied energy, location of product source, durability, end-of-life considerations, resource renewability, and environmental impact. No project will be composed of a perfectly green set of materials and strategies; rather, designers and owners must determine what the most important characteristics are for the particular project and the particular needs of the occupants. After establishing the top priorities in the selection of a building material, as many other green features should be incorporated as possible.

Green building design is an integrated, holistic process with a greater goal than the sum of its individual material components. Much more important than agonizing over the greenness of each and every material is the process of creating wonderful, healthy spaces that provide human contact to the natural environment while not over-using energy resources (perhaps even *producing* net energy), enhancing the surrounding environment, and supporting the local economy and culture.

[1] http://www.physics.otago.ac.nz/eman/403downloads/ AS4_EmbodiedEnergyCoeffs.pdf

[2] Triangle J. Council of Governments, *WasteSpec: Model Specifications for Construction Waste, Reduction, Reuse, and Recycling,* 1995.

[3] EPA Document No. EPA-832-R-92-005, Chapter 3.

[4] Texas Water Development Board and Center for Maximum Potential Building Systems, *Texas Guide to Rainwater Harvesting*, 1997.

[5] *Environmental Building News*, Vol 2, No. 2, March-April, 1993.

[6] Ibid

[7] American Institute of Architects, *Environmental Resource Guide*, John Wiley & Sons, 1996.

[8] http://www.epsea.org/adobe.html

[9] R-value is a measure of thermal resistivity, the opposite of conductivity. The higher a material's R-value, the better it will insulate against heat transfer. The overall R-value of a building envelope assembly (an exterior wall, for instance) is determined by adding up the individual R-values of the components of the assembly. If, however, a conductive material spans from one side of the assembly to the other, heat will travel along this "path of least resistance," just as it will rush through an open window in an otherwise sealed wall.

[10] *Environmental Building News*, Vol 3, No. 4, July-August, 1994.

[11] Ibid.

[12] Ibid.

[13] http://www.physics.otago.ac.nz/eman/403downloads/ AS4_EmbodiedEnergyCoeffs.pdf

[14] Truss Joist MacMillan product literature, 1998.

[15] Energy Design Update "How Thermal Shorts and Insulation Flaws Can Degrade and 'R-19' Stud Wall to a Measly 'R-11' "; Johns-Manville Research and Development Center "Effects of Insulation Gaps," Nov., 1979. Information cited at http://www.westerngreen.com/miscellany.htm

[16] Building Science Corporation and Energy Efficient Building Association, *Builder's Guide*, 1998.

[17] Ibid.

[18] Ibid.

[19] Mahone, Doug, *Inclusion of Coof Roofs in Title 24: California Building Energy Efficiency Standards, Revisions for July 2003 Adoption*, 2001.

[20] http://www.photonics.com/Content/Aug97/techMatsu.html

[21] *Design Handbook for Residential Woodburning Equipment*, Auburn, Alabama, June, 1981.

[22] *Environmental Building News*, Vol. 1, No. 2, September/October, 1992.

[23] Lyle, David, *The Book of Masonry Stove: Rediscovering an Old Way of Warming*, Brick House Publishing Co., Inc., 1984.

[24] Energy Educators of Ontario, *Energy Fact Sheet*, 1993; available at http://www.iclei.org/efacts/photovol.htm

[25] *Environmental Building News*, Vol. 6, No. 9, October, 1997.

[26] *Environmental Building News*, Vol. 7, No. 8, September, 1998.

[27] Light viewed during the night interrupts melatonin production, according to Nancy Clanton, PE, IESNA, President of Clanton Engineering, Board Member of the International Dark Skies Association.

[28] *Environmental Building News*, Vol. 7, No. 8, September, 1998

[29] Ibid.

[30] E Source, Inc., "Cooling Demands from Office Equipment and Other Plug Loads: Less than One Watt Per Square Foot," Report #TU-96-9, 1996.

Chapter

3 Efficient Use of Energy & Other Resources

James Armstrong, CPE, CEM

A green design team develops a vision of a facility that considers the entire building and how it interacts with its surroundings, its occupants, and internal operations. This chapter will explore the way in which the building systems design can drastically impact the consumables required to meet the desired design conditions, including occupant comfort. It will first review the factors to consider, then outline some strategies for reducing the use of energy and other natural resources. It should also be noted that energy equipment and building technologies improve regularly, and designers must make an extra effort to evaluate new alternatives rather than merely repeating the last successful design solution.

The Building Envelope & Systems Interactions

The building envelope must be considered as surrounding a dynamic and constantly changing environment, rather than as a static box in which architects and engineers tend to design systems to perform based on extreme conditions. The building has many processes and interactions going on within it every minute of every day. The concept of green design requires the designer to meet these varying conditions in an energy-efficient manner, using systems and or components that appropriately interact. These interactions can be as simple as daylight entering a space, or as complex as manufacturing processes running within the facility, and they affect the dynamics of the building's consumable resources (energy, water). The building's systems capability and/or reactions with other systems must be taken into account in order to achieve the desired design conditions.

The interaction processes can be divided into four categories:
1. Ventilation
2. Envelope
3. Occupancy
4. Process

Ventilation

Ventilation, or movement of air in and out of a building, is accomplished in one of two ways: **mechanical infiltration** and **ventilation.** Infiltration occurs even without a mechanical ventilation system installed. Infiltration is the entering and/or escaping of air from one space to another, usually due to pressure or temperature differential. Infiltration occurs in routes established during construction, and over time through cracks that form as the building settles.

The **temperature differential**—between different spaces within the building, or between the indoor and outdoor temperature—can cause the air to migrate through open doors, windows, and other means of egress or settlement cracks. The temperature differential causes a buoyant pressure difference and natural convection currents. Warm air tends to leak out the top of a building, while cold air comes in through lower openings. Infiltration is also caused by the pressure difference between the windward and leeward sides of a building.

Infiltration may be adequate to ventilate the space if there is no requirement for, or any existing, mechanical ventilation. Depending on the building type, mechanical ventilation may or may not be required. For example, infiltration augmented by operable windows is usually sufficient for residences.

Mechanical ventilation brings into the "box" outside air, which must be conditioned prior to entering the space (heated, cooled, humidified, or dehumidified) in order to meet the design criteria for the space. Depending on the era of construction, ventilation varies widely. The ASHRAE (American Society of Heating, Refrigerating, and Air-Conditioning Engineers) guidelines, such as ASHRAE 62, specify ventilation requirements for the building depending on usage, type, and or the projected occupancy for the space.

Proper ventilation is one of the cornerstones of a green building design. The key to achieving energy efficiency while maintaining a proper amount of fresh air (10-20 CFM of OA, or outside air, per person) is recovering the thermal energy from the exhausted air and using it to pre-heat or pre-cool the entering air. This energy recovery reduces the required consumable energy needed to condition the air. Desiccant wheels can exchange moisture between the fresh air and exhaust air, allowing "enthalpy" recovery as well. *(See "Heat Recovery Systems" later in this chapter.)*

Ventilation requirements are usually driven by human occupancy, and a control system that measures and responds to varying occupancy has the potential for tremendous savings. For example, most courtrooms are ventilated according to their design (maximum) occupancy, which might only occur once every five years. Installing controls to detect occupancy and modulate the ventilation rate can reduce significantly the amount of outside air that needs to be conditioned.

Often the movement of air is used for two purposes: to act as a flowing medium to heat and cool the space, and to provide fresh air (oxygen) to the occupants. A green design approach (advocated by Vivian Loftness of Carnegie Mellon University) is to separate the fresh air function from the space conditioning function, which enables the designer to optimize each independently and reduce the overall fan power.

The Building Envelope

The building envelope is a major determining factor in a building's energy consumption. The envelope controls the impact of outside conditions on the interior spaces, while the HVAC systems strive to maintain the specified design conditions. An example is sunlight entering the space through the windows, doors, and/or skylights. Sunlight adds solar heat to the space. Depending on the climate, the design set point for temperature can be exceeded due to the thermal solar gains. The building systems will then strive to achieve set point by attempting to condition, or cool, the space. In North America, a space with a south-facing façade with large window walls will require more cooling than a north-facing space with similar window walls. Heat must be added to the north-facing space and removed from the south-facing space. This is a normal dynamic for many office buildings in northern climates, even in the middle of the winter. Adding to this equation is the heat gain from building occupants, lighting, and computers or other equipment, which may require that the building needs be cooled year-round, and may never need heat. This is common in many southern climates. Solar gain through windows accounts for 32% of needed cooling energy in U.S. buildings (with 41% caused by heat from electric lighting, 17% from equipment, 7.5% from people, and the rest from heat conduction through roofs and walls).

The perimeters of these same buildings' may at times have too much light, and yet the buildings' lighting systems are still on. With green design, it is possible to shut off or dim the electrical lighting to maintain even lighting levels, and to incorporate skylight shafts, clerestory windows, glass interior walls, and other daylighting techniques, to bring natural light into more of the building. A green design would also transfer heat from the overheated to the under-heated sections and use outside air economizer systems to cool whenever the outdoor ambient temperature meets the design conditions without the use of mechanical cooling.

Green design also relies on trees to provide seasonal shade, thereby reducing the need for mechanical cooling. A deciduous, or leaf-bearing, tree planted on the south-facing wall will shade the light during the summer months with its leaves, and provide natural cooling. This tree will lose its leaves in the fall and allow the space to receive natural lighting and solar heat in the winter months. Trees also reduce the water consumption of the lawn underneath by two thirds. Trees are effective for shading west walls when the sun is low in the sky. This is true green design—using natural elements to reduce the consumable energy required to condition a space.

The insulation and vapor-retardant limitations of the envelope can also have a tremendous impact on the consumable energy required for a space. For years, wall and ceiling insulation has been touted as the best way to reduce the energy loss of a space. What has not been well explained are the limitations of insulation. Buildings need to breathe somewhat in order to provide fresh air for the occupants and remove moisture. Insulation, as part of the wall and roof systems, should be considered in context of all the building systems, including HVAC. Insulation materials also need to be examined for their effects on health, and the environmental impact of their production. *(See Chapter 2 for more on insulation choices.)*

Some designers have changed the function of the building skin by replacing conventional building materials, such as glass, with photovoltaic (PV) panel systems. The change in appearance from the outside may be acceptable, and the envelope becomes a part of the building's ability to self-generate electricity in a sustainable method. *(See Chapter 4 and the Appendix for photovoltaic systems.)*

Roof design has made major strides where sustainability is concerned. Because the roof is the most weather-impacted part of a building envelope, designers must consider long-term solutions to the conditions caused by weather exposure. Selection of roof materials for a green building involves health, environmental, and energy considerations. The available materials have pros and cons. Coal tar and gravel, for example, can be produced from recycled materials, whereas EPDM roofing is made from virgin materials. (LEED provides a listing of roofing materials with their environmental impacts that can be helpful in making selections.) Some green roofing approaches include changing the color of a roof to reduce the thermal gains by reflecting solar heat, using recycled or recyclable material (such as shingles manufactured from slate dust), and using material that has a longer life (such as metal or polymer roofing systems). A **protected-membrane roofing system** allows reuse of the rigid insulation during future re-roofing, substantially reducing material use.

Some roofs have become a resource as well as a shield. Rain can be collected by a roofing system connected to a cistern (collection tank) so that the water can be used for other purposes. *(See "Rainwater Collection Systems" later in this chapter.)* Living roofs become their own ecosystem, with plantings and grass contained within the membrane. This strategy provides insulation, alleviates run-off, and helps to meet the impervious surface requirements on some facilities so that more building can be accomplished with less land.

The key to understanding the impact of the envelope is the interactions and changes that occur within and through it. Changing the envelope to become a more dynamic component of the building is a critical part of green design.

Occupancy & Controls

This is the human impact on the space design conditions. The human body gives off heat at various rates depending on activity level and inherent characteristics. Human beings also require oxygen, the main reason for ventilation of a space. The higher the occupancy of a space, the more ventilation will be required, with less heat required in colder climates or seasons, and a higher cooling load in warmer climates or seasons.

Occupancy is also a variable that can be monitored in a facility's energy use. The type of usage of a facility can drastically change the energy requirements of a space. Typically the cubic feet of space per person is the main criterion for ventilation. In most residential situations, this factor has minimum impact, since the cubic feet per person tends to be much higher than in commercial spaces. An exception is a dormitory or bunkroom, which requires more air exchange than an apartment. Auditoriums, conference spaces, and gymnasiums are extreme examples. A conference room may have an occupancy capacity of 100 people. This same space may be normally occupied for only five hours per day, and is only at capacity on six occasions per year. The space has HVAC and lighting systems that were designed to maintain the entire space at peak, or design, conditions. This brings in too much fresh air and more lighting than is needed most of the time. This space could benefit from "smart controls," such as sensors, for a combined net impact of as much as one-third of the total required energy. The occupants are just as comfortable, yet the consumable energy required is reduced.

There is technology currently available that monitors the CO_2 levels of the return air, a good indicator of a space's occupancy. This sensor, when integrated into a building management system, can modulate the fresh air requirements based on desired conditions. Occupancy sensors can also be used to shut off lights in unoccupied spaces. Time clock systems shut down the air handlers and other mechanical systems (as well as lights) when a space is scheduled to be unoccupied. These interactions make the building more dynamic and more efficient.

Process

Many facilities in North America use vast quantities of consumable commodities in order to complete a process, whether it is making photocopies or manufacturing automobiles. The processes should be reviewed to reduce the waste by-products or reuse these products in some fashion. Many facilities require year-round air conditioning due to the heat gain from their internal processes. Existing facilities and planned new construction need to be reviewed as a whole. The interactions of each process should be considered, including water usage, heat requirements, emissions, cooling requirements, and ventilation requirements. All of these should be measured and catalogued. *(Chapter 14 provides information on available energy modeling programs.)*

Sub-metering of equipment and processes is a component of green building design and operation. It allows for the operator to better understand the various components of a facility and can be used to make further improvements and/or establish operating requirements in order to minimize the consumption of energy and natural resources.

Energy Efficiency Strategies

Roofs

The following paragraphs explore energy considerations related to roofing materials. Insulation for roofs and exterior walls is addressed in "Wall and Roof Insulation" later in this section.

Reflectivity

Research by energy service companies, product manufacturers, and entities such as the Lawrence Berkeley National Laboratory (LBNL) are demonstrating the potential of reflective roofing to conserve energy, mitigate "urban heat islands," and improve air quality. Development in areas such as the U.S. Sunbelt has resulted in increased temperature and smog, as green areas and shade trees have been replaced with dark paving and roofs. Black roofs (such as EPDM, asphalt, and modified bitumen) have been shown to have a 6% reflectivity and temperatures 75-100 degrees hotter than the ambient temperature, while white, reflective roof membranes can reflect 80% of the heat, with roof temperatures only 15-25 degrees warmer than the ambient temperature.

Cooler reflecting roofs not only release less heat into the environment, but have a major effect on the building's interior temperature, thereby reducing cooling costs by as much as 30%. The net yearly impact depends on the building's particular location. (In extreme northern conditions, lower reflectivity may be preferred, as heat gain may be required for other reasons, including snow melting.) In addition to saving energy by reducing solar heat gain, cooler roofing materials can increase the longevity of the roof system itself.

A variety of coatings and materials can provide light colors and reflectivity. Like all products, selection of these systems should include evaluation of demonstrated life cycle and maintenance costs and a good warranty, supported by a reliable manufacturer. The Energy Star® program has established specifications for roofing products, including a solar reflectance of at least 65% for low-slope and steep-slope use, and 81% for low-slope only, when the product is initially installed. (www.energystar.gov/products — click on "Roof Products.") It should be noted that durability and maintenance influence reflectance, as the percentage can be reduced by surface weathering and dirt accumulation.

Appearance may be a factor in selection of reflective roofing, particularly in residential applications where sloped roofs are more visible than the low-slope roofs more common on commercial buildings. Houses may also have attics to help reduce the effect of heat gain on air-cooling requirements.

Living Roof System

"Green Roofs" involve a waterproof membrane applied on a roof deck, then covered with earth that will grow grass or other vegetation to collect the rain and minimize the impact of the site's impervious surfaces. Living roofs also provide thermal insulation and generate oxygen, causing a net reduction in a facility's CO_2 generation.

Green roof considerations include:

- Structural requirements (the sod and plantings can weigh as little as 2 lbs./SF in some systems, or as much as 150 lbs./SF in others).
- Careful waterproofing (leaks being extremely difficult to pinpoint once the growing materials are in place).
- Maximum roof pitch of 17%.
- Best suited to wetter areas; can be a fire hazard in hot, dry climates.
- Maintenance requirements.
- Required certification by the contractor installing the membrane.

Green roofs can be as simple as 6" grass growing in sod, or as large and elaborate as a whole garden with seating areas. In addition to tremendous energy savings, green roofs provide aesthetic benefits, and, properly cared for, can last much longer than conventional roof decks, since the sod and plant materials protect the waterproof membrane from ultraviolet light. National and state green building organizations, such as can be found at **www.dnr.state.md.us/smartgrowth/ greenbuilding/roofing.html**, can be good sources of additional information.

Exterior Walls
"Active Walls"

In addition to using recycled framing, sheathing, and insulation materials, walls can be green by virtue of their energy efficiencies—both passive (sunspaces, for example, that collect and store heat) and active. Active walls act as a generator or collector of energy. An example is a double glass wall that collects solar energy and is designed to reflect the thermal energy when the interior envelope temperatures have been reached. This combination reduces the net heating and cooling loads of a facility. Another example of an active wall is one comprised of solar collectors. An office tower that might normally have a glass façade could instead be faced with active photovoltaic panels that generate electricity to be used in the building. This approach reduces the overall construction requirements because the engineered active panels replace the glass or brick typically used. (The Durst Building at 4 Times Square in New York City is an example of this design approach.)

Wall & Roof Insulation

Adding insulation to an existing building is the simplest of all measures and one that homeowners have been practicing for years. The insulation value of the building is increased to a point where its thermal energy remains in the building. The impact of outside environmental conditions on interior conditions is reduced. This approach has a limited opportunity in commercial facilities due to the volume of fresh air they require. Selecting appropriate insulation for a new, sustainable building is key to strategies to reduce energy use.

The many insulation systems available today offer a variety of R-values and other features. However, it is important to consider the entire building envelope, not just insulation, and to design it to eliminate moisture (from the wall pocket), while minimizing the thermal conductivity between the indoor and outdoor air. This is true for any design, not just green design. As designers establish the cross-section of a wall, its dew point must be considered. Water will condense in the coldest part of a wall. Since humid air can travel through the insulation but heat cannot, the vapor barrier is placed on the warm side of the insulation (outside in a cooling climate, inside in a heating climate). This is a sustainable design issue for other reasons besides energy efficiency, as a poorly designed wall will fail in 10-20 years, and the mold growth promoted by the moisture will be a source of indoor air quality problems. Constructing replacement walls can result in significant cost, disruption, and waste of natural resources. The design should consider and minimize the environmental impact over time, and allow for the building dynamics.

The thermal resistance of insulation is measured in **R-value**, which is the resistance to heat flow (in °F per hr/BTU/S.F., degrees of temperature difference divided by wall area and heat loss rate in BTU/hr). Common forms of insulation used in the building envelope are loose-fill, batt, rigid board stock, and foamed-in-place. Materials and corresponding R-values are listed in Figure 3.1. Material selection criteria should include cost and R-value, but also effects on indoor air quality and health, energy, and other environmental impacts during manufacturing. Cellulose, fiberglass, and cotton can all have high-recycled content, depending on the supplier. (Cotton batt insulation has the additional advantage of being easy to handle.) When selecting foam insulation, it is important to specify that no harmful gases (chlorofluorocarbons, or CFCs) be used to expand the foam. Any insulation selected should meet

Insulation R-values

Material	R-value per inch thickness (°F per hr/BTU/inch)
Mineral Fiber	3.3 to 4.3
Glass Fiber	4.0
Perlite	2.8 to 3.7
Polystyrene	3.8 (expanded) 5.0 (extruded)
Cellular Polyisocyanurate	5.6 to7.0
Cellulose, loose fill	3.1 to 3.7
Polyurethane, spray applied foam	5.6 to 6.2
Cotton, batt	3.4
Source: 1997 ASHRAE Fundamentals Handbook; cotton statistics from Environmental Building News	

Figure 3.1

all applicable fire rating, pest-resistance, and insulation value product standards set forth by ASTM and others. ASHRAE 90.1 specifies required insulation criteria for building envelope components, dependent on heating degree days and other factors.

Fenestration

Low-Emissivity (or Low-E) Glass

Emissivity is defined as the ability of a product to emit or receive radiant rays, thus decreasing the U-value. *(U-factors represent the heat loss per unit area per degree of temperature difference, BTU/S.F./°F. They are reported by the National Fenestration Rating Council, NFRC).* Most non-metallic solids can emit or receive radiant rays and, therefore, have a high degree of emissivity. Fenestrations that reflect radiant rays have a low emissivity. Use of low-E glass windows allows the daylight to enter the building, but reduces the amount of thermal energy from the sun that enters the building envelope. The result is a reduction in the facility's net cooling requirements.[1]

Heat Mirror Technology

This type of fenestration uses a low-emissivity coated film product suspended inside or between the panes of an insulating glass unit. This is a lower-cost alternative to low-E glass double-pane units.[2]

Window Films

Films can be applied to the surface of an existing window to change the optical properties. Unlike the wavy, bubbly polyester films of the past, today's acrylic films are hardly noticeable. These films are designed to reduce the amount of solar heat transmission through window glass by increasing the solar reflection (not necessarily visible reflection) and decreasing solar absorption of the glass.[3]

Opaque Insulated Fenestration

A composite fenestration that combines controlled, usable, natural daylight with highly energy-efficient properties. This product has R-values (insulation values) from R-4 through R-12. (Typical windows have an R-value of 1.) The translucent wall panels allow for natural lighting without the thermal energy loss normally associated with windows. The panels are lightweight and shatterproof, and have impressive structural integrity.[4]

Doors

In addition to seeking sustainable door materials made from recycled material or certified lumber, it is important to look for energy efficiency in the form of exterior door R-value and appropriate door seals. Jamb materials merit attention as they can also reduce conductive heat loss on exterior doors.

Vestibules

A vestibule is an area between two sets of doors, serving as an air lock at a building's entrance. Vestibules minimize the infiltration of exterior conditions into the space within the building envelope.

At Mount Wachussett Ski area base lodge, the building is heated with over 400 kW of electric resistance heat. A utility-sponsored energy study demonstrated that the building would be more comfortable and reduce its electric heating load by 40% with the installation of vestibules. Not only was the energy reduced, but the ticket agents no longer had to wear gloves because the existing systems could now keep up with the heat loss at the main door.[5]

Air Doors

Air doors, sometimes called *air walls*, are typically used for garage-type or larger doors to reduce infiltration and ex-filtration. An air door creates an invisible barrier of high-velocity air that separates different environments. Air enters the unit through the intake and is then compressed by scrolled fan housings and forced through a nozzle, which is directed at the open doorway. The system utilizes centrifugal fans mounted on direct-driven, dual-shafted motors. The result is a uniform air screen across the opening with enough force to stop winds up to 25 mph.[6]

Plastic Curtains

Plastic curtains reduce infiltration and ex-filtration. They are an economical solution for protecting employees and goods from adverse environmental conditions. Plastic curtain or strip doors are inexpensive, easy to install, and save energy.

HVAC Systems
Right-Sizing HVAC Systems

Buildings are typically designed based on extreme conditions. The heating system is sized based on a "design day" (the average coldest day in that location) and the design occupancy for the space. The cooling system is sized based on a "design day" (the average hottest day) with design occupancy for the space. Buildings may operate at these design conditions for only 1% of the year. When specifying equipment sizes, engineers might allow design conditions to be exceeded 1%, 2.5%, or 5% of the time. (For critical applications, such as artifact storage or hospitals, exceeding the design conditions might be allowed for only a very small fraction of the time, say 0.1%.) While the capacity of an HVAC system might be designed to be exceeded only 1% of the time, in reality there would be no consequences if it were exceeded 2.5% or even 5% of the time.

Right-sizing rather than over-sizing is essential for green design of mechanical systems. It is important for the designer to ascertain what the requirements are, and then to specify an efficient mechanical system to meet, but not exceed, those sizing requirements. To be fair, owners must agree to this in the contract: that the designer will be free from liability if the environmental conditions exceed the design conditions for some fraction of the year. Clearly, there are huge savings in first cost and operating cost if engineers would stop over-sizing equipment in order to avoid liability if indoor conditions stray slightly from desired conditions (too warm, too humid) for a limited number of hours per year.

Heating System Efficiency

In sizing boilers and furnaces to meet the building's actual load and operating requirements, two basic conditions need to be understood:

1. Standard efficiency units are more efficient when fully loaded.

2. Condensing units are more efficient when part-loaded.

Because engineers and facility managers depend on the reliability of heating systems, they have typically installed multiple units, often two or three boilers. One was supposed to be sufficient to heat the building, and the second was a backup. This evolved into a three-boiler system with two units sized for the peak load and the third as a backup for either base unit. With new energy code requirements, the over-sizing of systems is no longer permitted. Designers must now size systems for the actual conditions without backup factors. (The other method is to use staged systems to meet the peak load, especially with cooling systems.)

When selecting components for a facility, it is important to understand the types and efficiencies of available equipment. The most common way to obtain equipment efficiency is the ASHRAE efficiency rating, a measure of how effectively a gas or oil heating system converts fuel into useful heat. This measure is defined by the BTUs of fuel going into a unit as compared to the effective number of BTUs of heat output by a unit. The difference is the energy that goes up the stack. There are two common types of efficiency ratings:

- **Combustion Efficiency (CE):** The system's efficiency while it is running. Combustion efficiency is like the miles per gallon a car gets when it is cruising at a steady speed on the highway. This measurement is typically used to define boilers and hot water heaters.

- **Annual Fuel Utilization Efficiency (AFUE):** This seasonal efficiency rating is a more accurate estimation of fuel use. It is a measure of the system efficiency and accounts for start-up, cool-down, and other operating losses that occur under normal operating conditions. AFUE is like a car's mileage over all kinds of driving conditions, from stop-and-go traffic to highway driving. This measurement is typically applied to furnaces and direct-fired forced hot air systems.[7]

Following are brief system descriptions and operating efficiencies, which can vary by manufacturer.

Boilers: Hot Water

- Standard efficiency: 80% Combustion Efficiency (CE).
- High-efficiency oil/gas units: 84-87% CE. These boilers operate with lower stack temperatures.
- Condensing propane and natural gas boilers: 88-96% CE. Condensing boilers operate with stack temperatures below 246° F. At this temperature, the water in the exhaust gas condenses in the stack. The lower stack temperatures effectively cause less stack losses and a net increase in combustion efficiency.

Boilers: Steam

- Standard efficiency: 80% CE.
- High-efficiency oil/gas units: 82–84% CE.

Makeup Air & Air Side Systems

These are the building's fresh air systems that require some pre-treating or pre-heating.

High AFUE is a measure of the system efficiency.

- Standard-efficiency systems can range from 80-85% AFUE.
- High-efficiency systems can range from 85-95% AFUE.[8]

(Also consider solar preheat of ventilation air using the perforated collector described in Chapter 4.)

Efficiency Controls

Efficiency controls for boilers and furnaces include:

- **Pressure Reset Systems:** Used on steam systems to allow for wide fluctuations in pressure. As a result, the burners can be shut off longer and stay on longer, with fewer cycles. Avoiding short cycles increases the net system efficiency.
- **Dead Band Widening:** Used on steam systems to allow for a wide system dead band, or time delay, from the set point. Again, the burners can be shut off longer and stay on longer, with fewer cycles. Avoiding short boiler cycling increases the net system efficiency.

- **Reset Controls:** Used in hot water systems to inversely control the hot water loop set point as compared to the outdoor temperature. For example, the system may be set for 180° F when the outdoor temperature is 0° F and, inversely, the loop temperature could be 120° F when the outdoor air temp is 45° F. The lower water temperature setting allows more efficient heating when outdoor temperatures are less severe.

Other methods to improve boiler efficiency include:

- Decentralized systems (to reduce distribution losses).
- Modernize boiler controls (install feed-forward control-type systems). Feed-forward controls react more quickly by monitoring the entire system. Rather than reacting to swings in operating pressures or temperatures, these systems maintain the loads based on actual usage.
- Install an economizer heat exchanger in the flue to preheat the boiler feed water.
- Install an oxygen trim system to optimize the fuel/air ratio that monitors stack conditions and continuous stack gas analysis for combustion control.
- Reduce excess air-to-boiler combustion.
- Consider opportunities for cogeneration (combined heat and power), including the use of fuel cells and microturbines as the heat source.

Radiant Heat

Under-floor systems use much lower water temperatures (typically 110-120° F). These systems are tied to condensing boilers or other low-temperature systems, such as ground-source heat pumps. This approach takes advantage of lower water temperatures, which are otherwise only effective with oversized radiation systems. These systems maintain one of the most constant building temperatures, as the radiant system retains its heat for long periods of time. The floor becomes a large thermal mass or thermal storage system. This creates comfortable and more consistent space temperatures. The only downside to radiant systems is that you cannot reset the temperatures when a space is unoccupied, and they tend to be more expensive than traditional heating systems.

Heat Recovery Systems

Heat wheels, or enthalpy wheels, remove moisture from the ambient air, while also cooling the ventilated air by passing all incoming air over a desiccant-coated wheel. The wheel rotates, and this same desiccant migrates from the incoming air to the exhaust air, where the moisture is exhausted outdoors. This process removes up to 85% of the heat and moisture from the exhaust air and transfers that heat to the intake air in winter. These systems also remove heat from intake air in summer and transfer it to the exhaust air. In both conditions, the result is a reduction in the net load of the fresh air systems on the facility's energy requirement for conditioning. Heat recovery systems contribute in two different ways to a sustainable, healthy building. They reduce humidity to a level that is not conducive to dust mite and mold growth, and their ability to recover heat and moisture greatly reduces the energy required to heat or cool the ventilation air. Heat recovery systems also enable a reduction in the heating and cooling capacity of the system.[9]

Air-to-Air Heat Exchangers

An energy recovery ventilator (ERV) is a type of mechanical equipment that features a heat exchanger, combined with a ventilation system for providing controlled ventilation into a building. Typically this is an air-to-air, plate-type heat exchanger.[10]

Heat Sink Systems

This is also an ERV, but uses the principal of exhausting over a thermal heat sink, then switching the incoming air to travel over the heat sink that was heated by the exhaust air.[11]

Alternative Heating Systems

Infrared Heaters: Electric, propane, or natural gas units heat the materials and equipment, not the air within the space. These units typically have lower combustion efficiency, but a higher heat transfer or emissivity, yielding higher efficiency.

Solar Thermal Systems

Solar collectors gather energy when the sun is shining and use thermal storage or an auxiliary system to supplement the heat when the sun is not shining. Solar water heating is often cost-effective. For space heating, passive solar architecture is preferred over solar mechanical solutions.[12] *(See Chapter 4 and the Appendix for full coverage of solar electrical and heating and hot water systems.)*

Cooling Systems
Cooling & Refrigeration

Refrigeration is the process of lowering and maintaining the temperature in a given space for the purpose of chilling foods, preserving certain substances, or providing an atmosphere conducive to bodily comfort. Storing perishable foods, furs, pharmaceuticals, or other items under refrigeration is commonly known as **cold storage**. Such refrigeration prevents both bacterial growth and adverse chemical reactions that occur in the normal atmosphere.

In mechanical refrigeration, constant cooling is achieved by the circulation of a refrigerant in a closed system, in which it evaporates to a gas and then condenses back again to a liquid in a continuous cycle. If no leakage occurs, the refrigerant lasts indefinitely throughout the entire life of the system. All that is required to maintain cooling is a constant supply of power, and a method of dissipating waste heat. The two main types of mechanical refrigeration systems used are the **compression system,** used in domestic units for large cold-storage applications and for most air conditioning; and the **absorption system,** now employed largely for heat-operated air-conditioning units, but formerly also used for heat-operated domestic units.[13]

Three things must be considered when choosing a "green" cooling system.

1. **Refrigerant Type:** Depending on the type of cooling system, the refrigerant can be carcinogenic, flammable, ozone-depleting, or totally neutral and drinkable (water). For green systems, only the non-CFC type refrigerants are acceptable—whether for air conditioning or refrigeration of food products or process equipment. To establish the type of refrigerant and alternatives, check the following Web site: **http://www.epa.gov/ozone/index.html**

2. **Energy Usage:** One of the fundamentals of green building design is the use of energy-efficient equipment. A later section in this chapter will review typical energy usage for various types of energy use for delivered cooling. The actual usage should be supplied by the manufacturer and certified by the ARI (American Refrigeration Institute). Refer to the following Web site for an explanation of the calculations of efficiency ARI Standard 550/590-1998: **http://www.ari.org/pr/1999/990114-550.html**

3. **Waste Heat Removal:** All types of cooling remove heat from one space and convey it to another. The type of waste heat removal has a direct relationship to the energy efficiency. Following are the basic types of waste heat removal systems: air-cooled, evaporative-cooled, water-cooled, and air-cooled coil.

Air-Cooled Systems

The most common type of waste heat removal is air-cooled, which requires a fan to move air across a coil to remove heat. This method has the lowest temperature differential between the refrigerant and the atmosphere. Air is also a fair to poor heat transfer medium. This is not the preferred method for optimum energy efficiency. There are some oversized condensers that have a higher EER than smaller condenser systems; these are an allowable exception.

Evaporative Cooling

This method uses technology similar to air-cooled, except that water is added to the air stream and is allowed to evaporate in the cooling process. The result is a larger temperature differential. Introducing water into the air stream also creates a better heat transfer medium. The water is typically collected into a sump, and pumps are used to spray the water over the coils. Some of the water is evaporated, and some is re-circulated. The sump typically has a makeup water system for the water that has been evaporated. For green building design, gray water recovery can be used, as opposed to fresh water, for the makeup supply.

Water-Cooling

These systems are heat exchanger-based. The refrigerant passes through a heat exchanger on one side, and water is passed through the heat exchanger on the other. The water is then sent outside to a waste heat removal system.

Air-Cooled Coil

This method is most commonly used on smaller systems that require year-round operation (e.g., computer cooling systems). The cooling medium may have glycol added to allow the system to be operated throughout the seasons and to reduce the potential for freezing. If using this system in a green building, the designers should strive to recover this heat. In some facilities this waste heat is used to prehcat domestic water or the return lines from a hydronic heating system. In green design the air-cooled coil should only be used when all of the heat has been recovered for other uses. Excess heat must still be rejected from water and should only be used as a last resort.

Cooling Towers

Cooling towers take advantage of the evaporative properties of water. Water is sprayed over large surface areas, and large volumes of air are forced over the surfaces. The air and water mixture causes evaporation and latent heat removal. Depending on the cooling tower design and the ambient wet bulb temperature (outdoor temperature), the water temperature may actually become cooler than the ambient dry bulb temperature. In some manufacturing facilities, this process is used as the process thermal heat removal system. The following Web site provides more information regarding the evaporative cooling principle: http://www.piec.com/page3.htm

For green building design, recovered gray water (as opposed to fresh, potable water) can be used in the makeup supply. One of the keys to effective cooling tower design is increasing the surface area and using propeller-type fans. These fans use one half the energy of "squirrel cage fans," but require larger towers.

Mechanical Cooling Systems

Air-Cooled Direct Expansion Systems (DX): In DX systems, the refrigerant expands through the TXV (thermal expansion valve), then removes heat from the air stream by way of the DX coil. For DX systems to operate, the refrigerant must be compressed from a low-temperature, low-pressure gas to a high-temperature, high-pressure gas in the compressor, where the heat is then removed by air- or liquid-cooling. Gas coil-to-air heat exchange is not as efficient as gas coil-to-liquid heat exchange, as the thermal conductivity is typically lower than water. Therefore, in general terms, air-cooled refrigeration systems are not as efficient as water-cooled systems. However, some manufacturers have increased the efficiency of air-cooled equipment by increasing heat surface area and using larger fans.

Evaporative-cooled condenser systems will typically drop the energy usage of any compressor system by 10-20%, depending on weather conditions. Evaporative-cooling involves the spraying of water over the condenser of a refrigeration system and allowing the water to evaporate. This evaporation increases the system's ability to remove heat.[14]

Free Cooling Systems: Plate and frame heat exchangers, or "free cooling systems," are used when there are wide swings in outdoor conditions, and there is a building need for cooling most of the year. This system uses the evaporative cooling of the cooling tower system and a plate and frame heat exchanger to remove heat from the chilled water system directly to the condenser water system without the need for mechanical cooling.

Free cooling systems have also been described as "airside free cooling." They bring the cool outdoor air into the space and mix it with the treated air to achieve the desired conditions without mechanical cooling.

Compression-Type Refrigeration Technologies

- Electric scroll compressors: electric-powered rotary compressors for small 1-5 ton systems that use less electricity than conventional reciprocating refrigeration compressors, typically .9-1.4 kWh/ton Hr.[15]
- Electric screw compressors: electric-powered rotary compressors for larger 10-100 ton systems. These also use less

electricity than traditional reciprocating refrigeration compressors, typically .7-.95 kWh/ton Hr.[16]

Natural Gas-Fired Air-Conditioning Systems

Natural gas-fired air-conditioning systems are an option for green building designers due to their net energy savings. With any electric system there are inherent losses associated with the distribution of electricity. The average power plant has a heat rate or efficiency of 20-35% of energy output in kWh to energy input BTUs. There are also energy losses due to the transmission of electricity over wires over many miles. If a facility operates with gas-fired equipment, the heat rate for internal combustion equipment is typically 35%, with no transmission losses. Natural gas-fired units can have:

- Reciprocating compressors (used for 10-100 ton systems typically use 12-14 MBTU of natural gas per ton-hour of cooling[17]). These are equally efficient, yet have none of the electrical transmission losses associated with conventional electric power.
- Screw compressors (used for 10-100 ton systems typically use 12-14 MBTU of natural gas per ton-hour of cooling[18]).

Chilled Water Systems

In chilled water systems, the refrigerant expands through the TXV (thermal expansion valve), then removes heat from the chilled water medium, which is circulated through a facility and into the air stream by way of a chilled water coil. Like air-cooled DX systems, chilled water system refrigerant needs to be compressed from a low- to a high-temperature, high-pressure gas in the compressor, with the heat removed in the condenser. Again, the condenser can be air- or liquid-cooled. The system loses some efficiency due to the multiple heat exchanges; however, the heat exchange, typically liquid-to-liquid, is very efficient, as the thermal conductivity tends to be higher in water.

In general terms, water-cooled systems are more efficient than air-cooled systems. They are rated by their IPLV (integrated part load value). Refer to the following Web site for details: **http://www.trane.com/commercial/library/vol281/table2.asp**

IPLV Ratings

Air-Cooled Chillers:

- Chillers with Screw Compressors (25–100 tons), typical IPLV .9-.75 kWh/ton Hr.
- Air-Cooled Scroll Chillers (1–25 tons), typical IPLV .95-1.2 kWh/ton Hr.
- Evaporative-Cooled Chillers (25–100 tons), typical IPLV .85-.7 kWh/ton Hr.

Water-Cooled Chillers
- Screw Chillers (25–100 tons), typical IPLV .8-.60 kWh/ton Hr.
- Centrifugal Chillers (100–3,000 tons), typical IPLV .7-.5 kWh/ton Hr.
- Centrifugal Chillers with VFDs (100-3,000 tons), typical IPLV .6-.4.2 kWh/ton Hr.

Absorption Chillers

One of the oldest artificial cooling systems available, absorption cooling is a chemical reaction type of cooling system that uses heat to separate water from lithium bromide. Once the solutions have been separated, heat is rejected through a condenser heat exchanger, which condenses the steam and cools the lithium bromide. The two chemicals are then allowed to mix in the absorber where the lithium bromide absorbs the water, and an isothermal reaction causes cooling. This isothermal reaction is similar to an ice pack where the liquid (water) is mixed with a solid (lithium bromide), causing cooling. For green building design, absorption is a perfect heat sink or way to use waste heat. Some commercially available absorbers can use waste heat (under vacuum) as low as 140 degrees (lower than the waste heat temperature in many facilities). For more information, consult: **http://www.hydronics.com/yazaki.htm**

BCS Building Control System: Energy-Saving Strategies

1. **Discharge Reset** of hot water or air handling units based on the load requirements in the spaces.

2. **Static Pressure Reset**: Adjusts the system static pressure set point based on the area with the greatest load.

3. **Enthalpy-Based Economizer Controls**: Utilizes air with the lowest heat content for cooling, by controlling a space based on total heat, not just temperature. *(See Chapter 6 for more detail.)*

4. **CO_2 Control**: Modulates the fresh air into a space above the minimum required, depending on the CO_2 level in the space. This becomes a truly dynamic control and maintains the building CO_2 level within recommended parameters. This approach is very effective in spaces that have large fluctuations in occupancy.

5. **Energy Monitoring and Trending**: The BCS system can monitor energy usage to identify large energy users or spikes. This allows a facility manager and commissioning agent to identify anomalies in a building's energy usage, saving thousands of dollars in energy costs by identifying short cycling or changes in schedules that are normally missed by the operators.

6. **VFD (Variable Frequency Drives) Modulation:** Fans and pumps can be "slowed down" by the VFD with properly located sensors. This ensures that only the volume required is delivered and not re-circulated, thereby reducing wasted energy in the form of unnecessary recycling of air. VFDs are usually controlled by a combination of the above-mentioned strategies to deliver only the required volumes.

7. **Occupancy Control:** Occupancy sensors or supervisory access cards enable the fresh air louvers to open when people are in a space, a method similar to CO_2 control, but without the calculations. The outdoor air louvers are shut when there is no occupancy and opened when someone enters the space. This type of control is cost-effective when using smaller air handlers.

Lighting

Lighting uses between 20-25% of electricity in the U.S.—5-10% of it in households, and 20-30% in commercial facilities. In most of these buildings, at least 50% of this energy is wasted because of inefficient fixtures or equipment, poor maintenance, or inappropriate use. There are several approaches to saving energy expended on lighting. They include:

- **Daylighting:** Designing buildings for optimum use of natural light. Daylighting can save 40-60% of energy costs compared to conventional design practices. It involves strategies to avoid glare and excess heat gain, while reflecting light into the building. *(See Chapter 6 for more on daylighting.)*

- **Using lower wattage lamps** in existing or new fixtures, providing the illumination is adequate for the task, purpose, and users. Replacing lamps with new ones of a more appropriate (lower) wattage, smaller tungsten halogen lamps, or CFLs (compact fluorescent lamps) is one method. New fixtures with lower wattage lamps can be a better solution, since they are likely to be more efficient and reliable over time.

- **Controlling the amount of light and the time lights are on** through devices such as dimmers, occupancy sensors, photocells, or timers (clock or crank timers), or encouraging users to turn lights off when they are not needed. Occupancy timers are well-suited to spaces used infrequently and are effective as a security measure. Dimmers can be used with both incandescent and fluorescent lamps. They prolong the life of incandescent lamps, but reduce their lumen output, making them less efficient. Fluorescent lamps must have dimming ballasts and lamp holders that accommodate dimmers, but are no less efficient with dimming.

- **Proper maintenance:** Keeping fixtures dusted and cleaned and replacing yellowed lenses. Maintaining wall and ceiling finishes also increases light efficiency, since dirt decreases light reflection on the walls.

Types of Lighting[19]

The most common and newly emerging types of lighting include: incandescent, fluorescent, high-intensity discharge, low-pressure sodium, and light-emitting diode (LED).

Incandescent: These lamps, used primarily in homes, have the lowest purchase price, but the highest operating cost. Incandescent lamps have shorter lives and are less efficient than the other types of lighting, but can be made more efficient by choosing the most appropriate lamp for the situation. Common types of incandescent bulbs include:

- Standard, or Type A bulbs, which are the least efficient. "Long-Life" bulbs do have a longer service life, but are less efficient than the regular Type A bulbs.
- Reflector, or Type R bulbs are used for floodlighting and spotlighting, often in stores and theatres. They spread light over a wider area than Type A bulbs.
- Tungsten halogen bulbs, most often used in commercial settings, are more efficient than either standard or reflector bulbs, but also more costly.
- Parabolic aluminized reflectors (Type PAR) bulbs are used outdoors for floodlights.
- Ellipsoidal reflectors (Type ER) are used for projecting light downward from recessed fixtures, where they are twice as efficient as Type PAR bulbs.

Fluorescent: These lamps are used in commercial indoor lighting and to some extent, in homes, where they offer efficiency and produce less glare than incandescent bulbs. Fluorescent lamps are three to four times more efficient than incandescent bulbs and last ten times longer. They are best used in situations where they will be left on for at least a few hours at a time.

Fluorescent tube lamps are common, and are often seen in 4', 40-watt or 8', 75-watt sizes. Compact fluorescent lamps (CFLs) provide efficiency and convenience, since they fit into standard incandescent bulb fixtures and save as much as 75% of the energy incandescent bulbs would use. CFLs last 10-15 times as long as incandescent bulbs, and they cost about 10-20 times as much. Their long life and energy savings over time make them well worth the extra investment.

Fluorescent light efficiency can be improved by replacing the fixtures themselves with more efficient models, by replacing their lamps with lamps of a lower wattage (where appropriate), or by replacing their ballasts. Electronic ballasts have made a big difference in the conservation of electricity. However, designers must consider the effect of electronic noise that is produced when using large quantities of electronic ballasts or other electronic equipment. Harmonic mitigation (measures to control electronic noise) has become a requirement when the installed kW of electronic components exceeds 10% of the total harmonic load.

Low- or no-mercury fluorescent lamps should always be used in green construction to minimize the waste impact on the environment. Manufacturers' data should provide this information. (One of the best research organizations is the Illuminating Society of America: http://www.iesna.org) The tubes should be recycled and not disposed of in landfills. Existing fixtures are also potentially hazardous since the older tubes contained larger quantities of mercury, and older ballasts may contain PCBs (polychlorinated biphenyls).

High-Intensity Discharge (HID): These lamps, used for outdoor lighting in stadiums and other large spaces, provide the highest **efficacy** (ratio of light output from a lamp to the energy it consumes, measured in lumens per watt, LPW) of all the lighting types. HID lamps are 75-90% more efficient than incandescent lamps. HID lighting includes mercury vapor, metal halide, and high-pressure sodium.

- Mercury vapor, the oldest of the HID lighting types, casts a cool (blue-white) light. Often used for street lighting, they have been replaced in many indoor applications such as gymnasiums by metal halide systems, which are more efficient and have better color rendition.

- Metal halide lamps offer not only the superior color rendition advantage, but deliver a higher output of light with more lumens per watt than mercury vapor lights. Applications include indoor arenas and gymnasiums, as well as outdoor spaces where color rendition is a factor.

- High-pressure sodium lights, highly efficient at 90-150 lumens per watt, produce a warm white light, variable color rendition, and have long lives with good reliability.

Low-Pressure Sodium This is the most efficient type of lighting, with the added advantage of long service life. The applications are, however, limited to highways and security, where color rendition is not a factor, since the light produced is mostly yellow or gray.

LED (Light-Emitting Diodes) These lamps have a long life of up to 20 years and low energy usage. The problem is that they produce a low level of light. There are some LEDs in development that will allow for multiple lamps to be grouped together serving as one light source, increasing the light output.

Electrical Power Generation

Fuel Cells

These units provide electrical power for many of the manned space craft and unmanned space probes and have finally become commercially available. They are, however, very expensive. Fuel cells use hydrogen, while the only byproduct is hot water and a small amount of CO_2. Since hydrogen is not a common fuel, many fuel cells are equipped with "reformers" to produce hydrogen from natural gas, propane, or other fuels. Reformer systems have been demonstrated (Frieberg, Germany and Humbolt, California) to produce the hydrogen by solar electrolysis of water. While still largely dependent on fossil fuels, fuel cells utilize a non-combustion chemical process that produces no emissions (except carbon dioxide and water vapor). The chemical efficiency is not limited to the Carnot efficiency, which limits the efficiency of heat engines (spark ignition, diesel, rankine, or brayton cycle engines). Fuel cells are available in sizes from 0.5 kW to 200 kW. They are characterized by their electrochemistry: proton exchange membrane, alkaline fuel cell, phosphoric acid, molten carbonate, or solid oxide. Fuel cells may eventually replace heat engines as the prime movers of our society. The non-profit information center for all fuel cell manufacturers can be accessed at: **http://www.fuelcells.org**

Figure 3.2

Fuel Cell Types and Applications

Fuel Cell Type	Applications	Operating Temp.	Comments
Alkaline	Space	80 - 100° C	Needs pure fuel/oxidant
Phosphoric Acid	Stationary	200 - 220° C	Long life, useful heat
Proton Exchange Membrane	Stationary Transportation	80 - 100° C	Short start time, easily manufactured Small size/scalability Limited co-generation
Molten Carbonate	Stationary	600 - 650° C	High efficiency, good co-generation
Solid Oxide	Stationary	650 - 1000° C	High efficiency, good co-generation

Renewable Energy & Distributed Generation Technologies

Renewable energy is truly the best source of power for all of our project needs. Non-renewable energy forms, such as fossil fuels, are not sustainable over the long term. Each type of renewable energy outlined below has advantages and challenges, including initial installation expense. However, appropriate application of these technologies can be economically advantageous over the long run, as major corporations and homeowners alike are discovering in their facilities and homes.

Distributed Generation & Cogeneration

Distributed generation is a technology that is used to create the power required for a facility at the point of use. Cogeneration is a form of distributed generation. In cogeneration systems, the system produces power at the point of use and also uses the waste heat generated by the process for other purposes within a facility. In green design, we strive to minimize waste and effectively use as much of a process as possible. Examples of cogeneration are described in the chiller portion of this chapter. The combined heat and power challenge Web site offers other examples at: **http://www.aceee.org/chp**

Photovoltaic Systems (PV)

Photovoltaic systems produce DC power, which can easily be converted to AC through an inverter. *(See Chapter 4 and the Appendix for complete coverage of photovoltaic systems.)*

Wind Power

These systems generate AC power, which is then converted to DC, and back to AC to regulate the voltage. *(See Chapter 5 for an overview of wind power, its costs, requirements, and suitable applications.)*

Water Power (Hydroelectric)

These systems generate AC or DC power. They require a minimum of 3' of head (steady) to be buildable. Like wind turbine systems, permitting is often the biggest issue.[20]

Water Conservation

There are several practical approaches to conserving water, including reducing the quantity used—by such measures as low-flow plumbing fixtures and xeriscaping, and using drip- and finely-tuned irrigation systems with rain sensors; re-using process waste water for irrigation or HVAC systems; and collecting rainwater for similar uses, depending on the filtration methods. A green building project should incorporate as many of these methods as possible.

Potable Water Reduction

The first line of defense in any green building project is conservation. Therefore, any use of water must involve conservation equipment. These devices are required by code in many areas of the country.[21] They include:

1. Water-saving, low-flow shower heads and toilets.

2. Water-saving or automatic shut-off sinks.

3. Waterless urinals (uses a chemical seal and highly polished surface to eliminate the need for flushing water).

4. Re-circulating dishwashers for commercial applications.

5. Steam trap programs. (Water is the basic component of steam; therefore all steam trap programs inherently conserve water.) In commercial facilities that require steam for process, the steam condenses to become water. The percentage of water that is reused is a key component in water conservation.[22]

Non-Potable Substitution Systems

These systems collect and use by product water to replace potable water for various uses. Sources of substitution, reclaimed water include:

- Storm water systems: Rainwater collected in tanks for non-potable water usage. (Can be used as potable water in some cases if properly filtered, in areas where air or other pollution does not create toxicity.)
- Process water: Can be recycled and collected for non-potable systems.

Some of the uses for non-potable reclaimed water include:

- Cooling systems heat sink
- Irrigation systems
- Toilet flushing
- Process cooling

Storm Water Collection & Infiltration

This is the single most significant way we can preserve water for the future. For years, we have been letting water run off into rivers and streams and back to the ocean. Meanwhile, we are pumping it out of the ground faster than it can recharge. All green building designs must minimize the amount of run-off from impervious surfaces on a property. Rainwater falling on these surfaces should be collected and channeled to a recharge area, so it can go back into the ground, or should replace municipal water used for irrigation, cleaning, process cooling, or even drinking, if properly purified.[23]

Rainwater Collection Systems

Rainwater catchment or collection systems offer several advantages, in addition to saving water and money. The water has no minerals and is therefore "soft" and better for washing and watering plants. It also provides owners with an independent supply. The technology used for these systems is fairly simple and low-maintenance. Collecting rainwater also helps reduce the burden on municipal drainage systems and water treatment plants.

Suitability: Collection tanks have traditionally been used in locations such as islands with salt-contaminated ground, remote areas far from water sources, and tropical regions where annual rainfall is plentiful, but there is also a dry season. Recently, many have discovered that even in areas without those criteria, rainwater can be a money-saving source of high-quality water.

Some considerations include:

- Monthly rainfall. (Use data from national weather agencies for at least the previous ten years.)
- Total catchment area—the area of the roof that is available for collecting rain.
- Loss factor—the water that does not go into the tank.
- How much water is needed to accommodate building uses.

Tank Size, Type of System, & Cost: Rainwater collection tanks can range in size from 50 to 30,000 gallons. The need for water and amount of rainfall, as well as period of drought, will help determine the appropriate tank size. In areas of evenly distributed rainfall, the tank might be sized to hold a month's worth. In regions with both rainy and dry seasons, a bigger tank might be desirable to store water for times of drought. The intended purpose of the collected water is another key factor. A simple 50-gallon drum placed under the downspout might be adequate for watering plants, depending on the climate. (One-fourth inch of rainfall from an average home's roof would fill the barrel.) Larger needs will require a bigger tank. The planned use of the water will also determine the need for filtration systems and other features.

The cost of rainwater receptacles varies widely, depending on materials and size. A large, high-end, underground tank could cost roughly a dollar per gallon of capacity ($5,000 for a 5,000-gallon tank). Galvanized tanks are less expensive than polyethylene, but tend to rust and will need to be replaced at some point. Fiberglass tanks range in size from several hundred to 30,000 gallons. A 4,000-gallon fiberglass tank can be purchased for less than $2,000.

(See Chapter 6, "Water Quality," for more on the comfort and health benefits and precautions of using collected rainwater.)

Conclusion

Green design is not a bunch of gadgets one can acquire in order to reduce energy. Green design is an interactive, holistic approach that sets environmental standards for the building's operations and life cycle, while meeting the requirements of building users and owners. Passive systems are encouraged as they truly work without the impact of human or machine.

Increasing efficiency does not require drastic, high-tech, or expensive measures. What is needed is a conscious effort to incorporate healthy, resource-saving features into a facility design, but also to make sure the facility has the flexibility to change as its use changes. Green is very much a common sense approach to building design.

[1] http://www.askbuild.com/cgi-bin/column?097

[2] http://www.southwall.com/products/heatmirror.html

[3] http://www.3m.com/about3M/technologies/film_solutions/index.jhtml

[4] http://www.kalwall.com/about.htm

[5] http://www.wachussett.com

[6] http://www.tmi-pvc.com/air/index.html

[7] http://www.elpasoelectric.com/apogee/res_html/rehcomb.htm

[8] http://www.elpasoelectric.com/apogee/res_html/rehcomb.htm

[9] http://www.gri.org/pub/solutions/desiccant/tutorial/dw_dw_vs_enthalpy.html

[10] http://www.greenbuilder.com/sourcebook/EnergyRecoveryVent.html

[11] http://www.regenteco.com

[12] http://www.eren.doe.gov/erec/factsheets/solar.html

[13] http://www.ari.org/consumer/howdoesitwork

[14] http://www.achrnews.com/CDA/ArticleInformation/features/
BNP_Features_Item/0%2C1338%2C18149%2C00.html

[15] http://www.nypha.com/prodhp.htm http://www.engr.siu.edu/staff2/abrate/
scroll.htm

[16] http://www.york.com.sg/esg_chillYCWS.html

[17] http://www.tecogen.com/chiller.htm

[18] http://www.tecogen.com/chiller.htm

[19] U.S. Department of Energy, Office of Energy Efficiency and Renewable
Energy, Consumer Energy Information: EREC Fact Sheet, "Energy-Efficient
Lighting," available at http://www.eren.doc.gov/erec/factsheets/eelight.html

[20] http://www.fwee.org/TG/nwaterpwr.html

[21] http://wwwga.usgs.gov/edu

[22] http://www.geocities.com/RainForest/7575/#bath

[23] http://www.epa.gov/ow

Chapter 4

Solar Energy Systems

Andy Walker, Ph.D., PE

Worshipped by ancients, the sun delivers the light and heat upon which life on Earth depends. An early reference to solar energy use in buildings comes from Socrates, "In houses that face toward the south, the sun penetrates the portico in winter, while in summer the path of the sun is right over our heads and above the roof so that there is shade."[1] Historic buildings include hints for the use of solar energy, as effective designs evolved over centuries of experience. Old buildings often include numerous and high windows to admit daylight, a practical requirement because they were built before the advent of electric lights. In old sections of Denver, the floor plans of historic houses on the east side of the streets are reflections of those on the west side; the most-occupied rooms remain on the south side of every house. Many older homes have kitchens on the east side, where they benefit from morning light, and the dining room on the west side, to take in the early evening light.

Many of these strategies fell into disuse when electric lights were introduced, and automatic thermostats made occupants less aware of how much fuel they used. Large design firms with national and international influence promulgated signature building designs that did not take local climates into consideration, although some 20th century architects such as Wright, Le Corbusier, and Alvar Aalto, designed with solar energy in mind.

In recent decades, concern over the cost and environmental consequences of fossil fuel use, and a reawakened interest in the health and comfort benefits of natural systems has caused a revival of solar energy use in building design. New technologies—such as photovoltaics that convert solar energy cleanly and silently into electricity, and super-insulated windows that admit visible light while screening out ultraviolet and infrared—provide today's designer with powerful new tools in the utilization of solar energy in buildings. It is now technically feasible to provide all of a building's energy needs with solar energy (except perhaps in polar regions). In areas where delivery of fossil fuels or where the provision of electric power is expensive, solar energy is also an economically feasible choice. The largest markets for solar energy products are currently developing nations, where a major investment in a central utility infrastructure has not already been made, and solar energy is the least expensive option.

The sun is a nuclear reactor 93,000,000 miles from Earth, streaming radiant energy out into space. Enough solar energy reaches the Earth to power the world economy 13,000 times over.[2] In fact, 20 days worth of solar radiation is equal to the capacity of all our stored fossil fuel from gas, coal, and oil resources.[3] There is no question whether solar energy is of adequate quantity to meet our energy needs. The emphasis is rather on how solar energy technology can be integrated into building design, given the distributed and intermittent nature of the solar resource.

For better or worse, every building is solar-heated. While this can be positive, designers should be also concerned with consequences of excessive sun in the wrong places, producing glare and overheating, as they are with its benefits, such as daylighting or passive solar heating. Occupant discomfort can be common in occupied spaces with west-facing windows or in atriums. Even if energy were free, designers have to be well-versed in solar engineering in order to provide quality conditions.

Background: Energy, Economics, Environment, Health, & Security

The True Cost of Conventional Energy Sources

The first law of thermodynamics[4] tells us that energy is not created or destroyed, but may be converted from one form to another. For buildings, the important forms of energy are electric power and chemical energy stored in fuels, such as natural gas. The second law of thermodynamics[5] tells us that whenever energy is converted from one form to another, some fraction is irretrievably lost as heat. To generate electricity for building consumption, about twice as much energy is wasted as reject heat at the power plant, and losses also occur in transmitting and distributing the electricity over power lines. Partially as a consequence of these thermodynamic inefficiencies, electric energy costs an average of $0.077/kWh in 1999, about 3.8 times more than the $0.020/kWh for heat from natural gas.[6]

Energy provides comfort in buildings and powers our automated economy, but at a price. Expenditures for energy in the United States reached $581 billion in 1999; $100 billion of this for commercial buildings, and $135 billion for residential buildings. The remainder went toward transportation and industrial processes. Energy expenditures in homes averaged $1,293 per home per year in 1999, a significant 6.3% of the average household income. In commercial buildings, energy expenditures averaged $1.58 per square foot per year. While the price of energy has been affordable for most on average, volatile prices in recently deregulated markets have occasionally forced offices to close and factories to cease production. In the summer of 2000, for example, the price of power in San Diego tripled as a consequence of electric industry deregulation.[7] Estimates of the long term availability of fossil fuels vary widely, and are frequently revised as new reserves are discovered, as technologies to extract fuels improve, and as the needs for different fuels change. Current estimates of recoverable reserves in the United States include 125 billion barrels of crude oil (including oil offshore, bound up in shale, and estimated but yet undiscovered), 1,111 trillion cubic feet of natural gas, and 255 billion tons of coal.[8] At current rates of consumption these reserves might be expected to last 82 years. In order to secure our children's energy future, renewable energy technologies must be developed and deployed before these reserves are exhausted.

Not included in this accounting are the environmental impacts of energy use. In 1999, atmospheric emissions associated with energy use in U.S. buildings included 5.0 million tons of NOx, 9.1 million tons of SO_2, and 531 million metric tons of CO_2. U.S. buildings account for 35% of U.S. carbon emissions, and 9% of all global carbon emissions.[9] These emissions have demonstrated a negative effect on health, and threaten the stability of the ecosystem that nourishes us. Fuel cells (which use electrochemical reactions rather than combustion) have been suggested to avoid SOx and NOx emissions, but emission of the global warming gas CO_2 is unavoidable with the use of any hydrocarbon fuel. Unlike the combustion of fossil fuels, the use of solar energy emits no pollution. Environmental impacts of exploring for, extracting, refining, and delivering fossil fuels are also avoided, since solar energy is available in all locations.

A Renewable, Safe Alternative

The use of solar energy avoids many security and reliability problems. A striking example of the brittleness of our interconnected power systems is the massive power outage that occurred on August 10, 1996, with a sagging power line touching a tree limb in Oregon, cascading to affect millions of customers in Oregon, California, Washington, Idaho, Utah, Montana, Wyoming, Colorado, New Mexico, Alberta, British Columbia, Arizona, and Nevada.[10] Business was lost as customers were evacuated from darkened malls, and safety was threatened by the failure of traffic lights. Since solar energy can be produced and stored in a distributed fashion (e.g., at each building), it is not vulnerable to such an accident or to sabotage. Instead of panicking in the dark when the power goes out, occupants of daylit rooms can see, and perhaps even keep on working. Pipes are less likely to freeze in a home with passive solar heating. Solar energy provides a decentralized, robust energy source capable of withstanding local power interruptions. The homes of American aid workers in Haiti with solar energy systems were the only buildings with lights and refrigeration during the 1985 oil embargo of the island. Furthermore, global conflicts over energy supplies are certain if we acknowledge that energy supplies are crucial for any nation's interest and will be secured by military force. As an equitable resource available to all, the increased use of solar energy lessens global conflicts over energy resources.

Energy Use in Different Types of Buildings

Different building types use energy in different ways. Because commercial and residential buildings use energy differently, they require different solar energy strategies. *See Figure 4.1.* In an office building, lighting is paramount, occupancy is during the day, and daylighting will be a principal strategy. For a motel, water heating may be the largest use of energy, and daylighting may be less important, since primary

Figure 4.1
Energy end-uses in different types of commercial and residential buildings.

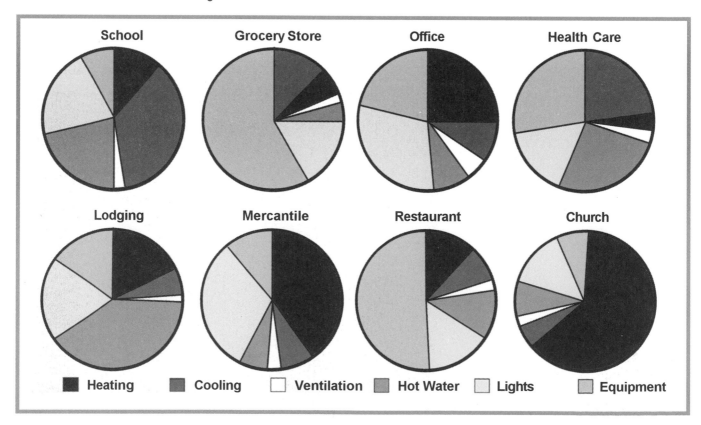

Green Building: Project Planning & Cost Estimating

occupancy is at night. While it might be appropriate to consider daylighting and solar water heating for all buildings, the differences of these end-uses have implications for the building design. The solar energy strategies used to address these differing requirements will influence both the building envelope and mechanical systems in different ways, as discussed in this chapter.

The Solar Resource

A solar power system can be designed to operate anywhere on Earth, or anywhere in the galaxy. A solar energy system design should include a solar collector area large enough to capture sunlight to meet the load, and storage capacity to span cloudy periods. The solar collectors should be oriented to optimize collection for the location and the climate.[11]

The Effect of Latitude

The path of the sun across the sky has implications for building layout, solar collector orientation, and shading geometries. The amount of sunlight on a surface throughout the day is factored into the design of solar energy systems. At lower latitudes, near the Equator, for example, the sun rises almost directly to the east, passes nearly overhead, and sets to the west, and this path does not change much throughout the year, so the seasons are less pronounced at lower latitudes. As we move north to higher latitudes, the path of the sun across the sky causes more seasonal variation. In summer, the sun rises slightly north of due east, passes a

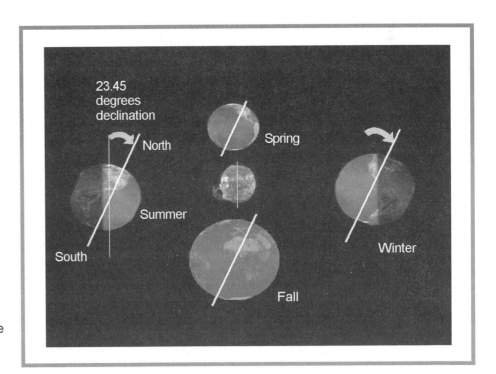

Figure 4.2
The tilt of 23.45 degrees between the Earth's own axis and its axis around the Sun causes the seasons to occur.

zenith which is south of directly overhead, and sets to the north of due west. In winter, the sun rises south of due east, cuts a low arc across the sky, and sets south of due west.

In the northern hemisphere, at low latitudes and in summer, east- and west-facing walls receive the most sun (east in the morning, west in the afternoon). At higher latitudes and in winter, the sun cuts a lower arc across the sky, and the south-facing wall receives the most sun. The north wall of a building receives sun only in the morning and evening in summer, and then only at a very oblique angle. Extending the long axis of a building in the east-west direction has two advantages: it limits overheating of west-facing exposures during summer afternoons, and it maximizes south-facing exposure for solar heating on winter days. (Low sun angles in the morning and evening are a source of glare when daylighting with east and west-facing windows.) For the southern hemisphere, the geometry would be reversed.

Solar Collectors in Photovoltaic & Thermal Systems

There are two types of collectors used to gather sunlight. Focusing collectors use only direct beam radiation and depend on specular optics. Flat plate collectors use both the direct and diffuse components of solar radiation.

Tracking Systems

For solar collectors in photovoltaic or solar thermal systems, it is possible to construct a tracker that rotates with both the azimuth of the sun from east to west and the altitude of the sun off the horizon throughout the day, thus keeping the collector facing directly toward the sun at all times. Tracking is more common with photovoltaic systems than with thermal systems since electrical connections are more flexible than plumbing connections. Tracking the sun from east to west

Figure 4.3

A building with the long axis stretched out in the east-west direction minimizes solar heat gain in summer, and maximizes solar heat gain in winter.

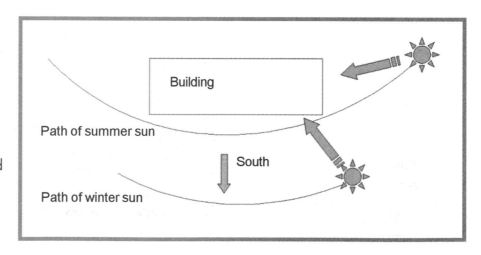

increases energy collection by as much as 40% in summer, but does not significantly improve performance in winter due to the path of the sun in the sky. This benefit of increased collection would be weighed against the cost of additional solar collector area in deciding whether tracking is appropriate for a particular application.

Fixed Systems

Fixed (non-tracking) systems are often favored for simplicity and lower cost. It is important to determine the best fixed angle at which to mount the collector. In general, a south-facing surface tilted up from the horizontal at an angle equal to the local latitude maximizes annual energy collection.

Passive Solar Heating

Every building with windows is solar-heated, whether to the benefit or detriment of occupant comfort and utility bills. In cold climates, the goal may be to capture and store as much solar heat as possible, while in warm climates the objective is to keep heat out. In general, a building must perform both functions, using solar heat in winter and rejecting it in summer. Passive solar features can be woven into any architectural theme, from New England Cape Cod style to Santa Fe Pueblo style. Figure 4.4 shows a passive solar home in the Victorian style.

In a typical commercial building, 16% of annual energy use is for space heating, while in a typical residential building, the fraction is much higher at 33%. The heating load can be significantly reduced by deliberate orientation of the building on the site and by careful design of the size and orientation of each window. Buildings designed in this way, using standard construction methods, are known as **sun-tempered.**

Figure 4.4
This Victorian-style passive solar home in Denver, Colorado, has a heating bill of only $50 per year. (Photo by Melissa Dunning, courtesy of NREL.)

Strategies to meet a higher percentage of the heating load through architectural design solutions are known as **passive solar heating.** The word "passive" means that the architectural elements, such as windows, insulation, and mass, operate as a system without the need for power input to mechanical equipment. Passive solar designs are categorized as **direct gain, sunspaces,** or **Trombe walls** (named after a French inventor). All three types have the same major components: windows to admit the solar radiation, mass to store the heat and avoid nights-too-cold and days-too-hot by smoothing out the temperature fluctuations, and a superior level of insulation in walls, roof, and foundation.

An understanding of solar radiation and of the position of the sun in the sky, as discussed in the Solar Resource Appendix, is essential to effective building design. In the northern hemisphere, winter sun is at its maximum on the south side of a structure, so this is the façade most affected by passive solar heating design, and all passive solar heating features have a southerly orientation. The building floor plan would be laid out to provide sufficient southern solar exposure, with the long axis of the building running from east to west. The extent of this elongation must be optimized for the climate, since it also increases surface area and associated heat loss. Some east-facing windows are also recommended in areas with cool mornings. One strategy to maintain a compact plan while also admitting solar gain into the northern rooms of a building, is to use high, south-facing clerestory windows, as illustrated in Figure 4.5. The fact that the clerestory windows are high up also ensures high-quality daylight, along with and passive solar heat gain. It is important to take into consideration any surrounding objects that might shade the solar features, such as hills, other buildings, and trees.

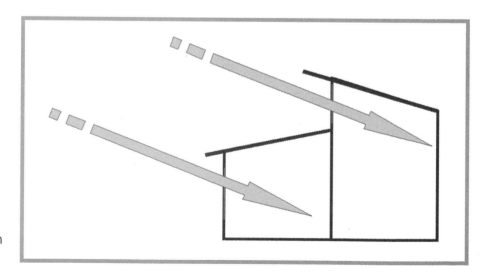

Figure 4.5
Clerestory windows offer a means to admit solar heat directly into rooms on the north side of a building.

Window Efficiencies

Advances in window technology have revolutionized passive solar heating design. Excessive heat loss from large window areas used to limit the application of passive solar heating to moderate climates. The well-insulated glass assemblies available today allow large windows even in very cold climates and high elevations, albeit at higher cost.

The designer may now select glass with a wide range of optical and thermal properties. The heat loss from a glazing assembly is described by the loss coefficient, or U-value.[12] The lower the U-value of a window, the less heat loss. Manufacturers construct windows with multiple layers of glass separated by gaps of air or other low-conductivity gas to reduce convective heat loss, and apply a low-emissivity (low-E) coating to reduce radiative heat loss. The U-value of a window ranges from 1.23 for single-pane with metal frame to as low as 0.24 for triple-pane with low-E coating and gas fill. Standard double-pane glass has a U-value between 0.73 and 0.49, depending on the type of frame.[13] Other properties to consider include the **Solar Heat Gain Coefficient (SHGC)**, and the **visible transmittance**. The SHGC is the fraction of solar heat that is transmitted directly through the glass, plus the fraction absorbed in the glazing and eventually convected to the room air. SHGC varies from 0.84 for single-pane clear glass to as low as zero for insulated opaque spandrel glass. Standard double-pane clear glass has an SHGC of 0.7.

The visible transmittance of glass is an important consideration for daylighting goals. Tints and reflective coatings would affect the appearance of a window and also diminish the solar heat gain. The selection of glass is important to system performance, and will depend on the system type and climate as discussed below, but double-pane clear glass is the most common for most passive solar heating applications.

Vertical south-facing windows are recommended over sloped or horizontal glazing for passive solar buildings in the northern hemisphere. Sloped glazing provides more heat in the cool spring, but this benefit is obviated by excessive heat gain in the warm autumn and also the additional maintenance caused by dirt accumulation and leaks. Overhangs admit the low winter sun while blocking the high summer sun, but since the ambient temperature lags behind the sun's position in the sky (cool on the spring equinox, warm on the autumnal equinox), there is no single fixed window overhang geometry that is perfect for performance. Therefore movable controls are often used. Controls include external awnings, plant trellises (which are usually fuller in autumn than in spring), or internal measures, such as drapes and blinds.

Thermal Storage Mass

Thermal storage mass is often provided by the structural elements of a building. It is important that the mass be situated such that the sun strikes it directly. Mass may consist of concrete slab floor, brick, concrete, masonry walls, or other features such as stone fireplaces. A way to add some mass to a sun-tempered space is to use a double-thickness of drywall. There are some exotic thermal storage materials including liquids and phase-change materials such as eutectic salts or paraffin compounds that store heat at a uniform temperature. Such materials are not commonly used, however, due to their cost and the need to reliably contain the material over the life of the building.

Optimum levels of insulation in a passive solar building are frequently double those used in standard construction, not only to reduce back-up fuel use, but also to help limit the size of the required passive solar heating features to reasonable proportions. The need to add insulation has implications for selection of wall section type and choice of cathedral versus attic ceiling, since an attic can accommodate more insulation. Insulation on slab edges and foundation walls is especially important, because these massive elements are often used to store solar heat. In all cases, the insulation should be applied to the outside of the mass in order to force the mass to stabilize the interior temperature. The mass should not be insulated from the occupied space, so that it easily heats the room air. Furring out from the mass wall or carpeting the floor slab is not recommended. Finished concrete or tile floors are preferred. Durable insulated finish systems are available for exterior application to concrete or block walls. Although advanced glazing assemblies are already well-insulated, drapes and movable insulation are sometimes used to provide additional insulation at times when solar gain is not a factor, such as at night.

It is not reasonable to expect passive solar energy to heat mass that is not directly in the sun, or to distribute widely throughout a building. The reason is that natural (passive) convection is caused by the temperature difference between the hot area and the cold area, and we want that temperature difference to be minimized for comfort reasons. Distribution to other parts of a building requires a mechanical solution involving pumps or fans.

Direct Gain

Direct gain spaces admit the solar radiation directly into the occupied space. This strategy is most effective in residences or within atriums and hallways of commercial buildings. Direct gain is generally not recommended for workspaces, or where people view computer screens or televisions, due to excessive glare and local heat gain. In a residence, occupants can move to a chair that is not directly in the sun, but in workspaces, people usually have to remain in place to accomplish a task.

The required window area varies from 10-20% of floor area for a temperate climate, to 20-30% for a cold climate.[14] Although they reduce the solar heat gain, glazings that absorb the ultraviolet portion of the solar spectrum are used in direct-gain spaces to avoid fading of fabrics. The percentage of the heating load that can be met with solar in a direct gain application is limited by the need to maintain comfortable conditions. The space cannot be allowed to get too hot, which limits the amount of solar heat that can be stored for night-time heating. Nor can it get too cold, which means it will require the use of a back-up heater at times.

Sunspaces

A sunspace avoids the limitations of a direct gain space by allowing the temperature to vary beyond comfort conditions. In sunspaces, the mass can overheat and store more energy when sun is available. Sunspaces can also re-use fuel by allowing the spaces to subcool at night or during storms. As a consequence, the sunspace may not be comfortable at all times, and its uses should be programmed accordingly. Appropriate uses for a sunspace include casual dining area, crafts workspace, or an area for indoor plants.

Figure 4.6
Direct-gain solar heating is provided by the south-facing windows in south offices, and by the clerestory windows in the high-bay north rooms of the Thermal Test Facility at National Renewable Energy Laboratory. (Photo by Warren Gretz, courtesy of NREL.)

Skylights or sloped glazing in sunspaces are common in practice, but are not recommended, since the high sun is not gladly received in summer, and since the sun hits the horizontal skylight only at an oblique angle in winter. (Two suppliers of skylights address this issue by incorporating shades and louvers to control direct heat gain in summer.) It is also common to see sunspaces that project out from the house wall, another approach that is not recommended. It is better to have the house partially surround the sunspace (except on the south side) to reduce heat loss from both the sunspace and the house. Thus, the sunspace differs from a direct gain space more in terms of temperature control and the use of the space than it does in terms of architecture.

The recommended amount of glazing in a sunspace varies from 30-90% of floor area in temperate climates to 65-150% of floor area for cold climates.[15] In most applications, the wall between the sunspace and the building acts as a massive thermal storage wall. In very cold climates or if the sunspace windows are poorly insulated (high U-value), it may be necessary to insulate this wall. Operable windows and doors between the sunspace and the building are opened and closed to provide manual control. Vents and fans are also used to extract heat from the sunspace under automatic control based on the temperature of the sunspace.

Trombe Wall

A Trombe wall is a sunspace without the space. It consists of a thermal storage wall directly behind vertical glazing. This passive solar heating

Figure 4.7

This sunspace at a home in Denver, Colorado incorporates extensive glazing and thermal storage mass. (Photo by Jim Cook, courtesy of Sunrooms of Colorado, Inc.)

strategy provides privacy and avoids glare and afternoon overheating. Over the course of the day, the wall heats up, and releases its heat to the space behind the wall over a 24-hour period. The outside surface becomes very hot during the day, but due to the thermal inertia of the mass, the interior surface remains at a rather constant temperature. Since the wall is not insulated, care must be taken to ensure that the heating cycle by the sun matches the cooling cycle of heat loss to the interior and exterior. Well-insulated glazing can reduce this heat loss, but multiple panes, low-E coatings, and ultraviolet filters also reduce the amount of solar heat that gets through the glass, so the trade-offs must be evaluated to optimize cost.

Trombe wall area varies from 25-55% of floor area in temperate climates, and from 50-85% of floor area in cold climates.[16] The wall is covered with a **selective surface,** which has a high absorbtivity in the short wavelengths solar spectrum, but a low emissivity in the long wavelength infrared spectrum, thus reducing radiant heat loss off the wall. The heat must conduct into the wall from the selective surface (a blackened metal foil), so proper adhesion to avoid blistering or peeling of the surface from the wall is critical to performance. Rather than hollow block, the wall should be solid to allow the heat to conduct through uniformly. Since the space between the mass wall and the window can exceed 180° F, all materials including paint and seals must

Figure 4.8
Thermal-storage trombe wall at the National Renewable Energy Laboratory, Colorado.

be able to tolerate high temperatures. Similar to direct gain spaces and sunspaces, an overhang over the glazed trombe wall reduces unwanted summertime heat gain.

Design Tools

Analysis techniques useful for passive solar design include rules-of-thumb, correlation tables, and computer simulations. Rules of thumb relate the size of windows and amount of mass (as well as details such as overhang dimensions and mass thickness) to the square footage of the space to be heated. Rules of thumb can be found in books on passive solar heating.[17] Correlation tables are the results of detailed calculations that relate passive solar design parameters to conditions such as average temperature, local latitude, and other factors that affect system performance. In recent years, computer simulations have overtaken these methods. Two popular simulations that analyze passive solar heating are Energy-10 and DOE-2. Both simulate solar gains, thermal losses, and resulting temperature of the indoor space for each of 8,760 hours of a typical year, using representative weather data for the site.

- **Energy-10** is very easy to use for direct gain and sunspaces, but currently does not have the feature of modeling Trombe walls.
- **DOE-2** can model any passive solar heating strategy in a large number of zones. Newer versions of DOE-2 include a geometric representation of the building and account for self-shading of building areas.

Both programs account for the interactions between solar heat gain, internal heat gain from lights, people, and equipment, mechanical system performance, and other simultaneous effects. *(See Chapter 13 for more on Energy-10 and DOE-2.)*

Cooling Load Avoidance

Since heat sources internal to the building, such as lighting and computers, are often constant throughout the year, the peak cooling load and the size of the air conditioning system required to meet this peak are often determined by solar heat gain on the building envelope. On a national average, space cooling represents 10% of annual energy use in residential buildings, and 12% in commercial buildings. In commercial buildings, 33% of the cooling load is due to solar heat gain through the windows (of the remainder, 42% is due to heat from lights, 18% to heat from equipment, and 7% to heat from the people inside).[18]

Since the sun cuts a high arc across the sky in summer, a building elongated along the east and west dimension is recommended for cooling load avoidance, as it was for solar heating in winter, when the sun cuts a much lower arc to the south. In the summer, the sun is at a maximum on the roof and on the west façade, which is why these faces deserve the most attention regarding strategies to reduce solar heat gain. While solar heat gain on well-insulated opaque surfaces is negligible, the size and orientation of windows is key. Solar heat-gain on west-facing windows is at a maximum on summer afternoons, so the size of these windows should be no more than what is required to take advantage of an important view or to meet daylighting goals.

Solar heat gain can also be controlled by careful selection of windows glazing properties. Glazing with a low Solar Heat Gain Coefficient (SHGC) attenuates solar heat gain. The low SHGC is achieved by absorbing the energy in the tint of the glass or reflecting it with a surface coating. Reflection is the more elegant way to reject solar heat, since some of the light absorbed in the tinted glass will be re-radiated or convected into the room air. If a clear appearance is desired, or if a high visible transmittance is required to meet daylighting goals, a **selective glazing** is recommended. Selective glazing screens out the infrared and ultraviolet portions of the solar spectrum, but allows much visible light to pass. A double-pane assembly of selective glazing typically has an SHGC of 0.35. Occupant comfort may be improved by the use of shades and blinds to block the sun. However, once solar heat makes it through the window glass, it must be removed by the building mechanical system, with associated energy cost and environmental impacts.

Several measures can be taken on the outside of the building to mitigate solar heat gain if it is unwanted. Deciduous trees provide shade in summer, but in winter they lose their leaves, allowing about 60% more

Figure 4.9
The overhangs of St. Benedict Child Care Center in Louisville, KY, provide shade over south-facing and clerestory windows in this photo taken during the summer. (Photo by Paul Torcellini, courtesy of NREL.)

sun to pass through for solar heating. Vegetation can also be provided on a trellis to block the sun from a window or porch. **Green roofs** are roofs with a thin layer of planted soil to dissipate solar heat, absorb water run-off, and give the roof space a pleasing garden-like appearance. *(See Chapter 3 for more on living or green roofs.)* Reflective white or aluminized coatings are also used to reflect solar heat. Water-spray systems have been demonstrated to cool the roof during the day and supply chilled water at night, when the roof is radiating heat. The drawback is significant water consumption.

Design Tools

Design tools for cooling load avoidance are the same as those already discussed for passive solar heating. Figure 4.10 shows an application of the DOE-2 computer program to evaluate external shades as a cooling load avoidance measure at a new GSA federal courthouse in Gulfport, Mississippi.

Photovoltaics

Photovoltaics (PV), as the name implies, are devices that convert sunlight directly into electricity. PVs generate power without noise, without pollution, and without consuming any fuel. These are compelling advantages for several applications, especially where utility power is not available (such as remote ranger stations) or inconvenient (such as watches and calculators). One disadvantage of photovoltaics is that they require a large surface area to generate any significant

Figure 4.10
The DOE-2 computer program (with PowerDOE interface) was used to model the performances of these louvers to provide shade over south-facing windows on a new GSA Courthouse in Gulfport, Mississippi. (Graphic by Andy Walker.)

amount of power. This is because the sunlight comes to us distributed over a wide area, and because today's PVs can only convert about 10% of the solar power to electricity. Efforts to make systems more efficient (to convert more sunlight to electricity) and to utilize unused roof space mitigate this problem. A second disadvantage is that PV is rather expensive due to the high-technology manufacturing processes. Still, in many applications they cost less initially than alternatives, and even when they cost more initially, they often recoup this investment in fuel and operations savings over time.

The PV industry has been growing tremendously as demand for the technology in niche applications and in developing countries far exceeds supply. U.S. production rose from 6,897 kW in 1980 to 13,837 kW in 1990 and to 76,787 kW in 1998. Value of PV shipments in 1999 was estimated at $185 million.[19] PV is used mostly in remote locations where utility power is not available. However, more and more utility customers are adding PV to buildings in order to realize the utility cost savings, the improved reliability and power quality, and the environmental benefits associated with not using utility power (which would most likely come from a gas- or coal-fired power plant).

Figure 4.11
The photovoltaic effect consumes no material, produces no pollution, and can continue as long as light is provided to the cell. (Graphic by Jim Leyshon.)

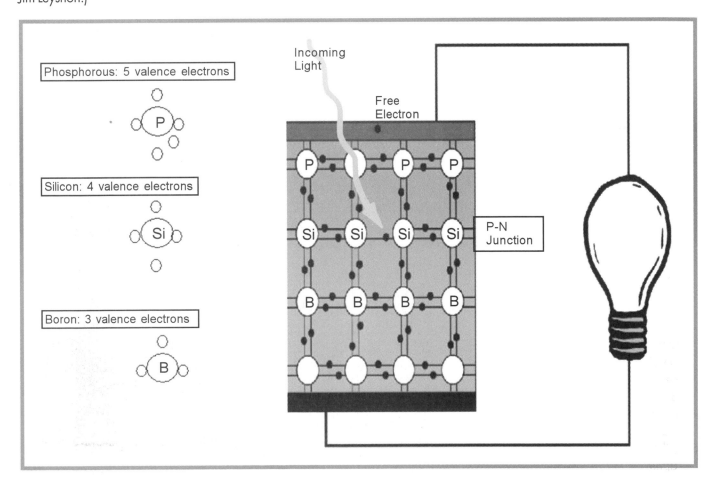

Photovoltaic Cells & Modules

The electric power that PV produces is DC (direct current), similar to that coming from a battery. The voltage of each cell depends on the material's band gap, or the energy required to raise an electron from the valence band to the conduction band. For silicon, each cell generates a voltage of about 0.5V. The voltage decreases gradually (logarithmically) with increasing temperature. The current generated by each cell depends on its surface area and intensity of incident sunlight. Cells are wired in series to achieve the required voltage, and series strings are wired in parallel to provide the required current. As increasing current is drawn from the cell, the voltage drops off, leading to a combination of current and voltage which maximizes the power output of the cell. This combination, called the **maximum power point** (MPP), changes slightly with temperature and intensity of sunlight. Most PV systems have power conditioning electronics, called a **maximum power point tracker** (MPPT) to constantly adjust the voltage in order to maximize power output. Simpler systems operate at a fixed voltage close to the optimal voltage.

Each "PV cell" is a wafer as thin and as fragile as a potato chip. In order to protect them from weather and physical damage, they are

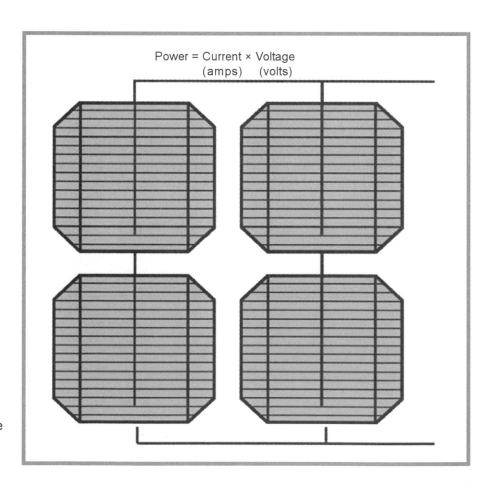

Figure 4.12

PV cells are wired in series, to provide the required voltage, and parallel to one another.

encapsulated in a "glue" called Ethyl Vinyl Acetate and sandwiched between a sheet of tempered glass on top and a layer of glass or other protective material underneath. A frame often surrounds the glass laminate to provide additional protection and mounting points. Such an assembly is known as a **PV module**. The current and voltage of the module will reflect the size and series-parallel arrangement of the cells inside. The **Rated Power** of a PV module is the output of the module under standard rating conditions (1 kW/m² light, 25° C, 1 m/s wind speed). Other standard tests conducted on PV modules include the "hi pot" test (where a high voltage is applied to the internal circuits, and the assembly dipped in electrolyte solution to detect imperfect insulation). Another test involves 1" iceballs fired at 55 mph at different parts of the module to evaluate hail-resistance.

Similarly, modules are wired in series to increase the voltage, and then series strings of modules are wired in series to provide the required current and overall power output from a **PV array**.

For small DC systems, 12V, 24V, and 48V configurations are common to match the voltage of lead-acid batteries often used in these systems. Higher voltage results in less current and less loss in the wiring. For large systems, voltage as high as 400 V is used to minimize line losses. There is a trade-off however, between line loss and reliability, since if any module in a series fails (by shading or damage), that whole series string is affected.

Figure 4.13
PV cells are arranged in modules, and modules into arrays to provide the required amount of power at the proper voltage.

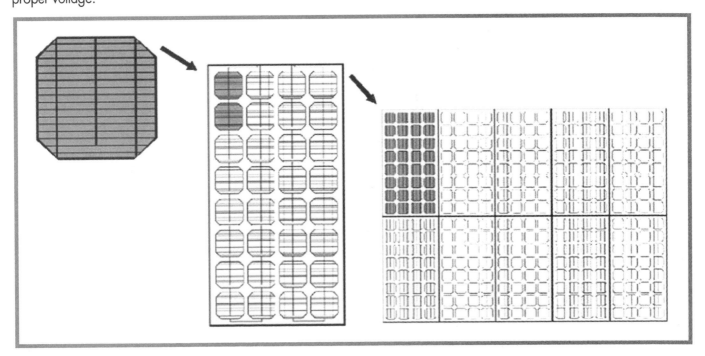

PV System Components

A PV system may consist of some or all of the following components, depending on the type of system and the applications:

- PV array to convert sunlight to electricity.
- Array support structure and enclosure to protect other equipment.
- Maximum Power Point Tracker to match load to optimal array voltage.
- Batteries to store charge for when it is needed.
- Charge controller to protect battery from over-charging.
- Low voltage disconnect to protect battery from over-discharging.
- Inverter to convert direct current (DC) to alternating current (AC).
- Wiring, combiner boxes, fuses, and disconnects.
- Automatic generator starter/stopper to start a generator when battery is too low, and a battery charger to re-charge the batteries with generator power.

Batteries

There is an acute need to store electrical energy for many purposes besides PV systems, and researchers are investigating alternatives. Battery manufacturers continue to implement innovations to improve

Figure 4.14
DC PV system with batteries

performance. But as one practitioner puts it, "battery technology is raging headlong into the 1700s. We keep coming back to the same old lead-acid technology because of its low cost."

Batteries do have some dangers. They contain several toxic materials, and care must be taken to ensure that they are recycled properly. In some cases batteries are shipped dry, with the electrolyte added on-site. During installation, care must be taken to ensure that battery electrolyte (battery acid) is not ingested by an installer or an unaware bystander. Storing battery electrolyte only in well-labeled child-proof containers can reduce this risk. Finally, batteries are capable of rapidly releasing their stored energy if they are shorted; care must be taken to avoid electrocution and fires caused by sparks.

The amount of battery capacity required depends on the magnitude of the load and the required reliability. A typical battery capacity is sufficient to meet the load for 3-5 days without sun, but in applications that require high reliability, 10 days of battery storage may be recommended.

Charge Controller

The function of the battery **charge controller** is very important for system performance and battery longevity. The charge controller modulates the charge current into the battery to protect against overcharging and an associated loss of electrolyte. The low-voltage disconnect protects the battery from becoming excessively discharged

Figure 4.15
Each of these parking lot lights in Honolulu, Hawaii is equipped with two 48 PV panels and a 90 Ah battery at the top of the pole (two per pole). The cost of $2,500 per lamp was less than the cost of trenching and repairing the parking lot to bring utility power to the poles.

by disconnecting the load. It seems unfortunate to disconnect the load, but doing so avoids damage to the battery, and not doing so would simply delay the inevitable, since the load would not be served by a ruined battery. The set point of the low-voltage disconnect involves a cost trade-off. For example, allowing the battery to get down to a 20% state of charge (80% discharged) would result in a short battery life. Limiting it to an 80% state of charge (20% discharged) would make the battery last considerably longer, but would also require 4 times as many batteries to provide the same storage capacity.

Inverter

Utility power in U.S. buildings is 120V or 240V AC (alternating current) of 60 Hz frequency (50 Hz in many countries overseas). Since many appliances are designed to operate with alternating current, PV systems

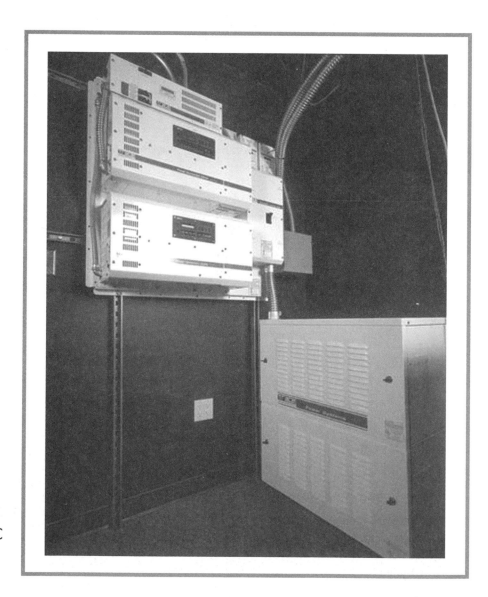

Figure 4.16
Each of these two inverters at the visitor center in Zion National Park is capable of converting 4 kW from DC to AC. (Photo by Paul Torcellini, courtesy of NREL.)

are often furnished with power conditioning equipment called an **inverter** to convert the DC power from the PV array or the battery to AC power for the appliances. A "rotary inverter" is a DC motor driving an AC generator, and might be used in a place where such simple equipment could be easily serviced, like a developing country. More common are "static inverters" which use power transistors to achieve the conversion electronically. Advances in inverter technology have resulted in systems that deliver a pure sine wave form and exceptional power quality. In fact, except for the PV array, the components of a PV system are the same as those of an uninterruptible power supply (UPS) system used to provide critical users of power with the highest power quality. Inverters are available with all controls and safety features built in.

Generator

For small stand-alone systems it is often cost-effective to meet the load using only solar power. However, during extended cloudy weather this approach requires a very large battery bank and solar array. To optimize cost, the PV system can incorporate a generator to run infrequently during periods when there is no sun. This **hybrid PV/ generator system** takes advantage of the low operating cost of the PV array and the on-demand capability of a generator. In this configuration the PV array and battery bank would ordinarily serve the load. If the battery becomes discharged, the generator automatically starts to serve the load, but also to power a battery charger to recharge the batteries.

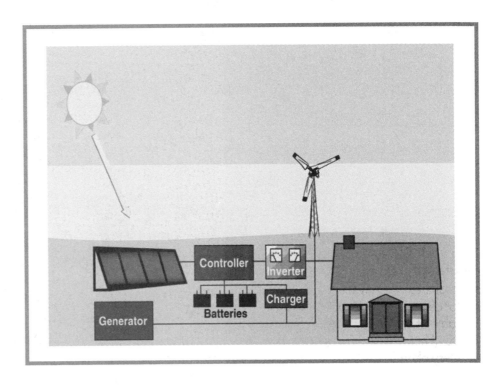

Figure 4.17
PV may be combined with other power sources in a hybrid configuration to benefit from the advantages each resource offers. (Graphic by Jim Leyshon.)

When the batteries are fully charged, the generator automatically turns off again. This system of cyclically charging batteries is cost-effective even without PV, as it keeps a large generator from running to serve a small load. A hybrid system would be designed to minimize life-cycle cost, with the PV array typically providing 70-90% of the annual energy, and the generator providing the remainder. PV is also often combined with wind power, under the hypothesis that if the sun is not shining, the wind may be blowing.

Note: **Grid Connected** systems don't require batteries because the utility provides power when solar is not available. Several utility and industry standards (most notably UL1741 and IEEE929) must be satisfied, and an agreement with the utility must be negotiated, before a customer's system can interact with the utility system.

Building-Integrated Photovoltaics (BIPV)

An exciting trend is **building-integrated photovoltaics,** or BIPV, where the photovoltaic material replaces a conventional part of the building construction. One-for-one replacements for shingles, standing seam metal roofing, spandrel glass, and overhead skylight glass are already on the market. The annual energy delivery of these components will be reduced if walls and roofs are not at the optimal orientation, but it has been demonstrated that PV installed within 45 degrees of the optimal tilt and orientation suffers only a slight reduction in annual performance.

Figure 4.18
Views of this hybrid PV/generator system at Joshua Tree National Park show the 20.5 kW PV array, the 613 kWh battery bank, and the 35 kW propane generator. The $273,000 cost was initially financed by Southern California Edison under a 15-year tariff.

Tilt less than optimal will increase summer gains, but decrease the annual total, and panels facing east will increase morning gains, but decrease the daily total.

Design Tools

Design tools for PV systems are simple hand calculations and hourly simulations of PV system performance. Hand calculations are facilitated by the fact that PV systems are rated at a solar radiation level of 1 kW/m², so a PV array can be expected to deliver its rated output for a number of hours (called **sunhours**) per day equal to the number of kWh/m²/day presented in the solar resource data *(see Appendix)*. For an example of a hand calculation for a system in Bettles, Alaska.

Solar Water Heating

Solar water heating systems are relatively simple extensions to buildings' plumbing systems, which impart heat from the sun to preheat service hot water. Water heating accounts for a substantial portion of a building's energy use, ranging from approximately 9% of total energy use in office buildings to 40% in lodging facilities. Averaged across all buildings, hot water represents 15% of energy use in residential buildings, and 8% in commercial buildings.[20]

Solar water heating systems are usually designed to provide about two thirds of a building's hot water needs, and more where fuel is very expensive or unavailable. Solar water heating applications include domestic water heating, pool and spa heating, industrial processes such as laundries and cafeterias, and air conditioning reheat in hot, humid

Figure 4.19
The house on the right, in Bowie, Maryland, incorporates 2.2 kW of BIPV in the standing seam metal roof, but is barely distinguishable from the other houses in the photo. (NAHB demonstration project, photo by Tim Ellison, courtesy of NREL.)

climates. Solar water heating is most effective when it serves a steady water heating load that is constant throughout the week and year (or at a maximum during the summer). For example, a prison that is occupied 7 days a week would accrue 40% more cost savings than a school open only 5 days a week.

In 1999, a total of 23,800 solar water heating systems were installed in the U.S., totaling 8,583,000 square feet of collector area. Swimming pool heating was by far the largest application, with 8,141,000 square feet. Systems to supply service hot water accounted for 373,000 square feet. Space heating employed 42,000 square feet, and 16,000 square feet were directed to systems that provide both space heating and hot water. Process heating accounted for 5,000 square feet, and 4,000 square feet was installed for electrical generation.[21]

Solar water heating can be used effectively in almost any geographic location, but is especially prevalent and effective at low latitudes, where the constant solar resource matches a constant water load. In 1999, 46% of solar thermal collectors were shipped to Florida, 27% to California, 5% to Arizona, 4% to Nevada, and 3% to Hawaii.[23] Appropriate near-south-facing roof area or nearby unshaded grounds would be required for installation of a collector. System types are available to accommodate freezing outdoor conditions, and systems have been installed as far north as the arctic and as far south as Antarctica.

There are different types of solar water heating systems; the choice depends on the temperature required and the climate. All types have the

Figure 4.20
This 75kW BIPV system at Hawaii's Mauna Lani Bay Hotel adds insulation to the roof. (Photo by Powerlight Corp., courtesy of NREL).

same simple operating principle. Solar radiation is absorbed by a wide-area "solar collector," or "solar panel," which heats the water directly or heats a non-freezing fluid which, in turn, heats the water by a heat exchanger. The heated water is stored in a tank for later use. A backup gas or electric water heater is used to provide hot water when the sun is insufficient, and to optimize the economical size of the solar system.

Solar water heating systems save the fuel otherwise required to heat the water, and avoid the associated cost and pollution. A frequently overlooked advantage of solar water heating is that the large storage volume increases the capacity to deliver hot water. As one residential system owner described it: "With 120 gallons of solar-heated water and the 40 gallon backup heater, I can take a shower, my wife can take a bath, we can have the dishwasher and the clothes washer going, and we never, never run out of hot water."

Types of Collectors for Solar Water Heating

Solar thermal collectors can be categorized by the temperature at which they efficiently deliver heat. **Low-temperature collectors** are unglazed and uninsulated. They operate at up to 18° F (10° C) above ambient temperature, and are most often used to heat swimming pools. At this low temperature, a cover glass would reflect or absorb solar heat more

Figure 4.21

Solar Collector Types: unglazed, flat plate, evacuated tube, and parabolic trough.

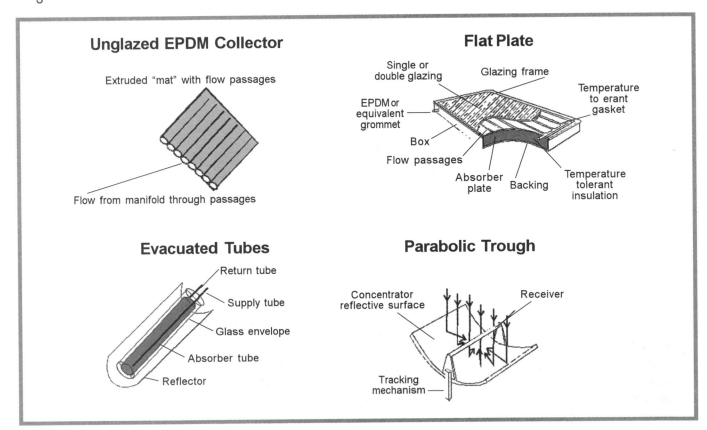

than it would reduce heat loss. Often, the pool water is colder than the air, and insulating the collector would be counter-productive. Low-temperature collectors are extruded from polypropylene or other polymers with UV stabilizers. Flow passages for the pool water are molded directly into the absorber plate, and pool water is circulated through the collectors with the pool filter circulation pump.

Mid-temperature systems place the absorber plate in an enclosure insulated with fiberglass or polyicocyanurate, and with a low-iron cover glass to reduce heat loss at higher temperatures. They produce water 18° to 129° F (10° to 50° C) above the outside temperature, and are most often used for heating domestic hot water (DHW). Reflection and absorption reduce the solar transparency of the glass and reduce the efficiency at low temperature differences, but the glass is required to retain heat at higher temperatures. A copper absorber plate with copper tubes welded to the fins is used. To reduce radiant losses from the collector, the absorber plate is often treated with a black nickel selective surface, which has a high absorptivity in the short-wave solar spectrum, but a low-emissivity in the long-wave thermal spectrum.

High-temperature collectors surround the absorber tube with an evacuated borosilicate glass tube to minimize heat loss, and often utilize mirrors curved in a parabolic shape to concentrate sunlight on the tube. Evacuating the air out of the tube eliminates conduction and convection as heat loss mechanisms, and using a selective surface minimizes radiation heat loss. High-temperature systems are required for absorption cooling or electricity generation, but are used for mid-temperature applications such as commercial or institutional water

Figure 4.22
Unglazed solar collectors for low-temperature swimming pool heating solar collectors on the roof of the Georgia Tech Aquatic Center, site of the 1996 Olympic swimming competition. (Photo courtesy of NREL.)

Green Building: Project Planning & Cost Estimating

heating as well. Due to the tracking mechanism required to keep the focusing mirrors facing the sun, high-temperature systems are usually very large and mounted on the ground adjacent to a facility.

Selecting the best type of collector will depend on the application. Figure 4.25 shows the efficiency of different types of collectors as a function of the temperature difference between the inside of the collector and the outdoor temperature, and the intensity of the solar radiation. Notice that at low temperatures, the inexpensive, unglazed collectors offer the highest efficiency, but efficiency drops off very quickly as temperature increases. Glazed collectors are required to efficiently achieve higher temperatures, and very high-temperature applications require an evacuated tube in order to deliver any useful heat.

Although solar water heating systems all use the same basic principle, they do so with a wide variety of specific technologies that distinguish different collectors and systems. The distinctions are important because certain types of collectors and systems best serve certain applications in various locations.

The following nomenclature describes types of solar water heating systems:

- Passive: Relies on buoyancy (natural convection) rather than electric power to circulate the water.
- Active: Requires electric power to activate pumps and/or controls.
- Direct: Heats potable water directly in the collector.

Figure 4.23
This 484 square-foot mid-temperature solar water heating system at Chickasaw National Recreation Area, Oklahoma uses flat plate collectors and a 1,000 gallon storage volume to deliver 18,194 kWh/year for showers and laundry. (Photo by Andy Walker.)

- Indirect: heats propylene glycol or other heat transfer fluid in the collector and transfers heat to potable water via a heat exchanger.

Design Tools

Solar water heating systems should be designed to minimize life-cycle cost. It is never cost-effective to design a system to provide 100% of the load with solar because of the excessive investment in collector area and storage volume. The economic optimum is usually on the order of 70% of the load met with solar. One strategy is to design a system that meets 100% of the load on the sunniest day of the year. This approach will ensure that the investment in solar hardware is always working to deliver energy savings, with no over-capacity. Other design considerations include maintenance, freeze protection, overheating protection, and aesthetics of the collector mount and orientation.

In the northern hemisphere, solar hot water collectors should be oriented to face toward the equator within 30° of true (not magnetic) South. Collectors tilted up from the horizontal at an angle of latitude plus 15° maximize winter solar gains and result in a solar delivery that is uniform throughout the year. This would be the appropriate tilt angle for a solar water-heating load that is also constant throughout the year. A collector tilted up from the horizontal at an angle of latitude minus 15° maximizes summer solar gains, and would be appropriate for a

Figure 4.24
Parabolic trough solar water heating system at Jefferson County Detention Facility, Golden, Colorado. (Photo by David Parsons, courtesy of NREL.)

summer-only applications, such as swimming pool heating or beach showers. It is usually acceptable to mount the collectors flush on a pitched roof as close to the optimal orientation as possible in order to reduce installed cost and improve aesthetics.

Design tools include simple hand calculations, correlation methods, and hourly computer simulations. Hand calculations are facilitated by the assumption that solar water heating systems have a typical efficiency of 40%. *(See Figure 4.26.)* Accurately accounting for the changing effects of solar radiation, ambient temperature, and even wind speed requires an hourly simulation. Correlations of simulation results, such as an F-Chart, were popular before computers were ubiquitous. FRESA[23] and RETScreen[24] are two computer programs used for preliminary analysis. Hourly simulation programs TRNSYS[25] and WATSUN[26] are widely used for precise engineering data and economic analysis and to optimize parameters of solar water heating system design.

Codes & Standards

The Solar Rating and Certification Corporation (SRCC) is an independent, nonprofit trade organization that creates and implements solar equipment certification programs and rating standards. SRCC ratings are used to estimate and compare the performance of different collectors and systems submitted to SRCC by manufacturers for testing. SRCC developed a solar water heating system rating and certification program, short-titled OG 300, to improve performance and reliability of solar products.[27]

Figure 4.25

At low temperatures, inexpensive unglazed collectors offer the highest performance. At higher temperatures or lower solar radiation, the superior insulation of flat plates, and ultimately evacuated tubes, is required. (Graphic by Jim Leyshon.)

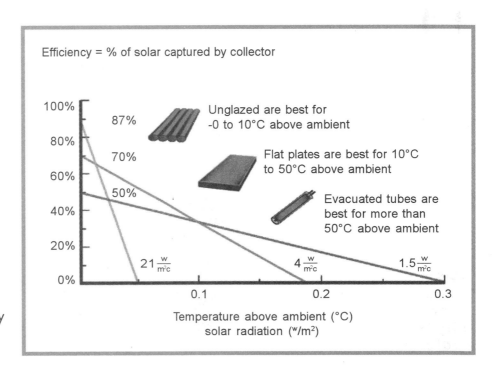

Other standards include the following from the American Society of Heating, Refrigerating, and Air Conditioning Engineers:

- ASHRAE 90003: Active Solar Heating Design Manual
- ASHRAE 90336: Guidance for Preparing Active Solar Heating Systems Operation and Maintenance Manuals
- ASHRAE 90342: Active Solar Heating Systems Installation Manual
- ASHRAE 93: Methods of Testing to Determine the Thermal Performance of Solar Collectors

From the American Water Works Association (AWWA):

- AWWA C651 Disinfecting Water Mains

From Factory Mutual Engineering and Research Corporation (FM):

- FM P7825 Approval Guide

From the National Fire Protection Association (NFPA):

- NFPA 70 National Electrical Code

- MIL-HDBK 1003/13A Solar Heating of Buildings and Domestic Hot Water

Solar Ventilation Air Heating

Solar ventilation air preheating is a cost-effective application of solar energy thanks to innovative transpired collector heat transfer technology that is both inexpensive and high-performance. Heating of ventilation air accounts for about 15% of the total heating load in an average commercial building, much more in buildings that require a lot of ventilation, like factories and laboratories. Preheating the air with solar energy before it is drawn into the space can save much of this

Figure 4.26

An example of a simple hand calculation of solar water heater size and annual energy savings.

Mass of hot water used each day, M

M = 4 person × 40 gal/person/day × 3.785 kg/gal = **606 kg/day**

Energy load to heat water each day, L

$L = MC (T_{hot}-T_{cold})$ = 606 kg/day × 0.001167 kWh/kgC × (50C-18C) = **22.6 kWh/day**

Divide load by peak solar resource and efficiency to size collector, Ac

For Denver, I_{max} = 6.1 and I_{ave} = 5.5 kWh/m²/day

$A_c = L / (\eta_{solar} I_{max})$ = 22.6 kWh/day / (0.4 × 6.1 kWh/m²/day) = **9.3 m²**

Multiply collector size by average solar resource and efficiency to estimate energy savings, and divide by boiler efficiency to estimate annual fuel savings, Es

$E_s = A_c I_{ave} \eta_{solar} 365/ \eta_{boiler}$ = 9.3 m² × 5.5 kWh/m²/day × 0.4 × 365 days/year/0.97 = **7,665 kWh/year** energy. Solar ventilation air preheating technology is simple, low-cost, extremely reliable (no moving parts except the fan), very low in maintenance requirements, and high in efficiency (up to 80%). There are no problems with freezing or fluid leaks, but there is also no practical way to store the heated ventilation air for night-time use. Well over one million square feet of transpired collectors have been installed since 1990.

Transpired Collector Principle

The key to low cost and high performance is an elegant solar technology known as **transpired collectors.** A painted metal plate is perforated with small holes about 1 mm in diameter and 3 mm apart. At this small scale, within 1 mm of the surface of the plate, flow within the laminar boundary layer is dominated by viscosity of the air, and heat transfer is dominated by conduction. This is in contrast to the air flow even a few more mm away from the plate where the flow is dominated by the momentum of the wind, and the heat transfer is dominated by convection. These two differences between the boundary layer of air within 1mm of the plate and the air farther away is key to the operating principle.

Sunlight strikes the black surface of the plate and is absorbed. Solar heat conducts from the surface to the thermal boundary layer of air 1 mm thick next to the plate. This boundary layer of air is drawn into a nearby hole before the heat can escape by convection, virtually eliminating heat loss off the surface of the plate. Since the plate operates at less than 20° C warmer than ambient air, heat loss by radiation is not overly consequential. There is no cover glass to reflect or absorb radiation.

To operate effectively, the fan-induced flow through the wall must be sufficient to continuously draw in the boundary layer. Consequently, efforts to increase the temperature of delivered air by reducing the flow rate will adversely affect performance. As one practitioner describes it, "Don't get greedy. They don't call it ventilation *preheating* for nothing." On cold winter days supplemental heating by gas or electricity will be required to ensure comfortable conditions.

Solar Ventilation Preheating System

The transpired collector is mounted about six inches away from the south wall of a building, forming a plenum between the wall and the collector. The collector is fastened to the wall, and the edges are sealed using standard metal building flashing techniques. A fan is installed in the wall to draw air from the plenum into the supply ductwork. The solar preheated air can be delivered to the air handler for the heater or directly into the space to be ventilated. The fan could be thermostatically controlled, or it could supply ventilation air continuously. Heat transmitted through the south wall of the building enters the air in the plenum, a form of heat recovery that works even at night. Introducing the ventilation air high in the space tends to destratify warm air near the ceiling, and pressurizing the space forces drafts outward, ensuring comfort for those working near leaky overhead doors.

In summertime, the sun is higher in the sky and shines primarily on the roof, not on the south wall. A by-pass damper is provided to bring outside air directly in, by-passing the solar wall. The stack effect causes outside air to enter the solar cladding along the bottom and rise to the top where it exits through holes in the outer skin. The net result is that any unwanted solar gain is transferred to the air and not to the interior of the wall. (The collector shades the south wall.)

The transpired collector makes an efficient sunlight-to-air heat exchanger that tempers the incoming fresh air. It is not possible to recirculate the room air back to the collector for reheating. The amount of temperature rise the air experiences coming through the collector depends on the air flow rate and on the incident solar radiation. The recommended air flow rate is about 4 CFM per square foot of collector area. At flow rates much less than this, the boundary layer can blow away before it is sucked through a hole, and at flow rates much higher, the required additional fan power begins to erode the cost savings.

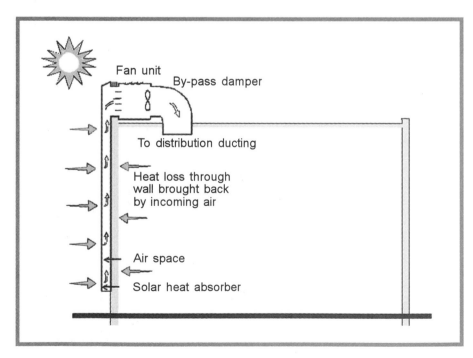

Figure 4.27
Solar ventilation air preheating system

Typical Applications for Solar Ventilation Air Preheating

The transpired collector technology is appropriate for preheating ventilation air in industrial and maintenance buildings, school and institutional buildings, apartment buildings, commercial buildings, and penthouse fans. Examples include factories, aircraft hangers, chemical storage buildings, and other facilities that require ventilation air. Industrial process uses for heated air, such as crop drying, can also be addressed with this technology.

Due to its metal construction, the transpired collector matches well with other metal construction, which is most common in industrial applications. The design of a new building is the best time to consider solar ventilation preheating, but it can be used in retrofit applications as well. It can even improve the appearance of a dilapidated façade. There must be sufficient south-facing vertical wall to mount the collector, and the wall must be largely unshaded by surrounding buildings, trees, hills, or other objects.

Design considerations for solar ventilation air preheating include some flexibility with wall orientation and color. A south-facing wall is best, but not absolutely necessary: +/- 20° of south gives 96-100%, of heat delivery, while +/- 45° of south gives 80-100% of the heat delivery of a south-facing wall. Black is best for absorbing solar radiation, but a wide choice of dark to medium colors may be used with efficiency loss of less than 10%.

Figure 4.28
The by-pass damper is clearly visible on this solar ventilation preheating system at the National Renewable Energy Laboratory, Colorado. The 300 S.F. system saves 14,310 kWh of electric heat per year. (Photo by Warren Gretz, courtesy of NREL.)

Design Tools

The solar resource information presented earlier in this chapter cannot be used directly to analyze solar ventilation preheating systems since performance depends not only on the solar resource, but also on the simultaneous need to heat the ventilation air. (Buildings in southern climates have great solar resource, but cannot use much of the heat.) The map in Figure 4.31 has been developed to assist in the design of solar ventilation air preheating systems. This map indicates energy savings including the effects of solar radiation and ambient air temperature. This map assumes that the building is occupied seven days a week. If it is occupied only on weekdays, multiply the savings by 5/7.

Conclusion

The effects of solar energy on a building are unavoidable. If we ignore the sun in building design, we are often left with complaints about glare, uncomfortable radiant conditions, and excessively high utility bills. On the other hand, if we harvest and control the useful daylight and solar heat, we can improve occupant comfort and health, enhance lighting quality, and reduce or even eliminate utility costs. The solar energy technologies described in this chapter provide a useful checklist for considering solar in building design: passive solar heating, cooling load avoidance, solar water heating, photovoltaics, and solar air ventilation preheating. Of course, these systems need to work together as part of a holistic building design, including mechanical and lighting systems, working in concert with the sun.

Figure 4.29
Solar ventilation preheating is incorporated into the south wall of the Bureau of Reclamation's water treatment plant in Leadville, Colorado. (Photo by Thomas Bunelle, courtesy of NREL.)

We can learn a lot about architectural measures, such as passive solar heating, cooling load avoidance, and daylighting, from quality historic buildings that were constructed before utilities were available. Solar water heating and photovoltaics, on the other hand, are evolving from space-age technology. Photovoltaics, for example, were initially developed to power spacecraft, but are finding more and more cost-effective applications on Earth. Many buildings, especially off-grid homes, now rely on solar energy for 100% of their space heating, water heating, and electricity needs.

In remote areas not served by a utility or with high costs to deliver fuel, solar energy can be the lowest-cost way of serving energy requirements. As the cost of solar technologies continues to decline, and as their performance continues to improve, there will come a day when clean, silent solar power is actually cheaper than the economic and environmental consequences of fossil fuel use. Many in the green building design industry believe that day is today.

Figure 4.30
This 5,000 square foot (465 m²) solar ventilation preheat system delivers 45,000 cfm of preheated air, saving 2,300 million BTUs per year. The system saves $12,000 per year in energy costs, and financing the cost of the system adds $4,800 per year to the annual lease payments for the building. Note that the color of the wall is not black. (Photo by Warren Gretz, courtesy of NREL.)

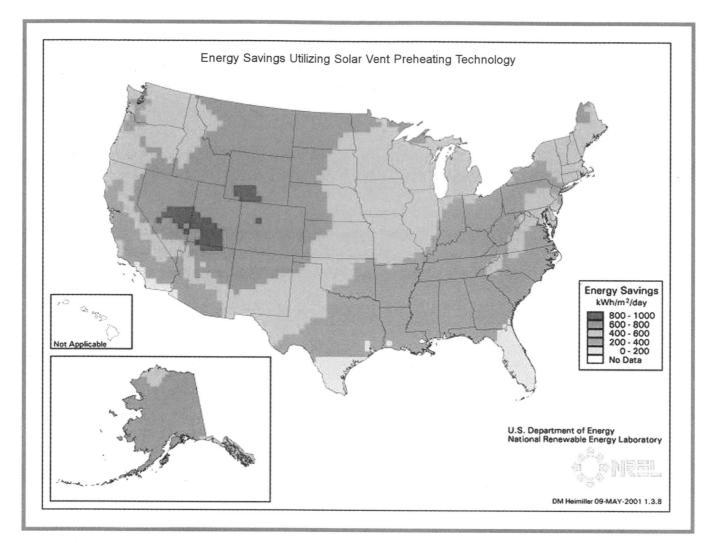

Energy Savings Utilizing Solar Vent Preheating Technology

Energy Savings
kWh/m²/day

800 - 1000
600 - 800
400 - 600
200 - 400
0 - 200
No Data

Not Applicable

U.S. Department of Energy
National Renewable Energy Laboratory

NREL

DM Heimiller 09-MAY-2001 1.3.8

Figure 4.31
Map shows annual energy savings of
solar ventilation air preheating
systems, including effects of solar
radiation and ambient air
temperature. (GIS map by Donna
Heimiller, NREL.)

[1] Butti, Ken and John Perlin *A Golden Thread, 2500 Years of Solar Architecture and Technology*, (Palo Alto: Cheshire Books).

[2] Assuming 1,353 W/m² solar radiation, 1.27 E7 m earth diameter, and 382 Quad annual global energy use.

[3] Brower, M., *Cool Energy: Renewable Solutions to Environmental Problems*, (Cambridge: MIT Press, 1992).

[4] Trying to save military budgets, Benjamin Thompson ("Count Rumford") observed the correlation between the food rations given to soldiers (chemical energy), and the clothing provided to them (insulation against the loss of heat energy), perhaps the first realization that these two seemingly disparate topics had something in common, energy.

[5] *International Energy Annual 1999, DOE/EIA-0219(99)*, Energy Information Agency, Washington DC, January 2001.

[6] Ibid

[7] Ibid

[8] *2001 BTS CORE DATABOOK*, Office of Energy Efficiency And Renewable Energy, U.S. Department of Energy, Washington DC. July 13, 2001. Available at **www.eren.doe.gov**

[9] Factories that manufacture solar energy equipment produce pollution, but in this context we refer to the fact that solar energy products do not cause emissions over their life cycle.

[10] *Western System Coordinating Council Disturbance Report for the Power System Outage that Occurred on the Western Interconnection August 10, 1996. 1548 PAST, October 18, 1996.*

[11] The solar energy resource is relatively uniform, varying in the mainland US from an annual average of 3.0 kWh/m²/day on a horizontal surface in Quillayute, Washington to 5.8 kWh per day in Daggett, California [1]. Other factors affecting feasibility vary by more than this, such as the cost of fuel delivery. Even north of the Arctic Circle or in Antarctica, it is possible to utilize solar energy for much of the year. Other weather parameters, such as temperature and wind speed, also affect the performance of solar energy systems.

[12] (W/m²/C or BTU/S.F./hour/F)

[13] *2001 BTS CORE DATABOOK, Office of Energy Efficiency And Renewable Energy*, U.S. Department of Energy, Washington DC. July 13, 2001. Available at **www.eren.doe.gov**

[14] *The Passive Solar Design and Construction Handbook* Steven Winter Associates, John Wiley and Sons.

[15] Ibid

[16] Ibid

[17] Ibid

[18] *2001 BTS CORE DATABOOK, Office of Energy Efficiency And Renewable Energy,* U.S. Department of Energy, Washington DC. July 13, 2001. Available at **www.eren.doe.gov**

[19] Ibid

[20] Ibid

[21] Ibid

[22] Ibid

[23] FRESA software available at **www.eren.doe.gov/femp**

[24] RETScreen software available at **www.retscreen.gc.ca**

[25] TRNSYS software available at **www.sel.me.wisc.edu/trnsys**

[26] WATSUN-PV software available from **www3.sympatico.ca/numlog/ watsunpv.htm**

[27] SRCC OG-300-91 Operating Guidelines and Minimum Standards for Certifying Solar Water Heating Systems, Solar Rating and Certification Corporation (SRCC), Florida.

[28] FRESA software available at **www.eren.doe.gov/femp**

People have been harnessing the energy of the wind in this country for more than a hundred years. In the late 1800s and early 1900s, millions of windmills were installed on farms to pump water from deep underground. Large-scale commercial wind energy development began in California in the early 1980s, and produced large arrays of turbines, generating power on windy ridges or passes, and more recently, on the prairie. Small wind electric systems—a single turbine, much smaller than the utility-scale models, were very common in the 1930s, producing clean, affordable electricity for a rural home, farm, or business. These small turbines with aerodynamic blades were much more efficient than the old fashioned windmill. The systems can still be found, but began disappearing when the Rural Electric Administration (REA) brought utility power to farms.

Why is wind energy gaining so much momentum? Spiraling utility bills, the need for uninterrupted service, the high cost of accessing the utility's electric grid from a remote location, and concerns over environmental impacts. Reducing dependence on potentially volatile prices for electrical power is another key motivator for many home-scale windsmiths.

Depending on the local wind resource and utility rates, a small wind energy system can reduce a customer's electricity bill by 50-90%. It can be installed as a stand-alone system, eliminating the high cost of extending utility power lines to a remote location, or it can be connected to the power grid, enabling the customer to sell excess power to the utility or buy additional power as needed. Over its 20- to 40-year life, a small residential wind turbine can offset approximately 1.2 tons of air pollutants and 200 tons of carbon dioxide and other "greenhouse" gases. And it can do so at one-third to one-half the installed cost of the most competitive solar electric technology.

Stand-alone or hybrid off-grid wind systems can be appropriate for homes, farms, or even entire villages that are far from the nearest utility lines. (The cost of running a power line to a remote site to connect with the utility grid can be prohibitive, ranging from $15,000 to more than $50,000 per mile, depending on the terrain.)

Many areas of the country qualify as having sufficient wind resources for small wind systems. Wind resource maps give only a rough estimate of whether a particular location is windy enough to make small wind energy economic. Local terrain and other factors also influence the wind power available at a specific site.

The map in Figure 5.1 provides an idea of the wind resources available in different parts of the United States. Annual average wind power is classified from lowest (Class 1, shown on this map in white) to highest

Figure 5.1

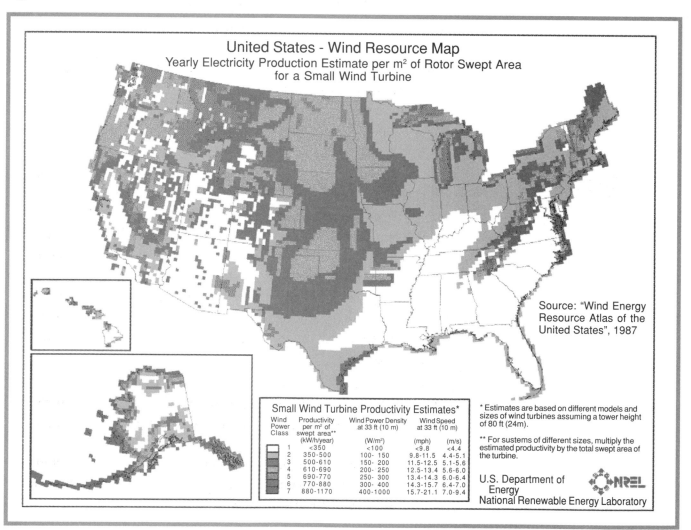

United States - Wind Resource Map
Yearly Electricity Production Estimate per m² of Rotor Swept Area for a Small Wind Turbine

Source: "Wind Energy Resource Atlas of the United States", 1987

Small Wind Turbine Productivity Estimates*

Wind Power Class	Productivity per m² of swept area** (kW/h/year)	Wind Power Density at 33 ft (10 m) (W/m²)	Wind Speed at 33 ft (10 m) (mph)	(m/s)
1	<350	<100	<9.8	<4.4
2	350-500	100- 150	9.8-11.5	4.4-5.1
3	500-610	150- 200	11.5-12.5	5.1-5.6
4	610-690	200- 250	12.5-13.4	5.6-6.0
5	690-770	250- 300	13.4-14.3	6.0-6.4
6	770-880	300- 400	14.3-15.7	6.4-7.0
7	880-1170	400-1000	15.7-21.1	7.0-9.4

* Estimates are based on different models and sizes of wind turbines assuming a tower height of 80 ft (24m).

** For sustems of different sizes, multiply the estimated productivity by the total swept area of the turbine.

U.S. Department of Energy
National Renewable Energy Laboratory

(Class 7). Large-scale turbines require a minimum of a Class 3 wind regime (and prefer a Class 5). However, small wind systems can be successfully installed in Class 2 or better wind regimes. Class 2 corresponds to average annual wind speeds of 9-11 miles per hour, or 4-5 meters per second.

Indicators of good topography include:

- Gaps, passes, gorges, and long valleys extending down from mountain ranges
- High elevation plains and plateaus
- Plains and valleys with persistent downslope winds associated with strong pressure gradients
- Exposed ridges and mountain summits
- Coastlines and immediate inland strips with minimum wind barriers and vegetation
- Upwind and crosswind corners of islands
- Wind-deformed vegetation: flagging of trees and shrubs
- Surface materials deposited by the wind to form playas, sand dunes, and other types of "eolian" landforms

Power generated by small wind systems is used to reduce the demand for utility-supplied electricity or is sold to the utility, often at retail prices. Thus the value of this widely available energy resource depends on the retail cost of electricity in a particular location. In general, the value of power generated by small wind energy systems ranges from 6 to 18 cents per kilowatt-hour.

Applications & Concerns: An Overview

Small wind energy systems are sometimes referred to as "residential" applications, and indeed they are. But they also can and do provide power to farms, schools, and other rural businesses. A small wind turbine along with solar photovoltaic panels can provide supplementary power for a grid-connected, all-electric home (which includes a heat pump and an electric car). However, small systems may also be installed to power a specific application, such as pumping water distant from the utility grid. The size of the system required to meet a given customer's needs depends on how much energy the customer uses and the annual average wind speed.

For example, a home or farm using 1,400 kWh per month in a location with Class 4 winds could cover virtually all its electricity needs with a 10 kW turbine. A larger ranch or facility using 10,000 kWh per month would require a 50-60 kW system to meet its electricity needs, depending on the wind resource available. Some commercial customers may even consider negotiating a power purchase agreement with their local utility to purchase back excess electricity generated.

Concerns that may arise regarding use of wind turbines include noise, aesthetics, potential harm to birds, and interference with television and radio signals. The noise level of most modern residential turbines is around 52-55 decibels. They are audible outdoors, but no noisier than the average refrigerator.

Because small turbines are mounted on tall towers, they are visible from a distance. To minimize any objection from neighbors, the wind industry recommends customer property sizes of ½ acre or more for turbines up to about 2 kW, and 1 acre or more for larger wind turbines.

While birds can collide with any structure, reports of small wind turbines killing birds are very rare. A sliding glass door is more dangerous to birds than a small wind turbine.

Small wind turbines have not been found to interfere with TV or radio reception. The rotors are made of fiberglass or wood; both materials are transparent to electromagnetic waves, such as radio or TV.

Wind can supply electricity during a utility power outage if the system includes storage batteries and a way to disconnect from the utility grid (for those that are connected).

Small wind turbines are equipped with overspeed protection and are designed to furl out of the wind during extreme gusts.

Other Considerations

Connecting to the Utility Grid

Whether or not to connect a wind system to the local utility grid depends on a number of factors. In general, grid-connected small wind systems can be practical if the following conditions exist:

- Average annual wind speed is at least 10 miles per hour (4.5 meters per second).
- The market rates for power are fairly high (10-15 cents/kWh).
- Utility requirements for connecting to the grid are not prohibitive.
- There are tax credits or rebates for the purchase of wind turbines or good incentives for the sale of excess electricity.

(Utility grid connection is discussed in more detail later in the chapter.)

Net Metering

The idea of net metering is to allow the electric meters of customers with generating facilities to turn backwards when their generators are producing more energy than the customers demand. Net metering allows customers to use their generation to offset their consumption over an entire billing period, not just at the time the electricity is produced. This way the customers can receive retail value for more of the electricity they generate.

Net metering programs vary by state and by utility company. Net excess generation (NEG) may be carried on a monthly basis, or it may be credited for up to a year. Annual NEG credits allow wind turbine owners to use energy produced in the winter, when weather tends to be windier, to displace large summer loads such as air-conditioning or pumping water for irrigation. *(Net metering is covered in more detail later in this chapter.)*

Basic Criteria for Using a Wind System

In considering whether to incorporate a small wind energy system into new construction or retrofit projects, the following factors should be reviewed:

- **A good wind resource.** Wind resource maps *(See Figure 5.1)* indicate whether a property is in a Class 2 zone or better, but terrain and other factors also affect windiness at a particular site. In general, the more exposed, the better.
- **Size of the property.** At least one-half acre is typically enough for the smallest small wind systems (up to 2 kW), but the general rule-of-thumb is one acre or more.
- **Average monthly electricity bill.** A monthly bill of $100 or more means small wind is more likely to be economic.
- **Local zoning codes or covenants.** If local codes specifically allow wind turbines, the permitting process can be expedited.
- **State or local incentive programs.** Incentive programs for small wind systems can help improve the economics.

Small Wind System Components

Wind is created by the unequal heating of the Earth's surface by the sun. Wind turbines convert the kinetic energy in the wind into mechanical power that runs a generator to produce clean, nonpolluting electricity. Today's small-scale turbines are versatile and modular. Their rotors consist of two or three blades that are aerodynamically designed to capture the maximum energy from the wind. The wind turns the blades, which spin a shaft connected to a generator that makes electricity. A mainframe supports the rotor, generator, and tail that aligns the rotor into the wind.

Turbines are mounted on towers—typically 80-120 feet high, which place the blades high enough to be exposed to the wind. There are many tower options, but in general the taller the tower, the more power the wind system can produce. The tower also raises the turbine above air turbulence created by objects (buildings, trees, etc.) closer to ground level. As a rule of thumb, the bottom of the rotor blades should be at least 30 feet above any obstacle within 300 feet of the tower. Towers may be self-supporting, but more commonly use guy wires. Some small tower models can be tilted down to facilitate maintenance work. Towers constructed as a lattice are strong and inexpensive, but attract birds by providing perches.

In addition to the tower and turbine, small wind energy systems require:

- A **foundation,** usually made of reinforced concrete.
- A **wire run,** to conduct electricity from the generator to the electronics.
- A **disconnect** (or safety switch,) which allows the electrical output to be isolated from the electronics.
- A **power processing** (or conditioning) unit, which makes the turbine power compatible with the utility power.
- A **system energy meter,** which records energy production.

If the system is designed to stand alone or operate during a power outage, it will need deep-cycle batteries (like the ones used for golf carts) to store power, and a charge controller to keep the batteries from overcharging. A grid-connected system not designed to operate during a power outage does not need batteries.

Evaluating the Local Wind Resource

Wind resources can vary significantly over an area of just a few miles due to local terrain influences on the wind flow. As a first step in evaluating whether there is enough wind on the site to make a small wind turbine system economically worthwhile, wind resource maps *(See Figure 5.1)* can be used to estimate the potential wind power density in the region. The highest average wind speeds in the U.S. are generally found along seacoasts, on ridgelines, and across the Great Plains; however many areas have wind resources strong enough to power a small wind turbine. The wind resource estimates on this map generally apply to terrain features that are well exposed to the wind, such as hilltops, ridge crests, and high plains.

New, high-resolution wind resource maps are being produced using state-of-the art computer modeling tools to give a better estimate of wind regimes at different heights above ground level. The models help predict daily and seasonal patterns which can be compared to on-site energy usage patterns. Other ways to indirectly quantify the wind resource include obtaining long-term wind speed information from a nearby airport and observing the project site's vegetation. (Trees, especially conifers or evergreens, can be permanently deformed by strong winds. For more information on the use of "flagging," see *A Siting Handbook for Small Wind Energy Conversion Systems*, available through the National Technical Information Service, at **www.ntis.gov**)

Green Building: Project Planning & Cost Estimating

Direct monitoring by a wind resource measurement system at a site provides the clearest picture of the available resource. Wind monitoring equipment can be purchased for $1200–$4,000, depending on tower height. This expense may not be justified for one small wind turbine project. The anemometers, or wind sensors, must be set high enough to avoid turbulence created by trees, buildings, and other obstructions. The most useful readings are taken at turbine hub-height, the elevation at the top of the tower where the blades will connect.

Finally, if there is already another small wind turbine system installed in the area, it may be possible to obtain information on the annual output from the owner.

Estimating the Cost of Wind Systems

Although wind energy systems involve a significant initial investment, they can be competitive with conventional energy sources when accounting for a lifetime of reduced or altogether avoided utility costs. The length of the payback period depends on the system selected, the wind resource at the site, electricity costs, and how the wind system will be used.

A guideline for estimating the cost of a small wind system is $2–$4 per installed watt, with larger turbines costing less. For example, a 10 kW system costs $30,000–$40,000 installed, and a 50 kW system costs $100,000–$150,000 installed. A comparable photovoltaic (PV) solar system would cost over $90,000 including wiring and installation. Wind turbines become more cost-effective as the rotor size increases in diameter. Although small wind systems cost less in initial outlay, they are proportionally more expensive than larger machines, unlike PV systems that have basically the same cost per watt independent of array size. At the 50 watt size level, a small wind turbine may cost up to $8/watt, compared to approximately $6/watt for a PV module.

Installed costs for small wind turbines are expected to decrease to $1.50/kW by 2010. Volume production is expected to drive overall costs down 15-30%, and new technology breakthroughs are further reducing manufacturing and installation costs.

It is important to evaluate the trade-off between the incremental cost of a taller tower and increased wind turbine performance. Wind speed increases with height above ground, and increasing speed increases wind power exponentially. Thus, relatively small investments in increased tower height can yield very high rates of return in power production. For instance, installing a 10 kW generator on a 100-foot tower rather than a 60-foot tower involves a 10% increase in overall system cost, but can result in 29% more power.

Determining Payback

A typical home consumes 830 kWh of electricity per month, and a 10 kW turbine could provide this, if wind in the location caused its rated output 12% of the time (also called 12% "capacity factor"). For customers paying 12 cents/kWh or more for electricity in an area with average wind speeds of 10 mph or more, payback periods will generally fall in the range of 8-16 years. After this payback period, the energy from the wind system will be virtually free (except for upkeep costs) for the remainder of the system's 20-50 year life.

Key factors in calculating payback are the cost and value of the electricity produced, and whether rebates, buy-down funds, or other financial incentives, such as net metering, tax exemptions, and tax credits, are available. For example, combining a California-type 50% buy-down program, net metering, and an average annual wind speed of 15 mph (6.7 m/s) would result in a simple payback of approximately 6 years.

Turbine manufacturers can help estimate the energy production and the expected payback period based on the particular wind turbine power curve, the average annual wind speed at the site, the height of the planned tower, and the wind frequency distribution—that is, the number of hours the wind blows at each speed during an average year. The calculation will be adjusted for the site's elevation, which affects air density and thus turbine power output.

Obstacles & Incentives

There are 21 million U.S. homes and 4.6 million commercial buildings located on properties of one or more acre, 60% of them in areas with Class 2 winds or better. Why, then, are there not more small wind energy systems already in place? Part of the reason is that low production volume and historic lack of public funding have led to relatively high costs for this technology. Efforts by the U.S. Department of Energy and state agencies to promote small wind have only recently begun to help.

Other barriers include zoning regulations with height restrictions of 35 feet and concerns about potential noise from turbines. The process of obtaining approval for interconnection with the utility grid can be expensive and time-consuming.

Fortunately, a number of promising developments are bringing down these barriers. The U.S. Department of Energy has made small wind a major emphasis of its current outreach efforts. DOE's Advanced Small Wind Turbine Program, combined with industry research and development, is improving small wind technology, while lowering the manufacturing costs.

As the market begins to expand, higher volume production is also expected to lower costs, perhaps by as much as 30%. New low-cost "micro" 1.5 kW systems are able to generate 100-300 kWh per month for a total installed cost of under $4,000.

A host of programs and policies are already in place to nurture the rural residential wind market. More are in development. At the federal level, the Public Utility Regulatory Policies Act of 1978 (PURPA) requires utilities to connect with and purchase power from small wind energy systems. However, there are currently no federal tax credits for small wind systems. (These expired in 1985.)

Economic Incentive Programs

State incentive programs include rebates, buy-down programs, and grants; loan funds and industry recruitment programs; sales tax and property tax exemptions; personal and corporate tax incentives; and net metering policies. Ten states (CA, IA, IL, IN, MA, MI, MT, and NJ), have rebates, grants, or buy-down programs which offer the strongest financial incentive for the small wind turbine market. Fifteen states (AK, AZ, CA, CT, ID, IA, MD, MN, MO, NE, NY, OR, TN, VA and WI) offer loan funds, and six (AZ, CA, CT, MT, NC, and WA) offer industry recruitment incentives. Ten states (AZ, IA, MA, MN, ND, NJ, OH, RI, VT, and WA) have sales tax incentives. Eighteen states (CT, IL, IN, IA, KS, MD, MN, MT, NV, NH, ND, OH, OR, RI, SD, TX, VT, and WI) have property tax incentives. Fourteen states (AZ, HI, ID, MA, MN, MT, NC, ND, OH, OR, RI, TX, UT, and WV) have personal or corporate tax credits, deductions, exemptions, and accelerated depreciation policies for installation of wind energy systems.

Zoning Ordinances

Other state polices include zoning ordinances allowing tall towers, wind access laws, and line extension requirements. FL, MN, MT, OR, and WI have wind access or easement rights laws to secure property owners' wind resources, which include restrictions against neighborhood covenants that prohibit the use of renewable energy systems. Texas has a unique line extension policy which requires utilities to provide information on on-site renewable energy technology options to customers required to pay for the construction of utility power lines to a remote location.

Net Metering Policies

Thirty-three states (AZ, AK, CA, CO, CT, DE, GA, ID, IL, IN, IA, ME, MD, MA, MN, MT, NV, NH, NJ, NM, NY, ND, OH, OK, OR, PA, RI, TX, VT, VA, WA, WI and WY) have net metering policies that allow customers to offset power consumption up to 100% at the full retail value over the billing period. Net metering rules are determined on a state-by-state basis and sometimes by individual utility. Some state laws apply only to private investor-owned utilities that are regulated by public utility commissions, and as a result many rural electric cooperatives are not required to offer the option to their customers. This is unfortunate, since small wind turbines have historically been used and have a larger market in rural settings.

Without net metering, small wind system owners are considered to be qualifying facilities under the Public Utility Regulatory Policies Act of 1978 (PURPA), and are paid only the utility's avoided fuel cost (often under 2 cents/kWh) for their "instantaneous" excess generation. Combined with requirements to purchase a second meter, this arrangement gives little financial incentive to consumers to install wind systems.

Building Permit Issues

Many jurisdictions restrict the height of structures permitted in residentially zoned areas, although variances are often obtainable. A conditional use permit may be required, which could specify a number of requirements the installation must meet. Most restrictions occur in populated areas where height, safety, or aesthetics are issues. In addition to zoning issues, neighbors might object to a wind turbine that blocks their view, or potential noise.

Most zoning and aesthetic concerns can be addressed by supplying objective data, such as the ambient noise level of 52-55 decibels, with sound dropping sharply with distance. In many cases, the perception of visual and noise impacts prior to wind turbine installation is worse than the actual impact.

Tower Height

County ordinances that restrict tower height may adversely affect optimum economics for small wind turbines. Unless the zoning jurisdiction has established small wind turbine as a "permitted" or "conditional" use, it may be necessary to obtain a variance or special use permit to erect an adequate tower.

The 35-foot height limit in many zoning ordinances dates back to the early 1900s as the height to which the typical firefighting engine could pump water, and is clearly not pertinent for modern residential wind turbines. Small wind advocates may want to encourage local governments to allow wind turbine towers up to at least 90-120 feet as a permitted use.

The Federal Aviation Administration (FAA) has regulations on the height of structures, particularly those near the approach path to runways at local airports. Objects that are higher than 200 feet (61 meters) above ground level must be reported, and beacon lights may be required. A proposed wind system within ten miles of an airport, no matter how tall the tower, requires contacting the local FAA office to determine if it is necessary to file for permission to erect a tower. A general rule of thumb for proper and efficient operation of a wind turbine is that the bottom of the turbine's blades should be at least 10 feet (3 meters) above the top of anything within 300 feet (about 100 meters).

Noise

The most characteristic sounds of a wind turbine are the "swish . . . swish . . . swish" of its turning blades and the whirring of the generator. Improved designs have made wind turbines much quieter over the last decade. Within several hundred feet of a machine, these sounds may be distinguishable from the background noise of local traffic or the wind blowing through the trees, but they usually are not disruptive or objectionable. The impact on any particular neighbor will depend on how close they live, whether they are upwind or downwind, and the level of other noise sources, such as traffic. Some permitting agencies have set up noise complaint resolution processes.

Visibility

The visibility of a particular wind system will depend on many factors, including tower height, proximity to neighbors and roadways, local terrain, and tree coverage. Some neighbors may object to a wind turbine being in their field of view, and this could be an issue when applying for a zoning permit. In most areas, modern wind turbines are an uncommon sight, so it is natural to expect some reservations about their introduction. Objections are more likely to occur in populated and tourist areas. Opposition is least likely to surface in rural settings and after some small turbines have been installed in the area.

Connecting Wind Systems to Utility Grids

Federal regulations under PURPA require utilities to connect with and purchase power from small wind energy systems. Local utilities should be contacted before connecting to their distribution lines to address any power quality and safety concerns.

A grid-connected wind turbine can reduce the home or business' consumption of utility-supplied electricity. When the wind system produces more electricity than is used, the excess is sent or sold to the utility. If the turbine cannot deliver the full amount of energy needed, the utility makes up the difference. A grid-connected system requires no batteries for storage; only a power conditioning unit (an inverter) or an induction generator is needed to make the turbine output electrically compatible with the utility grid. The output is connected to the household breaker panel on a dedicated breaker, just like a large appliance. In effect, the utility acts as a big battery bank, and the utility sees the wind turbine as a negative load.

Electrical code requirements emphasize proper wiring and installation and the use of components that have been certified for fire and electrical safety, such as Underwriters Laboratories (UL). Most local electrical code requirements are based on the *National Electrical Code* (NEC), published by the National Fire Protection Association.

The utility's principal concern will be that the wind turbine automatically stops delivering any electricity to power lines during an outage. Otherwise line workers and the public, thinking that the line is "dead," might not take normal precautions and might be injured. Another concern among utilities is that the power from the wind system synchronize properly with the utility's grid, and that it matches the utility's own power in terms of voltage, frequency, and power quality.

Most utilities and other electricity providers require a formal agreement before interconnecting a wind turbine to the utility grid. In states with retail competition for electricity service, such as California and Pennsylvania (where the utility operates the local wires, but the customer has a choice of electricity provider), it may be necessary to sign separate agreements with each company. These agreements are usually written by the utility or electricity supplier, and the terms and conditions of those with investor-owned utilities must be reviewed and approved by state regulatory authorities.

Several state governments are developing new standardized interconnection requirements for small renewable energy generating facilities. At least five states (CA, DE, NY, OH and TX) have conducted proceedings on interconnection of distributed generating facilities. In most cases the new requirements are based on standards and testing procedures developed by consensus through independent third-party authorities, such as the Institute of Electrical and Electronic Engineers (IEEE) and UL. Sixteen states (CA, DE, GA, MD, MT, NJ, NM, NV, NY, OH, OR, RI, VT, VA, WA, and WY) have adopted interconnection standards based on UL/IEEE. As existing safety standards developed specifically for photovoltaics, UL 1741 and IEEE 929 have been successfully used to certify inverters for small wind turbines. The IEEE is working on standard IEEE P1547 for inter-tied "distributed generation" technologies, including small wind turbines.

A number of states have also required utilities to develop simplified, streamlined agreements for interconnecting small-scale renewable generating facilities, including wind turbines. These shorter agreements are designed to be relatively consumer-friendly and avoid complicated legal or technical jargon.

Some utilities require small wind turbine owners to maintain liability insurance of $1 million or more, claiming this is necessary to protect the utility from liability for facilities it does not own and control. Such insurance requirements quickly make small wind turbine systems uneconomical. Since PURPA was enacted, requiring utilities to interconnect with the grid, there have been no liability claims relating to electrical safety of wind turbines anywhere in the U.S., in spite of over 400 million hours of interconnected operation.

In eight states (CA, GA, MD, NV, OH, OK, OR, and WA), laws or regulatory authorities prohibit utilities from imposing any insurance requirements on small wind systems that qualify for "net metering." In five other states (ID, NM, NY, VA, and VT), regulatory authorities have allowed utilities to impose insurance requirements, but have reduced the required coverage amounts to levels consistent with the conventional residential or commercial insurance policies (such as $100,000–$300,000).

Owners of small wind systems may be asked to indemnify their utility for any potential liability arising from the operation of the wind turbine. Indemnity provisions should be fair to both parties. Customer charges can take a variety of forms, including interconnection fees, metering fees, and standby fees, among others. PURPA prohibits utilities from assessing discriminatory charges to customers who have their own generation facilities.

Grid-connected small wind turbines can provide many benefits to utilities, as well as turbine owners. In rural areas with long power lines, they can improve power quality (by boosting voltage) and reduce line losses. They can also provide extra generating capacity and reduce power plant emissions.

Conclusion

Although important challenges exist for the domestic small wind market, small wind turbines have significant potential to contribute to the nation's electricity supply, and to reduce the environmental impacts of generating electricity. Approximately 21 million U.S. homes are built on one-acre and larger lots, and 24% of the U.S. population lives in rural areas. Recent reductions in costs and increased public, political, and institutional support for small wind energy systems are helping this potential to be realized. (For updated information on wind power, contact The American Wind Energy Association (AWGA), 122 C Street, NW, Suite 380, Washington, DC 20001, phone: (202) 383-2500, Web site: **www.awea.org**)

6 Health, Comfort, & Productivity

James Armstrong
Andy Walker, Ph.D., PE

To be adopted, any green building measure must enhance the mission of the building, and all green buildings have as a part of their mission the provision of quality conditions. Green building includes not only using energy-efficient, recycled, and recyclable materials and products, but also creating a healthy, comfortable indoor environment. The rewards have been demonstrated: higher property values on more desirable space, higher productivity among building users, enhanced ability to attract and retain employees, and valuable public relations for the owner and/or tenants.

There are many factors in the green indoor environment, including:

- Indoor air quality: healthy, properly humidified, odorless air—and operable windows to admit outside air.
- Thermal comfort, with individual control over one's space, including effects of air temperature, radiant heat gain from the sun or surroundings, air movement, and humidity.
- Views of the outdoors and ample natural light with task lighting, including effects of color rendition, and positioning of fixtures to avoid glare and reflections.
- Clean water.
- Comfortable noise levels and speech privacy.
- Comfortable, climate-appropriate furnishings.

Indoor Air Quality

Indoor air quality (IAQ) has been much discussed over the past several years. Today's buildings are more tightly constructed than ever. This means that less airborne dirt and dust can infiltrate buildings from outside, but it also means that airborne particles generated in the space or brought into a building on clothing or by other means, or from construction or other materials installed in the building, cannot get out and are recirculated over and over again. These particles can cause unnecessary physical discomfort and illness. Particulates can be a variety of substances, including dust, pollen, and mold spores. Some particulates harbor harmful bacteria and viruses, which can remain in the air stream.

Mold

Mold is the most common medium for growth and development of airborne bacteria. Molds are small organisms found almost everywhere, indoors and out, including on plants, foods, and dry leaves. They can be nearly any color, including white, orange, green, and black. Molds are beneficial to the environment and are needed to break down organic material. Very tiny and lightweight, mold spores travel easily through the air.

Most building surfaces provide adequate nutrients to support the growth of mold. When mold spores land on material that is damp (for example, walls, floors, carpets, furniture, or appliances such as humidifiers or air conditioners), they can begin to multiply. When molds are present in large numbers, they may cause allergic symptoms similar to those caused by plant pollen.

Mold needs a food source such as leaves, paper, wood, soil, or other organic material; a source of moisture; and a place to grow. There can be many sources of moisture in a facility including flooding, leaky roofs, humidifiers/air handlers, damp basements or crawl spaces, constant plumbing leaks (common under sinks and behind dishwashers and clothes washers), and clothes dryers that are vented indoors.

People are exposed to some mold every day, usually by touching, eating, or inhaling it. When mold is growing on a surface, spores can be released into the air, where they can be easily inhaled. A person who ingests or inhales a large number of spores may suffer adverse health effects, including asthma and allergic symptoms such as watery eyes, a runny nose, sneezing, nasal congestion, itching, coughing, wheezing, difficulty breathing, headache, and fatigue. The same amount of mold may cause health effects in one person, but not in another, because some people are more sensitive to molds than others. This group includes infants and children, elderly persons, immune-compromised patients (e.g., people with HIV infection, cancer, lung or liver disease, or who are undergoing chemotherapy), and individuals with existing respiratory conditions, such as allergies and asthma. Airborne mold spores in large numbers can also cause skin irritation and allergic reactions and infections. Exposure to high spore levels can actually stimulate the development of a mold allergy.

Mold is the natural process by which organic materials are broken down or decay. Many construction components (including structural elements) are derived from organic (carbon-based) materials, such as wood or pulp, and thus can be damaged by unchecked mold growth.

Stachybotrys

Stachybotrys is a greenish-black, slimy type of mold found only on cellulose products (such as wood or paper) that have remained wet for several days or longer. Stachybotrys does not grow on concrete, linoleum, or tile. According to the U.S. Centers for Disease Control and Prevention (CDC), all molds should be treated the same with respect to potential health risks and removal. In 1994, the CDC investigated whether exposure to Stachybotrys might be related to pulmonary hemorrhage, also known as "bleeding lungs," in infants in Cleveland, Ohio.[1]

Construction Problems & Solutions

Prevention of mold requires prevention of moisture intrusion from the outdoors, as well as attention to potential moisture leaks inside the building. Moisture can also accumulate as warm humid air condenses water on a cold surface (either the inside wall layer of a cooled building, or the outer layer of a heated building). Humidity can build up to high levels in a space due to tighter buildings with reduced air infiltration, the result of added insulation and better-fitting windows and doors. Another contributor is oversized cooling systems, which run less frequently, providing less opportunity to expel humidity from the building interior. Improper building maintenance or operating procedures, and compromised air filtration, can also lead to mold. Mold often grows in wall cavities, under impervious floors, or in cavities in cathedral ceilings where it is difficult to detect and treat.

Manufactured homes have had their share of moisture-inducing problems, including duct leakage and tears in the "belly board," the material that protects the structure from ground moisture. These homes also use nonporous finish treatments, such as vinyl and plastic, which encourage condensation.

Construction techniques to address moisture intrusion from outside include vapor diffusion retarders, airflow retarders, waterproofing and dampproofing, flashings (with special attention to HVAC equipment on rooftops), vented spaces with drainage planes, proper slopes in grading and use of granular backfill or drainage board next to the foundation, perimeter drains as needed, and low-VOC dampproofing coatings. *(See Chapter 2 for more on green approaches to prevention of moisture intrusion.)*

Careful planning can avoid the creation of conditions conducive to mold growth. For example, potentially problematic plumbing connections and floor drains should be accessible for easy cleaning and frequent detection of leaks.

Monitoring Humidity

Special-use buildings, such as schools, laboratories, libraries, and museums, may require humidity monitoring systems and control methods. Schools, especially in the southeastern part of the United States, experience mold problems related to shutting off the cooling/ventilation systems in summer or in the afternoon when the school day ends. Both humidity and contaminants tend to build up during those "off" periods. The additional problem with schools is that children are more susceptible to IAQ problems, including mold. Some studies recommend desiccant systems to remove moisture and reduce CO_2.

Cleanup of Mold

It is important to make sure that the source of moisture is stopped before mold is cleaned up. If this is not done, it will grow again. The appropriate cleanup measures will depend on the surface where mold is growing. A professional should be consulted if large areas (more than 30 square feet) are contaminated with mold. The first step is to clean surfaces with soap and water. When most of the staining has been removed, a water and bleach mixture (10:1 ratio) can be used to kill the mold spores. Bleach must not be mixed with any other chemicals or cleaners. The space should be well-ventilated, not only because of the bleach's toxicity, but to help dry the wet surfaces.

During the cleanup of molds, many spores may be released into the air. Mold counts in air are typically 10-1,000 times higher than their background levels prior to the cleaning and removal. To prevent health effects, several protective measures can be practiced. Anyone with a chronic illness, such as asthma or emphysema, should not perform the cleanup. A HEPA (high efficiency particulate air) filter respirator will reduce the mold spores that can be inhaled. Protective clothing should be worn, along with rubber gloves that are easily cleaned or discarded. Bystanders should not be present when the cleanup takes place. Work should be done over short time spans and breaks taken in a fresh-air location. Windows should be open and air handlers turned off, except for exhaust fans. Fans can also be used in windows to blow air out of the affected room to the outside during and after the cleanup. (Make sure the air is being blown outside the building, not into another room). Contaminated materials should be double-bagged before they are removed from the area.

Gases

Other threats to indoor air quality include noxious gases such as radon, carbon monoxide, propane, methane (natural gas), and formaldehyde—from natural sources and appliances and man-made construction materials. Hospitals, labs, parking garages, gas stations, sewage treatment plants, airports, and factories may additionally have to control exposure to hydrogen, ammonia, and fluorocarbons (Freon). Identifying such gases, their sources, and amounts enables professionals to determine an appropriate treatment. *(See also "Gas Detectors and Alarms" later in this chapter.)*

Off-Gassing of Construction Materials

Many forms of construction materials and products introduce contaminants into a facility, both initially and for many years after construction is completed. This is due to the off-gassing of contaminants over time until the product becomes stabilized, sometimes years later. Selecting natural carpeting, fabrics, flooring, and finish materials, including natural wall covering or, preferably, low- or no-VOC paints and wood floor finishes; and framing, sheathing, and cabinetry materials without harmful chemicals is the green approach. Materials constructed with potentially harmful chemicals, such as particleboard with formaldehyde resin, can sometimes be wrapped or sealed to reduce exposure (for example, millwork completely wrapped in laminate or coated with a nontoxic coating). Gypsum board and acoustic panels and ceiling tiles should also be investigated for toxic components before specifying. Natural floor materials, such as cork, bamboo, or linoleum are a better choice than vinyl, which contains potentially toxic chemicals.

Insulation is another potential source of indoor pollutants, from fibers and chemicals in materials such as cellulose, fiberglass, and mineral wool (which uses phenol formaldehyde binders), polyurethane spray foam, and polystyrene. Safer choices include Perlite, Icynene, and Air Krete, as well as scrap cotton. Formaldehyde-free fiberglass insulation was recently introduced.

Formaldehyde: Formaldehyde is a chemical used widely to manufacture building materials and products, such as glue in fiberboard. Formaldehyde is also a by-product of combustion and certain other natural processes. Thus, it may be present in substantial concentrations both indoors and out. Sources of formaldehyde include building materials; smoking; household products; and the use of un-vented, fuel-burning appliances, such as fork lifts, gas stoves, or kerosene space heaters. Formaldehyde, by itself or in combination with other chemicals, is used for a number of purposes in manufactured products. For example, it is used to add permanent-press qualities to clothing and draperies, as a component of glues and adhesives, and as a preservative in some paints and coating products.

In smaller facilities and homes, the most significant sources of formaldehyde are likely to be pressed wood products made using adhesives that contain urea-formaldehyde (UF) resins. Pressed wood products made for indoor use include: particleboard (used as sub-flooring and shelving and in cabinetry and furniture); hardwood plywood paneling (used for decorative wall covering and in cabinets and furniture); and medium-density fiberboard (used for drawer fronts, cabinets, and furniture tops). Medium-density fiberboard contains a higher resin-to-wood ratio than any other UF pressed wood product and is generally recognized as emitting the highest levels of formaldehyde.

Other pressed wood products, such as softwood plywood and flake or oriented strand board, are produced for exterior construction use and contain the dark, or red/black-colored phenol-formaldehyde (PF) resin. Although formaldehyde is present in both types of resins, pressed woods that contain PF resin generally emit formaldehyde at considerably lower rates than those containing UF resin.

Since 1985, the Department of Housing and Urban Development (HUD) has permitted the use of plywood and particleboard only if they conform to specified formaldehyde emission limits in the construction of prefabricated panels. In the past, some construction using prefabricated panels had elevated levels of formaldehyde because of the large amount of high-emitting pressed wood products used in their construction.

The rate at which products such as pressed wood or textiles release formaldehyde can change. Formaldehyde emissions generally decrease as products age. When products are new, high indoor temperatures or humidity can cause increased release of formaldehyde.

During the 1970s, many properties had urea-formaldehyde foam insulation (UFFI) installed in the wall cavities as an energy conservation measure. However, many of these properties were found to have relatively high indoor concentrations of formaldehyde soon after the UFFI installation.

Use of this product has been declining. Studies show that formaldehyde emissions from UFFI decrease with time; therefore, homes in which UFFI was installed many years ago are unlikely to have high levels of formaldehyde now.

Formaldehyde, a colorless, pungent-smelling gas, can cause eye, nose, and throat irritation; wheezing and coughing; fatigue; skin rash; and severe allergic reactions. High concentrations may trigger attacks in people with asthma. There is evidence that some people can develop a sensitivity to formaldehyde, which has also been shown to cause cancer in animals and may cause cancer in humans.[2]

The average concentration of formaldehyde in older properties without UFFI is generally below 0.1 PPM (parts per million). In properties with significant amounts of new pressed wood products, levels can be greater than 0.3 PPM. Coatings may reduce formaldehyde emissions for some period of time. To be effective, the coating must cover all surfaces and edges and remain intact.

Since release of formaldehyde may be affected by the humidity level (as well as heat), dehumidifiers and air conditioning can help reduce emissions. (Drain and clean dehumidifier collection trays frequently so that they do not become a breeding ground for microorganisms.) Increasing the rate of ventilation will also help reduce formaldehyde levels. *(See Chapters 2 and 10, and Part 5 for more on construction materials that minimize exposure to contaminants.)*

Tools for Improving Air Quality

Air Purification Systems

Operable windows are becoming more popular in a variety of facility types, as part of the movement toward a more comfortable, natural environment in workplaces and in homes. Being able to open a window to admit "fresh" outside air when the outdoor air temperature is comfortable, and having some control over one's immediate space conditions are valuable features, and can greatly enhance the quality of the indoor air. (Tuberculosis hospitals built early in the 20th century were located in the countryside at high altitudes, for fresh, healing air.)

More and more building managers are also using high-efficiency air filtration systems, increasing the amount of fresh air brought into a building, as well as the exhaust volumes. Of course, all of the air introduced into the facility must be conditioned (heated, cooled, filtered), processes that require large quantities of energy. Fortunately, the new generation of HVAC motors and controls allow more economical air cleaner operation, while also lowering overall operating costs, reducing noise, and providing greater levels of comfort.

A variety of systems are available for homes, offices, and other types of facilities, using HEPA filters and other methods, such as ionization, to remove particulates and odors from the air. The ionization method restores the negative ions in the air to a healthy level. (Clean-air environments, such as national forests, mountains, and waterfalls, have a negative ion level of roughly 2,000 per cubic centimeter, whereas typical urban indoor environments may have only 200 negative ions, due to the buildings' air-tightness, and the effect of man-made materials, such as concrete and asphalt.) It should be noted, however, that some ozone-generating, ion air purifiers may increase indoor ozone levels above federal health limits. Ozone at high levels has been shown to trigger asthma.

Cleaning the Air in Large Facilities

Larger facilities use technologies such as "hot process dynamics" (particles rising with hot air). Indoor air enters the base of the air purifier, which releases and recirculates clean air. Each system covers an area up to 1,600 square feet, and offers features such as adjustable louvers that enable users to customize the air flow patterns. Some other approaches include:

- **Activated charcoal filtration:** An air-side filtration system that can be activated to pull certain chemicals and components from the air stream.

- **Electrostatic precipitators:** Filtration systems that ionize the air. The ionized particles are attracted to an electric anode, which can be cleaned to remove the particulates.

- **Desiccant systems:** Moisture-removal systems that remove water-borne contaminants. An increasingly popular method for maintaining operating room air quality, while providing 100% outside air.

- **Ultraviolet lighting:** A system that kills mold and bacteria in the air stream. Ultraviolet systems require a switch to shut them off when the door is opened to prevent the UV rays from causing harm to people.

- **Providing more outside air:** The easiest method, made more efficient by the use of heat recovery to mitigate the requirement for air-side treatment (heating or cooling) of the fresh air.

Air Purification in Homes & Smaller Facilities

Residential and small commercial facilities can be treated with portable air cleaners. Factors to consider when selecting these devices include:

- **Capacity for removing particulates:** Typical systems remove particulates between 0.01-0.3 microns, the size that tends to cause asthma and allergic reactions.

- **Method used to purify air:** Negative ion, ozone air cleaners, HEPA filters.

- **Size:** Stationary filters clean the air only in their nearby surroundings. Even air cleaners with motors or fans require multiple units to purify the air in a whole house or similar space, since walls, floors, ceilings, and doors act as barriers. Another approach is an in-duct air purifier. In considering size, portability may be a factor, depending on the intended use of the system.

- **Type of system**: Filters can harbor mold and bacteria, and glass plates can be fragile, whereas ceramic plates are more durable. "Needlepoint" ionization is capable of producing a high density of negative ions, which increases its effectiveness in removing allergens. HEPA filters are disposable and can cost up to $170/year. Washable filters produce savings and avoid waste.
- **Cost**: To evaluate cost, one must consider not only the cost of filter replacements and other maintenance, but also the system's coverage in square feet, and its annual consumption of electricity. HEPA filters, ozone, and negative ion air cleaners may be priced in the same range, but the latter two tend to cover a larger area. The cost of replacement parts and maintenance are other considerations.
- **Noise**: Motors that draw air through a filter can produce significant noise. Negative ion and ozone generators use quieter fans. Some ionizers rely on natural air flow; they have no fans or motors and are very quiet. In small spaces, the purifier may be effective set on the lowest speed, which is also the quietest and uses less energy.
- **Warranty** (typically two years) and guarantee.

Whole-House Air Filters

For existing homes and spaces that have central air, pleated, electrostatic filters can be installed. For more stringent air cleaning, electronic precipitator cleaners can be used, collecting particulates on electrically charged plates.[3]

Gas Detectors & Alarms

Detectors and alarms are available to identify carbon monoxide, radon, propane, methane, and formaldehyde. These devices generally plug into 110-volt wall sockets, are UL-listed, and offer battery backups. Industrial air monitors are used in hospitals and labs, parking garages and gas stations, chemical and pharmaceutical industries, food and beverage industries, process plants, sewage treatment plans, and airports. These systems test for gases such as hydrogen, ammonia, carbon monoxide, and fluorocarbons (Freon).

Home Carbon Monoxide Detection & Alarms

The U.S. Consumer Product Safety Commission recommends a minimum of one carbon monoxide (CO) alarm in every home. This requirement is legislated in six states and eleven cities, including Chicago, Baltimore, and Des Moines. The UL standard for CO alarms requires that they activate within a period of 4 hours at 70 PPM.

Many HVAC contractors test for CO using hand-held instruments when maintaining or repairing systems. Some detection devices require training, available from manufacturers or industry institutes. These practices enable the contractor to identify and then repair any faulty equipment.

The capabilities and sensitivities of CO alarms vary significantly. Excessive false alarms have been a problem with many systems. Others have to be replaced frequently since their electrochemical sensors have a limited lifespan. Metal Oxide Semiconductor (MOS)-based detectors are capable of cross-sensitivity, which can lead to false alarms. The other drawback of MOS-based detectors is that they may be less sensitive over time, and are unable to read levels below 100 PPM. More sensitive equipment may be needed for buildings used by infants, seniors, and pregnant women, as well as people with compromised respiratory systems. Appropriate CO detection/alarm systems for this population should be capable of reading below 60 PPM. Manufacturers of digital carbon monoxide systems offer low-level alert and other features, including improved response time and accuracy, and a wider range of monitoring.[4]

Indoor Plants

Research has shown that indoor plants have a beneficial effect on indoor air quality, by increasing oxygen and humidity, and absorbing off-gassed chemicals. In *Your Naturally Healthy Home*, author Alan Berman suggests that at least one plant should be provided for each ten square yards of floor space with ceiling heights between eight and nine feet. The following types of plants are recommended for their particular effectiveness in improving air quality[5]:

- Areca, Reed, and dwarf date palms
- Boston and Australian sword ferns
- Janet Craig dracaena
- English ivy
- Peace lily
- Rubber plant
- Weeping fig

Proper watering and care of plants is required to ensure that the pots themselves do not become sources of mold.

Thermal Comfort

Perhaps the most urgent need that humans have of buildings is protection from the elements. The space inside a building provides conditions that allow us to survive freezing cold or blistering hot outdoor conditions. Clearly temperature is important, but several other factors also contribute to thermal comfort. Air temperature, humidity, and velocity all play a part, as do other sources of heat, such as solar radiation through a window or thermal radiation from a hot tin roof. Heat radiation from hot ceilings or other objects in the room can also cause discomfort, if they are more than 18-45° F (10-25° C) warmer than the other surfaces in the room. Drafts in excess of 0.25 m/s velocity (turbulent drafts greater than 0.1 m/s) can also cause discomfort.

Another factor in thermal comfort is the human metabolism, which generates heat. The amount of heat people generate depends on their level of activity, and varies from about 430 BTU/hr (125 W) for a resting adult, to as high as 1,700 BTU/hr (500 W) for strenuous activity. Comfort is a condition of the mind that depends on the physiological processes the body must perform (as controlled by the hypothalamus in the brain) to maintain a constant 98.6° F (37° C) body temperature. At low temperatures, blood vessels in the skin constrict, causing the skin to serve as a layer of insulation. The body can induce muscle activity, including noticeable shivering, to increase the rate of heat production. At high temperatures, blood vessels in the skin dilate and dissipate heat from the core of the body. Sweat glands in the skin pump water to cool the skin by evaporation. Indoor thermal comfort is achieved by providing a temperature that avoids the body's need to perform these physiological responses. ASHRAE Standard 55, "Thermal Environmental Conditions for Human Occupancy," specifies summer and winter comfort zones to account for differences in clothing. Most people are comfortable at an air temperature between 70-79° F (21-26° C).

Humidity influences human comfort because it affects the rate at which sweat can evaporate from the skin, but humidity has other effects too. Overly dry air can dry out mucous membranes, leading to more frequent colds, respiratory illness, and associated absenteeism. On the other hand, overly humid air causes sweat to accumulate on the skin and clothing. Relative humidity of 30-60% usually ensures comfort. Higher humidity is acceptable at low temperatures, and lower humidity is more comfortable at high temperatures. Most environments in North America are dry in the winter and humid in the summer. These conditions require humidification in the winter and dehumidification in the summer.

The HVAC system required to achieve comfortable conditions will depend on the local climate. In many areas and building types, for example, air conditioning is not required. In warm climates, heating might be needed only infrequently, and amply provided by a low-cost electric heater. A complete HVAC system would provide control of both temperature and humidity; air distribution systems would be designed to provide everyone with adequate ventilation air and positioned so as to avoid drafts. A new approach is to separately filter or otherwise purify outdoor ("fresh") and indoor air, in combination with energy recovery ventilators or heat exchangers, with an overall decrease in the amount of air that needs to be heated or cooled.

Tools for Thermal Comfort

Building envelope considerations, such as reflective roofing, low-E windows, and window tinting, are some of the tools that enable designers to optimize thermal comfort while also improving energy efficiency. Some strategies can be modified to suit the season, such as tinted window shades that can be up in winter and down in summer. Enthalpy-controlled HVAC systems (EMS) are dynamic and focus on humidity as well as temperature, as factors in human comfort. Siting the building according to seasonal heat gain and use is another key to thermal comfort, as is landscaping (e.g., shade trees). Individual control over one's space is also a key comfort item. Operable windows provide part of the solution.

Quality of Light Daylighting

Daylighting is more than just having windows. It is admitting natural light into the space, but it also includes controlling and distributing light for uniform lighting levels, avoiding glare and reflections, and controlling artificial light to achieve energy and cost savings.

Figure 6.1
Sealed for many years, this beautiful skylight in a historic Washington D.C. federal building has been restored to operation.

Daylight is very bright compared to the light we need in a built environment. As a result, small apertures in building walls and roofs are sufficient to meet daylighting goals. Daylighting works best in a task-ambient lighting strategy, where daylight is used to maintain a low ambient light level everywhere, and task lights (such as desk lamps) are used to provide a higher light level only when and where needed. Daylighting was a practical requirement in historic buildings built before the advent of electric lights, and much can be learned from the study of old office buildings and factories. In many cases, historic features, such as numerous high windows, clerestory windows, transom windows, skylights, and narrow floor plates to provide all rooms with perimeter windows, have been compromised by subsequent changes to the building. Restoring the daylighting system to its original intent could be both cost-effective and improve the quality of the space.

Daylighting has numerous benefits. Daylight allows us to dim or switch off artificial light, resulting in energy and cost savings. Our eyes, having evolved in sunlight, respond better to daylight than artificial light, which also may flicker and hum. Daylight also admits less heat into a space, than artificial light. Incandescent lamps are essentially electric heaters that happen to give off a little light, and fluorescent lights also introduce heat into a space, exacerbating cooling loads. Finally, it can be disturbing for people to work in windowless cubicles with no awareness of the weather and no connection to the outdoors. Occupants of daylit spaces are certainly happier, and evidence shows that they are more productive.

Cautions

It is important to discuss potential pitfalls related to daylighting so that they may be avoided. The pupil of the human eye constricts in response to bright light. If brightness is not uniform throughout the room, this constriction makes it hard to see in the darker areas, requiring people to install and use even more artificial light. A daylighting strategy should not admit more light than is needed for recommended lighting levels, so that additional artificial light is not needed in areas not daylit. Similarly, even in daylit areas, the difference in lighting level between the brightest spot and the darkest spot in a room must be minimized. This requires not only special measures to distribute light to the dark spots, but also to attenuate light in areas that are readily daylit. Computer screens, increasingly common in all environments, are best viewed in low ambient light levels. Surrounding sources of light are reflected to the eye from the surface of a computer screen, causing an annoying veil over the image on the screen. Computer workstations can be oriented to avoid reflections of windows and lighting fixtures. Fixtures with sharp cut-off angles may be specified so that reflections of light sources do not appear on computer screens. A person standing in front of a window appears only as a silhouette, and such backlighting should always be avoided.

The temperature a person feels is a combination of the surrounding air temperature and radiant heat gain. Radiant heat gain from sunlight is intense, and direct exposure to sunlight indoors almost always causes thermal discomfort. Direct sun may be acceptable in circulation spaces (such as an atrium or hallway) or in residential buildings where occupants can move out of the sun, but should be avoided on all workstations.

Building Layout for Daylighting

To achieve daylighting goals, the daylighting designer must be involved early in the programming phase of a project, when the relationships between spaces are being laid out. In general, daylight cannot be expected to penetrate more than 15-20 feet into a room from a perimeter window. Overhead skylights can provide light in areas farther from walls, but only on the top floor or in single-story buildings. Several devices have been invented to project daylight deep into the core of a building, including window reflectors, light pipes, and fiber optics. A building design that puts occupants in the proximity of perimeter windows results in high quality daylighting and high occupant satisfaction (by providing a visual connection to the outdoors). This

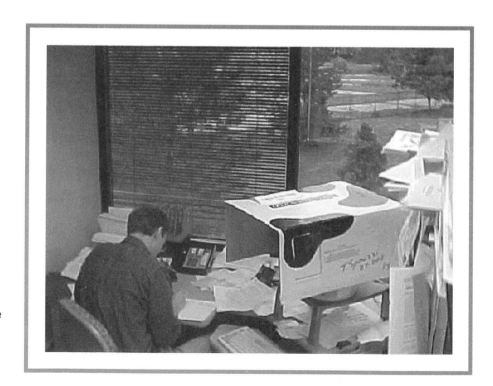

Figure 6.2
A cardboard box over the computer screen is an attempt to mitigate glare and reflections on the screen due to problems caused by a poorly designed daylighting system.

requires a more articulated plan, which may increase wall heating and cooling loads, but can also fit well with natural ventilation and passive solar heating objectives.

Historic buildings have provided a good lesson in effective daylighting, with designs such as the double-loaded corridor (two rows of rooms separated by a corridor, so that every room has an exterior wall). Premium daylight is available to all rooms through the outside wall, and the lower light level required in the hall is "borrowed" through transom windows between the hall and the room. Often these windows are high (above the doors) and translucent to provide privacy. While a double-loaded corridor with room windows facing north and south would be best, it can be configured around a courtyard, an E shape, or an infinite variety of other shapes.

Glazing Properties

A wide variety of window glass options are available, and careful selection of glass is an important element in any daylighting strategy. Developments in glazing technology have revolutionized architecture by addressing the limitations caused by excessive heat loss, and also by controlling the amount and nature of light passing through the window. Light striking a window is reflected off the surface, absorbed by the tint in the glass, or transmitted to the other side. These properties are described by the transmittance and reflectivity of the glass. The visible transmittance is the fraction of visible light that makes it through the glass, while the total transmittance includes the infrared and ultraviolet parts of the solar spectrum. Some of the heat absorbed in the glass is convected to the room air. The parameter used to describe the sum of transmitted solar radiation plus this absorbed heat that eventually makes it into the room air, is called the Solar Heat Gain Coefficient (SHGC).

For passive solar heating applications, it may be desirable to transmit as much sunlight as possible. It is also common to add a UV coating to protect occupants and items inside from ultraviolet radiation. Such coatings effectively remove 99% of ultraviolet radiation. If light is required for daylighting, but solar heat is not wanted, selective glazings are available that screen out the ultraviolet and infrared, but maximize visible transmittance. Selective glazings would be specified in cases where the control of solar heat gain is important, but a clear appearance is also desired. Selective glass can have a SHGC as low as 40%, but a visible transmittance in excess of 70%. A SHGC less than 40% usually requires attenuation of the visible spectrum by tint or reflective coating. The interior and exterior appearance (reflectivity and color tint), the daylighting and passive solar heating goals, and the orientation of the window are considerations when specifying glazing properties.

Heat loss through glazing is described by the Heat Loss Coefficient (U-value), which is multiplied by the indoor-outdoor temperature difference to calculate the heat loss rate. Multiple layers of glazing result in a lower heat loss coefficient, with air or a lower conductivity gas, like argon, used in the spaces between the layers. Low emissivity (low-E) coatings are applied to the interior surfaces to reduce the radiant heat transfer from one pane to another through the air gap. In some products, the low-E coating is applied to a thin film that serves as a third pane suspended between two glass panes. The glazing assemblies are sealed, often with a desiccant in the frame, to avoid unsightly water condensation between the panes.

Daylighting Apertures: Windows, Skylights, & Light Pipes

Windows are most effective when they introduce daylight very high into a space. Variations on windows include clerestory and roof-monitors, which are vertical windows installed in articulations in the roofline. The effectiveness of windows as daylighting apertures also depends on their orientation.

- North-facing windows are good sources of daylight. The sun hits north windows only in the early morning or late evening, and then only at a very oblique angle. The diffuse, indirect sunlight coming from the north prevents the glare and heat gain of other orientations, and no overhangs, shades, or special glazing treatments are required.

- South-facing windows require shades to control direct solar gain in the winter, when the sun is low in the sky. South-facing windows receive maximum sun at mid-day in winter, and are essential components of a passive solar heating strategy. In summer, overhangs over south-facing windows are effective at blocking direct solar gain. Specific overhang geometry is calculated using the sun angle equations (see Chapter 4).

- East-facing windows receive maximum sun and very low sun angles on summer mornings. West-facing windows receive maximum sun on summer afternoons. In general, low sun angles are a source of glare and unwanted heat gain, and east- and west-facing windows would be minimized depending on the views and other program requirements. However, in some climates, such as the high desert, some heat gain in the morning mitigates the night chill, and may be acceptable. Views can often be framed in small windows to avoid the problems that large windows or floor-to-ceiling glass would create on east or west faces. Where east or west windows are required, the most elegant way to reject the solar heat is with a highly reflective glass. Occupants would also use internal shades and drapes to achieve comfort.

Light shelves, such as those shown in Figure 6.3, are used to bounce light off the ceiling, project light deeper into the space, distribute it from above, and diffuse it to produce a uniform light level below. Like overhangs, light shelves are designed using the sun path geometry described in Chapter 4. The upper surface of the light shelf would have a high reflectivity, and may be specular (like a mirror). The ceiling in the space would also have a high reflectivity, but would be diffuse (like flat, white paint).

The sun is at its maximum on a roof during mid-day in summer. As a result, skylights were previously discouraged as sources of unwanted heat gain. However, new developments in glazing and shading designs, shown in Figure 6.4, have made it possible to use skylights to provide daylight above core zones in single-story buildings, or on the top floor of multi-story buildings.

Getting daylight into the core of large buildings has proved challenging. **Light pipes** are lined with highly reflective film to reflect light down the length of the pipe from a roof aperture to a room fixture. Light pipes are becoming popular in residential construction, and have found application in industrial facilities as well. Due to the relatively small size of each pipe, they seem to be best suited for small spaces like bathrooms or hallways. **Fiber optics** have also been demonstrated as a means to introduce light deep into the core of buildings, and may become feasible as glass fiber used for telecommunications become affordable.

Figure 6.3

Interior and exterior views of light shelves at a building at the National Renewable Energy Laboratory, Colorado. (Photo by Warren Gretz, courtesy of NREL.)

Daylighting Controls

Controls are required to realize the energy and cost savings of daylight by dimming or switching off the artificial lighting. Available daylighting controls are of two types: multi-level switching or continuous dimming.

Multi-level switching turns off some or all of the lights in response to daylight. Equipment consists of a light level sensor and relays. Standard lamps and ballasts are utilized. For example, a three-lamp fluorescent fixture with a one-lamp ballast and another two-lamp ballast would have four lighting levels: all off, one on, two on, or three on. The switching of circuits on and off is noticeable to occupants, and a potential cause for complaints. Lighting circuits must be laid out such that they correspond to the natural light levels in a room. Rows of lights would be laid out parallel to the windows such that lights near the windows could be off, while those far away from the windows are on. The difficulty and expense of reconfiguring lighting circuits limits the use of multiple-level switching in retrofit projects.

Continuous dimming controls address the shortcomings of multi-level switching, albeit at a higher cost. Equipment consists of a light level sensor, which supplies a low-voltage control signal to each electronic, dimmable ballast. The electronic controls within the ballast modulate light output in response to the signal from the sensor. Since the control wiring is independent of the power wiring, there is no need to reconfigure the power circuits in a retrofit project, although installation

Figure 6.4
Advanced solar luminaires use reflectors to increase light level and mitigate the glare and heat gain of horizontal skylights.

of the low-voltage control wiring is required. The cost of dimmable ballasts is significantly higher than non-dimmable electronic ballasts, as shown in the cost data in Part 5 of this book.

Placement and orientation of the light sensor is of paramount importance in daylighting system design. Usually, the light sensor is located in the ceiling overhead (measuring light reflected off the work surface below, between the windows and the light fixtures to prevent artificial light from causing control feedback). Daylighting sensors can

Figure 6.5
Skylights provide daylight in the cafeteria at Durant Middle School in Raleigh, North Carolina. "Daylit classrooms have increased the well-being of the students and teachers and are at least partly responsible for our record high attendance." –Tom Benton, Principal. (Photo by Robert Flynn, courtesy of NREL.)

Figure 6.6
NREL researcher Paul Torcellini checks the accuracy of the daylighting sensor that controls artificial light at the Thermal Test Facility in Golden, Colorado. Notice that the electric light in the background is turned off in this daylit photo. (Photo by Warren Gretz, courtesy of NREL).

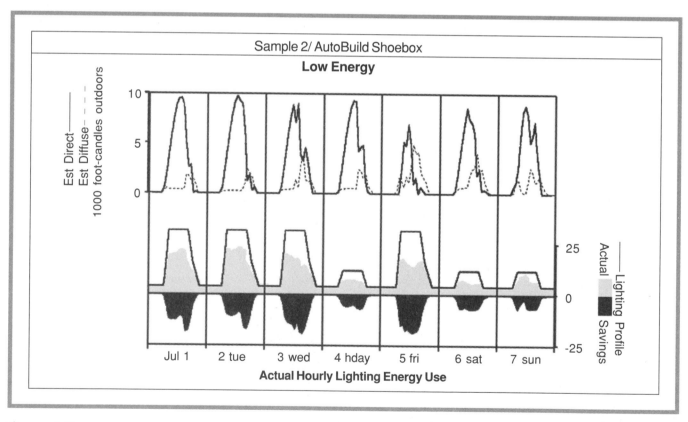

Figure 6.7
Savings due to daylighting in a small commercial building for the first week in July as calculated by the hourly simulation program Energy–10.

also be built into the switch plate, mounted on a vertical wall, providing an easy and inexpensive retrofit. The desired light level is selected by programming or dip switches on the sensor. Lower light level settings will result in higher energy and cost savings, since daylight will allow artificial light to be off for more hours of the year. (If necessary, task lights can augment daylight to provide the required light level on the work surface.)

Daylighting Design Tools

Daylighting design is complicated by the fact that sunlight varies in both magnitude and position throughout the day and year. Handbooks provide useful correlation of indoor to outdoor light levels for several

Figure 6.8
This photorealistic Radiance® simulation, at noon and at night, was done to evaluate daylighting and efficient electric lighting retrofit options for a historic office building in Washington D.C. Notice how the model correctly represents glare on the computer screen and reflection in the window glass. (Model by Lawrence Berkeley National Laboratory, photo courtesy of NREL.)

common window and room geometries. Sophisticated computer programs, such as those listed below, have been developed to analyze daylighting and the effects on building systems.

- **DOE-2** takes window and room geometry, wall reflectivity, and sensor placement into account to calculate electric light savings and effects on heating and cooling load in an hourly simulation. *(See Chapters 4 and 14 for more on DOE-2.)*
- **Energy-10** can automatically divide a small building into daylighting zones (north, south, east, west, and core) to calculate daylighting savings and effects on whole building energy use. *(See Chapter 14 for more on Energy-10.)*
- **Radiance®** is a ray-tracing program that displays light level contours and produces lifelike renderings. Radiance was developed by the U.S. Department of Energy and Lawrence Berkeley National Laboratory and is available from: **radsite.lbl.gov/radiance/HOME/html**

Because photons of light are so much smaller than the physical dimensions of a building or even of a small model of a building, physical models are very useful in predicting light levels in a building. The model can be placed on a rotating and tilting platform to replicate the sun's angles at different times of day and year.

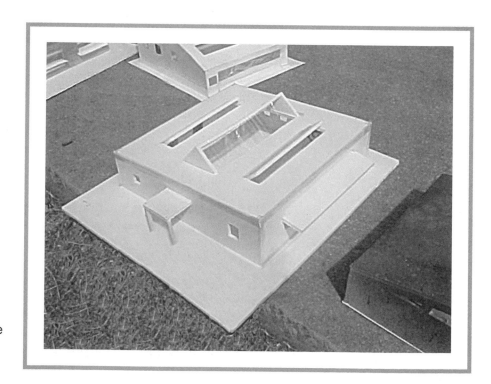

Figure 6.9
Models, such as these produced by students in the author's class at University of Colorado at Boulder, are useful for analyzing daylighting designs.

Water Quality

Water, even coming directly from a private well, can be contaminated with chemicals and particulates that can be unhealthy, foul-tasting, or malodorous. The minerals in water can make it too "hard" to use effectively for bathing or washing, and can be harmful to HVAC equipment and piping. A healthy indoor environment should include clean water, appropriate to all purposes.

Purification Systems

There are a variety of purification systems available to address water problems throughout the home or facility—for drinking, bathing/washing, and other purposes. Reverse osmosis filter systems are one option. Ultraviolet lamps may be incorporated to reduce contaminants by 90%, and biological hazards, such as anthrax, E. coli, Giardia, viruses, and salmonella, by up to 99.9%. These systems are capable of reducing compounds including chlorine, PCBs, VOCs, arsenic, copper, iron, cyanide, and lead, as well as filtering out particles and sediments. Shower head systems designed to remove chlorine are now available. Major faucet manufacturers now offer "filtering faucets," a convenient advantage over bulky home filtration systems. Some of these devices have two separate channels, one with filtered water, the other unfiltered. Pressing a button selects the desired channel. The filtered water tends to have a lower pressure. These units are priced from $200-$400, depending on the features and available types of filters, some of which filter out chlorine; microorganisms, such as Giardia; and lead.

Carbon Absorption

This system is most often used for residential water treatment as it is effective in removing the odor and unpleasant taste sometimes found in municipal water supplies. Carbon filters are not certified for removing VOCs, lead, coliform, or asbestos. Carbon systems use either granular activated carbon (which removes several chemicals, gases, and microorganisms) or solid block carbon (compressed carbon with binding medium). Potential problems with carbon systems include:

- **Bacteria growth** from accumulated impurities.
- **Chemical recontamination** of water from filters saturated with impurities.
- **Channeling,** or pathways that allow water to pass without proper filtering.

Carbon block systems avoid the above problems by providing complete filtration of organic impurities (no channeling). These filters are available with a fine filtering mechanism to remove coliform and other bacteria, and pathogenic cysts such as Giardia, as well as lighter-weight VOCs. Carbon block filter density does not permit bacteria growth. Carbon block filters, available in types to fit under the sink, on the faucet, or on the counter, need to be replaced more frequently than granular carbon filters.[6]

Typical water purification systems include a storage tank, special faucet, and filters, as well as the filtering mechanisms. Mechanisms include microfiltration, molecular (which captures broad spectrum adsorption), electrochemical separations, and ultraviolet light disinfection. Solar-powered systems are even available, used mostly for remote areas or emergency, power-outage situations. Larger systems can produce up to 1,000 gallons per day.

Maintaining water purification systems involves changing cartridges regularly (every 6-12 months for residential applications). The frequency depends on the area and water content.

Healthy Use of Gray Water

Gray water is wastewater recycled from showers, baths, and laundry. *(See Chapter 3 for more on equipment and other considerations.)* Gray water can be used, especially in warm months of the year when it is most needed, to provide moisture for plants. Using gray water as part of a healthy, green approach can reduce water utility expenses significantly, while decreasing demand on local water supplies. Some precautions are necessary, however, since gray water is not disinfected and could contain contaminants.

Gray water systems must be clearly labeled and must not have any cross-connects to potable water systems. Gray water should never be consumed as drinking water, nor should it be sprayed on anything that might be eaten. Gray water should not be used in a manner that would allow it to run off of the property, or to puddle. Recycled water should only come from bathing, the bathroom sink, or clothes washing. Water used to clean soiled diapers, or that has contacted meat or poultry should never be re-used. The same is true for water used by someone with an infectious disease. Laundry wastewater that contains chlorine bleach or phosphates should not be used to water plants. (Biodegradable soaps are recommended.) The following plants should never be watered with gray water:

- Vegetables and herbs
- Seedlings
- Potted plants
- Acid-loving plants, such as rhododendrons, azaleas, other evergreens, and begonias

Plants watered with gray water should be watered with clean water every other time to prevent any harmful build-up.

Using Rainwater

Landscape irrigation has been estimated to account for 40% of residential water consumption. While xeriscaping (use of native plants) is key to reducing landscape water demand, accumulated rainwater, in rain barrels or cisterns, is another resource- and money-saving approach that can help maintain the landscape. Chapter 3 includes a section on the equipment, and cost and design considerations for rainwater collection systems. Here we will address health and comfort issues.

Benefits

Water collected from rooftop runoff is free. It contains no chlorine, calcium, or lime and generally has far fewer salts and sediments than city or most well water. Rainwater is not "hard," so it feels better and cleans more effectively, with less soap or detergent. Collected rainwater can be used for organic vegetable gardening and potted plants (indoors and out), and is especially healthy for tropical plants such as orchids, as compared to chlorinated city water. Rainwater is also good for washing vehicles and windows. Stored rainwater can be especially valuable in an emergency and in locations frequently hit by storms or drought.

Precautions

In many areas of the country, and especially cities, collected rainwater should not be used as drinking water because of air pollution, which is slightly acidic and contains VOCs, lead, and petrochemicals. In an emergency, an appropriate filtration system could be used to make rainwater safer to drink. If rainwater in a particular location is deemed safe for drinking, it is still necessary to consider the roofing material to make sure no harmful contaminants are leaching from it. Many systems include a roof washer to dispose of the first water collected during a rain shower, as this will contain the most impurities, such as bird droppings, soot, and dirt. The rainwater must also be stored out of ultraviolet light to prevent growth of algae, and filtered to remove all debris.

It is important to provide barriers to mosquito infestation in the barrel or cistern by use of screens or plastic lids. Even with these barriers, there is a chance of mosquito eggs dropping into the receptacle from the gutters. Nontoxic water treatments can control this problem in an environmentally friendly way. Leaves and other forms of debris can also find their way into the rainwater collection barrel or cistern. Using a mesh or other gutter guard is helpful.

Other contaminants occurring in collected rainwater in some parts of the country can be identified through water testing. In some states, such as Hawaii, home test kits are available.

Plumbing Fixtures

There have been some claims that porcelain bathtubs emit lead, which can be particularly harmful to infants and children. Lead testing kits are available. Re-glazing is an option to contain potential lead emission.[7]

Noise Management

A healthy, comfortable indoor environment should be as free as possible from the stress of loud, distracting noise and lack of speech privacy. There are several approaches to this goal, most of them inherent in the design of new construction or remodeled space. Proper selection of windows, wall insulation, and wall framing and materials is essential to reducing noise from outside, such as traffic on major thoroughfares in suburban areas, or throughout urban areas. Some sound-insulating materials, such as acoustic ceiling tile and straw-bale construction, can offer the advantages of recycling or using natural materials as an added green benefit. Hard versus absorbent surfaces also have a major impact on noise level inside a space, as do interior wall framing and insulating techniques.

Acoustic or sound-absorption panels are effective in mitigating the noise in gathering spaces. A preferred design approach is to reduce the number of parallel surfaces, using more curved and angled walls to diminish the acoustic bounce and the noise.

Noise from HVAC Systems

Proper design of air duct systems can further reduce noise transmission. For example, one of the main sources of noise from HVAC duct registers results from balancing dampers just inside, or behind the grille. If the dampers are substantially closed in order to balance the system, noise levels can rise by as much as 5-20 decibels above their ratings. If dampers are installed farther upstream in the supply duct, noise is reduced. Small diffusers and large air intakes also tend to create more noise. Insulating elbows can help reduce noise, although other issues may also need to be investigated, such as vibrating turning vanes or bars, rattling dampers, or imbalances in fans and other rotating equipment. Placement of furnace closets is crucial in building design, as some noise is unavoidable in the adjacent areas.

The key to ductwork noise control is velocity control, which is achieved by designing the ductwork to reduce velocity throughout the distribution system, while maintaining constant velocity and balanced air distribution. Most mechanical engineering firms understand this, as do many contractors. Again, it is a key factor that must not be overlooked.

A commissioning plan should include checking for problems when the system is installed. The building management staff can respond to problems such as vibration and eliminate them, but it is important to prevent them wherever possible in the initial installation.

Selection of the type of mechanical system can also affect noise. For example, scroll compressors are significantly noisier than centrifugal compressors in cooling systems.[8]

Noise from Light Ballasts

Lighting designers must consider the electronic noise produced by numerous electronic fluorescent light ballasts, especially when combined with other electronic equipment. Harmonic mitigation is required when the installed kW of electronic components exceeds 10% of the total load. (Refer to **http://www.powerquality.net/problem.htm** for more detail.)

Audio Masking (or Sound Conditioning) Systems

In existing facilities, audio masking systems offer one solution to noise attenuation. These devices provide electronically generated background sound at a certain level and frequency. They can reduce the distraction of intrusive noise, such as speech or equipment noise. These systems also increase speech privacy—which can not only boost productivity, but also security, by protecting against eavesdropping. Some systems provide protection from laser beams and other high-tech sound detection devices. ASTM defines three levels of speech privacy:

- Confidential privacy: heard, but not understood.
- Normal privacy: sometimes heard and understood, but for the most part not intrusive.
- Poor privacy: all speech in the area can be heard and understood.

Privacy is sometimes measured in terms of the Privacy Index (PI), based on the Articulation Index (AI).

Audio masking systems can incorporate music and paging, and offer varying levels and types of masking. For example, *white noise* is thought to have more of a "hiss" sound, as compared to *pink noise*. Sound masking systems are typically wall- or shelf-mounted, but can also be installed above ceiling tiles in plenums with sound-masking speakers located at intervals (such as every 12-15 feet) in a large space.[9]

Furniture & Furnishings

The selection of ecologically friendly furnishings is no longer confined to futons, yoga mats, candles, and incense burners. This expanding market currently offers a wide array of interesting, comfortable furniture and fabrics for those with discerning tastes, environmental awareness, and chemical sensitivities.

Furniture

Green furniture choices include used furniture from flea markets and auctions and "new" pieces made from recycled and natural, nontoxic materials. Some furniture is made from old wood from recycled barns, 80-100 years old, and from shipping pallets, which are otherwise discarded in landfills. (It has been estimated that the amount of wood thrown away in pallets is equal to the quantity of framing lumber used annually in 300,000 average-size U.S. homes.) Picture frames and other furnishings from recycled wood are also available. Another green choice in wood furniture is certified wood, or second-growth, rather than old-growth, wood, often oak or maple. The finishes used on environmentally friendly wood furniture are typically water-based or traditional oils and waxes, and are nontoxic. Other materials are being recycled into furniture as well. Some creative examples include Adirondack chairs made from skis and snowboards, and tables, chairs, and shelving from bicycle parts.

The type of furniture and upholstery also affects thermal comfort. In general, un-upholstered wood or metal furniture is preferred in warm climates, and thick upholstery is favored in cold climates.

Qualities to Look for in Furniture[10]

- Longevity/durability (well-made furniture, preferably from local materials that can be repaired)
- Safely biodegradable materials
- Certified woods
- Organic fabrics
- Washable components
- Solid wood, rather than veneer, that can be refinished, if necessary

What to Avoid[11]

- Tropical hardwoods
- Particleboard containing urea or formaldehyde glue
- PVC, nylon, and other petroleum-based plastics
- Finishes with a high level of VOCs or other toxic chemicals
- Laminated and veneer finishes, which will eventually show wear and have to be replaced
- Plastic and foam
- Upholstered furniture that cannot be washed and therefore has a shortened life

- Bromines, formaldehyde, or halogens used for fireproofing
- Stain-resistant substances that contain formaldehyde, fluorocarbons, or PFOs (polymer, perfluorooctane suphonate)

Flooring & Wall Finishes

Ecological flooring options include reclaimed American antique hardwood, bamboo, linoleum, and ceramic tiles made with recycled glass. There are natural wall covering materials available, and while most adhesives contain harmful chemicals, healthy living Web sites and publications feature "recipes" for natural, nontoxic adhesives.[12]

Paints should be low- or no-VOC. Milk paint, also known as casein, has been found in many historic buildings, and was popular in the first half of the 20th century and until today in the paper industry and for painting theater scenery. Milk paint is gaining popularity again now as a natural coating. The original milk paint used the protein found in milk as a binder, with oil or other additives to increase durability.[13]

Carpeting, Rugs, & Mattresses

Epidemiologists have discovered a connection between asthma and exposure to wall-to-wall carpeting. Carpet made of wool is a safer, natural choice, along with area rugs made from wool, or braided hemp or cotton scraps, which can be removed for cleaning and airing.

Healthy mattresses are made with wool, pure latex, and organic cotton without chemical sizing or fabric softeners, and without metal, virgin paper cardboard cording, or mechanically tufted batting. Cotton mattress materials are often recommended for people with back and joint problems or chemical sensitivities. Some crib-size waterproof mattress covers made from polyvinyl chloride covered with cotton and/or polyester layers, or polyolefin, have been shown to emit toxic fumes. Wool offers several advantages as a mattress material:

- Absorbs and releases moisture
- Is naturally resistant to fire, mold, and dust mites
- Is resilient

Organic wool is recommended to avoid pesticides commonly used as a pesticide-control dip for sheep. Organic cotton is a better choice than standard cotton because no pesticides are used in its production. Fire-retardance, required by federal law for mattresses, can be achieved with boric acid, which is nontoxic and releases no vapors.

Standard mattresses can be enclosed in a barrier cloth made of tightly woven cotton.

Pillows are available in organic cotton and wool. Sheets, towels, shower curtains, and table linens are also available in organic cotton.

Office Furnishings

The EPA estimates that approximately three million tons of used office furniture are being discarded annually by U.S. businesses, much of it because of fabric wear, out-of-date appearance, or poor construction that rendered it irreparable. Fortunately, there are some good alternatives. Many organizations are saving 30-50% over new furniture costs by purchasing refurbished or remanufactured furniture for a new look or purpose, or having their own used furniture reconditioned. Others are purchasing new furniture made from recycled content, including metal, PVC, pressboard, and fabrics. The cost of new furniture made of recycled content is similar to new, non-recycled furniture.

The basic options are:

- **Re-used:** As is, without improvements or repairs.
- **Refurbished or remanufactured:** Disassembled, with the parts cleaned and repaired or replaced, then reassembled.
- **New, recycled content.**

Green office furnishings include such items as reupholstered chairs, refinished tables, and office partitions made with cores of recycled cellulose, recycled aluminum frames, and upholstery from recycled soda bottles. Other office items, such as appointment books, briefcases, bulletin boards, and mouse pads, are available in recycled rubber and other materials. Energy-saving devices, such as solar PC chargers, are additional ecological choices for the office. Specifications for refurbished office furniture could include indoor air quality issues, such as not allowing materials that off-gas toxic fumes or that require use of toxic cleaning solvents. The specifications might also require availability of replacement parts and accessories.

(The Office Furniture Recyclers Forum is a trade association for the recycling, refurbishing, and remanufacturing industry. OFRC has developed a standard for refurbished office furniture, which can be downloaded from **www.ofdanet.org/Documents/recycle.pdf** *Another resource is The Green Office, a monthly publication for facility managers, and designers of office space. 1-800-709-0012.)*

Green Cleaning & Maintenance

A healthy indoor environment also requires use of nontoxic cleaning and personal care products. The availability of these items is widespread and growing. Some traditional products have been proven unhealthy, such as ammonia, which is corrosive; poisonous; irritating to eyes, lungs, and nose; and produces lethal gases when combined with bleach. In addition, ammonia is explosive when exposed to flames.

Natural substances including essential oils, tannic acid powder, and boric acid can be used to neutralize allergens in dust mites and pet dander, and to repel insects and rodents.

There are *key words* used on product labels to define the risk to people and the environment. Being familiar with this terminology is important to selecting healthy products. Four key terms are:

- **Poison/Danger:** Highly toxic—a few drops could be fatal.
- **Warning:** Toxic—a teaspoonful could be fatal.
- **Caution:** Somewhat less toxic—two tablespoons to a cup could be fatal.
- **Strong Sensitizer:** Could cause allergic reactions.

According to The Environmental Research Foundation, the *most dangerous substances* that should be avoided are[14]:

- Pesticides
- Toxic gases, including chlorine and ammonia
- Heavy metals, such as lead and mercury
- VOCs (volatile organic compounds), such as formaldehyde

Conclusion

The holistic theme that permeates green building projects is evident in the indoor environment, where many different components must interact to create healthy and comfortable air, water, lighting, and furnishings. The interior space is where building owners and users are likely to spend the most time experiencing the long-term benefits of thoughtful, ecological design—and to enjoy an awareness that they are saving natural resources while taking care of their health.

[1] Morbidity and Mortality Weekly Report, 10 March 1999. http://www.cdc.gov/mmwr/preview/mmwrhtml/mm4909a3.htm

[2] The Environmental Protection Agency's Integrated Risk Information System profile, http://www.epa.gov/iris/subst/0419.htm

[3] *The Green Guide,* The Green Guide Institute.

[4] http://www.snipsmag.com

[5] Berman, Alan. *Your Naturally Healthy Home*. Rodale Press, 2001.

[6] Schaeffer, John, ed. *Real Goods Solar Living Source Book: The Complete Guide to Renewable Energy Technologies & Sustainable Living, 9th Edition*. Real Goods, 1996.

[7] http://www.leadcheck.com

[8] http://www.snipsmag.com/CDA/ArticleInformation/features/BNP_Features_Item/0,3374

[9] http://www.armstrong.com/commceilingsna/article831.html

[10] http://wwwcare2.com

[11] Ibid.

[12] Ibid. and Berge, Bjorn. *The Ecology of Building Materials*. Architectual Press, 2001

[13] Swanke Hayden Connell Architects. *Historic Preservation: Project Planning & Estimating*. R.S. Means Co., Inc., 2000.

[14] *Toxic Turnaround*, The Environmental Research Foundation.

Part

2 Phases of a Green Building Project

Chapter

7 Assembling the Project Team

Andy Walker, Ph.D., PE

One of the critical distinctions between a conventional and a sustainable design is the use of an integrated design process, whereby the full green team has input into the building's conceptual or schematic design. Normally, in conventional practice, the architect hands an already evolved building design to the mechanical engineer, who sizes a mechanical system to meet the peak load. By that time, decisions regarding building orientation, massing, and fenestration—all of which affect energy use—have already been made. This late in the process, there is limited or no opportunity to optimize the building as a system. The mechanical engineer can only optimize the HVAC subsystem, which is usually the task. Similarly, in order to have proper daylighting, the lighting designer would have to be consulted even as early as the building is being laid out on the site. Everybody involved in a building project may wish to coordinate closely at the outset, but the way competitive design fees are conventionally structured and procured, there is no financial incentive to participate in meetings and correspondence, evaluate alternatives, and reach a true consensus.

With green design, several trends promise better design integration. Owners are beginning to realize that the value of the team's time spent coordinating early in the design process is likely to be returned several times over in lower construction and operating costs. Several powerful new communication technologies enable design team members in different locations to share information, analyze data, and generate results efficiently. Many design and construction professionals are also making maximum use of collaborative Internet Web sites to share drawings and coordinate schedules. Finally, efforts are under way by industry and national laboratories to integrate computer-aided design drawings, energy analysis computer programs, cost estimating procedures, and all processes where information is shared. *(See Chapter 14 for more on computer programs for energy analysis.)*

There is not one design process that is "green" and another that is "not green." Rather there is continuous improvement in processes that results in better and better buildings. Key to the process is abandoning the idea of replicating what worked last time, and instead continuously evaluating new products and methods to seek improvement. Team members must have a common interpretation of what constitutes improvement. Defining measurements and setting goals are important aspects of team building.

The Design Team

Every project involves an **owner** or a developer with legal power to improve the property. The **architect** ascertains the owner's requirements, creates the building design, and administers the construction contract, and thus is the key determinate of the sustainability of the resulting building. The **landscape architect** affects sustainability of the grounds themselves, including water and chemical (insecticide, fertilizer) requirements, but may also impact energy use by siting and planting to provide shade and/or wind breaks.

The **structural engineer** integrates a variety of design requirements, including window openings, the storage of heat in mass, and the need to withstand physical forces. The **civil engineer** decides issues of site sustainability, in the sense that issues such as reduction of surface water run-off are addressed by this member of the team. The **mechanical engineer** calculates energy use and thus informs all the other team members of the life-cycle energy use implications of design decisions. In addition to designing an efficient system, the **electrical engineer** may have an opportunity to integrate use of innovative sources of power, such as co-generation or solar energy. The **plumbing engineer** can save resources initially, with fixture and pipe layouts and material selection, but also over the building life cycle by specifying low-flow fixtures and minimizing pumping power.

If consulted early in the process, the **interior designer** has an opportunity to specify recycled and recyclable furniture, furnishings, and fixtures, as well as appropriate colors and reflectivity, which allow a lower lighting level, and furniture upholstery options that are durable and comfortable over a wider range of temperatures.

The **lighting designer** makes decisions critical to both the occupants' well-being and life-cycle energy use. Recommendations of an **HVAC consultant** might include right-sizing the system or using innovative methods, such as displacement ventilation or solar or geothermal heat, that can save energy and improve indoor environmental quality. An environmental building consultant would make recommendations regarding the impact of building materials as they are produced, and the waste they generate in the construction process and over their product life cycle. A waste management consultant might have ideas on how to minimize construction waste and also how to enhance the facility's recycling capacity over its life.

The contractor and the trades should be consulted early, not only to ensure the constructability of the design, but also because the trades are often the best source of ideas for innovative improvements. The commissioning agent should be involved from the pre-design phase, beginning with the end in mind. *(See Chapter 11 for more on commissioning.)*

It is tempting to map out a process with each professional pigeonholed into his or her discreet discipline, but this approach would be disastrous to the sustainability of the result. With a team approach, the structural engineer would be responsible for ensuring that the structural members did not interfere with the distribution of daylight, and the landscape architect's job would include consideration of the effects of plantings on summer solar heat gain inside west rooms. Integration of these otherwise disparate activities requires more than communication. It requires that sustainability goals established in early program documents be shared across the team, and that the tasks required to integrate with the work of others be included in the contract documents.

Teamwork in the Design Process

Teamwork is collaboration and cooperation, and the priority of a shared goal. Team members work together better if they are all involved in setting the project goals early in the design process. Deliberate and planned efforts to communicate at each step help to ensure success in green design.

Pre-design planning includes project identification, a feasibility study, and programming. The healthier environment and lower operating cost of a green building are key features in a marketing plan, and would enhance the feasibility of a project by commanding higher rates and higher occupancy. Some non-profit organizations have discovered that donors are much more enthusiastic about supporting a project with superlative goals than a business-as-usual building. Environmental compliance, once seen as a barrier, now presents opportunities for green-minded designers, whether the project is a redevelopment of a brownfield or using solar energy to avoid running a new power line over pristine land.

Subsequent activities include the procurement of architectural and engineering services including preliminary or schematic design, design development, and construction document preparation. The Statement of

Work describing these services must include the additional work required to arrive at an exemplary design, such as:

- More specific research of the client's needs and the most effective way to meet them.
- Detailed energy modeling.
- Life-cycle analysis.
- Evaluation of alternative systems and materials.
- Development of documentation related to sustainability rating criteria.

The design process also involves complying with the National Historic Preservation Act and the National Environmental Policy Act. These processes, which involve people with diverse interests, must remain collaborative rather than confrontational to avoid impeding project implementation. Green design strategies may assuage the community's concern with pollution, noise, or inappropriate development. Measures that may be required to mitigate such impacts can be real assets to a green project. A good example is preservation of wetlands adjacent to a project.

Schematic design, design development, construction documents, bidding and negotiation with contractors, and construction contract administration are considered the architect's basic services.[1] A suite of comprehensive services would also include project analysis, feasibility studies, programming, land use studies, analysis of financing options, attending or facilitating meetings to set goals and monitor progress, management of construction, energy analysis, surveys of the sustainability attributes of various materials, or other special consulting services.

The Building Program

The building program is a document conveying the conditions and requirements of a project. Along with specifying the number of square feet of different types of space (office, assembly, laboratory, etc.), and the need to meet code requirements, the program should state clear and quantitative sustainability performance goals. For example, the building program may specify a desired LEED level (silver, gold, platinum), or it may specify a maximum $/S.F./year operating cost. Other goals frequently described in the program relate to achievement of a project that is beautiful, safe, reliable, comfortable, or that provides superior air and light quality.

Sustainability goals require a clear definition and criteria that can be used to determine whether we have succeeded in meeting the goal. Sustainability ratings provide a convenient means to do this. For example, the building program might set the goal of a Silver LEED rating. Other sustainability criteria include BREEAM/New Offices—

Building Research Establishment Environmental Assessment Method; BEPAC—Building Environmental Performance Assessment Criteria; and ISO 14000, ISO 14001 Environmental Management Standard—International Organization for Standardization.

Some organizations, such as federal agencies, have developed their own architectural guidelines regarding sustainability that would be referred to in the building program. The building program would also document the energy-related needs of users—a critical first step in designing systems to meet those needs efficiently, and an indicator of the suitability of various renewable energy sources.

Goal-setting should be considered a team activity. Team members must proceed with a keen awareness of, and commitment to, project goals. This is much more likely to happen if they have a sense of control by sharing in setting goals and also in determining how success will be measured. If a goal is stated very generally, as "to minimize life-cycle cost through sustainable design principles," it would be difficult to judge whether it was met in the end. This is why a more quantitative goal could be more useful.

Energy performance goals can be set with different objectives. Annual energy use per gross square foot (BTU/S.F./year) is a common metric among federal projects because that is the way progress toward statutory goals is tracked.[2] Shortcomings of BTU/S.F./year as a measurement standard are that BTUs supplied by different fuels have different costs, and there is no differentiation between time-of-use or demand rates.

Another option is to specify an energy use goal as a certain percentage less than that required by code. For example, a goal might be to use 25% less energy than allowed by 10CFR434/435 for federal projects, ASHRAE 90.1 for commercial buildings, or California Title 24. A useful metric is annual operating costs ($/year), which accounts for costs of different fuels, different time-of-use and demand savings, and integrates well as a figure of merit with all other annual costs, such as operation, maintenance, water, and disposal.

It is important to use the same yardstick to measure performance as was used to set the goal in the first place. Disputes often arise when goals set using a computer model are compared to actual utility bills. There are many variables, including schedules, occupancy, and plug loads, that affect energy use after a building is occupied. These are outside of the designer's control. Although the performance of the building will ultimately be evaluated by measuring the actual resource use (such as utility bills) of the completed building, the performance of the design team should be evaluated by simulating the final design with the same computer program and uncontrolled parameters (weather file, utility rates, occupancy, schedules, plug loads) that were used to set the goal.

How do you set an energy goal before you even know what the building looks like? One approach is to model a default building in the shape of a shoebox with the same floor area and number of floors, the same occupancy schedules, and the same kinds of space (office, circulation, kitchen, meeting rooms, storage, etc.) as called for in the building program. First, a **reference case** is defined to serve as a benchmark with which the performance of the evolving design will be compared. For the reference case shoebox model, the properties of walls, roofs, windows, and mechanical systems are the minimum required by applicable codes. The annual energy performance of the reference case shoebox model is evaluated using climate data and utility rates for the site. Then a suite of energy-efficiency measures is modeled using the shoebox to determine which strategies are most effective. For

Figure 7.1
The performance goal for a new courthouse in Miami was set by GSA at 550 MJ/gross square meter/yr (48k BTU/S.F./yr), or 21% less than an ASHRAE 90.1 prototype building, whichever is less. Rendering by ARQ/HOK, courtesy of General Services Administration.

Green Building: Project Planning & Cost Estimating

example, if evaporative cooling is effective on the shoebox model, it is likely to be effective for the actual design. Measures are evaluated in combination with each other to account for interactions.

The shoebox model with the most cost-effective package of measures implemented provides an estimate of what should be achievable in the design, but the goal is usually set above this level. For example, a reference case might be 100 KBTU/S.F./year, the shoebox with all ideal cost-effective measures implemented might be 30 KBTU/S.F./year, and the actual goal for the project might be set at 40 KBTU/S.F./year, a reasonable goal for the design team. The Energy-10 computer program has been developed especially to implement this pre-design analysis and to aid in setting energy-use goals.[3] *(See Chapter 14 for more on Energy-10 and other design programs.)*

Design Team Selection Criteria

Selection of capable, enthusiastic individuals to be on the design team is perhaps the most important step in green design. The right team will always strive for success; inclusion of disinterested people is a formula for failure. A good proposal:

- States commitment to superior performance.
- Includes a team that demonstrates capability to respond to sustainability and energy targets set in program documents.
- Includes a team that responds to sustainability rating and energy analysis results with an effective combination of communication and decision-making authority.
- Includes an energy/sustainability expert on the design team.
- Demonstrates familiarity with new materials and energy technology and familiarity with analysis tools (such as Energy-10 or DOE-2).
- Demonstrates proficiency with sustainability rating criteria (for example, includes a LEED-accredited professional).
- Demonstrates understanding of code requirements.
- Cites completed (and measured), successful projects. Advanced degrees and qualifications are good, but there is no substitute for an established track record of projects recognized as successful advancements in green design.

Design Team Statement of Work

To continuously improve sustainability, the design team must research new technology and rank many alternatives, as well as employ sophisticated methods of evaluating performance. These additional tasks must be included in the scope of work to ensure that they get done, and that the designer has enough hours budgeted for the additional analysis and design team meetings.

The **performance goals** from the building program should be written by the architect and owner or consultant into the statement of work for all subsequent architectural and engineering services. This establishes the contractual obligation to create a sustainable project and also creates a mutual understanding between parties of what that means in terms of specific tasks. The statement of work should involve the mechanical engineer and lighting designer as early as possible in the design process.

Green design can take 40-100% more effort on the part of the mechanical engineer or energy analyst over the work required to simply size the mechanical system. The mechanical engineer would use the shoebox model analysis to investigate various mechanical system strategies early in the design, then maintain an ongoing energy analysis of the evolving design in order to continuously inform designers of the energy use and cost implications of design decisions.

Energy modeling with hourly computer simulation programs is essential for green design, but energy modeling is a specialized field, and the programs are very detailed. Someday, computer-aided design software will link directly to an energy analysis program. In the meantime, the task of doing **takeoffs** (reading dimensions off plans and entering them into the energy program) falls on the mechanical engineer. The energy analysis requires several iterations to analyze multiple design alternatives, including:

- Building envelope and orientation.
- Size and type of HVAC plant.
- Type of distribution system.
- Control set points.
- Daylighting apertures and control.
- Efficient lighting.
- Renewable energy supplies.

Time must be budgeted to conduct regular meetings of the project designers to communicate energy use and cost implications and recommend alternatives. The task of investigating utility rates and programs should be included and should integrate with the hourly computer simulation. The statement of work for the energy analyst should include assistance with compiling the building commissioning handbook.

Whole-building analysis is needed to account for interactions between systems. Exploiting these interactions is a key strategy in green building design. For example, energy-efficient lighting reduces the heat gain from lights, resulting in a smaller chiller and significantly less energy required for cooling. On the other hand, competing measures suffer from the fact that you cannot save the same kWh twice. For example, a daylight sensor, which turns off the electric lights in a room whenever ample daylight is coming in the window, will not save anything if an occupancy sensor has already turned the light off because nobody is in the room. Most interactions are well-represented by hourly simulation computer programs such as DOE-2, Energy-10, and Blast. These programs are based on first principles (laws of physics), rather than correlation, enabling them to evaluate an infinite variety of design configurations. The hourly simulation consists of an equation balancing energy in and out of each and every building component, and these equations are solved simultaneously for each of the 8,760 hours of a typical year. Solving the system of equations at each hour accounts for interaction between envelope, heating, cooling, and lighting systems, as well as solar heat gain, heat gain from occupants in the space, and any other energy flows specified by the user.

During pre-design, the energy analyst develops the code-compliant reference case, identifies and evaluates energy efficiency and renewable energy strategies, and sets performance goals based on a case with all effective strategies implemented. During preliminary design, the task is to evaluate schemes and the sensitivity of results to variable inputs, such as utility rates, and then select strategies for further development. Schematic design will determine rough sizes of components (such as array, batteries, and inverter for a photovoltaic system). During design development, the analyst assists with determining precise sizes and complete descriptions of the designs, and will have the most input before the design is 35% complete. By the time it is 90% complete, the role of the analyst has been reduced to confirming that performance goals have been met.

Performance-Based Fee

While far from business-as-usual, several projects have piloted the concept of basing the professional fees on the level of performance as designed. Performance-based fees reward the effort of minimizing the project's life-cycle cost and reward the designer for not over-sizing equipment. The elements of a performance-based fee include:

- A clear goal, along with a specification, of how performance relative to that goal is to be measured.
- A schedule showing how the fee relates to success in meeting the goal.
- A method of evaluating the design.
- A protocol for resolving disputes without expensive litigation.

To mitigate the risk of this new approach, some projects have retained a minimum fee, and based a special incentive fee on the documented performance of the design.[4] Several efforts to develop performance-based fee contracts have been scuttled by contracting officers or legal advisors unfamiliar with the technology required to evaluate performance. It is essential to involve legal counsel in the very earliest stages of contract development.

Schematic/ Preliminary Design

In this phase, the team prepares schematic design studies showing the scale and relationship of the project components. Submittals include drawings, specifications, and a cost estimate. This package provides the owner with a description of the design for review and approval and addresses both the project requirements and cost. Clearly, any suitable sustainability measure must be included in the schematic design, because subsequent phases only develop these concepts and rarely add new ones.

The schematic design submittal should include the size of major energy system components and how strategies interact. In addition to floor

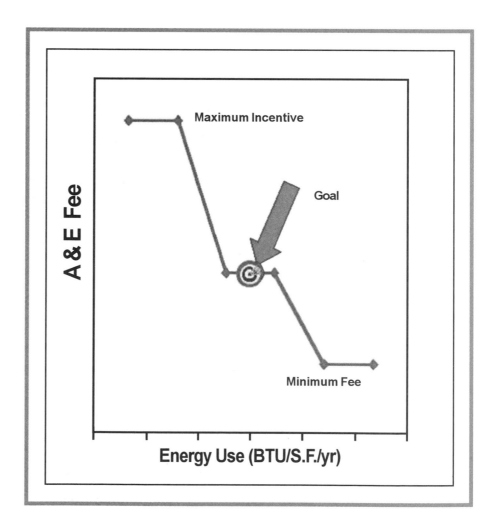

Figure 7.2
A performance-based fee might include a minimum fee plus an incentive up to a budgeted maximum.

plans, elevations, and type and size of mechanical system components, the following information should be included:

- **Building Plan:** Building dimensions and layout accommodating green building design strategies. For example, a double-loaded corridor often suits daylighting and natural ventilation. The design team would consider any strategies that affect the shape of the building (open or private offices, perimeter circulation spaces, orientation, earth-protection, articulated or compact plan, atrium, and sunspaces, to name a few).

- **Daylighting:** Size, number, and position of apertures (windows or roof monitors); relative dimensions of shading overhangs and light shelves; type of control (switching or dimming) number and location of light sensors; and requirements for room surface finishes and window glazing.

- **Passive Solar Heating:** Window areas and glazing properties, amount of thermal storage material and relative position of glazing and mass, optimal levels of envelope insulation, size and relative position of shading, and overheat protection.

- **Natural Ventilation:** Size and relative position of apertures (operable windows or vents), controls, and interface requirements for HVAC system.

- **Solar Energy Systems:** System type, solar collector area and orientation, amount of storage (water tank for solar hot water or batteries for photovoltaics), size of heat exchangers and pumps, controls, and power conditioning equipment.

For each energy savings measure, and for the optimal combination of measures, the schematic design should include estimates of energy use and operating cost, along with probable construction costs. This information informs decisions of features that should be included in the schematic design based on life-cycle cost effectiveness. Concepts included in the schematic design proceed to design development.

The energy analysis would include an hourly simulation to evaluate different schematic designs and the interaction between measures. Measures can be considered independently (single measure included). Elimination parametrics can also be used (single measure excluded) to evaluate the impact of a measure on the building as a whole system. The analyst can then rank strategies based on their performance and life-cycle cost.[5] The objective is to select systems for design development. As the design develops, it will be too late to add new strategies or technologies. Thus, it is important that complete information for decision-making, such as a design charette or advice of consultants, be sought prior to completion of the schematic design.

Design Charette

A design charette is an intense effort to complete a design in a short period of time. Charette participants first listen in order to understand the goals, needs, and limitations of a project, then envision creative, but realistic solutions. Charettes often consist of plenary sessions and specific break-out sessions. The break-out sessions might treat topics such as lighting, mechanical systems, material use, water and wastewater, site and landscape, or other specific areas of interest to charette participants. During plenary sessions, participants deliberately expose and exploit interactions between topics discussed in the break-out sessions, and bring discussion back to a whole-building perspective.

It is important to record ideas as they are mentioned, and to express these ideas effectively in a charette report. An independent recorder helps to ensure that the record includes not only the views of the most vocal, or of the facilitator, but every concept, no matter how timidly presented. The work of volunteer scribes rarely measures up to that of a professional recorder. The report will carry the ideas generated at the charette forward into the design process.

Since each aspect of the design affects all other aspects, and thus whole-building performance, it is best to involve a wide range of stakeholders in a charette. Often, charette topics do not end at the building walls. In addition to the owner and representatives of all disciplines and firms on the design team, a charette may include electric, gas, and water utilities; surrounding community associations; water quality and air quality management districts; industrial partners and technology experts; financial institutions; and environmental organizations.

Team Decision-Making

Disagreements between team members are inevitable, and are perhaps most acute in the schematic design phase. A structured approach to decision-making anticipates disagreement and enhances communication by stimulating team dialogue before competing options are identified, or before any team member falls in love with any design option.

Any decision-making process must evaluate priorities and goals. Sometimes, the team revises its initial goals in the schematic design phase. The dialogue about priorities should be kept alive throughout the design process. An effective decision-making process unites the team's focus and direction and fosters an awareness of effects on the building system as a whole, rather than just the sub-system (such as lighting or mechanical) that most concerns an individual team member. To evaluate the implications of a design option on whole-building performance, the team can establish a weighting system in order to evaluate dissimilar criteria, including cost, environmental impacts, noise, functionality, and resource use. One approach would be to convert all criteria to present-value dollars. Many costs, such as construction costs, are already in present-value dollars. Methods to convert life-cycle operating costs to present-value are well established. Assigning dollar values to emissions has been done,[6] but assigning dollar values to intangible attributes, such as architectural quality, has little precedent.

Documenting the decision-making process is important in order to maintain the awareness of how the design got to where it is and also to inform the owner or new team members, thus avoiding a need to revisit decisions that have been made. The dual needs of weighting criteria and documentation can be satisfied by setting up a bookkeeping system for priorities, numerical values of various weighting criteria, and a convenient format for reporting the rationale of design decisions.

The LEED rating criteria offers a method to quantify green building design measures, and may be useful as a system of weighting criteria for a team. Multi-Criteria Decision-Making (MCDM) is another process for which supporting software is available. The first step is to identify the criteria by which design options will be judged. Team members then vote on the weight, or significance, of each criterion. The evolving design is evaluated relative to these criteria, with numerical scores being determined for each. Criteria weights are used as scaling factors to relate the scores for one criterion to other criteria and aggregate all the scores into an overall measure of value. Figure 7.3 lists an example of criteria and weights used in the design of a new weather forecast office in Caribou, Maine. Performance of design options is determined relative to the overall score, accounting for all implications of design decisions on all building components. The MCDM software uses graphics to convey the results at a glance. On the hexagon-shaped charts of Figure 7.4, smaller is better (less cost, less resource use, less emissions).

Design Development

During design development, drawings and documents are developed to describe the entire project in detail. Drawings and specifications describe the architectural, structural, mechanical, electrical, materials, and site plan of the project. During design development, the team arrives at sustainability strategies and systems based on the brainstorming and selection that took place in the schematic design phase of the project. The energy analyst performs a more detailed analysis, including cost and performance trade-offs between alternative systems. The architect, mechanical engineer, and electrical engineer work together to place renewable energy sources (solar water heating, solar ventilation preheating, photovoltaics) in

Sample Criteria & Weights for Project Design

Criteria	Default Weight	Sub-Criteria	Default Sub-Weight
Life-cycle cost	1/6	Construction cost	.68
		Annual operation cost	19.4
		Annual maintenance cost	19.4
Resource use	1/6	Annual electricity, kWh/m^2	3
		Annual fuels, kWh/m^2 (of heat equivalent)	1
		Annual water, kg/m^2	0.15
		Construction materials, kg/m^2	0.03
		Land, m^2/m^2	300
Environmental	1/6	CO$_2$ emissions from construction, kg/m^2	1
		SO$_2$ emissions from construction, kg/m^2	90
		NO$_x$ emissions from construction, kg/m^2	45
		Annual CO$_2$ emissions from operation, kg/m^2	30
		Annual SO$_2$ emissions from operation, kg/m^2	3000
		Annual NO$_x$ emissions from operation, kg/m^2	1500
Architectural quality	1/6	Identity	0.25
		Scale/proportion	0.25
		Integrity/coherence	0.25
		Integration in urban context	0.25
Indoor quality	1/6	Air quality	0.35
		Lighting quality	0.25
		Thermal quality	0.20
		Acoustic quality	0.20
Functionality	1/6	Functionality	0.45
		Flexibility	0.15
		Maintainability	0.25
		Public relations value	0.15

Figure 7.3

such a way that they do not look like afterthought add-ons. Mechanical system options (thermal storage, economizer, night cooling, HVAC controls, evaporative cooling, ground-exchange) are specified at the component level. The lighting system design development integrates daylighting, equipment, fixtures, and controls. Communication during design development is key, since a change in any system, such as lighting power, could affect all other systems, such as the cooling load on the mechanical system.

It is wise to conduct design reviews that are both internal and external to the project team. The focus of design review efforts should be on the early schematic design submittals. By the time the design is 35% complete, it is usually too late to make major changes. An objective party who has not been involved in the design might be recruited to review it. These reviewers might include consultants, advocates from state and local governments or national laboratories, and experts on sustainability topics such as energy, materials, and indoor environmental conditions. Reviewers point out strengths as well as weaknesses, and try to be constructive with solutions to perceived problem areas.

It is important that reviewers do not put the designer on the defensive or embarrass him or her in front of the owner (their client). To do so would rupture the team approach and make sharing of information problematic in subsequent reviews. A reviewer without all the answers might take a Socratic, or questioning, approach. Design reviews can be

Figure 7.4

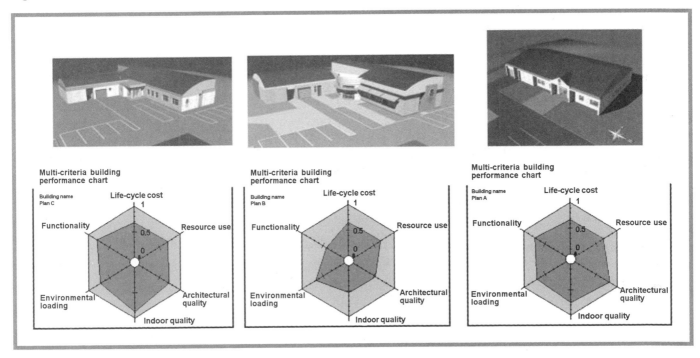

accomplished by marking up plans and specifications and by supplying product literature and other information to facilitate implementation of the recommendations. A meeting can be called where reviewers convey more complicated concepts from reviewers to the design team.

Value Engineering

During value engineering, the design is scrutinized to see how the same or better result can be achieved at a lower cost. Value engineering sometimes focuses on the functional mission of a building. It is important that sustainability goals key to the design intent not be compromised. Value engineering should be based on life-cycle cost rather than first cost. Energy analysis should be incorporated into the value engineering process to inform the value engineer of the consequences of deleting important energy features and to ensure that energy targets and goals are maintained through the value engineering process. The energy analyst would have to perform analysis and computer simulation as necessary to determine the effects of proposed cost cuts and to defend justified measures.

Value engineering is not always the enemy of the sustainability advocate. Sometimes it represents a final opportunity to include a sustainability measure that saves on first cost or has compelling benefits.

Construction Documents

During this phase of the project, the design team prepares working drawings and specifications from design development work approved by the owner and confirmed as meeting the sustainability goals set in the building program. In addition, the design team may prepare necessary bidding information, determine the form of contract with the contractor, and specify any special conditions of the contract. The construction documents contain all the information necessary for bid solicitation, and thus all the information that bidders need to provide an accurate costing of labor and materials. At this time, the team ensures that architectural, mechanical, and lighting details and specifications meet energy goals. They then perform a final energy analysis to confirm that the energy goals have been met, and also to provide necessary documentation required for LEED certification or other purposes.

The task of collecting documentation to evaluate environmental performance criteria must be planned and budgeted. There is a considerable amount of work involved in preparing green specifications. Certainly the detail that describes the green attributes of the specified material or method must be added, and often information must be included to find suppliers and assist the installing subcontractors in adopting a new material or technique. Careful specifications are key to keeping the cost down while promoting sustainable construction methods among suppliers and subcontractors.

The result of this final design effort is a package of drawings and specifications for use in the construction contract documents. Forms certifying that the construction documents comply with all applicable codes and standards (including those related to energy and environmental requirements) are signed, and the plans are stamped by the architect and professional engineer. Contract documents are often organized according to the structure presented in Figure 7.5.

Bid Solicitation & Contract Award

During the bidding phase of a project, bidders submit offers to perform the work described in the construction documents at a specified price. Bids describe the costs proposed for all construction described by the construction documents, as well as other direct construction costs. (Bids do not include design team fees, the cost of the land, rights of way or easements, or other costs defined as being the responsibility of the owner or otherwise outside of the scope of the construction contract.)

The design team supports the owner in bid solicitation and negotiation. This way, the team has an opportunity to maintain sustainability goals if cost cutting is required. Again, the energy analyst might have to perform studies to analyze trade-offs or substitutions. Also, since the contractor is providing all labor and materials to complete the construction, bidders may want to substitute materials they are familiar with or have easy access to for those specified for their sustainability benefits. In such cases, it is important that a sustainability expert and advocate remain involved in order to advise the owner toward a compromise that optimizes the benefits of material selection.

Construction

Administration of the construction contract is often included in the architect's and design team's basic services. The green design team specifically monitors sustainability and energy-related aspects during construction. The commissioning agent, although involved from the beginning, would be most active at this stage in order to correct problems early in construction. Many energy efficiency measures, such as insulation and vapor barriers, require special attention to detail during installation. The oversight of the commissioning agent helps to ensure that the benefits of these measures are realized. It is often too late to correct problems if they are discovered after installation. For example, it is much more expensive to correct sagging or missing insulation after the drywall and interior finish are installed. Again, the design team maintains adherence to sustainability goals as change orders are issued and if cost-cutting is required. Additional analysis may be required to evaluate cost and performance trade-offs.

Sometimes it is possible to include the construction contractor in the design process, but more often the contractor is not selected until the design is complete. In either case, it is important to get input from the trades early in the design process. Advice from the construction contractor, or a construction expert hired as a consultant, serves several

Elements of a Construction Contract

Bidding Requirements	Invitation Instructions Information Bid Form Bid Bond
Contract Forms	Agreement Performance Bond Payment Bond Certificates
Contract Conditions	General Supplementary
Specifications (in divisions)	General Site Construction Concrete Masonry Metals Wood and Plastics Thermal and Moisture Protection Doors and Windows Finishes Specialties Equipment Furnishings Special Construction Conveying Systems Mechanical Electrical Sustainabilty
Drawings	Site Architectural Electrical Mechanical

Figure 7.5

Green Building: Project Planning & Cost Estimating

useful purposes in the design process. The contractor can advise team members on the constructability of a design concept (e.g., how difficult or expensive it would be to implement). Trades are also an excellent source of ideas on how a design objective can be realized with less materials or at a lower cost, if they are made aware of the strategies being pursued.

Commissioning

Commissioning, addressed in more detail in Chapter 11, is the procedure used to confirm that building systems are installed according to the design intent. Commissioning should not be considered optional, as it provides the owner and design team with needed information and often uncovers problems that are easy to correct, but would have dire consequences if not detected. Unlike testing and balancing, which is part of the construction contract, commissioning is performed by a third-party **commissioning authority** on behalf of the owner. The commissioning authority should be involved very early in the design process. Early involvement will help the commissioning authority develop a record of the design intent with respect to energy efficiency and sustainability. The commissioning authority's recommendations to the design team will result in system designs that are not only easy to evaluate in field installations, but more reliable. The team should develop and implement a commissioning protocol with reference to *ASHRAE Commissioning Guidelines*.

Operations & Maintenance

Operations and maintenance staff from the owner's other buildings are usually available to advise the design team. If O&M staff members understand and support the sustainability goals of a project, they are more likely to make an extra effort to see that the systems perform. On the other hand, if the staff does not like a system, it will quickly be disabled and forgotten. Involving O&M staff in the design process gives them an understanding of the rationale behind system selection, the design intent of sustainability measures, and the importance of new or unusual systems to the performance of the building as a whole.

It is important to train both occupants and maintenance staff on the energy-related features of a building and also on sustainability features, such as recycling and gray water systems. Since staff change jobs frequently, the training should be videotaped, and good documentation (such as videos and manuals) should be well-organized and protected as a resource for new maintenance staff.

Measurement & Verification

Measurement and verification provides continuous post-occupancy evaluation of how systems are performing. This is a requirement for performance contracting, but provides critical information for all projects. Sustainability features often provide more than one way to meet a service. For example, if the solar water heater fails, the electrical system provides hot water; or if the recycling bins are full, a person can use the trash can. Managers are often unaware when these redundant sustainability features fail, because they get no complaints from the occupants. Measurement and verification provides diagnostic information so that systems continuously realize their intended benefits. The International Performance Measurement and Verification Protocol (**www.ipmvp.org**) describes options for structuring and implementing such a program.

Establishing a Green Team in an Existing Facility

Designing new buildings or major remodeling projects provides an excellent opportunity to create a facility that will benefit from green construction and operations practices. However, existing buildings—even without major renovations—can also become significantly greener, with a plan and an internal team to champion this effort. The American Society of Hospital Engineering published a monograph, "Green and Healthy Buildings for the Health Care Industry," which recommends a short- and long-term plan for implementing green practices into facilities operations. The short-term steps include:

- Establishing a "green team."
- Requiring project designers to specify cost-competitive green products for new projects, and requiring procurement managers to put in place procedures that include green attributes in procurement decisions for all supplies (paper products, cleaning materials, etc.).
- Providing seminars on healthy building practices and efficient resource management. Occupant awareness and behavior is credited with $500 million of the $1.2 billion energy savings achieved by the federal government from 1985 to 1995. Occupant cooperation helps ensure that efforts to optimize resource use are successful, and in fact, occupants hostile to changes can ensure that those measures fail.
- Expanding the Environmental Health & Safety department's responsibility to include monitoring air quality.
- Measuring resource consumption (energy and water), emissions, and waste generated, and establishing goals to improve efficiencies. Consider alternative financing, such as Energy Savings Performance Contracting (where the cost of a measure is paid back over time from energy cost savings) to fund projects that the facility does not have money for.
- Establishing recycling practices.
- Using LEED as an evaluation tool and modifying if appropriate.

The medium- and long-range recommended goals include:

- Establishing life-cycle measurements for environmental, human health, and natural resource performance.
- Designing for 50-year plus building life expectancy.
- Merging capital and O&M budgets to optimize life-cycle costing.
- Establishing procurement policies consistent with green practices, and review/revise annually.
- Establishing partnerships with regulators to review and revise regulations to reflect impacts on human health and environmental quality.
- Establishing an internal green building rating system.
- Establishing a permanent position to oversee compliance with green building standards.
- Providing ongoing green building training for staff.
- Integrating and balancing resource flows to enhance life-cycle efficiency.
- Designing for flexibility so that future changes can be implemented efficiently.

Conclusion

The procurement of architectural and engineering services is the best place to leverage the resources of an entire project toward increased resource efficiency. Designers respond to what the customer asks for, and careful specification of Statements of Work and deliverables for A&E teams is where owners tell the design community that they want green buildings. Requests for proposals that require and provide budgets for green design services will enhance interest and capability in green building among design firms. Owners sometimes say they want a green building, but then do not include the additional tasks or budget to allow the design team to truly pursue that goal. The Statement of Work, and its accompanying budget estimate, are necessary precursors to a successful green building project.

[1] Harris, Cyril M., ed. *Dictionary of Architecture and Construction 2nd Edition.* McGraw-Hill Inc., 1993.

[2] Energy Policy Act of 1992.

[3] Doug Balcomb, NREL, Personal communications. Energy10 available from Sustainable Buildings Industry Council, **www.sbic.org**

[4] Charles Eley, Eley and Associates.

[5] Doug Balcomb, NREL, Personal communications. Energy10 available from Sustainable Buildings Industry Council, **www.sbic.org**
EPA and NPS emissions factors

[6] Harris, Cyril M., ed. *Dictionary of Architecture and Construction 2nd Edition.* McGraw-Hill Inc., 1993.

Chapter

8 Economic Incentives & Funding Sources

Joseph Macaluso, CCC

Building professionals must constantly evaluate and manage cost issues to be successful in today's ultra-competitive world. Ideally, long-term value should be the criterion by which costs are evaluated. Analyzing building costs should include not only first costs, but also future costs that occur over the life of the facility, system, or component. These costs include operation, maintenance, disposal, and all the incidental expenses associated with an item. This life-cycle costing process, discussed in Chapter 12, is part of value engineering.

Understanding the Investment in Green Building

Many green building components have higher initial costs, but lower operating or maintenance costs, and have less environmental impact than comparable, conventional components. A high-efficiency boiler, for example, will increase the cost of a project, but using it saves money over time, because of reduced fuel consumption. A few green building components have lower initial costs, but higher maintenance costs. For example, leaving a natural habitat unpaved may cost less and reduce runoff, but it also increases gardening and maintenance costs. In some cases, a green building approach actually has both lower initial costs and lower future costs. For example, through integrated design, smaller chillers can be used in facilities, reducing both initial and operating costs. Finally, some green building components have both higher first costs and future costs, but the benefit to the building occupants and/or the environment may be deemed worth the investment. Newly developed coatings may in some instances cost more than those formulated with harmful compounds. They may also not last as long, increasing both first costs and future costs. The first and life-cycle costs and benefits of each green component should be evaluated both individually and as part of an entire system.

In the private sector, often the initial purchaser of a building component, or the builder of a facility, is not the ultimate user; therefore most of the emphasis is on first costs, not future costs. The exception is the owner-occupied building. In the public sector where the building is frequently owner-occupied, the entire life cycle cost of the facility will more likely be considered; in fact for federal agencies, life-cycle cost analysis is required by regulation 10CFR436. This is one of the reasons why green buildings are starting to be embraced in the public sector. Another factor is the voluntary, and sometimes mandatory, green design guidelines established by government agencies for their projects.

Even in the private sector, lower operating costs can, over time, more than offset the additional first costs of green components. In most cases, however, owners will probably stipulate an acceptable payback period that must be met for the overall green-related first cost increase.

Take the case of a builder who has a choice between two furnaces; they both cost the same to operate. The standard model complies with all current regulations and costs only $6,000. The green model not only complies with all current regulations, but also has a 10% higher efficiency rate by condensing water vapor from the exhaust. It costs $8,000. It is clear which would be an easier sell based on first cost, but life-cycle cost may indicate that the more expensive furnace is actually a better choice.

Much research has been done on the health and societal costs associated with pollution and resource use. Agencies such as the National Park Service assign dollar values to air pollution ($14 per ton of CO_2, $0.85 per lb. of SO_2, and $3.75 per lb. of NO_x)[1] for inclusion in the life-cycle cost analysis. In some cases, the value of these emissions can account for as much as half of the total operating costs. Still, our building industry has not developed a comprehensive mechanism for determining all of the environmental costs associated with a component.

There are various attempts by different groups to describe environmental impacts and ways of selecting components based on a set of environmental preferences. However, there is no uniform method to accurately put a dollar value on the amount of valuable resources used up or environmental damage that a building component causes. Therefore, there is no way of charging an "environmental tax" to building components, and no direct financial penalty for not building green.

Currently it is difficult for building industry purchasers to even make a determination on how green a product is. A group called the Sustainable Products Purchasers Coalition is actively trying to promote the use of green products by encouraging the use of standardized life-cycle analysis in order to be able to accurately and thoroughly understand the total environmental impact of a product. (For information, visit their Web site at **www.sppcoalation.org**)

The Value of Quality & Innovation

So why build green? Aside from the obvious hurdles and often higher initial costs, there are some compelling, albeit longer-term, financial advantages to building green. For institutions or corporations, building green can showcase the entity's environmental stewardship. A green building shows the world that the owner will spend more to invest in quality and innovation.

Today's green designers realize that any approach must improve quality, such as better control of temperature, humidity, lighting effectiveness, and indoor air quality. Gone are the days when conservationists ask people to put on a sweater and turn the thermostat down. The focus of today's green designers is on using integrated design and a high degree of equipment efficiency to provide superior conditions with less expenditure of natural resources.

Today's green buildings are still unique enough to enjoy notoriety. This is a valuable commodity that brings positive publicity not only to the building owner, but to all those involved with the project, including the architect, engineer, and contractors. The very concept of designing, building, and operating a green building pushes the designer, constructor, and owner to work in a collaborative way, often encouraging all three to "think outside the box." This process not only exposes the designer, constructor, and operator to new technology and alternate methods, but enables them to acquire unique and valuable knowledge, experience, and insight that they may not gain from "ordinary" projects. It also forces the owner to systematically assess the needs of the organization from different perspectives. Green building projects are truly learning experiences for all involved. The result is the delivery of a unique, energy-efficient, and comfortable building. A project like this can translate to increased profits for all down the line.

Insurance & Productivity

The insurance industry is moving toward rewarding green building approaches. To ensure stringent compliance with energy efficiency and indoor air quality requirements, green buildings require a more thorough commissioning process than conventional buildings. This process increases the likelihood that a building will operate trouble-free. On this premise, insurance companies are now considering lower premiums for owners, architects, and engineers associated with a fully commissioned green building.

Appraisers are starting to recognize that green buildings operate more efficiently. One method appraisers use to determine the value of a building is income capitalization. With this method, taking the net operating income and dividing it into the prevailing cap rate determines the value of a building. Reducing energy costs increases the net operating income, increasing the value of the building.[2]

Improved indoor air quality also creates a healthier indoor environment that may be linked to increased occupant productivity, and a reduction in absenteeism. The financial incentive in this case is to the facility owner and user.

Potential Drawbacks of Incentives & Rebates

Some would argue that tax credits and rebates are not necessary and may actually hinder the development of new green technologies. The argument is that the credits can create an artificial market; if the credit is taken away, it could be damaging to these fledgling industries. There is also concern that these credits send a subtle message to the public that these technologies are not yet cost-effective, when they may in fact be not only cost-effective, but cost-advantageous. Tax credits may also encourage fraud by encouraging sellers to artificially set the selling price of the product higher, to increase the tax credit amount to the seller, and then refund part of the inflated amount directly to the customer by means of a finder's fee, or some other gimmick.[3] In spite of these concerns, many feel that incentives are needed to offset the initial high cost of new technological advances until they become more cost-efficient.

Federal & State Government Incentive Programs

To encourage green practices, federal, state, and local governments have initiated programs that for the most part offer information, technical assistance, advice, consultation, and encouragement to builders and potential owners of green properties. Because of the higher initial costs of many green building components, financial incentives are made available to builders and owners to help defray these costs. Most of the incentives are offered for conserving energy and water resources, because by reducing the demand for these resources state and local governments can reduce infrastructure costs, and thereby reduce taxes.

Brownfields: Federal Assistance Program

One green approach available to developers is to remediate moderately polluted sites, known as "brownfields," and then build on them. This approach encourages the cleaning up of sites that may otherwise have been left polluted. It also prevents unnecessary development of natural environments and reduces urban sprawl, especially since most of these brownfield sites are located in urban or industrialized areas.

Hundreds of thousands of potential sites are currently considered brownfields. The Small Business Relief and Brownfields Revitalization Act signed by President George W. Bush increases the amount of federal assistance for the cleanup of brownfield sites to $200 million, and increases liability protection to developers who voluntarily clean up the site.

In addition, insurance companies are more willing to write environmental insurance policies than they were in the early 1990s because they have gathered more experience and confidence in this area. The insurance policies protect the developer from drastic increases in cleanup costs over the original estimate, and also cover the cost if additional pollution is found after the site is sold to the developer. The accuracy of technology used to determine the extent of the pollution has also improved, allowing developers and insurance companies to make more accurate assessments of the cleanup costs.

The Federal Brownfields Tax Incentive allows builders to fully deduct the remediation costs of a project in the year they were incurred, instead of having to capitalize these costs. The convergence of several factors has made brownfield development a lot more attractive to developers than it was in the recent past.[4]

State Incentive Programs

Most states offer rebates, loans, grants, and tax credits to encourage water and energy conservation or the use of renewable forms of energy. To find out more about these offers, visit the individual states' Web sites. Another good source is the Database of State Incentives for Renewable Energy at **www.dsireusa.org** The green building project team should include someone with expertise in tracking down, and skill in applying for, environmental and energy-related loans, grants, and funding from both government and private sources.

Tax incentives include those on income tax, property tax, and depreciation in the value of the equipment. Available incentive programs depend on the taxable status and liability of the parties, on the financing mechanism utilized, and on the technology employed. For example, solar distributed generation projects currently enjoy a 10% federal business investment tax credit.

Some Examples

New York: Signaling that it is willing to lend financial support to green building, New York State has signed into law the Green Building Tax Credit Legislation. The legislation allows tax credits for the utilization of green products and systems and for specific components. It is aimed at large commercial and multi-family projects. The state is formulating standards for the greening of facilities. This includes energy efficiency, indoor air quality, recycling, and compliance with existing regulations. The bill offers a tax credit of up to 7% of the allowable costs, capped at $150/square foot for the base building (sidewalks, parking areas, mechanical rooms, main lobbies, elevators, stairways, etc.), and $75/square foot for tenant areas.

For fuel cells that service green facilities, the applicant can receive a 30% tax credit of allowable costs. Allowable costs are capped at $1,000/kw of capacity.

For integrated photovoltaic modules, a 100% tax credit of the allowable incremental costs is offered. Allowable costs are capped at $3/watt capacity.

A 25% tax credit of the allowable incremental costs is available for non-integrated photovoltaic modules. Allowable costs are capped at $3/watt capacity.

For new air-conditioning equipment using non-ozone depleting refrigerant servicing green spaces, a tax credit is currently offered at 10% of the allowable cost.

The New York State Energy Resource Development Authority (NYSERDA) offers technical assistance for the Green Building Tax Credit and other loans, grants, and incentives for improving energy efficiency and installing green building components.

Maryland: Maryland has approved a tax credit bill similar to the New York bill. Maryland offers a tax credit of up to 8% of the allowable cost of the base building, capped at $120 per square foot and $60 per square foot for tenant spaces.

The fuel cell tax credit is 30% of the allowable cost, capped at $1,000/kw of capacity.

The integrated photovoltaic credit is 20% of the allowable cost, capped at $3/watt capacity.

The non-integrated photovoltaic credit is 25% of the allowable cost, capped at $3/watt capacity.

In addition, there is a wind turbine credit of 25% of the allowable cost.

Massachusetts: Massachusetts is also considering legislation with criteria similar to New York's and Maryland's Green Building Tax Credit legislation.

Oregon: The Portland, Oregon Commercial Sustainable Building Program is for large commercial, institutional, and mixed-use projects. It offers developers up to $20,000 for achieving the silver, gold, or platinum levels of the Portland Leadership in Energy & Environmental Design (LEED) standard. *(See Chapter 9 for a description of LEED.)* The Portland standard is a localized supplement to the U.S. Green Building Council standard. Portland's residential program, which is open to new and major remodeling of single-family homes, duplexes, and condominiums, offers incentives based on a scoring system similar to LEED that rates the sustainability of the site, energy efficiency of the building, materials resource efficiency, indoor air quality, and the use of innovative and new technology in the project.

Texas: The city of Austin, Texas not only provides technical assistance and free publicity to developers who incorporate green features, but offers rebates of up to $1,415. The project is reviewed by the Green Building Program, and receives a rating from one to four stars, depending on the design's degree of sustainability. The rebate is dependent on the completion of the project, and the amount of energy and water savings realized.

Virginia: Arlington County, Virginia has a program that, in lieu of tax incentives, rewards developers with allowances to build higher-density projects if they meet the LEED silver standard. The higher the density, the more units, the higher the rent. The increased rental income can offset the higher first costs of building green.[5] As with all regulations, check restrictions and requirements carefully. *(See the Resources section for more on state and municipal initiatives)*

The Advantage of Marketing Green

For residential developers, building green can increase demand for their homes over conventionally built homes. Many home buyers are interested in incorporating green features into their homes for altruistic reasons, as well as energy savings and a healthier indoor environment. The question is, how much is the home buyer willing to spend, and for what features? One survey conducted by a building industry group, The Cahners Residential Group, has shown that 55% of those buyers were willing to pay between $5,000–$10,000 more for green features in a new home.[6]

Mortgage Advantages

Building green often increases the construction cost of new homes, but building to an established green standard adds value to a house because purchasers are assured that they are getting a well-constructed, healthy, and energy-saving home—all of which increases the demand for these homes. Energy saving features make a new home more affordable by reducing monthly expenses. Mainstream consumer lending institutions like Countrywide Home Loans, Chase Manhattan Mortgage, and Bank of America are taking energy cost savings into account when determining the size loan for which the applicant is eligible.

Home mortgages have several advantages as a way of financing green construction projects. Interest rates are kept low by the operation of Federal Loan Associations, which implement federal policy. Interest rates on home mortgages are tax-deductible, resulting in a lower effective project cost. Terms of 15-30 years are much longer than available through other types of financing. (Most financers prefer a term of less than 10 years.) A disadvantage is that the cost of the green building measures may add to the appraised value of the house, increasing the mil levy property taxes.

All of the Federal Home Loan Associations have similar programs that promote energy efficiency or renewable energy measures. Federal National Mortgage Association (Fannie Mae) is a financial institution that works directly with banks to help provide funding for lower- and middle-income borrowers. Fannie Mae offers mortgages up to $240,000 at market interest rates that allow a 2% increase in debt-to-income ratio for energy-efficient homes secured over a 30-year term. Fannie Mae also has Residential Energy Efficiency Improvement Loans up to $15,000 (or up to 10% of the base loan) at below-market interest rates, unsecured, over a 10-year term. Federal Home Mortgage Loan Corp. (Freddie Mac) has mortgages for up to $240,000 at market interest rates or variable prime plus 2%, and allows up to 10% above the base loan amount with their Energy-Efficient Mortgage. The U.S. Department of Housing and Urban Development (HUD) allows up to 10% above the base loan amount with an Energy-Efficient Mortgage. The U.S. Department of Veterans Affairs (VA), for veterans, allows up to $230,000, up to 10% above the base loan amount with an Energy-Efficient Mortgage.

Fannie Mae also offers several mortgage programs that promote green building practices under the Home Performance Power Suite, which aims to encourage energy efficiency. The Energy-Efficient Mortgage^{SM} factors in the savings from improvements brought about by the increased efficiency to the home. A full 100% of the energy improvements of the home can be financed on one-family through four-family homes. To qualify, the borrower must obtain a Home Energy Rating System report. This report provides an energy rating of the home's efficiency and estimates the potential savings. These savings are used in the expense-to-income ratios to qualify borrowers. A favorable rating allows a borrower to qualify for a larger mortgage. The homes must exceed the 1993 *Model Energy Code* or a qualifying energy efficient guideline.

The Flexible Home Performance Power Fannie Mae mortgage program is available to buyers of new, one-family houses. This mortgage program is based on the increased efficiency in a green home, and resulting water and utility savings. The projected savings are counted as increased income in the calculations used to determine the borrower's qualification for the mortgage. This program features a low 3% downpayment that may also come from Community Seconds®, a second lien mortgage that can be combined with one of Fannie Mae's

Community Lending mortgage products to increase affordability. A federal, state, or local government agency, an employer, or a nonprofit organization typically provides this mortgage option. A home energy rater (someone who is qualified to rate the energy performance of a home) provides an energy efficiency rating, and the projected savings are used in the qualification calculations.

Colorado Built Green Mortgage is a Fannie Mae program offered in conjunction with the Colorado Association of Home Builders. This program is available for new or existing one-family through four-family houses. The house must be located in Colorado and registered with Built Green of Colorado. This program factors in the present value of the energy, water, and maintenance cost savings, or the actual cost of the resource efficiency improvements into the valuation of the house. The result is a more favorable loan-to-value ratio, an increase in the amount that can be borrowed. This mortgage program can be combined with other Fannie Mae programs.

Albuquerque DREEM is a low downpayment Fannie Mae mortgage available to borrowers with low incomes for properties that exceed the Model Energy Code and employ water and other resource conservation measures.

Fannie Mae has also teamed up with Natural Resources Defense Council and others to create the Location Efficient Mortgage. This mortgage features a low 3% downpayment, but requires the home to be located in a densely populated area near public transportation. The theory is that the money saved by using public transportation increases the borrower's qualifying income and home-buying power. This can be considered a green approach because the use of public transportation reduces pollution and urban sprawl.

Financing Green Projects

Financing can convert the future stream of savings into the required initial investment for green buildings, components, and systems. Whether the higher cost is justified by fuel cost savings or other benefits depends largely on the terms of the financing arrangement. Strategies to extend the term of financing and reduce the interest rate will speed the implementation of cleaner, more efficient technologies. Options for financing green building projects include:

- Appropriations (using an agency's or organization's own money)
- Debt (commercial bank loan)
- Mortgage and home equity loan
- Limited partnership
- Vendor financing

- General obligation bond
- Revenue bond
- Lease
- Energy savings performance contract
- Utility programs
- Chauffage (end-use purchase)
- Grants

The federal government uses appropriations for large construction projects, and bases decisions of cost-effectiveness on the requirements of regulation 10CFR436. Green measures would be considered cost-effective if the ratio of life-cycle savings to investment cost (Savings-to-Investment Ratio, or SIR) is greater than one. 10CFR436 requires agencies to implement the alternative with the lowest life-cycle cost, favoring energy-efficient options.

Local governments often use General Obligation Bonds (GOBs) to finance construction projects. These bonds are secured by the good faith and credit of the governments and are repaid by the taxpayers. Revenue bonds, on the other hand, are paid back by the revenue from the project, and are thus held to a lower level of approval.

Leases are an effective way to obtain energy-efficient equipment or green products without a large capital investment. For example, it might be possible to lease carpet, which would be recycled, rather than to purchase it outright. In an Energy Savings Performance Contract (ESPC), an Energy Services Company (ESCO) would pay for the initial cost of a measure in exchange for a share of the energy savings. ESPC is unusual for new construction because the utility bill, and thus the savings, have not been established for a new building. However, using a building modeling DOE-2 computer program, it is possible to estimate the savings and base the payments to the ESCO on that modeled amount.

Utilities should always be consulted when initiating a green building project. Utility companies often offer rebates for efficient equipment. They may also offer design assistance services and consultation on the effects of rate structures on the cost effectiveness of green options.

Chauffage is an arrangement that involves purchasing an end-result rather than purchasing the equipment to produce that end result. Examples include purchasing hot water (in $/BTU) from a solar water heating system or purchasing the electricity produced by a photovoltaic system. Such arrangements to purchase hot water from solar heating have been set up at several prisons, including Tehachapi California State Prison, Phoenix Federal Correctional Institution, and Jefferson County Jail in Colorado. *(See Chapter 4 for more on solar energy.)*

Conclusion There are numerous economic and financial incentives that can make green projects more viable. These incentives are usually linked to a set of guidelines to ensure that the project is in line with the funding partner's overall goals. There are many guidelines being promulgated, and the project team member responsible for the financial aspects of the project should become familiar with all applicable funding and incentive sources and their current, specific requirements.

[1] National Park Service Denver Service Center Guideline 94-04, revised September 1997.

[2] "Can Green be Gold?" David Kozlowsi, senior editor, **www.facilitiesnet.com**

[3] *Environmental Building News*, June 2000.

[4] *New York Times*, "For Developers Brownfields Look Less Risky," 4/21/02.

[5] Governing, January 2002.

[6] *Green Builder*, David Johnson, contributing editor, 9/1/00 **www.housingzone.com/green/index.asp**

Chapter
9 Standards & Guidelines

Joseph Macaluso, CCC

Green standards can be classified into two groups: those that relate to specific building components, and those that relate to the building as a whole entity. Many well-established trade organizations provide standards that relate to specific properties of individual building materials or systems. Other standards, relating to building components' overall environmental performance, are available from more recently formed, environmentally based organizations. Several standards, emerging from both environmental groups and environmental/industry/ government partnerships, can be applied to determine how green a building (or building design) is, as a whole.

The LEED™ (Leadership in Energy and Environmental Design) standard, developed by the U.S. Green Building Council, seems to be emerging as the most popular, all-encompassing, whole-building standard in the U.S. Energy Star® is another popular whole building standard, although its scope is limited to energy efficiency. Some private developers, architects, engineers, and contractors are incorporating energy efficiency standards like Energy Star® and other green standards into their own design guidelines.

Several states including Maryland, California, Pennsylvania, Connecticut, and Massachusetts have incorporated, or are in the process of incorporating, green architectural guidelines into the building requirements of state-owned facilities. Some of the standards have even found their way into government building codes and regulations. Municipalities are making similar moves. For example, the city of Frisco, Texas has recently mandated that all new homes must comply with the Energy Star Homes® program requirements. This clearly demonstrates that today's voluntary guideline may be tomorrow's legal requirement, raising the bar as to what is considered green.

There can be challenges incorporating green components into the design of a building. Building codes are usually prescriptive, which means that some green components may not be allowable in some locations, even if they accomplish the same functions as a standard component in a more earth-friendly way. If code officials are willing to consider green alternatives, a lengthy review process is often required. Some believe that to encourage innovation and the use of green building products, building codes should be more performance-oriented. In other words, a building component or system approval should be based on how well it performs a function, not based on exactly specified materials or components and how they must be installed.[1]

Building Component Standards

GreenSpec®
www.buildinggreen.com

GreenSpec® building products are included in the *GreenSpec® Directory*, a compilation of over 1,500 products selected by BuildingGreen, the editors of *Environmental Building News*. (*Environmental Building News* is a leading newsletter on environmentally responsible design and construction.) The products in the binder are arranged in CSI MasterFormat™ order. The compilation is available in print form or on the Internet as part of Green Spec's premium Web content subscription service. To be included in the compilation, products must meet at least one of the following criteria:

- Composed of recycled or salvaged materials.
- Reduces the impact of construction.
- Saves energy or water.
- Avoids toxic or other emissions.
- Promotes healthy indoor spaces.
- Preserves natural resources.

In the selection process, the editors apply quantifiable and verifiable standards, when possible. For example, the standard for domestic water heaters is an energy factor of .80 or higher. For appliances, the standard is typically higher than what is required by Energy Star®. For central air conditioners and heat pumps, the product line must have at least one model with a Seasonal Energy Efficiency Ratio (SEER) rating of 16 or greater. The standards are constantly evaluated and updated. When an applicable standard is not available, judgment calls are made based on the editors' knowledge. The staff considers not only specific benefits, but also overall environmental performance of a product or material.[2]

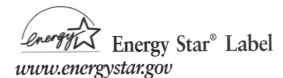 Energy Star® Label

www.energystar.gov

The U.S. Environmental Protection Agency created the Energy Star® label to promote energy-efficient products, recognizing that increased energy efficiency reduces carbon dioxide emissions. Since the creation of Energy Star®, the Department of Energy has also joined in the effort. Energy Star® is a voluntary program maintained by these two government agencies in cooperation with private industry. The program labels many products, ranging from appliances to traffic lights.

Figure 9.1

Energy Star® Building Components

CSI #	COMPONENT	KEY CRITERIA
07300	Low-slope roofs	• Initial solar reflectance of .65 or greater • Maintains reflectance of .50 or greater three years after installation
07300	Steep-slope roofs	• Initial solar reflectance of .25 or greater. • Maintains reflectance of .15 or greater three years after installation
08500	Windows	• Carries a National Fenestration Rating Council energy performance label. Northern regions, Maximum .35 U factor Central regions, Maximum .40 U factor Southern regions, Maximum .75 U factor
11454 11454	Refrigerators Clothes washers	• 10% more efficient than NAECA standards • MEF of 1.26 or greater
15510	Residential boilers	• Manufacturer sells at least one model with AFUE rating of at least 85%
15530	Furnaces	• Minimum AFUE rating of at least 90%
15730	Central air-conditioners	• Minimum SEER of 12
15730	Room air-conditioners	• Under 8,000 BTU – Min 10.7 EER • 8,000 - 13,999 BTU – Min 10.8 EER • 14,000-19,999 BTU – Min 10.7 EER • 20,000 or greater BTU – Min 9.4 EER
15740	Heat Pump	• Minimum seer of 12 • Minimum HSFP of 7.6
15740 15740 15740	Closed-loop geothermal heat pumps Open-loop geothermal heat pumps DX geothermal heat pumps	• Minimum EER of 14.1 and COP of 3.3 • Minimum EER of 16.2 and COP of 3.6 • Minimum EER of 15 and COP of 3.5
16270	Single-phase transformers	• Minimum efficiency levels that range from 97.7% for 15 kVa, to 98.9% for 333 kVa transformers
16270	Three-phase transformers	• Minimum efficiency levels that range from 97.0% for 15 kVa, to 98.9% for 1,000 kVa transformers

A substantial portion of this list covers building components. Figure 9.1 lists some of the Energy Star® rated building components and the key criteria that determine eligibility.

 ## The Forest Stewardship Council
www.fscus.org

The Forest Stewardship Council is concerned with ecological, social, and economic aspects of the forest management practices used to produce wood products. These products are tracked from the logging sites through to the end-user. The council has adopted criteria that a company must follow in order for its products to be certified. The company harvesting the product must:

- Meet all applicable laws.
- Have legally established rights to the harvest.
- Respect indigenous rights.
- Maintain community well being.
- Conserve economic resources.
- Protect biological diversity.
- Have a written management plan.
- Engage in regular monitoring.
- Maintain high conservation value forests.
- Manage plantations to alleviate pressures on natural forests.

Generally, the forest must be managed to maintain ecological productivity. Management must minimize waste and avoid damage to other forest resources. A complete environmental assessment must be performed before the start of any site-disturbing activities. Safeguards must be in place to protect endangered species. Environmentally friendly pest control should be used, and chemical pesticides avoided.

 ## Global Ecolabeling Network
www.gen.gr.jp

Ecolabeling is performed by individual organizations, using specific criteria to determine whether a product results in a lower environmental burden and impact in relation to comparable products. If the product meets these goals, it may display a label signifying that it meets the criteria set by the individual ecolabeling organization. The Global Ecolabeling Network is a nonprofit association composed of 26 ecolabeling organizations. Formed in 1994, its goal is to "improve, promote, and develop the ecolabeling of products and services." Members of the Global Ecolabeling Network must:

- Be based solely on voluntary participation for potential licensees.
- Run by not-for-profit organizations without commercial interests.
- Exhibit independence from undue commercial interests.
- Have a source of funding that will not create a conflict of interest.
- Seek advice from and consult with stakeholder interests.
- Have a legally protected logo.
- Determine criteria based on an assessment of the overall life of a product category.
- Open access to potential licensees from all countries.
- Establish criteria levels that encourage the production and use of products and services that are significantly less damaging to the environment than other products.
- Conduct periodic reviews, and if necessary, update both environmental criteria and categories, taking into account technological and market place developments.

EcoLogo Label – Global Ecolabel Network Member
www.environmentalchoice.com

The EcoLogo is issued on products that are certified by The Environmental Choice Program, a Canadian organization established in 1988 to "provide an incentive to manufacturers and suppliers of environmentally preferable products and services, thereby helping consumers identify products and services that are less harmful to the environment." The EcoLogo can be issued to a product or service that "improves energy efficiency, reduces hazardous products, uses recycled materials, is re-usable, or provides some other environmental benefit. Certified products or services should meet or exceed any applicable industry-specific safety and performance standards." Figure 9.2 lists EcoLogo building components and key criteria that determine eligibility.

Green Seal Label – Global Ecolabel Network Member
www.greenseal.org

Green Seal is a nonprofit organization that certifies a wide variety of products, including building components such as occupancy sensors,

Ecologo Building Components

CSI #	COMPONENT	KEY CRITERIA
01540	Safety fence, made from mixed recycled materials	• Contains over 90% recycled plastics
01540	Safety fence, made from single resin recycled materials	• Contains at least 25% recycled material
02520	Drainage pipe, made from single resin recycled materials	• Contains over 25% of recycled materials
07210	Insulation, fiberglass	• Contains over 35% recycled material
07210	Insulation, mineral board	• Contains over 45% recycled material
07210	Insulation, plastic foam	• Contains over 75% recycled material • Low impact on ozone and global warming
07210	Insulation, mineral wool, loose fill, and spray-on mineral	• Contains at least 50% recycled material
09250	Gypsum board	• Contains 10% recycled material or 20% flue gas desulphurization (FGD) gypsum B and 5% recycled material or 50% (FGD) gypsum B
09648	Wood floors	• Meets or exceeds ASTM D5230 "Taber Abrasion Test" • Meets or exceeds ASTM D1037 "Hardness Test" • Does not emit VOCs, including formaldehyde, at a rate greater than 0.5 mg/m²/hr in accordance with ASTM D5116-90 standard • Finish water-based or 100% solid UV curable coating • If finished with water-based coating, it must meet ECP-76. • Not coated with products that are manufactured or formulated with arsenic, cadmium, chromium, lead, mercury, nickel, or suspected carcinogens or mutagens • Guarantee of at least 10 years • Compliance with International Trade in Endangered Species Act • If manufactured from fast growing wood substitute, must be grown in accordance with sustainable harvest principles, sustainable forest management system, or programs run by FSC or INBAR
09680	Carpeting, commercial modular	• Sold as removable tiles using a peel-and-stick water-base adhesive • Sold with a service offering rotation and replacement of worn tiles • For carpet: TVOC emission rated of .25 mg/m² per hour or less after 24 hours. Formaldehyde emission rate of .02/m² per hour. • For adhesive: TVOC emission rated of .05 mg/m² per hour or less after 72 hours. Formaldehyde emission rate of .02/m² per hour. • Carpet backing contains at least 5% recycled material • Is not manufactured with topically applied biological inhibitors • Manufactured using closed loop water process

Figure 9.2

photovoltaic modules, residential central air conditioning systems, chillers, heat pumps, windows, window films, and paints. Green Seal-certified air conditioners, heat pumps, and chillers must meet minimum efficiency requirements. The chemical composition of paints is evaluated for substances that are harmful to the environment. Requirements are also set for the content of recycled material used in the packaging.

Figure 9.2 (continued)

Ecologo Building Components

CSI #	COMPONENT	KEY CRITERIA
09910	Low-VOC paints and surface coatings	• Not formulated with formaldehyde, halogenated or aromatic solvents, or heavy metals • Flashpoint of 61° C or greater • Does not contain VOCs in excess of 200 grams per liter • Does not contain VOCs in excess of 300 grams per liter for varnishes
13838	Thermostat control	• Fuel savings of at least 10% • States that unit must be professionally installed • States that unit is to be used with furnaces over 7 years old
15418	Compost toilets, residential	• Keeps composting material in an aerobic state • Includes a users' manual that explains proper use, uses for the compost, conditions, in which the process will not work, and ways to avoid problems with animals, rodents, and pathogens • 5 year warranty
15418	Shower heads, water conserving	• Maximum flow rate of less than 9.5 L/min at 5.5 kg/cm^2 • Trickle valves flow rate of 1.9 L/min in "trickle" mode • 3 year warranty • Meets CSA standards
15480	Hot water tanks, indirect fired	• Stand-by-loss of less than 60 watts/hr for tanks up to 200 liters, 120 watts/hr for tanks greater than 200 liters and less than 450 liters • Use polyurethane foam insulation blowing agents with zero ozone depletion potential • Performance requirements: IAZ Z-21 10.1b 1994 with input ratings of 75,000 BTU/h or less IAZ Z-21 10.3b 1994 with input ratings above 75,000 BTU/h • Manufacturer certified by International Approval Services
15530	Boilers	• Emission rates for NO$_x$ of 94 mg/kWh or less • Emission rates for CO of 40ppm or less • Combustion efficiency of 88% or greater • Conforms to ANSI Z21.13 • Conforms to ASME Standards for Class "H" • Certified by IAS

The Green Seal organization employs life cycle analysis when developing these standards. Green Seal also has created a set of standards specifically aimed at the environmental practices of lodging properties. Their mission is "to achieve a more sustainable world by promoting environmentally responsible production, purchasing, and products." Products that conform to these standards are allowed to display the Green Seal label. The Green Seal label meets the criteria for ISO 14020 and 14024 standards for Ecolabeling and the U.S. Environmental Protection Agency's criteria for third-party certifiers of environmentally preferable products.

Other Global Ecolabel Network Members
www.gen.gr.jp

There are many ecological labeling programs throughout the world that are members of the Global Ecolabel Network. The particular standards used for determining the award of a label vary, and are usually based on government or industry standards. These individual labels cover a variety of product categories, including building products. There are Ecolabel programs in 25 different countries.

Other international labeling standards include the European Union and Nordic Swan Ecolabels. The European Union label represents 27 different countries. The Nordic Swan label represents Denmark, Finland, Iceland, Norway, and Sweden.

Climate Cool™ Brand Label
www.climateneutral.com

Climate Cool™ brand is a trademark of the Climate Neutral™ Network, a non-profit organization "dedicated to helping companies, communities, and consumers achieve a net-zero impact on the earth's climate." The Climate Cool™ brand can be used only on products that have eliminated or offset greenhouse emissions associated with that product throughout their entire life cycle. To make that determination, an environmental review panel from the Climate Neutral™ Network requires the manufacturer to conduct an inventory of the greenhouse emissions associated with the production and use of the product throughout the entire product life cycle. This record is used as a baseline for implementing steps to reduce or eliminate greenhouse emissions associated with the product. If, after taking significant steps to reduce emissions, a company is still not able to totally comply with their elimination, it can offset those remaining emissions with efforts outside the product sphere, such as investing in other energy-efficient products, conservation, or other measures to protect the environment. Progress is evaluated to ensure the company is on target to meet its goals. In addition to certifying individual product lines, a certification can be earned for the entire company or "enterprise."

ASHRAE Standards

ASHRAE (American Society of Heating, Refrigerating, and Air-Conditioning Engineers, Inc.) publishes basic standards for heating, ventilation, and other mechanical building components. ASHRAE publications include standards that relate to green building construction, such as for airborne contaminants, CFC emission reduction, commissioning, energy management systems, energy conservation, indoor air environment, and solar energy.

Of special interest to those involved in green building construction is ASHRAE 90.1 *Energy Standard for Buildings Except Low-Rise Residential Buildings*. This code sets requirements for energy efficiency and methods for determining compliance. It covers the building envelope systems (walls, roofs, etc.), HVAC systems (heating, ventilation, and air-conditioning), lighting systems, and hot water systems for new building construction and major additions.

The code consists of basic requirements for these systems. After these requirements are met, additional ones must be complied with by choosing amongst three alternate methods: prescriptive, system performance, or energy cost budget methods. The **prescriptive method**, which is component-oriented, is the simplest method for demonstrating compliance. The **system performance method** allows some trade-offs between components, although it is more difficult to use than the prescriptive method. The **energy budget method** allows trade-offs between systems to arrive at an overall building performance, but is the most difficult to use, and requires computer modeling.[3]

(Note: The preceding description is a very simplistic summary. Those who need to use this code should read the actual code and other supporting materials, or attend courses that explain the code in detail.)

The current version is ASHRAE 90.1-2001. The *Model Energy* and the *International Energy Conservation Codes* reference ASHRAE 90.1 for commercial and high-rise residential buildings. The regulations regarding construction of new federal buildings, 10CFR 434 and 435, codify the ASHRAE 90.1 voluntary standards for private buildings and make them mandatory for federal projects. A number of states have adopted or incorporated the *Model Energy Code* or ASHRAE 90.1 into their building codes. To see which states have adopted these codes, check the Web site, **www.eere.energy.gov/EE/buildings_energy_codes.html**

Other ASHRAE standards applicable to green buildings include:

90003 –	Active Solar Heating Design Manual
90336 –	Guidance for Preparing Active Solar Systems Operation & Maintenance Manuals
90342 –	Active Solar Heating Systems Installation Manual
93 –	Methods of Testing to Determine the Thermal Performance of Solar Collectors
55-1992 –	Thermal Environmental Conditions for Human Occupancy
62-1989 –	Ventilation for Acceptable Indoor Air Quality

Whole Building Standards

Energy Star® Label for Commercial Buildings

www.energystar.gov

In addition to standards for individual building components, Energy Star® has developed standards for office buildings, hotels, motels, schools, supermarkets, computer data centers, and garages. Convenience stores, healthcare centers, and warehouses will be added to the list. Since the program started in 1999, over 1,400 commercial buildings have earned the Energy Star® label.

If a building is eligible, the applicant can log on to the Energy Star® Internet site and enter the pertinent information about a building into a program called the Portfolio Manager, or download a Microsoft® Excel spreadsheet template that can be used to enter the information. The program or spreadsheet is used to generate what is called a Statement of Energy Performance, which is required for the Energy Star® application. The building must score 75 points or higher on the Statement of Energy Performance. The building must not only meet the guidelines for energy efficiency, but also indoor air quality standards, and a professional engineer must verify this achievement. Additional information can be found in the "For Business" section of the Energy Star® Web site.

Energy Star® Label for Houses

www.energystar.gov

Houses can also receive an Energy Star® label. Since the Energy Star® for homes program started in 1997, over 200,000 houses have earned the Energy Star® label. Eligibility is accomplished by a scoring system called HERS (Home Energy Rating System). HERS compares the house to be rated to a computer-simulated house of the same dimensions and configuration that complies with the *Model Energy Code*. If the house to be rated is at least 30% more energy-efficient, it qualifies. As with the Energy Star® applications for commercial buildings, a qualified third party must verify the results.

LEED™ Green Building Rating System

www.usgbc.org

The U.S. Green Building Council is a well-respected and recognized proponent of sustainable building. It is a nonprofit organization composed of a broad spectrum of manufacturers, building professionals, building owners, and financial institutions.

The USGBC produces and maintains the LEED Green Building Rating System™, a nationally and internationally recognized benchmarking system, considered the definitive green building design standard. (LEED is an acronym for Leadership in Energy & Environmental Design.) LEED-NC is applicable to new commercial, institutional, and high-rise residential buildings. By early 2005, just five years after LEED was launched, there were over 150 certified projects with over 1,700 registered for certification. This number is sure to increase with the release of LEED-CI for commercial interiors, which covers tenant fit-outs, and LEED-EB for existing buildings, which includes criteria for maintenance, operations, and refurbishments. The planned release of LEED-CS for core and shell will cover speculative developments. The planned release of LEED-H for homes will be a collaborative effort with existing local green homes programs. The planned release of LEED-ND will cover neighborhood development programs. Also in discussions are versions tailored to retail, education, and other industry sectors.

The certification process starts with registering the project. It is recommended that registration be completed early in the process, so that the project is tracked along the way. Registration can be completed directly through the USGBC's Web site. Upon registration, applicants receive:

- Credit calculation and scorecard, as well as a Microsoft® Excel® spreadsheet "Letter Template," which has a built-in calculator that automatically calculates credits earned and expected LEED rating and cover sheet templates for credit requests.

- Two years of access to the LEED Credit Interpretation Ruling Web page.
- An allowance for two free interpretations of LEED credit criteria by the Green Building Council as part of the registration fee for applicants who encounter special or unusual conditions that require rulings by the Green Building Council on compliance with credit criteria. Additional interpretations are available on a "pay as you go" basis.

The scorecard consists of five weighted core sections relating to the project. Points can be earned in sections that relate to the efficiency, quality, and sustainability of the building's site; water efficiency; energy efficiency; pollution prevention; material and resource use; and quality of the indoor environment. In addition, some points can be earned for design innovations and having project team members successfully complete the LEED-accredited training workshop and exam. A total of 69 points are possible.

Four levels of certification can be achieved, depending on how many points are earned on the scorecard. The levels are:

- Certified: 26-32 points
- Silver: 33-38 points
- Gold: 39-51 points
- Platinum: over 51 points

Examples of a gold-rated project, the Jean Vollum Natural Center in Portland, Oregon, and a silver-rated one, the Steelcase Wood Plant in Michigan, are featured in the case studies section of this book.

Each core section has several subsections where points can be earned for different requirements. As an example, the Water Efficiency section has subsections on Water-Efficient Landscape, Innovative Wastewater Technology, and Water Use Reduction. Each one of these subsections clearly identifies the intent, the requirement, and the technology/ strategies that can be used to achieve the requirement. Some of the core sections contain prerequisites that must be met before additional credits can be earned. The Sustainable Sites core section, for example, has a prerequisite for Erosion and Sediment Control.

Points can be earned for green building strategies including the use of:

- Low-emitting materials, such as paint, carpeting, and composite wood.
- Materials that are manufactured locally.
- Materials that are recycled or salvaged.
- Electricity from renewable sources.
- Daylighting techniques.

- Operable windows.
- Controls to limit pollutants and indoor chemicals.
- Means of public transportation.

The system is flexible in that it is performance-based, and does not force the applicant into following a narrowly defined set of specifications. The entire scorecard can be downloaded, and other information can be obtained at the Web site.

BREEAM

BREEAM for Commercial, Retail, Industrial, and Large-Scale Residential Buildings
www.bre.co.uk

Internationally, BREEAM (Building Research Establishment Environmental Assessment Method) is one of the most widely used comprehensive methods of assessing energy, environmental, and indoor air qualities of buildings. This standard examines both design and management aspects of a building, covering nine categories:

- Management of the building
- Health and comfort
- Energy
- Transportation
- Water consumption
- Materials
- Land use
- Site ecology
- Pollution

BREEAM contains three modules. The **Core** module provides an assessment of the building's potential environmental performance. The **Design and Procurement** module is for assessing new buildings and refurbishment at the design stage, including land use and selection of materials. The **Management and Operation** module assesses buildings that are in use, and focuses on health and well-being issues. Specialists licensed by BRE perform the assessments. BREEAM reports are provided both before and after recommendations are implemented.

The BREEAM assessment method was established in 1988. To date, over 900 buildings have been rated, and BREEAM is currently used for approximately 30% of the new office construction in the United Kingdom alone.

As an alternative to the standard BREEAM rating system, the BREEAM/Green Leaf rating system was developed as a less expensive method of assessing a building, while still addressing the basic principles of BREEAM. The savings are achieved by enabling part of the assessment to be performed in-house. A successful rating is designated as between one and five leaves, as follows:

- One Green Leaf: Some measures to improve the environment have been initiated.
- Two Green Leaves: There has been some movement beyond basic awareness in all areas of operations and management.
- Three Green Leaves: There has been excellent progress in achieving eco-efficiency practices and management.
- Four Green Leaves: National industry leadership has been shown in eco-efficiency practices and management, and there are efforts toward continuous improvement.
- Five Green Leaves: The applicant is a world leader in eco-efficiency, and continually introduces policies and practices that can be adopted by others.[4]

 R-2000

www.oee.nrcan.gc.ca/r-2000

R-2000 is a voluntary Canadian standard established by Natural Resources Canada with a goal of constructing energy-efficient, new houses that do not compromise indoor or outdoor environments. To date, over 9,000 R-2000 homes have been built. The houses must be built by trained and licensed R-2000 builders. After completing the R-2000 builders' course, builders must register, build, and certify a demonstration home before becoming licensed R-2000 builders. R-2000 sets requirements that are often above basic for levels of insulation, air-tightness, window performance, HVAC sizing, venting, and standby loss. These requirements often exceed current Canadian building codes and regulations. For example, energy performance targets for the combined space and water heating is based on the size, location, and fuel types of the house. Compliance is calculated using HOT2000™ software by a licensed R-2000 plans evaluator. Water conservation requirements include water-saver or ultra-low flush toilets, low flow showerheads, and faucets.

In addition to the basic requirements, the builder must incorporate at least three R-2000 indoor air quality features from a list of nine features, which include:

- Low-emission carpeting
- Air filtration systems
- Low-emission paints and varnishes
- Low-emission floor adhesives
- Low-emission cabinets and vanities
- Low-emission flooring
- Low-emission particle board underlayment
- Sub-slab depressurization system
- Indoor moisture control measures

Each of these features contains specific R-2000 requirements. For example, paints and varnishes must be water based or meet/exceed Environmental Choice standards.

The R-2000 builder must also incorporate at least two environmental features from a list of features, which include:

- Recycled content insulation (choice of fiberglass, cellulose, mineral fiber, or plastic)
- Recycled content sheathing and drywall (choice of fiberboard, siding, or drywall)
- Recycled content steel studs, saw mill cut-off, and ureaformaldyhide-free wood studs and trim
- Foundation/under-slab drainage
- Energy-efficient appliances
- Reduced energy consumption (at least 15% less than the target amount)
- High-efficiency cooling systems

As with the indoor air quality features, each environmental feature has specific R-2000 requirements. For example, the high-efficiency cooling system must have a minimum SEER (Seasonal Energy Efficiency Ratio) of 12.0 for split systems air-cooled air conditioners, a minimum of 12.0 EER (Energy Efficiency Ratio) for single-package central air and heat pumps, a minimum EER of 10.5 for ground- or water-source closed loop air conditioners, and a minimum EER of 11.0 for others.

 EarthCraft House^{SM}

www.atlantahomebuilders.com/default.aspx

The National Home Builders Association, a leading, national building trade group, has several programs that offer a certificate of compliance, which designates that the house meets the programs' environmental standards. The EarthCraft House^{SM} is one such program. It requires member builders who join EarthCraft House℠ to attend a training program. The builder must then submit a preliminary worksheet, which offers several avenues to earn the required points. The worksheet includes sections on:

- Site planning
- Energy-efficient envelope and systems
- Energy-efficient lighting and appliances
- Resource-efficient design
- Resource-efficient building materials
- Waste management
- Indoor air quality
- Water conservation and quality
- Homebuyer education and opportunities
- Builder operations
- A section for bonus points

Bonus points are available for sites located near public transportation, sidewalks that connect houses to a business district, projects that are built on brownfield sites, solar electric systems, vehicle electric charging or natural gas pump stations, compliance with the Health House standards, and for exceeding Energy Star® requirements. Bonus points are also available for innovative features.

After the project is finished, the final worksheet is submitted, and a member of the EarthCraft House℠ program inspects the house.

Whole Building Standards in Other Countries

Individual whole building standards are established in:

Hong Kong – HK-BEAM

Norway – EcoProfile

France – ESCALE (under development)

Sweden – EcoEffect

Canada – EPACT

In addition to these standards, there is substantial interest in whole building standards in Argentina, Austria, Brazil, Belgium, Chile, Finland, Germany, Japan, Latvia, the Netherlands, Poland, South Africa, and Taiwan.

Natural Step

www.naturalstep.org

Dr. Karl-Henrik Roberts, a Swedish cancer researcher, developed the Natural Step program, which is based on four basic system conditions that form a framework for a sustainable society.

1. Substances from earth's crust must not systematically increase in the biosphere.

2. Substances produced by society must not systematically increase in the biosphere.

3. Nature's function and diversity must not be systematically impoverished by physical displacement, over-harvesting, or other forms of ecosystem manipulation.

4. Resources must be used fairly and efficiently in order to serve basic human needs globally.

This framework allows a business to test its practices against an overall goal of sustainability.[5]

Backcasting

In an attempt to apply the Natural Step principles to building construction practices, the Oregon Natural Step Network looked at current green building standards, which are all based on incrementally improving the level of sustainability using current methods and technology. In looking for an alternative to current rating systems, this group may be on its way to developing the green building standard of the future. Backcasting achieves results by visualizing the desired outcome. It works in four stages. In the case of a sustainable commercial building, the group produced the following results:

- A system flow chart of the current standard practices in producing a commercial building. The chart showed materials, transportation, and energy flowing in, products/services, and solid waste flowing out. Flowing both in and out are water, air, and habitat.

- A matrix indicating in detail how each in-flow and out-flow violates the four basic Natural Step principles. As an example, the incoming water to the building from wells and rivers, and water flowing out in the form of waste/storm water violates Natural Step principles 3 and 4.

- Visualizing a construction process that compliments the four Natural Step principles by modifying the existing in-flows and out-flows helped create new goals. The goal for water in-flow and out-flow, for example, is a water budget that does not exceed what naturally falls on the site. If the needs exceed the site limits, the difference may be purchased from other sites that have excess water, as long as the process has no damaging impact on the natural systems. The quality, temperature, and rate of flow on the grounds of the site and leaving the site must have no damaging impact on the natural systems of the watershed.

- With the goals established, the last stage is to develop a plan to realize the vision.[6]

Measurement, Management, & Reporting Standards

ISO 14000 Series Standards

ISO is not an acronym. The word is actually a Greek term that means equal. The full name for the organization is the International Organization for Standardization. Established in 1947, it is truly an international organization that consists of representatives throughout the world. Its purpose is to develop voluntary technical standards, which help promote fair trade. The 14000 series standard encompasses a wide range of environmental issues, as seen below.

14001 Environmental management systems specifications

14004 Environmental management systems guidelines, systems, and techniques

14010 Environmental auditing principles

14011 Environmental auditing procedures

14020 Environmental label and declaration principles

14040 Environmental management, life cycle assessment principles, and framework

14041 Environmental management, life cycle assessment goal and scope definition, and inventory analysis

14048 Environmental management, life cycle assessment data documentation format

14050 Environmental management vocabulary

ISO also publishes standard 7330, which is used for the determination of acceptable ranges for temperature, humidity, and air velocity for indoor environments.

ASTM Standards E 2114 & E 2129

ASTM (American Society for Testing and Materials), now ASTM International, is another venerable standards organization. It was formed in 1898 and is one of the largest standards development organizations in the world. ASTM Standard E 2114 encompasses standards for terminology and product selection for green buildings.

ASTM E 2129 sets standards for data collection for sustainability of green building products.

International Performance Measurement & Verification Protocol

The IPMVP protocol was developed with the help of 20 national organizations from 12 different countries for use as a framework for measuring and verifying energy and water conservation as well as indoor air quality measures.

Global Reporting Initiative Guidelines

Financial reporting must conform to certain standards that have evolved over the years. However, the reporting of a firm's "greenness" or ecological sustainability and other social issues are relatively new issues for most corporations. There are no standards in place for reporting this type of information. In the past, companies have simply selected the most favorable environmental aspects of their business practices and included them in their annual reports. However, as in financial reporting, guidelines are necessary in order to present the relevant information in a clear, balanced, reliable, manner in accordance with acceptable external reporting principles. To be useful, the format should also be easy to understand. The Global Reporting Initiative is a group formed in 1997 that has set out to formulate guidelines for reporting what it calls "environmental, social, and economic sustainability." Among the topics covered by the guidelines are frequency of reporting, graphics, and format. The guidelines recommend that reports embody these specific underlying principles:

- The boundaries of the organization must be defined.
- The scope of the report must be clear.
- The information must be properly allocated to the report period.
- The information must reflect the assumption that the firm is to continue operations into the foreseeable future.
- Achievements must be claimed only if they can be directly attributed to the firm.
- The information must be relevant.

Conclusion

Clearly there are many sustainability guidelines available that can be applied to a building project. In some cases, it may be more suitable to formulate a specific set of guidelines for an individual project. The choice of standards is important, as it will be used as a starting point for selecting systems, components, and individual products. It is, however, only the first step. A meticulous selection and specifying process ensures that the goals of the guidelines are achieved.

1 *Environmental Building News*, Volume 10, Number 9, September 2001.

2 *Environmental Building News*, Volume 9, Number 1, January 2000, revised February 2001.

3 ASHRAE/IES Standard 90.1-1989 Users Manual – November 1992.

4 **http://www.surveying.salford.ac.uk/bqtoolkit/tkpages/ass_meth/classes/all.htm**

5 *Environmental Design and Construction Magazine*, May/June 2002.

6 *Environmental Design and Construction Magazine*, May/June 2002.

Chapter 10
Specifying Green Building Products

Mark Kalin, FAIA, FCSI

Early in 1995, Kalin Associates set out to create a standard specification that could be used by design professionals to select and specify a wide range of green products. As a first step, they sent 6,500 letters to building product manufacturers asking them to send product literature on their "green products." Over 600 manufacturers responded, but primarily with their standard literature. After a long sorting process, 400 products were selected and compiled to create the first *GreenSpec – Specifications for Environmental Sustainability.*

There seemed to be a burgeoning interest in green building products, propelled by environmentalists, green architects, owners, and even President Clinton's Council on Sustainable Development, which had this mission statement:

"Our vision is of a life-sustaining earth. We are committed to the achievement of a dignified, peaceful, and equitable existence. We believe a sustainable United States will have an economy that equitably provides for satisfying livelihoods and a safe, healthy, high quality life for current and future generations. Our nation will protect its environment, its natural resource base, and the functions and viability of natural systems on which all life depends."

Nearly eight years later, what has happened? Truthfully, based on reviewing project specifications for over 1,000 projects, green battles are being won, but the war goes poorly. Not enough firms follow up on their green commitment in the specifications. Value engineering limits product selection. Lack of good information from product manufacturers is a real problem. Remember, specifications are the neck of the funnel for written communication between the designer and the contractor. The contractor needs to know what products to buy for the project.

This chapter provides information to help building design professionals specify green building products. Topics include:

- Building Product Manufacturers and Green Products
- What Are Green Products?
- Who Selects Green Products?
- When Are Green Products Selected?
- Green Product Checklist
- Green Specs
- Greening Your Firm

Building Product Manufacturers & Green Products

Claims by the product manufacturer that their products are environmentally friendly must be carefully evaluated. Several cases in point:

Claim 1: Sheet lead is a green product. When we requested information from product manufacturers, one of the first responses was from the Lead Institute. They maintained that lead was a green product because it was a natural material and had a successful history of long-term performance. They recommended we include lead in our list, but we didn't. Is lead a green product? Do we accept the claims of the supplier, which include that there are no EPA regulations against using lead in buildings? Or do we consider that lead content is regulated in commercial and residential paint products, as chips of lead paint are believed to cause brain damage in young children? Or that installers are required to regularly have their lead levels checked? Or that lead doesn't migrate in the soil, and its use for hundreds of years verifies the manufacturer's claims?

Opinion: Lead is okay (green or not), but perhaps not for the entrance canopy or columns on an elementary school.

Claim 2: Carpet pad manufactured from virgin urethane is greener than rebonded carpet cushion. Manufacturers of carpet cushion claim less energy is required to manufacture carpet pad from virgin urethane than the energy and adhesives required to fabricate rebonded carpet pads. Should we only recommend the use of virgin urethane pads?

Opinion: Virgin urethane pads have more uniform density. Don't feel compelled to use rebonded carpet pads. Depending on your green perspective, both may be seen as green.

Claim 3: Latex paints are the greener choice, compared to oil-based paints with higher VOC (volatile organic content) emissions. Water-based latex paints are considered greener than oil-based paints. However, manufacturers of oil-based paint claim longer service life and less repainting over the life cycle of the building. The cleanup of oil-based paints is controlled, while latex paint waste is frequently flushed down drains where the algicides and fungicides in the paint kill the bacteria at the sewage treatment plant. Should we use oil-based paints?

Opinion: Latex formulations have advanced significantly. Since a lot of commercial repainting is done for new tenants or a new color scheme, longer service life isn't necessarily the determining factor.

Claim 4: Linoleum is green, as natural components are used. The last linoleum plant in the U.S. closed in the 1930s, and now linoleum is manufactured only in Europe. Should we count the embodied energy in manufacturing as well as transportation in our product selection? The manufacturing process for linoleum is energy-intensive, and is the extra cost worth somewhat higher wear performance?

Opinion: Although an increase for the demand in linoleum may instigate manufacturing in the U.S., selection based on green criteria should include consideration of the point of origin. It's really the designer's choice.

Claim 5: Consider PVC for roofing. Use of PVC for roofing in Europe is considered a hazard, but high-performing PVC systems are readily available in the U.S. PVC didn't exist 80 years ago, and now every living organism on the planet has a measurable amount of PVC in its system. Do we know the answer?

Opinion: PVC roofing performs well, as the intended purpose of roofing is to keep the building dry. If your goal is to reduce the amount of PVC in your building, start on the inside with PVC-free computer cases, pens, chairs, and furniture (if you can find them).

Claim 6: Use certified wood for your projects. There's even a USGBC LEED point you can earn for using certified wood. However, certified wood has thus far been available only at a premium price (as much as 30% higher), most of the certified forests are mid-sized, and not all species are available. The program is excellent, but critics such as the Canadian Government believe they have been managing their forests for decades, and they are green without being certified. On a recent LEED project, the requirement to achieve the point included using certified wood throughout the project, including for concrete formwork and furniture. Since the design team didn't have control over the furnishings, they abandoned the point and used no certified wood.

Opinion: Should LEED points be dependent on the use of certified wood? The material seems an appropriate choice for casework, but it is still a new concept to most designers. Future LEED documentation will clarify that the formwork should be considered only if it remains in place, and that built-in furnishings (not movable items) will be part of the equation for achieving the point.

What Are Green Products?

Identifying green products, just like defining sustainability, is an exercise in subjectivity. There are those who define green as 100% recycled and recyclable; others define it as using less energy in manufacture; others as improving the building users' health through reduction in toxic materials; and others as employing more energy-efficient methodologies for heating, cooling, and lighting. *(See Chapters 1 and 2 for green building definitions, and more on green materials and products.)*

Green is all of the above and more. By our definition, green products are those which maintain or improve the human environment while diminishing the impact of their use on the natural environment—in other words, *sustainable*.

Materials in use for sustainable design run the gamut from cotton insulation to recycled asphalt paving to photovoltaics. Many of the products offer a green component that is at best incremental, offering performance or some other characteristic that is only slightly better than the conventional product. Use of these products by a small percentage of designers and contractors results in an effect that is not measurable; common usage can make the effect global and lasting.

In our experience, green products fall into six categories. Many products have benefits in multiple categories. Please note that these categories are somewhat subjective, and a product that falls into three categories is not necessarily any more green than a product that falls into only one category.

Green Process: The product is manufactured with consideration for exposure of workers to chemicals, source of materials, energy-efficient production methods, use of recycled materials in packaging, reclaiming manufacturing waste, and prudent use of energy. Since many of these approaches actually save the manufacturer money, these principles are incorporated as manufacturing facilities are upgraded. Even manufacturers of plastics can effectively claim their manufacturing as a green process. *(See Chapter 9 for more on green product rating standards.)*

Improved Sustainability: The product is renewable, and its selection considers the use of available resources. Use of wood from well-managed forests for building framing is an example of renewable and sustainable product selection. Sustainability considers the whole instead of specifics, emphasizing relationships rather than pieces in isolation. Sustainable design considers environmental and human health and well-being, in addition to the traditional criteria of function, cost, and aesthetics. While environmentalists have focused attention on the degradation of natural systems, advocates of sustainability generally believe in trading destructive behaviors for healthy ones, and developing in ways that make sense ecologically and economically.

Sustainability can be illustrated by systems as well as individual products, such as those used to improve the energy performance of the building. For example, the recent Energy Code Update to the *Massachusetts State Building Code* requires an air barrier in the exterior wall assembly and insulation located outboard of the metal studs in a brick veneer/steel stud wall assembly. An air barrier can be established simply by taping the joints and perimeter of the exterior gypsum sheathing, but only by using a tape with a very low permeability and a high-performing permanent adhesive. Many architects have chosen to put a continuous air and vapor barrier membrane over the entire wall, again improving the long-term energy performance of the building and reducing the risk of premature failure of the exterior wall. Since the insulation is outside of the membrane, this allows the elimination of fibrous insulation in the metal stud cavity and the vapor barrier behind the interior drywall. Some prefer to limit fibrous insulation, and most acknowledge that an interior vapor barrier is frequently breached during installation or by utility penetrations. (For details illustrating the concept, refer to **www.pacerepresentatives.com**, a manufacturer's collaborative Web site.) The assembly improves the longevity of the exterior wall, decreases the risk of mold in the exterior wall, and improves the energy performance of the building.

Recycled Content: The product is fabricated with post-consumer materials or post-industrial by-products. Many products, ranging from steel to finish materials to carpet cushion, are manufactured with recycled content. For example, synthetic gypsum board is manufactured from gypsum deposited on the inside of smokestacks at power plants. The gypsum is chemically the same as naturally occurring gypsum, and does not have to be mined. Considering the overall energy consumption and shipping costs of using synthetic gypsum board, it makes most sense to use it within 500 miles of its manufacturing location. One large gypsum manufacturer claims that 30% of its overall production is synthetic gypsum board. The company recommends that designers consider using their standard products if the project location is more than 500 miles from a synthetic gypsum plant, because the cost of shipping will outweigh the advantage of using recycled plastic. Post-consumer materials include items such as plastic wood products fabricated using recycled plastic bottles. Products such as steel are fabricated with both post-industrial (waste scrap) and post-consumer (salvaged steel) content.

Recyclable: The product can be reused or reprocessed after use and refabricated. We are most familiar with recyclable soda cans and bottles, but the same can apply to asphalt paving, masonry, metal framing, insulation, toilet compartments, and even carpet. Some extruded polystyrene manufacturers claim their product can be reused after roofing repairs, since the material is not affected by moisture.

Low Toxicity: The product is less toxic than comparable products used for the same purpose. Toxic fumes from site-mixed products, coatings, adhesives, and sealants containing such chemicals as formaldehyde and styrenes are a real threat to health, especially in remodeling projects where the structure may be occupied while the work is being performed. Exposure to such products as carpet adhesives and high-performance paints has caused problems ranging from discomfort, which disappears upon leaving the premises, to long-term disability. All products are now required to have Material Safety Data Sheets listing their components and potential hazards. Many hospitals and even computer companies require MSDS submittals before they will allow a product at their construction site or manufacturing facility. Wood particleboard manufactured with resins that do not contain formaldehyde offers a less toxic environment for chemically-sensitive individuals, and even for artwork stored in museums. *(See Chapter 6 for more on airborne toxins.)*

Biodegradable: The product returns to the earth naturally under exposure to the elements. The abandoned barn in the field eventually collapses and disappears. The subway car is dumped into the ocean as a marine habitat, and over time, the steel itself corrodes. We expect our buildings to last a lifetime, but it is not necessary that products last for thousands of years.

Who Selects Green Building Products?

Product selection is different than specification writing. The specifier may know the method to communicate product selection to the contractor, but cannot prepare the specification until a product is selected. A frequent criticism of specifications by contractors is that there are pages of specs, but no specific product.

Selection of building products is difficult. Considerations of cost, performance, and aesthetics are critical. For a detailed methodology for product selection by performance or prescriptive methods, refer to the *Construction Specifications Institute Manual of Practice* at **www.csinet.org**. The same methodology applies to green products. Who selects them?

The Owner: Corporate owners and owners of retail chains choose products frequently. Their experience with hundreds of locations gives them the perspective of what works. One retail chain might focus on carpet adhesive to deliver to contractors, as lawsuits from tripping hazards are a major concern. Individual building owners select products infrequently and usually allow the architect to make product selections. Institutional projects sometimes come with faculty or student committees who pass on their green product research.

The Architect: The architect's license addresses the need to protect the public's health, safety, and welfare. Product selection is largely the architect's responsibility. If a waterproofing material must withstand 50 feet of hydrostatic head, the architect must find a product that complies. If the building code requires fire-retardant treatment for roof sheathing, it is the architect's responsibility to specify a fire-retardant product. The contractor is not responsible for code compliance for product selection. Since most green products are relatively new, the architect must perform significant research or verification that the product is suitable and code-compliant.

The Specification Writer: There may be as many as 1,700 products in a project specification. The design architect generally selects the products with the most critical performance requirements or products of visual importance. In reality, the specification writer selects many of the other products, based on the materials already researched in their master specifications, recent projects, or field experience. For most manufacturers, it is important to have their name included in the specifications. A specifier who finds a green product that is suitable for use may incorporate that product into their master specification, and use it on every project. Otherwise, the specification writer shares the responsibility for specification writing with the architect.

The Contractor/Subcontractor: Contractors and subcontractors have significant product knowledge. They can assist the architect or specification writer during design, or suggest substitutions during construction. The value of their contribution to the product selection process should not be underestimated, as the same product can succeed or fail depending on the situation. A major building product manufacturer indicated that six out of seven product failures they investigate are attributed to inappropriate use of the product. For example, moisture-resistant gypsum board should not be used for ceilings in toilet rooms. The product was researched, specified, bid, purchased, and installed—and then failed because it was the wrong product for that purpose. There are no spec police, and product selection should be done by experienced people.

The Product Manufacturer: The product manufacturer is the expert. The architect, specifier, or contractor cannot know the product as intimately as its manufacturer. The manufacturer should assist in the recommendation of green products based on its knowledge of where and how the product is to be used. For example, a carpet installation on a slab-on-grade will require a vapor barrier, while a carpet installation on an elevated slab may not. A low-odor adhesive may have a more limited installation temperature range as compared to standard adhesives. Water-based epoxies may be suitable for toilet rooms, but not for the food service area.

When Are Green Products Selected?

There are five phases in the typical construction project, and selection requirements for green products depend on the phase. *(See Chapter 7 for more on the green project team and sequence.)* The following selections and specifications should be considered for green products.

1. **Schematic Design:** Prepare outline specifications or a project description. Determine the owner's requirements for green, any budget impact, and possible need for green products to meet industry green evaluation programs, such as the U.S. Green Building Council LEED Certification. Green products and alternative mechanical and electrical systems often involve an initial premium price, with justification usually based on life-cycle costs. *(See Chapter 12 for life-cycle cost evaluation methods.)*

2. **Design Development:** Update outline specifications or prepare a draft of full specifications. Verify project requirements, including the essential evaluation of the green products' performance requirements. Explore information on product options and features.

3. **Construction Documents:** Prepare full specifications, illustrating the requirements for green products. Re-evaluate detailed information, compatibility with adjacent materials, and material performance. If the contractor is not familiar with the product, additional details and installation instructions will be needed.

4. **Bid and Award:** Assist with sourcing green products and answering bidders' questions. The contractor may require phone numbers or sources for green products unfamiliar to them. Bidders must be advised that they are bidding the products specified, which may not be familiar to them.

5. **Construction Administration:** Enforce your specifications. Be wary of substitutions that, while meeting other performance criteria, cannot meet green requirements. Verify that green

products are ordered on time, and that the installers are factory-trained or acceptable to the manufacturer. For a USGBC project, maintain a project notebook for final submittal for LEED certification. This will require collection of specific manufacturer information on chemical content limits and recycled content, usually described in the manufacturer's MSDS (material safety data sheet). For items where the manufacturing location and source of materials is important, an affidavit from the manufacturer should be required.

A Green Product Checklist

One of the easiest ways to get started selecting green products is to develop a checklist of choices. While a checklist could be dozens of pages long, Figure 10.1 is limited to reasonable choices that can be used for most projects. The checklist is intended to help the design team select green products efficiently for construction projects. The 120 green choices are listed in CSI MasterFormat order. After completion of this checklist, the author (usually the designer or project architect) should circulate it to the project team and specification writer for comments. Since these choices might also be included in your firm's master specifications, refer to the specs for specific products, manufacturers, and telephone numbers for each item.

Greening Your Firm

How do you get to green? The following examples relate the relative success of five firms as they approach sustainable design and green product selection.

Firm 1: The principals of the architectural firm make a commitment to sustainable design and green products. They decide to evaluate internally all of their projects based on the LEED Rating System of the U.S. Green Building Council. Green review is added to their quality assurance program.

Six Months Later: The firm finds that the criteria for sustainable design closely matched their existing design policies. Sensitivity to context and energy efficiency have been considered in their projects for many years. The LEED rating system points out some new opportunities, but there is no major change in their design or document production processes. Green products selected for projects are frequently value-engineered out, and their corporate owners don't seem particularly committed to green, nor to the claims of increased productivity with sustainable design. Green grows slowly in the firm.

Firm 2: A firm specializing in government work notes that their clients are requiring evidence of experience with green design as a selection criterion for architects. The marketing principal convenes a meeting of

PROJECT NAME: _____ **DATE:** _____

PROJECT NUMBER: _____ **COMPLETED BY:** _____

DIVISION 1 - GENERAL

- Implement construction pollution controls.
- Implement a construction waste management system, including recycling.
- Require LEED certification: [basic] [silver] [gold] [platinum] level.

DIVISION 2 - SITE WORK

- Recycled subbase materials.
- Containment structures fabricated from recycled materials.
- Retaining walls fabricated from recycled plastic.
- Geomembrane liner fabricated with recycled geotextiles.
- Geotextiles fabricated from recycled materials.
- Soil stabilization mat fabricated from recycled plastic.
- Rubber paving manufactured from recycled tires.
- Porous paving manufactured of recycled plastic.
- Rubber paving fabricated from post-consumer recycled rubber.
- Brick paving fabricated from cleaned oil-contaminated soils.
- Glass pavers fabricated from recycled glass.
- Pavers fabricated from recycled glass.
- Rubber unit pavers fabricated from post-consumer vehicle tires.
- Stepping stones fabricated from recycled rubber.
- Gray water recycling system.
- Irrigation hosing fabricated from recycled vehicle tires.
- Play equipment fabricated from recycled components.
- Granulated rubber play surfacing fabricated from recycled tires.
- Fencing fabricated from recycled plastic.
- Erosion control mats fabricated from recycled fibers.
- Organic fertilizers.
- Landscape edging fabricated from recycled plastic.
- Landscape timbers fabricated from recycled plastic.
- Mulch fabricated from recycled hardwood blend.
- Mulch fabricated from recycled newspapers.
- Root barriers fabricated from recycled polypropylene.
- Soil amendments composed of recycled or composted materials.

DIVISION 3 - CONCRETE

- Permanent insulating concrete formwork.
- Rebar supports fabricated from recycled plastic.
- Cellular concrete.
- Coal fly ash in concrete mix.
- Low-VOC concrete hardening compounds.

DIVISION 4 - MASONRY

- Glass block fabricated from recycled glass.
- Glass bricks fabricated from recycled glass.
- Simulated stone fabricated from recycled materials.
- Concrete masonry units with integral insulation.
- Autoclaved aerated concrete masonry units.
- Brick fabricated from cleaned, petroleum-contaminated soils.
- Rubber blocks fabricated from recycled rubber.
- Masonry cavity drainage material fabricated from recycled materials.

DIVISION 5 - METALS

- Structural steel with recycled content.
- Cold-formed metal framing with recycled content.

DIVISION 6 - WOOD AND PLASTICS

- Certified wood, Forest Stewardship Council.
- Arsenic- and chromium-free pressure-treated wood.
- Engineered framing fabricated from small wood pieces.
- Sheathing fabricated from recycled waste paper.
- Sheathing fabricated from recycled waste paper, fire-retardant.
- Structural insulated panels.
- Floor decking fabricated from recycled wastepaper.
- Underlayment fabricated from recycled wastepaper.
- Underlayment fabricated from recycled materials.
- Medium density fiberboard fabricated without formaldehyde.
- Wood trim fabricated from veneered finger-jointed wood.
- Medium density fiberboard trim fabricated without formaldehyde.
- Wood panels fabricated with certified wood veneers.

Figure 10.1

DIVISION 7 - THERMAL AND MOISTURE PROTECTION

- Fiberglass insulation manufactured with recycled glass.
- Mineral wool insulation manufactured with recycled material.
- Cellulose insulation manufactured with recycled material.
- Foamed-in-place insulation.
- Extruded polystyrene insulation, non-ozone depleting.
- Polyisocyanurate insulation, non-ozone depleting.
- Exterior water-repellent sealers with low VOCs.
- Air and vapor barrier membrane at all exterior walls and soffits.
- Fiber-cement roofing shingles.
- Green roof systems.
- Roof walkway pads fabricated from recycled materials.
- Expanding foam sealants.
- Joint fillers fabricated from recycled materials.

DIVISION 8 - DOORS AND WINDOWS

- Steel doors and frames with recycled content.
- Wood doors with certified wood, Forest Stewardship Council.
- Wood doors fabricated from hardboard.
- Plastic doors fabricated from recycled plastic.
- High-performance wood windows.
- High-performance vinyl replacement windows.
- High-performance fiberglass windows.
- High-performance insulating glass.

DIVISION 9 - FINISHES

- Gypsum board fabricated with synthetic gypsum.
- Ceramic tile with recycled content.
- Ceramic tile adhesives, low-odor.
- Acoustical ceiling panels with recycled content.
- Wood flooring with certified wood, Forest Stewardship Council.
- Wood flooring adhesives, low-odor.
- Cork flooring.
- Linoleum tile flooring.
- Linoleum sheet flooring.
- Recycled rubber flooring.
- Flooring adhesives, low-odor.
- Carpet fabricated with recycled materials.
- Carpet fabricated with natural materials (wool).
- Carpet tile fabricated with recycled materials.
- Carpet cushion fabricated from recycled materials.
- Carpet adhesive, low-odor.
- Cork wallcovering.
- Recycled fiberboard wall panels.
- Sisal wallcoverings.
- Acoustical wall panels with recycled content.
- Sound control board fabricated from recycled newsprint.
- Interior paints with zero-VOC content.
- Interior water-based multi-color paints.
- Latex vapor barrier coating with low VOCs.

DIVISION 10 - SPECIALTIES

- Bulletin boards fabricated from cork.
- Toilet compartments fabricated from recycled HDPE plastic.
- Electric hand dryers in toilet rooms.
- Shower curtains fabricated of cotton.
- Shower doors fabricated with recycled architectural glass.

DIVISION 11 - EQUIPMENT

- Dock bumpers fabricated from recycled vehicle tires.

DIVISION 12 - FURNISHINGS

- Anti-fatigue mats fabricated from recycled materials.
- Entry mats fabricated from recycled vehicle tires.
- Entry mats fabricated from cocoa fibers.
- Furniture fabricated from certified wood, Forest Stewardship Council.
- Window treatment systems with photosensors, automated operation.

DIVISION 13 - SPECIAL CONSTRUCTION

- Solar water heaters.

DIVISION 14 - CONVEYING SYSTEMS

- Energy-efficient elevators.

DIVISION 15 - MECHANICAL

- Waterless urinals.
- Composting toilets.
- Heat-sensing flow consumption fittings.

DIVISION 16 - ELECTRICAL

- Energy efficient lighting fixtures and bulbs.
- Perimeter daylighting controls.

Figure 10.1 (cont.)

SECTION 01000—GREEN PRODUCT SHORTLIST

PART 1 GENERAL

1.1 SUMMARY

A. The green products included in this Section are provided for example only. No endorsement of individual products is intended. Verify product selections and current availability with the product manufacturer before including this text in a project specification. In a typical specification, these products would be included in the appropriate specification section, and not grouped together in a single section. This is a source list; additional product features and attributes would be listed in a full specification.

B. For a more comprehensive list of products and manufacturers, we suggest the Web site www.BuildingGreen.com provided by BuildingGreen Inc., publishers of *Environmental Building News*, the current GreenSpec, EBN Archives, and Green Building Advisor.

1.2 SUBMITTALS

A. Product Data: Submit manufacturer's product data and installation instructions for each material and product used.

B. Shop Drawings: Submit shop drawings indicating material characteristics, details of construction, connections, and relationship with adjacent construction.

C. Samples: Submit two representative samples of each material specified indicating visual characteristics and finish. Include range samples if variation of finish is anticipated.

1.3 QUALITY ASSURANCE

A. Comply with governing codes and regulations. Provide products of acceptable manufacturers which have been in satisfactory use in similar service for three years. Use experienced installers. Deliver, handle, and store materials in accordance with manufacturer's instructions.

PART 2 PRODUCTS

2.1 SYNTHETIC GYPSUM BOARD

A. Synthetic Gypsum Board: Provide synthetic gypsum board fabricated from gypsum reclaimed from manufacturing processes and recycled paper facings, manufactured by one of the following:
 1. Gypsum Wallboard, as manufactured by G-P Gypsum Corp. (Wheatfield, IN and Savannah, GA plants), Atlanta, GA, telephone 404/652-4000.
 2. Gold Bond Gypsum Wallboard, as manufactured by National Gypsum Company. (Shippingport, PA or Baltimore, MD plants), Charlotte, NC, telephone 800/628-4662.
 3. Sheetrock Brand Gypsum Panels, as manufactured by United States Gypsum Co. (Baltimore, MD and 5 other plants), Chicago, IL, telephone 800/606-4476.

2.2 MEDIUM DENSITY FIBERBOARD

A. Medium Density Fiberboard Fabricated from Wood Residuals and Without Formaldehyde: Provide Medite II for interior applications, Medex for use in high moisture applications, and Medite FR for Class 1 fire-rated applications as applicable, as manufactured by SierraPine Ltd, Roseville, CA, telephone 800/676-3339.

2.3 PRESERVATIVE TREATMENT

A. Pressure-Treated Wood, Arsenic- and Chromium-Free: Provide pressure-treated wood produced in accordance with AWPA standards as applicable, C1, C2, C4, C5, C9, C15, C17, C22, P5 and the following:
 1. Standard Product: Preserve Brand treated wood products with ACQ treatment.
 2. Water-Repellent Product: Preserve Plus, water-repellent, retention of 0.31 pounds per cubic foot.
 3. Manufacturer: CSI Chemical Products; telephone 704/522-0825; www.treatedwood.com
 4. Retention Rate:
  a. Above Ground Deck Support: 0.40 pounds per cubic foot for decking, fence boards, handrails, and similar items.
  b. Ground Contact Fresh Water: 0.40 pounds per cubic foot for fence posts, landscaping, piers, docks, and similar items.
  c. Permanent Wood Foundations: 0.60 pounds per cubic foot for wood foundations and crawl spaces.

Figure 10.1 (cont.)

d. Poles: 0.60 pounds per cubic foot for building and distribution poles.

2.4 CERTIFIED WOOD

A. Certified Wood: Provide wood products from managed forests complying with requirements of the Forest Stewardship Council Guidelines for certified wood building components; Forest Stewardship Council, Washington, DC, telephone 877/372-5646.

2.5 ACOUSTICAL CEILINGS

A. Acoustical Ceiling Panels-with Recycled Content: Provide acoustical ceiling tiles with percentage recycled content listed for mineral wool and cellulose fiber:
1. Manufacturer: Armstrong; telephone 888/234-5464; www.ceilings.com
    a. Product: Ultima, 79 percent recycled content, reclaimable.
    b. Product: Fire Guard Ceilings, 37-75 percent recycled content, reclaimable.
    c. Product: Crossgate, 72 percent recycled content, reclaimable.
    d. Product: Stratus, 72 percent recycled content, reclaimable.
    e. Product: Cirrus, 69 percent recycled content, reclaimable.
    f. Product: Sanserra, 69 percent recycled content, reclaimable.
    g. Product: Soundsoak Walls, 65 percent recycled content, reclaimable.
    h. Product: Fine Fissured Duratex, 54 percent recycled content, reclaimable.
    i. Product: Ceramaguard, 52 percent recycled content.
    j. Product: Graphis, 44 percent recycled content, reclaimable.
    k. Product: Random Fissured, 31 percent recycled glass content.
    l. Product: Optima, 28 percent recycled glass content.
    m. Product: Painted Nubby, 28 percent recycled glass content.
    n. Product: Cortega, 25 percent recycled content, reclaimable.
    o. Product: Steel Suspension Systems, 25 percent recycled content, recyclable.
2. Manufacturer: USG Corporation, Chicago, IL, telephone 312/606-4000; www.usg.com
    a. Product: X-Technology, 74 percent recycled content.
    b. Product: Acoustone, 68 percent recycled content.
    c. Product: Auratone, up to 62 percent recycled content.
3. Manufacturer: Celotex Corp., Tampa, FL, telephone 800/235-8639; www.celotex.com
    a. Products: Hytone, Softone, Celotone, high recycled content.

2.6 LINOLEUM

A. Linoleum Tile Flooring: Solidified mixture of linoleum cement binder and ground cork, wood flour, mineral fillers, and pigments bonded to a fibrous or other suitable backing so that backing is partially embedded in mixture. Patterns and colors extending through entire wear-layer thickness. Provide linoleum tile in color and pattern selected by the Architect and as follows:
1. Manufacturer: Armstrong World Industries, Inc., telephone 877/276-7876; www.commercial-floors.com
    a. Type: Marmorette; (2.0) (2.5) (3.2) mm thick, (48 by 48 cm) (60 by 60 cm) tile size; installed with S-240 epoxy adhesive.
    b. Type: Colorette; (2.5) (3.2) mm thick, (48 by 48 cm) (60 by 60 cm) tile size; installed with S-240 epoxy adhesive.
    c. Type: Linorette; 2.5 mm thick, (48 by 48 cm) (60 by 60 cm) tile size; installed with S-240 epoxy adhesive.
    d. Type: Uni Walton; (2.0) (2.5) (3.2) mm thick, (48 by 48 cm) (60 by 60 cm) tile size; installed with S-240 epoxy adhesive.
    e. Type: Linodur; 4.0 mm thick, (48 by 48 cm) (60 by 60 cm) tile size; installed with S-240 epoxy adhesive.
2. Manufacturer: Marmoleum Dual as manufactured by Forbo Industries, Hazleton, PA, telephone 800/842-7839;www.forbo-industries.com
B. Linoleum Sheet Flooring: ASTM F 2034. Provide linoleum sheet in color and pattern selected by the Architect and as follows:
1. Manufacturer: Armstrong World Industries, Inc., telephone 877/276-7876; www.commercial-floors.com
    a. Type: Marmorette; (2.0) (2.5) (3.2) mm thick; installed with heat-welded seams and S-235 adhesive.
    b. Type: Colorette; (2.5) (3.2) mm thick; installed with heat-welded seams and S-235 adhesive.
    c. Type: Linorette; 2.5 mm thick; installed with heat-welded seams and S-235 adhesive.
    d. Type: Uni Walton; (2.0) (2.5) (3.2) mm thick; installed with heat-welded seams and S-235 adhesive.

Figure 10.1 (cont.)

e. Type: Linodur; 4.0 mm thick; installed with heat-welded seams and S-235 adhesive.

f. Heat-Welding Bead: Solid-strand product of floor covering manufacturer. Color as selected by Architect.

g. Integral Cove Base: 1 inch radius cove strip provided or approved by floor covering manufacturer and square metal cap provided by or approved by floor covering manufacturer.

2. Manufacturer: Marmoleum and Artoleum as manufactured by Forbo Industries, Hazleton, PA, telephone 800/842-7839;www.forbo-industries.com

3. Manufacturer: Linosom Etrusco, Veneto and Narnidur by Domco, Inc. US, telephone 800/366-2689; www.domco.com

2.7 TILE WITH RECYCLED CONTENT

A. Tile with Recycled Content: Provide one of the following:

1. Ceramic Tiles, as manufactured by Crossville Ceramics, Crossville, TN, telephone 615/484-2110.

2. Armstone Confetti, as manufactured by PermaGrain Products, Inc., Newtown Square, PA, telephone 610/353-8801.

3. Traffic Tile, as manufactured by Stoneware Tile Co., Richmond, IN, telephone 317/935-4760.

4. Imperva, as manufactured by Summitville Tiles, Summitville, OH, telephone 330/223-1511.

5. Green Series, as manufactured by Terra Designs Tileworks, Dover, NJ, telephone 973/328-1135.

2.8 TILE ADHESIVE

A. Tile Adhesive, Low-Odor without Solvents: Provide tile adhesive recommended by tile manufacturer, or one of the following:

1. Advanced Air Tech Adhesives, as manufactured by Advanced Adhesive Technology Inc., Dalton, GA, telephone 706/226-0610.

2. CT-12, as manufactured by Capitol Adhesives, Dalton, GA.

3. Chapco Safe-Set 9, as manufactured by Chicago Adhesive Products Co., Chicago, IL, telephone 312/581-1300.

2.9 CARPET

A. Carpet Fabricated with Recycled Materials:
Provide one of the following:

1. Encore SD Ultima, as manufactured by J&J Industries, Dalton, GA, telephone 800/241-4586.

2. Metafloor by Lees Carpets Division of Burlington Industries, Greensboro, NC, telephone 800/523-5647.

3. Commercial Carpet with ColorStrand by Mohawk Industries, Calhoun, GA, telephone 800/622-6227.

4. EcoSolution Q and Ecoworx by Shaw Contract Group, Dalton, GA; telephone 800/441-7429.

B. Wool Carpet: Provide wool carpet by one of the following:

1. Classic Weavers, Dalton, GA, telephone 706/277-7767.

2. Dresso USA, Inc., Wayne, PA, telephone 215/526-9517.

3. Floorgraphix Inc., Cartersville, GA, telephone 404/386-0310.

4. Louis De Poortere, Atlanta, GA, telephone 404/688-6331.

5. U.S. Axminster, Greenville, MS, telephone 601/332-1581.

2.10 CARPET TILE

A. Carpet Tile Fabricated with Recycled Materials:
Provide one of the following:

1. Powerbond RS with ER3, as manufactured by Collins & Aikman Floorcoverings, Dalton, GA, telephone 800/248-2878.

2. Earth Square, as manufactured by Milliken Carpet, LaGrange, GA, telephone 877/327-3639.

3. Entropy, Sabi, and Prarie School as manufactured by Interface Flooring Systems, LaGrange, GA, telephone 706/882-1891.

2.11 CARPET CUSHION

A. Carpet Cushion Fabricated from Recycled Materials: Provide one of the following:

1. EcoSoft Carpet Cushion, as manufactured by DuPont Commercial Flooring, Kennesaw, GA, telephone 800/438-7668.

2. Syntex Carpet Cushion, as manufactured by Leggett & Platt, Inc., Chicago, IL, telephone 800/621-6907.

3. Endurance II, as manufactured by Shaw Contract Group, Dalton, GA, telephone 800/441-7429.

Figure 10.1 (cont.)

2.12 CARPET ADHESIVE

A. Carpet Adhesive, Low-Odor Type without Solvents: As recommended by carpet manufacturer or one of the following:
   1. Advanced Air Tech Adhesives, as manufactured by Advanced Adhesive Technology Inc., Dalton, GA, telephone 706/226-0610.
   2. Carpet Adhesive, as manufactured by Capitol Adhesives, Dalton, GA.
   3. Chapco Safe - Set, as manufactured by Chicago Adhesive Products Co., Chicago, IL, telephone 312/581-1300.

2.13 ZERO VOC PAINTS

A. Interior Paints with zero-VOC Content: Provide one of the following:
   1. Pristine Eco-Spec by Benjamin Moore & Co., Montvale, NJ, telephone 800/344-0400.
   2. Pure Performance by PPG Architectural Finishes, Pittsburgh, PA; telephone 800/441-9695.
   3. Harmony by Sherwin-Williams, Cleveland OH, telephone 800/321-8194.

2.14 MULTI-COLOR PAINTS

A. Interior Water-Based Multi-Color Paints: Provide one of the following:
   1. Polomyx Aegis, as manufactured by Surface Protection Industries International, North Billerica, MA, 978/988-9500.
   2. Zolatone Elites, as manufactured by Surface Protection Industries International, North Billerica, MA, 978/988-9500.

2.15 FIBERGLASS INSULATION

A. Fiberglass Insulation Manufactured with Recycled Glass: Provide one of the following:
   1. CertainTeed Building Insulation by CertainTeed Corp., Valley Forge, PA, telephone 800/233-8990.
   2. ComfortTherm and Fiberglass Building Insulation by Johns Manville Corp., Denver, CO, telephone 800/654-3103.
   3. Miraflex and Pink Fiberglass Building Insulation by Owens Corning, Toledo, OH, telephone 800/438-7465.
   4. Fiberglass Insulation by Ottawa Fibre, Inc., Ottawa, Canada, telephone 613/736-1215.

2.16 MINERAL WOOL INSULATION

A. Mineral Wool Insulation Manufactured with Recycled Material: Provide one of the following:
   1. Thermal-Pruf, Dendamix, and Sound-Pruf by American Sprayed Fibers, Inc., Merrillville, IN, telephone 800/824-2997.
   2. Sloss Blowing Wool by Sloss Industries Corp., Alexandria, IN, telephone 800/428-6404.
   3. Enviroguard Gold, Enviroguard 200, and ThermaTech Gold by ThermaFiber LLC, Wabash, IN, telephone 888/834-2371.
   4. Roxul Mineral Wool, by Roxul Inc., Milton, Canada, telephone 800/265-6878.
   5. Mineral Fiber Insulation, as manufactured by American Rockwool Inc., Nolanville, TX, telephone 817/698-2233.

2.17 CELLULOSE INSULATION

A. Cellulose Insulation Manufactured with Recycled Material: Provide K-13 and SonaSpray 'fc' Insulation by International Cellulose Corporation, Houston, TX, telephone 800/444-1252; or Cellulose Insulation by members of the Cellulose Insulation Manufacturers Association, Dayton, OH, telephone 888/881-2462.

2.18 FOAMED-IN-PLACE INSULATION

A. Foamed-In-Place Insulation: Provide one of the following:
   1. Air Krete Foam Insulation, as manufactured by Air Krete Inc., Weedsport, NY, telephone 315/834-6609.
   2. Sealection by Demilec USA, Grand Prairie, TX, telephone 972/647-0561.
   3. SuperGreen Foam by Foam-Tech, Div. of H.C. Fennell, N. Thetford, VT, telephone 802/333-4333.
   4. Icynene Insulation System by Icynene, Mississauga, Canada, telephone 888/946-7325.

2.19 RIGID INSULATION

A. Extruded Polystyrene Insulation, Non-Ozone Depleting Substances: Styrofoam High Performance by Dow Chemical Co., Midland, MI, telephone 800/441-4369.

B. Polyisocyanurate Foam Insulation, Non-Ozone Depleting Substances: ACFoam, as manufactured by Atlas Roofing Corp., Atlanta, GA, telephone 770/952-1442.

Figure 10.1 (cont.)

2.20 HIGH-PERFORMANCE INSULATING GLASS

A. High-Performance Insulating Glass: Provide products by the following:
   1. Comfort E2, Comfort T1, and Solar Glass by AFG Industries, Kingsport, TN, telephone 800/251-0441.
   2. INE Neutral Low-E Glass by Interpane, Clinton, NC, telephone 800/334-1797.
   3. Pilkington Energy Advantage by Pilkington NA, Toledo, OH, telephone 800/526-6557.
   4. Sungate 500, Solarban 60, and Azurlite by PPG Industries, Pittsburgh, PA, telephone 800/377-5267.
   5. Superwindow by Viracon, Owatonna, MN, telephone 800/533-2080.
   6. Superglass with Heat Mirror by Southwall Technologies, Palo Alto, CA, telephone 800/365-8794.

2.21 HIGH-PERFORMANCE WINDOWS

A. High-Performance Wood Windows: Provide high-performance windows as manufactured by one of the following:
   1. Heat Smart, as manufactured by Lowen Windows, Steinbach, Canada; telephone 800/563-9367; www.loewen.com
   2. High-Performance Wood Windows, as manufactured by Marvin Windows and Doors, Fargo, ND; telephone 800/346-5128; www.marvin.com
   3. Designer Series SmartSash, as manufactured by Pella Corporation, Pella, IA, telephone 800/847-3552; www.pella.com
   4. High-Performance Wood Windows, as manufactured by Weathershield Manufacturing Inc., Medford, WI, telephone 800/477-6808; www.weathershield.com

B. High-Performance Vinyl Replacement Windows: Provide high-performance windows as manufactured by one of the following:
   1. Gilkey Window Company, Cincinnati, OH, telephone 513/769-4527; www.gilkey.com
   2. Kensington Windows, Vandergrift, PA, telephone 800/444-4972.
   3. Stanek Vinyl Windows Corp., Cuyahoga Heights, OH, telephone 216/341-7700; www.stanekwindows.com
   4. Thermal Industries, Inc., Pittsburgh, PA, telephone 800/245-1540; www.thermalindustries.com

C. High-Performance Fiberglass Windows: Provide high-performance windows as manufactured by one of the following:
   1. Accurate Dorwin, Winnipeg, Canada; telephone 204/982-8370; www.accuratedorwin.com
   2. Fibertec Window Mfg. Ltd., Concord, Canada, telephone 905/660-7102; www.fibertec.com
   3. Marvin Windows and Doors, Fargo, ND, telephone 800/346-5128; www.marvin.com
   4. Thermotech Windows, Ltd., Ottawa, Canada; telephone 613/225-1101; www.thermotechwindows.com

2.22 CONCRETE MASONRY UNITS

A. Concrete Masonry Units with Integral Insulation: Provide units by one of the following:
   1. IMSI System, as manufactured by Insulated Masonry Systems, Inc., Scottsdale, AZ, telephone 602/970-0711.
   2. Sparfil Wall System II, as manufactured by Sparfil Blok Florida, Inc., Tampa, FL, telephone 813/963-3794.
   3. ThermaLock Concrete Block, as manufactured by ThermaLock Products, North Tonawanda, NY, telephone 716/695-6000.

B. Autoclaved Aerated Concrete Masonry Units: Provide lightweight insulating autoclaved concrete masonry by one of the following:
   1. ACCO Aerated Concrete Systems, Inc., Apopka, FL, telephone 888/901-2226.
   2. Babb International Inc., Smyrna, GA, telephone 770/308-1500.
   3. E-Crete, Scottsdale, AZ, telephone 480/596-3819.
   4. Texas Contec, Inc., San Juan, TX, telephone 956/783-5422.

2.23 CONCRETE CONTAINING COAL FLY ASH

A. Concrete Containing Coal Fly Ash: Provide coal fly ash in concrete mix, in percentage acceptable to project structural engineer. Provide coal fly ash from one of the following:
   1. Member, American Coal Ash Association, Syracuse, NY, telephone 315/428-2400.
   2. Boral Material Technologies, San Antonio, TX, telephone 210/349-4069.
   3. Hanson Aggregates South Central Region, Dallas, TX, telephone 800/441-0005.
   4. Mineral Solutions, Eagan, MN, telephone 800/437-5980.
   5. The SEFA Group, West Columbia, SC, telephone 800/884-7332.
   6. VFL Technology, Dagsboro, DE, telephone 302/934-8025.

Figure 10.1 (cont.)

2.24 HAND DRYERS

    A. Electric Hand Dryers: Provide electric hand dryers by one of the following:
       1. XLerator Electric Hand Dryer by Excel Dryer, Inc., East Longmeadow, MA, telephone 413/525-4531.
       2. Electric Hand Dryer by World Dryer, Berkeley, IL, telephone 800/323-0701.

2.25 GREEN ROOF SYSTEMS

    A. Green Roof Systems: Provide green roof system by one of the following:
       1. Garden Roof Assembly by American Hydrotech, Inc., Chicago, IL, telephone 800/877-6125.
       2. Green Roof-Roofscape by Barrett Company, Millington, NJ, telephone 800/647-0100.
       3. SopraNature by Soprema USA, Inc., Wadsworth, OH, telephone 800/356-3521.
       4. Green Roof System by The Garland Company, Cleveland, OH, telephone 800/321-9336.

2.26 GRAY WATER SYSTEM

    A. Graywater Recycling System: System shall recycle gray water from non-toilet bathroom and laundry waste water for exterior below-grade irrigation system. Provide system by one of the following:
       1. M-1000, M-100, as manufactured by Agwa Systems Inc., Burbank, CA, telephone 818/562-1449.
       2. ReWater System, as manufactured by ReWater Systems, Inc., Palo Alto, CA, telephone 415/324-1307.

PART 3 EXECUTION

3.01 INSTALLATION

    A. Install materials and systems in accordance with manufacturer's instructions and approved submittals. Install materials and systems in proper relation with adjacent construction and with uniform appearance. Coordinate with work of other sections.
    B. Restore damaged components. Clean and protect work from damage.

Figure 10.1 (cont.)

project managers, and an organized effort is made to LEED-certify a project and green their specifications. Designers and project managers in the firm are encouraged to learn green principles, so they can "talk the talk."

Six Months Later: Several LEED projects are under way, and the engineering disciplines in the firm are pleased to have the opportunity to do more energy modeling, and to work with the designers to improve overall performance of the buildings. However, green efforts are generally limited to key people, and the rest of the firm waits for the trickle-down influence of those in senior positions. The firm has established its green credentials, and use of the firm's green specifications gradually increases.

Firm 3: A committee of interior designers in a multidisciplinary firm meets monthly to discuss green topics. Speakers are invited, staff attends green seminars, and a consultant is hired to create a database of green products to be made available on the firm's intranet. Green articles in magazines are circulated to appropriate staff.

Six Months Later: The enthusiasm of the green committee spreads to most of the younger staff in the firm. Individuals contribute to a common database, and even small contributions build the firm's green deliverables. The firm subscribes to over 50 magazines, and the librarian routes articles to the interest areas expressed by individual staff. The green dynamic continues to grow in the firm, and a certain green pride develops.

Firm 4: The principal responsible for maintaining the firm's details on energy performance and exterior wall assemblies expands his long-standing commitment to building technology by adding sustainable design to his criteria. Green products are added to the firm's master specifications. LEED projects accelerate the process. The firm creates a position for a green researcher.

Six Months Later: All projects are reviewed during design for energy performance and green opportunities. The technology principal has much success requiring individual project architects to evaluate their projects for green. During bidding and construction, some contractors object to the special materials and increased inspections during construction, but the firm enforces its policies. Research backs up product selection and detailing. Buildings with improved energy performance and careful product selection are constructed and put into service.

Firm 5: A specifications consultant becomes LEED-certified, offering to be the LEED-trained person on the project (worth 1 LEED credit). Clients are made aware of the firm's credentials and commitment to green.

Six Months Later: As the design firm undertakes LEED projects, the architect's own staff becomes LEED-certified, and the marketing effort of the specifier has limited effect. However, the spec consultant has demonstrated his commitment to green, and architects look for advice as green projects are designed and specified. The product selection remains with the design professional, but more and more green products are included in the specifications based on a growing database.

Conclusion

The responsibility for selecting and specifying green building products and systems remains with the entire design team. Owners, architects, engineers, and contractors can all contribute based on their unique views of the project. Owners who make green credentials part of their designer selection process have the most success. Young architects with the energy to investigate and try new products move the green industry forward. Contractors who understand building technology embrace buildings that perform better. The imperative for green increases. Designing, specifying, and building green works with a concerted joint effort.

The construction industry is slow to change, as product selection and installation are based on the hands-on knowledge of design professionals and builders struggling to complete their projects on schedule and on budget. One industry researcher indicated that if the ultimate hammer was suddenly introduced into the marketplace, it would still take seventeen years before all carpenters had them on their belts. We are on our way with green products, but it will be a journey.

The transition to sustainable and green products will be won or lost over the next five years based on the actions of those responsible for the built environment. To quote the scholar, "If we fail to choose, we choose to fail." Excuse the hyperbole, but someday only the sun will be available as a power source; there won't be any more Third World countries to fabricate our most hazardous products; the ozone layer won't replenish itself. Be selfish for your great grandchildren. Specify green.

[1] Published by Kalin Associates in Boston in 1996 on recycled paper using soy ink in a post-consumer, reconstituted plastic binder.

Chapter 11
Commissioning the Green Building

Arthur Adler, PE, CEM

There is the potential for installation and operations problems in all newly constructed buildings. Green buildings may include special systems and equipment that are not familiar to the owner, maintenance staff, or some members of the design and construction team. Consulting an independent, qualified commissioning agent during the programming phase can save time and money, and perhaps most importantly, ensure that the building functions properly and is easy to maintain and operate as designed.

Commissioning is often thought of as a series of tests conducted on equipment prior to the turnover of systems to the building owner at the end of a construction project. Final testing of systems is only one aspect of the commissioning process. ASHRAE defines commissioning as the process of ensuring that systems are designed, installed, functionally tested, and capable of being operated and maintained to conform to the design intent. The process begins with planning and includes design, construction, start-up, acceptance, and training, and can be applied throughout the life of the building.[1]

There are a number of commissioning resources available that employ different methods of accomplishing the same goal, providing a building that operates as intended, with full documentation and training on all systems. The sources that are referred to most often by owners and commissioning providers are:

- University of Washington Commissioning Guidelines
- Portland Energy Conservation Incorporated (PECI)
- ASHRAE Commissioning Guideline
- Bonneville Power Administration
- SMACNA Commissioning Guidelines

Not all aspects of each of these guidelines are required. Owners may choose to have the commissioning agent perform some of these activities and eliminate others. Not surprisingly, cost is the primary reason for reducing the commissioning scope, although it can be argued that the less thorough the commissioning, the higher the costs will be in change orders, energy consumption, and maintenance over the life of the building.

The LEED green building rating system (described in Chapter 9) includes two levels of commissioning. The basic commissioning activities that are a prerequisite to achieving any rating are:

- Engaging a commissioning authority.
- Collecting and reviewing the design intent and basis of design documentation.
- Including commissioning requirements in the construction documents.
- Developing and utilizing a commissioning plan.
- Verifying the installation, functional performance, operational training, and maintenance documentation for each commissioned system.
- Completing a commissioning report.

To receive an additional credit for commissioning, the following additional activities must be performed:

- Conducting a focused review of the design prior to the construction documents phase.
- Conducting a focused review of the construction documents when close to completion.
- Conducting a selective review of contractor equipment submittal documents for equipment to be commissioned.
- Developing a recommissioning management manual.
- Having a contract in place for a near warranty end or post occupancy review.

Another stipulation to receive the additional credit is having the first three items performed by an independent commissioning agent. An independent third party can be an advantage because this person has no allegiance to any of the other companies involved and will be able to focus on aspects of the project that deal with operating and maintaining the equipment.

Commissioning tasks should be structured to meet the requirements of the project, and not just the points for a rating system. The more complex the components and systems, the more detailed the commissioning effort should be. For all projects that utilize the sustainable design approach, the commissioning agent should be hired during the programming phase so that he/she can provide input and help define what the building should and should not be able to do. In this way, attributes that may be deemed desirable by some may be negated by the commissioning agent prior to the design team spending any time incorporating these features into the design. The value added by the commissioning agent at this early stage of the process will depend greatly on his/her experience in both the sustainable design process and commissioning of various types of building elements and systems.

Approach

This chapter describes the commissioning-related activities that can be performed during each step of a *complete* commissioning process. (Previously mentioned, some owners may choose to perform only selected steps or equipment due mainly to cost considerations.) The primary steps in the life of a project are listed and described below, as they relate to building commissioning.

1. Programming
2. Design
3. Construction
4. Acceptance
5. Post-Acceptance

The Programming Phase

Hiring the Commissioning Agent (CA)

The owner or company procuring commissioning services should request the following information from each potential commissioning agent (CA).

1. A list of the green projects the company has worked on. (If a CA has done work on green projects, he/she may have a better understanding of the process and be able to add more value.)

2. A listing of the specific phases of the project that each team member was involved in.

3. A resumé for each individual who will be working on the project.

4. A copy of a final commissioning report completed by members of the commissioning team.

Commissioning Checklist

The purpose of the commissioning checklist, Figure 11.1, is to help plan and keep track of the activities that will be carried out by the commissioning agent. Depending on timing and budget, certain

Commissioning Checklist

	Check Items That Apply	Notes on Percent Testing, Hours of Training, etc.
Programming Phase		
CA Participation in the Sustainable Process		
Design Phase		
Design Intent Document		*(Created by A/E?)*
Commissioning Plan		
Commissioning Specifications		
Construction Documents Review		*(At which stages?)*
Construction Phase		
Coordinate and Direct Commissioning Activities		
Review Construction Meeting Minutes		
Review Equipment Submittals and Manufacturer		
Test Procedures		
Conduct Commissioning Scoping Meetings		*(Number of meetings)*
Create Test Procedures		*(List tests)*
O&M Manual Review		
Training		*(List systems and hours (video?))*
Equipment Start-up and Pre-Functional Testing		*(List systems to be witnessed and percent of each type)*
Acceptance Phase		
Conduct Commissioning Meetings		*(Number of meetings)*
Review of Control System Programming		*(Review for each system type)*
Functional Performance Testing		*(List equipment and percent of each type to be tested)*
Retesting		*(List percent allowance)*
Systems Manuals		*(List level of detail to be added)*
Final Commissioning Report		*(List topics to be included)*
Post-Acceptance Phase		
Seasonal Testing		
Interview Facility Staff and Recommend Improvements		
Trend Analysis		

Figure 11.1

commissioning activities may be eliminated or reduced in scope. This list can be helpful in planning which activities will be used, and then checking them off as they are completed.

The Design Phase

The commissioning agent must ensure that the owner understands all elements of the design proposed by the architect and engineer. The CA will have questions for all parties involved in systems to be commissioned during creation of the design intent and construction documents. Finally, the CA is responsible for making sure that all aspects of commissioning have been properly incorporated into the specifications.

The Design Intent Document

This document explains the ideas, concepts, and criteria considered important to the owner. It provides detailed design parameters that the systems must be able to attain when the project is complete. It clarifies the final goals of the system operation to the CA, as well as to all parties involved in the project's design. The design engineer is solicited for input and feedback to clarify the design intent. The document becomes the basis for functional testing and defining system performance.

The design intent is always evolving. For green buildings, it is critical to first document the basic conditions that the structure, systems, and products must meet. The following questions apply.

- What are the general and specific light level requirements for each type of space (e.g., classroom or office)?
- What are the temperature and humidity requirements of each type of space?
- What are the noise level requirements of the mechanical systems?

The design intent evolves into the basis of design and selection of system types and sizes. The architect, engineer, and owner begin to evaluate the performance requirements that will be required of each item. This is not a trivial exercise. Space heating and cooling loads are greatly affected by the design of the building envelope (insulation values of the roof, walls, and windows), and the internal loads (such as lighting, computers, and people). The CA should make sure that the design team has discussed all of the energy-saving options available.

Most high-performance equipment has an additional cost, which may be offset over the life of the equipment due to lower energy consumption. Selecting equipment with lower loads can also translate into space savings through smaller heating and cooling systems.

Some of the energy-related items that should be evaluated include:

- High-performance chillers and cooling towers.
- High-efficiency motors.
- Maximum allowable energy consumption per footcandle.
- Daylight harvesting.
- Energy-saving sequences, such as static pressure reset, condenser, and chilled and hot water reset enthalpy-based economizer.
- Double- or triple-pane glass with low-E coating.
- Additional insulation in the walls and ceilings.
- Energy Star-compliant office equipment.

After energy-related issues have been discussed, materials must be chosen for the building interior and exterior. The engineer and architect should work with the owner to define which elements are priorities relative to the budget. For materials that have a high-recycled or low-VOC (volatile organic compounds) content, there may be a premium to be paid. Items that fall into this category include:

- Wood products from properly managed forests.
- Locally harvested or manufactured materials.
- Recycling construction waste.
- Caulking and sealants. (Consider what the maximum allowable level of VOCs is and their lifespan.)
- Carpets. (Consider what the minimum requirement for recycled fiber is and the maximum VOC levels.)
- Paints (environmentally-friendly with low-VOC level).

The CA should ask questions about each item selected to determine if it will be maintainable, and if the product has been installed in other buildings. The level of effort at this stage of the process by the CA should be equivalent to that during the functional testing phase. Making changes to materials or systems at this stage of the process is always less expensive than later modifications.

Commissioning Plan

The commissioning plan is a document (or group of documents) prepared by the CA that defines the commissioning process in the various phases of the project. The plan is continually adjusted as the construction of the subsystems and other parts of the building progress. Every portion of the commissioning process is included in the commissioning plan. The plan includes schedules, responsibilities, documentation requirements, communication and reporting protocols, and the level of testing to be completed. Portions of the commissioning plan are incorporated into the commissioning specifications, including systems to be tested and the responsibility of each party relative to the commissioning process.

A draft commissioning plan is prepared prior to the start of the construction phase to ensure that commissioning activities are incorporated into the construction schedule. The CA must spend time with the Construction Manager (CM) to make sure that all commissioning activities are inserted into the construction schedule. This is critical to ensure that commissioning does not slow down the project.

The major categories addressed by the commissioning plan are:

- Introduction
- Systems to be commissioned
- Commissioning team
- Scope and team member responsibilities
- Documentation requirements
- Verification test procedures
- Operations and maintenance manuals
- Training
- Schedule

Commissioning Specifications

Detailed testing requirements must be incorporated into the specifications so that contractors can budget the proper amount of time for functional performance tests in their pricing. One source for this documentation is the Model Commissioning Plan adopted by the U.S. Department of Energy.[2] This document describes the specification sections where commissioning activities should be detailed:

0800   Supplementary Conditions

01700 Project Closeout

15010 Mechanical General

15990 Testing, Adjusting, and Balancing

15997 Mechanical Testing Requirements

16010 Electrical General

16997 Electrical Testing Requirements

17100 Commissioning Process

This is a partial list of section numbers. It is not complete and is not part of the CSI format as of this book's printing. CSI is in the process of developing a new numbering system, which should be followed when available.[3]

Construction Documents Review

The construction documents should be reviewed by the CA at the 50% and 95% completion stages to ensure that commissioning tasks have been properly coordinated, and to comment on accessibility of equipment for maintenance and adequacy of metering, as well as proper placement of devices. For green buildings, it is important to review not only individual systems and components, but their interrelationships. Conducting a thorough review and research of new products at this stage of a project can save a lot of time, money, and aggravation later.

For example, large atriums with lighting fixtures, smoke detectors, or fans installed high above the floor may require a lift for servicing. Tile specified for the finished flooring must be strong enough to support the concentrated wheel load of a lift without cracking.

Specified materials such as paints, sealants, ceiling tiles, carpeting, and furnishings may have certain characteristics that cause them to off-gas VOCs or other potentially harmful chemicals. Architects may inadvertently specify green products that are new and may be untested. The CA should ask the engineer and architect to determine if they have considered the possible side effects of the new products being specified. Have the MSDS (Material Safety Data Sheets) been requested as part of the submittal package? Have qualified material substitutions been identified?

If a system is being specified that has not been used extensively in the past, such as a well water heat pump system, a series of questions must be asked. Has all information been requested relative to the well flow rate capacity, conductivity, environmental permitting, filtration pipe size, and serviceability? Is the heat pump reliable? Does it have adequate heating capacity and temperature output? The engineer should have performed a "worst case" analysis to determine the heat available when both the well temperature and outside air temperature are cold. An additional heat source may be required. As with any other system that is not commonly installed in buildings, an expert may need to be consulted to discuss all the pros and cons.

Other areas that the commissioning agent should focus on include:

- Clear and rigorous design documentation, including detailed and complete sequences of operation.
- An HVAC, fire, and emergency power response matrix that lists all equipment and components (e.g., air handlers, dampers, and valves) with their status and action during a fire alarm and under emergency power.
- Access for reading gauges, entering doors and panels, and observing and replacing filters and coils.

- Required isolation valves, dampers, interlocks, piping, etc., to allow for manual overrides, and simulation of failures and seasonal, or other testing conditions.
- Sufficient monitoring points in the building automation systems (BAS), even beyond those necessary to control the systems, to facilitate performance verification and operation and maintenance (O&M).
- Adequate trending and reporting features in the BAS.
- Pressure and temperature plugs close to controlling sensors for verifying their calibration.
- Pressure gauges, thermometers, and flow meters in strategic areas to facilitate verification of system performance and ongoing O&M.
- Pressure and temperature plugs in less critical areas or on smaller equipment where gauges and thermometers would not be necessary.
- Specification of the locations and criteria for duct static pressure sensors and hydronic differential pressure sensors.
- Adequate balancing valves and dampers, flow metering, and control stations and control system functions to facilitate and verify reliable test and balance.
- Specification of required startup and testing functions to be performed by the manufacturer's field service personnel, such as generator load bank testing.
- Complete O&M documentation requirements in the specifications.
- Complete training requirements in the specifications.

The Construction Phase

During the construction phase of the project, the building systems are installed, started up, and undergo pre-functional performance testing. Weekly construction meeting minutes are reviewed by the CA to make note of punchlist items relative to maintenance and usability of the HVAC, electrical, plumbing, fire protection, and telecommunications systems. Topics related to commissioning checklists, training plans, and operation and maintenance data are also reviewed.

Coordinate and Direct Commissioning Activities

The CA coordinates and directs commissioning activities according to the approved commissioning plan. Regular communication between the CM and CA is critical to transfer scheduling information and provide up-to-date information on change orders, submittal status, and scheduled meetings. This allows commissioning activities to be carried out without delaying the project completion, while limiting formal written correspondence.

Review Construction Meeting Minutes

The CA reviews and comments, as appropriate, on all construction meeting minutes. It is important for the CA to be kept up-to-date on any changes being discussed so that he/she can provide input prior to the recommendation becoming a change in the scope.

Review Equipment Submittals and Manufacturer Test Procedures

The CA should review equipment submittals for compliance with the design intent and the specifications. It is especially important that any substitutions for green components be reviewed for compliance with the specification. Details of specific operational attributes of the equipment to be installed are incorporated into the pre-functional and functional test procedures. The items in the construction documents review section (listed previously in this chapter) also apply to the submittal review process. Request additional submittal data until all questions are answered, especially for products that are substitutions.

Manufacturers of major mechanical equipment, such as chillers, boilers, photovoltaic arrays, and emergency generators, have startup and test procedures that have been developed specifically for the equipment being installed. For this equipment, the CA does not need to develop pre-functional test procedures, but should review and understand how the equipment's operation will interface with other systems. This information will be used to write functional performance tests for integrated systems.

Conduct Commissioning Scoping Meetings

The CA calls commissioning scoping meetings with the contractors to review any outstanding documentation issues, as well as upcoming testing and training. These meetings are held as required during the construction phase to discuss issues that the CA has identified or items relating to equipment startup scheduling, O&M manuals, or training. Late in the construction phase when contractors are more familiar with their role in the commissioning process, it may be possible to incorporate these meetings into the weekly construction meeting. This approach shows respect for the contractors' time, which makes them more likely to support the commissioning process and provide the CA with the necessary information.

Create Test Procedures

The CA prescribes test procedures based on manufacturer recommendations or creates pre-functional and functional test procedures for all equipment that does not have manufacturers' test procedures. Test procedure forms should include space to record the following:

1. System and equipment or component name(s).

2. Equipment location and ID number.

3. Project name and date.

4. Participating parties.

5. A copy of the specification section describing the test requirements.

6. A copy of the specific sequence of operations or other specified parameters being verified.

7. Required pre-test field measurements.

8. Instructions for setting up the test.

9. Set points, alarm limits, and so forth.

10. Specific, step-by-step procedures to execute the test, in a clear, sequential, and repeatable format.

11. Acceptance criteria of proper performance with a Yes/No check box to allow for clearly marking whether proper performance of each part of the test was achieved.

12. A section for comments.

13. Signatures and date block for the CA.

O&M Manual & Contractor Test Procedure Review

Contractors will be requested to submit O&M manuals to the CM and CA as soon as the equipment submittals have been reviewed and approved. The CA should review and comment on the O&M manuals. Contractors are asked to submit for review any pre-functional test forms that meet the specifications and are typically used for the startup of major equipment and systems.

Training

Prior to scheduling training, the O&M manuals and a training plan must be submitted by the contractors to the CM, CA, and A/E. The training plan should indicate:

- Equipment to be included.
- Intended audience.

- Location.
- Objectives.
- Subjects covered (e.g., description, duration of discussion, and special methods).
- Duration of training on each subject.
- Instructor for each subject.
- Methods (e.g., classroom lecture, video, site walk-through, actual operational demonstrations, written handouts).
- Instructor and qualifications.

The CA reviews the manuals and plan, then audits the training sessions to ensure that the O&M personnel understands the operation of each system. Videotaping training sessions is recommended so that future operation and maintenance personnel can be easily introduced to the systems and the ways in which they were designed to operate. Each training session should have an agenda, a sign-up sheet with participant contact information, and an evaluation to provide feedback to the training organizers and instructors.

Equipment Start-Up and Pre-Functional Testing

Start-up and pre-functional testing of major equipment, such as boilers, chillers, and large fan and pumping systems, are performed by the contractor or manufacturer's representative and are typically witnessed by the CA. Test results are recorded by the contractor and included with the O&M manual. The contractors maintain a master deficiency list of tests that are either incomplete or have failed. The CA can comment on how the tests were executed and any open issues that prevented the tests from being completed successfully.

The Acceptance Phase

After the building systems have been started up, and pre-functional performance testing has been successfully completed, the contractors sign off on each system, stating that it is ready for functional performance testing. Prior to starting functional testing of any equipment associated with the building control system, it is recommended that the CA perform a review of the system programming.

Review of Control System Programming

This is a critical component of the standard commissioning procedure that can be used to minimize misunderstandings between the engineer's specified sequence of operation and that programmed by the controls contractor. After the controls contractor has completed programming and started up equipment, a field meeting is held between the CA and the controls programmer/technician. The CA asks the controls

Green Building: Project Planning & Cost Estimating

programmer how each sequence was programmed, and records the response. All interlocks, delays, and control routines are reviewed for each type of unit or system. Many issues are identified during this review, and the programmer is given the opportunity to revise the code, or the design engineer is asked if programming meets the original intent. As a result, there are fewer unexpected problems during functional testing, fewer deficiencies, and fewer retests (not to mention less paperwork and finger-pointing).

Functional Performance Testing

The purpose of functional performance tests is to determine if the performance defined in the design intent documentation has been met. Each system is tested through all modes of system operation (for example, seasonal, occupied/unoccupied, warm-up/cool-down, and so forth, as applicable). This includes every individual interlock and conditional control logic, all control sequences, both full- and part-load conditions, emergency conditions, and simulation of all abnormal conditions for which there is a required system or controls response.

Testing may be accomplished by traditional manual testing (for example, changing a set point and immediately observing a response) and short-term monitoring using the energy management system (EMS) trending capabilities. Portable data loggers may also be used to gather data. The best method, however, is to specify any points that provide energy consumption or temperature information and include them as part of the EMS. The monitoring requirements are detailed in the functional performance tests. As each individual check or test is accomplished, the CA observes and records the physical responses by the system and compares them to the specified sequences to verify the test results.

The verification of the Testing, Adjusting, and Balancing (TAB) report is an integral part of functional performance testing. The CA requests that the TAB contractor demonstrate the results of random balancing readings, which are recorded by the CA and compared to the TAB report values.

As an extension of actual tests, the controls contractor's trend logs, developed in the EMS, are evaluated by the CA for control, stability, and conformance with the design intent. This is a key element in evaluating the long-term operation and performance of the systems.

When individual system functional performance has been verified, the integrated or coordinated response between each system is checked. Fire and smoke alarm interactions with HVAC equipment in all modes must be part of the integrated testing.

Typically, the operation of all major and critical equipment is functionally tested. Usually, a percentage (typically 25%) of terminal equipment, such as variable air volume boxes, fan coil units, and radiation, is put through full functional testing. All systems that are either new or green should be fully tested to ensure optimum performance.

Retesting

Portions of systems that fail functional performance tests are retested after the contractor indicates in writing that the deficiency has been resolved. Typically, a budget is set aside for re-running functional tests. Actual failure rates cannot be predicted. However, for multiple equipment items such as rooftop units or VAV boxes, portions of the test that fail on more than one piece of equipment will not be executed on subsequent equipment until the contractor submits in writing that all equipment of this type has been reviewed for the deficiency. Clauses can and should be added to the specifications that limit the number of retests (usually one) for each type of equipment. Additional retests should be paid for by the responsible contractor. The CA is responsible for identifying the parties responsible for the failed tests.

Systems Manuals

Operation and maintenance manuals that are assembled by contractors are not always well-organized or easy to use. Systems or recommissioning manuals should be created by the CA using the O&M manuals and organizing the information by system. A brief description of how each system operates is typically added to the front of each section, along with a schematic diagram with all equipment identified, the operational sequence, and the maintenance requirements and frequency. The front of the manual should include contact information on contractors that were responsible for installing and testing each system. Manuals should also provide cut sheets and identify suppliers of major equipment and replacement parts. A troubleshooting guide is another important component, listing problems that may arise, possible causes and solutions, and criteria for deciding when equipment should be repaired, and when it must be replaced. Portland Energy Conservation Incorporated (PECI) publishes a series of O&M best practice manuals that can be helpful in defining how systems are maintained.[4]

Final Commissioning Report

The commissioning report is intended to be the primary record document for commissioning for each specific system and the building as a whole. Information in the report should include the following:

- Name, address, firm, and phone number of CA.

- Description of installed systems.
- List and description of commissioning tasks.
- Commissioning plan.
- Completed design intent document.
- Completed pre-functional test checklists.
- Completed functional performance tests.
- All non-compliance forms.
- Summary of commissioning findings.
- Recommendations for system recommissioning.
- Analysis of the performance of each system.
- Recommendations for system improvements.
- Summary of operator training.
- Sequence documentation.
- Site visit reports.
- Blank functional checklist forms for recommissioning.

The Post-Acceptance Phase

Perform Seasonal Testing

Portions of systems that are weather-dependent should be retested during the opposite season from the one in which they were originally tested. For example, if an air handling unit was commissioned during the summer, a follow-up test should be performed during the winter for items such as the heating valve and damper controls. These components would have been verified for proper operation during the summer, but their stability of control would not have been confirmed. One of the primary means of documenting the proper operation of each system over time is by plotting and reviewing trend data in a program such as Microsoft® Excel. Control of temperature and pressure loops can be demonstrated under all load conditions through summer and winter, occupied and unoccupied periods.

Interview Facility Staff

The facility operations and maintenance staff should be interviewed during quarterly operational reviews conducted through the first year of operation. These personnel are required to maintain a log of issues including:

- Changes in the building usage, installed equipment, and occupancy.
- Documentation of any changes in set points, control sequences, or overrides.
- Trouble finding or using equipment maintenance procedures.

- System servicing and maintenance documentation and problems.
- Documentation of comfort complaints.

This information will help the CA provide the building operations personnel with an understanding of the changes or issues and a more focused approach to addressing them. It is important to document and address problems as soon as possible while some equipment is still under warranty.

Recommend Improvements

During the warranty period, needed improvements and enhancements to the operation of commissioned systems are identified. The CA should make the recommendations based on a review of system operations and interviews with the operating personnel and building occupants. Any implemented changes should be documented in the O&M manual by the CA.

Conclusion

Commissioning of green buildings is more important than for any other type of structure due to the myriad of new products, systems, and technologies that are incorporated. Making sure that the operations personnel understand how to properly maintain and operate the building can mean the difference between having an environment in which people thrive; are happy, productive, and healthy; and one where the building is more costly to operate or makes occupants sick. The commissioning agent must put him/herself in the place of the building owners and occupants and ask more questions earlier in the design and construction process to help avoid problems.

[1] ASHRAE Guideline 1-1996 "The HVAC Commissioning Process."

[2] Complete Guide specifications, **www.peci.org**

[3] Construction Specifications Institute, **www.csinet.org**

[4] O&M Best Practice Series, **www.peci.org**

Economic & Environmental Analysis

Chapter *12* Evaluating Products Over Their Life Cycle

Barbara C. Lippiatt

Selecting building products based on minimum life-cycle economic impacts is relatively straightforward. Products are bought and sold in the marketplace, which established the first cost; and sound analytical procedures to quantify life-cycle cost have been developed and employed for over 20 years. In addition to initial cost, future costs that contribute to life-cycle cost include the cost of energy, operation and maintenance, labor and supplies, replacement parts, and eventually the cost of decommissioning or recycling the system. Chapter 13, "Economic Analysis & Green Buildings," addresses in detail the economic aspects of life-cycle costing.

But how do we include life-cycle environmental impacts in our purchase decisions? Environmental impacts, such as global warming, indoor air quality, water pollution, and resource depletion, are for the most part economic externalities. That is, their costs are not reflected in the market prices of the products that generated the impacts. Moreover, even if there were a mandate today to include environmental "costs" in market prices, it would be nearly impossible to do so due to difficulties in assessing these impacts in classical economic terms. How do you put a price on clean air and clean water? What, ultimately, is the price of human life, and how do we value the avoidance of its loss? Economists have debated these questions for decades, and a consensus does not appear imminent.

While environmental performance cannot be measured on a monetary scale, it can be quantified using the evolving, multi-disciplinary approach known as **environmental life-cycle assessment** (LCA). All stages in the life of a product are analyzed: raw material acquisition, manufacture, transportation, installation, use, and recycling and waste management. The National Institute of Standards and Technology BEES

(Building for Environmental and Economic Sustainability) tool[1] applies an LCA approach to measure the environmental performance of building products, following guidance in the International Organization for Standardization (ISO) 14040 series of standards for LCA.[2] BEES separately measures economic performance using the American Society for Testing and Materials (ASTM) standard life-cycle cost (LCC) approach.[3] These two performance measures are then synthesized into an overall performance measure using the ASTM standard for Multiattribute Decision Analysis.[4] For the entire BEES analysis, building products are defined and classified based on UNIFORMAT II, the ASTM standard classification for building elements.[5]

Measuring Environmental Performance

Environmental life-cycle assessment is a "cradle-to-grave" systems approach for measuring environmental performance. It is based on the belief that all stages in the life of a product generate environmental impacts and must therefore be analyzed. The stages include:

- Raw materials acquisition
- Product manufacture
- Transportation
- Installation
- Operation and maintenance
- Recycling and waste management

An analysis that excludes any of these stages is limited because it ignores the full range of upstream and downstream impacts of stage-specific processes.

The strength of environmental life-cycle assessment is its comprehensive, multi-dimensional scope. Many sustainable building claims and strategies are now based on a single life-cycle stage or a single environmental impact. A product is claimed to be green simply because it has recycled content, or accused of not being green because it emits volatile organic compounds (VOCs) during its installation and use. These single-attribute claims may be misleading because they ignore the possibility that other life-cycle stages, or other environmental impacts, may yield offsetting effects. For example, the recycled content product may have a high embodied energy content, leading to resource depletion, global warming, and acid rain impacts during the raw materials acquisition, manufacturing, and transportation life-cycle stages. LCA thus broadens the environmental discussion by accounting for shifts of environmental problems from one life-cycle stage to another, or one environmental medium (land, air, or water) to another. The benefit of the LCA approach is in implementing a trade-off analysis to achieve a genuine reduction in overall environmental impact, rather than a simple shift of impact.

The general LCA methodology involves four steps. The **goal and scope definition** step spells out the purpose of the study and its breadth and depth. The **inventory analysis** step identifies and quantifies the environmental inputs and outputs associated with a product over its entire life cycle. Environmental inputs include water, energy, land, and other resources; outputs include releases to air, land, and water. However, it is not these inputs and outputs, or *inventory flows*, that are of primary interest. We are more interested in their consequences, or impacts on the environment. Thus, the next LCA step, **impact assessment**, characterizes these inventory flows in relation to a set of environmental impacts. For example, impact assessment might relate carbon dioxide emissions, a *flow*, to global warming, an *impact*. Finally, the **interpretation** step combines the environmental impacts in accordance with the goals of the LCA study.

Goal & Scope Definition

The goal of the BEES LCA is to generate relative environmental performance scores for building product alternatives based on U.S. average data. These scores are combined with relative U.S. average economic scores to help the building community select environmentally and economically balanced building products.

The scoping phase of any LCA involves defining the boundaries of the product system under study. The manufacture of any product involves a number of unit processes (e.g., ethylene production for input to the manufacture of the styrene-butadiene bonding agent for stucco walls). Each unit process involves many inventory flows, some of which themselves involve other, subsidiary unit processes.

The first product system boundary determines which unit processes are included in the LCA. In the BEES approach, the boundary-setting rule consists of a set of three decision criteria. For each candidate unit process, mass and energy contributions to the product system are the primary decision criteria. In some cases, cost contribution is used as a third criterion.[6] Together, these criteria provide a robust screening process.

The second product system boundary determines which inventory flows are tracked for in-bounds unit processes. Quantification of *all* inventory flows is not practical for the following reasons:

- An ever-expanding number of inventory flows can be tracked. For instance, including the U.S. Environmental Protection Agency's Toxic Release Inventory (TRI) data would result in tracking approximately 200 inventory flows arising from polypropylene production alone. Similarly, including radionucleide emissions generated from electricity production would result in tracking more than 150 flows. Managing such large inventory flow lists adds to the complexity, and thus the cost, of carrying out and interpreting the LCA.

- Attention should be given in the inventory analysis step to collecting data that will be useful in the next LCA step, impact assessment. By restricting the inventory data collection to the flows actually needed in the subsequent impact assessment, a more focused, higher quality LCA can be carried out.

Therefore, in the BEES model, a focused, cost-effective set of inventory flows is tracked, reflecting flows that will actually be needed in the subsequent impact assessment step.

Defining the unit of comparison is another important task in the goal and scoping phase of LCA. The basis for all units of comparison is the **functional unit**, defined so that the products compared are true substitutes for one another. In the BEES model, the functional unit for most building products is 0.09 m² (1 S.F.) of product service for 50 years.[7] Therefore, for example, the functional unit for the BEES roof covering alternatives is covering 0.09 m² (1 S.F.) of roof surface for 50 years. The functional unit provides the critical reference point to which all inventory flows are scaled.

Scoping also involves setting data requirements. Data requirements for the BEES study include:

- **Geographic coverage:** The data is U.S. average data.
- **Time period:** The data is a combination of information collected specifically for BEES within the last 8 years, and from the well-known Ecobalance LCA database created in 1990.[8] Most of the Ecobalance data is updated annually. No data older than 1990 is used.
- **Technology:** When possible, the most representative technology is studied. Where data for the most representative technology is not available, an aggregated result is used based on the U.S. average technology for that industry.

Inventory Analysis

Inventory analysis entails quantifying the inventory flows for a product system. Inventory flows include inputs of water, energy, and raw materials, and releases to air, land, and water. Data categories are used to group inventory flows in LCAs. For example, in the BEES model, flows such as aldehydes, ammonia, and sulfur oxides are grouped under the air emissions data category. Figure 12.1 shows the categories under which data is grouped in the BEES system. For each product included in BEES, up to 400 inventory flow items are tracked.

A number of approaches may be used to collect inventory data for LCAs.[9] These range from:

- Unit process- and facility-specific: Data collected from a particular process within a given facility that is not combined in any way.
- Composite: Data collected from the same process combined across locations.
- Aggregated: Data collected combining more than one process.
- Industry-average: Data derived from a representative sample of locations believed to statistically describe the typical process across technologies.
- Generic: Data without known representatives, but that are qualitatively descriptive of a process.

Since the goal of the BEES LCA is to generate U.S. industry-average results, data is collected primarily using the industry-average approach. Data collection is done under contract with Environmental Strategies and Solutions (ESS) and PricewaterhouseCoopers/Ecobalance, using the Ecobalance LCA database, which covers more than 6,000 industrial processes gathered from actual site and literature searches from more

Figure 12.1
BEES Inventory Data Categories

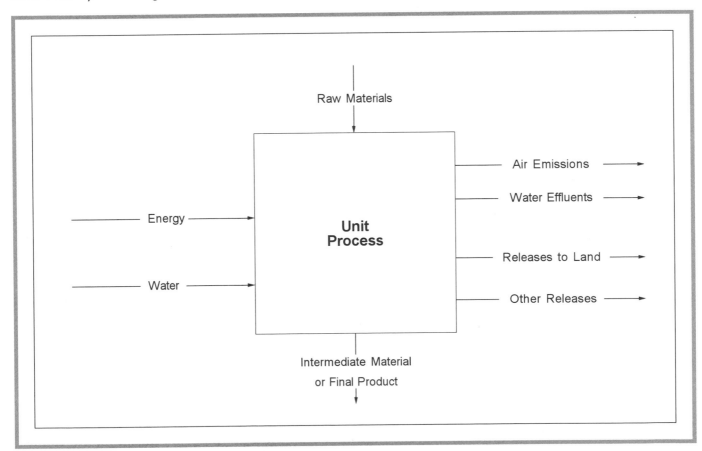

than 15 countries. Where necessary, the data is adjusted to be representative of U.S. operations and conditions. Approximately 90% of the data comes directly from industry sources, with about 10% from generic literature and published reports. The generic data includes inventory flows for electricity production from the average U.S. grid, and for selected raw material mining operations (e.g., limestone, sand, and clay mining operations). In addition, ESS and Ecobalance gathered additional LCA data to fill data gaps for the BEES products. Assumptions regarding the unit processes for each building product are verified through experts in the appropriate industry to assure the data is correctly incorporated in BEES.

Impact Assessment

The impact assessment step of LCA quantifies the potential contribution of a product's inventory flows to a range of environmental impacts. BEES takes a classification/characterization approach to impact assessment, as developed within the Society for Environmental Toxicology and Chemistry (SETAC). It involves a two-step process[10]:

1. **Classification** of inventory flows that contribute to specific environmental impacts. For example, greenhouse gases, such as carbon dioxide, methane, and nitrous oxide, are classified as contributing to global warming.

2. **Characterization** of the potential contribution of each classified inventory flow to the corresponding environmental impact. This results in a set of indices, one for each impact, that is obtained by weighting each classified inventory flow by its relative contribution to the impact. For instance, the Global Warming Potential index is derived by expressing each contributing inventory flow in terms of its equivalent amount of carbon dioxide.

The BEES model uses this classification/characterization approach because it enjoys some general consensus among LCA practitioners and scientists.[11] The following global and regional impacts are assessed using the classification/characterization approach:

- Global warming potential
- Acidification potential
- Eutrophication potential (unwanted addition of mineral nutrients to the soil or water, which can lead to undesirable ecosystem shifts)
- Natural resource depletion
- Indoor air quality
- Solid waste impacts

As part of its Framework for Responsible Environmental Decision-Making project, the EPA confirmed the validity of the six impacts included in BEES 1.0. In addition, the EPA suggested that four additional impacts be pilot-tested in the June 2000 release of BEES 2.0 for a select group of products:

- Smog
- Ecological toxicity
- Human toxicity
- Ozone depletion[12]

Note that the data and science underlying measurement of these four impacts are less certain than for the original six BEES impacts. The classification/characterization method does not offer the same degree of relevance for all environmental impacts. For global and regional effects (e.g., global warming and acidification), the method may result in an accurate description of the potential impact. For impacts dependent on local conditions (e.g., smog, ecological toxicity, and human toxicity), the classification/characterization method may result in an oversimplification of the actual impacts because the indices are not tailored to localities.

Interpretation

At the LCA interpretation step, the impact assessment results are combined. Few products are likely to dominate their competition in all impact categories. One product may outperform the competition in terms of natural resource depletion and solid waste, but may fall short relative to global warming and acidification, and fall somewhere in the middle on the basis of indoor air quality and eutrophication. To compare the overall environmental performance of competing products, the performance measures for all impact categories may be synthesized. *(Note that in BEES, synthesis of impact measures is optional.)*

Synthesizing the impact category performance measures involves combining "apples and oranges." Global warming potential is expressed in carbon dioxide equivalents, acidification in hydrogen equivalents, eutrophication in phosphate equivalents, and so on. How can these diverse measures of impact category performance be combined into a meaningful measure of overall environmental performance? The most appropriate technique is **Multiattribute Decision Analysis (MADA)**. MADA problems are characterized by tradeoffs, as is the case with the BEES impact assessment results. The BEES system follows the ASTM standard for conducting MADA evaluations of building-related investments.[13]

MADA first places all impact categories on the same scale by normalizing them. Within an impact category, each product's performance measure can be normalized by dividing by the highest measure for that category, as in the BEES model. All performance measures are thus translated to the same, dimensionless scale from 0-100, with the worst performing product in each category assigned the highest possible normalized score of 100. Note that the normalization procedure used by BEES results in relative environmental performance scores, meaning they indicate how much better or worse products perform with respect to one another. *Absolute* performance scores are more desirable, as they measure a product in relation to fixed benchmarks of environmental performance and will not fluctuate with changes in the product comparison set. With the impending release of fixed environmental performance benchmarks for the U.S., the next release of BEES will incorporate an absolute scoring system.

MADA then weights each impact category by its relative importance to overall environmental performance. In the BEES software, the set of importance weights is selected by the user. Several derived, alternative weight sets are provided as guidance, and may be used either directly or as a starting point for developing user-defined weights. The alternative weight sets are based on an EPA Science Advisory Board study, a Harvard University study, and a set of equal weights, representing a spectrum of ways in which people value various aspects of the environment.

Measuring Economic vs. Environmental Performance

Measuring the economic performance of building products is more straightforward than measuring environmental performance. Published economic performance data is readily available, and there are well-established ASTM standard methods for conducting economic performance evaluations. First, cost data is collected from the latest edition of the R.S. Means annual publication, *Building Construction Cost Data*, and future cost data is based on the latest data published by Whitestone Research in *The Whitestone Building Maintenance and Repair Cost Reference*, supplemented by industry interviews. The most appropriate method for measuring the economic performance of building products is the life-cycle cost (LCC) method. *(See Chapter 13 for full coverage of LCC.)* BEES follows the ASTM standard method for life-cycle costing of building-related investments.[14]

It is important to distinguish between the time periods used to measure environmental performance and economic performance, which are different. Recall that in environmental LCA, the time period begins with raw material acquisition and ends with product end-of-life. Economic performance, on the other hand, is evaluated over a fixed period (known as the *study period*) that begins with the purchase and installation of the product, and ends at some point in the future that does not necessarily correspond with product end-of-life.

Economic performance is evaluated beginning at product purchase and installation because this is when out-of-pocket costs begin to be incurred, and investment decisions are made based on out-of-pocket costs. The study period ends at a fixed date in the future. For a private investor, its length is set at the period of product or facility ownership. For society as a whole, the study period length is often set at the useful life of the longest-lived product alternative. However, when all alternatives have very long lives (e.g., more than 50 years), a shorter study period may be selected for three reasons:

- Technological obsolescence becomes an issue.
- Data becomes too uncertain.
- The further in the future, the less important the costs.

In the BEES model, economic performance is measured over a 50-year study period, as shown in Figure 12.2. This period is selected to reflect a reasonable period of time over which to evaluate economic performance for society as a whole. The same 50-year period is used to evaluate all products, even if they have different useful lives. This is one

Figure 12.2
BEES Study Periods for Measuring Building Product Environmental and Economic Performance.

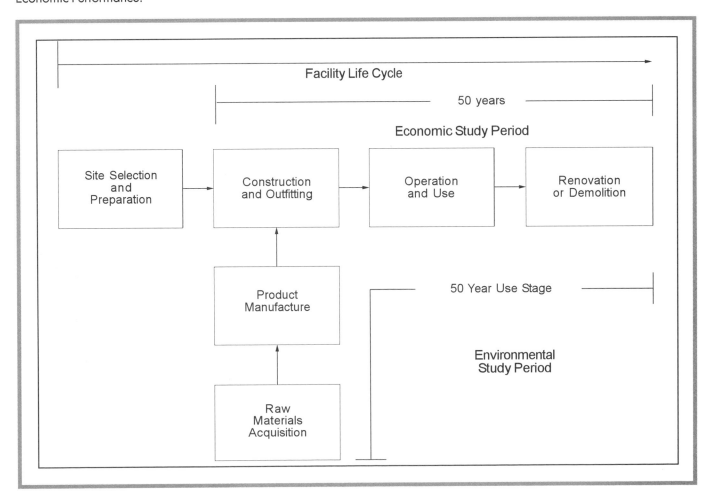

of the strengths of the LCC method. It adjusts for the fact that different products have different useful lives when evaluating them over the same study period.

For consistency, the BEES model evaluates the use stage of environmental performance over the same 50-year study period. Product replacements over this 50-year period are accounted for in the environmental performance score, and end-of-life solid waste is prorated to year 50 for products with partial lives remaining after the 50-year period.

The LCC method totals all relevant costs associated with a product over the study period. Alternative products for the same function, such as floor covering, can then be compared on the basis of their LCCs to determine which is the least costly means of providing that function over the study period. Categories of cost typically include costs for purchase, installation, maintenance, repair, and replacement. A negative cost item is the *residual value*. The residual value is the product value remaining at the end of the study period. In the BEES model, the residual value is computed by prorating the purchase and installation cost over the product life remaining beyond the 50-year period.[15]

The LCC method accounts for the time value of money by using a discount rate to convert all future costs to their equivalent present value. Future costs must be expressed in terms consistent with the discount rate used. There are two approaches. First, a *real* discount rate may be used with constant-dollar costs (e.g., Year 2000). Real discount rates reflect the portion of the time value of money attributable to the real earning power of money over time, and not to general price inflation. Even if all future costs are expressed in constant Year 2000 dollars, they must be discounted to reflect this portion of the time value of money. Second, a *market* discount rate may be used with current-dollar amounts (e.g., actual future prices). Market discount rates reflect the time value of money stemming from both inflation and the real earning power of money over time. When applied properly, both approaches yield the same LCC results. The BEES current version of the model computes LCCs using constant Year 2000 dollars and a real discount rate. As a default, it uses a real rate of 4.2%, the 2000 rate mandated by the U.S. Office of Management and Budget (OMB) for most federal projects.[16]

Overall Performance: Economic & Environmental

The BEES overall performance score combines the environmental and economic results into a single score, as illustrated in Figure 12.3. To combine them, the two results must first be placed on a common basis. The environmental performance score reflects *relative* environmental performance, or how much better or worse products perform with respect to one another. The economic performance score, the LCC, reflects *absolute* performance, regardless of the set of alternatives under analysis. Before combining the two, the life-cycle cost is converted to the same, relative basis as the environmental score by dividing by the highest life-cycle cost alternative. Then the environmental and economic performance scores are combined into an overall score by weighting environmental and economic performance by their relative importance values. Overall scores are thereby placed on a scale from 0-100; if a product performs worst with respect to all environmental impacts *and* has the highest life-cycle cost, it would receive the worst possible overall score of 100. The BEES user specifies the relative importance weights used to combine environmental and economic performance scores and may test the sensitivity of the overall scores to different sets of relative importance weights. Figures 12.4 through 12.6 show three BEES summary graphs illustrating how BEES reports environmental, economic, and overall performance, respectively, based on user-defined importance weights.

Figure 12.3
Deriving the BEES Overall
Performance Score

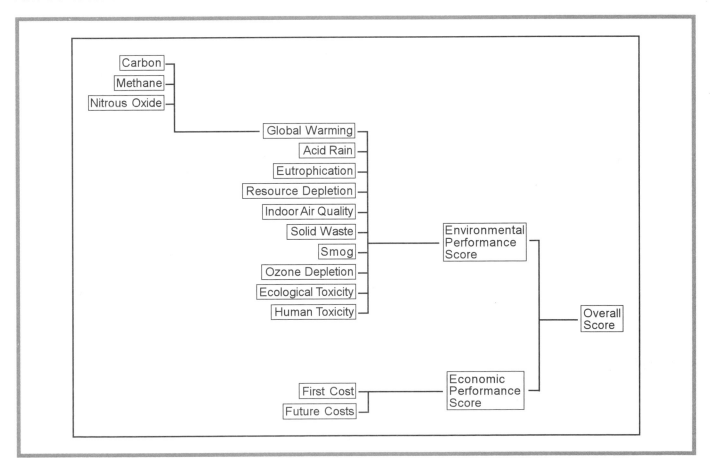

Limitations

Properly interpreting the BEES scores requires placing them in perspective. There are inherent limits to applying U.S. industry-average LCA and LCC results and in comparing building products outside the design context.

The BEES LCA and LCC approaches produce U.S. average performance results for generic product alternatives. The BEES results do not apply to products manufactured in other countries where manufacturing and agricultural practices, fuel mixes, environmental regulations, transportation distances, and labor and material markets may differ.[17] Furthermore, all products in an industry-average, generic product group, such as vinyl composition tile floor covering, are not created equal. Product composition, manufacturing methods, fuel mixes, transportation practices, useful lives, and cost can all vary for individual products in a generic product group. Thus, the BEES results for the generic product group do not necessarily represent the performance of an individual product.

Figure 12.4
Viewing BEES Environmental Performance Results

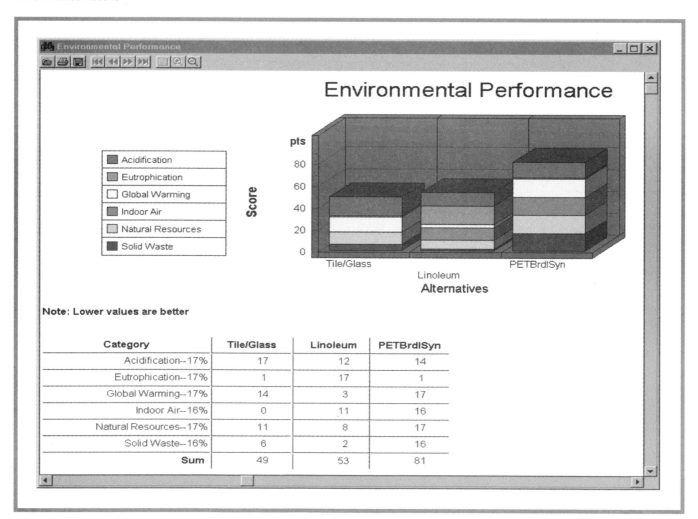

The BEES LCA uses selected inventory flows converted to selected local, regional, and global environmental impacts to assess environmental performance. Those inventory flows that currently do not have scientifically proven or quantifiable impacts on the environment are excluded. Examples are mineral extraction and wood harvesting, which are qualitatively thought to lead to loss of habitat and an accompanying loss of biodiversity, but whose impacts may not have been quantified. Ecological toxicity, human toxicity, ozone depletion, and smog impacts are included in BEES for a select set of products, but the science and data underlying their measurement are less certain. Finally, since BEES develops U.S. average results, some local impacts such as resource scarcity (e.g., water scarcity) are excluded even though the science is proven and quantification is possible. If the BEES user has important knowledge about these or other potential environmental impacts, this information should be brought into the interpretation of the BEES results.

Figure 12.5
Viewing BEES Economic
Performance Results

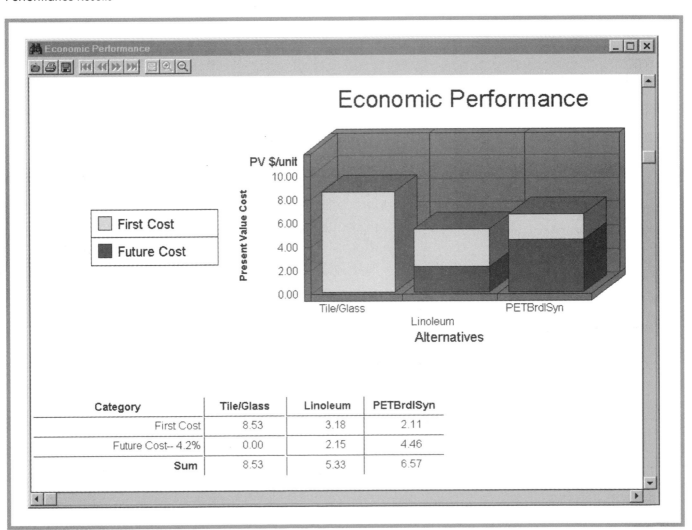

During the interpretation step of the BEES LCA, environmental impacts are optionally combined into a single environmental performance score using relative importance weights. These weights necessarily incorporate values and subjectivity. BEES users should routinely test the effects on the environmental performance scores of changes in the set of importance weights.

The BEES environmental scores do not represent *absolute* environmental damage. Rather, they represent proportional differences in damage, or *relative* damage, among competing alternatives. Consequently, the environmental performance score for a given product alternative can change if one or more competing alternatives are added to or removed from the set of alternatives under consideration. In rare instances, rank reversal, or a reordering of scores, is possible. Finally, since they are relative performance scores, no conclusions may be drawn by comparing scores across building elements. That is, if exterior wall

Figure 12.6
Viewing BEES Overall
Performance Results

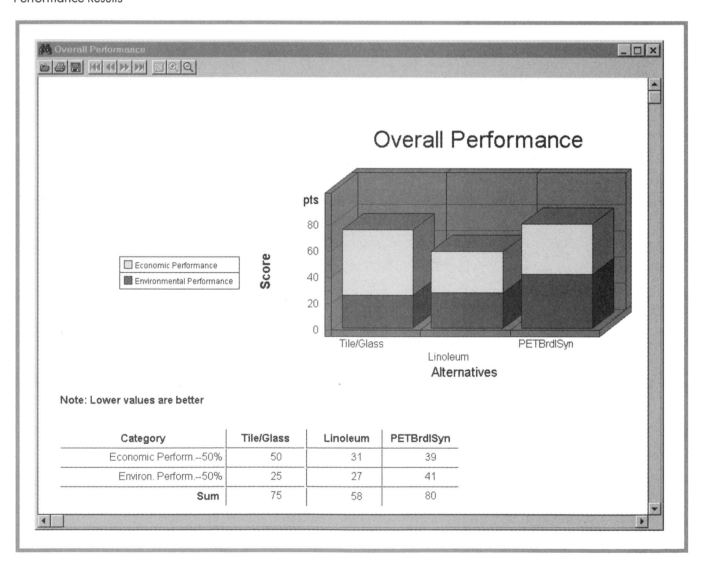

Note: Lower values are better

Category	Tile/Glass	Linoleum	PETBrdlSyn
Economic Perform.--50%	50	31	39
Environ. Perform.--50%	25	27	41
Sum	75	58	80

finish Product A has an environmental performance score of 60, and roof covering Product D has an environmental performance score of 40, Product D does not necessarily perform better than Product A (keeping in mind that lower performance scores are better). The same limitation relative to comparing environmental performance scores across building elements, of course, applies to comparing overall performance scores across elements.

There are inherent limits to comparing product alternatives without reference to the whole building design context. First, this approach may overlook important environmental and cost interactions among building elements. For example, the useful life of one building element (e.g., floor coverings), which influences both its environmental and economic performance scores, may depend on the selection of related building elements (e.g., subflooring). There is no substitute for good building design.

Environmental and economic performance are but two attributes of building product performance. The BEES model assumes that competing product alternatives all meet minimum technical performance requirements.[18] However, there may be significant differences in technical performance, such as acoustical performance, fire performance, or aesthetics, which may outweigh environmental and economic considerations.

Conclusion

Applying the BEES approach leads to several general conclusions. First, environmental claims based on single impacts, such as recycled content alone, should be viewed with skepticism. These claims do not account for the fact that one impact may have been improved at the expense of others. Second, measures must always be quantified on a functional unit basis as they are in BEES, so that the products being compared are true substitutes for one another. One roof covering product may be environmentally superior to another on a pound-for-pound basis, but if that product requires twice the mass as the other to cover one square foot of roof, the results may reverse. Third, a product may contain a negative-impact constituent, but if that constituent is a small portion of an otherwise relatively benign product, its significance decreases dramatically. Finally, a short-lived, low-first-cost product is often not the cost-effective alternative. A higher first cost may be justified many times over for a durable, maintenance-free product. In sum, the answers lie in the trade-offs.

1. BEES is developed by the National Institute of Standards and Technology (NIST) Building and Fire Research Laboratory with support from the U.S. EPA Environmentally Preferable Purchasing Program and the White House-sponsored Partnership for Advancing Technology in Housing (PATH). The current version, BEES 2.0, aimed at designers, builders, and product manufacturers, includes actual environmental and economic performance data for 65 building products spread across 15 building applications. The BEES software and manual may be downloaded free of charge from **www.bfrl.nist.gov/oae/software/bees.html**

2. International Organization for Standardization, *Environmental Management—Life-Cycle Assessment—Principles and Framework*, International Standard 14040, 1997; ISO *Environmental Management—Life-Cycle Assessment—Goal and Scope Definition and Inventory Analysis*, International Standard 14041, 1998; and ISO *Environmental Management—Life-Cycle Assessment—Life Cycle Impact Assessment*, International Standard 14042, 2000.

3. American Society for Testing and Materials, *Standard Practice for Measuring Life-Cycle Costs of Buildings and Building Systems*, ASTM Designation E 917-99, West Conshohocken, PA, 1999.

4. American Society for Testing and Materials, *Standard Practice for Applying the Analytic Hierarchy Process to Multiattribute Decision Analysis of Investments Related to Buildings and Building Systems*, ASTM Designation E 1765-98, West Conshohocken, PA, 1998.

5. American Society for Testing and Materials, *Standard Classification for Building Elements and Related Sitework—UNIFORMAT II*, ASTM Designation E 1557-97, West Conshohocken, PA, September 1997.

6. While a large cost contribution does not directly indicate a significant environmental impact, it may indicate scarce natural resources or numerous subsidiary unit processes potentially involving high energy consumption.

7. All product alternatives are assumed to meet minimum technical performance requirements (e.g., acoustic and fire performance).

8. Ecobalance, Inc., DEAM™ 3.0: Data for Environmental Analysis and Management, Bethesda, MD, 1999.

9. U.S. Environmental Protection Agency, Office of Research and Development, *Life Cycle Assessment: Inventory Guidelines and Principles*, EPA/600/R-92/245, February 1993.

10. SETAC-Europe, *Life Cycle Assessment*, B. DeSmet, et al. (eds.), 1992; SETAC, *A Conceptual Framework for Life Cycle Impact Assessment*, J. Fava, et al. (eds.), 1993; and SETAC, *Guidelines for Life Cycle Assessment: A Code of Practice*, F. Consoli, et al. (eds.), 1993.

[11] SETAC, *Life-Cycle Impact Assessment: The State-of-the-Art*, J. Owens, et al. (eds.), 1997.

[12] U.S. EPA, *Framework for Responsible Environmental Decision Making (FRED): Using Life Cycle Assessment to Evaluate Preferability of Products*, by Science Applications International Corporation, Research Triangle Institute, and EcoSense, Inc., EPA 600/R-00/095, 2000.

[13] American Society for Testing and Materials, *Standard Practice for Applying the Analytic Hierarchy Process to Multiattribute Decision Analysis of Investments Related to Buildings and Building Systems*, ASTM Designation E 1765-98, West Conshohocken, PA, 1998.

[14] American Society for Testing and Materials, *Standard Practice for Measuring Life-Cycle Costs of Buildings and Building Systems*, ASTM Designation E 917-99, West Conshohocken, PA, 1999. Note that the Building Life-Cycle Cost (BLCC) software discussed in the next chapter also follows this ASTM standard method in conducting its life-cycle costing evaluations.

[15] For example, a product with a 40-year life that costs $10 per 0.09 square meters ($10 per square foot) to install would have a residual value of $7.50 in year 50, considering replacement in year 40.

[16] Office of Management and Budget (OMB) Circular A-94, *Guidelines and Discount Rates for Benefit-Cost Analysis of Federal Programs*, Washington, DC, October 27, 1992 and OMB Circular A-94, Appendix C, February 2000.

[17] Since most linoleum manufacturing takes place in Europe, linoleum is modeled based on European manufacturing practices, fuel mixes, and environmental regulations. However, the BEES linoleum results are only applicable to linoleum imported into the United States because transport from Europe to the United States is built into the BEES linoleum data.

[18] Environmental and economic performance results for wall insulation, roof coverings, and concrete beams and columns do consider technical performance differences. For wall insulation and roof coverings, BEES accounts for differential heating and cooling energy use. For concrete beams and columns, BEES accounts for different compressive strengths.

13 Economic Analysis & Green Buildings

Sieglinde K. Fuller, Ph.D.

Building economics, value engineering, and cost engineering are the three main fields that explicitly include an economic evaluation in building-related project analyses. The common theme that ties the three disciplines together is that each is concerned with improving the allocation of resources by implementing only projects that are cost-effective. A number of methods can be used to measure economic efficiency. **Life-Cycle Cost** (LCC) analysis is one of the most straightforward and easily understandable methods of evaluation; it is used in all three of these fields. Certified value specialists and cost engineers also often present their economic analysis results in terms of **Payback Period** (PB) or **Internal Rate of Return** (IRR). Building economists usually also include measures of **Net Savings** (NS) and **Savings-to-Investment Ratio** (SIR) to cover all aspects of an economic analysis. Except for payback, all of these supplementary measures are consistent with the life-cycle costing principle of assessing the long-term costs of ownership. The payback measure usually ignores costs and benefits that are incurred after payback of initial costs is achieved.

LCC analysis has been widely recognized as a valuable tool for evaluating the economic performance of energy and water conservation and renewable energy projects undertaken by federal, state, and local governments and the private sector. The method applies to any project, public or private, where future operational cost savings are traded off against higher initial capital investment costs. This is usually the case also for green building components, which may cost more initially, but save money and have a positive impact on the environment in the long run by reducing energy use, resource depletion, and waste.

The LCC method described in this chapter is fully consistent with the *Standards on Building Economics* published by the American Society for Testing and Materials (ASTM).[1] These same standards are followed in the BLCC5[2] (Building Life-Cycle Cost Program) for evaluating energy and water conservation and renewable energy projects, and in BEES[3] (Building for Environmental and Economic Sustainability), a life-cycle assessment tool for evaluating the environmental and economic impact of building materials.

This chapter presents an overview of the principles and method of life-cycle costing. A reference section at the end of the book lists LCC publications, software, and workshop information for readers who wish to pursue the topic further.

Economic Efficiency

Figures 13.1a through 13.1c show three complementary concepts of economic efficiency.

Figure 13.1a displays total owning and operating costs associated with a range of energy efficiency levels. As the level increases, investment costs rise at an increasing rate. The cost of energy consumption is reduced, but at a decreasing rate. The total cost curve is the vertical

Figure 13.1a

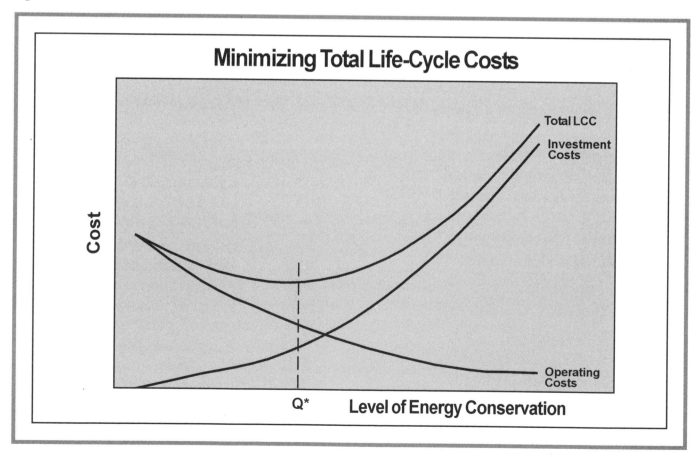

Minimizing Total Life-Cycle Costs

summation of the investment cost and operating costs associated with any level of energy efficiency. The lowest point on the total LCC cost curve, Q*, is the level of energy efficiency that minimizes life-cycle costs.

Figure 13.1b shows that the most cost-effective level of energy consumption can also be determined by maximizing net savings. The investment cost curve is the same as in Figure 13.1a. The savings curve is the difference between the operating cost at the zero level of investment and the operating cost at any other level of investment. The economically optimal level of energy efficiency is the level for which net savings are greatest, the level at which the curves are most distant, again at Q*.

The two curves in Figure 13.1c show that each additional unit of energy efficiency results in smaller and smaller increments in savings, and greater and greater additions to cost. The point at which the last increment in cost increases savings by the same amount is the economically optimal level, Q*.

In all three cases, it pays to increase investment if the level of energy efficiency is to the left of Q*. To the right of Q*, reducing investment lowers life-cycle costs and increases net savings. Economists refer to the

Figure 13.1b

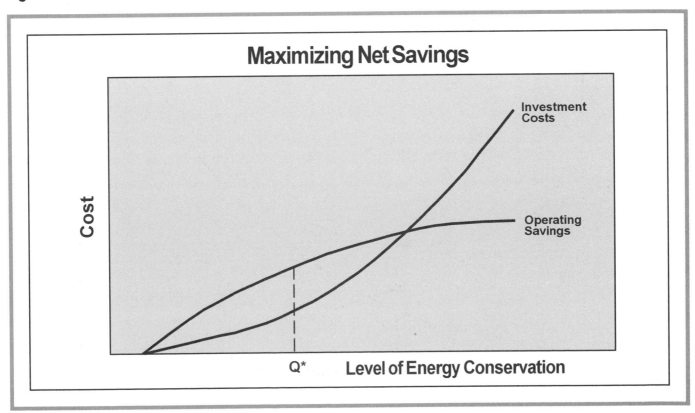

level of investment, Q*, where LCC is minimized, NS is maximized, and incremental investment is equal to incremental savings, as the "economically efficient level" of investment for a given project.

Discounting

Because of inflation and the real earning power of money, a dollar paid or received today is not valued the same as a dollar paid or received at some future date. For this reason, costs and savings occurring over time must be "discounted." **Discounting** adjusts cash flows to a common time, often the present, when an analysis is performed, or a decision has to be made. The conversion of all costs and savings to time-equivalent "present values" allows them to be added and compared in a meaningful way.

To make future costs and savings time-equivalent, they must be adjusted for both inflation and the real earning power of money. One approach is to first eliminate the effects of inflation from the estimated dollar amounts and state them in "constant dollars." The discount rate used to calculate present values needs to be a "real" discount rate, excluding

Figure 13.1c

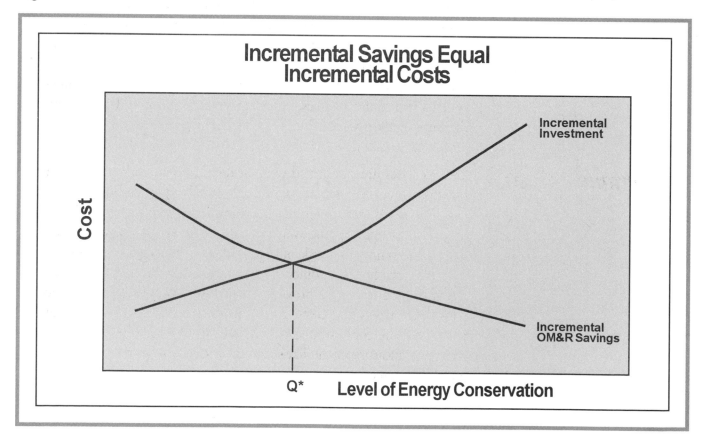

inflation; it adjusts only for the real earning power of money. A different approach, recommended when taxes are included in the analysis or when budget allocation is an issue, is the "current-dollar approach," where the rate of inflation is included in the dollar amounts, and the discount rate is a "nominal" rate that also includes inflation. Both approaches, if applied correctly and consistently to all cash flows in the analysis, yield the same present-value results.

Discount Rate

The discount rate used to adjust future costs and savings to present value is the rate of interest that makes the investor indifferent between cash amounts received or paid now or in the future. Most people would prefer receiving $100 today rather than later. There is an "opportunity cost" associated with deferring receipt of funds in that you give up the interim use of, or earnings on, the funds. By determining the future amount that makes you just willing to forego a present amount, it is possible to calculate your **Minimum Acceptable Rate of Return** (MARR) or the opportunity cost of money. The greater your earning opportunities from alternative investments, the higher your MARR will be. Individuals, firms, and institutions set the discount rate to reflect their MARR.

Study Period

The study period is the time over which the effects of a decision are of interest to a decision-maker. There is no one correct study period, but it must be long enough to enable a correct assessment of long-run economic performance. Often, the life of a building or system under analysis determines the length of the study period. Replacement costs and residual values are used to equalize the study period for buildings or systems with different lives. All alternatives have to be evaluated over the same study period.

Uncertainty & Risk

LCC analyses are performed early in the decision-making process, and the input data used is therefore inherently subject to uncertainty and risk. The results are presented deterministically, implying a level of accuracy that may not be warranted. Some simple techniques exist for taking uncertainty and risk into account. Sensitivity analysis, for example, tests how outcomes differ as the uncertain input values are changed. This technique provides a range of outcomes and break-even values for savings and costs. If probabilities can be attached to input values, a more sophisticated risk analysis can be performed that includes a measure of the likelihood of a deviation from the "best-guess" outcome.[4]

Measures of Economic Evaluation

Life-Cycle Cost

LCC analysis takes into account all costs of acquiring, operating, maintaining, and disposing of a building or building system. The LCC concept requires that all costs and savings be evaluated over a common study period and discounted to present value before they can be meaningfully compared. Figure 13.2 is a diagram of this process.

From a decision standpoint, the LCC of a design alternative has meaning only when it is compared to the LCC of a base case fulfilling the same basic performance requirements. *(See Figure 13.3.)* The basic criterion for determining whether a design alternative that increases capital investment and lowers future operating costs is cost-effective is that the savings generated by the investment must be greater than the additional investment cost. This will ensure that the total life-cycle cost

Figure 13.2
Life-Cycle Costing
at a Glance

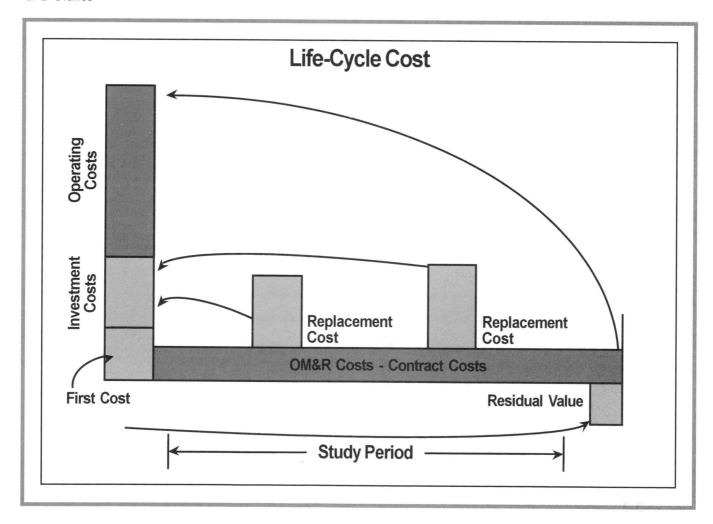

of the energy-saving or green alternative is lower than that of the base case. If several alternatives are being considered, the most cost-effective alternative is the one with the lowest life-cycle cost.

Supplementary Measures of Economic Evaluation

Lowest LCC is a measure of economic efficiency that is relatively easy to calculate and interpret. It is the method prescribed by the Federal Energy Management Program (FEMP) of the U.S. Department of Energy (DOE) and other government agencies to evaluate energy and water conservation projects. To supplement LCC, additional measures of economic performance can be used to determine the comparative cost-effectiveness of capital investments. Several widely used measures are Net Savings (NS), Savings-to-Investment Ratio (SIR), Internal Rate of Return (IRR), and Payback Period (PB). These measures are meaningful only in relation to a base case and are consistent with the LCC methodology if they use the same study period, discount rate, and escalation rates.

Net Savings

Net Savings (NS) is a measure of long-run profitability of an alternative relative to a base case. The NS can be calculated as an extension of the LCC method as the difference between the LCC of a base case and the LCC of an alternative. It can also be calculated directly from differences

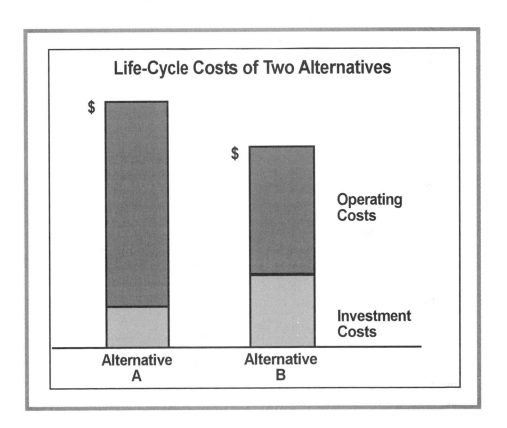

Figure 13.3

in the individual cash flows between a base case and an alternative. For a project alternative to be cost-effective with respect to the base case, it must have an NS greater than zero. Even with a zero NS, the minimum required rate of return has been achieved because it is accounted for in the NS computation through the discount rate.

Savings-to-Investment Ratio

The **Savings-to-Investment Ratio** (SIR) is a dimensionless measure of performance that expresses the ratio of savings to costs. The numerator of the ratio contains the operation-related savings; the denominator contains the increase in investment-related costs. An SIR greater than 1.0 means that an alternative is cost-effective relative to a base case. The SIR is recommended for setting priorities among projects when the budget is insufficient to fund all cost-effective projects. The projects are ranked in descending order of their SIRs.

Internal Rate of Return

Internal Rate of Return (IRR) measures solve for the interest rate that will equate the stream of costs and savings. The calculated interest rate is compared against a specified minimum acceptable rate of return, usually equal to the discount rate. The calculation of the traditional IRR assumes that any proceeds from the project can be reinvested at the calculated rate of return over the study period. A widely used version of the IRR is the Adjusted IRR (AIRR) or Overall IRR (OIRR); it uses the discount rate rather than the calculated rate of return as the reinvestment rate. The AIRR is used in the same way as the SIR.

Payback Period

The **Payback Period** (PB) measures the length of time until accumulated savings are sufficient to pay back the cost. **Discounted Payback** (DPB) takes into account the time value of money by using time-adjusted cash flows. If the discount rate is assumed to be zero, that is, if the opportunity cost of money is not taken into account, the method is called **Simple Payback** (SPB). Since both the DPB and the SPB ignore all costs and savings that occur after payback has been achieved, they are not entirely consistent with the LCC measure. They should be used only as a screening measure, followed up with a full LCC analysis.

Basic Steps in LCC Analysis

The basic steps in an LCC analysis are:
- Identify feasible alternatives.
- Establish assumptions and parameters.
- Specify costs and estimate in dollars.
- Discount costs to present values.
- Compute LCC for each alternative.

- Select the alternative with the lowest life-cycle cost.

Depending on the circumstances, one may also want to calculate supplementary measures of economic performance, perform an uncertainty assessment, and add a narrative describing non-monetary costs and savings.

Identify Feasible Alternatives

Only energy-saving or green alternatives that are technically sound and practical may be included in the set of candidates to be evaluated. This presumes that they satisfy the technical performance requirements set out in the project description, and that there are no physical or other constraints that would eliminate an alternative for reasons other than economics.

Establish Assumptions & Parameters

The assumptions and parameters that apply to all inputs should be clarified and documented at the outset. They include:

- Length of study period
- Base date
- Length of planning/construction period
- Service date
- Treatment of inflation
- Operational assumptions for building or building system
- Energy and water price schedules

Specify Costs & Estimate in Dollars

Relevant Effects

The most challenging part of an LCC analysis is determining the economic effects of a design change to a building or building system and estimating the associated costs. Only costs that are relevant to the decision and significant in amount need to be included. Because LCC analysis is performed early in the design process, engineers and analysts rely on estimating guides and databases for initial and operating cost estimates. Careful engineering judgment must be applied when determining the relevant effects of energy conservation and other green building features, and when estimating their costs.

Types of Costs

The cost components typical for building-related LCC analyses are:

- Initial investment costs
- Capital replacement costs
- Residual values, such as resale or salvage values or disposal costs

- Operating, maintenance, and repair costs
- Energy costs
- Water costs
- Taxes
- Non-monetary costs

All costs included in the analysis are expressed in base-year dollars. These base-year amounts will be multiplied by discount factors that incorporate the discount rate and any applicable escalation rate.

Cost Categories

The method used to classify the cost components of an LCC analysis will depend on what role they play in the mechanics of the methodology. The most important categories distinguish between investment-related and operational costs, annually recurring and non-annually recurring costs, and initial and future costs.

Investment-Related Costs & Operational Costs For the purpose of entering data for an LCC analysis, costs are usually divided into investment-related costs and operational costs. Acquisition costs, including costs for planning, design, and construction, are investment-related, as are residual values, such as resale value, salvage value, or disposal costs. Under the FEMP rule, capital replacement costs are also defined as investment-related. Energy and water costs, maintenance costs, and repair costs are considered operational. This distinction is useful when computing economic measures that evaluate long-run savings in operational costs in relation to the capital investment costs needed to implement the project.

Annually Recurring & Non-Annually Recurring Costs Some of the costs included in an LCC analysis are recurring, such as energy, routine maintenance, and repair. They are lumped together into annual amounts for the purpose of discounting. Non-annually recurring costs are those that may occur only one time during the life cycle, such as acquisition costs and residual values, or several times, such as replacement or major repair costs. This categorization is needed for choosing the appropriate pre-calculated discount factors used to convert future costs to present values.

Initial & Future Costs In a third classification, acquisition costs are designated as initial costs, and all other costs as future costs, a useful classification both for selecting discount factors and for relating a project's initial investment costs to its future operational costs.

Taxes In the case of private-sector projects, taxes may have an impact on the economic viability of projects in two ways:

- As a mechanism for providing direct financial subsidies.
- Through regular tax laws, such as property tax laws, sales taxes, and income tax laws.

In the case of conservation or green projects for federal, state or local governments, taxes can be disregarded in an LCC analysis.

Non-Monetary Costs & Benefits Non-monetary costs and benefits are project-related effects for which there may not be an objective way to assign a dollar value. Examples of non-monetary costs might include the loss of productivity due to noisy HVAC equipment or insufficient lighting. Examples of non-monetary benefits might include good employee morale because of a beautiful view, an indoor garden, or good public relations due to owning a green building. Even though these non-monetary costs and benefits cannot directly be included in the LCC calculations, they should be documented in narrative form and taken into consideration in the decision-making.

Discount Costs to Present Values

The basic equation for discounting dollar amounts to present values is

$$PV = F_t/(1+d)^t$$

where F_t = cost or savings in future year t, and d = a discount rate.

If a cost of $5,000 is to be incurred in 5 years, an amount of $3,918 will have to be included in the analysis as a present value if the (real) discount rate is 5%. The interest rate at which an investor feels adequately compensated for trading money now for money in the future is the appropriate rate to use as a discount rate.

Multiplicative discount factors for various types of discounting operations are available from look-up tables in cost engineering, economics, and finance textbooks and are usually included in LCC computer programs.

When performing an LCC analysis, three types of future cash flows are most commonly encountered, each requiring a different type of present-value factor:

1. A one-time amount is multiplied by the **Single Present Value** (SPV) factor to compute its present value. An example of a one-time amount is a replacement cost or a salvage value.

    Example: Find the present value of a replacement cost (C_0) of $5,000 (constant base-year dollars) occurring 8 years from the base date, using a real discount rate of 3.2%.

    $$PV = C_0 \times SPV_8$$
    $$PV = \$5,000 \times 0.777 = \$3,885$$

2. An annual amount as of the base-year is multiplied by the **Uniform Present Value** (UPV) factor to find the present value of a stream of costs over the study period. An example is an operating and maintenance cost that remains the same (apart from inflation) from year to year. Recurring costs are treated as annual amounts discounted to the base date from the year of their occurrence.

   Example: Find the present value of a series of maintenance costs (A_0) of $3,500 recurring annually over a time period of 15 years using a real discount rate of 3.2%.

   $$PV = A_0 \times UPV_{15}$$
   $$PV = \$3,500 \times 11.77 = \$41,195$$

3. An annual amount (A_0) that varies from year to year at some known rate is multiplied by the **Modified Uniform Present Value** (UPV*) factor. The rate of change can be either constant or variable from year to year. An amount changing at a constant rate may be an operating cost that increases annually due to expected higher maintenance costs. An example of an amount that changes at a variable rate each year is the energy cost of a building. The FEMP UPV*, for example, includes varying energy price projections published annually by DOE's Energy Information Administration (EIA) by U.S. region, energy type, and rate type.

   Example: Find the present value of an annual electricity cost of $12,000 for a project located in Maryland and priced at a commercial rate. The study period is 25 years.

   $$PV = A_0 \times UPV^*_{25} \text{ (FEMP 2002)}$$
   $$PV = \$12,000 \times 16.66 = \$199,920$$

Figure 13.4 is a summary of present-value factors.

Compute LCC for Each Alternative
LCC Formulas
The general formula for the LCC present-value model is

$$LCC = \sum_{t=0}^{N} \frac{C_t}{(1+d)^t}$$

where:

- **LCC** = Total LCC in present value dollars of a given alternative
- C_t = Sum of all relevant costs, including initial and future costs, less any positive cash flows occurring in time t
- **N** = Number of periods in the study period
- **d** = Discount rate used to adjust cash flows to present value

A simplified formula for building-related projects can be stated as follows:

$$LCC = I + Repl - Res + E + W + OM\&R$$

where

I = Investment costs

$Repl$ = Capital replacement costs

Res = Residual value (resale, salvage value) less disposal costs

E = Energy costs

W = Water costs

$OM\&R$ = Non-fuel operating, maintenance, and repair costs

and where all amounts are in present values.

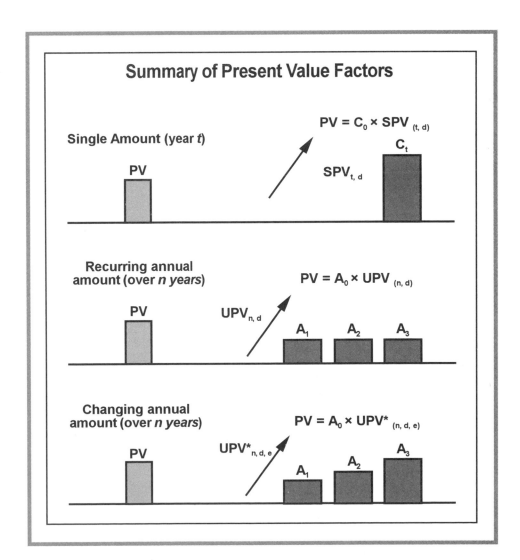

Figure 13.4
Summary of Present Value Factors

LCC Example

The following example applies the LCC method to the comparison of a conventional HVAC system base case with an energy-saving alternative. The system with the lower LCC will be accepted as the cost-effective system. The HVAC system is to be installed in a federal office building in Washington, D.C. The parameters and assumptions common to both the base case and the alternative are as follows:

Location: Washington, D.C.

Discount rate: Current FEMP discount rate: 3.2% real for constant-dollar analysis

Energy prices: Fuel type: Electricity at $0.08/kWh, local rate as of base date

Rate type: Commercial, FEMP UPV* factor, Region 3

Cash-flow convention: End-of-year occurrence for annually recurring amounts

Useful lives of systems: 20 years

Study period: 20 years

Base date: May 2002

The data summary and LCC calculation for conventional HVAC design, the base case, is as follows.

Cost Items (1)	Base Date Cost (2)	Year of Occurrence (3)	Discount Factor* (4)	Present Value (5)=(2)x(4)
Initial investment cost	$103,000	Base date	Already in PV	$103,000
Capital replacement (fan)	12,000	12	$SPV_{12}=0.685$	8,220
Residual value (salvage)	(3,500)	20	$SPV_{20}=0.533$	(1,865)
Electricity:				
250,000 kWh at $0.08	20,000	Annual	$FEMP\,UPV*_{20}=14.22$	284,400
OM&R	7,000	Annual	$UPV_{20}=14.61$	102,270
Total LCC				$496,025

In this example, the LCC of $496,025 for the conventional design serves as a baseline against which the LCC of the energy-saving alternative system will be compared.

The data summary and LCC calculation for energy-saving HVAC design, the alternative, is as follows.

Cost Items (1)	Base Date Cost (2)	Year of Occurrence (3)	Discount Factor* (4)	Present Value (5)=(2)x(4)
Initial investment cost	$110,000	Base date	Already in PV	$110,000
Capital replacement	12,500	12	$SPV_{12} = 0.685$	8,562
Residual value (salvage)	(3,700)	20	$SPV_{20} = 0.533$	(1,972)
Electricity:				
162,500 kWh at $0.08	13,000	Annual	FEMP $UPV*_{20} = 14.22$	184,860
OM&R	8,000	Annual	$UPV_{20} = 14.61$	116,880
Total LCC				$418,330

*The discount factors are calculated with a 3.2% real discount rate and, where appropriate, the DOE energy price escalation rates, as published in *Energy Price Indices and Discount Factors – April 2002, Annual Supplement to Handbook 135.*

Select Alternative With the Lowest Life-Cycle Cost
LCC Criterion

The LCC criterion for choosing one design over another is the lowest life-cycle cost. If one assumes that the input values are reasonably certain, and there are no non-monetary costs or benefits that need to be taken into account, one would select the energy-saving HVAC system for installation. If some of the input values are uncertain, sensitivity analysis can be used to calculate a range of possible LCCs.

Selection Criteria for Supplementary Measures

Since the Net Savings measure is simply the difference in present-value LCCs between a base case and an alternative, it can easily be calculated by subtracting the LCC of the alternative from the LCC of the base case. Thus the Net Savings for the alternative are:

$$NS_{Alt} = \$496,025 - \$418,330$$
$$NS_{Alt} = \$77,695$$

This means that the energy-saving design saves $77,695 in present-value dollars over the 20-year study period, over and above the 3.2% minimum acceptable real rate of return. If the LCC of an alternative is lower than the LCC of the relevant base case, it will have positive Net Savings, a Savings-to-Investment Ratio greater than one, an Internal Rate of Return greater than the discount rate, and a Payback Period shorter than the study period. An SIR of 11.77, an AIRR of 16.74%, and a PB period of two years have been computer-calculated for this example, as shown in the BLCC5 FEMP analysis in Figure 13.5.

Computer-Supported LCC Analysis

Various computer programs are available that greatly facilitate LCC analysis. NIST, under sponsorship of DOE/FEMP, developed the Building Life-Cycle Cost Program BLCC5. The program follows the LCC principles reviewed in this chapter and contains federal criteria established by legislation and recommended in Executive Order 13123 for "Greening the Government through Efficient Energy Management." Agency-specific discount rates, inflation rates, discounting conventions, and energy price escalation rates are built in as defaults for analyzing FEMP and MILCON (military construction) projects, funded either through appropriations or financed through private-sector energy savings performance contracts (ESPC) or utility energy services contracts (UESC). Since most of the default values in BLCC5 can be edited, the program can also be used by private-sector LCC practitioners. Specific private-sector modules that include tax and financial analyses will be added to BLCC5 in the future.

Figures 13.5 and 13.6 indicate how the LCC analysis may be approached in BLCC5.

The 2002 version of BLCC5 is BLCC5.1-02. It contains the following four modules with agency-specific defaults, which may be edited if not applicable to a particular project.

1. FEMP Analyses, for Energy Projects evaluated according to 10 CFR 436A.

2. Federal Analysis, for Financed Projects (ESPC, UESC as recommended in Executive Order 13123).

3. MILCON Analyses, for Energy Projects following the FEMP rules.

4. MILCON Analyses, for Department of Defense projects under the Energy Conservation Investment Program (ECIP).

The BLCC5 program calculates life-cycle costs, net savings, savings-to-investment ratio, internal rate of return, and payback period. The program's hierarchical data input structure serves as a guideline for data entry. Built-in defaults are provided for agency-specific discount rate, inflation rate, discounting convention, and inflation adjustment. DOE energy price forecasts are incorporated by region, along with fuel type and rate type. The program calculates region- and end-use-specific emissions reductions, and provides detailed reporting capability that can be used for project documentation.

Conclusion

Anybody concerned with the economic efficiency of buildings will recognize that making decisions on the basis of first cost only, or even on the basis of simple payback as it is generally used, does not optimize the allocation of the resources available for improving our built environment. Initial construction costs *and* future operational and repair costs determine the value of a building. The overview presented in this chapter introduces the concepts and techniques of life-cycle costing, a method of economic evaluation especially well suited to weigh future

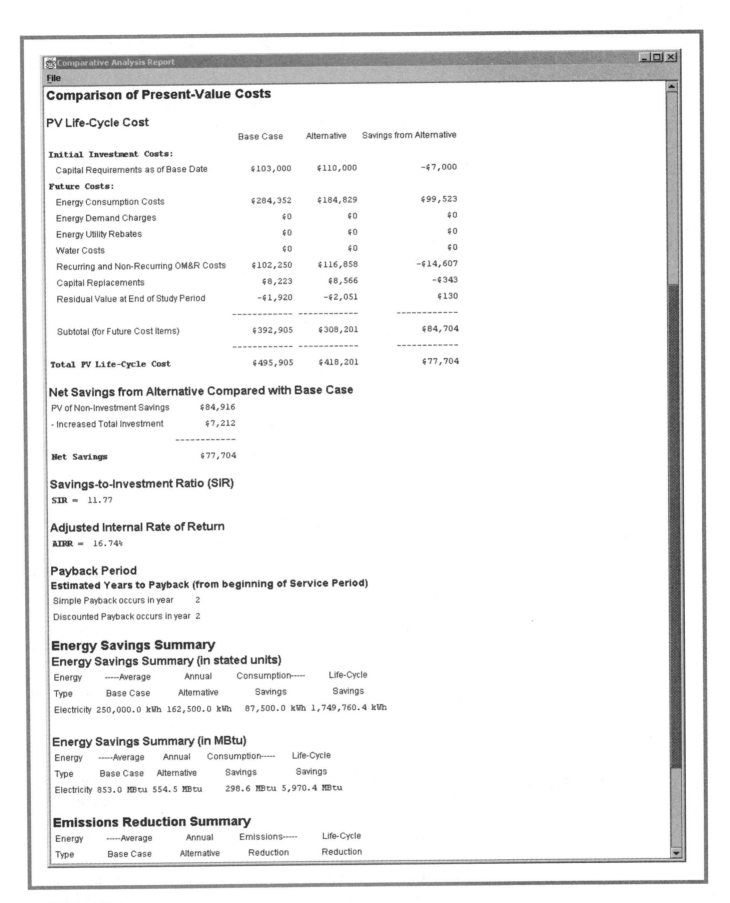

Comparison of Present-Value Costs

PV Life-Cycle Cost

	Base Case	Alternative	Savings from Alternative
Initial Investment Costs:			
Capital Requirements as of Base Date	$103,000	$110,000	-$7,000
Future Costs:			
Energy Consumption Costs	$284,352	$184,829	$99,523
Energy Demand Charges	$0	$0	$0
Energy Utility Rebates	$0	$0	$0
Water Costs	$0	$0	$0
Recurring and Non-Recurring OM&R Costs	$102,250	$116,858	-$14,607
Capital Replacements	$8,223	$8,566	-$343
Residual Value at End of Study Period	-$1,920	-$2,051	$130
	------------	------------	------------
Subtotal (for Future Cost Items)	$392,905	$308,201	$84,704
	------------	------------	------------
Total PV Life-Cycle Cost	$495,905	$418,201	$77,704

Net Savings from Alternative Compared with Base Case

PV of Non-Investment Savings	$84,916
- Increased Total Investment	$7,212

Net Savings	$77,704

Savings-to-Investment Ratio (SIR)

SIR = 11.77

Adjusted Internal Rate of Return

AIRR = 16.74%

Payback Period

Estimated Years to Payback (from beginning of Service Period)

Simple Payback occurs in year   2

Discounted Payback occurs in year 2

Energy Savings Summary

Energy Savings Summary (in stated units)

Energy Type	-----Average Base Case	Annual Alternative	Consumption----- Savings	Life-Cycle Savings
Electricity	250,000.0 kWh	162,500.0 kWh	87,500.0 kWh	1,749,760.4 kWh

Energy Savings Summary (in MBtu)

Energy Type	-----Average Base Case	Annual Alternative	Consumption----- Savings	Life-Cycle Savings
Electricity	853.0 MBtu	554.5 MBtu	298.6 MBtu	5,970.4 MBtu

Emissions Reduction Summary

Energy Type	-----Average Base Case	Annual Alternative	Emissions----- Reduction	Life-Cycle Reduction

Figure 13.5

FEMP Analysis on an Energy Project

cost reductions and benefits of green building features against higher initial investment costs. Supporting computer programs facilitate the application of an approach that is systematic, as well as practical, problem-solving. In combination with well-researched estimates of cost data, life-cycle costing leads to financially responsible decision making.

Figure 13.6

Energy Cost Screen in BLCC5 – HVAC selection

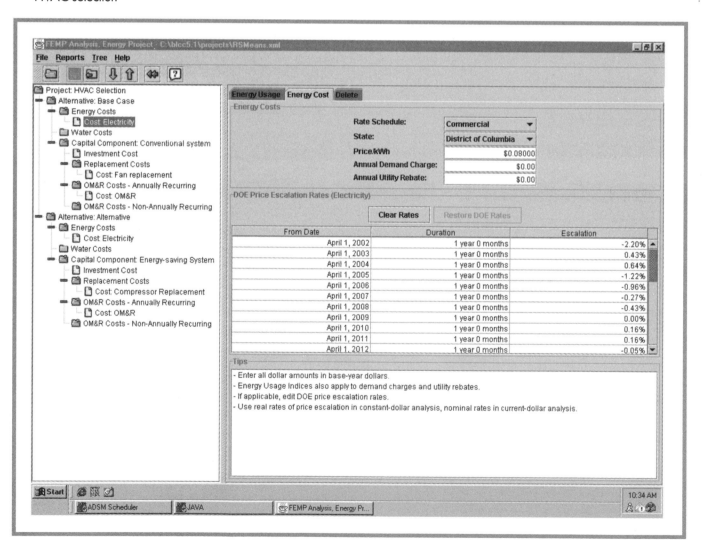

Green Building: Project Planning & Cost Estimating

1 *Standards on Building Economics, Fourth Edition*, 1999, American Society for Testing and Materials, 100 Barr Harbor Drive, West Conshohocken, PA 19428.

2 *Building Life-Cycle Cost Program*, BLCC5.1-02, 2002, National Institute of Standards and Technology, Gaithersburg, MD. 20899, updated annually on April 1.

3 *Building for Environmental and Economic Sustainability*, BEES2.0, 2000, National Institute of Standards and Technology, Gaithersburg, MD 20899.

4 See *Techniques for Treating Uncertainty and Risk in the Economic Evaluation of Building Investments*, 1995, National Institute of Standards and Technology Special Publication 757, Gaithersburg, MD 20899, for an in-depth description of how to account for uncertainty and risk in life-cycle cost analyses.

5 The discount factors used in the examples are from *Price Indices and Discount Factors for the Federal Energy Management Program*, April 2002. The factors are calculated with the 2002 FEMP discount rate of 3.2 percent (real) and the latest DOE energy price escalation rates.

Chapter

14 Compliance, Energy Modeling, & Decision-Making Tools

Joseph Macaluso, CCC / M. Magda Lelek, PE, CEM

One of the hallmarks of green building is the extra thought that needs to be given early on and throughout the design process. It means thinking beyond current codes and standards, traditional building design and construction procedures, and rules of thumb. Sustainable buildings, systems, and components must be analyzed and evaluated in greater detail and on more levels than most traditional buildings. Fortunately, many software tools are available that can assist the project team. These programs are available from government sources, environmental groups, and third-party software developers. Many of these programs can be obtained at no charge or a reasonable cost. Even product manufacturers are increasingly supplying software to assist architects, engineers, estimators, facility owners, managers, and other team members in evaluating energy efficiency and other environmental aspects of their products.

Cost analysis is an especially significant factor in green building design and construction, and costs are an important component in the software. The typically higher costs of many green approaches are weighed against future savings. Green buildings tend to have many departures from conventional designs, and this higher number of variables increases the chances of a large impact on the project budget. Green building features also tend to be more difficult to estimate because they are new to the marketplace, and there is little historical cost data available. In some cases, there are only a few manufacturers or suppliers of a particular green product.

Finally, because financing of green features is often tied to environmental impacts, energy savings, indoor air quality, and other attributes, cost issues are intertwined with architectural, engineering, and environmental issues. Most of the software that is being developed reflects the holistic approach of the green design philosophy. This chapter will review some of the more popular tools currently available to help with analysis, selection, and estimating of appropriate green building products and materials. Additional software can be found at the Energy Efficiency & Renewable Network Web site of the Department of Energy (DOE): **www.eere.energy.gov/buildings/ tools_directory**

Whole Building Simulation Software

DOE-2

DOE-2 software is designed to predict hourly energy use and energy cost of a building, given hourly weather data, a description of the building and its HVAC equipment, and the utility rates structure. It is widely recognized as the industry standard. DOE-2 is available with a range of user interfaces.

This software is used for building load analysis, and can be used for analysis of new design and existing buildings, residential and commercial facilities. It can calculate hourly, daily, weekly, monthly, seasonal, and annual load profiles, as well as peak loads and design loads for individual zones, systems, or the entire building. Daily, monthly, seasonal, and annual building energy consumption estimates can be calculated for individual building components or for the entire building.

The DOE programs are useful for comparing alternative building designs, systems, or components, including individual design features such as building geometry, location/orientation, construction materials, HVAC systems and controls, utility selection, and other design options.

DOE-2 can be used for LEED building analysis for the energy efficiency-related credits. It is also used for *Energy Code* compliance analysis, life cycle cost analysis (overall or individual building components), and pollution production/reduction analysis.

DOE-2 was first developed by the Simulation Research Group at Lawrence Berkeley Laboratory (LBL) in the 1970s. With major funding provided by the U.S. Department of Energy, numerous revisions were issued, most recently DOE-2.1E. Some of the commercial versions of DOE-2 include ADM-DOE-2, Compare-IT, DOE-PLUS, EnergyPro, EZDOE, FT1/DOE-2, PRC-DOE-2, and Visual DOE-3.0. Other commercial software derived from DOE-2 include DOE-2.2 and PowerDOE®. Released in the late 1990s, DOE-2.2 is a machine-independent batch execution. PowerDOE® is a Windows-based, interactive execution. Both tools share a common "simulation engine" core. Two types of reports are generated: standard and hourly.

Input for a building model can be grouped into three sections: loads, systems, and economics.

Loads:

- Building envelope: building location/orientation, building geometry, walls/roofs/floors, construction materials, and windows (shading-external, self-shading).
- Internal loads: occupants, plug loads, lights, other.
- Schedules: internal loads, shading devices, other.

Systems:

- HVAC

Figure 14.1
The DOE-2 computer program simulates building energy use for all 8,760 hours of a typical year and presents a summary of energy use and cost. User-friendly interfaces have been developed by private firms to display a graphical representation of the building and of the results of the analysis. This image of a new building to be built in Washington D.C. excludes the intermediate floors which are all identical. (Graphic courtesy of Sue Reilly, using EQuest.)

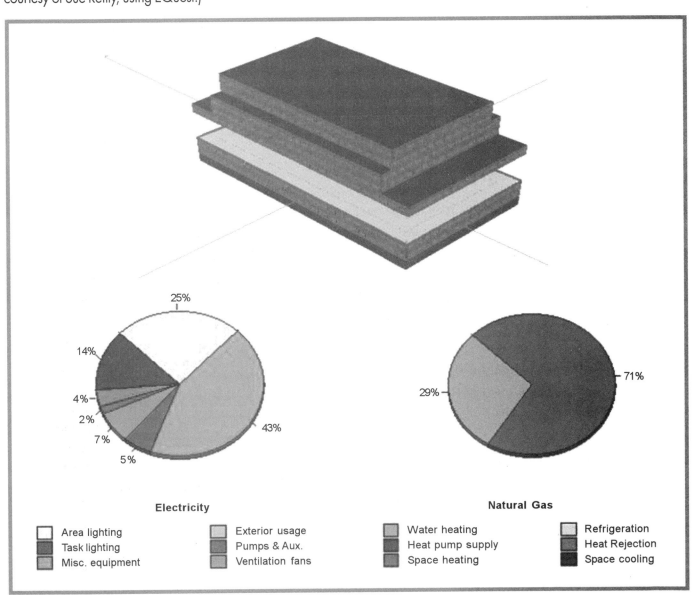

Electricity

Area lighting	Exterior usage	Water heating	Refrigeration
Task lighting	Pumps & Aux.	Heat pump supply	Heat Rejection
Misc. equipment	Ventilation fans	Space heating	Space cooling

Natural Gas

— Type/size/performance: DX, chilled water, constant volume, VAV, packaged, central stations, fan-coils, terminal units, etc.

— Control strategies: temperature control, fan control, schedules, setpoints, OA control, etc.

- Physical plant
- Equipment selection (type, size, performance)—chillers, boilers, cooling towers, district steam/CHW, domestic hot water heaters.
- Equipment control—schedules, setpoints, sequence of operation, etc.
- Process loads—Type (steam, hot water, chilled water, etc), size, schedules.

Economics:

- Utility rates/rate structures: electricity, natural gas, fuel oil, purchased steam, purchased chilled water, other.
- Equipment cost: first cost, maintenance costs, major overhaul costs.

The DOE program allows numerous design alternatives/iterations/comparisons to be performed at any level of design development. The program provides great flexibility in analysis, offering better system trade-off analysis as it takes into account interaction among all building components (e.g., fenestration area, lighting, daylighting, cooling load, cooling equipment size).

If required, the model can be very detailed and precise, although the time and effort involved in a high level of detail will have to be weighed against the potential impact of such a study. The time required will depend on the level of detail desired and on the objective/purpose of the model.

Once a model is created, some changes can be made with the "stroke of a key," a big advantage over "manual"/spreadsheet analysis. Building geometry/envelope input typically is considered the most time-consuming component, but again, the extent of the effort will depend on the level of detail required. The DOE software can also be helpful in later stages during project implementation, building commissioning, measurement, and verification and to quantify savings for potential monetary incentives from local utilities.

Energy-10 Energy-10 is a whole-building energy analysis software that helps to perform hourly energy simulations in order to quantify, analyze, assess, and illustrate the effects of changes in building insulation, windows, lighting systems, and mechanical systems, as well as daylighting, passive solar, and natural ventilation—individually and on the building in total. The program provides the results in the form of a summary table, as well as up to 20 graphics that compare the current design to a base design.

Energy-10 is the result of a collaboration between the National Renewable Energy Laboratory, Lawrence Berkley National Laboratory, and Berkeley Solar Group. It is easier to use and less expensive than DOE-2, but is not as robust. It is best used for analyzing small commercial and residential buildings, typically less than 10,000 square feet. Energy-10 is designed so that it can be used in the early stage of a building design. The cost of the software is approximately $250, as opposed to the $300-$2,000 range of the DOE-2 programs. The Energy-10 Web site is located at **www.nrel.gov/buildings/energy10**

Figure 14.2

Energy-10 simulates energy requirements for each hour of a typical year to account for variables such as occupancy and weather, as well as interactions between heating, lighting, and cooling systems. In this example of a new Ranger Station in New Mexico, the energy use of a code-compliant base case is compared to a case that includes many energy efficiency and passive solar features.

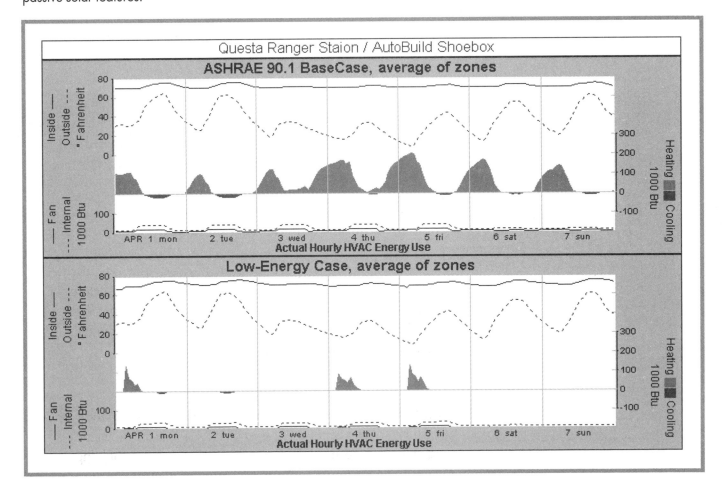

EnergyPlus

EnergyPlus (version 1.0.1) is a new generation simulation program that improves on DOE-2. It includes simulation time steps of less than an hour. The modular structure of the program will facilitate third-party development. The software is planned to produce ASCII output files that offer the advantage of being easy to adapt to spreadsheet and text for further development. Solar thermal, multi-zone airflow, photovoltaic, and fuel cell simulations are expected to be included. The basic program requires a degree of computer literacy. The software is available at no cost at the DOE Web site located at **www.eere.gov/buildings/energyplus/**

SPARK

SPARK (Simulation Problem Analysis Research Kernel) is a highly sophisticated program that can model more complex building envelopes and mechanical systems than DOE-2 or EnergyPlus. The software runs up to 10-20 times faster than other simulation programs. The basic program is available at no cost. The potential drawback is that it requires a high degree of computer literacy to use. To download the software, visit the Lawrence Berkeley National Laboratory Web site at **http://simulationresarch.lbl.gov**

HOT2000™

HOT2000™ simulation software is designed primarily for low-rise residential buildings. It evaluates the effectiveness of cooling and heating, including passive solar systems. It does not require a high level of computer literacy. The software generates detailed monthly and annual tables on heat loss HVAC loads and the cost of energy use. It can compare five different fuel types and several different HVAC systems. Four different types of houses can be compared. The cost of HOT2000 is approximately $300. It is available in both English and French, making it popular in Canada as well as the United States. The program has a following of over 1,400 users worldwide. To obtain the software, visit the Natural Resources Canada Web site at **http://buildingsgroup.nrcan.gc.ca**

Component Simulation Software

Programs such as RESFEN, WINDOW, and Therm are available at no charge from the Lawrence Berkeley National Laboratory for analysis of fenestration. Links to order these programs and for additional information can be found at **http://windows.lbl.gov/software/resfen/resfen.html** For solar water heating, FRESA and RETScreen® are two computer programs used for preliminary analysis for renewable energy applications. Both of these programs are available at no cost, FRESA at the DOE Web site, **www.eere.energy.gov/femp/information/download_fresa.efm** and RETScreen® at their Web site, **www.retscreen.net/ang/menu.php** The hourly energy simulation program, TRNSYS, is widely used for precise engineering data and economic analysis and to optimize parameters of solar water heating system design. The cost is $4,000 for commercial use and $2,000 for educational use. It is available at **http://sel.me.wisc.edu/trnsys/downloads/download.htm** These programs, along with Energy-10, are also used for photovoltaic modeling. PV*SOL, PVcad, and PV-DesignPro are some other popular programs used in photovoltaic systems. A free demonstration version of PV*SOL is available at **www.valentin.de** PVcad is available no cost at **www.iset.uni-kassel.de** PV-DesignPro costs approximately $160 and is available at **www.mauisolarsoftware.com**

Financial Analysis Software

BLCC 5.2-04 is a program developed by the National Institute of Standards and Technology (NIST) to perform life cycle analysis of buildings and building components. This program is useful for comparing alternate designs that have higher initial costs, but lower operating costs over the life of the building. BLCC is very useful in evaluating water and energy conservation projects, as well as renewable energy strategies. The software compares two or more competing alternate designs and determines which has the lowest LCC, and therefore which is the most economical in the long run. The software is Windows-based and is available at no cost through the DOE Web site (previously noted).

The next scheduled release of BLCC will include a module that will increase the type of cost/benefit analysis problems for which the software can be used. Also in the works is a module for private sector studies that will include tax and financial benefit analysis. Subsequent enhancements include sensitivity analysis and a feature that will allow customization of emission calculations.

BEES

As described in Chapters 12 and 13, the BEES model is a technique used to analyze both economic and environmental considerations and blend them into a rational decision-making scoring system. Based on practical, scientific methodology, the BEES model can be used to evaluate economic and environmental aspects of competing alternatives. The BEES (version 3.0) software contains pertinent data and the computational engine that generates the BEES score. The current version contains a database of 200 building products.

The BEES software produces graphics that combine the environmental and economic life cycle performance scores for user-selected alternate building products. Graphics also show individual environmental impact flows, as well as economic first and future costs. The Windows-based software is available at no cost from the DOE Web site.

This version of the BEES software includes generic and brand-specific items and EPA methods for evaluating environmental impacts. The new version will feature an absolute scoring system, as opposed to the relative scoring system used in the previous version. The new system allows comparisons across building elements.

Standards Compliance Software

REScheck, formerly MECcheck, is a quick and easy way to check to see if a typical single or multi-family residential building is in compliance with the 1992/1993/1995 *Model Energy Code* and the 1998/2000 *International Energy Conservation Code*. The program generates a report that lists project data and compliance results.

COMcheck-Plus is designed to check compliance with commercial building energy codes using whole-building performance methods, such as ASHRAE 90.1 and the *International Energy Conservation Code*. Knowledge of building modeling is helpful in using the software. The compliance report that is generated can be printed or copied to a file.

COMcheck-EZ, like COMcheck-Plus, is designed to check compliance with commercial building energy codes. While it is easier to use, it does not have as many features as COMcheck-Plus.

The REScheck and COMcheck series are Windows-based, and available at no charge at **www.energycodes.gov**

Database Software

The Green Building Advisor is available from Building Green, which publishes *Environmental Building News*, EBN archives, and *GreenSpec®*. *Environmental Building News* is a monthly newsletter devoted to sustainable building. It is independent because all of its revenue comes from subscriptions; the publication does not accept advertising. EBN archives is a searchable CD that contains all 77 back issues of *Environmental Building News*. *GreenSpec* is a directory of 1,500 green building products screened by the editors of *Environmental Building News* and a guideline specification for environmentally preferable products. *The Green Building Advisor* is interactive software, which generates a list of strategies by categories. Each strategy is linked so that additional details can be accessed, such as the relative cost of the strategy, when it should be considered, interrelationships with other strategies, and sources of additional information through actual case studies. The software is currently under $200 and is available at their Web site at **www.greenbuildingadvisor.com**

Green Developments is a CD-ROM available through the Rocky Mountain Institute, a nonprofit environmental organization with a seven million dollar budget that promotes efficient and restorative use of resources for a "more secure, prosperous, and life-sustaining world." The Rocky Mountain Institute is independent, non-adversarial, and trans-ideological, with an emphasis on market-based solutions. The CD contains over 200 case studies of green buildings. The case studies include project description, cost, size, date, location, owner, developer, design and engineering team, environmental issues addressed, and market performance. Case studies also include video and audio clips, and architectural, engineering, and financial community leadership resources. The cost of the CD is currently $20. Visit **www.rmi.org** for more information.

Capturing Cost Data for Future Projects

In addition to these software packages, the project team should use their customary spreadsheet and database software to create or add to their existing job cost database, capturing the actual job costs. Green building products, components, systems, and total project costs should all be captured in as much detail as possible. Total project cost should be broken down into CSI MasterFormat or UNIFORMAT II work breakdown structures to facilitate evaluation with other projects. Systems should follow the UNIFORMAT II work breakdown system, and individual line item costs should be recorded in CSI MasterFormat. Individual line item costs should be broken down into material costs, unit labor hours, composite wage rate, and equipment costs. Date and location of installation are also important factors to be recorded.

Maintaining accurate green cost data in the proper format is important so that it can be used in conjunction with the data in the cost section of this book (in addition to other Means cost data books and *CostWorks* software or other cost estimating programs). Breaking down the costs in this manner allows adjustments for factors such as material or labor cost escalation, and labor productivity. The resulting data can be used in future estimates and cost analysis. Standard spreadsheet software will also be useful for life cycle, value engineering, and other ad hoc analysis. Means *CostWorks* CDs and cost data books are good sources for conventional building costs that can be used for comparisons with green components. They are also useful because green building approaches often incorporate conventional building materials and components.

Conclusion

The software presented in this chapter represent useful tools in the analysis, evaluation, and storing of green building data. Often, because of the expense and time required to purchase and learn new programs, conventional wisdom dictates that the investment should only be made when it is needed for a particular project. However, it is recommended that software is purchased *before* it is determined that it is definitely needed for a particular project. This allows users to become familiar with it ahead of time, gaining valuable experience in a more relaxed atmosphere, instead of trying to figure out how features work with a deadline looming, thus avoiding the potential of missed deadlines or costly mistakes.

When using software for the first time, start off with a small job and have a contingency plan in place for performing the work manually, or even do it concurrently. As more experience is gained, users should experiment with some of the more advanced features of the software, even though they may not be required for a particular problem. Users will then become more comfortable with features that may be required on future projects. With a little time and experience, users will find that computer software can greatly enhance and streamline green building projects.

Case Studies

Case Study 1: California Environmental Protection Agency

Gordon Wright

California Environmental Protection Agency
Sacramento, California

by Gordon Wright, Editor

The new headquarters of the California Environmental Protection Agency (EPA) is notable for more than its abundance of "sustainable" features. The manner in which the 930,000-square foot building evolved was also atypical. It was developed by a public entity, the city of Sacramento, for lease to the EPA. The state of California has a 25-year lease, with an option to purchase the property.

The California Department of General Services (DGS) selected the city's proposal from a field that also included about 10 developers. Each submittal consisted of a proposal for both a building plan and a building site. A major strength of the city's proposal was its plan to use a strategically located site it owned across the street from City Hall.

The EPA worked closely with DGS to develop design criteria, according to Theresa Parsley, the EPA's assistant secretary for facilities.

The building's sustainable features can be grouped into three general categories: air quality; energy conservation and management; and recycling and recycled products.

Because offices housed in the building include those of the California Air Resources Board, which monitors air quality, the EPA was particularly sensitive to indoor air quality issues, and especially to the detrimental impact of volatiles and aldehydes, Parlsey says.

Floor-By-Floor HVAC System

The primary contributor to good interior air quality is an innovative, floor-by-floor HVAC system. Unlike a standard system that is fed by central ducts, each floor of the EPA building has at least two air intakes. Tower floors (nine through 25) have two mechanical rooms, and the first through eighth floors have three or more. Fan rooms, located at the northeast and northwest corners of the building, are positioned to prevent cross-contamination, which could occur if exhausted air is drawn back into the building. During the night, the building is flushed with outside night air, generally for at least five hours.

A lower noise level and reduced duct pressures are other advantages of the individual floor air distribution system compared to a central system, according to Anil Shenoy, president of the building's Santa Monica, California based mechanical engineer, Levine Seegel Associates.

The building was designed to be 30 percent more efficient than required by California's Title 24 energy code. However, Shenoy believes an analysis of operating data will show a performance that is about 40 percent better. This is a result in part of the use of dual glazing with a low-emissivity coating. Energy performance is also enhanced by varying the amount of exterior glass, which is used most extensively on the north wall. Precast concrete panels on the south and west sides of the building have integral sun shades.

Energy-Savings

David Martin, project designer with architect AC Martin Partners, emphasizes that the building's north-south orientation plays an important role in its efficient energy performance. "Because EPA was to be the tenant, we were as sensitive as we could be with respect to energy conservation," Martin says. Another objective of the design was to accommodate the building's massing so it would not detract from Sacramento's historic City Hall across the street.

Electric use for lighting is 0.9 watts per square foot as compared with 1.2 watts per square foot mandated by Title 24. Each workstation has a task light connected to a motion detector. The light is turned on when the station is entered, and off when an occupant leaves.

EPA Headquarters Design Highlights

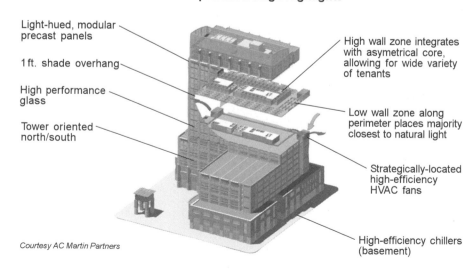

Light-hued, modular precast panels

1 ft. shade overhang

High performance glass

Tower oriented north/south

High wall zone integrates with asymetrical core, allowing for wide variety of tenants

Low wall zone along perimeter places majority closest to natural light

Strategically-located high-efficiency HVAC fans

High-efficiency chillers (basement)

Courtesy AC Martin Partners

PHOTOVOLTAIC TECHNOLOGY

Sun-Produced Electric Power

One indication of the California EPA's interest in the use of advanced technology to produce electricity is the photovoltaic system incorporated into the agency's new headquarters. It utilizes 736 solar collector units grouped into 15 panels on a ninth-floor roof.

The demonstration system generates less than 1 percent of the building's total electrical requirements. Although the system was integral to the building's original design concept, it was not included in the project's guaranteed maximum price. The system was financed in part by a rebate provided by Sacramento's city-owned electric utility.

"We were able to incorporate sustainable enhancements that at the time [of planning] were considered pretty far out, technologically speaking," says Gino Polizzotto, a construction manager with developer Thomas Development Partners. "But technology is moving so quickly that our 1998 goals would now be almost five years behind the curve."

A natural gas line will permit the future addition of a demonstration fuel cell system that would produce electricity through a chemical reaction process.

PROJECT SUMMARY

■ Building team

Owner: City of Sacramento
Development manager: Thomas Development Partners
Architect: AC Martin Partners
Interior architect: Interior Architects Inc.
Structural engineer: CBM Engineers
Mechanical/electrical engineer: Levine Seegel Associates
General contractor: Turner Construction

■ General information

Area: 930,000 gross square feet
Number of floors: 25
Construction time: June 1998 to December 2000
Delivery method: Design/build

■ Project suppliers

Roof insulation: Dow, Johns Manville, Apache
Skylights: Metcoe
Energy Management: Johnson Controls
Plumbing fixtures: Kohler
Door hardware: Corbin Russwin, Norton, Hager
Wall and floor tile: Dal-Tile
Ceilings: USG
Interior partitions: National Gypsum

■ Construction Costs

Core and shell:	$ 82,000,000
Sitework:	2,950,000
Off-site park improvement:	1,000,000
Tenant improvements	29,750,000
Total	**$ 115,700,000**

Electrical use is monitored both on a floor-by-floor basis and according to whether it is used to operate the mechanical system, lights, or power outlets. It is thus possible to check the performance of particular equipment. Computers with a reduced electrical requirement were installed on two floors, for example, and readings on those floors were compared with those for floors with less efficient computers. "We're validating that systems do what they're claimed to do," Parsley says.

Low VOCs and Recycled Materials

Interior finishes that do not contain volatile organic compounds (VOCs) were specified. Parsley says the only negative feature of non-VOC-containing paint discovered so far is that it appears to have a shorter shelf life – a disadvantage when it is stored for future maintenance use.

EPA had more than an academic interest in learning about the products used in its headquarters. "We're a regulatory agency," Parsley explains. "Before we apply regulations, we want to find out how the products perform."

Carpet tiles used in the EPA building have a recycled content of 53 percent. ("You can get a 100 percent recycling content if you want to go ugly," Parsley notes). The 18-inch square tiles have a sticky backing that does not require glue for application. Another factor that was considered in awarding the carpet tile contract to Collins & Aikman was the company's pledge that any returned used tiles would be recycled, and not placed in landfills, according to Parsley.

In some instances the recycled product proved to be less expensive than the virgin material version. This was the case, for example, for an 82 percent recycled content ceiling tile that has the same noise reduction property.

Although the procurement of sustainable components required planning, it did not hinder the construction schedule, says Terry Richards, project executive with general contractor Turner Construction Co. "If you need 770,000 square feet of carpeting, you can quickly tax a manufacturer's production capacity," he notes.

"The developer brought expertise in knowing how to buy a job, and how to get it designed right – in keeping the numbers competitive and the quality high," Richards says. "The result is a building of private-sector quality for a public-sector client."

Building Design & Construction magazine, published in Oak Brook, Illinois by Reed Business Information, is a monthly national architectural trade magazine serving members of the design and building team — architects, engineers, contractors, and owners — involved in commercial, industrial, institutional, and multifamily residential building construction.

Case Study 2: The Jean Vollum Natural Capital Center

Larry Flynn

The Jean Vollum Natural Capital Center:
Portland, Oregon

by Larry Flynn, Senior Editor

The Jean Vollum Natural Capital Center, a $12.5 million renovation of a historic warehouse into a mixed-use office and retail building, was named for a founding Ecotrust board member who financed the 1998 purchase of the site. In January of 2002, the center became the first building in the western United States to receive a LEED gold rating.

The Center houses 17 retail, office, and agency tenants, as well as Ecotrust offices. Tenants include Patagonia, an outdoor retailer known for its environmental ethic; the Certified Forest Products Council, a trade association promoting sustainably harvested

woods; the nonprofit Wild Salmon Center; Shorebank Pacific, the nation's first environmental bank; World Cup Coffee, a maker of state-grown coffees and teas; and Hot Lips, a pizzeria that uses its ovens to heat its own water supply.

"The green restoration is part of a larger vision of bringing people together to encourage a conservation economy, one that is respectful of communities and the natural world," said Spencer Beebe, Ecotrust founder and president, at the Center's opening. In accordance with its goal, Ecotrust chose to renovate the 70,000 square foot warehouse, built in 1895. The building is located in the Pearl District north of downtown Portland, which is being redeveloped.

Because many of the warehouses have been demolished in recent years, Jeff Stuhr, principal in charge of the project for local designer Holst Architecture, says there was a desire by the building team, which included the Portland office of contractor Walsh Construction Co., Chicago, to preserve the historic building.

Re-used & Renewed

During renovation, though many sustainable techniques were used in water and energy conservation and materials recycling, the re-use of the existing structure was perhaps the project's single biggest sustainable feature. "One of the most important decisions we made was to renovate an existing warehouse instead of building on a green field," says Bettina von Hagen, Ecotrust's Project Manager for the redevelopment, citing the building's location adjacent to rail transportation and bicycle paths as additional benefits.

The brick and timber building, however, was not in good condition. "It was a brittle old building that had settled in a lot of areas. It had dry rot and pigeons had been living in it," says Stuhr, adding that numerous parties had looked at it previously and concluded that it wasn't economically feasible to renovate.

A great deal of structural and seismic strengthening was performed on the building, with KPFF Consulting Engineers, Portland, as the designer. The condition of the building and the fact that its design called for the interior to be exposed, made the seismic upgrade and structural renovation the most challenging, as well as some of the most expensive ($2 million), parts of the project, says Carrington Barrs, Walsh's superintendent on the project.

Green & Eco-Friendly

Holst concentrated on four areas of green design: social equity, water, light, and air. To promote public participation, a large atrium and other public spaces were designed into the renovation of the structure. A 10,000 square foot third floor addition to the center, which contains a 3,000 square foot roof terrace with an open-air deck and fireplace, and a 7,000 square foot eco roof, was built with salvaged timber, mostly taken from the demolition of an annex. Ecotrust conducts weekly tours of the center, and more than 120 events have been booked at the building since it opened.

To protect the salmon-filled Willamette River, a system was devised to reduce stormwater runoff. The system is comprised of the eco roof, which can be seen by visitors to the third-floor terrace, and bioswales, which resemble drainage ditches, but contain native, drought-resistant plants that filter runoff from the building and parking lot before returning it to the earth. "Stormwater runoff is endangering the river and the salmon in it," says von Hagen.

Portland's aged sewer system combines stormwater runoff with the sewer. During heavy storms, the runoff diverts into the river, says Stuhr. The Vollum Center's stormwater management system reclaims 95% of the runoff, says Ralph DiNola, Green Building Services' senior design consultant for the project.

The eco roof, which contains groundcover and native, drought-resistant plants, offers many benefits, according to Stuhr. It reduces heat-island effects, slows down runoff, and acts as a carbon sink, absorbing carbon dioxide and producing oxygen.

A city record 98% of construction debris from the project was recycled by the construction team. "We set out with a goal to recycle 75% of the debris to get the two LEED points available. But we wanted to see how high the bar could be raised," says Barrs, adding that the construction team was "blown away" at the end result of its recycling effort.

Debris was source-separated onsite into seven dumpsters. In all, only nine-and-a-half dumpsters were hauled away during the nearly two-year project. DiNola credits Barrs for his championing of the recycling effort by "dumpster diving" at lunchtime to further separate incorrectly sorted material.

Because the warehouse's window apertures were small, the team took license with the historic building by adding new apertures to its west side. One large atrium skylight and 12 smaller skylights above the second floor work spaces were installed.

"The general lighting concept for the building was to have low lighting levels, a minimum number of fixtures and to have the lighting be responsive to the daylighting," says Robert Dupuy, lighting design team leader for Interface Engineering, Milwaukie, Ore., the project's M/E/P engineer.

Photocell Sensors Save Energy

In the skylit atrium and outside the building, photocell sensors adjust the brightness of fluorescent lamps in correspondence to the amount of daylight. The sensors in the atrium continually adjust the level of electric light in response to the amount of daylight. Outside, the lights are timed to go on and off. In the building corridors, two compact fluorescent T8 lamps in each fixture are controlled by occupancy sensors and automatically respond to the presence of people. When no one is in the area, one of the lamps is switched off automatically.

Lighting levels in the tenant spaces are 30 footcandles instead of the typical 50 footcandles for an office. Upper floor offices are equipped with direct and indirect fluorescent luminaries.

The air component of Holst's dictate dealt primarily with low-toxic and recycled interior materials. The team used low-VOC and recycled paint, installed wheatboard cabinets, recycled carpet, and flooring made from recycled tires. FSC-certified sustainably harvested wood was used throughout, on the outdoor terrace, in construction plywood and in new windows and office furniture.

A 30% energy saving was achieved through the use of energy-efficient operable windows, fixtures, and a heating ventilation and air conditioning system, according to Green Building Services. Minimizing the mechanical cooling system also saved the project $25,000 to $30,000 in first costs, says Andy Frichtel, project manager for Interface Engineering. "We saved money and energy because the system isn't oversized and runs more efficiently," Frichtel says.

"We're thrilled with the building," says von Hagen. "Its performance and people's interaction with it have far exceeded expectations."

PROJECT SUMMARY

■ Building team

Owner and developer: Ecotrust
Project manager: Ecotrust
Architect: Holst Architecture
Structural designer: KPFF Consulting Engineers
M/E/P: Interface Engineering
LEED certification manager: Green Building Services

■ Construction Costs

General conditions	$ 493,000
Sitework	902,000
Concrete	268,000
Masonry	661,000
Metals	1,048,000
Wood/plastics	968,000
Thermal/moisture protection	235,000
Doors and windows	387,000
Finishes	428,000
Specialties	64,000
Furnishings	3,000
Conveying systems	86,000
Mechanical	669,000
Electrical	454,000
Site purchase	2,500,000
Tenant improvements	1,373,000
Miscellaneous costs	2,261,000
Total	**$12,500,000**

Building Design & Construction magazine, published in Oak Brook, Illinois by Reed Business Information, is a monthly national architectural trade magazine serving members of the design and building team — architects, engineers, contractors, and owners — involved in commercial, industrial, institutional, and multifamily residential building construction.

Case Study 3: Chesapeake Bay Foundation

C.C. Sullivan

Chesapeake Bay Foundation:
Annapolis, Maryland

by C.C. Sullivan

Starting with a three-day retreat on the shores of the Chesapeake Bay, this unique building team was heading into an unusual project, says Charles D. Foster, director of facilities for the Chesapeake Bay Foundation (CBF). "We decided the building would be a culmination of everything we've learned in all our other buildings. We knew this wasn't going to be a design-and-bid-it-out building."

As a result, the general contractor was the first to be hired. "Green projects are where a GC can get into trouble," says Foster. "So you want to make sure the contractor has the wherewithal to deal with all the unusual materials and equipment that may not be stocked in the U.S."

The contractor joined a tightly knit team of designers, CBF staff and the owner's representative. "Because this was a green project, we took an integrated, team approach," says Greg Mella of the SmithGroup. "If you let the engineers have a say in very early decisions, they can actually make the project much more efficient and sustainable."

To develop a highly sustainable project, "Everyone really has to be conversing," explains Donna McIntire, a former SmithGroup architect and now with the U.S. Green Building Council's rating program, called LEED. "The LEED process really integrates everyone on the project team. We recommend the charrette process to open discussion and get everybody on the same page."

"There's nothing in this building that we did not discuss," recalls Foster of the team interaction. "It made the process much smoother."

In spite of the cost-cutting and other issues of feasibility, the team worked with a seemingly endless list of sustainable concepts and equipment. Team interaction was critical in ensuring they would work as expected, especially novel materials such as PSL. Other examples follow.

■ **Siting.** Located on a rather remote site of a defunct inn and beach club, the plan required minimal landscaping and the felling of only one tree. Yet, "It was not clear at all that the site would serve CBF's purposes," says T. James Truby, principal of Synthesis Inc. "While it was large at 33 acres, it had little developable land and included wetlands and unstable soils." In addition, accessing and building on the site was a concern for contractors and for CBF, as was future employee travel to and from the offices.

Based on advice from the GC, engineers, and environmental experts, CBF found the location suitable. "It was better than cutting down upland trees, and we knew we could control the impact of the building by controlling rainwater ... and through created wetlands," William C. Baker, president of CBF, explains.

■ **Mechanical & Electrical Systems.** What Foster terms "bleeding-edge technologies" were considered for mechanical, electrical, and plumbing systems, including automatic dimming controls for lighting, a total energy-management system, and a desiccant dehumidification and cooling system.

"What's really impressive is how they're integrated and tied together design-wise. Everyone from the contractor to the engineer to the landscaper was involved," says Foster, citing coordination of envelope design and mechanical system

sizing as an example. "So we made more informed design decisions."

SmithGroup's Mella recalls a similar example. "To figure out what thickness of structural insulated panels [SIPs] to use, we worked with the mechanical engineer to get the desired R-values for the roof and with the structural engineer to determine the span of the SIP," he says. In the end, a 12 inch thick panel with an astronomical R-45 gave way to an 8 inch panel with a still respectable R-34. The thinner SIP was less expensive, but necessitated the addition of timber purlins for support.

■ **Waste and Toxin Management.** Follow-through on material selection and job-site practices was critical to the construction phase, says Tom Eichbaum, principal of SmithGroup. "It's one thing to write a specification that all waste materials be recycled, or that all materials be free of VOCs, but the notion can be totally foreign to contractors, and they have to pass that on to all their suppliers," he notes.

Fortunately, Clark Construction had experience in those areas. "We're seeing a lot of recycling programs for construction waste. You have to make sure you're not comingling debris and that you use demolished materials where you can," says Barbara C. Wagner, vice president of Clark Construction, noting that concrete from the demolished inn was used as roadbed.

■ **Structure.** Concrete was also a favored material for the foundation, a conventional slab-and-beam deck with spread footings, adds Steven E. Colby, project manager for structural consultant Shemro Engineering, Bethesda, MD.

Offering an effective fire separation between the timber structure and parking area below, concrete also helped support heavy offset loads. "Exposure to salt water and air did not favor a steel structure," adds Colby. "And some environmental aspects are better with concrete."

"The project required more coordination than a typical job, because the structure is the architecture and the architecture is the structure, and everything is coated naturally," adds Colby, noting that hot-dipped galvanized steel was specified for most connections on timber joists and beams to help prevent rust.

■ **Interior Finishes.** Inside the structure, the lack of commercial finishes and fixtures is striking, but the austere approach is considered an environmental plus. Offices can be reconfigured without sending materials back to the landfill, says Baker, and there are fewer barriers to staff interaction. "We also learned that by not having walls and doors, the energy efficiency of the building really improves," he adds.

Interior trim is mostly SIPs and pressed wood fiberboard, materials that are new to most carpenters and building inspectors. The solid expanded polystyrene insulation in the exterior walls meant that electric chases were not possible, making coordination with the electrical trades all the more important. For flooring, the team settled on a mix of materials: old-fashioned cork and trendy imported bamboo, which is rapidly renewable.

■ **What's Not There.** Like the rest of the project, the interiors are most remarkable for what's not there. In seeking to make their office shed "invisible" to the habitat of the bay, this project team earned high honors:

the world's first "platinum rating" from the U.S. Green Building Council's environmental rating system, LEED.

Why is it the first top-rated green project? "Because the team understood the mission," says Donna McIntire, a program manager for the council and formerly a project manager for the CBF headquarters. "The owner had a huge role in that. It does take a strong client, and we're finding that long-term owners of buildings are leading the way."

Baker and the CBF seem to attribute their success to the project itself, as if it were another building team member. "We got led along by the mission of the project, and that's what happens when you're a goal-driven organization," Baker explains. "We weren't looking to do something that ambitious, but it grew from being a way to

have everybody under one roof to a teaching tool for everything from energy efficiency to environmental sensitivity."

The project does instruct, mainly by raising questions. For example, will the products and techniques employed become more cost-effective, workable and readily available? Or, like solar power, will it be decades before they can be applied across the commercial construction market? Where, for example, can composting toilets be used, and how do existing codes prevent their use? How much energy is required to make PSL or SIPs, and how clean are the manufacturing processes?

By provoking such thought, the CBF headquarters proves that it is more than mere design and construction: it is study of what is possible and what is true.

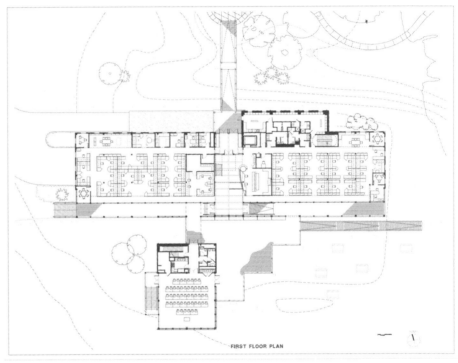

FIRST FLOOR PLAN

Case Study 4:
Adam Joseph Lewis Center at Oberlin College

Dave Barista

Adam Joseph Lewis Center at Oberlin College: Oberlin, Ohio

by Dave Barista, Associate Editor

Imagine a building that produces more energy than it needs to operate, that recycles its own water. A building that breathes and changes with the seasons like a tree. That was the goal for the building team that designed and built the Adam Joseph Lewis Center for Environmental Studies at Oberlin College, a 2,600-student liberal arts university located not far from Cleveland in Oberlin, Ohio.

Spearheaded by David Orr, professor of environmental studies at Oberlin, and funded with contributions from its namesake environmental philanthropist, the 13,600-square-foot, $6.61 million building was completed in January 2000. It was designed by a renowned practitioner of sustainable architecture, William McDonough & Partners of Charlottesville, Va.

Beauty Through Simplicity

The Lewis Center consists of two structures: a two-story main building that houses classrooms, faculty offices, and a two-story atrium; and a connected structure that hosts a 100-seat auditorium and a solarium.

Its brick exterior makes reference to the campus' turn-of-the-century building style, while its use of glass curtain wall and its curved roofs add a touch of modernism. Dominating the interior is an exposed curved ceiling, which is supported by 13 arched glulam wood beams and sheathed with white fir plywood panels. Interior walls do not extend to the ceiling, creating open space throughout the upper portions of the building for light to pass and to further expose the timber ceiling.

"Everyone who visits the building looks up and comments on the exposed beams and roof deck," adds Orr.

All wood used throughout the center – from the beams and ceiling panels to the trim and auditorium seat armrests – was harvested from forests managed according to sustainable practices. Other ecologically sensitive materials include low-VOC paints, adhesives and carpet, and materials with recycled content such as structural steel, brick, aluminum curtain-wall frame, ceramic tile in the restrooms, and even the toilet partitions. The materials were also selected for their durability and low maintenance.

McDonough & Partners even created a custom biodegradable fabric for the auditorium seats. The material degrades in sunlight over about three years and is actually edible, says William McDonough, principal of the 40-person firm, who admits to having actually taste-tested the fabric.

Specifying environmentally conscious materials, however, was just one component of this dynamic project, which is also meant to serve as a working lesson in sustainability.

"Oberlin represents probably the most ambitious program we've ever been involved with," says Kevin Burke, project architect with McDonough & Partners. "It stretched to include energy, water, wastewater, materials – everything."

Net Energy Exporter

To meet the goal of having the building be a net energy exporter – to create more energy than it uses – the building team had to employ a mix of simple and complex design concepts to minimize the energy needed to heat, cool and illuminate the interior space.

■ **Solar Energy.** Photovoltaic (PV) panels were installed on the main building's south-facing roof to power the building. The 3,700 square feet of PV panels are expected to collect about 64,500 kilowatt-hours (kW) of solar energy annually – enough energy for the entire building, which is calculated to consume 63,609 kW-hours a year. The array began operation in mid-November 2000, and as of Feb. 1 has generated approximately 3,280 kW-hours of energy. When more efficient solar cells become available – and affordable – the existing PV panels will be replaced, says Burke.

■ **Building Siting.** The building is oriented on an east-west axis to take advantage of daylight and solar heat gain. All the major classrooms are situated along the southern exposure to maximize daylight.

"I taught the first class in this building, and the natural light was so nice that we didn't even have to turn the lights on,"

Courtesy Oberlin College

adds McDonough. Even with the lights turned on, the energy-efficient fluorescent fixtures require just 0.9 watts per square foot, and occupancy sensors make sure they're operating only when needed.

■ **Solar Heat Gain.** The thermal mass of the building's concrete floors and exposed masonry walls helps to retain and reradiate heat. The walls have an R-21 energy performance rating while the standing-seam metal roof, which utilizes rigid polystyrene foam insulation, boasts an R-30 rating. Overhanging eaves and a vine-covered trellis on the south elevation help to shade the building, and an earth berm along the north wall further insulates the wall. The atrium's glass curtain wall features low-emissivity glass with an R-value of 7.1.

■ **Fresh Air.** Natural ventilation is utilized in all occupied spaces via operable windows to supplement conditioned air supplied through the heating, ventilation, and air-conditioning (HVAC) system. Energy consultants Steven Winter Associates of Norwalk, Conn., performed computational fluid dynamics (CFD) analysis to optimize air flow. For instance, says Adrian Tuluca, principal engineer with the firm, "In the atrium, CFD simulation proved that the most effective convection air flow would be achieved by introducing air at low-level windows on the south side and exhausting it through clerestory windows on the north face."

As part of the HVAC control system, the building's ventilation rates are based on carbon dioxide (CO_2) levels in the building. As more students enter the building the CO_2 levels rise, triggering the HVAC system or automatically opening clerestory windows. "Basically, it ensures that the building is not being ventilated more than it needs to be," says Andrew Persily, Indoor Air Quality group leader for the National Institute of Standards and Technology (NIST), which is conducting research to evaluate the center's ventilation rates, airflow patterns and emission rates of VOCs.

■ **Geothermal Energy.** The center utilizes 24 geothermal wells to heat and cool the space. Water circulates through closed-loop pipes to water-source heat pumps located in each space throughout the building. In addition, two larger heat pumps serve the ventilation needs for the building.

Each heat pump is controlled individually, allowing each unit to either reject or extract heat from the circulating water as needed. This reduces energy use by enabling simultaneous heating and cooling within the building.

Loop water temperature is between 30° F and 105° F. When the water is warmer than 105° F, it is circulated into the wells to reject the excess heat. When cooler than 30° F, it is supplemented with heat generated by an electric boiler.

The HVAC system also incorporates a heat-recovery system, which recycles heat from exhausted air and radiant coils – powered by a 120,000 BTU/hour electric boiler – underneath the concrete slab in the atrium to assist in heating the space.

More Than Energy Efficiency

For McDonough, the notion of sustainable design isn't limited to a laundry list of efficiency measures. "A sustainable building is much richer than a green building," he says. "Sustainable design incorporates culture, art, society, economics – a quality of life. It's not just a simple issue of energy efficiency."

To illustrate, McDonough points to a sundial outside the south entrance that traces the solar year and a pond on the east side that supplies irrigation water. Another example is a waste-water-treatment system that uses natural organic processes to recycle wastewater.

A Work In Progress

Of course, the building's merits have yet to be fully tested. Currently in the commissioning phase, McDonough admits that the team's original energy-use projection of 63,609 kW-hours annually has not been met. In fact, according to statistics provided by Oberlin professor John H. Scofield, through the first 10 months of operation, the building used 184,380 kW-hours of energy – which was 3.6 times the projected amount.

"There were quite a few things that were not done according to design that are currently being fixed," adds Tuluca. "For example, certain lights were put on to a circuit that always kept them on, even though they're not security lighting." Another example that Tuluca points to is the specification of the electric boiler that supplies heat for the radiant coils in the atrium floor, which is "a very expensive source of energy," he adds. Plans are to replace the boiler with a more energy-efficient natural-gas boiler.

Both McDonough and Tuluca believe that when commissioning is completed, energy expenditure levels will significantly drop and the building will indeed be a net energy exporter. Orr insists that the project is a long-term work in progress.

"While we can be proud of what's been accomplished, there's more to do," says Orr. "We intended for the building to improve, adapt, and change over time – in effect, a building that learns. This is a beginning, not the conclusion."

Future plans for the center include the integration of a fuel cell with the PV panels to provide energy at night and on overcast days. Moreover, a monitor in the atrium will display all of the building's vital signs, including temperature, CO_2 levels, PV power generation, and energy consumption.

Courtesy Oberlin College

PROJECT SUMMARY

Adam Joseph Lewis Center
at Oberlin College
Oberlin, Ohio

■ **Building team**
Owner: Oberlin College
Architect: William McDonough + Partners
General contractor: Mosser Construction
Structural & mechanical/electrical engineer: Lev Zetlin Associates
Energy consultant: Steven Winter Associates

■ **General information**
Area: 13,600 gross square feet
Number of floors: 2
Construction time: September 1998 to January 2000
Construction cost: $6.61 million
Delivery method: Design/bid/build

■ **Project suppliers**
Photovoltaic panels: BP Solarex
Access flooring: Interface
Wastewater treatment: Living Technologies Inc.
Sustainable wood: Collins Cos., Kane Hardwood, Columbia Forest Products

Building Design & Construction magazine, published in Oak Brook, Illinois by Reed Business Information, is a monthly national architectural trade magazine serving members of the design and building team — architects, engineers, contractors, and owners — involved in commercial, industrial, institutional, and multifamily residential building construction.

Case Study 5: The Steelcase Wood Plant

Larry Flynn

The Steelcase Wood Plant:
Dutton, Michigan

by Larry Flynn, Senior Editor

When the Steelcase furniture manufacturing company decided to build a new wood furniture facility in nearby Dutton, Michigan, the Grand Rapids, Michigan-based company turned to some familiar faces. The company awarded a design/build contract to the Grand Rapids-based contracting firm of Owen-Ames-Kimball Co. (OAK), which partnered with the Grand Rapids office of A/E/CM and contractor URS Corp.

The three entities knew each other well, having worked on previous projects. This time, however, they were faced with a new challenge: building the first industrial facility to be certified by the U.S. Green Building Council (USGBC) under its Leadership in Energy and Environmental Design (LEED) program.

At a ceremony in October in which the plant was awarded a silver rating, USGBC officials called the 600,000-square-foot plant one of the most environmentally friendly industrial facilities in the United States.

Sustainable Solutions

Out of necessity, the building team took a road less traveled on its way to certification, one that was paved with sustainable materials and innovative systems.

Faced with having to make the facility operational by April 2001, less than two years after work had commenced on the project, the team sought ways to speed the pace of construction. Enclosure of the building space and construction of floor slabs was of primary importance to enable crews to work on the project during the winter and because the owner had to have access to the building to begin installing the manufacturing equipment.

According to Max Blake, plant manager for Steelcase's wood division, team members visited a Steelcase plant in Atlanta to examine its use of insulated precast concrete wall panels as the building's exterior. The visit resulted in the team's selection of the same wall system for the Dutton facility. "When we decided to go for LEED certification we used all natural substrates in making the panels; no volatile organic chemicals in the manufacture of the panels or in the facility itself," says Blake.

The system not only helped the building meet energy efficiency standards, it shortened erection time. In all, 500 panels were erected, totalling 83,246 square feet. An average of 25 28-foot-tall panels were installed a day.

"Phased precast erection and steel erection helped us get into the building and start pouring floors so we could gain access for the owner," says Brad McAvoy, project manager of OAK.

A ribbed or raked finish to the panels adds an aesthetic quality to the building. "It's a beautiful precast project. You can't tell where the panels start and stop," says McAvoy.

An eight-foot-wide modular window system was planned in coordination with the wall system to ensure proper placement. The large windows allow significant amounts of daylight to enter the building. "You can see outside from any spot in the building," Blake says.

Thirteen 10 by 30-foot skylights placed at entryways and other key areas of the building also provide daylighting. "The skylighting and the windows in the facility are something that you don't see in most manufacturing facilities," says Bernard Wernette, architectural production manager for URS.

The nerve center for the building's systems is its energy management and temperature control system. Known as the BEAST (building enterprise automation system technology) to the team, the system was commissioned to ensure it uses the minimum required electrical current levels. Seven dust collectors, which exhaust hot air, cool the facility in the summer. According to Steelcase, the action of pulling air from the facility through the dust collectors heats it to 78° F. The air is then filtered, tested and released through 62-in. ductwork to heat the plant.

Steelcase's desire to achieve LEED certification added between 3.5 and 5 percent to the cost of the $26 million project, according to team members. But the added cost is worth it, according to its owner. "This site represents the most advanced wood production facility in the world. It's achieved many of the economic attributes we expected, but it also has achieved much in the area of environmental advancement and enablement," said James P. Hackett, Steelcase's president and CEO, during the LEED certification award ceremony. "The development of this new manufacturing facility represents our commitment to promoting a healthy environment for our community."

Teamwork Touted

Building team members stressed the importance of the team's established working relationship as the key to obtaining the LEED certification and completing the project on time and under budget.

"Both the architect and OAK have a long-lasting relationship with Steelcase, and all the parties know what to expect as far as quality and performance," says Ronald Bieber, general superintendent for OAK.

"Up front, we met with the contractors and told them exactly what we were after," says Blake. "The communication factor was important in ensuring that everyone was on the same page for meeting the LEED criteria," says Bieber. "That needed to happen in order to meet the point systems for certification."

Criteria Pose Challenges

Meeting the LEED criteria for certification was challenging on several levels. Because the project represented the first time that any member of the building team had been involved with LEED, Steelcase, OAK, and URS each designated staff members to undergo LEED training.

LEED certification is based on a point system awarded in five areas: energy efficiency, water management, materials and resource management, indoor environmental air quality, and site planning. Following completion, LEED personnel review the project and decide whether to award the building a rating of bronze (22-26 credits; 50-60% of total), gold (31-35 credits; 71-80% of total) or platinum (36 or more credits; 81% or more of total).

"Steelcase wanted to obtain a minimum bronze rating. They gave us something to shoot for from the start," say McAvoy. "The LEED program gives you a destination, but there are many different roads that you can take to get there. We had to figure out what path to take."

A First For An Industrial Facility

The project also was a milestone for the LEED program in that its criteria had never before been applied to an industrial facility. "The program is not set up for manufacturing facilities," says Wernette.

"We had to forge our own way," say McAvoy. "You have to start the documentation in the planning process because it needs to be in the project specifications. The parties involved in the project need to know what to expect up front."

Randy Bosler was appointed LEED coordinator for Steelcase and acted as the main go-between for the building team in working with the LEED program to ensure the project met the criteria. "There was a lot of documentation available to us," he says.

According to Peter Templeton, LEED program manager, the program is structured so that a level playing field exists across all building types. "There weren't any adjustments made in terms of credits for the project," he says. "The program is structured to be flexible."

But according to Bosler, some adjustments were made to accommodate the certification of a facility as large as the plant, which occupies 66 acres. For instance, an exception was made for the rule prohibiting disturbance of the site farther than 50 feet from the building perimeter. LEED also set guidelines on requirements in meeting ASHRAE standard 90.1-1989 for energy efficiency. Manufacturing facilities are exempt from having to meet the ASHRAE standard, but LEED requires its buildings to meet the standard. Though LEED required that only the cafeteria and the office space above it meet the ASHRAE standard, Bosler says the team went beyond the guidelines.

Another unusual aspect of the plant's certification process was that the team was required to remove the plant's manufacturing process loads from the building's energy modeling.

"From our standpoint, it was actually a very straightforward review process for the project," says Templeton. "The difficulty for Steelcase was that they had no model to learn from."

Since completion, Templeton says the LEED program has received many requests to speak with team members from others seeking certification of industrial facilities. As for Steelcase, the company has gained a green facility, and a productive one as well. "We are seeing great gains in production from our employees," says Blake.

Building Design & Construction magazine, published in Oak Brook, Illinois by Reed Business Information, is a monthly national architectural trade magazine serving members of the design and building team — architects, engineers, contractors, and owners — involved in commercial, industrial, institutional, and multifamily residential building construction.

PROJECT SUMMARY

■ Building team

Owner/developer: Steelcase Inc.
Architect/interior architect: URS Corp.
Mechanical/structural/ electrical engineer: URS Corp.
General contractor: Owen-Ames-Kimball

■ General information

Area: 606,416 gross sq. ft.
Number of floors: 1
Construction time: January 00 to April 01
Construction cost: $26.4 million
Delivery method: Design/build

■ Construction Costs

Sitework/landscaping:	$ 3,327,595
Footings, foundations, flatwork:	2,122,196
Precast concrete:	820,068
Masonry:	481,208
Structural steel/metals:	3,397,154
General trades:	376,093
Membrane roofing:	1,148,920
Metal roofing/wall panels:	167,472
Hollow metal/hardware:	59, 117
Overhead doors:	119, 119
Glass/glazing:	669,447
Finishes:	484,970
Mechanical:	7,225,014
Electrical:	3,267,110
General conditions:	2,707,673
Total:	**$ 26,373,156**

Case Study 6: MaGrann Associates Demonstration House

Edward Howard

MaGrann Associates Demonstration House: Medford, New Jersey

by Edward Howard

As there were no uniform standards for building green in New Jersey, MaGrann Associates developed its Demonstration House according to criteria used by other states. The results were submitted to the New Jersey Green Homes Office of the Department of Community Affairs (NJDCA), a state agency that promotes green building practices in the Garden State. The NJDCA is currently in the process of developing a Green Home Construction Standard that will be unique to New Jersey.

House & Site Features

The MaGrann Associates Demonstration House, a 1-1/2 story "Low Country" style home, features 3,500 square feet of living space, a full basement, and a two-car garage. Construction with green/sustainable materials added 9% to the cost of standard construction. The site is characterized by run-off retention areas/barriers, including a "Rain Garden" and earth berms. There are protected wetlands on the site, as well as plantings that are drought-resistant and indigenous to the Pinelands.

Neighborhood

The neighborhood is located in an in-fill development within the Pinelands Restricted Growth area. The community provides access to a natural lake, a beach, and 560 acres of Green Space at YMCA Camp Ockanickon. The existing streets are narrow with no sidewalks or streetlights, and residents of the community are able to walk or bike to the town's commercial area.

Challenges

Some of the challenges faced by MaGrann Associates and MaGrann Construction, the project managers, during the design and construction of the Demonstration House included lack of information and standardization criteria for building green. Other concerns involved securing vendors/distibutors of green building materials, pricing issues, and retaining subcontractors who were knowledgeable in green building concepts and sustainable construction techniques.

Building Green Design Standards & Evaluation Results

Colorado and Florida are among the states that have developed standards and adopted statewide Built Green Certification Programs. The MaGrann Associates Demonstration House would meet the Colorado and Florida Built Green Program standards achieving a 5-Star HERS (86-point minimum) rating and also exceeding the standards for MEC 93. The Florida program operates on a points system, 200 being the baseline. The Demonstration House scored 266 points in this program. For the Colorado Program, the house achieved 78 out of a possible 158 points, doubling the options needed to qualify.

Construction Materials

- Cementitious siding (HardiPlank™) and trim
- Recycled plastic decking (EPOCH, Tendura)
- OSB Sheathing/lam beams/truss joists
- Recyclable waste container on site
- Finger-jointed studs
- Low-E windows (Weather Shield®)

Finish Materials

- Low-water-use plumbing fixtures (Kohler®)
- Reycled carpet (Earthguard, P.E.T.) and pad
- Low-/no-VOC paints and adhesives
- Molded cementitious "stone"
- New growth pine floors
- Central vacuum system
- Finger-jointed trim
- Built-in recycling center

Energy Star® Features

- Geothermal heating and cooling (2 systems/3 zones by Water Furnace)
- R-11 insulated basement walls
- R-38/R-30 insulated ceilings (BIBS by Certain Teed)
- Energy Star® appliances
- High-Efficiency (.62 EF) hot water system
- Energy® Star ventilation/thermostat
- Energy® Star lighting

Construction Costs

Total Construction Cost: $400,000
Green building techniques represented a net increase in hard construction costs of $36,000, or 9% over the projected cost using all conventional building materials. Anticipated savings are expected to pay back the initial investment in energy-conserving components within 10-15 years.

MaGrann Associates is an energy consulting and engineering firm working with residential, commercial, and light industrial builders, as well as architects, utility companies, and government agencies. MaGrann provides innovative and cost-effective engineering services that maximize both energy and cost savings.

MaGrann Associates
15000 Commerce Parkway
Mt. Laurel, New Jersey 08054
856-722-9799
www.magrann.com

Case Study 7: Phillips Eco-Enterprise Center

LHB Engineers & Architects

Phillips Eco-Enterprise Center
Minneapolis, Minnesota

Architect: LHB Engineers & Architects

Photo Courtesy of Brian Droege

From its inception, the Phillips Eco-Enterprise Center's (PEEC) intent was to be a sustainably designed facility that would house environmentally conscious businesses and provide employment for the residents of its community. The Green Institute, a nonprofit organization based in the Phillips Neighborhood of Minneapolis, Minnesota, selected LHB Engineers & Architects in Minneapolis to help them design a facility on a restored inner-city brownfield site that would meet their goals. The site, already owned by The Green Institute, is conducive to sustainable transportation, since it is central to a densely populated urban neighborhood and adjacent to an inner-city bike path, major bus routes, and a future light rail line.

The Green Institute determined goals for the project after holding a charrette sponsored by the University of Minnesota's College of Architecture and Landscape Architecture and having a master plan created by Partners & Sirny LLP. Due to their practiced knowledge of sustainable design and ability to incorporate community participation, LHB was selected by The Green Institute to design PEEC.

Most of the goals for the project were met or exceeded. The design features can be categorized into three main areas: energy performance, resource conservation, and reduction of the ecological impact of the building. Another primary goal for the project was to design for indoor air quality.

A primary goal was the reduction of energy use by 50 percent versus traditional code-compliant buildings by using a variety of design methods. An air-to-air heat exchange system allows fresh air to be brought in and warmed by the outgoing air, and operable windows allow for natural cooling and improved indoor air quality. Next to the building, a restored prairie field filters roof runoff and covers the geothermal wells that heat and cool the office portion of the building. Future plans call for a 10 kilowatt Jacob's wind turbine to generate some electricity for the facility. The west-facing solar orientation of the building allows for the use of daylight in the space. Sun-tracking daylighting systems reflect light into the facility, and an advanced glazing system was utilized on the windows. Daylight sensors regulate if artificial light is needed from the high-efficiency light fixtures.

When a building is constructed, often the use of new materials deplete natural resources

and contributes to waste during construction. To help reduce this waste and conserve resources, goals were set to use construction materials from salvaged sources (a minimum of 10 percent) and recycled materials (a minimum of 25 percent). Salvaged materials included steel joists, wood decking, brick, sinks, and cabinets. An aggressive construction site recycling program was put into place, and the use of interior finish materials was minimized.

Finishes used were selected based on their long life span, recycled material content, recyclability (such as 100 percent recyclable resilient-textile carpet), and low VOC content. Spaces were designed for adaptability with deconstructable elements, such as stair towers that can be disassembled and reused in the future. Low flow showers for bike commuters and waterless urinals were placed in the design. Locally-produced materials were selected to avoid pollution caused by transporting materials and to help the local markets.

In addition to the restored prairie field benefitting from the rain water runoff from the roof, a roof top garden will also be cultivated. The garden will help to cool the building and provide a recreational area for the tenants. Parking lots on the north side of the building are fitted with biofiltration strips that double as parking lot islands. Instead of using traditional curb and gutter design, storm water from the parking lots is filtered through the strips, which help remove oil and sediment before the water enters the sewer system.

Currently, the building is leased almost to capacity, and The Green Institute intends to utilize PEEC as a teaching tool for designers, construction firms, and the public. The Green Institute and LHB hope that by showcasing this project as a working example of sustainable design, other facility owners, architects, and construction firms will consider environmental issues in future building projects.

MANUFACTURERS/SUPPLIERS

Exterior Walls — *Aluminum Windows, Curtainwall:* Tru-Therm; *Glass:* HGP Industries; *Gasket/Caulking:* Tremco; *Steel Doors:* Amweld; *Overhead Doors:* Midland Garage Door. **Roof** — *Metal:* Copper Sales. **Floors** — *Floor Grilles, Mats & Frames:* Construction Specialties. **Interior Walls** — *Acoustical Treatment:* Armstrong; *Paint:* Sherwin Williams, Valspar; *Hardware:* Schlage. **Elevators** — Schindler.

Design Cost Data/Sept-Oct 2000

ARCHITECT
LHB ENGINEERS & ARCHITECTS
250 3rd Avenue North, #450
Minneapolis, MN 55401

FILE UNDER
COMMERCIAL
Minneapolis, Minnesota

CONSTRUCTION TEAM

GENERAL CONTRACTOR: Kraus-Anderson
525 South 8th Street, Minneapolis, MN 55404

STRUCTURAL ENGINEER: LHB Engineers & Architects
250 3rd Avenue North, #450, Minneapolis, MN 55401

ELECTRICAL & MECHANICAL ENGINEER:
Sebesta Blomberg
5075 Wayzata Blvd., #200, Minneapolis, MN 55416

LANDSCAPE ARCHITECT: LHB Engineers & Architects
250 3rd Avenue North, #450, Minneapolis, MN 55401

ENERGY CONSULTANT: The Weidt Group
1497 Sargent Avenue, St. Paul, MN 55105

GENERAL DESCRIPTION

SITE: 3.4 acres, 148,104 square feet.
NUMBER OF BUILDINGS: One.
BUILDING SIZES: First floor, 52,000; second floor, 10,000; third floor, 2,000; covered walkways, 1,200; total, 65,200* square feet.
BUILDING HEIGHT: Total, 40'.
BASIC CONSTRUCTION TYPE: New.
FOUNDATION: Poured-in-place, precast, block.
EXTERIOR WALLS: Brick, curtainwall.
ROOF: Metal, membrane.
FLOORS: Vinyl, resilient.
INTERIOR WALLS: Gypsum.

PHILLIPS ECO-ENTERPRISE CENTER

Date Bid: Aug 1998 • Construction Period: Nov 1998 to Aug 1999 • Total Square Feet: 65,200*

C.S.I. Divisions (1 through 16)	COST	% OF COST	SQ.FT. COST		SPECIFICATIONS
BIDDING REQUIREMENTS	398,945	10.02	6.18		General conditions, bonds & certificates, supplementary conditions, insurance, tenant improvements.
1. GENERAL REQUIREMENTS	560,582	14.09	8.68	1	Modification procedures, contractors fee, tenant improvements.
3. CONCRETE	819,251	20.59	12.68	3	Cast-in-place, precast, cementitious decks & underlayment, tenant improvements.
4. MASONRY	—	—	—	4	—
5. METALS	390,434	9.81	6.05	5	Reconditioned steel joint, fabrications, expansion joint covers.
6. WOOD & PLASTICS	251,463	6.32	3.89	6	Rough carpentry, heavy timber construction, finish carpentry, plastic fabrications, tenant improvements.
7. THERMAL & MOIST. PROTECT	260,675	6.55	4.04	7	Dampproofing, firestopping, membrane roofing, manufactured roofing & siding, skylights.
8. DOORS & WINDOWS	306,943	7.71	4.75	8	Metal doors & frames, special doors, metal windows, tenant improvements.
9. FINISHES	225,492	5.67	3.49	9	Gypsum board, tile, sheet vinyl, acoustical treatment, resilient flooring, paints, wall coverings, tenant improvements.
10. SPECIALTIES	11,785	0.30	0.18	10	Compartments & cubicles, louvers & vents, signage, fire protection, bath & toilet accessories, tenant improvements.
11. EQUIPMENT	12,286	0.31	0.19	11	Dock levelers.
12. FURNISHING	11,518	0.29	0.18	12	Rugs & mats, tenant improvements.
13. SPECIAL CONSTRUCTIONS	—	—	—	13	—
14. CONVEYING SYSTEMS	31,900	0.80	0.49	14	Elevators (1).
15. MECHANICAL	450,421	11.32	6.97	15	Fire protection, HVAC, geo thermal wells, tenant improvements.
16. ELECTRICAL	247,523	6.22	3.83	16	Electrical, testing, tenant improvements.
TOTAL BUILDING COST	**3,979,218**	**100%**	**$61.60**		
2. SITE WORK	286,581			2	Demolition, preparation, utility piping materials, site concrete, tenant improvements.
LANDSCAPING & OFFSITE WORK	—				
TOTAL PROJECT COST	**4,265,799**		*(Excluding architectural and engineering fees)*		

* These calculations are based on covered walkways divided in half, giving the total square footage to calculate from of 64,600, according to AIA document D-101.

Case Study 8:
Environmental Living & Learning Center, Northland College

LHB Engineers & Architects

Environmental Living & Learning Center, Northland College

Ashland, Wisconsin

Architect: LHB Engineers & Architects/Associate Architect: Hammel Green & Abrahamson

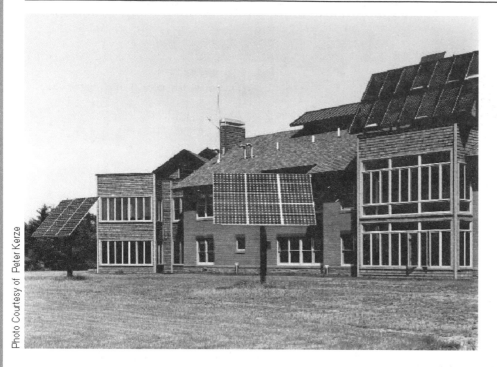

Photo Courtesy of Peter Kerze

MANUFACTURERS/SUPPLIERS

Roof — Copper Sales.
Floors — *Vinyl:* Armstrong.
Interior Walls — *Gypsum Board:*
Louisiana Pacific.

This new student housing complex is two stories high with a partial basement storage and mechanical space. Three different styles of housing rooms were created: standard double rooms; suites sharing a bathroom between two rooms; and six-person apartments which include full kitchens, living rooms as well as private and double bedrooms. The building includes 114 beds: 24 in apartments, 32 in suites, and 58 in double rooms. Common areas, kitchens, toilet/shower rooms, laundry, recycling rooms, and study/seminar rooms are provided for all students to use. The apartment wing includes a two-story greenhouse for use in growing food year round.

Renewable energy systems were utilized to demonstrate their contribution potential. The building includes supplemental photo voltaic and wind power generation; solar preheated water; a greenhouse; passive solar design in one wing; high efficiency gas boiler heating system with two heat recovery units. Op-

timum insulation values and wall to window ratios were utilized for the exterior envelope. Windows are high performance units with low-emissivity coated glass (Hp-4 for south facing glass and Hp-5 elsewhere). High efficiency lighting and energy efficient appliances were used throughout. Students have been encouraged to use a meter to measure the energy consumption of various appliances they bring into the building such as a stereo or television.

During the design phase, the architects evaluated all of the major materials, which would be used in the construction, and operation of the building. Questions of embodied energy, harvest practices of timber, recyclability, material life cycles, product durability, maintenance, transportation impacts, reuse/disposal and the overall budget were weighed for hundreds of materials. The decisions made were part of the learning process for all involved, but particularly for the students, who are mostly majoring in environmental studies.

Students encouraged the use of water saving composting toilets in the apartments — 2 such units were provided with design for expansion to 4 units. The rich compost created by these units will be used to fertilize site landscape plantings. Low volume showers, toilets, and sinks were specified to conserve water.

A variance from the Wisconsin code requirement to have an elevator was sought and received. This was issued primarily on the basis of a duplicate use on each floor. Not having to install an elevator is a significant resource saver for the environment and the college.

The new residence hall meets the needs and interests of students, models the school's environmental mission, and provides a living and learning laboratory for environmental studies. The facility educates its residents on energy costs through unique components of their "home". Since the facility is a teaching tool as well as a residence, students were involved in the design from concept to completion.

GENERAL DESCRIPTION

SITE: 2.64 acres.

NUMBER OF BUILDINGS: One.

BUILDING SIZES: Basement, 7,620; first floor, 16,187; second floor, 16,187; total, 39,994 square feet.

BUILDING HEIGHT: Basement, 9'; first floor, 9'; second floor to mid roof, 14'; total, 32'.

BASIC CONSTRUCTION TYPE: New.

FOUNDATION: Concrete.

EXTERIOR WALLS: Wood frame, brick veneer.

ROOF: Metal, asphalt shingles.

FLOORS: Linoleum, carpet, ceramic tile.

INTERIOR WALLS: Gypsum board, wood wainscoting.

CONSTRUCTION TEAM

GENERAL CONTRACTOR:
Frank Tomlinson Company, Inc.
411 11th Avenue West, Ashland, WI 54806

STRUCTURAL, MECHANICAL & ELECTRICAL ENGINEER:
Hammel Green & Abrahamson
1201 Harmon Place, Minneapolis, MN 55403

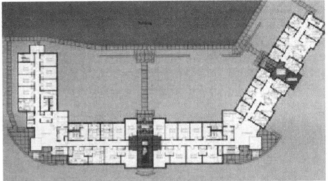

Plan Courtesy of Hammel Green & Abrahamson

ENVIRONMENTAL LIVING & LEARNING CENTER, NORTHLAND COLLEGE

Date Bid: Aug 1997 • Construction Period: Oct 1997 to Oct 1998 • Total Square Feet: 39,994

C.S.I. Divisions (1 through 16)	COST	% OF COST	SQ.FT. COST		SPECIFICATIONS
BIDDING REQUIREMENTS	203,996	6.00	5.10		General conditions.
1. GENERAL REQUIREMENTS	—	—	—	1	—
3. CONCRETE	249,605	7.34	6.25	3	Reinforcement, cast-in-place, precast, cementitious decks & toppings.
4. MASONRY	346,908	10.20	8.67	4	Unit.
5. METALS	27,332	0.80	0.68	5	Structural framing.
6. WOOD & PLASTICS	571,538	16.81	14.29	6	Rough carpentry, finish carpentry, architectural woodwork.
7. THERMAL & MOIST. PROTECT	102,274	3.01	2.56	7	Waterproofing, insulation, manufactured roofing & siding, membrane roofing, skylights.
8. DOORS & WINDOWS	136,031	4.00	3.40	8	Metal doors & frames, wood & plastic doors, special doors, wood & plastic windows.
9. FINISHES	719,212	21.16	17.98	9	Gypsum board, tile, acoustical treatment, resilient flooring, carpet, special coatings.
10. SPECIALTIES	35,813	1.06	0.90	10	Louvers & vents, identifying devices, fire protection, partitions, toilet & bath accessories.
11. EQUIPMENT	—	—	—	11	—
12. FURNISHING	—	—	—	12	—
13. SPECIAL CONSTRUCTIONS	212,416	6.25	5.31	13	Solar energy, wind energy.
14. CONVEYING SYSTEMS	—	—	—	14	—
15. MECHANICAL	600,185	17.65	15.01	15	Basic materials & methods, mechanical insulation, plumbing, HVAC, air distribution.
16. ELECTRICAL	194,481	5.72	4.86	16	Basic materials & methods, service & distribution, lighting, special systems.
TOTAL BUILDING COST	**3,399,791**	**100%**	**$85.01**		
2. SITE WORK	268,342			2	Excavation support systems, earthwork, paving & surfacing. Landscaping.
LANDSCAPING & OFFSITE WORK	18,117				
TOTAL PROJECT COST	**3,686,250**		*(Excluding architectural and engineering fees)*		

Cost Data

The costs in this section include green building components appearing for the first time in Means data and researched specifically for this book, along with some conventional building components that are either required elements in green building systems, or themselves have sustainable characteristics.

The selection of items is the result of the editors' opinions as to the likelihood of a particular material or component being specified for a green building project. Inclusion of a product was not based on any other standards, criteria, or guidelines, and should not be considered an endorsement of a component or of the use of one alternative over another.

Green building is much more than a collection of green components. The key to a successful project is how its elements work together as systems, and how these systems function as a whole building. Thus, individual components that may not normally be touted as green can be a part of a green system (or assembly). For example, concrete prepared using conventional materials may not be hailed as a green building product in itself, but used as part of a passive solar space for thermal storage, it becomes a component in a green building system. Conversely, the green attributes of a component designed specifically to deliver sustainable benefits may be lost if it is not used properly within the system, or in harmony with other building systems and materials.

While the editors have used their best judgment in identifying products and materials that may be specified for sustainable building projects, we recognize that criteria for sustainable design can vary widely among practitioners in the AEC industry. Factors such as energy consumed in manufacture and transport; durability versus natural, no-VOC materials; waste and disposal impacts; and many others must be considered by the design team and the owner.

The following pages provide information on the development of Means cost data and guidance for applying it.

Cost Data Table of Contents

Quick Start

If you feel you are ready to use this book and don't think you need the detailed instructions that begin on the following page, this Quick Start section is for you.

These steps will allow you to get started estimating in a matter of minutes.

1 First, decide whether you require a Unit Price or Assemblies type estimate. Unit price estimating requires a breakdown of the work to individual items. Assemblies estimates combine individual items or components into building systems.

If you need to estimate each line item separately, follow the instructions for **Unit Prices.**

If you can use an estimate for the entire assembly or system, follow the instructions for **Assemblies.**

2 Find each cost data section you need in the Table of Contents (either for Unit Prices or Assemblies).

Unit Prices: The cost data for Unit Prices has been divided into 16 divisions according to the CSI MasterFormat.

Assemblies: The cost data for Assemblies has been divided into 7 divisions according to the UNIFORMAT II.

3 Turn to the indicated section and locate the line item or assemblies table you need for your estimate. Portions of a sample page layout from both the Unit Price Listings and the Assemblies Cost Tables appear below.

Unit Prices: If there is a reference number listed at the beginning of the section, it refers to additional information you may find useful. See the referenced section for additional information.

- Note the crew code designation. You'll find full descriptions of crews in the Crew Listings including labor-hour and equipment costs.

Assemblies: The Assemblies (*not* shown in full here) are generally separated into three parts: 1) an illustration of the system to be estimated; 2) the components and related costs of a typical system; and 3) the costs for similar systems with dimensional and/or size variations. The Assemblies Section also contains reference numbers for additional useful information.

4 Determine the total number of units your job will require.

Unit Prices: Note the unit of measure for the material you're using is listed under "Unit."

- Bare Costs: These figures show unit costs for materials and installation. Labor and equipment costs are calculated according to crew costs and average daily output. Bare costs do not contain allowances for overhead, profit or taxes.

- "Labor-hours" allows you to calculate the total labor-hours to complete that task. Just multiply the quantity of work by this figure for an estimate of activity duration.

Assemblies: Note the unit of measure for the assembly or system you're estimating is listed in the Assemblies Table.

5 Then multiply the total units by . . .

Unit Prices: "Total Incl. O&P" which stands for the total cost including the installing contractor's overhead and profit. (See the "How To Use the Unit Price Pages" for a complete explanation.)

Assemblies: The "Total" in the right-hand column, which is the total cost **including the installing contractor's overhead and profit.** (See the "How To Use the Assemblies Cost Tables" section for a complete explanation.)

Material and equipment cost figures include a 10% markup. For labor markups, see the inside back cover of this book. If the work is to be subcontracted, add the general contractor's markup, approximately 10%.

6 The price you calculate will be an estimate for either an individual item of work or a completed assembly or *system.*

7 Compile a list of all items or assemblies included in the total project. Summarize cost information, and add project overhead.

Localize costs by using the Location Factors found in the Reference Section.

For a more complete explanation of the way costs are derived, please see the following sections.

Editors' Note: We urge you to spend time reading and understanding all of the supporting material and to take into consideration the reference material such as Crews Listing.

Unit Price Pages

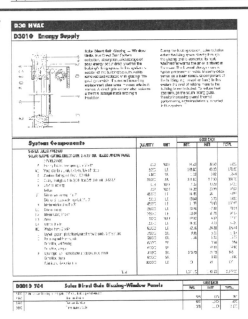

Assemblies Pages

How to Use the Cost Data: The Details

What's Behind the Numbers? The Development of Cost Data

The staff at R.S. Means continuously monitors developments in the construction industry in order to ensure reliable, thorough and up-to-date cost information.

While *overall* construction costs may vary relative to general economic conditions, price fluctuations within the industry are dependent upon many factors. Individual price variations may, in fact, be opposite to overall economic trends. Therefore, costs are continually monitored and complete updates are published yearly. Also, new items are frequently added in response to changes in materials and methods.

Costs—$ (U.S.)

All costs represent U.S. national averages and are given in U.S. dollars. The Means City Cost Indexes can be used to adjust costs to a particular location. The City Cost Indexes for Canada can be used to adjust U.S. national averages to local costs in Canadian dollars.

Material Costs

The R.S. Means staff contacts manufacturers, dealers, distributors, and contractors all across the U.S. and Canada to determine national average material costs. If you have access to current material costs for your specific location, you may wish to make adjustments to reflect differences from the national average. Included within material costs are fasteners for a normal installation. R.S. Means engineers use manufacturers' recommendations, written specifications and/ or standard construction practice for size and spacing of fasteners. Adjustments to material costs may be required for your specific application or location. Material costs do not include sales tax.

Labor Costs

Labor costs are based on the average of wage rates from 30 major U.S. cities. Rates are determined from labor union agreements or prevailing wages for construction trades for the current year.

- If wage rates in your area vary from those used in this book, or if rate increases are expected within a given year, labor costs should be adjusted accordingly.

Labor costs reflect productivity based on actual working conditions. These figures include time spent during a normal workday on tasks other than actual installation, such as material receiving and handling, mobilization at site, site movement, breaks, and cleanup.

Productivity data is developed over an extended period so as not to be influenced by abnormal variations and reflects a typical average.

Equipment Costs

Equipment costs include not only rental, but also operating costs for equipment under normal use. The operating costs include parts and labor for routine servicing such as repair and replacement of pumps, filters and worn lines. Normal operating expendables such as fuel, lubricants, tires and electricity (where applicable) are also included. Extraordinary operating expendables with highly variable wear patterns such as diamond bits and blades are excluded. These costs are included under materials. Equipment rental rates are obtained from industry sources throughout North America—contractors, suppliers, dealers, manufacturers, and distributors.

Crew Equipment Cost/Day—The power equipment required for each crew is included in the crew cost. The daily cost for crew equipment is based on dividing the weekly bare rental rate by 5 (number of working days per week), and then adding the hourly operating cost times 8 (hours per day).

General Conditions

Cost data in this book is presented in two ways: Bare Costs and Total Cost including O&P (Overhead and Profit). General Conditions, when applicable, should also be added to the Total Cost including O&P. The costs for General Conditions are listed in Division 1. General Conditions for the *Installing Contractor* may range from 0% to 10% of the Total Cost including O&P. For the *General* or *Prime Contractor*, costs for General Conditions may range from 5% to 15% of the Total Cost including O&P, with a figure of 10% as the most typical allowance.

Overhead and Profit

Total Cost including O&P for the *Installing Contractor* is shown in the last column on the Unit Price pages of this book. This figure is the sum of the bare material cost plus 10% for profit, the base labor cost plus total overhead and profit, and the bare equipment cost plus 10% for profit. (See the "How To Use the Unit Price Pages" for an example of this calculation.)

Factors Affecting Costs

Costs can vary depending upon a number of variables. Here's how we have handled the main factors affecting costs.

Quality—The prices for materials and the workmanship upon which productivity is based represent sound construction work. They are also in line with U.S. government specifications.

Overtime—We have made no allowance for overtime. If you anticipate premium time or work beyond normal working hours, be sure to make an appropriate adjustment to your labor costs.

Productivity—The productivity, daily output, and labor-hour figures for each line item are based on working an eight-hour day in daylight hours in moderate temperatures. For work that extends beyond normal work hours or is performed under adverse conditions, productivity may decrease. (See the section in "How To Use the Unit Price Pages" for more on productivity.)

Size of Project—The size, scope of work, and type of construction project will have a significant impact on cost. Economies of scale can reduce costs for large projects. Unit costs can often run higher for small projects. Costs for projects of a significantly different size or type should be adjusted accordingly.

Location—Material prices in this book are for metropolitan areas. However, in dense urban areas, traffic and site storage limitations may increase costs. Beyond a 20-mile radius of large cities, extra trucking or transportation charges may also increase the material costs slightly. On the other hand, lower wage rates may be in effect. Be sure to consider both these factors when preparing an estimate, particularly if the job site is located in a central city or remote rural location.

In addition, highly specialized subcontract items may require travel and per diem expenses for mechanics.

Other factors—
- season of year
- contractor management
- weather conditions
- local union restrictions
- building code requirements
- availability of:
  - adequate energy
  - skilled labor
  - building materials
- owner's special requirements/restrictions
- safety requirements
- environmental considerations

Unpredictable Factors—General business conditions influence "in-place" costs of all items. Substitute materials and construction methods may have to be employed. These may affect the installed cost and/or life cycle costs. Such factors may be difficult to evaluate and cannot necessarily be predicted on the basis of the job's location in a particular section of the country. Thus, where these factors apply, you may find significant, but unavoidable cost variations for which you will have to apply a measure of judgment to your estimate.

Rounding of Costs

In general, all unit prices in excess of $5.00 have been rounded to make them easier to use and still maintain adequate precision of the results. The rounding rules we have chosen are in the following table.

Prices from ...	Rounded to the nearest ...
$.01 to $5.00	$.01
$5.01 to $20.00	$.05
$20.01 to $100.00	$.50
$100.01 to $300.00	$1.00
$300.01 to $1,000.00	$5.00
$1,000.01 to $10,000.00	$25.00
$10,000.01 to $50,000.00	$100.00
$50,000.01 and above	$500.00

Final Checklist

Estimating can be a straightforward process provided you remember the basics. Here's a checklist of some of the items you should remember to do before completing your estimate.

Did you remember to . . .

- take into consideration which items have been marked up and by how much
- mark up the entire estimate sufficiently for your purposes
- read the background information on techniques and technical matters that could impact your project time span and cost
- include all components of your project in the final estimate
- double check your figures to be sure of your accuracy
- call R.S. Means if you have any questions about your estimate or the data you've found in our publications

Remember, R.S. Means stands behind its publications. If you have any questions about your estimate . . . about the costs you've used from our books . . . or even about the technical aspects of the job that may affect your estimate, feel free to call the R.S. Means editors at 1-800-334-3509.

How to Use the Unit Price Pages

The following is a detailed explanation of a sample entry in the Unit Price Section. Next to each bold number below is the item being described with appropriate component of the sample entry following in parenthesis. Some prices are listed as bare costs, others as costs that include overhead and profit of the installing contractor. In most cases, if the work is to be subcontracted, the general contractor will need to add an additional markup (R.S. Means suggests using 10%) to the figures in the column "Total Incl. O&P."

Description (Wall Panel, etc.)

Each line item is described in detail. Sub-items and additional sizes are indented beneath the appropriate line items. The first line or two after the main item (in boldface) may contain descriptive information that pertains to all line items beneath this boldface listing.

Division Number/Title (03400/Precast Concrete)

Use the Unit Price Section Table of Contents to locate specific items. The sections are classified according to the CSI MasterFormat (1995 Edition).

Line Numbers (03450 850 0100)

Each unit price line item has been assigned a unique 12-digit code based on the CSI MasterFormat classification.

Level One - CSI-MasterFormat Division
Level Two - CSI

03400
03450-850-0100

Means 12-digit Line Number
Level Four - Means
Level Three - CSI

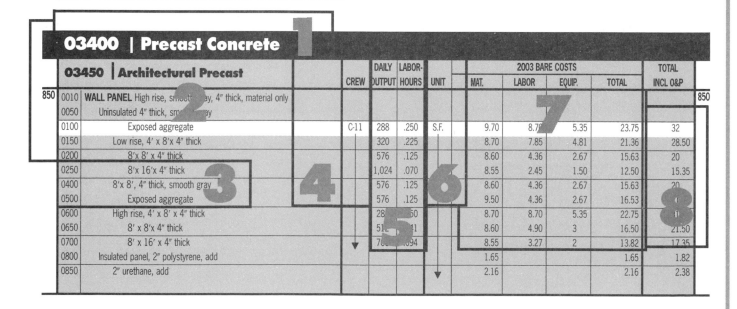

03400 | Precast Concrete

03450 | Architectural Precast

			CREW	DAILY OUTPUT	LABOR-HOURS	UNIT	MAT.	LABOR	EQUIP.	TOTAL	TOTAL INCL O&P
850	0010	**WALL PANEL** High rise, smooth gray, 4" thick, material only									850
	0050	Uninsulated 4" thick, smooth gray									
	0100	Exposed aggregate	C-11	288	.250	S.F.	9.70	8.70	5.35	23.75	32
	0150	Low rise, 4' x 8'x 4" thick		320	.225		8.70	7.85	4.81	21.36	28.50
	0200	8'x 8' x 4" thick		576	.125		8.60	4.36	2.67	15.63	20
	0250	8'x 16'x 4" thick		1,024	.070		8.55	2.45	1.50	12.50	15.35
	0400	8'x 8', 4" thick, smooth gray		576	.125		8.60	4.36	2.67	15.63	20
	0500	Exposed aggregate		576	.125		9.50	4.36	2.67	16.53	
	0600	High rise, 4' x 8' x 4" thick		288	.250		8.70	8.70	5.35	22.75	
	0650	8' x 8'x 4" thick		512	.141		8.60	4.90	3	16.50	21.50
	0700	8' x 16' x 4" thick		700	.094		8.55	3.27	2	13.82	17.35
	0800	Insulated panel, 2" polystyrene, add					1.65			1.65	1.82
	0850	2" urethane, add					2.16			2.16	2.38

(2003 BARE COSTS)

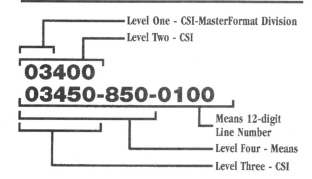

Crew (C-11)

The "Crew" column designates the typical trade or crew used to install the item. If an installation can be accomplished by one trade and requires no power equipment, that trade and the number of workers are listed (for example, "2 Carpenters"). If an installation requires a composite crew, a crew code designation is listed (for example, "C-11"). You'll find full details on all composite crews in the Crew Listings.

• For a complete list of all trades utilized in this book and their abbreviations, see the inside back cover.

Crew C-11	Hr.	Daily	Hr.	Daily	Bare Costs	Incl. O&P
1 Struc. Steel Foreman	$37.65	$301.20	$68.35	$546.80	$34.84	$61.19
6 Struc. Steel Workers	35.65	1711.20	64.75	3108.00		
1 Equip. Oper. (crane)	33.70	269.60	51.00	408.00		
1 Equip. Oper. Oiler	28.30	226.40	42.85	342.80		
1 Truck Crane, 150 Ton		1538.00		1691.80	21.36	23.50
72 L.H., Daily Totals		$4046.40		$6097.40	$56.20	$84.69

Productivity: Daily Output (288)/Labor-Hours (0.25)

The "Daily Output" represents the typical number of units the designated crew will install in a normal 8-hour day. To find out the number of days the given crew would require to complete the installation, divide your quantity by the daily output. For example:

Quantity	÷	Daily Output	=	Duration
4320 S.F.	÷	288/ Crew Day	=	15 Crew Days

The "Labor-Hours" figure represents the number of labor-hours required to install one unit of work. To find out the number of labor-hours required for your particular task, multiply the quantity of the item times the number of labor-hours shown. For example:

Quantity	x	Productivity Rate	=	Duration
4320 S.F.	x	0.250 Labor-Hours/ S.F.	=	1080 Labor-Hours

Unit (S.F.)

The abbreviated designation indicates the unit of measure upon which the price, production, and crew are based (S.F. = Square Foot). For a complete listing of abbreviations refer to the Abbreviations Listing in the Reference Section of this book.

Bare Costs:

Mat. (Bare Material Cost) (9.70)

The unit material cost is the "bare" material cost with no overhead and profit included. *Costs shown reflect national average material prices for January of the current year and include delivery to the job site. No sales taxes are included.*

Labor (8.70)

The unit labor cost is derived by multiplying bare labor-hour costs for Crew C-11 by labor-hour units. The bare labor-hour cost is found in the Crew Section under C-11.

Labor-Hour Cost Crew C-11	x	Labor-Hour Units	=	Labor
$34.84	x	0.25	=	$8.70

Equip. (Equipment) (5.35)

Equipment costs for each crew are listed in the description of each crew. The unit equipment cost is derived by multiplying the bare equipment hourly cost by the labor-hour units.

Equipment Cost Crew C-11	x	Labor-Hour Units	=	Equip.
$21.36	x	0.25	=	$5.35

Total (23.75)

The total of the bare costs is the arithmetic total of the three previous columns: mat., labor, and equip.

Material	+	Labor	+	Equip.	=	Total
$9.70	+	$8.70	+	$5.35	=	$23.75

Total Costs Including O&P

This figure is the sum of the bare material cost plus 10% for profit; the bare labor cost plus total overhead and profit; and the bare equipment cost plus 10% for profit.

Material is Bare Material Cost + 10% = 9.70 + 0.97	=	$10.67
Labor for Crew C-11 = Labor-Hour Cost (61.19) x Labor-Hour Units (0.25)	=	$15.30
Equip. is Bare Equip. Cost + 10% = 5.35 + 0.54	=	$ 5.89
Total (Rounded)	=	$32

01100 | Summary

		01107	**Professional Consultant**	CREW	DAILY OUTPUT	LABOR-HOURS	UNIT	2003 BARE COSTS				TOTAL INCL O&P	
								MAT.	LABOR	EQUIP.	TOTAL		
100	0011	**ARCHITECTURAL FEES**											**100**
	2000		For "Greening" of building				Project					5%	
300	0010	**ENGINEERING FEES**											**300**
	4000		Consultant, using DOE software energy analysis, small bldg, min				SF Flr.					.25	
	4010		Maximum									.45	
	4020		Medium buillding, minimum									.15	
	4030		Maximum									.35	
	4040		Large building, minimum									.05	
	4050		Maximum				↓					.25	

01400 | Quality Requirements

		01450	**Quality Control**	CREW	DAILY OUTPUT	LABOR-HOURS	UNIT	2003 BARE COSTS				TOTAL INCL O&P	
								MAT.	LABOR	EQUIP.	TOTAL		
500	0010	**FIELD TESTING**											**500**
	9000		Thermographic testing, for bldg envelope heat loss, average 2,000 S.F.	"			Ea.					500	

01800 | Facility Operation

01810		Commissioning	CREW	DAILY OUTPUT	LABOR-HOURS	UNIT	2003 BARE COSTS				TOTAL INCL O&P	
							MAT.	LABOR	EQUIP.	TOTAL		
100	0010	**COMMISSIONING** Including documentation of design intent										100
	0100	performance verification, O&M, training, min				Project					.50%	
	0150	Maximum				"					.75%	

01832		Facilities Maintenance										
350	0010	**MECHANICAL FACILITIES MAINTENANCE**										350
	0100	Air conditioning system maintenance										
	0800	Ductwork, clean										
	0810	Rectangular										
	0820	6"	1 Shee	187.50	.043	L.F.		1.58		1.58	2.44	
	0830	8"		140.63	.057			2.10		2.10	3.25	
	0840	10"		112.50	.071			2.63		2.63	4.06	
	0850	12"		93.75	.085			3.16		3.16	4.88	
	0860	14"		80.36	.100			3.68		3.68	5.70	
	0870	16"	▼	70.31	.114	▼		4.21		4.21	6.50	
	0900	Round										
	0910	4"	1 Shee	358.10	.022	L.F.		.83		.83	1.28	
	0920	6"		238.73	.034			1.24		1.24	1.92	
	0930	8"		179.05	.045			1.65		1.65	2.55	
	0940	10"		143.24	.056			2.07		2.07	3.19	
	0950	12"		119.37	.067			2.48		2.48	3.83	
	0960	16"	▼	89.52	.089	▼		3.31		3.31	5.10	

2

SITE CONSTRUCTION

02050 | Basic Site Materials & Methods

02065	Cement & Concrete	CREW	DAILY OUTPUT	LABOR-HOURS	UNIT	2003 BARE COSTS				TOTAL INCL O&P
						MAT.	LABOR	EQUIP.	TOTAL	
0010	**ASPHALTIC CONCRETE** plant mix (145 lb. per C.F.)				Ton	31.50			31.50	35
2000	Reclaimed pavement in stockpile					13			13	14.30
2100	Recycled pavement, at plant, ratio old: new, 70:30					19.30			19.30	21
2120	Ratio old: new, 30:70					27.50			27.50	30.50

300   300

02100 | Site Remediation

02115	Underground Tank Removal	CREW	DAILY OUTPUT	LABOR-HOURS	UNIT	2003 BARE COSTS				TOTAL INCL O&P
						MAT.	LABOR	EQUIP.	TOTAL	
0010	**REMOVAL OF UNDERGROUND STORAGE TANKS**									
0011	Petroleum storage tanks, non-leaking									
0100	Excavate & load onto trailer									
0110	3000 gal. to 5000 gal. tank	B-14	4	12	Ea.		315	54.50	369.50	545
0120	6000 gal to 8000 gal tank	B-3A	3	13.333			350	243	593	805
0130	9000 gal to 12000 gal tank	"	2	20			525	365	890	1,225
0190	Known leaking tank add				%				100%	100%
0200	Remove sludge, water and remaining product from tank bottom									
0201	of tank with vacuum truck									
0300	3000 gal to 5000 gal tank	A-13	5	1.600	Ea.		50	98	148	184
0310	6000 gal to 8000 gal tank		4	2			62	123	185	229
0320	9000 gal to 12000 gal tank		3	2.667			83	163	246	305
0390	Dispose of sludge off-site, average				Gal.					4.40
0400	Insert inert solid CO2 "dry ice" into tank									
0401	For cleaning/transporting tanks (1.5 lbs./100 gal. cap)	1 Clab	500	.016	Lb.	1.40	.39		1.79	2.16
0403	Insert solid carbon dioxide, 1.5 lbs./100 gal.	"	400	.020	"	1.40	.49		1.89	2.31
0503	Disconnect and remove piping	1 Plum	160	.050	L.F.		1.87		1.87	2.82
0603	Transfer liquids, 10% of volume	"	1,600	.005	Gal.		.19		.19	.28
0703	Cut accessway into undg stor tank	1 Clab	5.33	1.501	Ea.		37		37	58
0813	Remove sludge, wash and wipe tank, 500 gal	1 Plum	8	1			37.50		37.50	56.50
0823	3,000 gal		6.67	1.199			45		45	67.50
0833	5,000 gal		6.15	1.301			48.50		48.50	73.50
0843	8,000 gal		5.33	1.501			56		56	84.50
0853	10,000 gal		4.57	1.751			65.50		65.50	98.50
0863	12,000 gal		4.21	1.900			71		71	107
1020	Haul tank to certified salvage dump, 100 miles round trip									
1023	3000 gal. to 5000 gal. tank				Ea.				550	690
1026	6000 gal. to 8000 gal. tank								650	825
1029	9,000 gal. to 12,000 gal. tank								875	1,100
1100	Disposal of contaminated soil to landfill									
1110	Minimum				C.Y.					110
1111	Maximum				"					330
1120	Disposal of contaminated soil to									
1121	bituminous concrete batch plant									
1130	Minimum				C.Y.					55
1131	Maximum				"					110
1203	Excavate, pull, & load tank, backfill hole, 8,000 gal +	B-12C	.50	32	Ea.		990	1,900	2,890	3,600
1213	Haul tank to certified dump, 100 miles rt, 8,000 gal +	B-34K	1	8			205	600	805	970
1223	Excavate, pull, & load tank, backfill hole, 500 gal	B-11C	1	16			460	219	679	945
1233	Excavate, pull, & load tank, backfill hole, 3-5,000 gal	B-11M	.50	32			915	490	1,405	1,925
1243	Haul tank to certified dump, 100 miles rt, 500 gal	B-34L	1	8			249	120	369	505
1253	Haul tank to certified dump, 100 miles rt, 3-5,000 gal	B-34M	1	8			249	138	387	525

200   200

02100 | Site Remediation

02115	Underground Tank Removal	CREW	DAILY OUTPUT	LABOR-HOURS	UNIT	2003 BARE COSTS MAT.	LABOR	EQUIP.	TOTAL	TOTAL INCL O&P	
200											**200**
2010	Decontamination of soil on site incl poly tarp on top/bottom										
2011	Soil containment berm, and chemical treatment										
2020	Minimum	B-11C	100	.160	C.Y.	5.60	4.58	2.19	12.37	15.60	
2021	Maximum	"	100	.160		7.25	4.58	2.19	14.02	17.45	
2050	Disposal of decontaminated soil, minimum									66	
2055	Maximum									135	

02200 | Site Preparation

02220	Site Demolition	CREW	DAILY OUTPUT	LABOR-HOURS	UNIT	2003 BARE COSTS MAT.	LABOR	EQUIP.	TOTAL	TOTAL INCL O&P	
200											**200**
0010	**BUILDING DECONSTRUCTION** For salvage										
0225	Avg 2 story, pre 1970 house, 1400 SF, labor for all salv mat, min	6 Clab	25	1.920	SF Flr.		47.50		47.50	74	
0230	Maximum	"	15	3.200	"		79		79	123	
0235	Salvage of carpet, tackless	2 Clab	2,400	.007	S.F.		.16		.16	.26	
0240	Wood floors, incl denailing and packaging	3 Clab	270	.089	"		2.19		2.19	3.42	
0260	Wood doors and trim, standard	1 Clab	16	.500	Ea.		12.35		12.35	19.25	
0280	Base or cove mouldings, incl denailing and packaging		500	.016	L.F.		.39		.39	.62	
0320	Closet shelving and trim, incl denailing and packaging		18	.444	Set		10.95		10.95	17.10	
0340	Kitchen cabinets, uppers and lowers, prefab type	2 Clab	24	.667	L.F.		16.45		16.45	25.50	
0360	Kitchen cabinets, uppers and lowers, built-in		12	1.333	"		33		33	51.50	
0370	Bath fixt, incl toilet, tub, vanity, and med cabinet		3	5.333	Set		131		131	205	

02300 | Earthwork

02340	Soil Stabilization	CREW	DAILY OUTPUT	LABOR-HOURS	UNIT	2003 BARE COSTS MAT.	LABOR	EQUIP.	TOTAL	TOTAL INCL O&P	
500											**500**
0010	**SOIL STABILIZATION** Including scarifying and compaction										
1500	Geotextile fabric, woven, 200 lb. tensile strength	2 Clab	2,500	.006	S.Y.	1.79	.16		1.95	2.22	
1510	Heavy Duty, 600 lb. tensile strength		2,400	.007		1.60	.16		1.76	2.02	
1550	Non-woven, 120 lb. tensile strength		2,500	.006		.91	.16		1.07	1.25	

02360	Soil Treatment										
800											**800**
0010	**TERMITE PRETREATMENT**										
0030	SS mesh, no chemicals, avg 1400 home, min	1 Skwk	1,000	.008	SF Flr.	.25	.26		.51	.68	
0040	Max	"	500	.016	"	.25	.52		.77	1.09	

02370	Erosion & Sedimentation Control										
550											**550**
0010	**EROSION CONTROL** Jute mesh, 100 S.Y. per roll, 4' wide, stapled	B-80A	2,400	.010	S.Y.	.64	.25	.06	.95	1.15	
1400	Barriers, w/degradeable component, 3' H, incl wd stakes	2 Clab	1,600	.010	L.F.	1.50	.25		1.75	2.04	

02450 | Foundation & Load Bearing Elements

02455 | Driven Piles

		CREW	DAILY OUTPUT	LABOR-HOURS	UNIT	2003 BARE COSTS				TOTAL INCL O&P	
						MAT.	LABOR	EQUIP.	TOTAL		
900	0011	**PILES**										900
	5000	Marine pilings, recycled plastic w/steel reinf, up to 90' long, 8" dia	B-19	500	.128	V.L.F.	20	4.04	3.38	27.42	32
	5010	10" dia		500	.128		30	4.04	3.38	37.42	43
	5020	13" dia		400	.160		42.50	5.05	4.23	51.78	60
	5030	16" dia		400	.160		52.50	5.05	4.23	61.78	71
	5040	20" dia		350	.183		82	5.75	4.83	92.58	105
	5050	24" dia	↓	350	.183	↓	125	5.75	4.83	135.58	153

02500 | Utility Services

02530 | Sanitary Sewerage

		CREW	DAILY OUTPUT	LABOR-HOURS	UNIT	2003 BARE COSTS				TOTAL INCL O&P	
						MAT.	LABOR	EQUIP.	TOTAL		
100	0010	**SEWAGE TREATMENT** Plant, not incl. fencing or external piping										100
	0020	Steel packaged, blown air aeration plants									
	0100	1,000 GPD				Gal.				16.05	18.45
	0200	5,000 GPD								10.70	12.30
	0300	15,000 GPD								5.90	6.75
	0600	100,000 GPD								3.75	4.28
	0700	200,000 GPD								2.68	3.08
	0800	500,000 GPD				↓				2.62	3
	1000	Concrete, extended aeration, primary and secondary treatment									
	1010	10,000 GPD				Gal.				11.77	13.55
	1100	30,000 GPD								5.90	6.80
	1200	50,000 GPD								4.81	5.55
	1400	100,000 GPD								3.75	4.33
	1500	500,000 GPD				↓				2.68	3.10
	1700	Municipal wastewater treatment facility									
	1720	1.0 MGD				Gal.				4.60	5.30
	1740	1.5 MGD								4.55	5.25
	1760	2.0 MGD								3.91	4.50
	1780	3.0 MGD								3.05	3.53
	1800	5.0 MGD				↓				2.78	3.21
	2000	Holding tank system, not incl. excavation or backfill									
	2010	Recirculating chemical water closet	2 Plum	4	4	Ea.	720	149		869	1,025
	2100	For voltage converter, add	"	16	1		191	37.50		228.50	267
	2200	For high level alarm, add	1 Plum	7.80	1.026	↓	109	38.50		147.50	178

02600 | Drainage & Containment

02660 | Ponds & Reservoirs

		CREW	DAILY OUTPUT	LABOR-HOURS	UNIT	2003 BARE COSTS				TOTAL INCL O&P	
						MAT.	LABOR	EQUIP.	TOTAL		
500	0010	**GARDEN PONDS** made from 100% recycled plastic										500
	4000	185 gal, 18" deep				Ea.	214			214	236
	4010	245 gal, 36" deep					305			305	335
	4020	Pump kit for				↓	148			148	163

02700 | Bases, Ballasts, Pavements & Appurtenances

		02720	Unbound Base Courses & Ballasts	CREW	DAILY OUTPUT	LABOR-HOURS	UNIT	2003 BARE COSTS				TOTAL INCL O&P	
								MAT.	LABOR	EQUIP.	TOTAL		
200	0010		BASE COURSE For roadways and large paved areas										200
	0025		Red brick dust, from recycled brick, for bases/ballasts, mat only				C.Y.	27			27	29.50	
	0035		3/8" nuggets, recycled brick, bases/ballast, mat only					27			27	29.50	
	0045		1-1/4" nuggets, recyc brick, bases/ballasts, mat only				↓	41			41	45	
		02740	Flexible Pavement										
300	0010		ASPHALTIC CONCRETE PAVEMENT for highways										300
	0600		Porous pvmnt, 1" open graded friction course over 3" bitum course	B-25	7,725	.011	S.Y.	2.40	.31	.25	2.96	3.39	
315	0010		PAVING Asphaltic concrete										315
	2000		From 60% recycled content, base course 3" thick	B-25	800	.110	Ton	8	2.97	2.37	13.34	16	
		02780	Unit Pavers										
200	0011		BRICK PAVING										200
	1810		Brick paving, reprocessed clay and soil, 4" x 8" x 2-1/4"	D-1	110	.145	S.F.	2.50	4.15		6.65	9.10	
		02785	Flexible Pavement Coating										
500	0010		SURFACE TREATMENT										500
	5500		Recycle asphalt pavement at site										
	5520		Remove, rejuvenate and spread 4" deep	B-72	2,500	.026	S.Y.	2.14	.74	3.35	6.23	7.15	
	5521		6" deep	"	2,000	.032	"	3.21	.92	4.19	8.32	9.55	

02800 | Site Improvements and Amenities

		02810	Irrigation System	CREW	DAILY OUTPUT	LABOR-HOURS	UNIT	2003 BARE COSTS				TOTAL INCL O&P	
								MAT.	LABOR	EQUIP.	TOTAL		
900	0010		SUBSURFACE DRIP IRRIGATION, looped grid, pressure compensating										900
	0100		Preinserted emitter, line, hand bury, irregular area, small	3 Skwk	1,200	.020	L.F.	.32	.65		.97	1.36	
	0150		Medium		1,800	.013		.32	.43		.75	1.02	
	0200		Large		2,520	.010		.32	.31		.63	.83	
	0250		Rectangular area, small		2,040	.012		.32	.38		.70	.94	
	0300		Medium		2,640	.009		.32	.29		.61	.81	
	0350		Large		3,600	.007		.32	.22		.54	.69	
	0400		Install in trench, irregular area, small		4,050	.006		.32	.19		.51	.65	
	0450		Medium		7,488	.003		.32	.10		.42	.51	
	0500		Large		16,560	.001		.32	.05		.37	.42	
	0550		Rectangular area, small		8,100	.003		.32	.10		.42	.50	
	0650		Large	↓	33,264	.001		.32	.02		.34	.39	
	0700		Trenching and backfill	B-53	500	.016			.50	.16	.66	.92	
	0750		For vinyl tubing, 1/4", add to above					10%					
	0800		Vinyl tubing, 1/4", material only					.06			.06	.07	
	0850		Supply tubing, 1/2", material only, 100' coil					.11			.11	.12	
	0900		500' coil				↓	.10			.10	.11	
	0950		Compression fittings	1 Skwk	90	.089	Ea.	.68	2.87		3.55	5.25	
	1000		Barbed fittings, 1/4"		360	.022		.16	.72		.88	1.30	
	1100		Flush risers		60	.133		.74	4.30		5.04	7.55	
	1150		Flush ends, figure eight		180	.044		.13	1.43		1.56	2.38	
	1200		Ball valve, 4-1/2"		20	.400		5.80	12.90		18.70	26.50	
	1250		4-3/4"		20	.400		6.85	12.90		19.75	27.50	
	1300		Auto flush, spring loaded		90	.089		1.84	2.87		4.71	6.50	
	1350		Volumetric		90	.089		5.80	2.87		8.67	10.85	
	1400		Air relief valve, inline with compensation tee, 1/2"	↓	45	.178	↓	6.20	5.75		11.95	15.80	

2

SITE CONSTRUCTION

02800 | Site Improvements and Amenities

02810 | Irrigation System

			CREW	DAILY OUTPUT	LABOR-HOURS	UNIT	2003 BARE COSTS MAT.	LABOR	EQUIP.	TOTAL	TOTAL INCL O&P	
900	1450	1"	1 Skwk	30	.267	Ea.	17.20	8.60		25.80	32.50	900
	1500	Round box for flush ends, 6"		30	.267		3.41	8.60		12.01	17.20	
	1550	Fertilizer injector, non-proportional		4	2		3.31	64.50		67.81	105	
	1600	Screen filter, 3/4" screen		12	.667		18.40	21.50		39.90	53.50	
	1650	1" disk		8	1		48.50	32.50		81	104	
	1700	1-1/2" disk		4	2		116	64.50		180.50	228	
	1750	2" disk	▼	3	2.667	▼	231	86		317	390	
	1800	Typical installation 18" O.C., small, minimum				S.F.				.75	.86	
	1850	Maximum								1.39	1.60	
	1900	Large, minimum								.55	.64	
	2000	Maximum				▼				.92	1.07	
	2100	For non-pressure compensating systems, deduct								10%	10%	

02816 | Rainwater Harvesting Systems

			CREW	DAILY OUTPUT	LABOR-HOURS	UNIT	MAT.	LABOR	EQUIP.	TOTAL	TOTAL INCL O&P	
200	0010	**RAINWATER COLLECTION SYSTEM**										200
	1000	Potable, complete for average size home, minimum				System					15,000	
	1010	Maximum									30,000	
	1020	Non-potable, complete for average size home, min									3,000	
	1030	Maximum				▼					8,000	
	1040	Irrigation tape, for subsurface/surface, vinyl, flat, material only, 1-1/2"				L.F.	.18			.18	.20	
	1050	2"					.21			.21	.23	
	1060	3"					.37			.37	.41	
	1070	8 mil					.01			.01	.01	
	1080	10 mil					.01			.01	.01	
	1090	15 mil				▼	.01			.01	.01	
	1100	Couplings for	1 Clab	32	.250	Ea.	.78	6.15		6.93	10.50	
	1110	Batt oper moisture sensor and control valve for	"	8	1	"	20	24.50		44.50	60.50	

02820 | Fences & Gates

			CREW	DAILY OUTPUT	LABOR-HOURS	UNIT	MAT.	LABOR	EQUIP.	TOTAL	TOTAL INCL O&P	
925	0011	**FENCES, PLASTIC**										925
	9015	Fence rail, made from recycled plastic, various colors, 2 rail	B-1	150	.160	L.F.	3.90	4.05		7.95	10.65	
	9018	3 rail		150	.160		5.20	4.05		9.25	12.05	
	9020	4 rail		150	.160	▼	6.30	4.05		10.35	13.30	
	9030	Fence pole, made from recycled plastic, various colors, 7'		96	.250	Ea.	15	6.35		21.35	26.50	
	9040	Stockade fence, made from recycled plastic, various colors, 4' high		160	.150	L.F.	26	3.80		29.80	34.50	
	9050	6' high		160	.150	"	32	3.80		35.80	41	
	9060	6' pole		96	.250	Ea.	16	6.35		22.35	27.50	
	9070	9' pole		96	.250	"	24	6.35		30.35	36.50	
	9080	Picket fence, made from recycled plastic, various colors, 3' high		160	.150	L.F.	26	3.80		29.80	34.50	
	9090	4' high		160	.150	"	32	3.80		35.80	41	
	9100	3' high gate		8	3	Ea.	50	76		126	174	
	9110	4' high gate		8	3		58	76		134	183	
	9120	5' high pole		96	.250		9	6.35		15.35	19.80	
	9130	6' high pole	▼	96	.250		11	6.35		17.35	22	
	9140	Pole cap only					3			3	3.30	
	9150	Keeper pins only				▼	.20			.20	.22	

02840 | Walk/Road/Parking Appurtenances

			CREW	DAILY OUTPUT	LABOR-HOURS	UNIT	MAT.	LABOR	EQUIP.	TOTAL	TOTAL INCL O&P	
700	0011	**PARKING BARRIERS**										700
	1600	Bollards, recycled plastic, 5" x 5" x 5' L	B-6	20	1.200	Ea.	37	32	10.95	79.95	102	
	1610	Wheel stops, recycled plastic, yellow, 4" x 6" x 6' L		20	1.200		37	32	10.95	79.95	102	
	1620	Speed bumps, recycled plastic, yellow, 3"H x 10" W x 6' L		20	1.200		80	32	10.95	122.95	150	
	1630	3"H x 10" W x 9' L	▼	20	1.200	▼	110	32	10.95	152.95	183	

02800 | Site Improvements and Amenities

02870 | Site Furnishings

			CREW	DAILY OUTPUT	LABOR-HOURS	UNIT	2003 BARE COSTS				TOTAL INCL O&P	
							MAT.	LABOR	EQUIP.	TOTAL		
610	0011	**BENCHES & TABLES**										610
	1000	Picnic tables, recycled plastic, various colors, 4'	2 Clab	5	3.200	Ea.	490	79		569	665	
	1010	6'		5	3.200		520	79		599	695	
	1020	8'		4	4		590	98.50		688.50	805	
	1030	Classic park bench, recycled plastic, various colors, 4' long		5	3.200		220	79		299	365	
	1040	6' long		5	3.200		330	79		409	490	
	1050	8' long		4	4		420	98.50		518.50	615	
	1060	Backless mall bench, recycled plastic, various colors, 4' long		5	3.200		200	79		279	345	
	1070	6' long		5	3.200		295	79		374	450	
	1080	8' long		4	4		345	98.50		443.50	535	
	1200	Trash recep, recycled plastic, var colors, round, 32 Gal, 28" x 38" H		5	3.200		210	79		289	355	
	1210	32 Gal, 31" x 32" H	▼	5	3.200	▼	260	79		339	410	

02880 | Playfield Equipment

			CREW	DAILY OUTPUT	LABOR-HOURS	UNIT	MAT.	LABOR	EQUIP.	TOTAL	TOTAL INCL O&P	
700	0011	**PLAYGROUND EQUIPMENT**										700
	0200	Bike rack, 10' long, permanent	B-1	12	2	Ea.	400	50.50		450.50	515	

02900 | Planting

02910 | Plant Preparation

			CREW	DAILY OUTPUT	LABOR-HOURS	UNIT	2003 BARE COSTS				TOTAL INCL O&P	
							MAT.	LABOR	EQUIP.	TOTAL		
500	0010	**MULCH**										500
	1760	Landscape mulch, 100% recycld tires, var colors, hand spread, 3" deep	B-1	10	2.400	C.Y.	120	61		181	227	

02912 | General Planting

			CREW	DAILY OUTPUT	LABOR-HOURS	UNIT	MAT.	LABOR	EQUIP.	TOTAL	TOTAL INCL O&P	
280	0010	**GROUND COVER AND VINES** Planting only, no preparation										280
	0100	Ajuga, 1 year, bare root	B-1	9	2.667	C	63.50	67.50		131	175	
	0150	Potted, 2 year		6	4	"	233	101		334	415	
	0160	Andora Creeping Juniper, 2 gal. container		62	.387	Ea.	15.85	9.80		25.65	33	
	0200	Berberis, potted, 2 year		6	4	C	260	101		361	445	
	0250	Cotoneaster, 15" to 18", shady areas, B & B		.60	40		745	1,025		1,770	2,400	
	0300	Boston ivy, on bank, 1 year, bare root		6	4		117	101		218	286	
	0350	Potted, 2 year		6	4		292	101		393	480	
	0400	English ivy, 1 year, bare root		9	2.667		70.50	67.50		138	183	
	0450	Potted, 2 year		6	4	▼	145	101		246	320	
	0460	12" - 15" runners		496	.048	Ea.	14.40	1.23		15.63	17.70	
	0500	Halls honeysuckle, 1 year, bare root		5	4.800	C	78	122		200	276	
	0550	Potted, 2 year		4	6	"	375	152		527	650	
	0560	Liriope, Big Blue, 1 gal. container		94	.255	Ea.	3.08	6.45		9.53	13.50	
	0600	Memorial rose, 9" to 12", 1 gallon container		3	8	C	178	203		381	510	
	0650	Potted, 2 gallon container		2	12	"	320	305		625	825	
	0660	Oregon Holly-grape, 2' - 3'		62	.387	Ea.	17.45	9.80		27.25	34.50	
	0700	Pachysandra, 1 year, bare root		10	2.400	C	13.50	61		74.50	110	
	0750	Potted, 2 year		6	4	"	95.50	101		196.50	263	
	0760	Variegated Liriope, 1 gal. container		94	.255	Ea.	2.54	6.45		8.99	12.90	
	0770	Viburnum, Sweet, 24" - 30"		62	.387	"	15.60	9.80		25.40	32.50	
	0800	Vinca minor, 1 year, bare root		10	2.400	C	78	61		139	181	
	0850	Potted, 2 year		6	4		90	101		191	257	
	0900	Woodbine, on bank, 1/2 year, bare root		6	4		106	101		207	275	
	0950	Potted, 2 year	▼	4	6	▼	278	152		430	540	
	2000	Alternate method of figuring										

02900 | Planting

02912	General Planting	CREW	DAILY OUTPUT	LABOR-HOURS	UNIT	2003 BARE COSTS				TOTAL INCL O&P	
						MAT.	LABOR	EQUIP.	TOTAL		
280 2100	Ajuga, field division, 4000/M.S.F.	B-1	.23	104	M.S.F.	2,175	2,650		4,825	6,500	**280**
2300	Boston ivy, 1 year, 60/M.S.F.		10	2.400		69.50	61		130.50	171	
2400	English ivy, 1 yr., 500/M.S.F.		1.80	13.333		299	340		639	855	
2500	Halls honeysuckle, 1 yr., 333/M.S.F.		1.50	16		167	405		572	820	
2600	Memorial rose, 9"-12", 1 gal., 333/M.S.F.		.90	26.667		555	675		1,230	1,650	
2700	Pachysandra, 1 yr., 4000/M.S.F.		.25	96		580	2,425		3,005	4,450	
2800	Vinca minor, rooted cutting, 2000/M.S.F.		1	24		1,200	610		1,810	2,275	
2900	Woodbine, 1 yr., 60/M.S.F.		10	2.400		69.50	61		130.50	171	

02930	Exterior Plants										
050 0010	**SHRUBS AND TREES** Evergreen, in prepared beds, B & B										**050**
0100	Arborvitae pyramidal, 4'-5'	B-17	30	1.067	Ea.	42.50	28.50	17.50	88.50	110	
0150	Globe, 12"-15"	B-1	96	.250		10.40	6.35		16.75	21.50	
0200	Balsam, fraser, 6' - 7'	B-17	30	1.067		103	28.50	17.50	149	176	
0300	Cedar, blue, 8'-10'		18	1.778		113	47	29	189	229	
0350	Japanese, 4' - 5'		55	.582		79	15.40	9.55	103.95	121	
0400	Cypress, hinoki, 15" - 18"	B-1	80	.300		54	7.60		61.60	71.50	
0500	Hemlock, canadian, 2-1/2'-3'		36	.667		16.75	16.90		33.65	45	
0550	Holly, Savannah, 8' - 10' H		9.68	2.479		515	63		578	665	
0560	Yaupon, 6' - 7'	B-17	10	3.200		11.75	85	52.50	149.25	201	
0570	Burford, 3' - 4'		37	.865		12.55	23	14.20	49.75	65	
0580	Dwarf Burford, 2' - 3'		21	1.524		14.75	40.50	25	80.25	106	
0590	Dwarf Chinese, 2' - 3'		40	.800		13.15	21	13.10	47.25	61.50	
0600	Juniper, andorra, 18"-24"	B-1	80	.300		15	7.60		22.60	28.50	
0620	Wiltoni, 15"-18"	"	80	.300		11.65	7.60		19.25	24.50	
0640	Skyrocket, 4-1/2'-5'	B-17	55	.582		45.50	15.40	9.55	70.45	84	
0660	Blue pfitzer, 2'-2-1/2'	B-1	44	.545		20	13.80		33.80	43.50	
0670	Repandens holly, 15" to 18" high, in place		37	.649		18.15	16.40		34.55	45.50	
0675	Pfitzer juniper, 18" - 24"		26	.923		24	23.50		47.50	62.50	
0680	Ketleerie, 2-1/2'-3'		50	.480		30	12.15		42.15	52	
0700	Pine, black, 2-1/2'-3'		50	.480		31.50	12.15		43.65	53.50	
0720	Mugo, 18"-24"		60	.400		32	10.15		42.15	51.50	
0740	White, 4'-5'	B-17	75	.427		47	11.30	7	65.30	76.50	
0750	5' - 6'	B-1	22	1.091		52	27.50		79.50	101	
0760	Jack, 5' - 6'	B-17	22	1.455		86	38.50	24	148.50	180	
0800	Spruce, blue, 18"-24"	B-1	60	.400		31	10.15		41.15	50	
0820	Dwarf alberta, 18" - 24"	"	60	.400		26	10.15		36.15	44.50	
0840	Norway, 4'-5'	B-17	75	.427		58.50	11.30	7	76.80	89.50	
0900	Yew, denisforma, 12"-15"	B-1	60	.400		22	10.15		32.15	40.50	
1000	Capitata, 18"-24"		30	.800		18.80	20.50		39.30	52	
1100	Hicksi, 2'-2-1/2'		30	.800		27	20.50		47.50	61.50	
410 0010	**SHRUBS** Broadleaf evergreen, planted in prepared beds										**410**
0100	Andromeda, 15"-18", container	B-1	96	.250	Ea.	16.50	6.35		22.85	28	
0150	Aucuba, 3' - 4'		32	.750		15.60	19		34.60	46.50	
0200	Azalea, 15" - 18", container		96	.250		21	6.35		27.35	33.50	
0300	Barberry, 9"-12", container		130	.185		9.75	4.67		14.42	18.05	
0400	Boxwood, 15"-18", B & B		96	.250		20	6.35		26.35	32	
0450	Cast Iron Plant, 12" - 15" H		41.92	.573		13.55	14.50		28.05	37.50	
0470	Cleyera, 3' - 4' H, B & B		32.48	.739		25	18.70		43.70	56.50	
0480	Creeping gardenia, 2 gal. cont.		98.48	.244		10.05	6.15		16.20	20.50	
0500	Euonymus, emerald gaiety, 12" to 15", container		115	.209		13.75	5.30		19.05	23.50	
0520	Glossy Abelia, 2' - 3'		33	.727		14.40	18.40		32.80	45	
0600	Holly, 15"-18", B & B		96	.250		15	6.35		21.35	26.50	
0650	Indian Hawthorn, 18" - 24"		29.40	.816		15.30	20.50		35.80	49.50	
0700	Leucothoe, 15" - 18", container		96	.250		13.40	6.35		19.75	24.50	

02930 | Exterior Plants

		CREW	DAILY OUTPUT	LABOR-HOURS	UNIT	2003 BARE COSTS				TOTAL INCL O&P
						MAT.	LABOR	EQUIP.	TOTAL	
410	0800	Mahonia, 18" - 24", container	B-1	80	.300	Ea.	23	7.60		30.60	37.50
	0900	Mount laurel, 18" - 24", B & B		80	.300		69.50	7.60		77.10	88.50
	1000	Paxistema, 9 - 12" high		130	.185		14.65	4.67		19.32	23.50
	1100	Rhododendron, 18"-24", container		48	.500		33.50	12.65		46.15	56.50
	1200	Rosemary, 1 gal container		600	.040		57.50	1.01		58.51	65
	1300	Wax Myrtle, 3' - 4'		32	.750		23.50	19		42.50	55.50
	2000	Deciduous, amelanchier, 2'-3', B & B		57	.421		83	10.65		93.65	108
	2100	Azalea, 15"-18", B & B		96	.250		19.15	6.35		25.50	31
	2120	Kurume, 18" - 24"		29.80	.805		15.55	20.50		36.05	49
	2200	Barberry, 2' - 3', B & B		57	.421		19.95	10.65		30.60	38.50
	2300	Bayberry, 2'-3', B & B		57	.421		24	10.65		34.65	43
	2400	Boston ivy, 2 year, container	↓	600	.040		15.10	1.01		16.11	18.20
	2500	Corylus, 3' - 4', B & B	B-17	75	.427		29	11.30	7	47.30	57
	2600	Cotoneaster, 15"-18", B & B	B-1	80	.300		12.90	7.60		20.50	26
	2650	Crape Myrtle, 8' - 9'	B-17	10.50	3.048		44	81	50	175	227
	2700	Deutzia, 12" - 15", B & B	B-1	96	.250		7.90	6.35		14.25	18.55
	2800	Dogwood, 3'-4', B & B	B-17	40	.800		21	21	13.10	55.10	70.50
	2900	Euonymus, alatus compacta, 15" to 18", container	B-1	80	.300		21	7.60		28.60	35.50
	3000	Flowering almond, 2' - 3', container	"	36	.667		16.50	16.90		33.40	44.50
	3100	Flowering currant, 3' - 4', container	B-17	75	.427		18.95	11.30	7	37.25	46
	3200	Forsythia, 2'-3', container	B-1	60	.400		13.95	10.15		24.10	31
	3300	Hibiscus, 3'-4', B & B	B-17	75	.427		12.90	11.30	7	31.20	39.50
	3400	Honeysuckle, 3'-4', B & B	B-1	60	.400		16.75	10.15		26.90	34
	3500	Hydrangea, 2'-3', B & B	"	57	.421		19.50	10.65		30.15	38
	3550	Ligustrum, 2' - 3'	B-17	10.50	3.048		12.15	81	50	143.15	192
	3600	Lilac, 3'-4', B & B	"	40	.800		24.50	21	13.10	58.60	73.50
	3700	Mockorange, 3' - 4', B & B	B-1	36	.667		14.25	16.90		31.15	42
	3800	Osier willow, 2' - 3', B & B		57	.421		16.25	10.65		26.90	34.50
	3850	Pampas Grass, 3' - 4'		58	.414		14.65	10.50		25.15	32.50
	3900	Privet, bare root, 18"-24"		80	.300		9.85	7.60		17.45	22.50
	4000	Pyracantha, 2' - 3', container		80	.300		34	7.60		41.60	49.50
	4100	Quince, 2'-3', B & B	↓	57	.421		18.95	10.65		29.60	37.50
	4200	Russian olive, 3'-4', B & B	B-17	75	.427		20.50	11.30	7	38.80	47.50
	4300	Snowberry, 2' - 3', B & B	B-1	57	.421		11.25	10.65		21.90	29
	4400	Spirea, 3'-4', B & B	"	70	.343		26	8.70		34.70	42.50
	4500	Viburnum, 3'-4', B & B	B-17	40	.800		19.30	21	13.10	53.40	68
	4510	12" - 15"	"	62	.516		19.30	13.70	8.45	41.45	51.50
	4600	Weigela, 3' - 4', B & B	B-1	70	.343	↓	17.25	8.70		25.95	32.50
900	0010	**TREES** Deciduous, in prep. beds, balled & burlapped (B&B)									
	0100	Ash, 2" caliper	B-17	8	4	Ea.	110	106	65.50	281.50	355
	0200	Beech, 5'-6'		50	.640		215	16.95	10.50	242.45	275
	0300	Birch, 6'-8', 3 stems		20	1.600		154	42.50	26	222.50	264
	0400	Cherry, 6' - 8', 1" caliper		24	1.333		78.50	35.50	22	136	165
	0500	Crabapple, 6'-8'		20	1.600		141	42.50	26	209.50	251
	0600	Dogwood, 4'-5'		40	.800		59	21	13.10	93.10	111
	0610	Kousa, 6' - 8'		10	3.200		90.50	85	52.50	228	288
	0700	Eastern redbud 4'-5'		40	.800		114	21	13.10	148.10	172
	0710	5' - 6'		9	3.556		60.50	94.50	58.50	213.50	276
	0800	Elm, 8'-10'		20	1.600		108	42.50	26	176.50	214
	0810	Camperdown, 12' - 15', 3" caliper		4	8		282	212	131	625	780
	0900	Ginkgo, 6'-7'		24	1.333		160	35.50	22	217.50	255
	1000	Hawthorn, 8'-10', 1" caliper		20	1.600		123	42.50	26	191.50	230
	1100	Honeylocust, 10'-12', 1-1/2" caliper		10	3.200		131	85	52.50	268.50	335
	1200	Laburnum, 6' - 8', 1" caliper		24	1.333		53.50	35.50	22	111	138
	1300	Larch, 8'		32	1		86.50	26.50	16.40	129.40	154
	1400	Linden, 8'-10', 1" caliper	↓	20	1.600	↓	110	42.50	26	178.50	215

02900 | Planting

2
SITE CONSTRUCTION

02930 | Exterior Plants

			CREW	DAILY OUTPUT	LABOR-HOURS	UNIT	MAT.	LABOR	EQUIP.	TOTAL	TOTAL INCL O&P	
900	1450	Loquat, 7' - 8'	B-17	10	3.200	Ea.	15.10	85	52.50	152.60	205	900
	1500	Magnolia, 4'-5'		20	1.600		59	42.50	26	127.50	160	
	1510	10' - 12'		4	8		96	212	131	439	575	
	1600	Maple, red, 8'-10', 1-1/2" caliper		10	3.200		146	85	52.50	283.50	350	
	1610	16' - 18', 4" caliper		2.82	11.348		275	300	186	761	975	
	1700	Mountain ash, 8'-10', 1" caliper		16	2		144	53	33	230	276	
	1800	Oak, 2-1/2"-3" caliper		6	5.333		209	141	87.50	437.50	545	
	1810	Laurel, 18' - 22', 3" caliper		2	16		165	425	262	852	1,125	
	1820	18' - 22', 5" caliper		2	16		274	425	262	961	1,250	
	1830	Live, 15' - 20', 4" caliper		2	16		750	425	262	1,437	1,775	
	1840	Willow, 14' - 16'		3.56	8.989		225	238	147	610	775	
	1900	Pagoda, 6' - 8'		20	1.600		78.50	42.50	26	147	181	
	2000	Pear, 6' - 8', 1" caliper		20	1.600		129	42.50	26	197.50	237	
	2100	Planetree, 9'-11', 1-1/4" caliper		10	3.200		96.50	85	52.50	234	295	
	2200	Plum, 6'-8', 1" caliper		20	1.600		91	42.50	26	159.50	195	
	2300	Poplar, 9'-11', 1-1/4" caliper		10	3.200		44.50	85	52.50	182	238	
	2310	14' - 16'		4	8		197	212	131	540	685	
	2400	Shadbush, 4' - 5'		60	.533		69	14.15	8.75	91.90	108	
	2500	Sumac, 2'-3'		75	.427		23	11.30	7	41.30	50	
	2600	Tupelo, 5' - 6'		40	.800		47	21	13.10	81.10	98.50	
	2700	Tulip, 5'-6'		40	.800		46.50	21	13.10	80.60	98	
	2710	14' - 16'		6	5.333		200	141	87.50	428.50	535	
	2800	Willow, 6'-8', 1" caliper		20	1.600		50.50	42.50	26	119	150	
	2810	Weeping, 10' - 12', 2" caliper		6	5.333		98.50	141	87.50	327	420	
	9000	Minimum labor/equipment charge	1 Clab	4	2	Job		49.50		49.50	77	

02945 | Planting Accessories

			CREW	DAILY OUTPUT	LABOR-HOURS	UNIT	MAT.	LABOR	EQUIP.	TOTAL	TOTAL INCL O&P	
310	0010	**EDGING**										310
	0780	Landscape timbers, 100% recycled plastic, var colors, 4" x 4" x 8'	2 Carp	250	.064	L.F.	1.50	2.02		3.52	4.81	
	0790	6" x 6" x 8'	"	250	.064		2.50	2.02		4.52	5.90	
	1020	Edging, lawn, made from recycled tires, black, 1" x 6"	B-1	390	.062		1.14	1.56		2.70	3.68	
500	0011	**SIDEWALK GRATES**				Ea.	515			515	570	500
	1710	Tree grates, recycled plastic, 2-piece, black, 4' x 4' square	B-6	25	.960		505	25.50	8.75	539.25	605	
	1720	5' x 5' square		25	.960		560	25.50	8.75	594.25	665	
	1730	3' round		25	.960		440	25.50	8.75	474.25	535	
	1740	4' round		25	.960		445	25.50	8.75	479.25	540	
	1750	5' round		25	.960		610	25.50	8.75	644.25	720	

02950 | Site Restoration & Rehabilitation

02990 | Structure Moving

			CREW	DAILY OUTPUT	LABOR-HOURS	UNIT	MAT.	LABOR	EQUIP.	TOTAL	TOTAL INCL O&P	
300	0010	**MOVING BUILDINGS** One day move, up to 24' wide										300
	0020	Reset on new foundation, patch & hook-up, average move				Total					9,300	
	0040	Wood or steel frame bldg., based on ground floor area	B-4	185	.259	S.F.		6.55	2.07	8.62	12.45	
	0060	Masonry bldg., based on ground floor area	"	137	.350			8.80	2.80	11.60	16.80	
	0200	For 24' to 42' wide, add									15%	
	0220	For each additional day on road, add	B-4	1	48	Day		1,200	385	1,585	2,300	
	0240	Construct new basement, move building, 1 day										
	0300	move, patch & hook-up, based on ground floor area	B-3	155	.310	S.F.	6	8.25	10.80	25.05	31	

03050 | Basic Concrete Materials & Methods

03060	Basic Concrete Materials	CREW	DAILY OUTPUT	LABOR-HOURS	UNIT	2003 BARE COSTS				TOTAL INCL O&P	
						MAT.	LABOR	EQUIP.	TOTAL		
100	0010 **CONCRETE ADMIXTURES & SURFACE TREATMENTS**										100
	1590 Concrete forms, release agent, 100% biodegradeable, zero VOC, 5 Gal				Gal.	8.80			8.80	9.70	
	1595 55 Gal				"	8			8	8.80	

CONCRETE 3

03100 | Concrete Forms & Accessories

3 CONCRETE

03110	Structural C.I.P. Forms	CREW	DAILY OUTPUT	LABOR-HOURS	UNIT	2003 BARE COSTS				TOTAL INCL O&P
						MAT.	LABOR	EQUIP.	TOTAL	
410	**0010 FORMS IN PLACE, COLUMNS**									**410**
	2010 Concrete form tubes, recycled paper and fiber, single use, 8″ dia	C-1	155	.206	L.F.	1.81	6.15		7.96	11.60
	2020 10″ dia		155	.206		2.12	6.15		8.27	11.95
	2030 12″ dia		150	.213		2.24	6.35		8.59	12.40
	2040 14″ dia		145	.221		3.95	6.60		10.55	14.65
	2050 16″ dia		145	.221		5.15	6.60		11.75	15.95
	2060 20″ dia		145	.221		7.80	6.60		14.40	18.90
	2070 24″ dia		135	.237		10	7.05		17.05	22
	2080 30″ dia		130	.246		13.55	7.35		20.90	26.50
	2090 36″ dia		110	.291		15.30	8.70		24	30.50
	2100 42″ dia		100	.320		36	9.55		45.55	54.50
	2110 48″ dia		85	.376		53	11.25		64.25	76
460	**0010 FORMS IN PLACE, INSULATING CONCRETE**									**460**
	0020 Forms left in place, S.F. is for both sides									
	1000 Panel system, flat cavity, minimum	2 Carp	960	.017	S.F.	1.80	.53		2.33	2.80
	1010 Maximum		960	.017		2.70	.53		3.23	3.79
	1020 Grid cavity, minimum		960	.017		2	.53		2.53	3.02
	1030 Maximum		960	.017		3	.53		3.53	4.12
	1040 Post and beam cavity, minimum		960	.017		2.20	.53		2.73	3.24
	1050 Maximum		960	.017		3.30	.53		3.83	4.45
	1060 Plank system, flat cavity, minimum		1,920	.008		2	.26		2.26	2.61
	1070 Maximum		1,920	.008		3	.26		3.26	3.71
	1080 Grid cavity, minimum		1,920	.008		1.80	.26		2.06	2.39
	1090 Maximum		1,920	.008		2.70	.26		2.96	3.38
	1100 Post and beam cavity, minimum		1,920	.008		2	.26		2.26	2.61
	1110 Maximum		1,920	.008		3	.26		3.26	3.71
	1120 Block system, flat cavity, minimum		480	.033		1.80	1.05		2.85	3.62
	1130 Maximum		480	.033		2.70	1.05		3.75	4.61
	1140 Grid cavity, minimum		480	.033		2	1.05		3.05	3.84
	1150 Maximum		480	.033		3	1.05		4.05	4.94
	1160 Post and beam cavity, minimum		480	.033		1.80	1.05		2.85	3.62
	1170 Maximum		480	.033		2.70	1.05		3.75	4.61

03150 | Concrete Accessories

		CREW	DAILY OUTPUT	LABOR-HOURS	UNIT	MAT.	LABOR	EQUIP.	TOTAL	TOTAL INCL O&P
250	**0011 JOINTS**									**250**
	2140 Concrete expansion joint, recycled paper and fiber, 1/2″ x 6″	1 Carp	390	.021	L.F.	.31	.65		.96	1.35
	2150 1/2″ x 12″	″	360	.022	″	.62	.70		1.32	1.78
350	**0011 REBAR ACCESSORIES**									**350**
	9000 Rebar supports, recycled plastic, various shapes & sizes, minimum				Ea.	.07			.07	.08
	9010 Maximum				″	.14			.14	.15

03200 | Concrete Reinforcement

03210	Reinforcing Steel	CREW	DAILY OUTPUT	LABOR-HOURS	UNIT	2003 BARE COSTS				TOTAL INCL O&P
						MAT.	LABOR	EQUIP.	TOTAL	
100	**0010 ACCESSORIES** Materials only									**100**
	0013 Rebar, A615, sizes #3-8, from recycled steel, mat only				Lb.	.28			.28	.31

03200 | Concrete Reinforcement

03220	Welded Wire Fabric	CREW	DAILY OUTPUT	LABOR-HOURS	UNIT	2003 BARE COSTS MAT.	LABOR	EQUIP.	TOTAL	TOTAL INCL O&P	
200	**0010** WELDED WIRE FABRIC ASTM A185										**200**
	0065 Recycled steel, 6x6, 4x4, mat only				C.S.F.	10			10	11	

03300 | Cast-In-Place Concrete

03310	Structural Concrete	CREW	DAILY OUTPUT	LABOR-HOURS	UNIT	2003 BARE COSTS MAT.	LABOR	EQUIP.	TOTAL	TOTAL INCL O&P	
220	**0010** CONCRETE, READY MIX Normal weight										**220**
	6000 Concrete ready-mix additives, recycled coal fly ash, mixed at plant				Ton	45			45	49.50	
	6010 Recycled blast furnace slag, mixed at plant				"	75			75	82.50	

03400 | Precast Concrete

03450	Architectural Precast	CREW	DAILY OUTPUT	LABOR-HOURS	UNIT	2003 BARE COSTS MAT.	LABOR	EQUIP.	TOTAL	TOTAL INCL O&P	
850	**0010** WALL PANEL High rise, smooth gray, 4" thick, material only										**850**
	0050 Uninsulated 4" thick, smooth gray										
	0100 Exposed aggregate	C-11	288	.250	S.F.	9.70	8.70	5.35	23.75	32	
	0150 Low rise, 4' x 8'x 4" thick		320	.225		8.70	7.85	4.81	21.36	28.50	
	0200 8'x 8' x 4" thick		576	.125		8.60	4.36	2.67	15.63	20	
	0250 8'x 16'x 4" thick		1,024	.070		8.55	2.45	1.50	12.50	15.35	
	0400 8'x 8', 4" thick, smooth gray		576	.125		8.60	4.36	2.67	15.63	20	
	0500 Exposed aggregate		576	.125		9.50	4.36	2.67	16.53	21	
	0600 High rise, 4' x 8' x 4" thick		288	.250		8.70	8.70	5.35	22.75	31	
	0650 8' x 8'x 4" thick		512	.141		8.60	4.90	3	16.50	21.50	
	0700 8' x 16' x 4" thick	▼	768	.094		8.55	3.27	2	13.82	17.35	
	0800 Insulated panel, 2" polystyrene, add					1.65			1.65	1.82	
	0850 2" urethane, add				▼	2.16			2.16	2.38	

04200 | Masonry Units

04220 | Concrete Masonry Units

			CREW	DAILY OUTPUT	LABOR-HOURS	UNIT	2003 BARE COSTS				TOTAL INCL O&P	
							MAT.	LABOR	EQUIP.	TOTAL		
180	0010	**AUTOCLAVED AERATED CONCRETE BLOCK** Scaffolding not incl										180
	0050	Solid, 4" x 12" x 24", incl mortar	D-8	600	.067	S.F.	2.38	1.95		4.33	5.60	
	0060	6" x 12" x 24"		600	.067		2.86	1.95		4.81	6.15	
	0070	8" x 8" x 24"		575	.070		3.18	2.04		5.22	6.60	
	0080	10" x 12" x 24"		575	.070		3.83	2.04		5.87	7.35	
	0090	12" x 12" x 24"		550	.073		4.75	2.13		6.88	8.45	

04290 | Adobe Masonry Units

			CREW	DAILY OUTPUT	LABOR-HOURS	UNIT	MAT.	LABOR	EQUIP.	TOTAL	TOTAL INCL O&P	
100	0010	**ADOBE BRICK** Semi-stabilized, with cement mortar										100
	0060	Brick, 10" x 4" x 14", 2.6/S.F.	D-8	560	.071	S.F.	2.01	2.09		4.10	5.40	
	0080	12" x 4" x 16", 2.3/S.F.		580	.069		3.10	2.02		5.12	6.50	
	0100	10" x 4" x 16", 2.3/S.F.		590	.068		2.69	1.99		4.68	6	
	0120	8" x 4" x 16", 2.3/S.F.		560	.071		2.14	2.09		4.23	5.55	
	0140	4" x 4" x 16", 2.3/S.F.		540	.074		2.21	2.17		4.38	5.75	
	0160	6" x 4" x 16", 2.3/S.F.		540	.074		1.56	2.17		3.73	5.05	
	0180	4" x 4" x 12", 3.0/S.F.		520	.077		2.14	2.25		4.39	5.80	
	0200	8" x 4" x 12", 3.0/S.F.		520	.077		2.21	2.25		4.46	5.90	

04400 | Stone

04420 | Collected Stone

			CREW	DAILY OUTPUT	LABOR-HOURS	UNIT	2003 BARE COSTS				TOTAL INCL O&P	
							MAT.	LABOR	EQUIP.	TOTAL		
500	0011	**LIGHTWEIGHT NATURAL STONE** Lava type										500
	0100	Veneer, rubble face, sawed back, irregular shapes	D-10	130	.308	S.F.	5.50	9.20	3.80	18.50	24.50	
	0200	Sawed face and back, irregular shapes	"	130	.308	"	5.50	9.20	3.80	18.50	24.50	
750	0011	**ROUGH STONE WALL**, Dry										750
	0100	Random fieldstone, under 18" thick	D-12	60	.533	C.F.	8.35	15.45		23.80	33	
	0150	Over 18" thick	"	63	.508	"	10	14.75		24.75	33.50	
	0500	Field stone veneer	D-8	120	.333	S.F.	7.25	9.75		17	23	
	0510	Valley stone veneer		120	.333		7.25	9.75		17	23	
	0520	River stone veneer		120	.333		7.25	9.75		17	23	
	0600	Rubble stone walls, in mortar bed, up to 18" thick	D-11	75	.320	C.F.	10.05	9.75		19.80	26	
	9000	Minimum labor/equipment charge	D-1	2	8	Job		228		228	350	

04710 | Simulated Brick

			CREW	DAILY OUTPUT	LABOR-HOURS	UNIT	MAT.	LABOR	EQUIP.	TOTAL	TOTAL INCL O&P	
600	0010	**SIMULATED BRICK** Aluminum, baked on colors	1 Carp	200	.040	S.F.	2.50	1.26		3.76	4.72	600
	0050	Fiberglass panels		200	.040		2.75	1.26		4.01	5	
	0100	Urethane pieces cemented in mastic		150	.053		4.75	1.68		6.43	7.90	
	0150	Vinyl siding panels		200	.040		1.90	1.26		3.16	4.06	
	0160	Cement base, brick, incl. mastic	D-1	100	.160		3	4.56		7.56	10.30	
	0170	Corner		50	.320	V.L.F.	7.50	9.10		16.60	22.50	
	0180	Stone face, incl. mastic		100	.160	S.F.	7.25	4.56		11.81	15	
	0190	Corner		50	.320	V.L.F.	8	9.10		17.10	23	

04730 | Simulated Stone

			CREW	DAILY OUTPUT	LABOR-HOURS	UNIT	MAT.	LABOR	EQUIP.	TOTAL	TOTAL INCL O&P	
600	0010	**SIMULATED STONE**										600
	0100	Insulated fiberglass panels, 5/8" ply backer	L-4	200	.120	S.F.	9	3.53		12.53	15.40	

4
MASONRY

06050 | Basic Wood / Plastic Materials / Methods

06055 | Countertops

		CREW	DAILY OUTPUT	LABOR-HOURS	UNIT	2003 BARE COSTS				TOTAL INCL O&P	
						MAT.	LABOR	EQUIP.	TOTAL		
740	0011	**COUNTERTOPS**									**740**
	6000	Countertops, recy glass, steel/brass chips, w/binder, 1-1/2" T x 25"w	1 Carp	40	.200	S.F.	100	6.30		106.30	120	
	6010	Countertops, recycled waste paper, 1-1/2" Thick x 25" Deep	↓	40	.200	L.F.	75	6.30		81.30	92.50	
	6020	Backsplash for, 1" x 4"		60	.133	"	4	4.21		8.21	10.95	

06073 | Wood Treatment

		CREW	DAILY OUTPUT	LABOR-HOURS	UNIT	MAT.	LABOR	EQUIP.	TOTAL	TOTAL INCL O&P	
400	0011	**LUMBER TREATMENT**									**400**
	0700	Salt treated, water borne, .40 lb. retention			M.B.F.	129			129	142	
600	0010	**PLYWOOD TREATMENT** Fire retardant, 1/4" thick			M.S.F.	215			215	237	**600**
	0500	Salt treated water borne, .25 lb., wet, 1/4" thick				118			118	130	
	0530	3/8" thick				124			124	136	
	0550	1/2" thick				129			129	142	
	0570	5/8" thick				140			140	154	
	0600	3/4" thick			↓	146			146	160	

06090 | Wood & Plastic Fastenings

		CREW	DAILY OUTPUT	LABOR-HOURS	UNIT	MAT.	LABOR	EQUIP.	TOTAL	TOTAL INCL O&P	
680	0010	**NAILS** Prices of material only, based on 50# box purchase									**680**
	2000	Recycled steel, dbl hot-dipped galv., box nail, 3-20D			Lb.	1.90			1.90	2.09	
	2010	Common, 3-20D				1.90			1.90	2.09	
	2020	Annular/spiral thread, 3-20D				1.90			1.90	2.09	
	2030	Drywall nails				2.20			2.20	2.42	
	2040	Finish nails, 4-10D				2			2	2.20	
	2050	Flooring nails, 4-10D				2.61			2.61	2.87	
	2060	Masonry nails, plain shank				2.15			2.15	2.37	
	2070	Roofing nails, plain shank				1.80			1.80	1.98	
	2080	Roofing nails, spiral shank				1.90			1.90	2.09	
	2090	Siding nails, plain shank				2.10			2.10	2.31	
	2100	Siding nails, spiral shank			↓	2.30			2.30	2.53	
	2110	For air guns, carton of 1800, 6D			Ea.	40			40	44	
	2120	For air guns, carton of 1500, 8D				44			44	48.50	
	2130	For air guns, carton of 1200, 10D				40			40	44	
	2140	For air guns, carton of 1100, 16D			↓	44			44	48.50	
900	0010	**SHIMS**									**900**
	5000	Made from recycled plastic, 8"L x 1-1/4"W			Ea.	.15			.15	.17	
	5010	Case of 360			"	55.50			55.50	61	

06100 | Rough Carpentry

06110 | Wood Framing

		CREW	DAILY OUTPUT	LABOR-HOURS	UNIT	2003 BARE COSTS				TOTAL INCL O&P	
						MAT.	LABOR	EQUIP.	TOTAL		
050	0010	**LUMBER**									**050**
	8500	100% recycled plastic, var colors, NLB, 2" x 2"			L.F.	.90			.90	.99	
	8510	2" x 4"				1.80			1.80	1.98	
	8520	2" x 6"				2.60			2.60	2.86	
	8530	2" x 8"				3.50			3.50	3.85	
	8540	2" x 10"				4.50			4.50	4.95	
	8550	5/4" x 4"				1.70			1.70	1.87	
	8560	5/4" x 6"				2			2	2.20	
	8570	1" x 6"				2			2	2.20	
	8580	1/2" x 8"			↓	2.40			2.40	2.64	

WOOD & PLASTICS 6

06100 | Rough Carpentry

06110 | Wood Framing

		CREW	DAILY OUTPUT	LABOR-HOURS	UNIT	2003 BARE COSTS				TOTAL INCL O&P	
						MAT.	LABOR	EQUIP.	TOTAL		
050	8590	2" x 10" T & G				L.F.	5.50			5.50	6.05	**050**
	8600	3" x 10" T & G					8.05			8.05	8.85	
	8610	Add for premium colors					20%			20%	22%	
	8620	Mailbox post, recycled plastic, black/green , 4"x 4"x 6' H, incl. box	1 Clab	3	2.667	Ea.	58	65.50		123.50	167	
	9000	Lumber, wood, finger-jointed 2"x 4"s, add as a premium				M.B.F.	20			20	22	
	9400	Certified lumber, for flooring, decking, etc. S4S, add as premium				"	10%			10%	11%	
590	0010	**FRAMING, WALLS**										**590**
	5966	Prefab headers, w/EPS core, 12" H, for 3-1/2" wide wall	2 Carp	400	.040	L.F.	5.50	1.26		6.76	8	
	5967	For 5-1/2" wide wall		400	.040		5.75	1.26		7.01	8.30	
	5968	For 7-1/2" wide wall		400	.040		6	1.26		7.26	8.55	
	5969	For 9-1/2" wide wall		350	.046		6.25	1.44		7.69	9.15	

06120 | Structural Panels

		CREW	DAILY OUTPUT	LABOR-HOURS	UNIT	MAT.	LABOR	EQUIP.	TOTAL	TOTAL INCL O&P	
800	0010	**STRESSED SKIN PLYWOOD ROOF PANELS** 3/8" group 1 top										**800**
	0020	skin, 3/8" exterior AD bottom skin										
	0030	1150f stringers, 4' x 8' panels										
	0100	4-1/4" deep	F-3	2,075	.019	SF Roof	2.75	.62	.31	3.68	4.33	
	0200	6-1/8" deep		1,725	.023		2.95	.74	.37	4.06	4.81	
	0300	8-1/8" deep		1,475	.027		2.75	.87	.43	4.05	4.85	
	0500	3/8" top skin, no bottom skin, 5-3/4" deep		1,725	.023		2.51	.74	.37	3.62	4.32	
	0600	7-3/4" deep		1,475	.027		2.83	.87	.43	4.13	4.93	
	0800	For 3-1/2" factory fiberglass insulation, add					.36			.36	.40	
	1000	For 1/2" thick top skin, add					.36			.36	.40	
	1500	Floor panels, substitute 5/8" underlayment as										
	1510	top skin, add to roof panels above				SF Flr.	.42			.42	.46	
	2000	Curved roof panels, 3/8" structural 1 top skin,										
	2010	3/8" exterior AC bottom skin, laminated ribs										
	2200	8' radius, 2-1/4" deep, tie rods not req'd.	F-3	1,150	.035	SF Flr.	5.80	1.11	.55	7.46	8.75	
	2400	10' radius, 1-1/2" deep, tie rods are included		950	.042		4.57	1.35	.67	6.59	7.90	
	2600	10' radius, 3-3/8" deep, tie rods not req'd.		1,150	.035		7.95	1.11	.55	9.61	11.10	
	2800	12' radius, 2" deep, tie rods are included		950	.042		4.72	1.35	.67	6.74	8.05	
	3000	12' radius, 4-1/2" deep, tie rods not req'd.		1,150	.035		8.25	1.11	.55	9.91	11.40	
	6000	Box beams, structural 1 web										
	6200	24" deep, 2-2" x 4" flanges, 2 webs @ 3/8"	F-3	295	.136	L.F.	8.70	4.34	2.16	15.20	18.70	
	6400	24" deep, 3-2" x 4" flanges, 2 webs @ 1/2"		260	.154		10.85	4.92	2.45	18.22	22.50	
	6600	48" deep, 3-2" x 6" flanges, 2 webs @ 3/4"		140	.286		18.80	9.15	4.54	32.49	39.50	
	6800	48" deep, 6-2" x 6" flanges, 4 webs @ 3/8",										
	6810	including 2 interior webs	F-3	115	.348	L.F.	38	11.10	5.55	54.65	65.50	
	7000	For exterior AC outer webs, add					1.01			1.01	1.11	
	7200	For medium density overlaid outer webs, add					1.51			1.51	1.66	

06160 | Sheathing

		CREW	DAILY OUTPUT	LABOR-HOURS	UNIT	MAT.	LABOR	EQUIP.	TOTAL	TOTAL INCL O&P	
800	0011	**SHEATHING**, 60% Recycled Content										**800**
	3000	Wood fiber, regular, no vapor barrier, 1/2" thick	2 Carp	1,200	.013	S.F.	.53	.42		.95	1.24	
	3100	5/8" thick		1,200	.013		.71	.42		1.13	1.44	
	4000	Wafer board on roof, 1/2" thick		1,455	.011			.35		.35	.54	
	4100	5/8" thick		1,330	.012			.38		.38	.59	
900	0009	**UNDERLAYMENT**										**900**
	0955	Particleboard, 100% recycled straw/wheat, 4' x 8' x 1/4"	2 Carp	1,450	.011	S.F.	.26	.35		.61	.83	
	0960	4' x 8' x 3/8"		1,450	.011		.39	.35		.74	.97	
	0965	4' x 8' x 1/2"		1,350	.012		.52	.37		.89	1.15	
	0970	4' x 8' x 5/8"		1,300	.012		.62	.39		1.01	1.29	
	0975	4' x 8' x 3/4"		1,250	.013		.72	.40		1.12	1.42	

06160	Sheathing	CREW	DAILY OUTPUT	LABOR-HOURS	UNIT	2003 BARE COSTS				TOTAL INCL O&P	
						MAT.	LABOR	EQUIP.	TOTAL		
900	0980	4' x 8' x 1"	2 Carp	1,150	.014	S.F.	.97	.44		1.41	1.76	**900**
	0985	4' x 8' x 1-1/4"	↓	1,100	.015	↓	1.14	.46		1.60	1.97	

06180	Glued-Laminated Construction										
400	0010	**LAMINATED FRAMING** Not including decking										**400**
	0200	Straight roof beams, 20' clear span, beams 8' O.C.	F-3	2,560	.016	SF Flr.	1.56	.50	.25	2.31	2.77	
	0300	Beams 16' O.C.		3,200	.013		1.13	.40	.20	1.73	2.08	
	0500	40' clear span, beams 8' O.C.		3,200	.013		3	.40	.20	3.60	4.14	
	0600	Beams 16' O.C.	↓	3,840	.010		2.45	.33	.17	2.95	3.40	
	0800	60' clear span, beams 8' O.C.	F-4	2,880	.017		5.15	.52	.40	6.07	6.90	
	0900	Beams 16' O.C.	"	3,840	.013		3.83	.39	.30	4.52	5.15	
	1100	Tudor arches, 30' to 40' clear span, frames 8' O.C.	F-3	1,680	.024		6.70	.76	.38	7.84	9	
	1200	Frames 16' O.C.	"	2,240	.018		5.25	.57	.28	6.10	7	
	1400	50' to 60' clear span, frames 8' O.C.	F-4	2,200	.022		7.25	.68	.53	8.46	9.65	
	1500	Frames 16' O.C.		2,640	.018		6.15	.57	.44	7.16	8.15	
	1700	Radial arches, 60' clear span, frames 8' O.C.		1,920	.025		6.75	.78	.60	8.13	9.30	
	1800	Frames 16' O.C.		2,880	.017		5.20	.52	.40	6.12	7	
	2000	100' clear span, frames 8' O.C.		1,600	.030		7	.94	.72	8.66	9.95	
	2100	Frames 16' O.C.		2,400	.020		6.15	.63	.48	7.26	8.30	
	2300	120' clear span, frames 8' O.C.		1,440	.033		9.35	1.05	.80	11.20	12.75	
	2400	Frames 16' O.C.	↓	1,920	.025		8.50	.78	.60	9.88	11.20	
	2600	Bowstring trusses, 20' O.C., 40' clear span	F-3	2,400	.017		4.20	.53	.27	5	5.75	
	2700	60' clear span	F-4	3,600	.013		3.77	.42	.32	4.51	5.15	
	2800	100' clear span		4,000	.012		5.35	.38	.29	6.02	6.80	
	2900	120' clear span	↓	3,600	.013		5.75	.42	.32	6.49	7.30	
	3000	For less than 1000 B.F., add					20%					
	3050	For over 5000 B.F., deduct					10%					
	3100	For premium appearance, add to S.F. prices					5%					
	3300	For industrial type, deduct					15%					
	3500	For stain and varnish, add					5%					
	3900	For 3/4" laminations, add to straight					25%					
	4100	Add to curved				↓	15%					
	4300	Alternate pricing method: (use nominal footage of										
	4310	components). Straight beams, camber less than 6"	F-3	3.50	11.429	M.B.F.	2,325	365	182	2,872	3,325	
	4400	Columns, including hardware		2	20		2,500	640	320	3,460	4,100	
	4600	Curved members, radius over 32'		2.50	16		2,550	510	254	3,314	3,875	
	4700	Radius 10' to 32'	↓	3	13.333		2,525	425	212	3,162	3,675	
	4900	For complicated shapes, add maximum					100%					
	5100	For pressure treating, add to straight					35%					
	5200	Add to curved				↓	45%					
	6000	Laminated veneer members, southern pine or western species										
	6050	1-3/4" wide x 5-1/2" deep	2 Carp	480	.033	L.F.	2.69	1.05		3.74	4.60	
	6100	9-1/2" deep		480	.033		3.35	1.05		4.40	5.35	
	6150	14" deep		450	.036		4.99	1.12		6.11	7.25	
	6200	18" deep	↓	450	.036	↓	6.75	1.12		7.87	9.20	
	6300	Parallel strand members, southern pine or western species										
	6350	1-3/4" wide x 9-1/4" deep	2 Carp	480	.033	L.F.	3.34	1.05		4.39	5.30	
	6400	11-1/4" deep		450	.036		4.10	1.12		5.22	6.25	
	6450	14" deep		400	.040		4.89	1.26		6.15	7.35	
	6500	3-1/2" wide x 9-1/4" deep		480	.033		8.10	1.05		9.15	10.60	
	6550	11-1/4" deep		450	.036		10.05	1.12		11.17	12.80	
	6600	14" deep		400	.040		11.90	1.26		13.16	15.05	
	6650	7" wide x 9-1/4" deep		450	.036		16.95	1.12		18.07	20.50	
	6700	11-1/4" deep		420	.038		21	1.20		22.20	25.50	
	6750	14" deep	↓	400	.040	↓	25.50	1.26		26.76	30	

06200 | Finish Carpentry

06220 | Millwork

			CREW	DAILY OUTPUT	LABOR-HOURS	UNIT	2003 BARE COSTS				TOTAL INCL O&P	
							MAT.	LABOR	EQUIP.	TOTAL		
100	0011	**BOARDS, USED FOR**										100
	3000	Lumber, from submerged logs, maple, beech, birch, S2S, 15/16" T, #1				M.B.F.	7,000			7,000	7,700	
	3010	S2S, 15/16" Thick, #2 com					6,000			6,000	6,600	
	3020	S2S, 15/16" Thick, #1 com					10,000			10,000	11,000	
	3030	S2S, 15/16" Thick, #2 com					9,000			9,000	9,900	
	3040	Flooring, 3/4" thick, maple, random widths				S.F.	8.30			8.30	9.15	
	3050	Birch, random widths					7.95			7.95	8.75	
	3060	Beech, random widths					8.30			8.30	9.15	
	3070	Red/white oak, random widths					10.95			10.95	12.05	
700	0010	**MOLDINGS, TRIM**										700
	3750	Lattice, recycled plastic, white, 4' x 8' x 1/4"	2 Carp	400	.040	S.F.	.47	1.26		1.73	2.49	

06250 | Prefinished Paneling

			CREW	DAILY OUTPUT	LABOR-HOURS	UNIT	2003 BARE COSTS				TOTAL INCL O&P	
							MAT.	LABOR	EQUIP.	TOTAL		
200	0011	**PANELING**										200
	4000	Sheeting, recycled plastic, black or white, 4' x 8' x 1/8"	2 Carp	1,100	.015	S.F.	.57	.46		1.03	1.35	
	4010	4' x 8' x 3/16"		1,100	.015		.91	.46		1.37	1.72	
	4020	4' x 8' x 1/4"		950	.017		1.13	.53		1.66	2.07	
	4030	4' x 8' x 3/8"		950	.017		1.69	.53		2.22	2.69	
	4040	4' x 8' x 1/2"		900	.018		2.25	.56		2.81	3.36	
	4050	4' x 8' x 5/8"		900	.018		3.10	.56		3.66	4.29	
	4060	4' x 8' x 3/4"		850	.019		3.38	.59		3.97	4.65	
	4070	Add for colors				Ea.	5%			5%	6%	
500	0010	**PANELING, PLYWOOD**										500
	6400	Bamboo, unfinished, 4' x 8' x 3/4"T	2 Carp	320	.050	S.F.	5.70	1.58		7.28	8.70	
	6410	1' W x 6' L x 3/4"T		250	.064		5.50	2.02		7.52	9.20	
	6420	Finished, 1' W x 6' L x 3/4"T		250	.064		5.85	2.02		7.87	9.60	
	8000	Construction adhesive for, 99% VOC free, 10.5 oz tube				Ea.	2.75			2.75	3.03	

06400 | Architectural Woodwork

06410 | Custom Cabinets

			CREW	DAILY OUTPUT	LABOR-HOURS	UNIT	2003 BARE COSTS				TOTAL INCL O&P	
							MAT.	LABOR	EQUIP.	TOTAL		
230	0010	**CABINET HARDWARE**										230
	6000	Cabinet door/drawer pulls, 100% recycled glass, var colors, 1" sq	1 Carp	40	.200	Ea.	7	6.30		13.30	17.55	
	6010	2" square		40	.200		8.40	6.30		14.70	19.10	
	6020	1" round		40	.200		7	6.30		13.30	17.55	
	6030	2" round		40	.200		8.40	6.30		14.70	19.10	
	6040	Various colors & shapes		40	.200		7	6.30		13.30	17.55	
	6050	Door/window trim rosettes, 100% recycled glass, various colors, 3"sq		40	.200		5.60	6.30		11.90	16	
	6060	4" x 4"sq		40	.200		9.80	6.30		16.10	20.50	

6 WOOD & PLASTICS

07200 | Thermal Protection

07210 | Building Insulation

			CREW	DAILY OUTPUT	LABOR-HOURS	UNIT	2003 BARE COSTS				TOTAL INCL O&P	
							MAT.	LABOR	EQUIP.	TOTAL		
150	0010	**BLOWN-IN INSULATION** Ceilings, with open access										150
	0020	Cellulose, 3-1/2" thick, R13	G-4	5,000	.005	S.F.	.13	.12	.04	.29	.38	
	0030	5-3/16" thick, R19		3,800	.006		.21	.16	.05	.42	.54	
	0050	6-1/2" thick, R22		3,000	.008		.26	.20	.07	.53	.69	
	0100	8-11/16" thick, R30		2,600	.009		.34	.23	.08	.65	.83	
	0120	10-7/8" thick, R38	▼	1,800	.013	▼	.43	.34	.11	.88	1.13	
200	0010	**RADIANT BARRIER**										200
	2000	Radiant barrier, double sided aluminum over bubble-wrap core, 16" wide	1 Carp	1,500	.005	S.F.	.50	.17		.67	.81	
	2010	24" wide		1,500	.005		.44	.17		.61	.74	
	2020	48" wide	▼	1,500	.005	▼	.39	.17		.56	.69	
950	0010	**WALL OR CEILING INSUL., NON-RIGID**										950
	1700	Non-rigid insul, recycled blue cotton fiber, unfaced batts, R-13, 16" wide	1 Carp	1,600	.005	S.F.	.60	.16		.76	.91	
	1710	R-19, 16" wide		1,600	.005		.72	.16		.88	1.04	
	1720	Non-rigid insul, encapsul fiberglass batts, recycled glass, R-13, 16" wide	▼	1,600	.005		.35	.16		.51	.64	
	1740	Sprayed on soft foam insulation, installed cost, for 2" x 4" stud wall								2	2.20	
	1750	For 2" x 6" stud wall				▼				2.80	3.08	

07260 | Vapor Retarders

			CREW	DAILY OUTPUT	LABOR-HOURS	UNIT	2003 BARE COSTS				TOTAL INCL O&P	
							MAT.	LABOR	EQUIP.	TOTAL		
100	0010	**BUILDING PAPER** Aluminum and kraft laminated, foil 1 side	1 Carp	37	.216	Sq.	3.64	6.80		10.44	14.65	100
	0100	Foil 2 sides	"	37	.216	"	6.40	6.80		13.20	17.65	
	0450	Housewrap, exterior, spun bonded polypropylene										
	0470	Small roll	1 Carp	3,800	.002	S.F.	.16	.07		.23	.28	
	0480	Large roll	"	4,000	.002	"	.10	.06		.16	.21	
	0500	Material only, 3' x 111.1' roll				Ea.	55			55	60.50	
	0520	9' x 111.1' roll				"	100			100	110	
	0600	Polyethylene vapor barrier, standard, .002" thick	1 Carp	37	.216	Sq.	1.11	6.80		7.91	11.85	
	0700	.004" thick		37	.216		2.19	6.80		8.99	13.05	
	0880	Vapor retarder, recycled plastic, clear, 4 mil, 10' x 100' roll		36	.222		1.45	7		8.45	12.55	
	0890	6 mil, 10' x 100' roll		36	.222		2.16	7		9.16	13.35	
	0900	.006" thick		37	.216		2.93	6.80		9.73	13.85	
	1200	.010" thick		37	.216		5.75	6.80		12.55	16.95	
	2800	Asphalt felt, 50% recycled content, 15 lb, 4 sq per roll		36	.222		4	7		11	15.35	
	2810	30 lb, 2 sq per roll	▼	36	.222	▼	7.50	7		14.50	19.20	

07300 | Shingles, Roof Tiles & Roof Coverings

07310 | Shingles

			CREW	DAILY OUTPUT	LABOR-HOURS	UNIT	2003 BARE COSTS				TOTAL INCL O&P	
							MAT.	LABOR	EQUIP.	TOTAL		
800	0010	**SLATE**, Buckingham, Virginia, black										800
	0100	3/16" - 1/4" thick	1 Rots	1.75	4.571	Sq.	545	128		673	820	
	0200	1/4" thick		1.75	4.571		720	128		848	1,000	
	0900	Pennsylvania black, Bangor, #1 clear		1.75	4.571		435	128		563	700	
	1200	Vermont, unfading, green, mottled green		1.75	4.571		445	128		573	705	
	1300	Semi-weathering green & gray		1.75	4.571		310	128		438	560	
	1400	Purple		1.75	4.571		390	128		518	650	
	1500	Black or gray		1.75	4.571		345	128		473	600	
	1600	Red		1.75	4.571		1,125	128		1,253	1,450	
	1800	Roofing tiles, imitation slate, recycled plastic, grey or black		1.75	4.571		315	128		443	565	
	1810	Green		1.75	4.571		360	128		488	615	
	1820	Mulberry	▼	1.75	4.571	▼	415	128		543	675	

THERMAL & MOISTURE PROTECTION **7**

07300 | Shingles, Roof Tiles & Roof Coverings

07310 | Shingles

			CREW	DAILY OUTPUT	LABOR-HOURS	UNIT	MAT.	LABOR	EQUIP.	TOTAL	TOTAL INCL O&P	
800	1850	Roofing tiles, recycled composite of slate, clay and binders	1 Rots	1.75	4.571	Sq.	260	128		388	505	800
	1880	Roofing tiles, slate, salvaged, various colors, minimum		1.75	4.571		250	128		378	495	
	1890	Maximum		1.75	4.571		400	128		528	660	
	2500	Slate roof repair, extensive replacement		1	8	↓	540	224		764	975	
	2600	Repair individual pieces, scattered		19	.421	Ea.	5.40	11.75		17.15	26	
	9000	Minimum labor/equipment charge	↓	3	2.667	Job		74.50		74.50	127	
980	0010	**WOOD** 16″ No. 1 red cedar shingles, 5″ exposure, on roof	1 Carp	2.50	3.200	Sq.	151	101		252	325	980
	2051	Shingles, white cedar, Certified, dipped, A grade, 16″ long, 5″ exposure		2	4	″	215	126		341	435	
	2052	B grade, 16″ long, 5″ exposure		2	4	Sq.	197	126		323	415	
	2053	Undipped, A grade, 16″ long, 5″ exposure		2	4		180	126		306	395	
	2054	Undipped, B grade, 16″ long, 5″ exposure		2	4		160	126		286	375	
	8900	Roof shingles, imitation wood shakes, from recycled plastic		1.75	4.571	↓	180	144		324	425	
	8910	Ridge cap for	↓	170	.047	L.F.	27	1.48		28.48	32	
	8920	Roof shingles, imitation wood shakes, from recycled aluminum, installed				Sq.	200			200	220	
	8930	Roof shingles, imitation wood shingles, from recycled steel, installed				″	200			200	220	

07320 | Roof Tiles

			CREW	DAILY OUTPUT	LABOR-HOURS	UNIT	MAT.	LABOR	EQUIP.	TOTAL	TOTAL INCL O&P	
300	0011	**METAL**										300
	4000	Roof tiles, 100% recycled copper, 9″ x 15″	1 Carp	2.50	3.200	Sq.	350	101		451	545	
	4010	Starter strip for, 8′		50	.160	Ea.	13.75	5.05		18.80	23	
	4020	Gable end strip for, 8′		38	.211		13.75	6.65		20.40	25.50	
	4030	Sidewall or end strip for, 8′		38	.211		18.50	6.65		25.15	31	
	4040	Pipe flashing tile w/rubber boot, for 1-1/2″ pipe		16	.500		25.50	15.80		41.30	52.50	
	4050	For 2-1/2″ pipe		16	.500		29	15.80		44.80	56	
	4060	For 3-1/2″ pipe		16	.500		33	15.80		48.80	61	
	4070	For 4-1/2″ pipe		16	.500		35	15.80		50.80	63	
	4080	Continuous valley strip for, 10′	↓	24	.333		42	10.50		52.50	62.50	
	4090	16″ x 50′ copper roll, material only				↓	190			190	209	
	4100	Roof tiles, 100% recycled aluminum, 9″ x 15″	1 Carp	2.50	3.200	Sq.	163	101		264	335	
	4110	Starter strip for, 8′		50	.160	Ea.	10	5.05		15.05	18.90	
	4120	Gable end strip for, 8′		38	.211		13.75	6.65		20.40	25.50	
	4130	End or sidewall strip for, 8′		38	.211		12.60	6.65		19.25	24.50	
	4140	Flashing tile w/rubber boot, for 1-1/2″ pipe		16	.500		13.30	15.80		29.10	39	
	4150	For 2-1/2″ pipe		16	.500		14.20	15.80		30	40	
	4160	For 3-1/2″ pipe		16	.500		16.40	15.80		32.20	42.50	
	4170	For 4-1/2″ pipe		16	.500		16.90	15.80		32.70	43	
	4180	Continuous valley strip for, 10′	↓	24	.333		17.75	10.50		28.25	36	
	4190	16″ x 50′ roll, material only					72			72	79	
	4200	Bay window roof kit, 100% recycled copper, 8′ wide opening	1 Carp	3	2.667	↓	270	84		354	430	

07330 | Roof Coverings

			CREW	DAILY OUTPUT	LABOR-HOURS	UNIT	MAT.	LABOR	EQUIP.	TOTAL	TOTAL INCL O&P	
900	0010	**THATCHED ROOFING**										900
	2000	Thatched Roofing, 10-12″ thick, straw/wheat reed, tied bdles	2 Rofc	100	.160	S.F.	5.10	4.42		9.52	13.15	

07400 | Roofing & Siding Panels

07410 | Metal Roof & Wall Panels

			CREW	DAILY OUTPUT	LABOR-HOURS	UNIT	MAT.	LABOR	EQUIP.	TOTAL	TOTAL INCL O&P	
700	0011	**STEEL ROOFING**										700
	4000	Roof tiles, imitation clay, recycled steel various colors, installed				Sq.				180	198	

07400 | Roofing & Siding Panels

07420 | Plastic Roof & Wall Panels

			CREW	DAILY OUTPUT	LABOR-HOURS	UNIT	2003 BARE COSTS				TOTAL INCL O&P	
							MAT.	LABOR	EQUIP.	TOTAL		
770	0011	**CORRUGATED ROOF PANELS**										770
	2000	Corrugated roof panels, recycled plastic, various colors, 4' x 79" panel	G-3	10	.800	Ea.	13	24.50		37.50	53	
	2010	Closure strips for, 44" long		70	.457		2	14.10		16.10	24	
	2020	Ridge vents for, 79" long		70	.457		9	14.10		23.10	32	
	2030	Clear, 4' x 79" panel		40	.800		11	24.50		35.50	50.50	
	2040	Pipe flashing panel, 2' x 2'	↓	30	1.067	↓	3	33		36	54.50	
	2050	3" washered nails for				Lb.	3			3	3.30	

07500 | Membrane Roofing

07555 | ROOF COVERING

			CREW	DAILY OUTPUT	LABOR-HOURS	UNIT	2003 BARE COSTS				TOTAL INCL O&P	
							MAT.	LABOR	EQUIP.	TOTAL		
400	0010	**GREEN ROOF SYSTEMS**										400
	8000	Vegetated roof covering systems, flat or low pitch roof, minimum				S.F.					5	
	8010	Maximum				"					50	

07590 | Roof Maintenance & Repairs

			CREW	DAILY OUTPUT	LABOR-HOURS	UNIT	2003 BARE COSTS				TOTAL INCL O&P	
							MAT.	LABOR	EQUIP.	TOTAL		
300	0011	**ROOF COATINGS**										300
	1600	Reflective roof coating, white, elastomeric, approx. 50 SF per gal				Gal.	15			15	16.50	

07720 | Roof Accessories

			CREW	DAILY OUTPUT	LABOR-HOURS	UNIT	2003 BARE COSTS				TOTAL INCL O&P	
							MAT.	LABOR	EQUIP.	TOTAL		
800	0011	**ROOF WALKWAYS**										800
	0600	100% recycled rubber, 3' x 4' x 3/8"	1 Rofc	400	.020	L.F.	4	.55		4.55	5.35	
	0610	3' x 4' x 1/2"		400	.020		4.33	.55		4.88	5.70	
	0620	3' x 4' x 3/4"	↓	400	.020	↓	5.40	.55		5.95	6.90	

08600 | Skylights

08620 | Unit Skylights

		CREW	DAILY OUTPUT	LABOR-HOURS	UNIT	2003 BARE COSTS MAT.	LABOR	EQUIP.	TOTAL	TOTAL INCL O&P
100	0011 **SKYLIGHTS**									**100**
	0020 Skylight, fixed dome type, 22" x 22"	G-3	12	2.667	Ea.	42	82		124	174
	0030 22" x 46"		10	3.200		94.50	98.50		193	257
	0040 30" x 30"		12	2.667		79	82		161	215
	0050 30" x 46"		10	3.200		137	98.50		235.50	305
	0110 Fixed, double glazed, 22" x 27"		12	2.667		201	82		283	350
	0120 22" x 46"		10	3.200		252	98.50		350.50	430
	0130 44" x 46"		10	3.200		360	98.50		458.50	550
	0210 Operable, double glazed, 22" x 27"		12	2.667		299	82		381	460
	0220 22" x 46"		10	3.200		350	98.50		448.50	540
	0230 44" x 46"	↓	10	3.200	↓	475	98.50		573.50	675
	0235 Skylight, operable, double glazing, 14 S.F.				S.F.	34			34	37
	9000 Minimum labor/equipment charge	G-3	2	16	Job		495		495	765
400	0010 **PREFABRICATED** Glass block with metal frame, minimum	G-3	265	.121	S.F.	41	3.72		44.72	51	**400**
	0100 Maximum	"	160	.200	"	81.50	6.15		87.65	99.50
800	0010 **SKYLIGHT** Plastic domes, flush or curb mounted, ten or										**800**
	0100 more units, curb not included									
	0300 Nominal size under 10 S.F., double	G-3	130	.246	S.F.	19.10	7.60		26.70	33
	0400 Single		160	.200		13.25	6.15		19.40	24
	0600 10 S.F. to 20 S.F., double		315	.102		15.45	3.13		18.58	22
	0700 Single		395	.081		7.90	2.50		10.40	12.55
	0900 20 S.F. to 30 S.F., double		395	.081		14.25	2.50		16.75	19.50
	1000 Single		465	.069		10	2.12		12.12	14.30
	1200 30 S.F. to 65 S.F., double		465	.069		10.70	2.12		12.82	15.05
	1300 Single	↓	610	.052		13.80	1.62		15.42	17.70
	1500 For insulated 4" curbs, double, add					25%				
	1600 Single, add				↓	30%				
	1800 For integral insulated 9" curbs, double, add					30%				
	1900 Single, add					40%				
	2120 Ventilating insulated plexiglass dome with									
	2130 curb mounting, 36" x 36"	G-3	12	2.667	Ea.	360	82		442	525
	2150 52" x 52"		12	2.667		535	82		617	720
	2160 28" x 52"		10	3.200		420	98.50		518.50	615
	2170 36" x 52"	↓	10	3.200	↓	455	98.50		553.50	655
	2180 For electric opening system, add					269			269	295
	2200 Field fabricated, factory type, aluminum and wire glass	G-3	120	.267	S.F.	13.85	8.20		22.05	28
	2210 Operating skylight, with thermopane glass, 24" x 48"		10	3.200	Ea.	515	98.50		613.50	720
	2220 32" x 48"		9	3.556	"	540	110		650	765
	2300 Insulated safety glass with aluminum frame	↓	160	.200	S.F.	81	6.15		87.15	98.50
	2305 Skylight system w/ aluminum frame & glazing				"	46			46	50.50
	2310 Non venting insulated plexiglass dome skylight with									
	2320 Flush mount 22" x 46"	G-3	15.23	2.101	Ea.	292	65		357	420
	2330 30" x 30"		16	2		269	61.50		330.50	390
	2340 46" x 46"		13.91	2.300		495	71		566	655
	2350 Curb mount 22" x 46"		15.23	2.101		257	65		322	385
	2360 30" x 30"		16	2		245	61.50		306.50	365
	2370 46" x 46"		13.91	2.300	↓	460	71		531	615
	2400 Sandwich panels, fiberglass, for walls, 1-9/16" thick, to 250 SF		200	.160	S.F.	14.65	4.93		19.58	24
	2500 250 SF and up		265	.121		13.15	3.72		16.87	20.50
	2700 As above, but for roofs, 2-3/4" thick, to 250 SF		295	.108		21	3.34		24.34	28.50
	2800 250 SF and up	↓	330	.097	↓	17.30	2.99		20.29	23.50
	4000 Skylight, solar tube kit, incl dome, flashing, diffuser, 1 pipe, 9" dia.	1 Carp	2	4	Ea.	205	126		331	420
	4010 13" dia.		2	4		273	126		399	495
	4020 21" dia.		2	4		485	126		611	725
	4030 Accessories for, 1' long x 9" dia pipe	↓	24	.333	↓	27.50	10.50		38	46.50

8 DOORS & WINDOWS

08600 | Skylights

		08620	Unit Skylights	CREW	DAILY OUTPUT	LABOR-HOURS	UNIT	2003 BARE COSTS MAT.	LABOR	EQUIP.	TOTAL	TOTAL INCL O&P	
800	4040		2' long x 9" dia pipe	1 Carp	24	.333	Ea.	41	10.50		51.50	61.50	800
	4050		4' long x 9" dia pipe		20	.400		68.50	12.60		81.10	94.50	
	4060		1' long x 13" dia pipe		24	.333		33.50	10.50		44	53.50	
	4070		2' long x 13" dia pipe		24	.333		53.50	10.50		64	75.50	
	4080		4' long x 13" dia pipe		20	.400		93.50	12.60		106.10	123	
	4090		2' long x 21" dia pipe		16	.500		90.50	15.80		106.30	124	
	4100		4' long x 21" dia pipe		12	.667		153	21		174	202	
	4110		45 degree elbow, 9"		16	.500		63	15.80		78.80	94	
	4120		13"		16	.500		77.50	15.80		93.30	110	
	4130		Interior decorative ring, 9"		20	.400		17.85	12.60		30.45	39.50	
	4140		13"	▼	20	.400	▼	19.95	12.60		32.55	41.50	

08800 | Glazing

		08810	Glass	CREW	DAILY OUTPUT	LABOR-HOURS	UNIT	2003 BARE COSTS MAT.	LABOR	EQUIP.	TOTAL	TOTAL INCL O&P	
300	0010	**GLAZING VARIABLES**											300
	4000	Super efficient glazing, triple glazed with low-e glass, argon filled, min		2 Glaz	75	.213	S.F.	11	6.60		17.60	22	
	4010	Maximum		"	75	.213	"	16.50	6.60		23.10	28	
460	0010	**INSULATING GLASS** 2 lites 1/8" float, 1/2" thk, under 15 S.F.											460
	0020	Clear		2 Glaz	95	.168	S.F.	6.65	5.20		11.85	15.20	
	0100	Tinted			95	.168		9.90	5.20		15.10	18.80	
	0150	2 lites, 3/8" thick, clear, glass sealed edges			76	.211		10.25	6.50		16.75	21	
	0200	2 lites 3/16" float, for 5/8" thk unit, 15 to 30 S.F., clear			90	.178		8	5.50		13.50	17.15	
	0300	Tinted			90	.178		8.25	5.50		13.75	17.40	
	0400	1" thk, dbl. glazed, 1/4" float, 30-70 S.F., clear			75	.213		11.35	6.60		17.95	22.50	
	0500	Tinted			75	.213		13.75	6.60		20.35	25	
	0600	1" thick double glazed, 1/4" float, 1/4" wire			75	.213		17.15	6.60		23.75	29	
	0700	1/4" float, 1/4" tempered			75	.213		16.65	6.60		23.25	28.50	
	0800	1/4" wire, 1/4" tempered			75	.213		23	6.60		29.60	35.50	
	0900	Both lites, 1/4" wire			75	.213		22	6.60		28.60	34	
	2000	Both lites, light & heat reflective			85	.188		18.30	5.85		24.15	29	
	2500	Heat reflective, film inside, 1" thick unit, clear			85	.188		16.05	5.85		21.90	26.50	
	2600	Tinted			85	.188		17.25	5.85		23.10	28	
	3000	Film on weatherside, clear, 1/2" thick unit			95	.168		11.45	5.20		16.65	20.50	
	3100	5/8" thick unit			90	.178		14.20	5.50		19.70	24	
	3200	1" thick unit		▼	85	.188		15.75	5.85		21.60	26	
	3350	Minimum		1 Glaz	50	.160		8.75	4.95		13.70	17.15	
	3360	Maximum		"	25	.320		9.50	9.90		19.40	25.50	
	3370	Reflective or tinted, add						2.41			2.41	2.65	
	5000	Spectrally selective film, on ext, blocks solar gain/allows 70% of light		2 Glaz	95	.168	▼	6.80	5.20		12	15.40	
	9000	Minimum labor/equipment charge		1 Glaz	2	4	Job		124		124	188	
675	0010	**REFLECTIVE GLASS** 1/4" float with fused metallic oxide, tinted		2 Glaz	115	.139	S.F.	9.55	4.31		13.86	17.05	675
	0500	1/4" float glass with reflective applied coating			115	.139	"	7.95	4.31		12.26	15.30	
	2000	Solar film on glass, not including glass, minimum			180	.089	S.F.	3.84	2.75		6.59	8.40	
	2050	Maximum		▼	225	.071	"	8.90	2.20		11.10	13.10	

09300 | Tile

09310	Ceramic Tile	CREW	DAILY OUTPUT	LABOR-HOURS	UNIT	2003 BARE COSTS				TOTAL INCL O&P	
						MAT.	LABOR	EQUIP.	TOTAL		
100	0010 **CERAMIC TILE**										100
	9300 Ceramic tiles, recycled glass, var colors, 2" x 2" thru 6" x 6"	D-7	190	.084	S.F.	34	2.29		36.29	41	

09500 | Ceilings

09510	Acoustical Ceilings	CREW	DAILY OUTPUT	LABOR-HOURS	UNIT	2003 BARE COSTS				TOTAL INCL O&P	
						MAT.	LABOR	EQUIP.	TOTAL		
700	0011 **ACOUSTIC CEILING TILES**										700
	5000 Acoustic ceiling tiles, 100% recycled glass, excl susp syst, min	1 Carp	600	.013	S.F.	.75	.42		1.17	1.49	
	5010 Maximum	"	600	.013	"	1.50	.42		1.92	2.31	

09600 | Flooring

09648	Wood Strip Flooring	CREW	DAILY OUTPUT	LABOR-HOURS	UNIT	2003 BARE COSTS				TOTAL INCL O&P	
						MAT.	LABOR	EQUIP.	TOTAL		
100	0009 **WOOD**										100
	8600 Flooring, wood, bamboo strips, unfinished, 5/8" x 4" x 3'	1 Carp	255	.031	S.F.	3.95	.99		4.94	5.90	
	8610 5/8" x 4" x 4'		275	.029		4.10	.92		5.02	5.95	
	8620 5/8" x 4" x 6'		295	.027		4.50	.86		5.36	6.30	
	8630 5/8" x 4" x 3'		255	.031		4.35	.99		5.34	6.35	
	8640 5/8" x 4" x 4'		275	.029		4.55	.92		5.47	6.45	
	8650 5/8" x 4" x 6'		295	.027		4.60	.86		5.46	6.40	
	8660 Accessories, stair treads, 1-1/16" x 11-1/2" x 4'		18	.444	Ea.	38	14		52	64	
	8670 Finished, accessories, stair treads, 1-1/16" x 11-1/2" x 4'		18	.444		58	14		72	86	
	8680 Accessories, stair risers, 5/8" x 7-1/2" x 4'		18	.444		14	14		28	37.50	
	8690 Finished, accessories, stair risers, 5/8" x 7-1/2" x 4'		18	.444		26.50	14		40.50	51	
	8700 Unfinished, access, stair nosing, 6' long		16	.500		31	15.80		46.80	58.50	
	8710 Finished, access, stair nosing, 6' long		16	.500		39	15.80		54.80	67.50	

09651	Resilient Base & Access.	CREW	DAILY OUTPUT	LABOR-HOURS	UNIT	MAT.	LABOR	EQUIP.	TOTAL	TOTAL INCL O&P	
100	0012 **STAIR TREADS**										100
	3000 Rubber stair treads, black, recycled rubber, sq nose, 12" D x 36" W	1 Tilf	125	.064	L.F.	12.25	1.95		14.20	16.35	
	3010 12" D x 42" W		128	.063		11	1.90		12.90	14.90	
	3020 12" D x 48" W		136	.059		9.95	1.79		11.74	13.55	

09658	Resilient Tile Flooring	CREW	DAILY OUTPUT	LABOR-HOURS	UNIT	MAT.	LABOR	EQUIP.	TOTAL	TOTAL INCL O&P	
100	0010 **RESILIENT FLOORING**										100
	2200 Cork tile, standard finish, 1/8" thick	1 Tilf	315	.025	S.F.	3.47	.77		4.24	4.96	
	2250 3/16" thick		315	.025		3.50	.77		4.27	4.99	
	2300 5/16" thick		315	.025		4.17	.77		4.94	5.75	
	2350 1/2" thick		315	.025		5.55	.77		6.32	7.30	
	2500 Urethane finish, 1/8" thick		315	.025		4.42	.77		5.19	6	
	2550 3/16" thick		315	.025		4.15	.77		4.92	5.70	
	2600 5/16" thick		315	.025		5.65	.77		6.42	7.40	

9

FINISHES

09600 | Flooring

			CREW	DAILY OUTPUT	LABOR-HOURS	UNIT	2003 BARE COSTS				TOTAL INCL O&P	
							MAT.	LABOR	EQUIP.	TOTAL		
09658		**Resilient Tile Flooring**										
100	2650	1/2" thick	1 Tilf	315	.025	S.F.	8.35	.77		9.12	10.30	100
	9000	Linoleum, sheet goods		360	.022		4	.68		4.68	5.40	
	9010	Tiles	↓	300	.027	↓	4	.81		4.81	5.60	
09680		**Carpet**										
905	0010	**RECYCLED PADDING AND CARPET LEASING**										905
	2000	Carpet padding, recycled waste carpet, 5/16" thick	1 Tilf	150	.053	S.Y.	1.20	1.62		2.82	3.71	
	2010	3/8" thick		150	.053		1.60	1.62		3.22	4.15	
	2020	7/16" thick	↓	150	.053		2	1.62		3.62	4.59	
	2300	Carpet leasing, avg 5 year lease, install, maint & removal, min									18	
	2310	Maximum				↓					22	
09720		**Wall Coverings**										
100	0010	**WALL COVERING** Including sizing, add 10%-30% waste at takeoff										100
	5400	Wallpaper, 100% recycled content, textured, paintable, average	1 Pape	540	.015	S.F.	.50	.42		.92	1.18	
09910		**Paints & Coatings**										
920	0011	**PAINT, INTERIOR**										920
	8500	Paint, latex, interior, recycled, white, grey, beige, brown	1 Pord	1,800	.004	S.F.	.03	.12		.15	.22	
	8600	Paint, interior, latex and oil base, zero VOC, minimum		2,200	.004		.05	.10		.15	.21	
	8610	Maximum	↓	1,500	.005	↓	.17	.15		.32	.41	

10150 | Compartments & Cubicles

10155	Toilet Compartments	CREW	DAILY OUTPUT	LABOR-HOURS	UNIT	2003 BARE COSTS				TOTAL INCL O&P
						MAT.	LABOR	EQUIP.	TOTAL	
100	0010 **PARTITIONS, TOILET**										100
	3600 Toilet partition, recycl plastic, head rail braced, floor mtd, per cubicle	2 Carp	6	2.667	Ea.	675	84		759	875
	8500 Urinal screen, recycled plastic, head rail braced, floor mtd	"	10	1.600	"	145	50.50		195.50	239

10270 | Access Flooring

10275	Access Flooring	CREW	DAILY OUTPUT	LABOR-HOURS	UNIT	2003 BARE COSTS				TOTAL INCL O&P
						MAT.	LABOR	EQUIP.	TOTAL	
150	0010 **PEDESTAL ACCESS FLOORS** Computer room application, metal										150
	0020 Particle board or steel panels, no covering, under 6,000 S.F.	2 Carp	400	.040	S.F.	10.45	1.26		11.71	13.45
	0300 Metal covered, over 6,000 S.F.		450	.036		7.55	1.12		8.67	10.05
	0350 Perforated steel, 24" panels		500	.032		27	1.01		28.01	31.50
	0400 Aluminum, 24" panels		500	.032		25.50	1.01		26.51	30
	0500 For carpet covering, add					5.35				
	0510 For vinyl floor covering, add					4.82				
	0600 For carpet covering, add					5.45			5.45	5.95
	0700 For vinyl floor covering, add					5.50			5.50	6.05
	0900 For high pressure laminate covering, add					3.67			3.67	4.04
	0910 For snap on stringer system, add	2 Carp	1,000	.016		1.25	.50		1.75	2.17
	0950 Office applications, to 8" high, steel panels,									
	0960 no covering, over 6,000 S.F.	2 Carp	500	.032	S.F.	8	1.01		9.01	10.40
	1000 Machine cutouts after initial installation	1 Carp	10	.800	Ea.	41	25		66	84.50
	1050 Pedestals, 6" to 12"	2 Carp	85	.188		7.70	5.95		13.65	17.80
	1100 Air conditioning grilles, 4" x 12"	1 Carp	17	.471		48.50	14.85		63.35	76
	1150 4" x 18"	"	14	.571		66.50	18.05		84.55	101
	1200 Approach ramps, minimum	2 Carp	85	.188	S.F.	24	5.95		29.95	36
	1300 Maximum		60	.267	"	29.50	8.40		37.90	45
	1400 Stringers, 2' long		200	.080	L.F.	2.42	2.52		4.94	6.60
	1450 6' long		200	.080	"	4.88	2.52		7.40	9.30
	1475 Elevated floor assembly		200	.080	S.F.	5.40	2.52		7.92	9.90
	1500 Handrail, 2 rail, aluminum	1 Carp	15	.533	L.F.	86.50	16.85		103.35	122
	1600 Fascia plate	2 Carp	100	.160	"	22	5.05		27.05	32.50

10300 | Fireplaces & Stoves

10320	Stoves	CREW	DAILY OUTPUT	LABOR-HOURS	UNIT	2003 BARE COSTS				TOTAL INCL O&P
						MAT.	LABOR	EQUIP.	TOTAL	
100	0011 **WOODBURNING STOVES**										100
	2000 Stoves, wood/gas burning, free standing, recycled cast iron, minimum	2 Clab	2	8	Ea.	800	197		997	1,200
	2010 Maximum	"	1	16	"	1,800	395		2,195	2,600

10 SPECIALTIES

10615 | Demountable Partitions

		CREW	DAILY OUTPUT	LABOR-HOURS	UNIT	2003 BARE COSTS				TOTAL INCL O&P
						MAT.	LABOR	EQUIP.	TOTAL	
100	0010	**PARTITIONS, MOVABLE OFFICE** Demountable, add for doors									100
	0100	Do not deduct door openings from total L.F.								
	0900	Demountable gypsum system on 2" to 2-1/2"								
	1000	steel studs, 9' high, 3" to 3-3/4" thick								
	1200	Vinyl clad gypsum	2 Carp	48	.333	L.F.	39.50	10.50		50	60
	1300	Fabric clad gypsum		44	.364		98.50	11.45		109.95	126
	1500	Steel clad gypsum		40	.400		107	12.60		119.60	137
	1600	1.75 system, aluminum framing, vinyl clad hardboard,								
	1800	paper honeycomb core panel, 1-3/4" to 2-1/2" thick								
	1900	9' high	2 Carp	48	.333	L.F.	66.50	10.50		77	89.50
	2100	7' high		60	.267		59.50	8.40		67.90	78.50
	2200	5' high		80	.200		50.50	6.30		56.80	65.50
	2250	Unitized gypsum system								
	2300	Unitized panel, 9' high, 2" to 2-1/2" thick								
	2350	Vinyl clad gypsum	2 Carp	48	.333	L.F.	85.50	10.50		96	110
	2400	Fabric clad gypsum	"	44	.364	"	141	11.45		152.45	173
	2500	Unitized mineral fiber system								
	2510	Unitized panel, 9' high, 2-1/4" thick, aluminum frame								
	2550	Vinyl clad mineral fiber	2 Carp	48	.333	L.F.	85	10.50		95.50	110
	2600	Fabric clad mineral fiber	"	44	.364	"	127	11.45		138.45	157
	2800	Movable steel walls, modular system								
	2900	Unitized panels, 9' high, 48" wide								
	3100	Baked enamel, pre-finished	2 Carp	60	.267	L.F.	96.50	8.40		104.90	119
	3200	Fabric clad steel		56	.286	"	139	9		148	167
	5310	Trackless wall, cork finish, semi-acoustic, 1-5/8" thick, minimum		325	.049	S.F.	28	1.55		29.55	33.50
	5320	Maximum		190	.084		26.50	2.66		29.16	33
	5330	Acoustic, 2" thick, minimum		305	.052		22.50	1.66		24.16	27.50
	5340	Maximum		225	.071		39	2.24		41.24	46.50
	5500	For acoustical partitions, add, minimum					1.63			1.63	1.79
	5550	Maximum					7.60			7.60	8.35
	6100	In-plant modular office system, w/prehung hollow core door								
	6200	3" thick polystyrene core panels								
	6250	12' x 12', 2 wall	2 Clab	3.80	4.211	Ea.	3,050	104		3,154	3,500
	6300	4 wall		1.90	8.421		4,375	208		4,583	5,125
	6350	16' x 16', 2 wall		3.60	4.444		4,275	110		4,385	4,875
	6400	4 wall		1.80	8.889		6,050	219		6,269	7,025

10674 | Storage Shelving

		CREW	DAILY OUTPUT	LABOR-HOURS	UNIT	2003 BARE COSTS				TOTAL INCL O&P
						MAT.	LABOR	EQUIP.	TOTAL	
500	0012	**SHELVING, PLASTIC**									500
	6000	Shelving, industrial, recycled plastic, 2 shelf kit, 16"W x 27"H x 8' L	1 Clab	350	.023	SF Shlf	13.20	.56		13.76	15.40
	6010	1 shelf add-on kit, 16"W x 24"H x 8' L		350	.023		9.50	.56		10.06	11.35
	6020	Extra shelf, 16"W x 8' L		350	.023		5.70	.56		6.26	7.15
	6030	2 shelf kit, 24"W x 27"H x 8' L		350	.023		13.90	.56		14.46	16.15
	6040	1 shelf add-on kit, 24"W x 24"H x 8' L		350	.023		6.95	.56		7.51	8.55
	6050	Extra shelf, 24"W x 8' L		350	.023		3.17	.56		3.73	4.37
	6060	2 shelf kit, 36"W x 27"H x 8' L		350	.023		10.75	.56		11.31	12.75
	6070	1 shelf add-on kit, 36"W x 24"H x 8' L		350	.023		7.40	.56		7.96	9.05
	6080	Extra shelf, 36"W x 8' L		350	.023		4.40	.56		4.96	5.70

SPECIALTIES 10

10670 | Storage Shelving

		10674	Storage Shelving	CREW	DAILY OUTPUT	LABOR-HOURS	UNIT	2003 BARE COSTS				TOTAL INCL O&P	
								MAT.	LABOR	EQUIP.	TOTAL		
500	6090		2' H post for	1 Clab	32	.250	Ea.	6	6.15		12.15	16.25	500
	6100		3' H post for		32	.250		9	6.15		15.15	19.55	
	6110		4' H post for	↓	32	.250	↓	11	6.15		17.15	22	

10800 | Toilet/Bath/Laundry Accessories

		10820	Bath Accessories	CREW	DAILY OUTPUT	LABOR-HOURS	UNIT	2003 BARE COSTS				TOTAL INCL O&P	
								MAT.	LABOR	EQUIP.	TOTAL		
100	0010	**BATH ACCESSORIES**											100
	2300		Hand dryer, surface mounted, electric, 115 volt, 20 amp	1 Carp	4	2	Ea.	485	63		548	630	
	2400		230 volt, 10 amp	"	4	2	"	485	63		548	630	

10 SPECIALTIES

11010 | Maintenance Equipment

11013	Floor/Wall Cleaning Equipment	CREW	DAILY OUTPUT	LABOR-HOURS	UNIT	2003 BARE COSTS				TOTAL INCL O&P	
						MAT.	LABOR	EQUIP.	TOTAL		
800	0010 **VACUUM CLEANING**										800
	0020 Central, 3 inlet, residential	1 Skwk	.90	8.889	Total	580	287		867	1,100	
	0200 Commercial		.70	11.429		1,075	370		1,445	1,775	
	0400 5 inlet system, residential		.50	16		870	515		1,385	1,775	
	0600 7 inlet system, commercial		.40	20		980	645		1,625	2,075	
	0800 9 inlet system, residential		.30	26.667		1,175	860		2,035	2,650	
	4010 Rule of thumb: First 1200 S.F., installed									1,125	
	4020 For each additional S.F., add				S.F.					.18	

11160 | Loading Dock Equipment

11161	Loading Dock Equipment	CREW	DAILY OUTPUT	LABOR-HOURS	UNIT	2003 BARE COSTS				TOTAL INCL O&P	
						MAT.	LABOR	EQUIP.	TOTAL		
400	0010 **LOADING DOCK**										400
	1200 Bumpers, recycled rubber, incl. hdwe, 18" x 18" x 4-1/2" Thick	1 Carp	26	.308	Ea.	80	9.70		89.70	103	
	1210 18" x 18" x 10-1/2" Thick		24	.333		160	10.50		170.50	192	
	1220 18" x 18" x 12-1/2" Thick		22	.364		220	11.45		231.45	260	
	1230 Add for galvanized hardware					20			20	22	

11300 | Fluid Waste Treatment & Disposal Equipment

11355	Greywater Recovery Systems	CREW	DAILY OUTPUT	LABOR-HOURS	UNIT	2003 BARE COSTS				TOTAL INCL O&P	
						MAT.	LABOR	EQUIP.	TOTAL		
100	0010 **GREYWATER RECOVERY SYSTEMS**, for ext irrigation										100
	1000 Resi syst, for avg home, incl tank, pump & dist lines, inst costs, min				System					5,000	
	1010 Maximum				"					10,000	

11450 | Residential Equipment

11454	Residential Appliances	CREW	DAILY OUTPUT	LABOR-HOURS	UNIT	2003 BARE COSTS				TOTAL INCL O&P	
						MAT.	LABOR	EQUIP.	TOTAL		
500	0010 **RESIDENTIAL APPLIANCES**										500
	3100 Dishwasher, built-in, energy-star qualified, minimum	L-1	4	4	Ea.	340	150		490	600	
	3110 Maximum	"	2	8		520	300		820	1,025	
	6750 Washing machine, automatic, front-loading, energy-star qualified, min	1 Plum	3	2.667		800	99.50		899.50	1,025	
	6760 Maximum	"	1	8		1,475	299		1,774	2,075	
	6770 Dryer, electric, automatic, front-loading, energy-star qualified, minimum	L-2	3	5.333		500	147		647	780	
	6780 Maximum	"	2	8		700	221		921	1,125	
	6790 Refrigerator, energy-star qualified, 18 CF, minimum	2 Carp	4	4		800	126		926	1,075	
	6795 Maximum	"	2	8		1,100	252		1,352	1,600	

EQUIPMENT 11

12400 | Furnishings & Accessories

12460	Furnishing Accessories	CREW	DAILY OUTPUT	LABOR-HOURS	UNIT	2003 BARE COSTS				TOTAL INCL O&P	
						MAT.	LABOR	EQUIP.	TOTAL		
900	0010	**ASH/TRASH RECEIVERS**									900
5550	Plastic recycling barrel, w/lid & wheels, 32 gal	1 Clab	60	.133	Ea.	105	3.29		108.29	121	
5560	65 gal		60	.133		125	3.29		128.29	143	
5570	95 gal	↓	60	.133	↓	310	3.29		313.29	345	

12492	Blinds and Shades										
600	0010	**SHADES**									600
0900	Mylar, single layer, non-heat reflective	1 Carp	685	.012	S.F.	5.20	.37		5.57	6.30	
1000	Double layered, heat reflective		685	.012		5.75	.37		6.12	6.95	
1100	Triple layered, heat reflective	↓	685	.012		7.95	.37		8.32	9.30	
1200	For metal roller instead of wood, add per				Shade	3			3	3.30	
5011	Insulative shades	1 Carp	125	.064	S.F.	8.10	2.02		10.12	12.05	
6011	Solar screening, fiberglass	"	85	.094	"	3.75	2.97		6.72	8.75	
8011	Interior insulative shutter										
8111	Stock unit, 15" x 60"	1 Carp	17	.471	Pr.	8.10	14.85		22.95	32	

12800 | Interior Plants & Planters

12830	Interior Planters	CREW	DAILY OUTPUT	LABOR-HOURS	UNIT	2003 BARE COSTS				TOTAL INCL O&P	
						MAT.	LABOR	EQUIP.	TOTAL		
600	0010	**PLANTERS**									600
1000	Fiberglass, hanging, 12" diameter, 7" high				Ea.	38			38	42	
1100	15" diameter, 7" high					57			57	63	
1200	36" diameter, 8" high					252			252	277	
1500	Rectangular, 48" long, 16" high x 15" wide					224			224	246	
1550	16" high x 24" wide					320			320	350	
1600	24" high x 24" wide					465			465	515	
1650	60" long, 30" high, 28" wide					570			570	625	
1700	72" long, 16" high, 15" wide					465			465	510	
1750	21" high, 24" wide					690			690	760	
1800	30" high, 24" wide					630			630	690	
2000	Round, 12" diameter, 13" high					75			75	82.50	
2050	25" high					83			83	91	
2150	14" diameter, 15" high					75			75	82.50	
2200	16" diameter, 16" high					85			85	93.50	
2250	18" diameter, 19" high					101			101	111	
2300	23" high					147			147	162	
2350	20" diameter, 16" high					99.50			99.50	109	
2400	18" high					102			102	112	
2450	21" high					144			144	159	
2500	22" diameter, 10" high					72.50			72.50	80	
2550	24" diameter, 16" high					141			141	156	
2600	19" high					194			194	213	
2650	25" high					271			271	299	
2700	36" high					239			239	263	
2750	48" high					350			350	385	
2800	30" diameter, 16" high					217			217	238	
2850	18" high					223			223	246	
2900	21" high					227			227	249	
3000	24" high				↓	250			250	275	

12 FURNISHINGS

12830	Interior Planters	CREW	DAILY OUTPUT	LABOR-HOURS	UNIT	2003 BARE COSTS				TOTAL INCL O&P
						MAT.	LABOR	EQUIP.	TOTAL	
3350	27" high				Ea.	269			269	296
3400	36" diameter, 16" high					282			282	310
3450	18" high					310			310	340
3500	21" high					315			315	345
3550	24" high					335			335	370
3600	27" high					365			365	405
3650	30" high					405			405	445
3700	48" diameter, 16" high					450			450	495
3750	21" high					480			480	530
3800	24" high					550			550	605
3850	27" high					585			585	640
3900	30" high					620			620	680
3950	36" high					530			530	585
4000	60" diameter, 16" high					565			565	625
4100	21" high					575			575	635
4150	27" high					700			700	770
4200	30" high					860			860	950
4250	33" high					720			720	790
4300	36" high					880			880	970
4400	39" high					895			895	985
5000	Square, 10" side, 20" high					101			101	111
5100	14" side, 15" high					105			105	116
5200	18" side, 19" high					137			137	151
5300	20" side, 16" high					148			148	163
5320	18" high					175			175	192
5340	21" high					171			171	188
5400	24" side, 16" high					217			217	238
5420	21" high					248			248	273
5440	25" high					264			264	290
5460	30" side, 16" high					289			289	320
5480	24" high					370			370	410
5490	27" high					475			475	525
6000	Metal bowl, 32" diameter, 8" high, minimum					300			300	330
6050	Maximum					385			385	425
6100	Rectangle, 30" long x 12" wide, 6" high, minimum					291			291	320
6200	Maximum					340			340	375
6300	36" long 12" wide, 6" high, minimum					360			360	400
6400	Maximum					365			365	400
6500	Square, 15" side, minimum					360			360	400
6600	Maximum					360			360	395
6700	20" side, minimum					570			570	630
6800	Maximum					540			540	595
6900	Round, 6" diameter x 6" high, minimum					26.50			26.50	29.50
7000	Maximum					32			32	35
7100	8" diameter x 8" high, minimum					35.50			35.50	39
7200	Maximum					38			38	42
7300	10" diameter x 11" high, minimum					63.50			63.50	69.50
7400	Maximum					73.50			73.50	80.50
7420	12" diameter x 13" high, minimum					64			64	70.50
7440	Maximum					75			75	82.50
7500	14" diameter x 15" high, minimum					84			84	92
7550	Maximum					106			106	117
7580	16" diameter x 17" high, minimum					85.50			85.50	94.50
7600	Maximum					109			109	119
7620	18" diameter x 19" high, minimum					95			95	105
7640	Maximum					132			132	146

FURNISHINGS 12

12800 | Interior Plants & Planters

12830	**Interior Planters**	CREW	DAILY OUTPUT	LABOR-HOURS	UNIT	2003 BARE COSTS				TOTAL INCL O&P
						MAT.	LABOR	EQUIP.	TOTAL	
7680	22" diameter x 20" high, minimum				Ea.	131			131	144
7700	Maximum					187			187	206
7750	24" diameter x 21" high, minimum					242			242	266
7800	Maximum					249			249	274
7850	31" diameter x 18" high, minimum					500			500	550
7900	Maximum					745			745	820
7950	38" diameter x 24" high, minimum					885			885	975
8000	Maximum					910			910	1,000
8050	48" diameter x 24" high, minimum					880			880	965
8150	Maximum					1,275			1,275	1,400
8500	Plastic laminate faced, fiberglass liner, square									
8520	14" sq., 15" high				Ea.	268			268	295
8540	24" sq., 16" high					340			340	375
8580	36" sq., 21" high					480			480	525
8600	Rectangle 36" long, 12" wide, 10" high					290			290	320
8650	48" long, 12" wide, 10" high					325			325	355
8700	48" long, 12" wide, 24" high					480			480	525
8750	Wood, fiberglass liner, square									
8780	14" square, 15" high, minimum				Ea.	194			194	213
8800	Maximum					238			238	262
8820	24" sq., 16" high, minimum					238			238	262
8840	Maximum					315			315	345
8860	36" sq., 21" high, minimum					305			305	335
8880	Maximum					460			460	505
9000	Rectangle, 36" long x 12" wide, 10" high, minimum					213			213	235
9050	Maximum					277			277	305
9100	48" long x 12" wide, 10" high, minimum					230			230	253
9120	Maximum					290			290	320
9200	48" long x 12" wide, 24" high, minimum					277			277	305
9300	Maximum					405			405	445
9400	Plastic cylinder, molded, 10" diameter, 10" high					7.85			7.85	8.65
9500	11" diameter, 11" high					25			25	27.50
9600	13" diameter, 12" high					32.50			32.50	36
9700	16" diameter, 14" high					34			34	37.50

12 FURNISHINGS

13010 | Air Supported Structures

13011	Air Supported Structures	CREW	DAILY OUTPUT	LABOR-HOURS	UNIT	2003 BARE COSTS				TOTAL INCL O&P	
						MAT.	LABOR	EQUIP.	TOTAL		
100	0010	**AIR SUPPORTED STORAGE TANK COVERS** Vinyl polyester										100
	0100	scrim, double layer, with hardware, blower, standby & controls										
	0200	Round, 75' diameter	B-2	4,500	.009	S.F.	6.30	.22		6.52	7.25	
	0300	100' diameter		5,000	.008		5.65	.20		5.85	6.55	
	0400	150' diameter		5,000	.008		4.28	.20		4.48	5	
	0500	Rectangular, 20' x 20'		4,500	.009		13.90	.22		14.12	15.65	
	0600	30' x 40'		4,500	.009		13.90	.22		14.12	15.65	
	0700	50' x 60'		4,500	.009		13.90	.22		14.12	15.65	
	0800	For single wall construction, deduct, minimum					.40			.40	.44	
	0900	Maximum					1.32			1.32	1.45	
	1000	For maximum resistance to atmosphere or cold, add					.56			.56	.62	
	1100	For average shipping charges, add				Total	1,075			1,075	1,200	
200	0010	**AIR SUPPORTED STRUCTURES**										200
	0020	Site preparation, incl. anchor placement and utilities	B-11B	2,000	.008	SF Flr.	.73	.23	.53	1.49	1.73	
	0050	Warehouse, polyester/vinyl fabric, 28 oz., over 10 yr. life, welded										
	0060	Seams, tension cables, primary & auxiliary inflation system,										
	0070	airlock, personnel doors and liner										
	0100	5000 S.F.	4 Clab	5,000	.006	SF Flr.	15.55	.16		15.71	17.35	
	0250	12,000 S.F.	"	6,000	.005		11.25	.13		11.38	12.55	
	0400	24,000 S.F.	8 Clab	12,000	.005		8.25	.13		8.38	9.25	
	0500	50,000 S.F.	"	12,500	.005		7.10	.13		7.23	8	
	0700	12 oz. reinforced vinyl fabric, 5 yr. life, sewn seams,										
	0710	accordian door, including liner										
	0750	3000 S.F.	4 Clab	3,000	.011	SF Flr.	8.10	.26		8.36	9.30	
	0800	12,000 S.F.	"	6,000	.005		6	.13		6.13	6.80	
	0850	24,000 S.F.	8 Clab	12,000	.005		5.95	.13		6.08	6.75	
	0950	Deduct for single layer					.64			.64	.70	
	1000	Add for welded seams					.93			.93	1.02	
	1050	Add for double layer, welded seams included					1.91			1.91	2.10	
	1250	Tedlar/vinyl fabric, 28 oz., with liner, over 10 yr. life,										
	1260	incl. overhead and personnel doors										
	1300	3000 S.F.	4 Clab	3,000	.011	SF Flr.	15.05	.26		15.31	17	
	1450	12,000 S.F.	"	6,000	.005		10.60	.13		10.73	11.85	
	1550	24,000 S.F.	8 Clab	12,000	.005		8.25	.13		8.38	9.25	
	1700	Deduct for single layer					1.33			1.33	1.46	
	2250	Greenhouse/shelter, woven polyethylene with liner, 2 yr. life,										
	2260	sewn seams, including doors										
	2300	3000 S.F.	4 Clab	3,000	.011	SF Flr.	6.10	.26		6.36	7.10	
	2350	12,000 S.F.	"	6,000	.005		6.20	.13		6.33	7	
	2450	24,000 S.F.	8 Clab	12,000	.005		5.15	.13		5.28	5.85	
	2550	Deduct for single layer					.58			.58	.64	
	2600	Tennis/gymnasium, polyester/vinyl fabric, 28 oz., over 10 yr. life,										
	2610	including thermal liner, heat and lights										
	2650	7200 S.F.	4 Clab	6,000	.005	SF Flr.	14.50	.13		14.63	16.15	
	2750	13,000 S.F.	"	6,500	.005		10.90	.12		11.02	12.15	
	2850	Over 24,000 S.F.	8 Clab	12,000	.005		9.85	.13		9.98	11.05	
	2860	For low temperature conditions, add					.66			.66	.73	
	2870	For average shipping charges, add				Total	2,875			2,875	3,175	
	2900	Thermal liner, translucent reinforced vinyl				SF Flr.	.90			.90	.99	
	2950	Metalized mylar fabric and mesh, double liner				"	1.45			1.45	1.60	
	3050	Stadium/convention center, teflon coated fiberglass, heavy weight,										
	3060	over 20 yr. life, incl. thermal liner and heating system										
	3100	Minimum	9 Clab	26,000	.003	SF Flr.	37	.07		37.07	41	
	3110	Maximum	"	19,000	.004	"	43.50	.09		43.59	47.50	
	3400	Doors, air lock, 15' long, 10' x 10'	2 Carp	.80	20	Ea.	13,600	630		14,230	16,000	
	3600	15' x 15'	"	.50	32		19,600	1,000		20,600	23,200	

SPECIAL CONSTRUCTION 13

13010 | Air Supported Structures

13011 | Air Supported Structures

		CREW	DAILY OUTPUT	LABOR-HOURS	UNIT	2003 BARE COSTS				TOTAL INCL O&P	
						MAT.	LABOR	EQUIP.	TOTAL		
200	3700	For each added 5' length, add				Ea.	2,825			2,825	3,125	200
	3900	Revolving personnel door, 6' diameter, 6'-6" high	2 Carp	.80	20	↓	9,950	630		10,580	11,900	
	4200	Double wall, self supporting, shell only, minimum				SF Flr.					21	
	4300	Maximum				"					39	

13080 | Sound, Vibration & Seismic Control

13081 | Sound Control

		CREW	DAILY OUTPUT	LABOR-HOURS	UNIT	2003 BARE COSTS				TOTAL INCL O&P	
						MAT.	LABOR	EQUIP.	TOTAL		
100	0011	**AUDIO MASKING**										100
	3100	Audio masking system, including speakers, amplification										
	3110	and signal generator										
	3200	Ceiling mounted, 5,000 S.F.	2 Elec	2,400	.007	S.F.	1.09	.25		1.34	1.57	
	3300	10,000 S.F.		2,800	.006		1	.21		1.21	1.42	
	3400	Plenum mounted, 5,000 S.F.		3,800	.004		.81	.16		.97	1.13	
	3500	10,000 S.F.	↓	4,400	.004	↓	.54	.14		.68	.79	

13120 | Pre-Engineered Structures

13120 | Natural Fiber Construction

		CREW	DAILY OUTPUT	LABOR-HOURS	UNIT	2003 BARE COSTS				TOTAL INCL O&P	
						MAT.	LABOR	EQUIP.	TOTAL		
200	0010	**STRAW BALE CONSTRUCTION**										200
	2000	Straw bales wall, incl labor & material complete, minimum				S.F.					130	
	2010	Maximum									160	
	2020	Straw bales in walls w/ modified post and beam frame	2 Carp	320	.050	↓	1.28	1.58		2.86	3.87	

13128 | Pre-Engineered Structures

		CREW	DAILY OUTPUT	LABOR-HOURS	UNIT	2003 BARE COSTS				TOTAL INCL O&P	
						MAT.	LABOR	EQUIP.	TOTAL		
340	0010	**GEODESIC DOME** Shell only, interlocking plywood panels										340
	0400	30' diameter	F-5	1.60	20	Ea.	12,100	640		12,740	14,300	
	0500	34' diameter		1.14	28.070		14,700	900		15,600	17,600	
	0600	39' diameter	↓	1	32		16,600	1,025		17,625	19,800	
	0700	45' diameter	F-3	1.13	35.556		20,300	1,125	565	21,990	24,800	
	0750	55' diameter		1	40		29,100	1,275	635	31,010	34,700	
	0800	60' diameter		1	40		37,800	1,275	635	39,710	44,300	
	0850	65' diameter	↓	.80	50	↓	45,800	1,600	795	48,195	54,000	
	1100	Aluminum panel, with 6" insulation										
	1200	100' diameter				SF Flr.					30	
	1300	500' diameter				"					25	
	1600	Aluminum framed, plexiglass closure panels										
	1700	40' diameter				SF Flr.					82.50	
	1800	200' diameter				"					77	
	2100	Aluminum framed, aluminum closure panels										
	2200	40' diameter				SF Flr.					55	
	2300	100' diameter				↓					31	
	2400	200' diameter				↓					33	

13 SPECIAL CONSTRUCTION

13128 | Pre-Engineered Structures

		Description	CREW	DAILY OUTPUT	LABOR-HOURS	UNIT	MAT.	LABOR	EQUIP.	TOTAL	TOTAL INCL O&P	
340	2500	For VRP faced bonded fiberglass insulation, add				SF Flr.					10	340
	2700	Aluminum framed, fiberglass sandwich panel closure										
	2800	6' diameter	2 Carp	150	.107	SF Flr.	33	3.37		36.37	42	
	2900	28' diameter	"	350	.046	"	25	1.44		26.44	30	
540	0010	GREENHOUSE Shell only, stock units, not incl. 2' stub walls,										540
	0020	foundation, floors, heat or compartments										
	0300	Residential type, free standing, 8'-6" long x 7'-6" wide	2 Carp	59	.271	SF Flr.	37	8.55		45.55	54.50	
	0400	10'-6" wide		85	.188		28.50	5.95		34.45	41	
	0600	13'-6" wide		108	.148		25.50	4.67		30.17	35.50	
	0700	17'-0" wide		160	.100		28.50	3.16		31.66	36.50	
	0900	Lean-to type, 3'-10" wide		34	.471		33	14.85		47.85	59	
	1000	6'-10" wide		58	.276		25.50	8.70		34.20	41.50	
	1050	8'-0" wide	↓	60	.267	↓	23.50	8.40		31.90	38.50	
	1100	Wall mounted, to existing window, 3' x 3'	1 Carp	4	2	Ea.	355	63		418	490	
	1120	4' x 5'	"	3	2.667	"	530	84		614	715	
	1200	Deluxe quality, free standing, 7'-6" wide	2 Carp	55	.291	SF Flr.	73	9.20		82.20	95	
	1220	10'-6" wide		81	.198		68	6.25		74.25	84.50	
	1240	13'-6" wide		104	.154		63.50	4.85		68.35	77.50	
	1260	17'-0" wide		150	.107		54	3.37		57.37	65	
	1400	Lean-to type, 3'-10" wide		31	.516		85	16.30		101.30	119	
	1420	6'-10" wide		55	.291		79.50	9.20		88.70	102	
	1440	8'-0" wide	↓	97	.165	↓	74	5.20		79.20	89.50	
	1500	Commercial, custom, truss frame, incl. equip., plumbing, elec.,										
	1510	benches and controls, under 2,000 S.F., minimum				SF Flr.					30	
	1550	Maximum									40.50	
	1700	Over 5,000 S.F., minimum									24.50	
	1750	Maximum				↓					30	
	2000	Institutional, custom, rigid frame, including compartments and										
	2010	multi-controls, under 500 S.F., minimum				SF Flr.					77	
	2050	Maximum									105	
	2150	Over 2,000 S.F., minimum									41.50	
	2200	Maximum									65	
	2400	Concealed rigid frame, under 500 S.F., minimum									90	
	2450	Maximum									110	
	2550	Over 2,000 S.F., minimum									68	
	2600	Maximum									79	
	2800	Lean-to type, under 500 S.F., minimum									80	
	2850	Maximum									120	
	3000	Over 2,000 S.F., minimum									44	
	3050	Maximum				↓					73	
	3600	For 1/4" clear plate glass, add				SF Surf	1.48			1.48	1.63	
	3700	For 1/4" tempered glass, add				"	3.34			3.34	3.67	
	3900	For cooling, add, minimum				SF Flr.	2.23			2.23	2.45	
	4000	Maximum					5.50			5.50	6.05	
	4200	For heaters, 13.6 MBH, add					4.24			4.24	4.66	
	4300	60 MBH, add				↓	1.59			1.59	1.75	
	4500	For benches, 2' x 3'-6", add				SF Hor.	18.95			18.95	21	
	4600	3' x 10', add				S.F.	10.30			10.30	11.30	
	4800	For controls, add, minimum				Total	1,900			1,900	2,100	
	4900	Maximum				"	11,300			11,300	12,500	
	5100	For humidification equipment, add				M.C.F.	4.88			4.88	5.35	
	5200	For vinyl shading, add				S.F.	1.03			1.03	1.13	
	6000	Geodesic hemisphere, 1/8" plexiglass glazing										
	6050	8' diameter	2 Carp	2	8	Ea.	2,150	252		2,402	2,750	
	6150	24' diameter		.35	45.714		11,000	1,450		12,450	14,400	
	6250	48' diameter	↓	.20	80	↓	29,900	2,525		32,425	36,900	

SPECIAL CONSTRUCTION 13

13600 | Solar and Wind Energy Equipment

13625 | Solar Collectors, Hi-Temp

		CREW	DAILY OUTPUT	LABOR-HOURS	UNIT	2003 BARE COSTS				TOTAL INCL O&P
						MAT.	LABOR	EQUIP.	TOTAL	
200	0010	**SOLAR ENERGY**									200
	9000	Alt energy sources, evac tube solar collector, 20 tube unit, excl labor				System	1,475			1,475	1,625
	9010	30 tube unit, excl labor					2,250			2,250	2,475
	9020	Simple inst only, incl. collector, piping, pump, wiring & tank, min						5,000		5,000	5,500
	9030	Maximum						6,000		6,000	6,600
	9040	Complex inst only, incl. collector, piping, pump, wiring & tank, min						7,000		7,000	7,700
	9050	Maximum						8,000		8,000	8,800
	9060	Parabolic trough type, complete installation only, min				S.F.					25
	9070	Maximum				"					40

13630 | Solar Collector Components

		CREW	DAILY OUTPUT	LABOR-HOURS	UNIT	2003 BARE COSTS				TOTAL INCL O&P
						MAT.	LABOR	EQUIP.	TOTAL	
200	0010	**SOLAR ENERGY**									200
	0020	System/Package prices, not including connecting									
	0030	pipe, insulation, or special heating/plumbing fixtures									
	0500	Hot water, standard package, low temperature									
	0540	1 collector, circulator, fittings, 65 gal. tank	Q-1	.50	32	Ea.	1,350	1,075		2,425	3,125
	0560	2 collectors, circulator, fittings, 100 gal. tank	1 Plum	.22	36.364		1,850	1,350		3,200	4,075
	0580	2 collectors, circulator, fittings, 120 gal. tank	Q-1	.40	40		1,925	1,350		3,275	4,150
	0620	3 collectors, circulator, fittings, 120 gal. tank	"	.34	47.059		2,350	1,575		3,925	4,975
	0700	Medium temperature package									
	0720	1 collector, circulator, fittings, 80 gal. tank	Q-1	.50	32	Ea.	1,450	1,075		2,525	3,225
	0740	2 collectors, circulator, fittings, 120 gal. tank		.40	40		2,075	1,350		3,425	4,325
	0780	3 collectors, circulator, fittings, 120 gal. tank		.30	53.333		3,775	1,800		5,575	6,850
	0980	For each additional 120 gal. tank, add					660			660	730
	2250	Controller, liquid temperature	1 Plum	5	1.600		92	60		152	191
	2300	Circulators, air									
	2310	Blowers									
	2330	100-300 S.F. system, 1/10 HP	Q-9	16	1	Ea.	128	33.50		161.50	193
	2340	300-500 S.F. system, 1/5 HP		15	1.067		177	35.50		212.50	249
	2350	Two speed, 100-300 S.F., 1/10 HP		14	1.143		128	38		166	200
	2400	Reversible fan, 20" diameter, 2 speed		18	.889		102	29.50		131.50	158
	2520	Space & DHW system, less duct work		.50	32		1,400	1,075		2,475	3,200
	2550	Booster fan 6" diameter, 120 CFM		16	1		33	33.50		66.50	88
	2570	6" diameter, 225 CFM		16	1		40.50	33.50		74	96
	2580	8" diameter, 150 CFM		16	1		37	33.50		70.50	92.50
	2590	8" diameter, 310 CFM		14	1.143		57	38		95	122
	2600	8" diameter, 425 CFM		14	1.143		64	38		102	130
	2650	Rheostat		32	.500		13.95	16.65		30.60	41
	2660	Shutter/damper		12	1.333		45	44.50		89.50	118
	2670	Shutter motor		16	1		97	33.50		130.50	159
	2800	Circulators, liquid, 1/25 HP, 5.3 GPM	Q-1	14	1.143		139	38.50		177.50	211
	2820	1/20 HP, 17 GPM		12	1.333		146	45		191	229
	2850	1/20 HP, 17 GPM, stainless steel		12	1.333		230	45		275	320
	2870	1/12 HP, 30 GPM		10	1.600		315	54		369	425
	3000	Collector panels, air with aluminum absorber plate									
	3010	Wall or roof mount									
	3040	Flat black, plastic glazing									
	3080	4' x 8'	Q-9	6	2.667	Ea.	600	89		689	795
	3100	4' x 10'		5	3.200	"	740	107		847	980
	3200	Flush roof mount, 10' to 16' x 22" wide		96	.167	L.F.	146	5.55		151.55	170
	3210	Manifold, by L.F. width of collectors		160	.100	"	27	3.33		30.33	34.50
	3300	Collector panels, liquid with copper absorber plate									
	3320	Black chrome, tempered glass glazing									
	3330	Alum. frame, 4' x 8', 5/32" single glazing	Q-1	9.50	1.684	Ea.	545	56.50		601.50	685
	3360	Solar panel liq 3'-8x6' copr 5/32" gls		9	1.778		445	60		505	575

13 SPECIAL CONSTRUCTION

		13630	Solar Collector Components	CREW	DAILY OUTPUT	LABOR-HOURS	UNIT	2003 BARE COSTS				TOTAL INCL O&P	
								MAT.	LABOR	EQUIP.	TOTAL		
200	3390		Alum. frame, 4' x 10', 5/32" single glazing	Q-1	6	2.667	Ea.	650	89.50		739.50	845	200
	3450		Flat back, alum. frame, 3' x 8'		9	1.778		430	60		490	565	
	3500		4' x 8.5'		5.50	2.909		490	98		588	690	
	3520		4' x 10.5'		10	1.600		595	54		649	735	
	3540		4' x 12.5'	▼	5	3.200	▼	735	108		843	975	
	3550		Liquid with fin tube absorber plate										
	3560		Alum. frame 4' x 8' tempered glass	Q-1	10	1.600	Ea.	495	54		549	625	
	3580		Liquid with vacuum tubes, 4' x 6'-10"		9	1.778		845	60		905	1,025	
	3600		Liquid, full wetted, plastic, alum. frame, 3' x 10'	▼	5	3.200	▼	195	108		303	380	
	3610		Price per S.F. (collector panels)	1 Plum	152	.053	S.F.	17.05	1.97		19.02	21.50	
	3650		Collector panel mounting, flat roof or ground rack	Q-1	7	2.286	Ea.	64.50	77		141.50	187	
	3670		Roof clamps	"	70	.229	Set	1.61	7.70		9.31	13.35	
	3700		Roof strap, teflon	1 Plum	205	.039	L.F.	9.50	1.46		10.96	12.65	
	3900		Differential controller with two sensors										
	3930		Thermostat, hard wired	1 Plum	8	1	Ea.	92	37.50		129.50	158	
	3950		Line cord and receptacle		12	.667		77.50	25		102.50	123	
	4050		Pool valve system		2.50	3.200		199	120		319	400	
	4070		With 12 VAC actuator		2	4		256	149		405	510	
	4080		Pool pump system, 2" pipe size		6	1.333		160	50		210	251	
	4100		Five station with digital read-out	▼	3	2.667	▼	202	99.50		301.50	370	
	4150		Sensors										
	4200		Brass plug, 1/2" MPT	1 Plum	32	.250	Ea.	16.60	9.35		25.95	32.50	
	4210		Brass plug, reversed		32	.250		22.50	9.35		31.85	39	
	4220		Freeze prevention		32	.250		20	9.35		29.35	36	
	4240		Screw attached		32	.250		10.15	9.35		19.50	25.50	
	4250		Brass, immersion	▼	32	.250	▼	24.50	9.35		33.85	41	
	4300		Heat exchanger										
	4330		Fluid to air coil, up flow, 45 MBH	Q-1	4	4	Ea.	279	135		414	510	
	4380		70 MBH		3.50	4.571		315	154		469	575	
	4400		80 MBH	▼	3	5.333	▼	420	179		599	730	
	4580		Fluid to fluid package includes two circulating pumps										
	4590		expansion tank, check valve, relief valve										
	4600		controller, high temperature cutoff and sensors	Q-1	2.50	6.400	Ea.	695	215		910	1,100	
	4650		Heat transfer fluid										
	4700		Propylene glycol, inhibited anti-freeze	1 Plum	28	.286	Gal.	8.80	10.65		19.45	26	
	4800		Solar storage tanks, knocked down										
	4810		Air, galvanized steel clad, double wall, 4" fiberglass										
	4820		insulation, 20 Mil PVC lining										
	4870		4' high, 4' x 4', = 64 C.F./450 gallons	Q-9	2	8	Ea.	1,775	266		2,041	2,350	
	4880		4' x 8' = 128 C.F./900 gallons		1.50	10.667		2,250	355		2,605	3,025	
	4890		4' x 12' = 190 C.F./1300 gallons		1.30	12.308		3,000	410		3,410	3,925	
	4900		8' x 8' = 250 C.F./1700 gallons	▼	1	16		3,350	535		3,885	4,500	
	5010		6'-3" high, 7' x 7' = 306 C.F./2000 gallons	Q-10	1.20	20		8,150	690		8,840	10,000	
	5020		7' x 10'-6" = 459 C.F./3000 gallons		.80	30		10,300	1,025		11,325	12,900	
	5030		7' x 14' = 613 C.F./4000 gallons		.60	40		12,000	1,375		13,375	15,300	
	5040		10'-6" x 10'-6" = 689 C.F./4500 gallons		.50	48		12,400	1,650		14,050	16,200	
	5050		10'-6" x 14' = 919 C.F./6000 gallons	▼	.40	60		14,600	2,075		16,675	19,200	
	5060		14' x 14' = 1225 C.F./8000 gallons	Q-11	.40	80		17,100	2,825		19,925	23,200	
	5070		14' x 17'-6" = 1531 C.F./10,000 gallons		.30	106		19,200	3,775		22,975	26,900	
	5080		17'-6" x 17'-6" = 1914 C.F./12,500 gallons		.25	128		22,600	4,525		27,125	31,900	
	5090		17'-6" x 21' = 2297 C.F./15,000 gallons		.20	160		25,200	5,650		30,850	36,500	
	5100		21' x 21' = 2756 C.F./18,000 gallons	▼	.18	177	▼	28,900	6,275		35,175	41,500	
	5120		30 Mil reinforced Chemflex lining,										
	5140		4' high, 4' x 4' = 64 C.F./450 gallons	Q-9	2	8	Ea.	1,750	266		2,016	2,325	
	5150		4' x 8' = 128 C.F./900 gallons		1.50	10.667		2,650	355		3,005	3,475	
	5160		4' x 12' = 190 C.F./1300 gallons	▼	1.30	12.308	▼	3,525	410		3,935	4,500	

SPECIAL CONSTRUCTION 13

13600 | Solar and Wind Energy Equipment

13630 | Solar Collector Components

		CREW	DAILY OUTPUT	LABOR-HOURS	UNIT	2003 BARE COSTS				TOTAL INCL O&P
						MAT.	LABOR	EQUIP.	TOTAL	
5170	8' x 8' = 250 C.F./1700 gallons	Q-9	1	16	Ea.	3,925	535		4,460	5,150
5190	6'-3" high, 7' x 7' = 306 C.F./2000 gallons	Q-10	1.20	20		8,700	690		9,390	10,700
5200	7' x 10'-6" = 459 C.F./3000 gallons		.80	30		10,600	1,025		11,625	13,300
5210	7' x 14' = 613 C.F./4000 gallons		.60	40		12,300	1,375		13,675	15,700
5220	10'-6" x 10'-6" = 689 C.F./4500 gallons		.50	48		12,700	1,650		14,350	16,600
5230	10'-6" x 14' = 919 C.F./6000 gallons		.40	60		15,000	2,075		17,075	19,700
5240	14' x 14' = 1225 C.F./8000 gallons	Q-11	.40	80		17,500	2,825		20,325	23,700
5250	14' x 17'-6" = 1531 C.F./10,000 gallons		.30	106		19,600	3,775		23,375	27,400
5260	17'-6" x 17'-6" = 1914 C.F./12,500 gallons		.25	128		23,100	4,525		27,625	32,400
5270	17'-6" x 21' = 2297 C.F./15,000 gallons		.20	160		26,000	5,650		31,650	37,300
5280	21' x 21' = 2756 C.F./18,000 gallons		.18	177		29,800	6,275		36,075	42,500
5290	30 Mil reinforced Hypalon lining, add					.02%				
7000	Solar control valves and vents									
7050	Air purger, 1" pipe size	1 Plum	12	.667	Ea.	41	25		66	82.50
7070	Air eliminator, automatic 3/4" size		32	.250		27	9.35		36.35	43.50
7090	Air vent, automatic, 1/8" fitting		32	.250		8.80	9.35		18.15	24
7100	Manual, 1/8" NPT		32	.250		1.94	9.35		11.29	16.25
7120	Backflow preventer, 1/2" pipe size		16	.500		58.50	18.70		77.20	92
7130	3/4" pipe size		16	.500		59	18.70		77.70	93
7150	Balancing valve, 3/4" pipe size		20	.400		22.50	14.95		37.45	47
7180	Draindown valve, 1/2" copper tube		9	.889		187	33		220	256
7200	Flow control valve, 1/2" pipe size		22	.364		49.50	13.60		63.10	75
7220	Expansion tank, up to 5 gal.		32	.250		58	9.35		67.35	78
7250	Hydronic controller (aquastat)		8	1		41.50	37.50		79	102
7400	Pressure gauge, 2" dial		32	.250		21	9.35		30.35	37
7450	Relief valve, temp. and pressure 3/4" pipe size		30	.267		7.90	9.95		17.85	23.50
7500	Solenoid valve, normally closed									
7520	Brass, 3/4" NPT, 24V	1 Plum	9	.889	Ea.	212	33		245	283
7530	1" NPT, 24V		9	.889		212	33		245	283
7750	Vacuum relief valve, 3/4" pipe size		32	.250		25	9.35		34.35	41.50
7800	Thermometers									
7820	Digital temperature monitoring, 4 locations	1 Plum	2.50	3.200	Ea.	135	120		255	330
7900	Upright, 1/2" NPT		8	1		25.50	37.50		63	84.50
7970	Remote probe, 2" dial		8	1		29	37.50		66.50	88.50
7990	Stem, 2" dial, 9" stem		16	.500		19	18.70		37.70	49
8250	Water storage tank with heat exchanger and electric element									
8270	66 gal. with 2" x 2 lb. density insulation	1 Plum	1.60	5	Ea.	650	187		837	995
8300	80 gal. with 2" x 2 lb. density insulation		1.60	5		745	187		932	1,100
8320	100 gal. with 2" x 1/2 lb. density insulation		1.50	5.333		700	199		899	1,075
8380	120 gal. with 2" x 2 lb. density insulation		1.40	5.714		840	213		1,053	1,250
8400	120 gal. with 2" x 2 lb. density insul., 40 S.F. heat coil		1.40	5.714		965	213		1,178	1,400
8460	Insulated wrap for water heater, 2" x 1/2 lb		32	.250		64.50	9.35		73.85	84.50
8500	Water storage module, plastic									
8600	Tubular, 12" diameter, 4' high	1 Carp	48	.167	Ea.	76	5.25		81.25	91.50
8610	12" diameter, 8' high		40	.200		116	6.30		122.30	138
8620	18" diameter, 5' high		38	.211		127	6.65		133.65	150
8630	18" diameter, 10' high		32	.250		167	7.90		174.90	196
8640	58" diameter, 5' high	2 Carp	32	.500		460	15.80		475.80	535
8650	Cap, 12" diameter					12			12	13.20
8660	18" diameter					15			15	16.50
9000	Minimum labor/equipment charge	1 Plum	2	4	Job		149		149	226

13640 | Photovoltaics

		CREW	DAILY OUTPUT	LABOR-HOURS	UNIT	2003 BARE COSTS				TOTAL INCL O&P
						MAT.	LABOR	EQUIP.	TOTAL	
0010	**SOLAR ENERGY–PHOTOVOLTAICS**									
0200	Module system, 10 kW, grid connected, incl labor & material complete				System					100,000

13600 | Solar and Wind Energy Equipment

13640 | Photovoltaics

		CREW	DAILY OUTPUT	LABOR-HOURS	UNIT	2003 BARE COSTS				TOTAL INCL O&P
						MAT.	LABOR	EQUIP.	TOTAL	
0210	Non-grid connected, incl labor & material complete				System					150,000
0220	Alt energy source, photovoltaic module, 6 watt, 15V	1 Elec	8	1	Ea.	75	37.50		112.50	139
0230	10 watt, 16.3 volts		8	1		100	37.50		137.50	166
0240	20 watt, 14.5 volts		8	1		150	37.50		187.50	221
0250	36 watt, 17 volts		8	1		280	37.50		317.50	365
0260	55 watt, 17 volts		8	1		350	37.50		387.50	440
0270	75 watt, 17 volts		8	1		400	37.50		437.50	495
0280	130 watt, 33 volts		8	1		700	37.50		737.50	825
0290	140 watt, 33 volts		8	1		750	37.50		787.50	880
0300	150 watt, 33 volts		8	1		800	37.50		837.50	935
0310	DC to AC inverter for, 12V, 2,000 watt		4	2		1,900	75		1,975	2,200
0320	12V, 2,500 watt		4	2		2,175	75		2,250	2,475
0330	24V, 2,500 watt		4	2		2,175	75		2,250	2,475
0340	12V, 3,000 watt		2.67	2.996		2,600	113		2,713	3,025
0350	24V, 3,000 watt		2.67	2.996		2,850	113		2,963	3,325
0360	24V, 4,000 watt		2	4		3,500	150		3,650	4,075
0370	48V, 4,000 watt		2	4		3,500	150		3,650	4,075
0380	48V, 5,500 watt		2	4		4,000	150		4,150	4,625
0390	PV components, combiner box, 10 lug, NEMA 3R encl		4	2		161	75		236	289
0400	Fuse, 15 A for combiner box		40	.200		7	7.50		14.50	18.95
0410	Battery charger controller w/temp sensor		4	2		161	75		236	289
0420	Digital readout panel, displays hours, volts, amps, etc		4	2		80.50	75		155.50	201
0430	Deep cycle solar battery, 6V, 180 Ah (C/20)		8	1		330	37.50		367.50	415
0440	Battery intercon, 15" AWG #2/0, sld w/copp ring lugs		16	.500		8.40	18.80		27.20	37.50
0442	Batt connec, 24" AWG #2/0, sealed w/copper ring lugs		16	.500		9.80	18.80		28.60	39
0444	Batt connec, 60" AWG #2/0, sealed w/copper ring lugs		16	.500		14.70	18.80		33.50	44
0446	Batt temp computer probe, RJ11 jack, 15' cord		16	.500		20.50	18.80		39.30	50.50
0450	System disconnect, DC 175 Amp circuit breaker		8	1		231	37.50		268.50	310
0460	Conduit box for inverter		8	1		66	37.50		103.50	129
0470	Low voltage disconnect		8	1		137	37.50		174.50	206
0480	Vented battery enclosure, wood	1 Carp	2	4		140	126		266	350
0490	Roof mounting frame, metal, for 6 modules	1 Rofc	4	2		116	55.50		171.50	222

13660 | Wind Turbines

		CREW	DAILY OUTPUT	LABOR-HOURS	UNIT	2003 BARE COSTS				TOTAL INCL O&P
						MAT.	LABOR	EQUIP.	TOTAL	
0010	**WIND TURBINES & COMPONENTS**									
1000	Complete package, 20 kW, 220 V 50-60 Hz, incl labor & material, min				System					32,000
1010	Maximum				"					55,000
1040	Alt energy sources, wind turbines, 400 watt, 12/24 V, turbine only				Ea.	650			650	715
1045	DC to AC inverter for, 48V, 4,000 watt	1 Elec	2	4	"	3,500	150		3,650	4,075

13800 | Building Automation & Control

13832 | Direct Digital Controls

		CREW	DAILY OUTPUT	LABOR-HOURS	UNIT	2003 BARE COSTS				TOTAL INCL O&P
						MAT.	LABOR	EQUIP.	TOTAL	
0010	**CONTROL COMPONENTS / DDC SYSTEMS** (Sub's quote incl. M & L)									
0100	Analog inputs									
0110	Sensors (avg. 50' run in 1/2" EMT)									
0120	Duct temperature				Ea.					346.80
0130	Space temperature									622.20
0140	Duct humidity, +/- 3%									652.80

13800 | Building Automation & Control

13832	Direct Digital Controls	CREW	DAILY OUTPUT	LABOR-HOURS	UNIT	2003 BARE COSTS				TOTAL INCL O&P
						MAT.	LABOR	EQUIP.	TOTAL	
200											200
0150	Space humidity, +/- 2%				Ea.					999.60
0160	Duct static pressure									530.40
0170	C.F.M./Transducer									714
0172	Water temp. (see 15120 for well tap add)									612
0174	Water flow (see 15120 for circuit sensor add)									2,244
0176	Water pressure differential (see 15120 for tap add)									918
0177	Steam flow (see 15120 for circuit sensor add)									2,244
0178	Steam pressure (see 15120 for tap add)									958.80
0180	K.W./Transducer									1,275
0182	K.W.H. totalization (not incl. elec. meter pulse xmtr.)									586
0190	Space static pressure				▼					1,000
1000	Analog outputs (avg. 50' run in 1/2" EMT)									
1010	P/I Transducer				Ea.					591.60
1020	Analog output, matl. in MUX									285.60
1030	Pneumatic (not incl. control device)									601.80
1040	Electric (not incl control device)				▼					357
2000	Status (Alarms)									
2100	Digital inputs (avg. 50' run in 1/2" EMT)									
2110	Freeze				Ea.					408
2120	Fire									367.20
2130	Differential pressure, (air)									561
2140	Differential pressure, (water)									795.60
2150	Current sensor									408
2160	Duct high temperature thermostat									535.50
2170	Duct smoke detector				▼					663
2200	Digital output (avg. 50' run in 1/2" EMT)									
2210	Start/stop				Ea.					326.40
2220	On/off (maintained contact)				"					561
3000	Controller M.U.X. panel, incl. function boards									
3100	48 point				Ea.					4,947
3110	128 point				"					6,783
3200	D.D.C. controller (avg. 50' run in conduit)									
3210	Mechanical room									
3214	16 point controller (incl. 120v/1ph power supply)				Ea.					3,060
3229	32 point controller (incl. 120v/1ph power supply)				"					5,100
3230	Includes software programming and checkout									
3260	Space									
3266	V.A.V. terminal box (incl. space temp. sensor)				Ea.					790.50
3280	Host computer (avg. 50' run in conduit)									
3281	Package complete with PC, keyboard,									
3282	printer, color CRT, modem, basic software				Ea.					9,180
4000	Front end costs									
4100	Computer (P.C.)/software program				Ea.					6,120
4200	Color graphics software									3,672
4300	Color graphics slides									459
4350	Additional dot matrix printer				▼					918
4400	Communications trunk cable				L.F.					3.57
4500	Engineering labor, (not incl. dftg.)				Point					77.52
4600	Calibration labor									77.52
4700	Start-up, checkout labor				▼					117.30
4800	Drafting labor, as req'd									
5000	Communications bus (data transmission cable)									
5010	#18 twisted shielded pair in 1/2" EMT conduit				C.L.F.					357
8000	Applications software									
8050	Basic maintenance manager software (not incl. data base entry)				Ea.					1,836
8100	Time program				Point					6.43

13832	Direct Digital Controls	CREW	DAILY OUTPUT	LABOR-HOURS	UNIT	2003 BARE COSTS				TOTAL INCL O&P	
						MAT.	LABOR	EQUIP.	TOTAL		
200 8120	Duty cycle				Point					12.80	200
8140	Optimum start/stop									38.76	
8160	Demand limiting									19.18	
8180	Enthalpy program				↓					38.76	
8200	Boiler optimization				Ea.					1,147.50	
8220	Chiller optimization				"					1,530	
8240	Custom applications										
8260	Cost varies with complexity										

13834	Electric/Electronic Control	CREW	DAILY OUTPUT	LABOR-HOURS	UNIT	MAT.	LABOR	EQUIP.	TOTAL	TOTAL INCL O&P	
200 0010	CONTROL SYSTEMS, ELECTRONIC										200
0020	For electronic costs, add to division 13836-200				Ea.					15%	
9000	Minimum labor/equipment charge	1 Plum	8	1	Job		37.50		37.50	56.50	

13836	Pneumatic Controls	CREW	DAILY OUTPUT	LABOR-HOURS	UNIT	MAT.	LABOR	EQUIP.	TOTAL	TOTAL INCL O&P	
200 0010	CONTROL SYSTEMS, PNEUMATIC (Sub's quote incl. mat. & labor)										200
0011	and nominal 50 Ft. of tubing. Add control panelboard if req'd.										
0100	Heating and Ventilating, split system										
0200	Mixed air control, economizer cycle, panel readout, tubing										
0220	Up to 10 tons	Q-19	.68	35.294	Ea.	2,825	1,250		4,075	5,000	
0240	For 10 to 20 tons		.63	37.915		3,025	1,325		4,350	5,325	
0260	For over 20 tons		.58	41.096		3,275	1,450		4,725	5,775	
0270	Enthalpy cycle, up to 10 tons		.50	48.387		3,125	1,700		4,825	6,000	
0280	For 10 to 20 tons		.46	52.174		3,375	1,825		5,200	6,475	
0290	For over 20 tons	↓	.42	56.604	↓	3,650	1,975		5,625	7,025	
0300	Heating coil, hot water, 3 way valve,										
0320	Freezestat, limit control on discharge, readout	Q-5	.69	23.088	Ea.	2,100	780		2,880	3,475	
0500	Cooling coil, chilled water, room										
0520	Thermostat, 3 way valve	Q-5	2	8	Ea.	935	271		1,206	1,425	
0600	Cooling tower, fan cycle, damper control,										
0620	Control system including water readout in/out at panel	Q-19	.67	35.821	Ea.	3,725	1,250		4,975	6,000	
1000	Unit ventilator, day/night operation,										
1100	freezestat, ASHRAE, cycle 2	Q-19	.91	26.374	Ea.	2,050	925		2,975	3,675	
2000	Compensated hot water from boiler, valve control,										
2100	readout and reset at panel, up to 60 GPM	Q-19	.55	43.956	Ea.	3,850	1,550		5,400	6,575	
2120	For 120 GPM		.51	47.059		4,125	1,650		5,775	7,000	
2140	For 240 GPM		.49	49.180		4,325	1,725		6,050	7,350	
3000	Boiler room combustion air, damper to 5 SF, controls		1.36	17.582		1,850	615		2,465	2,975	
3500	Fan coil, heating and cooling valves, 4 pipe control system		3	8		840	281		1,121	1,350	
3600	Heat exchanger system controls	↓	.86	27.907	↓	1,800	980		2,780	3,475	
3900	Multizone control (one per zone), includes thermostat, damper										
3910	motor and reset of discharge temperature	Q-5	.51	31.373	Ea.	1,850	1,050		2,900	3,650	
4000	Pneumatic thermostat, including controlling room radiator valve	"	2.43	6.593		560	223		783	950	
4040	Program energy saving optimizer	Q-19	1.21	19.786		4,650	695		5,345	6,175	
4060	Pump control system	"	3	8		860	281		1,141	1,375	
4080	Reheat coil control system, not incl coil	Q-5	2.43	6.593	↓	730	223		953	1,125	
4500	Air supply for pneumatic control system										
4600	Tank mounted duplex compressor, starter, alternator,										
4620	piping, dryer, PRV station and filter										
4630	1/2 HP	Q-19	.68	35.139	Ea.	6,925	1,225		8,150	9,450	
4640	3/4 HP		.64	37.383		7,250	1,300		8,550	9,950	
4650	1 HP		.61	39.539		7,925	1,400		9,325	10,800	
4660	1-1/2 HP		.57	41.739		8,450	1,475		9,925	11,500	
4680	3 HP		.55	43.956		11,500	1,550		13,050	15,000	
4690	5 HP	↓	.42	57.143		20,100	2,000		22,100	25,100	

SPECIAL CONSTRUCTION 13

13800 | Building Automation & Control

13836 | Pneumatic Controls

		CREW	DAILY OUTPUT	LABOR-HOURS	UNIT	MAT.	LABOR	EQUIP.	TOTAL	TOTAL INCL O&P
						2003 BARE COSTS				
4800	Main air supply, includes 3/8" copper main and labor	Q-5	1.82	8.791	C.L.F.	233	298		531	705
4810	If poly tubing used, deduct									30%
7000	Static pressure control for air handling unit, includes pressure									
7010	sensor, receiver controller, readout and damper motors	Q-19	.64	37.383	Ea.	5,500	1,300		6,800	8,025
7020	If return air fan requires control, add									70%
8600	VAV boxes, incl. thermostat, damper motor, reheat coil & tubing	Q-5	1.46	10.989		865	370		1,235	1,500
8610	If no reheat coil, deduct									204

13838 | Pneumatic/Electric Controls

		CREW	DAILY OUTPUT	LABOR-HOURS	UNIT	MAT.	LABOR	EQUIP.	TOTAL	TOTAL INCL O&P
						2003 BARE COSTS				
0010	**CONTROL COMPONENTS**									
0700	Controller, receiver									
0730	Pneumatic, panel mount, single input	1 Plum	8	1	Ea.	268	37.50		305.50	350
0740	With conversion mounting bracket		8	1		277	37.50		314.50	360
0750	Dual input, with control point adjustment		7	1.143		370	42.50		412.50	470
0850	Electric, single snap switch	1 Elec	4	2		360	75		435	505
0860	Dual snap switches	"	3	2.667		450	100		550	645
1000	Enthalpy control, boiler water temperature control									
1010	governed by outdoor temperature, with timer	1 Elec	3	2.667	Ea.	199	100		299	370
2000	Gauges, pressure or vacuum									
2100	2" diameter dial	1 Stpi	32	.250	Ea.	14.55	9.40		23.95	30
2200	2-1/2" diameter dial		32	.250		16.95	9.40		26.35	33
2300	3-1/2" diameter dial		32	.250		21	9.40		30.40	37
2400	4-1/2" diameter dial		32	.250		31.50	9.40		40.90	48.50
2700	Flanged iron case, black ring									
2800	3-1/2" diameter dial	1 Stpi	32	.250	Ea.	66.50	9.40		75.90	87.50
2900	4-1/2" diameter dial		32	.250		91	9.40		100.40	114
3000	6" diameter dial		32	.250		72.50	9.40		81.90	93.50
3300	For compound pressure-vacuum, add					18%				
3350	Humidistat									
3390	Electric operated	1 Shee	8	1	Ea.	30	37		67	90
3400	Relays									
3430	Pneumatic/electric	1 Plum	16	.500	Ea.	184	18.70		202.70	230
3440	Pneumatic proportioning		8	1		100	37.50		137.50	167
3450	Pneumatic switching		12	.667		88.50	25		113.50	135
3460	Selector, 3 point		6	1.333		63.50	50		113.50	145
3470	Pneumatic time delay		8	1		235	37.50		272.50	315
3500	Sensor, air operated									
3520	Humidity	1 Plum	16	.500	Ea.	208	18.70		226.70	257
3540	Pressure		16	.500		47	18.70		65.70	79.50
3560	Temperature		12	.667		99.50	25		124.50	147
3600	Electric operated									
3620	Humidity	1 Elec	8	1	Ea.	26	37.50		63.50	85
3650	Pressure		8	1		830	37.50		867.50	970
3680	Temperature		10	.800		96	30		126	150
4000	Thermometers									
4100	Dial type, 3-1/2" diameter, vapor type, union connection	1 Stpi	32	.250	Ea.	97.50	9.40		106.90	121
4120	Liquid type, union connection		32	.250		136	9.40		145.40	164
4500	Stem type, 6-1/2" case, 2" stem, 1/2" NPT		32	.250		55.50	9.40		64.90	75
4520	4" stem, 1/2" NPT		32	.250		76	9.40		85.40	97.50
4600	9" case, 3-1/2" stem, 3/4" NPT		28	.286		92.50	10.75		103.25	117
4620	6" stem, 3/4" NPT		28	.286		98	10.75		108.75	124
4640	8" stem, 3/4" NPT		28	.286		121	10.75		131.75	149
4660	12" stem, 1" NPT		26	.308		133	11.55		144.55	165
5000	Thermostats									
5030	Manual	1 Shee	8	1	Ea.	27	37		64	87

13 **SPECIAL CONSTRUCTION**

		CREW	DAILY OUTPUT	LABOR-HOURS	UNIT	2003 BARE COSTS				TOTAL INCL O&P
	13838	Pneumatic/Electric Controls				MAT.	LABOR	EQUIP.	TOTAL	
200	5040	1 set back, electric, timed	1 Shee	8	1	Ea.	81	37		118	146
	5050	2 set back, electric, timed	↓	8	1		111	37		148	179
	5100	Locking cover					14.05			14.05	15.45
	5200	24 hour, automatic, clock	1 Shee	8	1		109	37		146	177
	5205	"Smart" type, via phone/Internet link, utility suppl some areas	1 Elec	8	1		200	37.50		237.50	276
	5220	Electric, low voltage, 2 wire		13	.615		18	23		41	54.50
	5230	3 wire	↓	10	.800	↓	22	30		52	69.50
	5300	Transmitter, pneumatic									
	5320	Temperature averaging element	Q-1	8	2	Ea.	95.50	67.50		163	207
	5350	Pressure differential	1 Plum	7	1.143		560	42.50		602.50	680
	5370	Humidity, duct		8	1		187	37.50		224.50	263
	5380	Room		12	.667		170	25		195	225
	5390	Temperature, with averaging element	↓	6	1.333		107	50		157	193
	5420	Electric operated, humidity	1 Elec	8	1		50.50	37.50		88	112
	5430	DPST	"	8	1	↓	71	37.50		108.50	134
	6000	Valves, motorized zone									
	6100	Sweat connections, 1/2" C x C	1 Stpi	20	.400	Ea.	67.50	15.05		82.55	97
	6110	3/4" C x C		20	.400		72.50	15.05		87.55	102
	6120	1" C x C		19	.421		84.50	15.85		100.35	117
	6140	1/2" C x C, with end switch, 2 wire		20	.400		71.50	15.05		86.55	101
	6150	3/4" C x C, with end switch, 2 wire		20	.400		76	15.05		91.05	106
	6160	1" C x C, with end switch, 2 wire		19	.421		86	15.85		101.85	119
	6180	1-1/4" C x C, w/end switch, 2 wire	↓	15	.533	↓	103	20		123	145
	7090	Valves, motor controlled, including actuator									
	7100	Electric motor actuated									
	7200	Brass, two way, screwed									
	7210	1/2" pipe size	L-6	36	.333	Ea.	182	12.50		194.50	219
	7220	3/4" pipe size		30	.400		276	14.95		290.95	330
	7230	1" pipe size		28	.429		330	16.05		346.05	390
	7240	1-1/2" pipe size		19	.632		355	23.50		378.50	425
	7250	2" pipe size	↓	16	.750	↓	530	28		558	620
	7350	Brass, three way, screwed									
	7360	1/2" pipe size	L-6	33	.364	Ea.	212	13.60		225.60	254
	7370	3/4" pipe size		27	.444		238	16.65		254.65	286
	7380	1" pipe size		25.50	.471		210	17.60		227.60	258
	7384	1-1/4" pipe size		21	.571		266	21.50		287.50	325
	7390	1-1/2" pipe size		17	.706		300	26.50		326.50	370
	7400	2" pipe size	↓	14	.857	↓	465	32		497	565
	7550	Iron body, two way, flanged									
	7560	2-1/2" pipe size	L-6	4	3	Ea.	355	112		467	560
	7570	3" pipe size		3	4		470	150		620	740
	7580	4" pipe size	↓	2	6	↓	655	225		880	1,075
	7850	Iron body, three way, flanged									
	7860	2-1/2" pipe size	L-6	3	4	Ea.	770	150		920	1,075
	7870	3" pipe size		2.50	4.800		930	180		1,110	1,300
	7880	4" pipe size	↓	2	6	↓	1,200	225		1,425	1,675
	8000	Pneumatic, air operated									
	8050	Brass, two way, screwed									
	8060	1/2" pipe size, class 250	1 Plum	24	.333	Ea.	100	12.45		112.45	129
	8070	3/4" pipe size, class 250		20	.400		133	14.95		147.95	169
	8080	1" pipe size, class 250		19	.421		151	15.75		166.75	190
	8090	1-1/4" pipe size, class 125		15	.533		217	19.90		236.90	268
	8100	1-1/2" pipe size, class 125		13	.615		251	23		274	310
	8110	2" pipe size, class 125	↓	11	.727	↓	285	27		312	355
	8180	Brass, three way, screwed									
	8190	1/2" pipe size, class 250	1 Plum	22	.364	Ea.	110	13.60		123.60	142

SPECIAL CONSTRUCTION 13

13800 | Building Automation & Control

		13838	Pneumatic/Electric Controls	CREW	DAILY OUTPUT	LABOR-HOURS	UNIT	2003 BARE COSTS				TOTAL INCL O&P	
								MAT.	LABOR	EQUIP.	TOTAL		
200	8200		3/4" pipe size, class 250	1 Plum	18	.444	Ea.	134	16.60		150.60	172	200
	8210		1" pipe size, class 250		17	.471		153	17.60		170.60	196	
	8214		1-1/4" pipe size, class 250		14	.571		210	21.50		231.50	263	
	8220		1-1/2" pipe size, class 125		11	.727		246	27		273	310	
	8230		2" pipe size, class 125	▼	9	.889	▼	310	33		343	390	
	8450		Iron body, two way, flanged										
	8460		2-1/2" pipe size, 250 lb. flanges	Q-1	5	3.200	Ea.	2,775	108		2,883	3,225	
	8470		3" pipe size, 250 lb. flanges		4.50	3.556		2,950	120		3,070	3,425	
	8480		4" pipe size, 250 lb. flanges	▼	3	5.333	▼	3,600	179		3,779	4,225	
	8560		Iron body, three way, flanged										
	8570		2-1/2" pipe size, class 125	Q-1	4.50	3.556	Ea.	680	120		800	925	
	8580		3" pipe size, class 125		4	4		845	135		980	1,125	
	8590		4" pipe size, class 125	▼	2.50	6.400		1,700	215		1,915	2,200	
	8600		6" pipe size, class 125	Q-2	3	8		2,325	279		2,604	2,975	

13850 | Detection & Alarm

		13851	Detection & Alarm	CREW	DAILY OUTPUT	LABOR-HOURS	UNIT	2003 BARE COSTS				TOTAL INCL O&P	
								MAT.	LABOR	EQUIP.	TOTAL		
065	0010		**DETECTION SYSTEMS**, not including wires & conduits										065
	8700		Carbon monoxide detector, battery operated, wall mounted	1 Elec	16	.500	Ea.	35	18.80		53.80	66.50	
	8710		Carbon dioxide detector, hard wired, wall mounted		8	1		120	37.50		157.50	188	
	8720		Duct mounted	▼	8	1	▼	140	37.50		177.50	210	

15100 | Building Services Piping

			DAILY	LABOR-		2003 BARE COSTS				TOTAL
15140	**Domestic Water Piping**	CREW	OUTPUT	HOURS	UNIT	MAT.	LABOR	EQUIP.	TOTAL	INCL O&P
100	0010	**BACKFLOW PREVENTER** Includes valves									100
	0020	and four test cocks, corrosion resistant, automatic operation									
	1000	Double check principle									
	1010	Threaded, with ball valves									
	1020	3/4" pipe size	1 Plum	16	.500	Ea.	191	18.70		209.70	238
	1030	1" pipe size		14	.571		194	21.50		215.50	245
	1040	1-1/2" pipe size		10	.800		340	30		370	415
	1050	2" pipe size	▼	7	1.143	▼	405	42.50		447.50	510
	1080	Threaded, with gate valves									
	1100	3/4" pipe size	1 Plum	16	.500	Ea.	620	18.70		638.70	710
	1120	1" pipe size		14	.571		645	21.50		666.50	735
	1140	1-1/2" pipe size		10	.800		735	30		765	855
	1160	2" pipe size	▼	7	1.143	▼	905	42.50		947.50	1,050
	1200	Flanged, valves are gate									
	1210	3" pipe size	Q-1	4.50	3.556	Ea.	1,425	120		1,545	1,750
	1220	4" pipe size	"	3	5.333		1,800	179		1,979	2,250
	1230	6" pipe size	Q-2	3	8		3,025	279		3,304	3,750
	1240	8" pipe size		2	12		5,625	420		6,045	6,825
	1250	10" pipe size	▼	1	24	▼	8,000	835		8,835	10,100
	1300	Flanged, valves are OS&Y									
	1370	1" pipe size	1 Plum	5	1.600	Ea.	675	60		735	835
	1374	1-1/2" pipe size		5	1.600		770	60		830	940
	1378	2" pipe size	▼	4.80	1.667		940	62.50		1,002.50	1,125
	1380	3" pipe size	Q-1	4.50	3.556		1,525	120		1,645	1,850
	1400	4" pipe size	"	3	5.333		2,175	179		2,354	2,675
	1420	6" pipe size	Q-2	3	8		3,425	279		3,704	4,200
	1430	8" pipe size	"	2	12	▼	6,350	420		6,770	7,625
	4000	Reduced pressure principle									
	4100	Threaded, valves arc ball									
	4120	3/4" pipe size	1 Plum	16	.500	Ea.	715	18.70		733.70	815
	4140	1" pipe size		14	.571		760	21.50		781.50	865
	4150	1-1/4" pipe size		12	.667		1,050	25		1,075	1,200
	4160	1-1/2" pipe size		10	.800		1,025	30		1,055	1,175
	4180	2" pipe size	▼	7	1.143	▼	1,100	42.50		1,142.50	1,275
	4500	Minimum labor/equipment charge	▼	4	2	Job		74.50		74.50	113
	5000	Flanged, bronze, valves are OS&Y									
	5060	2-1/2" pipe size	Q-1	5	3.200	Ea.	2,750	108		2,858	3,200
	5080	3" pipe size		4.50	3.556		3,425	120		3,545	3,950
	5100	4" pipe size	▼	3	5.333		4,850	179		5,029	5,625
	5120	6" pipe size	Q-2	3	8	▼	10,300	279		10,579	11,700
	5200	Flanged, iron, valves are gate									
	5210	2-1/2" pipe size	Q-1	5	3.200	Ea.	1,775	108		1,883	2,125
	5220	3" pipe size		4.50	3.556		1,975	120		2,095	2,350
	5230	4" pipe size	▼	3	5.333		2,525	179		2,704	3,050
	5240	6" pipe size	Q-2	3	8		3,875	279		4,154	4,700
	5250	8" pipe size		2	12		8,350	420		8,770	9,800
	5260	10" pipe size	▼	1	24	▼	11,000	835		11,835	13,400
	5600	Flanged, iron, valves are OS&Y									
	5660	2-1/2" pipe size	Q-1	5	3.200	Ea.	1,900	108		2,008	2,275
	5680	3" pipe size		4.50	3.556		2,025	120		2,145	2,400
	5700	4" pipe size	▼	3	5.333		2,675	179		2,854	3,225
	5720	6" pipe size	Q-2	3	8		4,200	279		4,479	5,050
	5740	8" pipe size		2	12		8,500	420		8,920	9,975
	5760	10" pipe size	▼	1	24	▼	11,700	835		12,535	14,100

MECHANICAL 15

15400 | Plumbing Fixtures & Equipment

15410	Plumbing Fixtures	CREW	DAILY OUTPUT	LABOR-HOURS	UNIT	2003 BARE COSTS				TOTAL INCL O&P
						MAT.	LABOR	EQUIP.	TOTAL	
300 0010	**FAUCETS/FITTINGS**									**300**
0971	Automatic flush sensor and operator for									
0972	urinals or water closets	1 Plum	5.33	1.501	Ea.	330	56		386	450
2810	Automatic sensor and operator, with faucet head	"	6.15	1.301	"	293	48.50		341.50	395

15411	Commercial/Indust Fixtures									
700 0010	**URINALS**									**700**
8000	Waterless (no flush) urinal									
8010	Wall hung									
8020	Standard unit	Q-1	21.30	.751	Ea.	385	25.50		410.50	460
8030	ADA compliant unit	"	21.30	.751		400	25.50		425.50	480
8070	For solid color, add					60			60	66
8080	For 2" brass flange, (new const.), add	Q-1	96	.167		19.20	5.60		24.80	29.50
8090	Rough-in, supply, waste & vent	"	3.86	4.145		80.50	139		219.50	299
8100	Trap liquid									
8110	1 quart				Ea.	12.80			12.80	14.10
8120	1 gallon				"	51			51	56.50
9000	Minimum labor/equipment charge	Q-1	4	4	Job		135		135	203

15418	Resi/Comm/Industrial Fixtures									
500 0010	**SHOWERS**									**500**
5500	Head, water economizer, 3.0 GPM	1 Plum	24	.333	Ea.	63	12.45		75.45	88.50
600 0011	**KITCHEN/BATH FAUCETS**									**600**
9400	Kitchen/bath faucet aerator, water saving	1 Clab	24	.333	Ea.	7	8.20		15.20	20.50
900 0010	**WATER CLOSETS**									**900**
3700	Toilets, composting, material only, minimum				Ea.	1,025			1,025	1,125
3710	Maximum				"	1,450			1,450	1,600
4000	Water conserving systems									
4900	2 quart flush, residential	Q-1	5.40	2.963	Ea.	500	99.50		599.50	700
4980	For rough-in, supply, waste and vent		1.94	8.247		144	277		421	580
5100	2 quart flush		4.60	3.478		520	117		637	745
5200	For remote valve, add		24	.667		153	22.50		175.50	202
5300	For residential air compressor		6	2.667		705	89.50		794.50	910
5400	For light industrial air compressor		4	4		1,125	135		1,260	1,450
5500	For heavy duty industrial air compressor		1	16		1,675	540		2,215	2,650
5600	For dual compressor alternator		20	.800		565	27		592	660
5800	Wax ring allowance					1.07			1.07	1.18
7000	Toilets, water-saving dams for tank	1 Clab	24	.333		2.25	8.20		10.45	15.35

15470	Domstc Water Filt Equip									
400 0010	**WATER FILTERS** Purification and treatment									**400**
1000	Cartridge style, dirt and rust type	1 Plum	12	.667	Ea.	29	25		54	69.50
1200	Replacement cartridge		32	.250		9.85	9.35		19.20	25
1600	Taste and odor type		12	.667		29	25		54	69
1700	Replacement cartridge		32	.250		23	9.35		32.35	39.50
3000	Central unit, dirt/rust/odor/taste/scale		4	2		665	74.50		739.50	845
3100	Replacement cartridge, standard		20	.400		127	14.95		141.95	163
3600	Replacement cartridge, heavy duty		20	.400		143	14.95		157.95	181
8000	Commercial, fully automatic or push button automatic									
8200	Iron removal, 660 GPH, 1" pipe size	Q-1	1.50	10.667	Ea.	1,575	360		1,935	2,300
8240	1500 GPH, 1-1/4" pipe size		1	16		2,675	540		3,215	3,725
8280	2340 GPH, 1-1/2" pipe size		.80	20		2,925	675		3,600	4,250
8320	3420 GPH, 2" pipe size		.60	26.667		5,400	895		6,295	7,300
8360	4620 GPH, 2-1/2" pipe size		.50	32		8,575	1,075		9,650	11,100
8500	Neutralizer for acid water, 780 GPH, 1" pipe size		1.50	10.667		1,525	360		1,885	2,225
8540	1140 GPH, 1-1/4" pipe size		1	16		1,725	540		2,265	2,700

T5 MECHANICAL

15400 | Plumbing Fixtures & Equipment

15470 | Domstc Water Filt Equip

			CREW	DAILY OUTPUT	LABOR-HOURS	UNIT	2003 BARE COSTS MAT.	LABOR	EQUIP.	TOTAL	TOTAL INCL O&P	
400	8580	1740 GPH, 1-1/2" pipe size	Q-1	.80	20	Ea.	2,500	675		3,175	3,775	400
	8620	2520 GPH, 2" pipe size		.60	26.667		3,250	895		4,145	4,925	
	8660	3480 GPH, 2-1/2" pipe size		.50	32		5,400	1,075		6,475	7,575	
	8800	Sediment removal, 780 GPH, 1" pipe size		1.50	10.667		1,450	360		1,810	2,150	
	8840	1140 GPH, 1-1/4" pipe size		1	16		1,750	540		2,290	2,725	
	8880	1740 GPH, 1-1/2" pipe size		.80	20		2,325	675		3,000	3,575	
	8920	2520 GPH, 2" pipe size		.60	26.667		3,350	895		4,245	5,025	
	8960	3480 GPH, 2-1/2" pipe size		.50	32		5,250	1,075		6,325	7,400	
	9200	Taste and odor removal, 660 GPH, 1" pipe size		1.50	10.667		2,050	360		2,410	2,800	
	9240	1500 GPH, 1-1/4" pipe size		1	16		3,550	540		4,090	4,700	
	9280	2340 GPH, 1-1/2" pipe size		.80	20		3,400	675		4,075	4,775	
	9320	3420 GPH, 2" pipe size		.60	26.667		6,100	895		6,995	8,075	
	9360	4620 GPH, 2-1/2" pipe size	↓	.50	32	↓	9,600	1,075		10,675	12,200	

15480 | Domestic Water Heaters

			CREW	DAILY OUTPUT	LABOR-HOURS	UNIT	2003 BARE COSTS MAT.	LABOR	EQUIP.	TOTAL	TOTAL INCL O&P	
200	0010	**WATER HEATERS**										200
	9400	Water heaters, tankless, on-demand, electric, 22 KW, 220V	1 Plum	3	2.667	Ea.	440	99.50		539.50	635	
	9410	Natural gas/propane, incl vent	"	2	4		490	149		639	765	
	9420	Fiberglass insulation blanket kit for 30 gal unit	1 Clab	10	.800	↓	15	19.70		34.70	47.50	

15500 | Heat Generation Equipment

15510 | Heating Boilers and Accessories

			CREW	DAILY OUTPUT	LABOR-HOURS	UNIT	2003 BARE COSTS MAT.	LABOR	EQUIP.	TOTAL	TOTAL INCL O&P	
400	0010	**BOILERS, GAS FIRED** Natural or propane, standard controls										400
	8000	Pulse combustion, standard controls / trim, 44,000 BTU	Q-5	1.50	10.667	Ea.	2,350	360		2,710	3,125	
	8050	88,000 BTU		1.40	11.429		2,775	385		3,160	3,625	
	8080	134,000 BTU	↓	1.20	13.333	↓	3,600	450		4,050	4,625	

15700 | Heating/Ventilating/Air Conditioning Equipment

15740 | Heat Pumps

			CREW	DAILY OUTPUT	LABOR-HOURS	UNIT	2003 BARE COSTS MAT.	LABOR	EQUIP.	TOTAL	TOTAL INCL O&P	
100	0010	**HEAT PUMPS** (Not including interconnecting tubing)										100
	1000	Air to air, split system, not including curbs, pads, or ductwork										
	1015	1.5 ton cooling, 7 MBH heat @ 0°F	Q-5	1.22	13.115	Ea.	1,225	445		1,670	2,025	
	1020	2 ton cooling, 8.5 MBH heat @ 0°F		1.20	13.333		1,275	450		1,725	2,075	
	1030	2.5 ton cooling, 10 MBH heat @ 0°F		1	16		1,425	540		1,965	2,375	
	1040	3 ton cooling, 13 MBH heat @ 0°F		.80	20		1,575	675		2,250	2,750	
	1050	3.5 ton cooling, 18 MBH heat @ 0°F		.75	21.333		1,775	720		2,495	3,050	
	1054	4 ton cooling, 24 MBH heat @ 0°F		.60	26.667		2,000	905		2,905	3,550	
	1060	5 ton cooling, 27 MBH heat @ 0°F		.50	32		2,300	1,075		3,375	4,150	
	1080	7.5 ton cooling, 33 MBH heat @ 0°F	↓	.30	53.333		7,775	1,800		9,575	11,300	
	1100	10 ton cooling, 50 MBH heat @ 0°F	Q-6	.38	63.158		10,800	2,225		13,025	15,300	
	1120	15 ton cooling, 64 MBH heat @ 0°F	↓	.26	92.308	↓	14,100	3,250		17,350	20,400	

MECHANICAL 15

15700 | Heating/Ventilating/Air Conditioning Equipment

	15740	Heat Pumps	CREW	DAILY OUTPUT	LABOR-HOURS	UNIT	2003 BARE COSTS				TOTAL INCL O&P	
							MAT.	LABOR	EQUIP.	TOTAL		
100	1130	20 ton cooling, 85 MBH heat @ 0°F	Q-6	.20	120	Ea.	19,700	4,200		23,900	28,100	100
	1140	25 ton cooling, 119 MBH heat @ 0°F	↓	.20	120	↓	23,400	4,200		27,600	32,100	
	1300	Supplementary electric heat coil, included										
	1500	Single package, not including curbs, pads, or plenums										
	1502	1/2 ton cooling, supplementary heat not incl.	Q-5	8	2	Ea.	1,200	67.50		1,267.50	1,425	
	1504	3/4 ton cooling, supplementary heat not incl.		6	2.667		1,300	90.50		1,390.50	1,550	
	1506	1 ton cooling, supplementary heat not incl.		4	4		1,375	135		1,510	1,725	
	1510	1.5 ton cooling, 5 MBH heat @ 0°F		1.55	10.323		3,100	350		3,450	3,925	
	1520	2 ton cooling, 6.5 MBH heat @ 0°F		1.50	10.667		3,175	360		3,535	4,025	
	1540	2.5 ton cooling, 8 MBH heat @ 0°F		1.40	11.429		3,325	385		3,710	4,225	
	1560	3 ton cooling, 10 MBH heat @ 0°F		1.20	13.333		3,625	450		4,075	4,650	
	1570	3.5 ton cooling, 11 MBH heat @ 0°F		1	16		3,950	540		4,490	5,150	
	1580	4 ton cooling, 13 MBH heat @ 0°F		.96	16.667		4,275	565		4,840	5,550	
	1620	5 ton cooling, 27 MBH heat @ 0°F		.65	24.615		4,875	835		5,710	6,600	
	1640	7.5 ton cooling, 35 MBH heat @ 0°F	↓	.40	40		8,025	1,350		9,375	10,900	
	1648	10 ton cooling, 45 MBH heat @ 0°F	Q-6	.40	60		10,800	2,100		12,900	15,100	
	1652	12 ton cooling, 50 MBH heat @ 0°F	"	.36	66.667	↓	13,200	2,350		15,550	18,000	
	1696	Supplementary electric heat coil incl., except as noted										
	2000	Water source to air, single package										
	2100	1 ton cooling, 13 MBH heat @ 75°F	Q-5	2	8	Ea.	1,725	271		1,996	2,300	
	2120	1.5 ton cooling, 17 MBH heat @ 75°F		1.80	8.889		2,050	300		2,350	2,700	
	2140	2 ton cooling, 19 MBH heat @ 75°F		1.70	9.412		2,100	320		2,420	2,800	
	2160	2.5 ton cooling, 25 MBH heat @ 75°F		1.60	10		2,175	340		2,515	2,900	
	2180	3 ton cooling, 27 MBH heat @ 75°F		1.40	11.429		2,375	385		2,760	3,175	
	2190	3.5 ton cooling, 29 MBH heat @ 75°F		1.30	12.308		2,450	415		2,865	3,325	
	2200	4 ton cooling, 31 MBH heat @ 75°F		1.20	13.333		2,850	450		3,300	3,825	
	2220	5 ton cooling, 29 MBH heat @ 75°F		.90	17.778		3,450	600		4,050	4,700	
	2240	7.5 ton cooling, 35 MBH heat @ 75°F		.60	26.667		3,900	905		4,805	5,675	
	2250	8.5 ton cooling, 40 MBH heat @ 75°F		.58	27.586		11,200	935		12,135	13,700	
	2260	10 ton cooling, 50 MBH heat @ 75°F	↓	.53	30.189		12,300	1,025		13,325	15,100	
	2280	15 ton cooling, 64 MBH heat @ 75°F	Q-6	.47	51.064		13,500	1,800		15,300	17,600	
	2300	20 ton cooling, 100 MBH heat @ 75°F		.41	58.537		15,100	2,050		17,150	19,700	
	2320	30 ton cooling, (twin 15 ton units)		.23	102		27,000	3,575		30,575	35,100	
	2340	40 ton cooling, (twin 20 ton units)		.20	117		30,200	4,100		34,300	39,400	
	2360	50 ton cooling, (twin 15 + 20 ton unit)	↓	.15	160	↓	42,100	5,625		47,725	55,000	
	3960	For supplementary heat coil, add					10%					
	4000	For increase in capacity thru use										
	4020	of solar collector, size boiler at 60%										
	9010	Geothermal heat pump, open loop, 4 ton, incl piping, well & ctrl, min				System					20,000	
	9020	Maximum				"					26,000	

15750 | Humidity Control Equipment

			CREW	DAILY OUTPUT	LABOR-HOURS	UNIT	MAT.	LABOR	EQUIP.	TOTAL	TOTAL INCL O&P	
300	0010	**DEHUMIDIFIERS**										300
	6000	Self contained with filters and standard controls										
	6040	1.5 lb/hr, 50 cfm	1 Plum	8	1	Ea.	2,950	37.50		2,987.50	3,300	
	6060	3 lb/hr, 150 cfm	Q-1	12	1.333		3,350	45		3,395	3,775	
	6065	6 lb/hr, 150 cfm		9	1.778		6,200	60		6,260	6,925	
	6070	16 to 20 lb/hr, 600 cfm		5	3.200		12,400	108		12,508	13,800	
	6080	30 to 40 lb/hr, 1125 cfm		4	4		20,400	135		20,535	22,700	
	6090	60 to 75 lb/hr, 2250 cfm		3	5.333		26,800	179		26,979	29,800	
	6100	120 to 155 lb/hr, 4500 cfm		2	8		49,000	269		49,269	54,500	
	6110	240 to 310 lb/hr, 9000 cfm	↓	1.50	10.667		69,000	360		69,360	76,500	
	6120	400 to 515 lb/hr, 15,000 cfm	Q-2	1.60	15		94,000	525		94,525	104,000	
	6130	530 to 690 lb/hr, 20,000 cfm		1.40	17.143		101,500	600		102,100	113,000	
	6140	800 to 1030 lb/hr, 30,000 cfm		1.20	20		116,000	695		116,695	128,500	
	6150	1060 to 1375 lb/hr, 40,000 cfm	↓	1	24	↓	161,500	835		162,335	179,500	

15 MECHANICAL

15750 | Humidity Control Equipment

		CREW	DAILY OUTPUT	LABOR-HOURS	UNIT	2003 BARE COSTS				TOTAL INCL O&P
						MAT.	LABOR	EQUIP.	TOTAL	
500	0010	**HUMIDIFIERS**									**500**
	0520	Steam, room or duct, filter, regulators, auto. controls, 220 V								
	0540	11 lb. per hour	Q-5	6	2.667	Ea.	2,050	90.50		2,140.50	2,375
	0560	22 lb. per hour		5	3.200		2,250	108		2,358	2,650
	0580	33 lb. per hour		4	4		2,325	135		2,460	2,750
	0600	50 lb. per hour		4	4		2,850	135		2,985	3,325
	0620	100 lb. per hour		3	5.333		3,400	181		3,581	4,025
	0640	150 lb. per hour		2.50	6.400		4,500	217		4,717	5,275
	0660	200 lb. per hour	▼	2	8	▼	5,575	271		5,846	6,550
	0700	With blower								
	0720	11 lb. per hour	Q-5	5.50	2.909	Ea.	2,850	98.50		2,948.50	3,300
	0740	22 lb. per hour		4.75	3.368		3,075	114		3,189	3,550
	0760	33 lb. per hour		3.75	4.267		3,125	144		3,269	3,675
	0780	50 lb. per hour		3.50	4.571		3,775	155		3,930	4,375
	0800	100 lb. per hour		2.75	5.818		4,250	197		4,447	4,975
	0820	150 lb. per hour		2	8		6,300	271		6,571	7,325
	0840	200 lb. per hour	▼	1.50	10.667	▼	7,375	360		7,735	8,675
	5000	Furnace type, wheel bypass								
	5020	10 GPD	1 Stpi	4	2	Ea.	129	75		204	255
	5040	14 GPD		3.80	2.105		171	79		250	310
	5060	19 GPD	▼	3.60	2.222	▼	198	83.50		281.50	345

15768 | Infrared Heaters

		CREW	DAILY OUTPUT	LABOR-HOURS	UNIT	MAT.	LABOR	EQUIP.	TOTAL	TOTAL INCL O&P
600	0010	**INFRARED UNIT**									**600**
	0020	Gas fired, unvented, electric ignition, 100% shutoff.								
	0030	Piping and wiring not included								
	0060	Input, 15 MBH	Q-5	7	2.286	Ea.	350	77.50		427.50	500
	0100	30 MBH		6	2.667		365	90.50		455.50	535
	0120	45 MBH		5	3.200		430	108		538	640
	0140	50 MBH		4.50	3.556		450	120		570	675
	0160	60 MBH		4	4		465	135		600	715
	0180	75 MBH		3	5.333		540	181		721	870
	0200	90 MBH		2.50	6.400		545	217		762	925
	0220	105 MBH		2	8		680	271		951	1,150
	0240	120 MBH	▼	2	8	▼	895	271		1,166	1,400
	2000	Electric, single or three phase								
	2010	1 kW, 3400 BTU	1 Elec	2.40	3.333	Ea.	147	125		272	350
	2020	3.2 kW, 10,900 BTU		2.40	3.333		158	125		283	360
	2050	6 kW, 20,478 BTU		2.30	3.478		360	131		491	595
	2100	13.5 KW, 40,956 BTU		2.20	3.636		565	137		702	830
	2150	24 KW, 81,912 BTU	▼	2	4	▼	1,225	150		1,375	1,575
	3000	Oil fired, pump, controls, fusible valve, oil supply tank								
	3050	91,000 BTU	Q-5	2.50	6.400	Ea.	5,225	217		5,442	6,075
	3080	105.000 BTU		2.25	7.111		5,475	241		5,716	6,400
	3110	119,000 BTU	▼	2	8	▼	5,775	271		6,046	6,750

15770 | Floor-Heating & Snow-Melting Eq.

		CREW	DAILY OUTPUT	LABOR-HOURS	UNIT	MAT.	LABOR	EQUIP.	TOTAL	TOTAL INCL O&P
200	0010	**ELECTRIC HEATING**, not incl. conduit or feed wiring									**200**
	5300	Infrared quartz heaters, 120 volts, 1000 watts	1 Elec	6.70	1.194	Ea.	119	45		164	198
	5350	1500 watt		5	1.600		119	60		179	221
	5400	240 volts, 1500 watt		5	1.600		119	60		179	221
	5450	2000 watt		4	2		119	75		194	243
	5500	3000 watt		3	2.667		139	100		239	300
	5550	4000 watt		2.60	3.077		139	116		255	325
	5570	Modulating control	▼	.80	10	▼	72.50	375		447.50	640

MECHANICAL 15

15700 | Heating/Ventilating/Air Conditioning Equipment

15770	Floor-Heating & Snow-Melting Eq.	CREW	DAILY OUTPUT	LABOR-HOURS	UNIT	2003 BARE COSTS				TOTAL INCL O&P
						MAT.	LABOR	EQUIP.	TOTAL	
500	0010	**RADIANT FLOOR HEATING**										500
	0100	Tubing, PEX (cross-linked polyethylene)									
	0110	Oxygen barrier type for systems with ferrous materials									
	0120	1/2"	Q-5	800	.020	L.F.	.49	.68		1.17	1.56
	0130	3/4"		535	.030		.62	1.01		1.63	2.21
	0140	1"		400	.040		1.25	1.35		2.60	3.43
	0200	Non barrier type for ferrous free systems									
	0210	1/2"	Q-5	800	.020	L.F.	.27	.68		.95	1.32
	0220	3/4"		535	.030		.44	1.01		1.45	2.01
	0230	1"		400	.040		.77	1.35		2.12	2.90
	1000	Manifolds									
	1110	Brass									
	1120	Valved									
	1130	1", 2 circuit	Q-5	13	1.231	Ea.	37.50	41.50		79	105
	1140	1", 3 circuit		11	1.455		51	49		100	131
	1150	1", 4 circuit		9	1.778		69	60		129	167
	1160	1-1/4", 3 circuit		10	1.600		58	54		112	146
	1170	1-1/4", 4 circuit		8	2		70.50	67.50		138	180
	1300	Valveless									
	1310	1", 2 circuit	Q-5	14	1.143	Ea.	18.75	38.50		57.25	79
	1320	1", 3 circuit		12	1.333		25.50	45		70.50	96
	1330	1", 4 circuit		10	1.600		33	54		87	119
	1340	1-1/4", 3 circuit		11	1.455		31.50	49		80.50	109
	1350	1-1/4", 4 circuit		9	1.778		36	60		96	131
	1400	Manifold connector kit									
	1410	Mounting brackets, couplings, end cap, air vent, valve, plug									
	1420	1"	Q-5	8	2	Ea.	64.50	67.50		132	173
	1430	1-1/4"	"	7	2.286	"	77.50	77.50		155	202
	1610	Copper, (cut to size)									
	1620	1" x 1/2" x 72" Lg, 2" sweat drops, 24 circuit	Q-5	3.33	4.805	Ea.	65.50	163		228.50	320
	1630	1-1/4" x 1/2" x 72" Lg, 2" sweat drops, 24 circuit		3.20	5		77.50	169		246.50	340
	1640	1-1/2" x 1/2" x 72" Lg, 2" sweat drops, 24 circuit		3	5.333		94	181		275	375
	1650	1-1/4" x 3/4" x 72" Lg, 2" sweat drops, 24 circuit		3.10	5.161		82.50	175		257.50	355
	1660	1-1/2" x 3/4" x 72" Lg, 2" sweat drops, 24 circuit		2.90	5.517		99	187		286	390
	1710	Copper, (modular)									
	1720	1" x 1/2", 2" sweat drops, 2 circuit	Q-5	17.50	.914	Ea.	6.15	31		37.15	54
	1730	1" x 1/2", 2" sweat drops, 3 circuit		14.50	1.103		9.25	37.50		46.75	66.50
	1740	1" x 1/2", 2" sweat drops, 4 circuit		12.30	1.301		10.70	44		54.70	78.50
	1750	1-1/4" x 1/2", 2" sweat drops, 2 circuit		17	.941		7.15	32		39.15	56
	1760	1-1/4" x 1/2", 2" sweat drops, 3 circuit		14	1.143		10.70	38.50		49.20	70.50
	1770	1-1/4" x 1/2", 2" sweat drops, 4 circuit		11.80	1.356		14.25	46		60.25	85
	3000	Valves									
	3110	Motorized zone valve operator, 24V	Q-5	30	.533	Ea.	40	18.05		58.05	71
	3120	Motorized zone valve with operator complete, 24V									
	3130	3/4"	Q-5	35	.457	Ea.	68.50	15.45		83.95	99
	3140	1"		32	.500		77.50	16.95		94.45	111
	3150	1-1/4"		29.60	.541		95.50	18.30		113.80	133
	3200	Flow control/isolation valve, 1/2"		32	.500		22	16.95		38.95	49.50
	3300	Thermostatic mixing valves									
	3310	1/2"	Q-5	26.60	.601	Ea.	71.50	20.50		92	110
	3320	3/4"		25	.640		87	21.50		108.50	128
	3330	1"		21.40	.748		93	25.50		118.50	140
	3400	3 Way mixing / diverting valve, manual, brass									
	3410	1/2"	Q-5	21.30	.751	Ea.	91	25.50		116.50	139
	3420	3/4"		20	.800		94	27		121	144
	3430	1"		17.80	.899		110	30.50		140.50	166

15 MECHANICAL

15770	Floor-Heating & Snow-Melting Eq.	CREW	DAILY OUTPUT	LABOR-HOURS	UNIT	2003 BARE COSTS				TOTAL INCL O&P
						MAT.	LABOR	EQUIP.	TOTAL	
500	3500	4 Way mixing / diverting valve, manual, brass									500
3510	1/2"	Q-5	16	1	Ea.	95.50	34		129.50	156
3520	3/4"		15	1.067		107	36		143	172
3530	1"		13.30	1.203		119	40.50		159.50	193
3540	1-1/4"		11.40	1.404		131	47.50		178.50	216
3550	1-1/2"		10.60	1.509		176	51		227	270
3560	2"		10	1.600		189	54		243	290
3570	2-1/2"		8	2		520	67.50		587.50	675
3800	Motor control, 3 or 4 way, for valves up to 1-1/2"	▼	30	.533	▼	131	18.05		149.05	172
5000	Radiant floor heating, zone control panel									
5110	6 Zone control									
5120	For zone valves	Q-5	16	1	Ea.	125	34		159	188
5130	For circulators	"	16	1	"	176	34		210	245
7000	PEX tubing fittings, compression type									
7110	PEX tubing to brass valve conn., 1/2"	Q-5	54	.296	Ea.	2.12	10.05		12.17	17.50
7200	PEX x male NPT									
7210	1/2" x 1/2"	Q-5	54	.296	Ea.	4.13	10.05		14.18	19.70
7220	3/4" x 3/4"		46	.348		6.95	11.75		18.70	25.50
7230	1" x 1"	▼	40	.400	▼	16.90	13.55		30.45	39
7300	PEX coupling									
7310	1/2" x 1/2"	Q-5	50	.320	Ea.	5	10.85		15.85	22
7320	3/4" x 3/4"		42	.381		14.45	12.90		27.35	35.50
7330	1" x 1"	▼	36	.444	▼	19.50	15.05		34.55	44
7400	PEX x copper sweat									
7410	1/2" x 1/2"	Q-5	38	.421	Ea.	3.62	14.25		17.87	25.50
7420	3/4" x 3/4"		34	.471		7.70	15.95		23.65	32.50
7430	1" x 1"	▼	29	.552	▼	16.90	18.70		35.60	46.50

15780	Energy Recovery Equipment	CREW	DAILY OUTPUT	LABOR-HOURS	UNIT	MAT.	LABOR	EQUIP.	TOTAL	TOTAL INCL O&P
100	0010	**HEAT RECOVERY PACKAGES**									100
0100	Air to air									
4000	Enthalpy recovery wheel									
4010	1000 max CFM	Q-9	1.20	13.333	Ea.	3,825	445		4,270	4,875
4020	2000 max CFM		1	16		4,475	535		5,010	5,750
4030	4000 max CFM		.80	20		5,175	665		5,840	6,725
4040	6000 max CFM	▼	.70	22.857		6,050	760		6,810	7,825
4050	8000 max CFM	Q-10	1	24		6,700	830		7,530	8,625
4060	10,000 max CFM		.90	26.667		8,000	920		8,920	10,200
4070	20,000 max CFM		.80	30		14,500	1,025		15,525	17,600
4080	25,000 max CFM		.70	34.286		17,700	1,175		18,875	21,300
4090	30,000 max CFM		.50	48		19,700	1,650		21,350	24,200
4100	40,000 max CFM		.45	53.333		27,100	1,850		28,950	32,700
4110	50,000 max CFM	▼	.40	60	▼	31,500	2,075		33,575	37,900
9000	Minimum labor/equipment charge	1 Shee	4	2	Job		74		74	114
9005	Drainwater heat recov unit, copp coil type, for 1/2" supply, 3" waste	1 Plum	3	2.667	Ea.	300	99.50		399.50	480
9010	For 1/2" supply, 4" waste		3	2.667		400	99.50		499.50	590
9020	For 3/4" supply, 3" waste		3	2.667		400	99.50		499.50	590
9030	For 3/4" supply, 4" waste		3	2.667		425	99.50		524.50	620
9040	For 1" supply, 4" waste, double manifold	▼	3	2.667	▼	980	99.50		1,079.50	1,225

MECHANICAL 15

15800 | Air Distribution

15830		Fans	CREW	DAILY OUTPUT	LABOR-HOURS	UNIT	2003 BARE COSTS				TOTAL INCL O&P
							MAT.	LABOR	EQUIP.	TOTAL	
100	0010	**FANS**										100
	3000	Paddle blade air circulator, 3 speed switch									
	3020	42", 5,000 CFM high, 3000 CFM low	1 Elec	2.40	3.333	Ea.	73	125		198	267
	3040	52", 6,500 CFM high, 4000 CFM low	"	2.20	3.636	"	74	137		211	286
	3100	For antique white motor, same cost									
	3200	For brass plated motor, same cost									
	3300	For light adaptor kit, add				Ea.	27			27	30
	8150	Attic fan, roof mtd, solar powered w/panel, 800 CFM, w/control	1 Carp	2	4	"	205	126		331	425

15860 | Air Cleaning Devices

			CREW	DAILY OUTPUT	LABOR-HOURS	UNIT	MAT.	LABOR	EQUIP.	TOTAL	TOTAL INCL O&P
100	0010	**AIR FILTERS**										100
	2000	Electronic air cleaner, duct mounted									
	2150	400 - 1000 CFM	1 Shee	2.30	3.478	Ea.	660	129		789	925
	2200	1000 - 1400 CFM		2.20	3.636		685	135		820	965
	2250	1400 - 2000 CFM		2.10	3.810		760	141		901	1,050
	2260	2000 - 2500 CFM	↓	2	4	↓	780	148		928	1,100
	2950	Mechanical media filtration units									
	3000	High efficiency type, with frame, non-supported				MCFM	45			45	49.50
	3100	Supported type					55			55	60.50
	4000	Medium efficiency, extended surface					5			5	5.50
	4500	Permanent washable					20			20	22
	5000	Renewable disposable roll				↓	120			120	132
	5500	Throwaway glass or paper media type				Ea.	4.60			4.60	5.05

16100 | Wiring Methods

16136	Boxes	CREW	DAILY OUTPUT	LABOR-HOURS	UNIT	2003 BARE COSTS				TOTAL INCL O&P	
						MAT.	LABOR	EQUIP.	TOTAL		
620	0010 **OUTLET BOXES, PLASTIC**										620
	4000 Air/vapor barrier boxes, plastic, for electrical work boxes	1 Elec	40	.200	Ea.	2.90	7.50		10.40	14.45	

16140 | Wiring Devices

		CREW	DAILY OUTPUT	LABOR-HOURS	UNIT	MAT.	LABOR	EQUIP.	TOTAL	TOTAL INCL O&P	
910	0010 **WIRING DEVICES**										910
	1650 Dimmer switch, 120 volt, incandescent, 600 watt, 1 pole	1 Elec	16	.500	Ea.	10.80	18.80		29.60	40	
	1700 600 watt, 3 way		12	.667		8.50	25		33.50	47	
	1750 1000 watt, 1 pole		16	.500		44.50	18.80		63.30	77	
	1800 1000 watt, 3 way		12	.667		64	25		89	108	
	2000 1500 watt, 1 pole		11	.727		87	27.50		114.50	137	
	2100 2000 watt, 1 pole		8	1		130	37.50		167.50	199	
	2110 Fluorescent, 600 watt		15	.533		67	20		87	104	
	2120 1000 watt		15	.533		83.50	20		103.50	122	
	2130 1500 watt	↓	10	.800	↓	157	30		187	218	

16200 | Electrical Power

16220	Motors & Generators	CREW	DAILY OUTPUT	LABOR-HOURS	UNIT	2003 BARE COSTS				TOTAL INCL O&P	
						MAT.	LABOR	EQUIP.	TOTAL		
900	0010 **VARIABLE FREQUENCY DRIVES/ADJUSTABLE FREQUENCY DRIVES**										900
	0100 Enclosed (NEMA 1), 460 volt, for 3 HP motor size	1 Elec	.80	10	Ea.	1,475	375		1,850	2,150	
	0110 5 HP motor size		.80	10		1,600	375		1,975	2,300	
	0120 7.5 HP motor size		.67	11.940		1,875	450		2,325	2,750	
	0130 10 HP motor size	↓	.67	11.940		1,875	450		2,325	2,750	
	0140 15 HP motor size	2 Elec	.89	17.978		2,175	675		2,850	3,400	
	0150 20 HP motor size		.89	17.978		3,225	675		3,900	4,550	
	0160 25 HP motor size		.67	23.881		3,750	900		4,650	5,475	
	0170 30 HP motor size		.67	23.881		4,575	900		5,475	6,375	
	0180 40 HP motor size		.67	23.881		6,700	900		7,600	8,725	
	0190 50 HP motor size	↓	.53	30.189		7,300	1,125		8,425	9,725	
	0200 60 HP motor size	R-3	.56	35.714		8,000	1,325	291	9,616	11,100	
	0210 75 HP motor size		.56	35.714		11,000	1,325	291	12,616	14,400	
	0220 100 HP motor size		.50	40		11,200	1,475	325	13,000	14,900	
	0230 125 HP motor size		.50	40		12,400	1,475	325	14,200	16,200	
	0240 150 HP motor size		.50	40		15,800	1,475	325	17,600	20,000	
	0250 200 HP motor size	↓	.42	47.619		19,600	1,775	390	21,765	24,600	
	1100 Custom-engineered, 460 volt, for 3 HP motor size	1 Elec	.56	14.286		2,425	535		2,960	3,450	
	1110 5 HP motor size		.56	14.286		2,550	535		3,085	3,600	
	1120 7.5 HP motor size		.47	17.021		3,050	640		3,690	4,300	
	1130 10 HP motor size	↓	.47	17.021		3,050	640		3,690	4,300	
	1140 15 HP motor size	2 Elec	.62	25.806		3,350	970		4,320	5,125	
	1150 20 HP motor size		.62	25.806		4,575	970		5,545	6,475	
	1160 25 HP motor size		.47	34.043		4,950	1,275		6,225	7,350	
	1170 30 HP motor size		.47	34.043		6,750	1,275		8,025	9,325	
	1180 40 HP motor size		.47	34.043		7,550	1,275		8,825	10,200	
	1190 50 HP motor size	↓	.37	43.243		7,550	1,625		9,175	10,700	
	1200 60 HP motor size	R-3	.39	51.282		11,300	1,900	420	13,620	15,700	
	1210 75 HP motor size		.39	51.282		13,000	1,900	420	15,320	17,600	
	1220 100 HP motor size		.35	57.143		13,600	2,125	465	16,190	18,600	
	1230 125 HP motor size		.35	57.143		14,300	2,125	465	16,890	19,400	
	1240 150 HP motor size	↓	.35	57.143	↓	16,100	2,125	465	18,690	21,400	

ELECTRICAL 16

16200 | Electrical Power

16220	Motors & Generators	CREW	DAILY OUTPUT	LABOR-HOURS	UNIT	2003 BARE COSTS				TOTAL INCL O&P	
						MAT.	LABOR	EQUIP.	TOTAL		
900	1250	200 HP motor size	R-3	.29	68.966	Ea.	22,200	2,550	565	25,315	28,800	**900**
	2000	For complex & special design systems to meet specific										
	2010	requirements, obtain quote from vendor.										

16221	Fuel Cells	CREW	DAILY OUTPUT	LABOR-HOURS	UNIT	MAT.	LABOR	EQUIP.	TOTAL	TOTAL INCL O&P	
950	0010	**FUEL CELLS**										**950**
	2000	Large comm units, 200KW, 480/277V, burns natural gas, unit only				System	860,000			860,000	946,000	
	2001	Complete system, natural gas, installed, 200 kW									1,050,000	
	2002	400 kW									1,980,000	
	2003	600 kW									2,795,000	
	2004	800 kW									3,660,000	
	2005	1000 kW									4,575,000	
	2010	Comm type, 100 watt, 12V, for battery charging, uses hydrogen				Ea.	2,175			2,175	2,400	
	2020	500 watt, 12V, for battery charging, uses hydrogen					4,450			4,450	4,900	
	2030	1000 watt, 48V, for battery charging, uses hydrogen					7,250			7,250	7,975	
	2040	Small, for demonstration or battery charging units, 12V					108			108	119	
	2050	Spare anode set for					33.50			33.50	36.50	
	2060	3 watts, uses hydrogen gas					450			450	495	
	2070	6 watts, uses hydrogen gas					810			810	890	
	2080	10 watts, uses hydrogen gas					1,175			1,175	1,275	
	2090	One month rental of 261 CF hydrogen gas cylinder for, min					14.40			14.40	15.85	
	2100	Maximum					36			36	39.50	

16500 | Lighting

16510	Interior Luminaires	CREW	DAILY OUTPUT	LABOR-HOURS	UNIT	2003 BARE COSTS				TOTAL INCL O&P	
						MAT.	LABOR	EQUIP.	TOTAL		
440	0010	**INTERIOR LIGHTING FIXTURES** Including lamps, mounting										**440**
	0030	hardware and connections										
	6250	LED lamp & fixture, 18 LED 110/220VAC or 12VDC, equals 15 watt	1 Elec	4	2	Ea.	90	75		165	211	
	6260	36 LED 110/220VAC or 12VDC, equals 30 watt	"	4	2	"	145	75		220	272	
	7500	Ballast replacement, by weight of ballast, to 15' high										
	7520	Indoor fluorescent, less than 2 lbs.	1 Elec	10	.800	Ea.		30		30	45	
	7540	Two 40W, watt reducer, 2 to 5 lbs.		9.40	.851		18.90	32		50.90	69	
	7630	Electronic ballast for two tubes		8	1		32.50	37.50		70	92	
	7640	Dimmable ballast one lamp		8	1		45	37.50		82.50	106	
	7650	Dimmable ballast two-lamp		7.60	1.053		73	39.50		112.50	140	

16520	Exterior Luminaires	CREW	DAILY OUTPUT	LABOR-HOURS	UNIT	MAT.	LABOR	EQUIP.	TOTAL	TOTAL INCL O&P	
300	0009	**EXTERIOR FIXTURES, HOODED,** w/lamps, non night sky polluting										**300**
	1950	Metal halide, 175 watt	1 Elec	2.70	2.963	Ea.	300	111		411	495	
	2000	400 watt	2 Elec	4.40	3.636		350	137		487	590	
	2200	1000 watt		4	4		470	150		620	740	
	2210	1500 watt		3.70	4.324		500	163		663	795	
	2250	Low pressure sodium, 55 watt	1 Elec	2.70	2.963		485	111		596	700	
	2270	90 watt		2	4		535	150		685	815	
	2290	180 watt		2	4		680	150		830	975	
	2340	High pressure sodium, 70 watt		2.70	2.963		193	111		304	380	
	2360	100 watt		2.70	2.963		198	111		309	385	

16 ELECTRICAL

		16520	Exterior Luminaires	CREW	DAILY OUTPUT	LABOR-HOURS	UNIT	2003 BARE COSTS				TOTAL INCL O&P	
								MAT.	LABOR	EQUIP.	TOTAL		
300	2380		150 watt	1 Elec	2.70	2.963	Ea.	220	111		331	410	300
	2400		400 watt	2 Elec	4.40	3.636		340	137		477	575	
	2600		1000 watt	"	4	4		500	150		650	775	
	9005		Solar powered floodlight, w/motion det, incl batt pack for cloudy days	1 Elec	8	1		120	37.50		157.50	188	
	9020		Battery pack for		8	1		12	37.50		49.50	69	
	9100		LED street lamp & fix, 72W, 110/220VAC or 12VDC, equal to 60W		4	2		450	75		525	605	
	9110		108 watt, 110/220VAC or 12VDC, equal to 90 watt		4	2		675	75		750	855	
	9120		144 watt, 110/220VAC or 12VDC, equal to 120 watt		4	2		830	75		905	1,025	
	9130		252 watt, 110/220VAC or 12VDC, equal to 210 watt	↓	4	2	↓	1,150	75		1,225	1,375	
500	0011	**EXTERIOR FIXTURES** With lamps											500
	0960		Landscape lights, solar powered, 6" dia x 12" h, one piece w/stake	1 Clab	80	.100	Ea.	22	2.47		24.47	28	

		16530	Emergency Lighting										
320	0010	**EXIT AND EMERGENCY LIGHTING**											320
	0080		Exit light ceiling or wall mount, incandescent, single face	1 Elec	8	1	Ea.	37.50	37.50		75	97.50	
	0200		L.E.D. standard, single face		8	1		62	37.50		99.50	124	
	0220		double face		6.70	1.194		65	45		110	139	
	0240		L.E.D. w/battery unit, single face		4.40	1.818		105	68.50		173.50	218	
	0260		double face		4	2		107	75		182	230	
	0290		L.E.D. retrofit kits	↓	60	.133	↓	34	5		39	45	

		16580	Lighting Accessories										
200	0010	**ENERGY SAVING LIGHTING DEVICES**											200
	0100		Occupancy sensors infrared, ceiling mounted	1 Elec	7	1.143	Ea.	85	43		128	158	
	0150		Automatic wall switches		24	.333		49	12.55		61.55	72.50	
	0200		Remote power pack		10	.800		22	30		52	69	
	0250		Photoelectric control, S.P.S.T. 120 V		8	1		11.95	37.50		49.45	69	
	0300		S.P.S.T. 208 V/277 V		8	1		15.15	37.50		52.65	72.50	
	0350		D.P.S.T. 120 V		6	1.333		116	50		166	203	
	0400		D.P.S.T. 208 V/277 V		6	1.333		120	50		170	207	
	0450		S.P.D.T. 208 V/277 V		6	1.333		143	50		193	233	
	0460		Daylight level sensor, ceiling mtd, automatically dims up to 50 ballasts	↓	8	1	↓	120	37.50		157.50	188	

		16585	Lamps										
600	0011	**ENERGY SAVING, COMPACT FLOURESCENTS, LEDs, ETC**											600
	0170		4' long, 34 watt energy saver	1 Elec	.90	8.889	C	435	335		770	980	
	0176		2' long, T8, 17 W engergy saver		1	8		380	300		680	870	
	0178		3' long, T8, 25 W energy saver		.90	8.889		380	335		715	920	
	0180		4' long, T8, 32 watt energy saver		.90	8.889		238	335		573	760	
	0350		8' long, 60 watt energy saver		.80	10		555	375		930	1,175	
	0512		2' long, T5, 14 watt energy saver		1	8		1,025	300		1,325	1,575	
	0514		3' long, T5, 21 watt energy saver		.90	8.889		1,025	335		1,360	1,625	
	0516		4' long, T5, 28 watt energy saver		.90	8.889		875	335		1,210	1,475	
	0560		Twin tube compact lamp		.90	8.889		495	335		830	1,050	
	0570		Double twin tube compact lamp		.80	10		1,200	375		1,575	1,875	
	0580		Compact flourescents, 15 watt, replaces standard 25 watt bulb		.90	8.889		600	335		935	1,150	
	0582		20 watt, replaces standard 75 watt bulb		.90	8.889		630	335		965	1,200	
	0584		23 watt, replaces standard 90 watt bulb		.90	8.889		660	335		995	1,225	
	0586		26 watt, replaces standard 100 watt bulb		.90	8.889	↓	700	335		1,035	1,275	
	8070		LED lamp, 18 watt, 110/220VAC or 12VDC, equal to 15W		32	.250	Ea.	54	9.40		63.40	73.50	
	8071		36 watt, 110/220VAC or 12V DC, equal to 30W		32	.250		126	9.40		135.40	153	
	8072		72 watt, 110/220VAC or 12VDC, equal to 60W		32	.250		189	9.40		198.40	222	
	8073		108 watt, 110/220VAC or 12VDC, equal to 90W		32	.250		305	9.40		314.40	350	
	8074		144 watt flood, 110/220VAC or 12VDC, equal to 150W	↓	32	.250	↓	380	9.40		389.40	430	

How to Use the Assemblies Cost Tables

The following is a detailed explanation of a sample Assemblies Cost Table. Most Assembly Tables are separated into three parts: 1) an illustration of the system to be estimated; 2) the components and related costs of a typical system; and 3) the costs for similar systems with dimensional and/or size variations. For costs of the components that comprise these systems or "assemblies" refer to the Unit Price Section. Next to each bold number below is the item being described with the appropriate component of the sample entry following in parenthesis. In most cases, if the work is to be subcontracted, the general contractor will need to add an additional markup (R.S. Means suggests using 10%) to the "Total" figures.

System/Line Numbers (D3010 784 2600)

Each Assemblies Cost Line has been assigned a unique identification number based on the UniFormat classification sytem.

UNIFORMAT II Major Group

D3010   784   2600

UNIFORMAT II Level 3

Means Major Classification

Means Individual Line Number

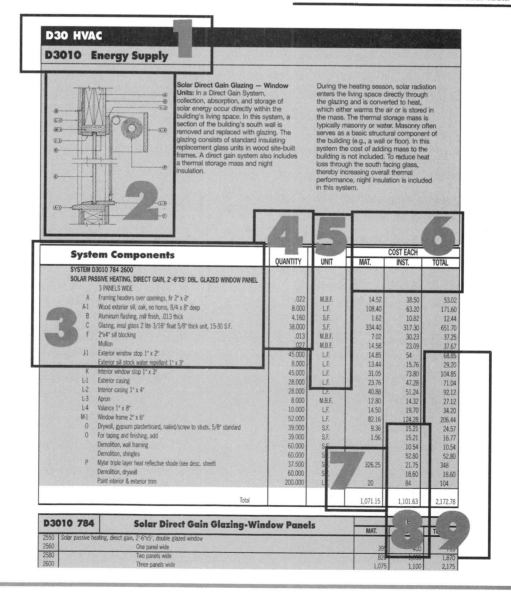

D30 HVAC
D3010   Energy Supply

Solar Direct Gain Glazing — Window Units: In a Direct Gain System, collection, absorption, and storage of solar energy occur directly within the building's living space. In this system, a section of the building's south wall is removed and replaced with glazing. The glazing consists of standard insulating replacement glass units in wood site-built frames. A direct gain system also includes a thermal storage mass and night insulation.

During the heating season, solar radiation enters the living space directly through the glazing and is converted to heat, which either warms the air or is stored in the mass. The thermal storage mass is typically masonry or water. Masonry often serves as a basic structural component of the building (e.g., a wall or floor). In this system the cost of adding mass to the building is not included. To reduce heat loss through the south facing glass, thereby increasing overall thermal performance, night insulation is included in this system.

System Components	QUANTITY	UNIT	COST EACH MAT.	COST EACH INST.	COST EACH TOTAL
SYSTEM D3010 784 2600					
SOLAR PASSIVE HEATING, DIRECT GAIN, 2'-6"X5' DBL. GLAZED WINDOW PANEL					
3 PANELS WIDE					
A Framing headers over openings, fir 2" x 8"	.022	M.B.F.	14.52	38.50	53.02
A-1 Wood exterior sill, oak, no horns, 8/4 x 8" deep	8.000	L.F.	108.40	63.20	171.60
B Aluminum flashing, mill finish, .013 thick	4.160	S.F.	1.62	10.82	12.44
C Glazing, insul glass 2 lite 3/16" float 5/8" thick unit, 15-30 S.F.	38.000	S.F.	334.40	317.30	651.70
F 2"x4" sill blocking	.013	M.B.F.	7.02	30.23	37.25
Mullion	.027	M.B.F.	14.58	23.09	37.67
J-1 Exterior window stop 1" x 2"	45.000	L.F.	14.85	54	68.85
Exterior sill stock water repellent 1" x 3"	8.000	L.F.	13.44	15.76	29.20
K Interior window stop 1" x 3"	45.000	L.F.	31.05	73.80	104.85
L-1 Exterior casing	28.000	L.F.	23.76	47.28	71.04
L-2 Interior casing 1" x 4"	28.000	L.F.	40.88	51.24	92.12
L-3 Apron	8.000	M.B.F.	12.80	14.32	27.12
L-4 Valance 1" x 8"	10.000	L.F.	14.50	19.70	34.20
M-1 Window frame 2" x 6"	52.000	L.F.	82.16	124.28	206.44
O Drywall, gypsum plasterboard, nailed/screw to studs, 5/8" standard	39.000	S.F.	9.36	15.21	24.57
O For taping and finishing, add	39.000	S.F.	1.56	15.21	16.77
Demolition, wall framing	60.000	S.F.		10.54	10.54
Demolition, shingles	60.000	S.F.		52.80	52.80
P Mylar triple layer heat reflective shade (see desc. sheet)	37.500	S.F.	326.25	21.75	348
Demolition, drywall	60.000	S.F.		18.60	18.60
Paint interior & exterior trim	200.000	L.F.	20	84	104
Total			**1,071.15**	**1,101.63**	**2,172.78**

D3010 784	Solar Direct Gain Glazing-Window Panels		MAT.	INST.	Total
2550	Solar passive heating, direct gain, 2'-6"x5', double glazed window				
2560	One panel wide		395	400	795
2580	Two panels wide		820	1,050	1,870
2600	Three panels wide		1,075	1,100	2,175

Illustration

At the top of most assembly pages is an illustration, a brief description, and the design criteria used to develop the cost.

System Components

The components of a typical system are listed separately to show what has been included in the development of the total system price. The table below contains prices for other similar systems with dimensional and/or size variations.

Quantity

This is the number of line item units required for one system unit.

Unit of Measure for Each Item

The abbreviated designation indicates the unit of measure, as defined by industry standards, upon which the price of the component is based. For example, baseboard radiation is priced by the linear foot.

Unit of Measure for Each System (Cost Each)

Costs shown in the three right hand columns have been adjusted by the component quantity and unit of measure for the entire system. In this example, "Cost Each" is the unit of measure for this system or "assembly."

Materials (1,071.15)

This column contains the Materials Cost of each component. These cost figures are bare costs plus 10% for profit.

Installation (1,101.63)

Installation includes labor and equipment plus the installing contractor's overhead and profit. Equipment costs are the bare rental costs plus 10% for profit. The labor overhead and profit is defined on the inside back cover of this book.

Total (2,172.78)

The figure in this column is the sum of the material and installation costs.

Material Cost	+	Installation Cost	=	Total
$1,071.15	+	$1,101.63	=	$2,172.78

Skylight

B3020 210	Skylights	COST PER S.F.		
		MAT.	INST.	TOTAL
5100	Skylights, plastic domes, insul curbs, nom. size to 10 S.F., single glaze	14.55	9.55	24.10
5200	Double glazing	21	11.75	32.75
5300	10 S.F. to 20 S.F., single glazing	8.70	3.87	12.57
5400	Double glazing	17	4.86	21.86
5500	20 S.F. to 30 S.F., single glazing	11	3.29	14.29
5600	Double glazing	15.65	3.87	19.52
5700	30 S.F. to 65 S.F., single glazing	15.20	2.51	17.71
5800	Double glazing	11.75	3.29	15.04
6000	Sandwich panels fiberglass, 9-1/16"thick, 2 S.F. to 10 S.F.	16.10	7.65	23.75
6100	10 S.F. to 18 S.F.	14.45	5.80	20.25
6200	2-3/4" thick, 25 S.F. to 40 S.F.	23.50	5.20	28.70
6300	40 S.F. to 70 S.F.	19.05	4.64	23.69

D30 HVAC

D3010 Energy Supply

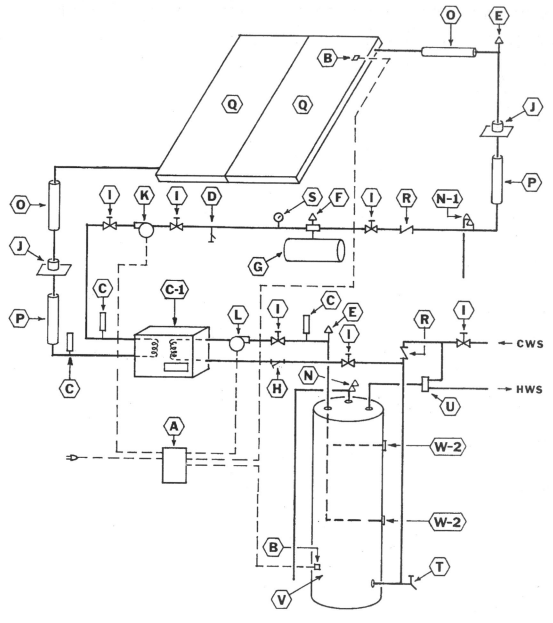

In this closed-loop indirect collection system, fluid with a low freezing temperature, such as propylene glycol, transports heat from the collectors to water storage. The transfer fluid is contained in a closed-loop consisting of collectors, supply and return piping, and a remote heat exchanger. The heat exchanger transfers heat energy from the

fluid in the collector loop to potable water circulated in a storage loop. A typical two-or-three panel system contains 5 to 6 gallons of heat transfer fluid.

When the collectors become approximately 20° F warmer than the storage temperature, a controller activates the circulator on the collector and storage

loops. The circulators will move the fluid and potable water through the heat exchanger until heat collection no longer occurs. At that point, the system shuts down. Since the heat transfer medium is a fluid with a very low freezing temperature, there is no need for it to be drained from the system between periods of collection.

D3010 Energy Supply

System Components	QUANTITY	UNIT	COST EACH		
			MAT.	INST.	TOTAL
SYSTEM D3010 715 2760					
SOLAR, CLOSED LOOP, ADD-ON HOT WATER SYS., EXTERNAL HEAT EXCHANGER					
3/4" TUBING, TWO 3'X7' BLACK CHROME COLLECTORS					
A,B,G,L,K,M Heat exchanger fluid-fluid pkg incl 2 circulators, expansion tank,					
Check valve, relief valve, controller, hi temp cutoff, & 2 sensors	1.000	Ea.	765	325	1,090
C Thermometer, 2" dial	3.000	Ea.	63	84	147
D, T Fill & drain valve, brass, 3/4" connection	1.000	Ea.	5.20	18.80	24
E Air vent, manual, 1/8" fitting	2.000	Ea.	4.26	28.20	32.46
F Air purger	1.000	Ea.	45	37.50	82.50
H Strainer, Y type, bronze body, 3/4" IPS	1.000	Ea.	19.15	24	43.15
I Valve, gate, bronze, NRS, soldered 3/4" diam	6.000	Ea.	120	135	255
J Neoprene vent flashing	2.000	Ea.	19.60	45	64.60
N-1, N Relief valve temp & press, 150 psi 210°F self-closing 3/4" IPS	1.000	Ea.	8.65	15.05	23.70
O Pipe covering, urethane, ultraviolet cover, 1" wall 3/4" diam	20.000	L.F.	33.40	86.60	120
P Pipe covering, fiberglass, all service jacket, 1" wall, 3/4" diam	50.000	L.F.	82.50	173	255.50
Q Collector panel solar energy blk chrome on copper, 1/8" temp glass 3'x7'	2.000	Ea.	1,200	171	1,371
Roof clamps for solar energy collector panels	2.000	Set	3.54	23.20	26.74
R Valve, swing check, bronze, regrinding disc, 3/4" diam	2.000	Ea.	71	45	116
S Pressure gauge, 60 psi, 2" dial	1.000	Ea.	23	14.10	37.10
U Valve, water tempering, bronze, sweat connections, 3/4" diam	1.000	Ea.	59.50	22.50	82
W-2, V Tank water storage w/heating element, drain, relief valve, existing	1.000	Ea.			
Copper tubing type L, solder joint, hanger 10' OC 3/4" diam	20.000	L.F.	39	119	158
Copper tubing, type M, solder joint, hanger 10' OC 3/4" diam	70.000	L.F.	114.10	406	520.10
Sensor wire, #22-2 conductor multistranded	.500	C.L.F.	4.70	22.50	27.20
Solar energy heat transfer fluid, propylene glycol anti-freeze	6.000	Gal.	58.20	96.60	154.80
Wrought copper fittings & solder, 3/4" diam	76.000	Ea.	86.64	1,824	1,910.64
Total			2,825.44	3,716.05	6,541.49

D3010 715	Solar, Closed Loop, Add-On Hot Water Systems	COST EACH		
		MAT.	INST.	TOTAL
2550	Solar, closed loop, add-on hot water system, external heat exchanger			
2700	3/4" tubing, 3 ea 3'x7' black chrome collectors	3,425	3,825	7,250
2720	3 ea 3'x7' flat black absorber plate collectors	3,050	3,825	6,875
2740	2 ea 4'x9' flat black w/plastic glazing collectors	2,700	3,850	6,550
2760	2 ea 3'x7' black chrome collectors	2,825	3,725	6,550
2780	1" tubing, 4 ea 2'x9' plastic absorber & glazing collectors	4,075	4,275	8,350
2800	4 ea 3'x7' black chrome absorber collectors	4,300	4,300	8,600
2820	4 ea 3'x7' flat black absorber collectors	3,800	4,325	8,125

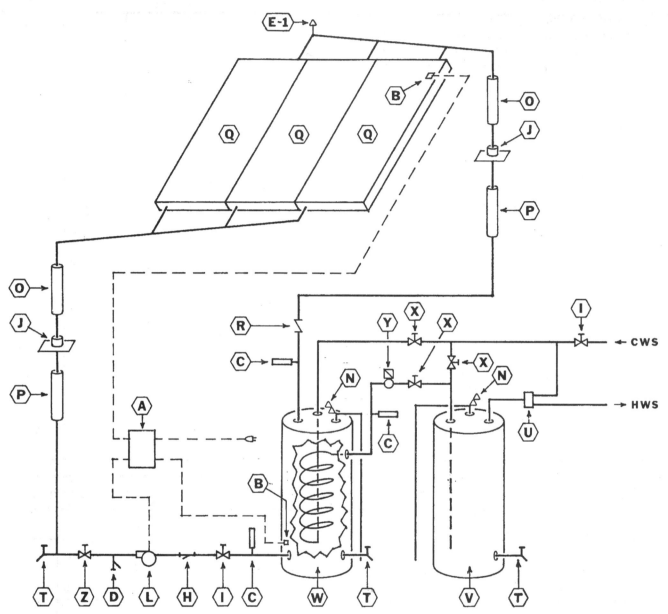

In the drainback indirect-collection system, the heat transfer fluid is distilled water contained in a loop consisting of collectors, supply and return piping, and an unpressurized holding tank. A large heat exchanger containing incoming potable water is immersed in the holding tank. When a controller activates solar collection, the distilled water is pumped through the collectors and heated and pumped back down to the holding tank. When the temperature differential between the water in the collectors and water in storage is such that collection no longer occurs, the pump turns off and gravity causes the distilled water in the collector loop to drain back to the holding tank. All the loop piping is pitched so that the water can drain out of the collectors and piping and not freeze there. As hot water is needed in the home, incoming water first flows through the holding tank with the immersed heat exchanger and is warmed and then flows through a conventional heater for any supplemental heating that is necessary.

D3010 Energy Supply

System Components	QUANTITY	UNIT	COST EACH		
			MAT.	INST.	TOTAL
SYSTEM D3010 720 2760					
SOLAR, DRAINBACK, ADD ON, HOT WATER, IMMERSED HEAT EXCHANGER					
3/4" TUBING, THREE EA 3'X7' BLACK CHROME COLLECTOR					
A, B Differential controller 2 sensors, thermostat, solar energy system	1.000	Ea.	85.50	37.50	123
C Thermometer 2" dial	3.000	Ea.	63	84	147
D, T Fill & drain valve, brass, 3/4" connection	1.000	Ea.	5.20	18.80	24
E-1 Automatic air vent 1/8" fitting	1.000	Ea.	9.70	14.10	23.80
H Strainer, Y type, bronze body, 3/4" IPS	1.000	Ea.	19.15	24	43.15
I Valve, gate, bronze, NRS, soldered 3/4" diam	2.000	Ea.	40	45	85
J Neoprene vent flashing	2.000	Ea.	19.60	45	64.60
L Circulator, solar heated liquid, 1/20 HP	1.000	Ea.	161	67.50	228.50
N Relief valve temp. & press. 150 psi 210°F self-closing 3/4" IPS	1.000	Ea.	8.65	15.05	23.70
O Pipe covering, urethane, ultraviolet cover, 1" wall, 3/4" diam	20.000	L.F.	33.40	86.60	120
P Pipe covering, fiberglass, all service jacket, 1" wall, 3/4" diam	50.000	L.F.	82.50	173	255.50
Q Collector panel solar energy blk chrome on copper, 1/8" temp glas 3'x7'	3.000	Ea.	1,800	256.50	2,056.50
Roof clamps for solar energy collector panels	3.000	Set	5.31	34.80	40.11
R Valve, swing check, bronze, regrinding disc, 3/4" diam	1.000	Ea.	35.50	22.50	58
U Valve, water tempering, bronze sweat connections, 3/4" diam	1.000	Ea.	59.50	22.50	82
W Tank, water storage immersed heat exchr elec 2"x1/2# insul 120 gal	1.000	Ea.	925	320	1,245
V Tank, water storage w/heating element, drain, relief valve, existing	1.000	Ea.			
X Valve, globe, bronze, rising stem, 3/4" diam, soldered	3.000	Ea.	153	67.50	220.50
Y Flow control valve	1.000	Ea.	54.50	20.50	75
Z Valve, ball, bronze, solder 3/4" diam, solar loop flow control	1.000	Ea.	12.20	22.50	34.70
Copper tubing, type L, solder joint, hanger 10' OC 3/4" diam	20.000	L.F.	39	119	158
Copper tubing, type M, solder joint, hanger 10' OC 3/4" diam	70.000	L.F.	114.10	406	520.10
Sensor wire, #22-2 conductor, multistranded	.500	C.L.F.	4.70	22.50	27.20
Wrought copper fittings & solder, 3/4" diam	76.000	Ea.	86.64	1,824	1,910.64
Total			3,817.15	3,748.85	7,566

D3010 720	Solar, Drainback, Hot Water Systems	COST EACH		
		MAT.	INST.	TOTAL
2550	Solar, drainback, hot water, immersed heat exchanger			
2560	3/8" tubing, 3 ea. 4' x 4'-4" vacuum tube collectors	4,600	3,350	7,950
2760	3/4" tubing, 3 ea 3'x7' black chrome collectors, 120 gal tank	3,825	3,750	7,575
2780	3 ea. 3'x7' flat black absorber collectors, 120 gal tank	3,450	3,775	7,225
2800	2 ea. 4'x9' flat blk w/plastic glazing collectors 120 gal tank	3,100	3,775	6,875
2840	1" tubing, 4 ea. 2'x9' plastic absorber & glazing collectors, 120 gal tank	4,500	4,225	8,725
2860	4 ea. 3'x7' black chrome absorber collectors, 120 gal tank	4,725	4,225	8,950
2880	4 ea. 3'x7' flat black absorber collectors, 120 gal tank	4,225	4,250	8,475

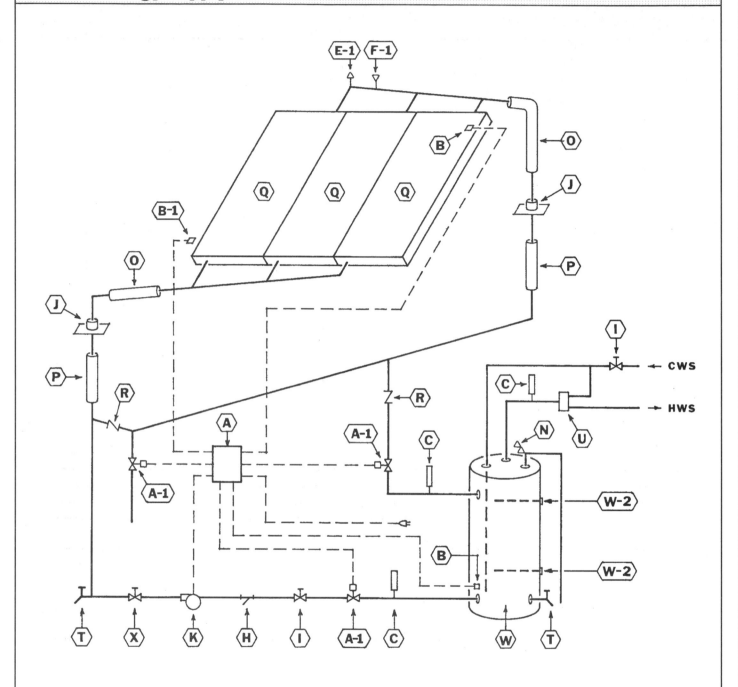

In the draindown direct-collection system, incoming domestic water is heated in the collectors. When the controller activates solar collection, domestic water is first heated as it flows through the collectors and is then pumped to storage. When conditions are no longer suitable for heat collection, the pump shuts off and the water in the loop drains down and out of the system by means of solenoid valves and properly pitched piping.

D3010 Energy Supply

System Components	QUANTITY	UNIT	COST EACH		
			MAT.	INST.	TOTAL
SYSTEM D3010 730 2760					
SOLAR, DRAINDOWN, HOT WATER, DIRECT COLLECTION					
3/4" TUBING, THREE 3'X7' BLACK CHROME COLLECTORS					
A, B Differential controller, 2 sensors, thermostat, solar energy system	1.000	Ea.	85.50	37.50	123
A-1 Solenoid valve, solar heating loop, brass, 3/4" diam, 24 volts	3.000	Ea.	699	150	849
B-1 Solar energy sensor, freeze prevention	1.000	Ea.	22	14.10	36.10
C Thermometer, 2" dial	3.000	Ea.	63	84	147
E-1 Vacuum relief valve, 3/4" diam	1.000	Ea.	27.50	14.10	41.60
F-1 Air vent, automatic, 1/8" fitting	1.000	Ea.	9.70	14.10	23.80
H Strainer, Y type, bronze body, 3/4" IPS	1.000	Ea.	19.15	24	43.15
I Valve, gate, bronze, NRS, soldered, 3/4" diam	2.000	Ea.	40	45	85
J Vent flashing neoprene	2.000	Ea.	19.60	45	64.60
K Circulator, solar heated liquid, 1/25 HP	1.000	Ea.	153	58	211
N Relief valve temp & press 150 psi 210°F self-closing 3/4" IPS	1.000	Ea.	8.65	15.05	23.70
O Pipe covering, urethane, ultraviolet cover, 1" wall, 3/4" diam	20.000	L.F.	33.40	86.60	120
P Pipe covering, fiberglass, all service jacket, 1" wall, 3/4" diam	50.000	L.F.	82.50	173	255.50
Roof clamps for solar energy collector panels	3.000	Set	5.31	34.80	40.11
Q Collector panel solar energy blk chrome on copper, 1/8" temp glass 3'x7'	3.000	Ea.	1,800	256.50	2,056.50
R Valve, swing check, bronze, regrinding disc, 3/4" diam, soldered	2.000	Ea.	71	45	116
T Drain valve, brass, 3/4" connection	2.000	Ea.	10.40	37.60	48
U Valve, water tempering, bronze, sweat connections, 3/4" diam	1.000	Ea.	59.50	22.50	82
W-2, W Tank, water storage elec elem 2"x1/2# insul 120 gal	1.000	Ea.	925	320	1,245
X Valve, globe, bronze, rising stem, 3/4" diam, soldered	1.000	Ea.	51	22.50	73.50
Copper tubing, type L, solder joints, hangers 10' OC 3/4" diam	20.000	L.F.	39	119	158
Copper tubing, type M, solder joints, hangers 10' OC 3/4" diam	70.000	L.F.	114.10	406	520.10
Sensor wire, #22-2 conductor, multistranded	.500	C.L.F.	4.70	22.50	27.20
Wrought copper fittings & solder, 3/4" diam	76.000	Ea.	86.64	1,824	1,910.64
Total			4,429.65	3,870.85	8,300.50

D3010 730	Solar, Draindown, Hot Water Systems	COST EACH		
		MAT.	INST.	TOTAL
2550	Solar, draindown, hot water			
2580	1/2" tubing, 4 ea. 4' x 4'-4" vacuum tube collectors, 80 gal tank	6,100	3,775	9,875
2760	3/4" tubing, 3 ea 3'x7' black chrome collectors, 120 gal tank	4,425	3,875	8,300
2780	3 ea 3'x7' flat collectors, 120 gal tank	4,050	3,875	7,925
2800	2 ea. 4'x9' flat black & plastic glazing collectors, 120 gal tank	3,700	3,900	7,600
2840	1" tubing, 4 ea. 2'x9' plastic absorber & glazing collectors, 120 gal tank	5,075	4,325	9,400
2860	4 ea 3'x7' black chrome absorber collectors, 120 gal tank	5,300	4,350	9,650
2880	4 ea 3'x7' flat black absorber collectors, 120 gal tank	4,800	4,375	9,175

D30 HVAC

D3010 Energy Supply

This draindown pool system uses a differential thermostat similar to those used in solar domestic hot water and space heating applications. To heat the pool, the pool water passes through the conventional pump-filter loop and then flows through the collectors. When collection is not possible, or when the pool temperature is reached, all water drains from the solar loop back to the pool through the existing piping. The modes are controlled by solenoid valves or other automatic valves in conjunction with a vacuum breaker relief valve, which facilitates draindown.

D3010 Energy Supply

System Components	QUANTITY	UNIT	COST EACH MAT.	COST EACH INST.	COST EACH TOTAL
SYSTEM D3010 760 2640					
SOLAR SWIMMING POOL HEATER, ROOF MOUNTED COLLECTORS					
TEN 4' X 10' FULLY WETTED UNGLAZED PLASTIC ABSORBERS					
A Differential thermostat/controller, 110V, adj pool pump system	1.000	Ea.	282	226	508
A-1 Solenoid valve, PVC, normally 1 open 1 closed (included)	2.000	Ea.			
B Sensor, thermistor type (included)	2.000	Ea.			
E-1 Valve, vacuum relief	1.000	Ea.	27.50	14.10	41.60
Q Collector panel, solar energy, plastic, liquid full wetted, 4' x 10'	10.000	Ea.	2,150	1,630	3,780
R Valve, ball check, PVC, socket, 1-1/2" diam	1.000	Ea.	75	22.50	97.50
Z Valve, ball, PVC, socket, 1-1/2" diam	3.000	Ea.	262.50	67.50	330
Pipe, PVC, sch 40, 1-1/2" diam	80.000	L.F.	241.60	1,004	1,245.60
Pipe fittings, PVC sch 40, socket joint, 1-1/2" diam	10.000	Ea.	11	225	236
Sensor wire, #22-2 conductor, multistranded	.500	C.L.F.	4.70	22.50	27.20
Roof clamps for solar energy collector panels	10.000	Set	17.70	116	133.70
Roof strap, teflon for solar energy collector panels	26.000	L.F.	271.70	57.20	328.90
TOTAL			3,343.70	3,384.80	6,728.50

D3010 760	Solar Swimming Pool Heater Systems	COST EACH MAT.	COST EACH INST.	COST EACH TOTAL
2530	Solar swimming pool heater systems, roof mounted collectors			
2540	10 ea. 3'x7' black chrome absorber, 1/8" temp. glass	7,200	2,600	9,800
2560	10 ea. 4'x8' black chrome absorber, 3/16" temp. glass (RD3010 -600)	8,300	3,100	11,400
2580	10 ea. 3'8"x6' flat black absorber, 3/16" temp. glass	5,950	2,650	8,600
2600	10 ea. 4'x9' flat black absorber, plastic glazing	6,600	3,225	9,825
2620	10 ea. 2'x9' rubber absorber, plastic glazing	12,100	3,500	15,600
2640	10 ea. 4'x10' fully wetted unglazed plastic absorber	3,350	3,375	6,725
2660	Ground mounted collectors			
2680	10 ea. 3'x7' black chrome absorber, 1/8" temp. glass	7,350	3,000	10,350
2700	10 ea. 4'x8' black chrome absorber, 3/16" temp glass	8,450	3,500	11,950
2720	10 ea. 3'8"x6' flat blk absorber, 3/16" temp. glass	6,100	3,050	9,150
2740	10 ea. 4'x9' flat blk absorber, plastic glazing	6,750	3,625	10,375
2760	10 ea. 2'x9' rubber absorber, plastic glazing	12,300	3,775	16,075
2780	10 ea. 4'x10' fully wetted unglazed plastic absorber	3,500	3,775	7,275

D30 HVAC

D3010   Energy Supply

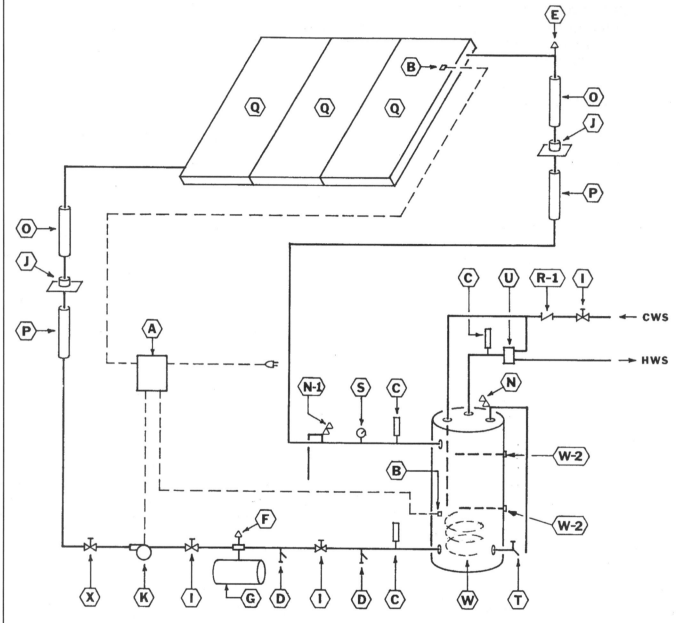

In this closed-loop indirect collection system, fluid with a low freezing temperature, such as propylene glycol, transports heat from the collectors to water storage. The transfer fluid is contained in a closed-loop consisting of collectors, supply and return piping, and a heat exchanger immersed in the storage tank. A typical two-or-three panel system contains 5 to 6 gallons of heat transfer fluid.

When the collectors become approximately 20° F warmer than the storage temperature, a controller activates the circulator. The circulator moves the fluid continuously through the collectors until the temperature difference between the collectors and storage is such that heat collection no longer occurs; at that point, the circulator shuts off. Since the heat transfer fluid has a very low freezing temperature, there is no need for it to be drained from the collectors between periods of collection.

D3010 Energy Supply

System Components	QUANTITY	UNIT	COST EACH		
			MAT.	INST.	TOTAL
SYSTEM D3010 780 2760					
SOLAR, CLOSED LOOP, HOT WATER SYSTEM, IMMERSED HEAT EXCHANGER					
3/4" TUBING, THREE 3' X 7' BLACK CHROME COLLECTORS					
A, B Differential controller, 2 sensors, thermostat, solar energy system	1.000	Ea.	85.50	37.50	123
C Thermometer 2" dial	3.000	Ea.	63	84	147
D, T Fill & drain valves, brass, 3/4" connection	3.000	Ea.	15.60	56.40	72
E Air vent, manual, 1/8" fitting	1.000	Ea.	2.13	14.10	16.23
F Air purger	1.000	Ea.	45	37.50	82.50
G Expansion tank	1.000	Ea.	64	14.10	78.10
I Valve, gate, bronze, NRS, soldered 3/4" diam	3.000	Ea.	60	67.50	127.50
J Neoprene vent flashing	2.000	Ea.	19.60	45	64.60
K Circulator, solar heated liquid, 1/25 HP	1.000	Ea.	153	58	211
N-1, N Relief valve, temp & press 150 psi 210°F self-closing 3/4" IPS	2.000	Ea.	17.30	30.10	47.40
O Pipe covering, urethane ultraviolet cover, 1" wall, 3/4" diam	20.000	L.F.	33.40	86.60	120
P Pipe covering, fiberglass, all service jacket, 1" wall, 3/4" diam	50.000	L.F.	82.50	173	255.50
Roof clamps for solar energy collector panel	3.000	Set	5.31	34.80	40.11
Q Collector panel solar blk chrome on copper, 1/8" temp glass, 3'x7'	3.000	Ea.	1,800	256.50	2,056.50
R-1 Valve, swing check, bronze, regrinding disc, 3/4" diam, soldered	1.000	Ea.	35.50	22.50	58
S Pressure gauge, 60 psi, 2-1/2" dial	1.000	Ea.	23	14.10	37.10
U Valve, water tempering, bronze, sweat connections, 3/4" diam	1.000	Ea.	59.50	22.50	82
W-2, W Tank, water storage immersed heat exchr elec elem 2"x2# insul 120 Gal	1.000	Ea.	925	320	1,245
X Valve, globe, bronze, rising stem, 3/4" diam, soldered	1.000	Ea.	51	22.50	73.50
Copper tubing type L, solder joint, hanger 10' OC 3/4" diam	20.000	L.F.	39	119	158
Copper tubing, type M, solder joint, hanger 10' OC 3/4" diam	70.000	L.F.	114.10	406	520.10
Sensor wire, #22-2 conductor multistranded	.500	C.L.F.	4.70	22.50	27.20
Solar energy heat transfer fluid, propylene glycol, anti-freeze	6.000	Gal.	58.20	96.60	154.80
Wrought copper fittings & solder, 3/4" diam	76.000	Ea.	86.64	1,824	1,910.64
TOTAL			3,842.98	3,864.80	7,707.78

D3010 780	Solar, Closed Loop, Hot Water Systems	COST EACH		
		MAT.	INST.	TOTAL
2550	Solar, closed loop, hot water system, immersed heat exchanger			
2560	3/8" tubing, 3 ea. 4' x 4'-4" vacuum tube collectors, 80 gal. tank	4,650	3,500	8,150
2580	1/2" tubing, 4 ea. 4' x 4'-4" vacuum tube collectors, 80 gal. tank	5,525	3,750	9,275
2600	120 gal. tank	5,625	3,800	9,425
2640	2 ea. 3'x7' black chrome collectors, 80 gal. tank	2,975	3,600	6,575
2660	120 gal. tank	3,100	3,575	6,675
2760	3/4" tubing, 3 ea. 3'x7' black chrome collectors, 120 gal. tank	3,850	3,875	7,725
2780	3 ea. 3'x7' flat black collectors, 120 gal. tank	3,475	3,875	7,350
2840	1" tubing, 4 ea. 2'x9' plastic absorber & glazing collectors 120 gal. tank	4,475	4,300	8,775
2860	4 ea. 3'x7' black chrome collectors, 120 gal. tank	4,675	4,325	9,000
2550	Solar passive heating, direct gain, 3'x6'8", double glazed door			
2560	One panel wide	980	325	1,305
2580	Two panels wide	1,500	470	1,970
2600	Three panels wide	1,975	605	2,580

D30 HVAC

D3010 Energy Supply

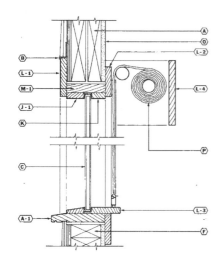

Solar Direct Gain Glazing — Window Units: In a Direct Gain System, collection, absorption, and storage of solar energy occur directly within the building's living space. In this system, a section of the building's south wall is removed and replaced with glazing. The glazing consists of standard insulating replacement glass units in wood site-built frames. A direct gain system also includes a thermal storage mass and night insulation.

During the heating season, solar radiation enters the living space directly through the glazing and is converted to heat, which either warms the air or is stored in the mass. The thermal storage mass is typically masonry or water. Masonry often serves as a basic structural component of the building (e.g., a wall or floor). In this system the cost of adding mass to the building is not included. To reduce heat loss through the south facing glass, thereby increasing overall thermal performance, night insulation is included in this system.

System Components		QUANTITY	UNIT	COST EACH		
				MAT.	INST.	TOTAL
SYSTEM D3010 784 2600						
SOLAR PASSIVE HEATING, DIRECT GAIN, 2'-6"X5' DBL. GLAZED WINDOW PANEL						
3 PANELS WIDE						
A	Framing headers over openings, fir 2" x 8"	.022	M.B.F.	14.52	38.50	53.02
A-1	Wood exterior sill, oak, no horns, 8/4 x 8" deep	8.000	L.F.	108.40	63.20	171.60
B	Aluminum flashing, mill finish, .013 thick	4.160	S.F.	1.62	10.82	12.44
C	Glazing, insul glass 2 lite 3/16" float 5/8" thick unit, 15-30 S.F.	38.000	S.F.	334.40	317.30	651.70
F	2"x4" sill blocking	.013	M.B.F.	7.02	30.23	37.25
	Mullion	.027	M.B.F.	14.58	23.09	37.67
J-1	Exterior window stop 1" x 2"	45.000	L.F.	14.85	54	68.85
	Exterior sill stock water repellent 1" x 3"	8.000	L.F.	13.44	15.76	29.20
K	Interior window stop 1" x 3"	45.000	L.F.	31.05	73.80	104.85
L-1	Exterior casing	28.000	L.F.	23.76	47.28	71.04
L-2	Interior casing 1" x 4"	28.000	L.F.	40.88	51.24	92.12
L-3	Apron	8.000	M.B.F.	12.80	14.32	27.12
L-4	Valance 1" x 8"	10.000	L.F.	14.50	19.70	34.20
M-1	Window frame 2" x 6"	52.000	L.F.	82.16	124.28	206.44
O	Drywall, gypsum plasterboard, nailed/screw to studs, 5/8" standard	39.000	S.F.	9.36	15.21	24.57
O	For taping and finishing, add	39.000	S.F.	1.56	15.21	16.77
	Demolition, wall framing	60.000	S.F.		10.54	10.54
	Demolition, shingles	60.000	S.F.		52.80	52.80
P	Mylar triple layer heat reflective shade (see desc. sheet)	37.500	S.F.	326.25	21.75	348
	Demolition, drywall	60.000	S.F.		18.60	18.60
	Paint interior & exterior trim	200.000	L.F.	20	84	104
	Total			1,071.15	1,101.63	2,172.78

D3010 784	Solar Direct Gain Glazing-Window Panels		COST EACH		
			MAT.	INST.	TOTAL
2550	Solar passive heating, direct gain, 2'-6"x5', double glazed window				
2560	One panel wide		395	400	795
2580	Two panels wide		820	1,050	1,870
2600	Three panels wide		1,075	1,100	2,175
2550	Solar passive heating, indirect gain				
2560	3'x6'8", double glazed thermal storage wall, one panel wide		209	370	579

D3010 Energy Supply

D3010 784	Solar Direct Gain Glazing-Window Panels	COST EACH		
		MAT.	INST.	TOTAL
2580	Two panels wide	395	655	1,050
2600	Three panels wide	583.51	959.09	1,543.30

D30 HVAC

D3010 Energy Supply

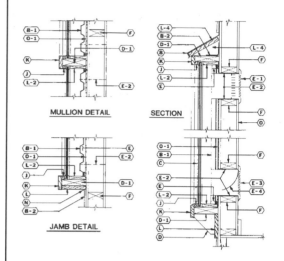

MULLION DETAIL

SECTION

JAMB DETAIL

Solar Indirect Gain — Thermosyphon Panel: The Thermosyphon Air Panel (TAP) System is an indirect gain system used primarily for daytime heating because it does not include thermal mass. This site-built TAP System makes use of double glazing and a ribbed aluminum absorber plate. The panel is framed in wood and attached to the south side of a building. Solar radiation passes through the glass and is absorbed by the absorber plate. As the absorber plate heats, the air between it and the glass also heats. Vents cut through the building's south wall and the absorber plate near the top and bottom of the TAP allow hot air to circulate into the building by means of natural convection.

System Components

		QUANTITY	UNIT	COST EACH MAT.	COST EACH INST.	COST EACH TOTAL
	SYSTEM D3010 788 2600					
	SOLAR PASSIVE HEATING, INDIRECT GAIN, THERMOSYPHON PANEL					
	3'X6'8" DOUBLE GLAZED PANEL, THREE PANELS WIDE					
B	Aluminum flashing and sleeves, mill finish, .013 thick	8.000	S.F.	8.97	59.80	68.77
B-1	Aluminum ribbed, 4" pitch, on steel frame .032" mill finish	45.000	S.F.	68.40	88.65	157.05
B-2	Angle brackets	9.000	Ea.	5.31	20.25	25.56
C	Glazing, insul glass 2 lite 3/16" float 5/8" thick unit, 15-30 S.F.	45.000	S.F.	396	375.75	771.75
D	Support brackets, fir 2"x6"	.003	M.B.F.	1.62	6.98	8.60
D-1	Framing fir 2" x 6"	.040	M.B.F.	33.60	79	112.60
E	Corrugated end closure	15.000	L.F.	8.70	28.65	37.35
E-1	Register, multilouvre operable 6" x 30"	3.000	Ea.	165	76.50	241.50
E-3	Grille 6" x 30"	3.000	Ea.	76.50	59.70	136.20
E-4	Back draft damper	.038	C.S.F.	.23	.40	.63
F	House wall blocking 2" x 4"	.012	M.B.F.	21.60	38	59.60
J	Absorber supports & glass stop	54.000	L.F.	18.36	78.84	97.20
K	Exterior & bottom trim & interior glazing stop	40.000	L.F.	62.98	148.52	211.50
L	Support ledger & side trim	24.000	L.F.	28.32	37.92	66.24
L-2	Trim cap	8.000	L.F.	11.60	15.76	27.36
N	Caulking/sealants, silicone rubber, cartridges	.250	Gal.	11.13		11.13
O	Drywall, nailed & taped, 5/8" thick	60.000	S.F.	14.40	23.40	37.80
O	For taping and finishing, add	60.000	S.F.	2.40	23.40	25.80
O-1	Insulation foil faced exterior wall	45.000	S.F.	16.20	13.05	29.25
	Demolition, framing	60.000	S.F.		13.02	13.02
	Demolition, drywall	60.000	S.F.		18.60	18.60
	Paint absorber plate black	45.000	S.F.	3.60	38.25	41.85
	Finish paint	125.000	S.F.	12.50	52.50	65
	Paint walls & ceiling with roller, primer & 1 coat	60.000	S.F.	6	21	27
	Total			973.42	1,317.94	2,291.36

D3010 788	Passive Solar Indirect Gain Panel	COST EACH MAT.	COST EACH INST.	COST EACH TOTAL
2550	Solar passive heating, indirect gain			
2560	3'x6'8", double glazed thermosyphon panel, one panel wide	340	465	805
2580	Two panels wide	655	890	1,545
2600	Three panels wide	975	1,325	2,300

D3010 Energy Supply

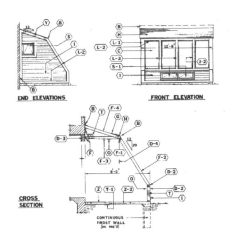

END ELEVATIONS   **FRONT ELEVATION**

CROSS SECTION

CONTINUOUS FROST WALL (as req'd)

Solar Attached Sunspace: The attached sunspace, a room adjacent to the south side of a building, is designed solely for heat collection. During the heating season, solar radiation enters the sunspace through south facing glass. Radiation is absorbed by elements in the space and converted to heat. This sunspace is thermally isolated from the building. A set of sliding glass doors connecting the sunspace to the building space is closed to prevent night heat losses from the living space. This attached sunspace uses standard size, double glazed units and has a concrete slab floor. Since the required depth of footings (if required) is dependent on local frost conditions, costs of footings at depths of 2′, 3′ and 4′ are provided with the base cost of system as shown.

System Components		QUANTITY	UNIT	COST EACH MAT.	COST EACH INST.	COST EACH TOTAL
SYSTEM D3010 790 2560						
SOLAR PASSIVE HEATING, DIRECT GAIN, ATTACHED SUNSPACE						
WOOD FRAMED, SLAB ON GRADE						
B	Aluminum, flashing, mill finish	21.000	S.F.	8.19	54.60	62.79
C	Glazing, double, tempered glass	72.000	S.F.	633.60	601.20	1,234.80
D-2-4	Knee & end wall framing	.188	M.B.F.	108.10	148.52	256.62
F	Ledgers, headers and rafters	.028	M.B.F.	97.74	171.95	269.69
	Building paper, asphalt felt sheathing paper 15 lb	240.000	S.F.	5.88	25.56	31.44
G	Sheathing plywood on roof CDX 1/2″	240.000	S.F.	129.60	134.40	264
H	Asphalt shingles inorganic class A 210-235 lb/sq	1.000	Sq.	32	68.50	100.50
I	Wood siding, match existing	164.000	S.F.	300.12	259.12	559.24
	Window stop, interior or external	96.000	L.F.	63.36	230.40	293.76
L-1	Exterior trim	44.000	L.F.	43.56	69.52	113.08
L-2, L-3	Exterior trim 1″ x 4″	206.000	L.F.	138.02	405.82	543.84
O	Drywall, taping & finishing joints	200.000	S.F.	8	78	86
O	Drywall, 1/2″ on walls, standard, no finish	200.000	S.F.	48	78	126
S, S-1	Windows, wood, awning type, double glazed, with screens	4.000	Ea.	1,720	198	1,918
T	Insulation batts, fiberglass, faced	210.000	S.F.	94.50	60.90	155.40
T-1	Polyethylene vapor barrier, standard, .004″ thick	2.500	C.S.F.	4.82	21.30	26.12
Y	Button vents	6.000	Ea.	9.30	39.30	48.60
Z	Concrete floor, reinforced, 10′ x 10′ x 4″	1.234	C.Y.	114.15	75.59	189.74
	Floor finishing, steel trowel	100.000	S.F.		65	65
Z-2	Mesh, welded wire 6 x 6, #10/10	1.000	C.S.F.	7.90	27.50	35.40
	Paint interior, exterior and trim	330.000	S.F.	36.30	188.10	224.40
	Total			3,603.14	3,001.28	6,604.42

D3010 790	Passive Solar Sunspace		COST EACH MAT.	COST EACH INST.	COST EACH TOTAL
2550	Solar passive heating, direct gain, attached sunspace, 100 S.F.				
2560	Wood framed, slab on grade		3,600	3,000	6,600
2580	2′ deep frost wall		3,925	3,700	7,625
2600	3′ deep frost wall		4,025	3,950	7,975
2620	4′ deep frost wall		4,150	4,225	8,375

F10 Special Construction

F1030 Special Construction Systems

PV power system, stand alone, AC and DC loads

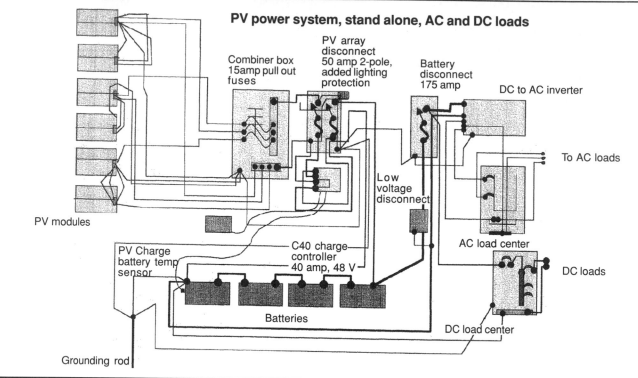

Photovoltaic System, EACH			COST EACH		
	QUANTITY	UNIT	MAT.	INST.	TOTAL
SYSTEM F1030 410 0400					
PHOTOVOLTAIC POWER SYSTEM, STAND ALONE					
Alternative energy sources, photovoltaic module, 75 watt, 17 volts	12.000	Ea.	4,800	672	5,940
DC to AC inverter for, 48V, 4,000 watt	1.000	Ea.	3,500	56	4,075
Alt energy sources, PV comp, combiner box, 10 lug, NEMA 3R encl	1.000	Ea.	177	112	289
Alternative energy sources, PV components, fuse, 15 A for combiner box	10.000	Ea.	77	112.50	189.50
Battery charger controller w/temp sensor	1.000	Ea.	177	112	289
Digital readout panel, displays hours, volts, amps, etc	1.000	Ea.	88.50	112	200.50
Deep cycle solar battery, 6V, 180 Ah (C/20)	4.000	Ea.	1,440	224	1,664
Battery intercon, 15" AWG #2/0, sld w/copp ring lugs	3.000	Ea.	27.75	84	111.75
Batt connec, 24" AWG #2/0, sealed w/copper ring lugs	2.000	Ea.	21.60	56	77.60
Batt connec, 60" AWG #2/0, sealed w/copper ring lugs	2.000	Ea.	32.30	56	88.30
Batt temp computer probe, RJ11 jack, 15' cord	1.000	Ea.	22.50	28	50.50
System disconnect, DC 175 Amp circuit breaker	1.000	Ea.	254	56	310
Conduit box for inverter	1.000	Ea.	72.50	56	128.50
Low voltage disconnect	1.000	Ea.	150	56	206
Vented battery enclosure, wood	1.000	Ea.	154	197	351
Grounding, rod, copper clad, 8' long, 5/8" diameter	1.000	Ea.	19.95	81.50	101.45
Grounding, clamp, bronze, 5/8" dia	1.000	Ea.	4.71	14.05	18.76
Bare copper wire, #8 stranded	1.000	C.L.F.	10.65	41	51.65
Wire, 600 volt, type THW, copper, stranded, #12	3.600	C.L.F.	20.52	147.60	168.12
Wire, 600 volt, type THW, copper, stranded, #8	1.050	C.L.F.	15.12	58.80	73.92
Rigid galvanized steel conduit, 3/4", including fittings	120.000	L.F.	259.20	672	931.20
Conduit,to 15' H,incl 2 termn,2 elb&11 bm clp per 100',(EMT), 1" dia	30.000	L.F.	32.70	117.30	150
Lightning surge suppressor	1.000	Ea.	43.50	14.05	57.55
General duty 240 volt, 2 pole NEMA 1, nonfusible, NEMA 3R, 60 amp	1.000	Ea.	177	195	372
Load centers, 3 wire, 120/240V, 100 amp main lugs, indoor, 8 circuits	2.000	Ea.	260	640	900
Plug-in panel or load center, 120/240 volt, to 60 amp, 1 pole	5.000	Ea.	45.25	187.50	232.75
Fuses, dual element, time delay, 250 volt, 50 amp	2.000	Ea.	12.80	18	30.80
Roof-mounting frame for 6 modules, metal	2.000	Ea.	232	111	444
Total			11,676.35	4,287.30	17,502.85

B20 Exterior Enclosure   RB2010-030   "U" & "R" Factors

Table B2010-031   Example Using 14″ Masonry Cavity Wall with 1″ Plaster for the Exterior Closure

Total Heat Transfer is found using the equation
$Q = AU(T_2 - T_1)$ where:

Q = Heat flow, BTU per hour
A = Area, square feet
U = Overall heat transfer coefficient
$(T_2 - T_1)$ = Difference in temperature of the air on each side of the construction component in degrees Fahrenheit

Coefficients of Transmission ("U") are expressed in BTU per (hour) (square foot) (Fahrenheit degree difference in temperature between the air on two sides) and are based on 15 mph outside wind velocity.

The lower the U-value the higher the insulating value.

$U = 1/R$ where "R" is the summation of the resistances of air films, materials and air spaces that make up the assembly.

Figure B2010-031   Example Using 14″ Masonry Cavity Wall with 1″ Plaster for the Exterior Closure

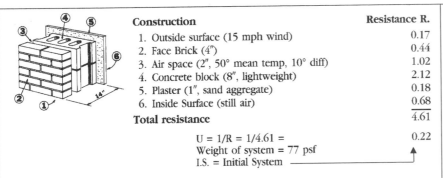

Construction	Resistance R.
1. Outside surface (15 mph wind)	0.17
2. Face Brick (4″)	0.44
3. Air space (2″, 50° mean temp, 10° diff)	1.02
4. Concrete block (8″, lightweight)	2.12
5. Plaster (1″, sand aggregate)	0.18
6. Inside Surface (still air)	0.68
Total resistance	4.61

$U = 1/R = 1/4.61 =$ 0.22
Weight of system = 77 psf
I.S. = Initial System

Replace item 3 with 2″ smooth rigid polystyrene insulation and item 5 with 3/4″ furring and 1/2″ drywall.

Total resistance		**4.61**
Deduct 3. Airspace	1.02	
5. Plaster	0.18	
	1.20	
Difference 4.61 — 1.20 =		3.41
Add rigid polystyrene insulation		10.00
3/4″ air space		1.01
1/2″ gypsum board		0.45
Total resistance		14.87

$U = 1/R = 1/14.87 =$ 0.067
Weight of system = 70 psf
M.S. = Modified System

Assume 20,000 S.F. of wall in Boston, MA (5600 degree days) Table L1030-501
Initial system effective $U = U_w \times M = 0.22 \times 0.905 = 0.20$
  (M = weight correction factor from Table L1030-203)
Modified system effective $U = U_w \times M = 0.067 \times 0.915 = 0.06$
Initial systems: $Q = 20{,}000 \times 0.20 \times (72° - 10°) = 248{,}000$ BTU/hr.
Modified system: $Q = 20{,}000 \times 0.06 \times (72° - 10°) = 74{,}400$ BTU/hr.

Reduction in BTU/hr. heat loss; $\dfrac{\text{I.S.} - \text{M.S.}}{\text{I.S.}} \times 100 = \dfrac{248{,}000 - 74{,}400}{248{,}000} \times 100 = 70\%$

Consult the ASHRAE standards for R- and U-values.

B20 Exterior Enclosure | RB2010-030 | "U" & "R" Factors

Table B2010-032 Thermal Coefficients of Exterior Closures

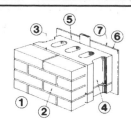

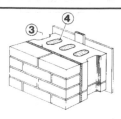

EXAMPLE:

Construction	Resistance R
1. Outside surface (15 MPH wind)	0.17
2. Common brick, 4"	0.80
3. Nonreflective air space, 0.75"	1.01
4. Concrete block, S&G aggregate, 8"	1.46
5. Nonreflective air space, 0.75"	1.01
6. Gypsum board, 0.5"	0.45
7. Inside surface (still air)	0.68
Total resistance	5.58

U = 1/R = 1/5.58 = 0.18

System weight = 97 psf

Substitution

Replace item 3 with perlite loose fill insulation and fill block cavities with the same.

Total resistance (Example)		R = 5.58
Deduct 3. Air space	1.01	
4. Concrete block	1.46	
	2.47	− 2.47
Difference		3.11
Add 0.75" perlite cavity fill		2.03
Perlite filled 8" block		2.94
Net total resistance		8.08

U = 1/R = 1/8.08 = 0.12

System weight = 97 psf

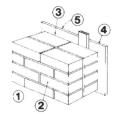

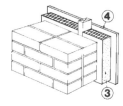

EXAMPLE:

Construction	Resistance R
1. Outside surface (15 MPH wind)	0.17
2. Common brick, 8"	1.60
3. Nonreflective air space, 0.75"	1.01
4. Gypsum board, 0.625"	0.56
5. Inside surface (still air)	0.68
Total resistance	4.02

U = 1/R = 1/4.02 = 0.25

System weight = 82 psf

Substitution

Replace item 3 with 4" blanket insulation and item 4 with 0.75" Gypsum plaster (sand agg.).

Total resistance (Example)		R = 4.02
Deduct 3. Air space	1.01	
4. Gypsum board	0.56	
	1.57	− 1.57
Difference		2.45
ADD Blanket insulation		13.00
Gypsum plaster		0.14
Net total resistance		15.59

U = 1/R = 1/15.59 = 0.06

System weight = 87 psf

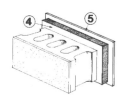

EXAMPLE:

Construction	Resistance R
1. Outside surface (15 MPH wind)	0.17
2. Cement stucco, 0.75"	0.15
3. Concrete block, 8" light weight	2.12
4. Reflective air space, 0.75"	2.77
5. Gypsum board, 0.5"	0.45
6. Inside surface (still air)	0.68
Total resistance	6.34

U = 1/R = 1/6.34 = 0.16

System weight = 47 psf

Substitution

Replace item 4 with 2" insulation board and item 5 with 0.75" Perlite plaster.

Total resistance (Example)		R = 6.34
Deduct 4. Air space	2.77	
5. Gypsum board	0.45	
	3.22	− 3.22
Difference		3.12
Add Insulation board 2" (polyurethane)		12.50
Perlite plaster		1.34
Net total resistance		16.96

U = 1/R = 1/16.96 = 0.06

System weight = 48 psf

Table B3010-011   Thermal Coefficients for Roof Systems

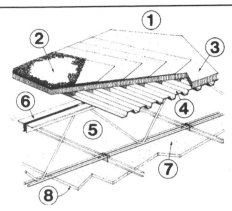

EXAMPLE:

Construction	Resistance R
1. Outside surface (15 MPH wind)	0.17
2. Built up roofing .375" thick	0.33
3. Rigid roof insulation, 2"	5.26
4. Metal decking	0.00
5. Air space (non reflective)	1.14
6. Structural members	0.00
7. Gypsum board ceiling 5/8" thick	0.56
8. Inside surface (still air)	0.61
Total resistance	8.07

$$U = 1/R = 1/8.07 = 0.12$$

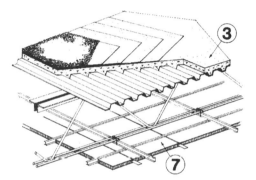

Substitution

Replace item 3 with Perlite lightweight concrete and item 7 with acoustical tile.

Total resistance (Example)		R =	8.07
Deduct 3. Rigid insulation	5.26		
7. Gypsum board ceiling	0.05		
	5.31		-5.31
			2.76
Difference			
Add Perlite concrete, 4"			4.32
Acoustical tile, 3/4"			1.56
		Total resistance	8.64

$$U = 1/R = 1/8.64 = 0.12$$

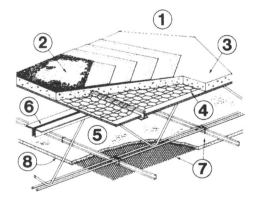

EXAMPLE

Construction	Resistance R
1. Outside surface (15 MPH wind)	0.17
2. Built up roofing .375" thick	0.33
3. Rigid roof insulation, 2" thick	1.20
4. Form bd., 1/2" thick	0.45
5. Air space (non reflective)	1.14
6. Structural members	0.00
7. Gypsum board ceiling 3/4" thick	0.14
8. Inside surface (still air)	0.61
Total resistance	4.04

$$U = 1/R = 1/4.04 = 0.25$$

(for modified system see next page)

B30 Roofing | RB3010-010 | "U" & "R" Factors

Table B3010-011 Thermal Coefficients for Roof Systems

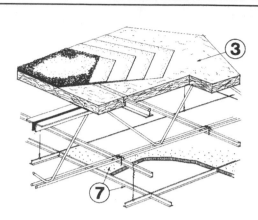

Substitution

Replace item 3 with Tectum board and item 7 with acoustical tile.

Total resistance (Example)		**R =**	4.04
Deduct 3. Gypsum concrete	1.20		
4. Form bd.	0.45		
7. Plaster	0.14		
	1.79	<-1.79>	
Difference		2.25	
Add Tectum bd. 3" thick		5.25	
Acoustical tile, 3/4"		1.56	
Total resistance		9.06	

$U = 1/R = 1/9.06 = 0.11$

(for limited system see previous page)

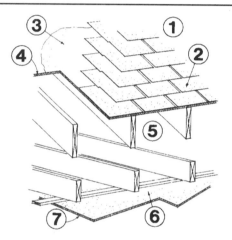

EXAMPLE:

Construction	Resistance R
1. Outside surface (15 MPH wind)	0.17
2. Asphalt shingle roof	0.44
3. Felt building paper	0.06
4. Plywood sheathing, 5/8" thick	0.78
5. Reflective air space, 3-1/2"	2.17
6. Gypsum board, 1/2" foil backed	0.45
7. Inside surface (still air)	0.61
Total resistance	4.68

$U = 1/R = 1/4.68 = 0.21$

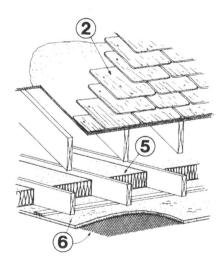

Substitution

Replace item 2 with slate, item 5 with insulation and item 6 with gypsum plaster

Total resistance (Example)		**R =**	4.68
Deduct 2. Asphalt shingles	0.44		
5. Air space	2.17		
6. Gypsum board	0.45		
	3.06	<-3.06>	
Difference		1.62	
Add Slate, 1/4" thick		0.03	
Insulation, 6" blanket		19.00	
Gypsum sand plaster 3/4"		0.14	
Total resistance		20.79	

$U = 1/R = 1/20.79 = 0.05$

Table D2020-101 Hot Water Consumption Rates

Type of Building	Size Factor	Maximum Hourly Demand	Average Day Demand
Apartment Dwellings	No. of Apartments: Up to 20 21 to 50 51 to 75 76 to 100 101 to 200 201 up	 12.0 Gal. per apt. 10.0 Gal. per apt. 8.5 Gal. per apt. 7.0 Gal. per apt. 6.0 Gal. per apt. 5.0 Gal. per apt.	 42.0 Gal. per apt. 40.0 Gal. per apt. 38.0 Gal. per apt. 37.0 Gal. per apt. 36.0 Gal. per apt. 35.0 Gal. per apt.
Dormitories	Men Women	3.8 Gal. per man 5.0 Gal. per woman	13.1 Gal. per man 12.3 Gal. per woman
Hospitals	Per bed	23.0 Gal. per patient	90.0 Gal. per patient
Hotels	Single room with bath Double room with bath	17.0 Gal. per unit 27.0 Gal. per unit	50.0 Gal. per unit 80.0 Gal. per unit
Motels	No. of units: Up to 20 21 to 100 101 Up	 6.0 Gal. per unit 5.0 Gal. per unit 4.0 Gal. per unit	 20.0 Gal. per unit 14.0 Gal. per unit 10.0 Gal. per unit
Nursing Homes		4.5 Gal. per bed	18.4 Gal. per bed
Office buildings		0.4 Gal. per person	1.0 Gal. per person
Restaurants	Full meal type Drive-in snack type	1.5 Gal./max. meals/hr. 0.7 Gal./max. meals/hr.	2.4 Gal. per meal 0.7 Gal. per meal
Schools	Elementary Secondary & High	0.6 Gal. per student 1.0 Gal. per student	0.6 Gal. per student 1.8 Gal. per student

For evaluation purposes, recovery rate and storage capacity are inversely proportional. Water heaters should be sized so that the maximum hourly demand anticipated can be met in addition to allowance for the heat loss from the pipes and storage tank.

Table D2020-102 Fixture Demands in Gallons Per Fixture Per Hour

Table below is based on 140°F final temperature except for dishwashers in public places (*) where 180°F water is mandatory.

Fixture	Apartment House	Club	Gym	Hospital	Hotel	Indust. Plant	Office	Private Home	School
Bathtubs	20	20	30	20	20			20	
Dishwashers, automatic	15	50-150*		50-150*	50-200*	20-100*		15	20-100*
Kitchen sink	10	20		20	30	20	20	10	20
Laundry, stationary tubs	20	28		28	28			20	
Laundry, automatic wash	75	75		100	150			75	
Private lavatory	2	2	2	2	2	2	2	2	2
Public lavatory	4	6	8	6	8	12	6		15
Showers	30	150	225	75	75	225	30	30	225
Service sink	20	20		20	30	20	20	15	20
Demand factor	0.30	0.30	0.40	0.25	0.25	0.40	0.30	0.30	0.40
Storage capacity factor	1.25	0.90	1.00	0.60	0.80	1.00	2.00	0.70	1.00

To obtain the probable maximum demand multiply the total demands for the fixtures (gal./fixture/hour) by the demand factor. The heater should have a heating capacity in gallons per hour equal to this maximum. The storage tank should have a capacity in gallons equal to the probable maximum demand multiplied by the storage capacity factor.

D30 HVAC — RD3020-010 — Heating

Table D3020-011
Heating Systems

The basic function of a heating system is to bring an enclosed volume up to a desired temperature and then maintain that temperature within a reasonable range. To accomplish this, the selected system must have sufficient capacity to offset transmission losses resulting from the temperature difference on the interior and exterior of the enclosing walls in addition to losses due to cold air infiltration through cracks, crevices and around doors and windows. The amount of heat to be furnished is dependent upon the building size, construction, temperature difference, air leakage, use, shape, orientation and exposure. Air circulation is also an important consideration. Circulation will prevent stratification which could result in heat losses through uneven temperatures at various levels. For example, the most

Heat Transmission

Heat transfer is an important parameter to be considered during selection of the exterior wall style, material and window area. A high rate of transfer will permit greater heat loss during the wintertime with the resultant increase in heating energy costs and a greater rate of heat gain in the summer with proportionally greater cooling cost. Several terms are used to describe various aspects of heat transfer. However, for general estimating purposes this book lists U valves for systems of construction materials. U is the "overall heat transfer coefficient." It is defined as the heat flow per hour through one square foot when the temperature difference in the air on either side of the structure wall, roof, ceiling or floor is one degree Fahrenheit. The structural segment may be a single homogeneous material or a composite.

efficient use of unit heaters can usually be achieved by circulating the space volume through the total number of units once every 20 minutes or 3 times an hour. This general rule must, of course, be adapted for special cases such as large buildings with low ratios of heat transmitting surface to cubical volume. The type of occupancy of a building will have considerable bearing on the number of heat transmitting units and the location selected. It is axiomatic, however, that the basis of any successful heating system is to provide the maximum amount of heat at the points of maximum heat loss such as exposed walls, windows, and doors. Large roof areas, wind direction, and wide doorways create problems of excessive heat loss and require special consideration and treatment.

Total heat transfer is found using the following equation:

$Q = AU(T_2 - T_1)$ where
$\quad Q$ = Heat flow, BTU per hour
$\quad A$ = Area, square feet
$\quad U$ = Overall heat transfer coefficient
$(T_2 - T_1)$ = Difference in temperature of air on each side of the construction component. (Also abbreviated TD)

Note that heat can flow through all surfaces of any building and this flow is in addition to heat gain or loss due to ventilation, infiltration and generation (appliances, machinery, people).

D30 HVAC — RD3010-600 — Solar Collectors

Table D3010-601 Collector Tilt for Domestic Hot Water

Optimum collector tilt is usually equal to the site latitude. Variations of plus or minus 10 degrees are acceptable and orientation of 20 degrees on either side of true south is acceptable; however, local climate and collector type may influence the choice between east or west deviations.

Flat plate collectors consist of a number of components as follows: Insulation to reduce heat loss through the bottom and sides of the collector. The enclosure which contains all the components in this assembly is usually weatherproof and prevents dust, wind and water from coming in contact with the absorber plate. The cover plate usually consists of one or more layers of a variety of glass or plastic and reduces the reradiation. It creates an air space which traps the heat by reducing radiation losses between the cover plate and the absorber plate.

The absorber plate must have a good thermal bond with the fluid passages.

The absorber plate is usually metallic and treated with a surface coating which improves absorptivity. Black or dark paints or selective coatings are used for this purpose, and the design of this passage and plate combination helps determine a solar system's effectiveness.

Heat transfer fluid passage tubes are attached above and below or integral with an absorber plate for the purpose of transferring thermal energy from the absorber plate to a heat transfer medium. The heat exchanger is a device for transferring thermal energy from one fluid to another. The rule of thumb of space heating sizing is one S.F. of collector per 2.5 S.F. of floor space.

For domestic hot water the rule of thumb is 3/4 S.F. of collector for one gallon of water used per day, on an average use of twenty-five gallons per day per person, plus ten gallons per dishwasher or washing machine.

Table D3020-021 Factor for Determining Heat Loss for Various Types of Buildings

General: While the most accurate estimates of heating requirements would naturally be based on detailed information about the building being considered, it is possible to arrive at a reasonable approximation using the following procedure:

1. Calculate the cubic volume of the room or building.
2. Select the appropriate factor from Table D3020-021 below. Note that the factors apply only to inside temperatures listed in the first column and to 0°F outside temperature.

3. If the building has bad north and west exposures, multiply the heat loss factor by 1.1.
4. If the outside design temperature is other than 0°F, multiply the factor from Table D3020-021 by the factor from Table D3020-022.
5. Multiply the cubic volume by the factor selected from Table D3020-021. This will give the estimated BTUH heat loss which must be made up to maintain inside temperature.

Building Type	Conditions	Qualifications	Loss Factor*
Factories & Industrial Plants General Office Areas at 70°F	One Story	Skylight in Roof	6.2
		No Skylight in Roof	5.7
	Multiple Story	Two Story	4.6
		Three Story	4.3
		Four Story	4.1
		Five Story	3.9
		Six Story	3.6
	All Walls Exposed	Flat Roof	6.9
		Heated Space Above	5.2
	One Long Warm Common Wall	Flat Roof	6.3
		Heated Space Above	4.7
	Warm Common Walls on Both Long Sides	Flat Roof	5.8
		Heated Space Above	4.1
Warehouses at 60°F	All Walls Exposed	Skylights in Roof	5.5
		No Skylight in Roof	5.1
		Heated Space Above	4.0
	One Long Warm Common Wall	Skylight in Roof	5.0
		No Skylight in Roof	4.9
		Heated Space Above	3.4
	Warm Common Walls on Both Long Sides	Skylight in Roof	4.7
		No Skylight in Roof	4.4
		Heated Space Above	3.0

*Note: This table tends to be conservative particularly for new buildings designed for minimum energy consumption.

Table D3020-022 Outside Design Temperature Correction Factor (for Degrees Fahrenheit)

Outside Design Temperature	50	40	30	20	10	0	−10	−20	−30
Correction Factor	0.29	0.43	0.57	0.72	0.86	1.00	1.14	1.28	1.43

Figure D3020-023 and D3020-024 provide a way to calculate heat transmission of various construction materials from their U values and the TD (Temperature Difference).

1. From the exterior Enclosure Division or elsewhere, determine U values for the construction desired.
2. Determine the coldest design temperature. The difference between this temperature and the desired interior temperature is the TD (temperature difference).

3. Enter Figure D3020-023 or D3020-024 at correct U value. Cross horizontally to the intersection with appropriate TD. Read transmission per square foot from bottom of figure.
4. Multiply this value of BTU per hour transmission per square foot of area by the total surface area of that type of construction.

D30 HVAC | RD3020-020 | Heat Transfer

Table D3020-023   Transmission of Heat

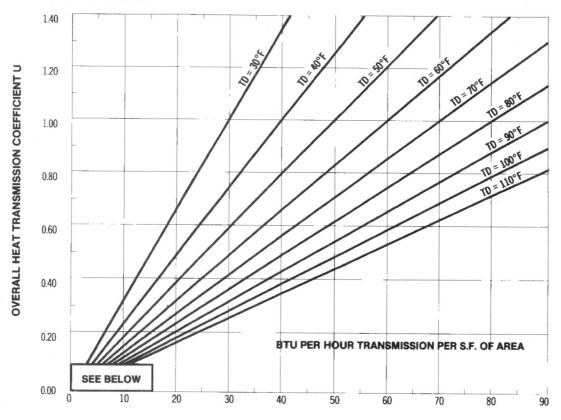

Table D3020-024   Transmission of Heat (Low Rate)

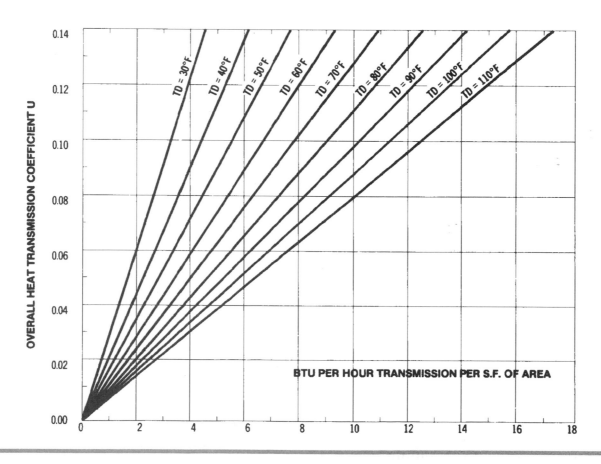

Table D3030-012 Air Conditioning Requirements

BTU's per hour per S.F. of floor area and S.F. per ton of air conditioning.

Type of Building	BTU per S.F.	S.F. per Ton	Type of Building	BTU per S.F.	S.F. per Ton	Type of Building	BTU per S.F.	S.F. per Ton
Apartments, Individual	26	450	Dormitory, Rooms	40	300	Libraries	50	240
Corridors	22	550	Corridors	30	400	Low Rise Office, Exterior	38	320
Auditoriums & Theaters	40	300/18*	Dress Shops	43	280	Interior	33	360
Banks	50	240	Drug Stores	80	150	Medical Centers	28	425
Barber Shops	48	250	Factories	40	300	Motels	28	425
Bars & Taverns	133	90	High Rise Office—Ext. Rms.	46	263	Office (small suite)	43	280
Beauty Parlors	66	180	Interior Rooms	37	325	Post Office, Individual Office	42	285
Bowling Alleys	68	175	Hospitals, Core	43	280	Central Area	46	260
Churches	36	330/20*	Perimeter	46	260	Residences	20	600
Cocktail Lounges	68	175	Hotel, Guest Rooms	44	275	Restaurants	60	200
Computer Rooms	141	85	Corridors	30	400	Schools & Colleges	46	260
Dental Offices	52	230	Public Spaces	55	220	Shoe Stores	55	220
Dept. Stores, Basement	34	350	Industrial Plants, Offices	38	320	Shop'g. Ctrs., Supermarkets	34	350
Main Floor	40	300	General Offices	34	350	Retail Stores	48	250
Upper Floor	30	400	Plant Areas	40	300	Specialty	60	200

*Persons per ton
12,000 BTU = 1 ton of air conditioning

Table D3030-013 Psychrometric Table

Dewpoint or Saturation Temperature (F)

	32	35	40	45	50	55	60	65	70	75	80	85	90	95	100
100	32	35	40	45	50	55	60	65	70	75	80	85	90	95	100
90	30	33	37	42	47	52	57	62	67	72	77	82	87	92	97
80	27	30	34	39	44	49	54	58	64	68	73	78	83	88	93
70	24	27	31	36	40	45	50	55	60	64	69	74	79	84	88
60	20	24	28	32	36	41	46	51	55	60	65	69	74	79	83
50	16	20	24	28	33	36	41	46	50	55	60	64	69	73	78
40	12	15	18	23	27	31	35	40	45	49	53	58	62	67	71
30	8	10	14	18	21	25	29	33	37	42	46	50	54	59	62
20	6	7	8	9	13	16	20	24	28	31	35	40	43	48	52
10	4	4	5	5	6	8	9	10	13	17	20	24	27	30	34

Dry bulb temperature (F)

This table shows the relationship between RELATIVE HUMIDITY, DRY BULB TEMPERATURE AND DEWPOINT. As an example, assume that the thermometer in a room reads 75°F, and we know that the relative humidity is 50%. The chart shows the dewpoint temperature to be 55°. That is, any surface colder than 55°F will "sweat" or collect condensing moisture. This surface could be the outside of an uninsulated chilled water pipe in the summertime, or the inside surface of a wall or deck in the wintertime. After determining the extreme ambient parameters, the table at the left is useful in determining which surfaces need insulation or vapor barrier protection.

Table D3030-014 Recommended Ventilation Air Changes

Table below lists range of time in minutes per change for various types of facilities.

Assembly Halls	2-10	Dance Halls	2-10	Laundries	1-3
Auditoriums	2-10	Dining Rooms	3-10	Markets	2-10
Bakeries	2-3	Dry Cleaners	1-5	Offices	2-10
Banks	3-10	Factories	2-5	Pool Rooms	2-5
Bars	2-5	Garages	2-10	Recreation Rooms	2-10
Beauty Parlors	2-5	Generator Rooms	2-5	Sales Rooms	2-10
Boiler Rooms	1-5	Gymnasiums	2-10	Theaters	2-8
Bowling Alleys	2-10	Kitchens-Hospitals	2-5	Toilets	2-5
Churches	5-10	Kitchens-Restaurant	1-3	Transformer Rooms	1-5

CFM air required for changes = Volume of room in cubic feet ÷ Minutes per change.

D50 Electrical · RD5010-110 · Electrical Systems Estimating

Figure D5010-114 Office Building 90' x 210', 3 story, w/garage

Garage Area = 18,900 S.F.
Office Area = 56,700 S.F.
Elevator = 2 @ 125 FPM

Tables	Power Required	Watts
D5010-1151	Garage Lighting .5 Watt/S.F.	9,450
	Office Lighting 3 Watts/S.F.	170,100
D5010-1151	Office Receptacles 2 Watts/S.F.	113,400
D5010-1151, RD5020-602	Low Rise Office A.C. 4.3 Watts/S.F.	243,810
D5010-1152, 1153	Elevators - 2 @ 20 HP = 2 @ 17,404 Watts/Ea.	34,808
D5010-1151	Misc. Motors + Power 1.2 Watts/S.F.	68,040
	Total	639,608 Watts

Voltage Available
277/480V, 3 Phase, 4 Wire

Formula

D5010-116

$$\text{Amperes} = \frac{\text{Watts}}{\text{Volts x Power Factor x 1.73}} = \frac{639,608}{480V \times .8 \times 1.73} = 963 \text{ Amps}$$

Use 1200 Amp Service

System	Description	Unit Cost	Unit	Total
D5020 210 0200	Garage Lighting (Interpolated)	$.94	S.F.	$ 17,766
D5020 210 0280	Office Lighting	5.62	S.F.	318,654
D5020 115 0880	Receptacle-Undercarpet	3.08	S.F.	174,636
D5020 140 0280	Air Conditioning	.40	S.F.	22,680
D5020 135 0320	Misc. Pwr.	.23	S.F.	13,041
D5020 145 2120	Elevators - 2 @ 20HP	2,075.00	Ea.	4,150
D5010 120 0480	Service-1200 Amp (add 25% for 277/480V)	13,875.00	Ea.	17,344
D5010 230 0480	Feeder - Assume 200 Ft.	176.00	Ft.	35,200
D5010 240 0320	Panels - 1200 Amp (add 20% for 277/480V)	22,650.00	Ea.	27,180
D5030 810 0400	Fire Detection	23,200.00	Ea.	23,200
	Total			$653,851
	or			$653,900

Table D5010-1151 Nominal Watts Per S.F. for Electric Systems for Various Building Types

Type Construction	1. Lighting	2. Devices	3. HVAC	4. Misc.	5. Elevator	Total Watts
Apartment, luxury high rise	2	2.2	3	1		
Apartment, low rise	2	2	3	1		
Auditorium	2.5	1	3.3	.8		
Bank, branch office	3	2.1	5.7	1.4		
Bank, main office	2.5	1.5	5.7	1.4		
Church	1.8	.8	3.3	.8		
College, science building	3	3	5.3	1.3		
College, library	2.5	.8	5.7	1.4		
College, physical education center	2	1	4.5	1.1		
Department store	2.5	.9	4	1		
Dormitory, college	1.5	1.2	4	1		
Drive-in donut shop	3	4	6.8	1.7		
Garage, commercial	.5	.5	0	.5		
Hospital, general	2	4.5	5	1.3		
Hospital, pediatric	3	3.8	5	1.3		
Hotel, airport	2	1	5	1.3		
Housing for the elderly	2	1.2	4	1		
Manufacturing, food processing	3	1	4.5	1.1		
Manufacturing, apparel	2	1	4.5	1.1		
Manufacturing, tools	4	1	4.5	1.1		
Medical clinic	2.5	1.5	3.2	1		
Nursing home	2	1.6	4	1		
Office building, hi rise	3	2	4.7	1.2		
Office building, low rise	3	2	4.3	1.2		
Radio-TV studio	3.8	2.2	7.6	1.9		
Restaurant	2.5	2	6.8	1.7		
Retail store	2.5	.9	5.5	1.4		
School, elementary	3	1.9	5.3	1.3		
School, junior high	3	1.5	5.3	1.3		
School, senior high	2.3	1.7	5.3	1.3		
Supermarket	3	1	4	1		
Telephone exchange	1	.6	4.5	1.1		
Theater	2.5	1	3.3	.8		
Town Hall	2	1.9	5.3	1.3		
U.S. Post Office	3	2	5	1.3		
Warehouse, grocery	1	.6	0	.5		

Rule of Thumb: 1 KVA = 1 HP (Single Phase)

Three Phase:

Watts = 1.73 x Volts x Current x Power Factor x Efficiency

$$\text{Horsepower} = \frac{\text{Volts x Current x 1.73 x Power Factor}}{746 \text{ Watts}}$$

Table D5010-1152 Horsepower Requirements for Elevators with 3 Phase Motors

Type	Maximum Travel Height in Ft.	Travel Speeds in FPM	Capacity of Cars in Lbs.		
			1200	1500	1800
Hydraulic	70	70	10	15	15
		85	15	15	15
		100	15	15	20
		110	20	20	20
		125	20	20	20
		150	25	25	25
		175	25	30	30
		200	30	30	40
Geared Traction	300	200			
		350			
			2000	2500	3000
Hydraulic	70	70	15	20	20
		85	20	20	25
		100	20	25	30
		110	20	25	30
		125	25	30	40
		150	30	40	50
		175	40	50	50
		200	40	50	60
Geared Traction	300	200	10	10	15
		350	15	15	23
			3500	4000	4500
Hydraulic	70	70	20	25	30
		85	25	30	30
		100	30	40	40
		110	40	40	50
		125	40	50	50
		150	50	50	60
		175	60		
		200	60		
Geared Traction	300	200	15		23
		350	23		35

The power factor of electric motors varies from 80% to 90% in larger size motors. The efficiency likewise varies from 80% on a small motor to 90% on a large motor.

Table D5010-1153 Watts per Motor

90% Power Factor & Efficiency @ 200 or 460V			
HP	Watts	HP	Watts
10	9024	30	25784
15	13537	40	33519
20	17404	50	41899
25	21916	60	49634

D50 Electrical | RD5010-110 | Electrical Systems Estimating

General: Variations in the following square foot costs are due to the type of structural systems of the buildings, geographical location, local electrical codes, designer's preference for specific materials and equipment, and the owner's particular requirements.

Figure D5010-117 Cost per S.F. for Total Electric Systems for Various Building Types (cont.)

Type Construction	Basic Description	Total Floor Area in Square Feet	Total Cost per Square Foot for Total Electric Systems
Apartment building, luxury high rise	All electric, 18 floors, 86 1 B.R., 34 2 B.R.	115,000	$ 7.86
Apartment building, low rise	All electric, 2 floors, 44 units, 1 & 2 B.R.	40,200	5.31
Auditorium	All electric, 1200 person capacity	28,000	15.68
Bank, branch office	All electric, 1 floor	2,700	18.46
Bank, main office	All electric, 8 floors	54,900	12.28
Church	All electric, incl. Sunday school	17,700	7.79
*College, science building	All electric, 3-1/2 floors, 47 rooms	27,500	14.84
*College, library	All electric	33,500	7.97
*College, physical education center	All electric	22,000	9.23
Department store	Gas heat, 1 floor	85,800	7.16
*Dormitory, college	All electric, 125 rooms	63,000	8.86
Drive-in donut shop	Gas heat, incl. parking area lighting	1,500	18.12
Garage, commercial	All electric	52,300	3.02
*Hospital, general	Steam heat, 4 story garage, 300 beds	540,000	20.96
*Hospital, pediatric	Steam heat, 6 stories	278,000	32.84
Hotel, airport	All electric, 625 guest rooms	536,000	12.54
Housing for the elderly	All electric, 7 floors, 100 1 B.R. units	67,000	7.53
Manufacturing, food processing	Electric heat, 1 floor	9,600	14.00
Manufacturing, apparel	Electric heat, 1 floor	28,000	6.79
Manufacturing, tools	Electric heat, 2 floors	42,000	12.86
Medical clinic	Electric heat, 2 floors	22,700	7.45
Nursing home	Gas heat, 3 floors, 60 beds	21,000	11.86
Office building	All electric, 15 floors	311,200	12.66
Radio-TV studio	Electric heat, 3 floors	54,000	15.24
Restaurant	All electric	2,900	18.25
Retail store	All electric	3,000	5.76
School, elementary	All electric, 1 floor	39,500	12.30
School, junior high	All electric, 1 floor	49,500	11.11
*School, senior high	All electric, 1 floor	158,300	11.81
Supermarket	Gas heat	30,600	10.41
*Telephone exchange	Gas heat, 300 kW emergency generator	24,800	13.93
Theater	Electric heat, twin cinema	14,000	12.40
Town Hall	All electric	20,000	9.91
*U.S. Post Office	All electric	495,000	14.10
Warehouse, grocery	All electric	96,400	5.70

*Includes cost of primary feeder and transformer.

General: The cost of the lighting portion of the electrical costs is dependent upon:
1. The footcandle requirement of the proposed building.
2. The type of fixtures required.
3. The ceiling heights of the building.
4. Reflectance value of ceilings, walls and floors.
5. Fixture efficiencies and spacing vs. mounting height ratios.

Footcandle Requirements: See Table D5020-204 for Footcandle and Watts per S.F. determination.

Table D5020-201 I.E.S. Recommended Illumination Levels in Footcandles

Commercial Buildings			Industrial Buildings		
Type	Description	Footcandles	Type	Description	Footcandles
Bank	Lobby	50	Assembly Areas	Rough bench & machine work	50
	Customer Areas	70		Medium bench & machine work	100
	Teller Stations	150		Fine bench & machine work	500
	Accounting Areas	150	Inspection Areas	Ordinary	50
Offices	Routine Work	100		Difficult	100
	Accounting	150		Highly Difficult	200
	Drafting	200	Material Handling	Loading	20
	Corridors, Halls, Washrooms	30		Stock Picking	30
Schools	Reading or Writing	70		Packing, Wrapping	50
	Drafting, Labs, Shops	100	Stairways	Service Areas	20
	Libraries	70	Washrooms	Service Areas	20
	Auditoriums, Assembly	15	Storage Areas	Inactive	5
	Auditoriums, Exhibition	30		Active, Rough, Bulky	10
Stores	Circulation Areas	30		Active, Medium	20
	Stock Rooms	30		Active, Fine	50
	Merchandise Areas, Service	100	Garages	Active Traffic Areas	20
	Self-Service Areas	200		Service & Repair	100

| **D50 Electrical** | **RD5020-200** | **Illumination** |

Table D5020-202 General Lighting Loads by Occupancies

Type of Occupancy	Unit Load per S.F. (Watts)
Armories and Auditoriums	1
Banks	5
Barber Shops and Beauty Parlors	3
Churches	1
Clubs	2
Court Rooms	2
*Dwelling Units	3
Garages — Commercial (storage)	½
Hospitals	2
*Hotels and Motels, including apartment houses without provisions for cooking by tenants	2
Industrial Commercial (Loft) Buildings	2
Lodge Rooms	1½
Office Buildings	5
Restaurants	2
Schools	3
Stores	3
Warehouses (storage)	¼
*In any of the above occupancies except one-family dwellings and individual dwelling units of multi-family dwellings:	
Assembly Halls and Auditoriums	1
Halls, Corridors, Closets	½
Storage Spaces	¼

Table D5020-203 Lighting Limit (Connected Load) for Listed Occupancies: New Building Proposed Energy Conservation Guideline

Type of Use	Maximum Watts per S.F.
Interior	
Category A: Classrooms, office areas, automotive mechanical areas, museums, conference rooms, drafting rooms, clerical areas, laboratories, merchandising areas, kitchens, examining rooms, book stacks, athletic facilities.	3.00
Category B: Auditoriums, waiting areas, spectator areas, restrooms, dining areas, transportation terminals, working corridors in prisons and hospitals, book storage areas, active inventory storage, hospital bedrooms, hotel and motel bedrooms, enclosed shopping mall concourse areas, stairways.	1.00
Category C: Corridors, lobbies, elevators, inactive storage areas.	0.50
Category D: Indoor parking.	0.25
Exterior	
Category E: Building perimeter: wall-wash, facade, canopy.	5.00 (per linear foot)
Category F: Outdoor parking.	0.10

Table D5020-204 Procedure for Calculating Footcandles and Watts Per Square Foot

1. Initial footcandles = No. of fixtures × lamps per fixture × lumens per lamp × coefficient of utilization ÷ square feet
2. Maintained footcandles = initial footcandles × maintenance factor
3. Watts per square foot = No. of fixtures × lamps × (lamp watts + ballast watts) ÷ square feet

Example: To find footcandles and watts per S.F. for an office 20′ x 20′ with 11 fluorescent fixtures each having 4–40 watt C.W. lamps.

Based on good reflectance and clean conditions:

Lumens per lamp = 40 watt cool white at 3150 lumens per lamp (Table R16510-120)

Coefficient of utilization = .42 (varies from .62 for light colored areas to .27 for dark)

Maintenance factor = .75 (varies from .80 for clean areas with good maintenance to .50 for poor)

Ballast loss = 8 watts per lamp. (Varies with manufacturer. See manufacturers' catalog.)

1. Initial footcandles:

$$\frac{11 \times 4 \times 3150 \times .42}{400} = \frac{58,212}{400} = 145 \text{ footcandles}$$

2. Maintained footcandles:

$$145 \times .75 = 109 \text{ footcandles}$$

3. Watts per S.F.

$$\frac{11 \times 4 (40 + 8)}{400} = \frac{2,112}{400} = 5.3 \text{ watts per S.F.}$$

Table D5020-205 Approximate Watts Per Square Foot for Popular Fixture Types

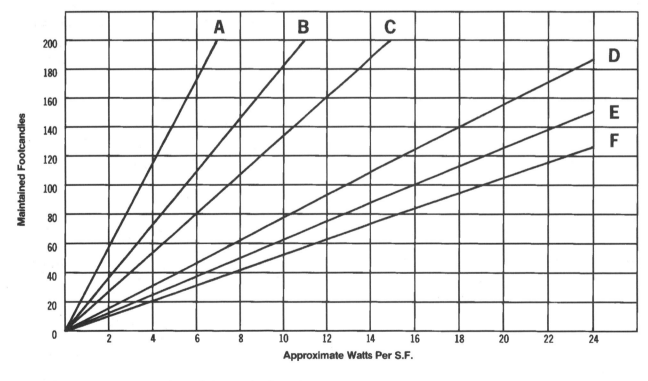

Due to the many variables involved, use for preliminary estimating only:

  a. Fluorescent – industrial System D5020 208
  b. Fluorescent – lens unit System D5020 208 Fixture types B & C
  c. Fluorescent – louvered unit
  d. Incandescent – open reflector System D5020 214, Type D
  e. Incandescent – lens unit System D5020 214, Type A
  f. Incandescent – down light System D5020 214, Type B

D50 Electrical | RD5020-240 | High Intensity Discharge

Table D5020-241   Comparison - Cost of Operation of High Intensity Discharge Lamps

Lamp Type	Wattage	Life (Hours)	1 Circuit Wattage	Average Initial Lumens	2 L.L.D.	3 Mean Lumens	4 One Year (4000 Hr.) Cost of Operation
M.V.	100 DX	24,000	125	4,000	61%	2,440	$ 40.00
L.P.S.	SOX-35	18,000	65	4,800	100%	4,800	20.80
H.P.S.	LU-70	12,000	84	5,800	90%	5,220	26.90
L.H.	No Equivalent						
M.V.	175 DX	24,000	210	8,500	66%	5,676	67.20
M.V.	250 DX	24,000	295	13,000	66%	7,986	94.40
L.P.S.	SOX-55	18,000	82	8,000	100%	8,000	26.25
H.P.S.	LU-100	12,000	120	9,500	90%	8,550	38.40
L.H.	No Equivalent						
M.V.	400 DX	24,000	465	24,000	64%	14,400	148.80
L.P.S.	SOX-90	18,000	141	13,500	100%	13,500	45.10
H.P.S.	LU-150	16,000	188	16,000	90%	14,400	60.15
L.H.	LH-175	7,500	210	14,000	73%	10,200	67.20
M.V.	No Equivalent						
L.P.S.	SOX-135	18,000	147	22,500	100%	22,500	47.05
H.P.S.	LU-250	20,000	310	25,500	92%	23,205	99.20
L.H.	LH-250	7,500	295	20,500	78%	16,000	94.40
M.V.	1000 DX	24,000	1,085	63,000	61%	37,820	347.20
L.P.S.	SOX-180	18,000	248	33,000	100%	33,000	79.35
H.P.S.	LU-400	20,000	480	50,000	90%	45,000	153.60
L.H.	LH-400	15,000	465	34,000	72%	24,600	148.80
H.P.S.	LU-1000	15,000	1,100	140,000	91%	127,400	352.00

1. Includes ballast losses and average lamp watts
2. Lamp lumen depreciation (% of initial light output at 70% rated life)
3. Lamp lumen output at 70% rated life (L.L.D. x initial)
4. Based on average cost of $.080 per k. W. Hr.

M.V.   = Mercury Vapor

L.P.S. = Low pressure sodium

H.P.S. = High pressure sodium

L.H.   = Metal halide

Table D5020-242   For Other than Regular Cool White (CW) Lamps

	Multiply Material Costs as Follows:				
Regular Lamps	Cool white deluxe (CWX)	x 1.35	Energy Saving Lamps	Cool white (CW/ES)	x 1.35
	Warm white deluxe (WWX)	x 1.35		Cool white deluxe (CWX/ES)	x 1.65
	Warm white (WW)	x 1.30		Warm white (WW/ES)	x 1.55
	Natural (N)	x 2.05		Warm white deluxe (WWX/ES)	x 1.65

Table D5020-251   Lamp Comparison Chart with Enclosed Floodlight, Ballast, & Lamp for Pole

Type	Watts	Initial Lumens	Lumens per Watt	Lumens @ 40% Life	Life (Hours)
Incandescent	150	2,880	19	85	750
	300	6,360	21	84	750
	500	10,850	22	80	1,000
	1,000	23,740	24	80	1,000
	1,500	34,400	23	80	1,000
Tungsten	500	10,950	22	97	2,000
Halogen	1,500	35,800	24	97	2,000
Fluorescent	40	3,150	79	88	20,000
Cool	110	9,200	84	87	12,000
White	215	16,000	74	81	12,000
Deluxe	250	12,100	48	86	24,000
Mercury	400	22,500	56	85	24,000
	1,000	63,000	63	75	24,000
Metal	175	14,000	80	77	7,500
Halide	400	34,000	85	75	15,000
	1,000	100,000	100	83	10,000
	1,500	155,000	103	92	1,500
High	70	5,800	83	90	20,000
Pressure	100	9,500	95	90	20,000
Sodium	150	16,000	107	90	24,000
	400	50,000	125	90	24,000
	1,000	140,000	140	90	24,000
Low	55	4,600	131	98	18,000
Pressure	90	12,750	142	98	18,000
Sodium	180	33,000	183	98	18,000

Color: High Pressure Sodium — Slightly Yellow
    Low Pressure Sodium — Yellow
    Mercury Vapor — Green-Blue
    Metal Halide — Blue White

Note: Pole not included.

Table D5020-602   Central Air Conditioning Watts per S.F., BTU's per Hour per S.F. of Floor Area and S.F. per Ton of Air Conditioning

Type Building	Watts per S.F.	BTUH per S.F.	S.F. per Ton	Type Building	Watts per S.F.	BTUH per S.F.	S.F. per Ton	Type Building	Watts per S.F.	BTUH per S.F.	S.F. per Ton
Apartments, Individual	3	26	450	Dormitory, Rooms	4.5	40	300	Libraries	5.7	50	240
Corridors	2.5	22	550	Corridors	3.4	30	400	Low Rise Office, Ext.	4.3	38	320
Auditoriums & Theaters	3.3	40	300/18*	Dress Shops	4.9	43	280	Interior	3.8	33	360
Banks	5.7	50	240	Drug Stores	9	80	150	Medical Centers	3.2	28	425
Barber Shops	5.5	48	250	Factories	4.5	40	300	Motels	3.2	28	425
Bars & Taverns	15	133	90	High Rise Off.-Ext. Rms.	5.2	46	263	Office (small suite)	4.9	43	280
Beauty Parlors	7.6	66	180	Interior Rooms	4.2	37	325	Post Office, Int. Office	4.9	42	285
Bowling Alleys	7.8	68	175	Hospitals, Core	4.9	43	280	Central Area	5.3	46	260
Churches	3.3	36	330/20*	Perimeter	5.3	46	260	Residences	2.3	20	600
Cocktail Lounges	7.8	68	175	Hotels, Guest Rooms	5	44	275	Restaurants	6.8	60	200
Computer Rooms	16	141	85	Public Spaces	6.2	55	220	Schools & Colleges	5.3	46	260
Dental Offices	6	52	230	Corridors	3.4	30	400	Shoe Stores	6.2	55	220
Dept. Stores, Basement	4	34	350	Industrial Plants, Offices	4.3	38	320	Shop'g. Ctrs., Sup. Mkts.	4	34	350
Main Floor	4.5	40	300	General Offices	4	34	350	Retail Stores	5.5	48	250
Upper Floor	3.4	30	400	Plant Areas	4.5	40	300	Specialty Shops	6.8	60	200

*Persons per ton

12,000 BTUH = 1 ton of air conditioning

Site Construction	R029	Landscaping

R02920-500　Seeding

The type of grass is determined by light, shade and moisture content of soil plus intended use. Fertilizer should be disked 4″ before seeding. For steep slopes disk five tons of mulch and lay two tons of hay or straw on surface per acre after seeding. Surface mulch can be staked, lightly disked or tar emulsion sprayed. Material for mulch can be wood chips, peat moss, partially rotted hay or straw, wood fibers and sprayed emulsions. Hemp seed blankets with fertilizer are also available. For spring seeding, watering is necessary. Late fall seeding may have to be reseeded in the spring. Hydraulic seeding, power mulching, and aerial seeding can be used on large areas.

Site Construction	R029	Landscaping

R02920-520　Trees and Plants by Environment and Purposes

Dry, Windy, Exposed Areas
Barberry
Junipers, all varieties
Locust
Maple
Oak
Pines, all varieties
Poplar, Hybrid
Privet
Spruce, all varieties
Sumac, Staghorn

Lightly Wooded Areas
Dogwood
Hemlock
Larch
Pine, White
Rhododendron
Spruce, Norway
Redbud

Total Shade Areas
Hemlock
Ivy, English
Myrtle
Pachysandra
Privet
Spice Bush
Yews, Japanese

Cold Temperatures of Northern U.S. and Canada
Arborvitae, American
Birch, White
Dogwood, Silky
Fir, Balsam
Fir, Douglas
Hemlock
Juniper, Andorra
Juniper, Blue Rug
Linden, Little Leaf
Maple, Sugar
Mountain Ash
Myrtle
Olive, Russian

Pine, Mugho
Pine, Ponderosa
Pine, Red
Pine, Scotch
Poplar, Hybrid
Privet
Rosa Rugosa
Spruce, Dwarf Alberta
Spruce, Black Hills
Spruce, Blue
Spruce, Norway
Spruce, White, Engelman
Yellow Wood

Wet, Swampy Areas
American Arborvitae
Birch, White
Black Gum
Hemlock
Maple, Red
Pine, White
Willow

Poor, Dry, Rocky Soil
Barberry
Crownvetch
Eastern Red Cedar
Juniper, Virginiana
Locust, Black
Locust, Bristly
Locust, Honey
Olive, Russian
Pines, all varieties
Privet
Rosa Rugosa
Sumac, Staghorn

Seashore Planting
Arborvitae, American
Juniper, Tamarix
Locust, Black
Oak, White
Olive, Russian
Pine, Austrian
Pine, Japanese Black

Pine, Mugho
Pine, Scotch
Privet, Amur River
Rosa Rugosa
Yew, Japanese

City Planting
Barberry
Fir, Concolor
Forsythia
Hemlock
Holly, Japanese
Ivy, English
Juniper, Andorra
Linden, Little Leaf
Locust, Honey
Maple, Norway, Silver
Oak, Pin, Red
Olive, Russian
Pachysandra
Pine, Austrian
Pine, White
Privet
Rosa Rugosa
Sumac, Staghorn
Yew, Japanese

Bonsal Planting
Azaleas
Birch, White
Ginkgo
Junipers
Pine, Bristlecone
Pine, Mugho
Spruce,k Engleman
Spruce, Dwarf Alberta

Street Planting
Linden, Little Leaf
Oak, Pin
Ginkgo

Fast Growth
Birch, White
Crownvetch
Dogwood, Silky

Fir, Douglas
Juniper, Blue Pfitzer
Juniper, Blue Rug
Maple, Silver
Olive, Autumn
Pines, Austrian, Ponderosa, Red
　Scotch and White
Poplar, Hybrid
Privet
Spruce, Norway
Spruce, Serbian
Texus, Cuspidata, Hicksi
Willow

Dense, Impenetrable Hedges
Field Plantings:
　Locust, Bristly,
　Olive, Autumn
　Sumac
Residential Area:
　Barberry, Red or Green
　Juniper, Blue Pfitzer
　Rosa Rugosa

Food for Birds
Ash, Mountain
Barberry
Bittersweet
Cherry, Manchu
Dogwood, Silky
Honesuckle, Rem Red
Hawthorn
Oaks
Olive, Autumn, Russian
Privet
Rosa Rugosa
Sumac

Erosion Control
Crownvetch
Locust, Bristly
Willow

RO2920-530 Zones of Plant Hardiness

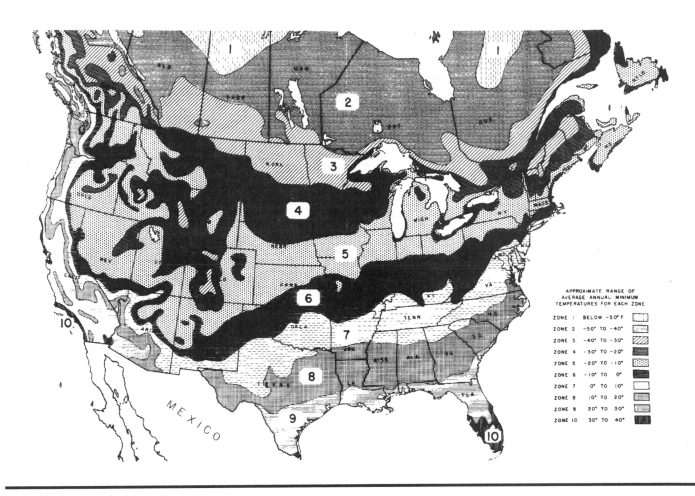

Special Construction | R130 | Air Supported Structures

R13011-110   Air Supported Structures

Air supported structures are made from fabrics that can be classified into two groups: temporary and permanent. Temporary fabrics include nylon, woven polyethylene, vinyl film, and vinyl coated dacron. These have lifespans that range from five to fifteen plus years. The cost per square foot includes a fabric shell, tension cables, primary and back-up inflation systems and doors. The lower cost structures are used for construction shelters, bulk storage and pond covers. The more expensive are used for recreational structures and warehouses.

Permanent fabrics are teflon coated fiberglass. The life of this structure is twenty plus years. The high cost limits its application to architectural designed structures which call for a clear span covered area, such as stadiums and convention centers. Both temporary and permanent structures are available in translucent fabrics which eliminates the need for daytime lighting.

Areas to be covered vary from 10,000 S.F. to any area up to 1000 foot wide by any length. Height restrictions range from a maximum of 1/2 of

width to a minimum of 1/6 of the width. Erection of even the largest of the temporary structures requires no more than a week.

Centrifugal fans provide the inflation necessary to support the structure during application of live loads. Airlocks are usually used at large entrances to prevent loss of static pressure. Some manufacturers employ propeller fans which generate sufficient airflow (30,000 CFM) to eliminate the need for airlocks. These fans may also be automatically controlled to resist high wind conditions, regulate humidity (air changes), and provide cooling and heat.

Insulation can be provided with the addition of a second or even third interior liner, creating a dead air space with an "R" value of four to nine. Some structures allow for the liner to be collapsed into the outer shell to enable the internal heat to melt accumulated snow. For cooling or air conditioning, the exterior face of the liner can be aluminized to reflect the sun's heat.

Special Construction | R131 | Pre-Engin. Struct. & Aquatic Facil.

R13128-310   Dome Structures

Steel — The four types are Lamella, Schwedler, Arch and Geodesic. For maximum economy, rise should be about 15 to 20% of diameter. Most common diameters are in the 200' to 300' range. Lamella domes weigh about 5 P.S.F. of floor area less than Schwedler domes. Schwedler dome weight in lbs. per S.F. approaches .046 times the diameter. Domes below 125' diameter weigh .07 times diameter and the cost per ton of steel is higher. See R05120-220 for estimating weight.

Wood — Small domes are of sawn lumber, larger ones are laminated. In larger sizes, triaxial and triangular cost about the same; radial domes cost more. Radial domes are economical in the 60' to 70' diameter range. Most economical range of all types is 80' to 200' diameters. Diameters can

run over 400'. All costs are quoted above the foundation. Prices include 2" decking and a tension tie ring in place.

Plywood — See division 06120-800 for stressed skin and folded plates. Stock prefab geodesic domes are available with diameters from 24' to 60'.

Fiberglass — Aluminum framed translucent sandwich panels with spans from 5' to 45' are commercially available.

Aluminum — Stressed skin aluminum panels form geodesic domes with spans ranging from 82' to 232'. An aluminum space truss, triangulated or nontriangulated, with aluminum or clear acrylic closure panels can be used for clear spans of 40' to 415'.

Table L1010-302 Design Wind Load in PSF for Glass at Various Elevations (BOCA Code)

Height From Grade	Velocity in Miles per Hour and Design Load in Pounds per S.F.																			
	Vel.	PSF	Vel.	PSF	Vel.	PSF	Vel.	PSF	Vel.	PSF	Vel.	PSF	Vel.	PSF	Vel.	PSF	Vel.	PSF	Vel.	PSF
To 10 ft.	42	6	46	7	49	8	52	9	55	10	59	11	62	12	66	14	69	15	76	19	83	22
10-20	52	9	58	11	61	11	65	14	70	16	74	18	79	20	83	22	87	24	96	30	105	35
20-30*	60	12	67	14	70	16	75	18	80	20	85	23	90	26	95	29	100	32	110	39	120	46
30-60	66	14	74	18	77	19	83	22	88	25	94	28	99	31	104	35	110	39	121	47	132	56
60-120	73	17	82	21	85	12	92	27	98	31	104	35	110	39	116	43	122	48	134	57	146	68
120-140	81	21	91	26	95	29	101	33	108	37	115	42	122	48	128	52	135	48	149	71	162	84
240-480	90	26	100	32	104	35	112	40	119	45	127	51	134	57	142	65	149	71	164	86	179	102
480-960	98	31	110	39	115	42	123	49	131	55	139	62	148	70	156	78	164	86	180	104	197	124
Over 960	98	31	110	39	115	42	123	49	131	55	139	62	148	70	156	78	164	86	180	104	197	124

*Determine appropriate wind at 30' elevation Fig. L1010-303 below.

Table L1010-303 Design Wind Velocity at 30 Ft. Above Ground

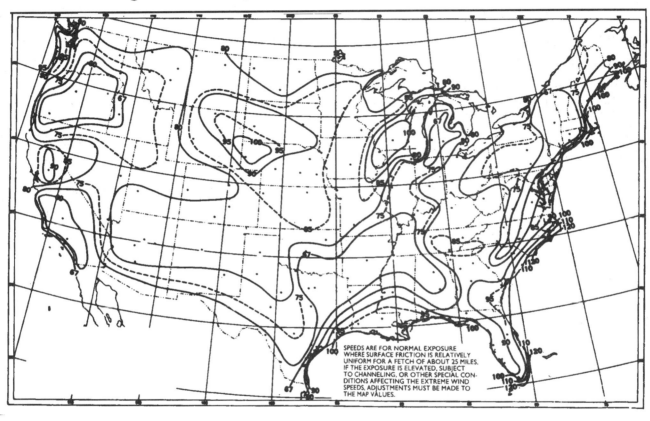

SPEEDS ARE FOR NORMAL EXPOSURE WHERE SURFACE FRICTION IS RELATIVELY UNIFORM FOR A FETCH OF ABOUT 25 MILES. IF THE EXPOSURE IS ELEVATED, SUBJECT TO CHANNELING, OR OTHER SPECIAL CONDITIONS AFFECTING THE EXTREME WIND SPEEDS, ADJUSTMENTS MUST BE MADE TO THE MAP VALUES.

Table L1030-101 "U" Values for Type "A" Buildings

Type A buildings shall include:

A1 Detached one and two family dwellings

A2 All other residential buildings, three stories or less, including but not limited to:
multi-family dwellings, hotels and motels.

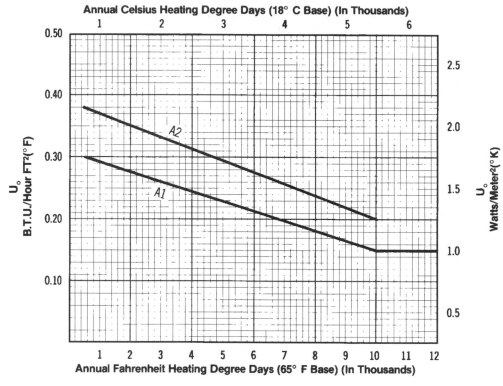

Table L1030-102 "U" Values for Type "B" Buildings

For all buildings Not Classified Type "A"

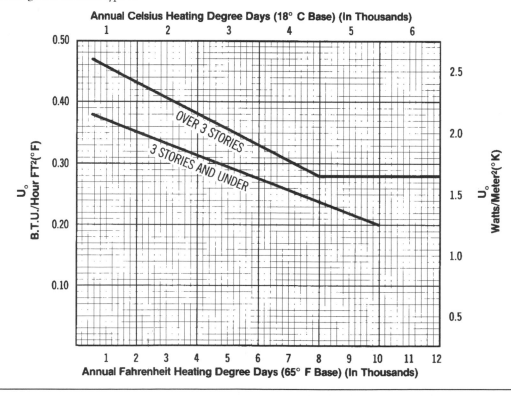

Table L1030-203   Influence of Wall and Roof Weight on "U" Value Correction for Heating Design

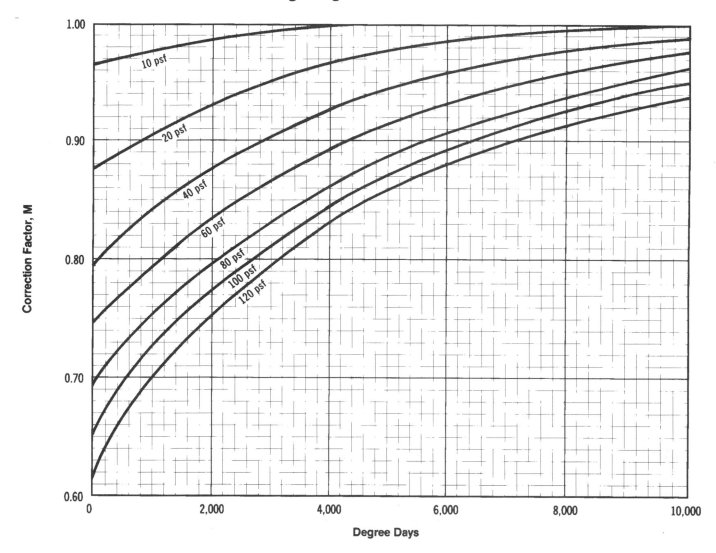

Effective "U" for walls: $Uw = Uw_{ss} \times M$ (similarly, Ur for roofs)

where   Uw = effective thermal transmittance of opaque wall area BTU/h x Ft.^{2} x °F

Uw_{ss} = steady state thermal transmittance of opaque wall area BTU/h x Ft.^{2} x °F

        (steady state "U" value)

        M = weight correction factor

Example: Uw_{ss} = 0.20 with wall weight = 120 psf in Providence, R.I.
(6000 degree days)
Enter chart on bottom at 6000, go up to 120 psf curve, read to the left .88 M = .88
and Uw = 0.20 x 0.88 = 0.176

Table L1030-204   "U" Values for Type "A" Buildings

One and two family dwellings and residential buildings of three stories or less shall have an overall U value as follows:

A. For roof assemblies in which the finished interior surface is essentially the underside of the roof deck, such as exposed concrete slabs, joist slabs, cored slabs, or cathedral ceilings or wood-beam construction.

$$U_{or} = 0.08 \text{ Btu/hr./ft.}^2/\text{°F. (all degree days)}$$

B. For roof-ceiling assemblies, such as roofs with finished ceilings attached to or suspended below the roof deck.

$$U_{or} = 0.05 \text{ for below 8,000 degree days}$$
$$= 0.04 \text{ for 8,000 degree days and greater.}$$

Table L1030-205   "U" Values for Type "B" Buildings*

For all buildings not classified type "A".

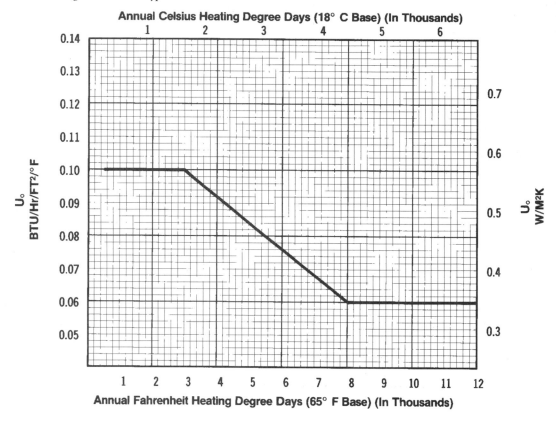

*Minimum requirements for thermal design, ASHRAE Standard 90-75

Table L1030-303   Insulation Requirements for Slabs on Grade for all Buildings

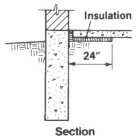

Section

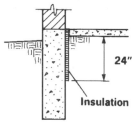

Section (alternate)

Table L1030-401   Resistances ("R") of Building and Insulating Materials

Material	Wt./Lbs. per C.F.	R per Inch	R Listed Size
Air Spaces and Surfaces			
Enclosed non-reflective spaces, E=0.82			
50°F mean temp., 30°/10°F diff.			
.5″			.90/.91
.75″			.94/1.01
1.50″			.90/1.02
3.50″			.91/1.01
Inside vert. surface (still air)			0.68
Outside vert. surface (15 mph wind)			0.17
Building Boards			
Asbestos cement, 0.25″ thick	120		0.06
Gypsum or plaster, 0.5″ thick	50		0.45
Hardboard regular	50	1.37	
Tempered	63	1.00	
Laminated paper	30	2.00	
Particle board	37	1.85	
	50	1.06	
	63	0.85	
Plywood (Douglas Fir), 0.5″ thick	34		0.62
Shingle backer, .375″ thick	18		0.94
Sound deadening board, 0.5″ thick	15		1.35
Tile and lay-in panels, plain or acoustical, 0.5″ thick	18		1.25
Vegetable fiber, 0.5″ thick	18		1.32
	25		1.14
Wood, hardwoods	48	0.91	
Softwoods	32	1.25	
Flooring Carpet with fibrous pad			2.08
With rubber pad			1.23
Cork tile, 1/8″ thick			0.28
Terrazzo			0.08
Tile, resilient			0.05
Wood, hardwood, 0.75″ thick			0.68
Subfloor, 0.75″ thick			0.94
Glass			
Insulation, 0.50″ air space			2.04
Single glass			0.91
Insulation Blanket or Batt, mineral, glass or rock fiber, approximate thickness			
3.0″ to 3.5″ thick			11
3.5″ to 4.0″ thick			13
6.0″ to 6.5″ thick			19
6.5″ to 7.0″ thick			22
8.5″ to 9.0″ thick			30
Boards			
Cellular glass	8.5	2.63	
Fiberboard, wet felted			
Acoustical tile	21	2.70	
Roof insulation	17	2.94	
Fiberboard, wet molded			
Acoustical tile	23	2.38	
Mineral fiber with resin binder	15	3.45	
Polystyrene, extruded,			
cut cell surface	1.8	4.00	
smooth skin surface	2.2	5.00	
	3.5	5.26	
Bead boards	1.0	3.57	
Polyurethane	1.5	6.25	
Wood or cane fiberboard, 0.5″ thick			1.25

Material	Wt./Lbs. per C.F.	R per Inch	R Listed Size
Insulation Loose Fill			
Cellulose	2.3	3.13	
	3.2	3.70	
Mineral fiber, 3.75″ to 5″ thick	2-5		11
6.5″ to 8.75″ thick			19
7.5″ to 10″ thick			22
10.25″ to 13.75″ thick			30
Perlite	5-8	2.70	
Vermiculite	4-6	2.27	
Wood fiber	2-3.5	3.33	
Masonry Brick, Common	120	0.20	
Face	130	0.11	
Cement mortar	116	0.20	
Clay tile, hollow			
1 cell wide, 3″ width			0.80
4″ width			1.11
2 cells wide, 6″ width			1.52
8″ width			1.85
10″ width			2.22
3 cells wide, 12″ width			2.50
Concrete, gypsum fiber	51	0.60	
Lightweight	120	0.19	
	80	0.40	
	40	0.86	
Perlite	40	1.08	
Sand and gravel or stone	140	0.08	
Concrete block, lightweight			
3 cell units, 4″-15 lbs. ea.			1.68
6″-23 lbs. ea.			1.83
8″-28 lbs. ea.			2.12
12″-40 lbs. ea.			2.62
Sand and gravel aggregates,			
4″-20 lbs. ea.			1.17
6″-33 lbs. ea.			1.29
8″-38 lbs. ea.			1.46
12″-56 lbs. ea.			1.81
Plastering Cement Plaster,			
Sand aggregate	116	0.20	
Gypsum plaster, Perlite aggregate	45	0.67	
Sand aggregate	105	0.18	
Vermiculite aggregate	45	0.59	
Roofing			
Asphalt, felt, 15 lb.			0.06
Rolled roofing	70		0.15
Shingles	70		0.44
Built-up roofing .375″ thick	70		0.33
Cement shingles	120		0.21
Vapor-permeable felt			0.06
Vapor seal, 2 layers of mopped 15 lb. felt			0.12
Wood, shingles 16″-7.5″ exposure			0.87
Siding			
Aluminum or steel (hollow backed) oversheathing			0.61
With .375″ insulating backer board			1.82
Foil backed			2.96
Wood siding, beveled, ½″ x 8″			0.81

Reference Aids | RL1030-500 | Weather Information

Table L1030-501 Weather Data and Design Conditions

City	Latitude (1) °	Latitude (1) 1'	Winter Temperatures (1) Med. of Annual Extremes	Winter Temperatures (1) 99%	Winter Temperatures (1) 97½%	Winter Degree Days (2)	Summer (Design Dry Bulb) Temperatures and Relative Humidity 1%	Summer (Design Dry Bulb) Temperatures and Relative Humidity 2½%	Summer (Design Dry Bulb) Temperatures and Relative Humidity 5%
UNITED STATES									
Albuquerque, NM	35	0	5.1	12	16	4,400	96/61	94/61	92/61
Atlanta, GA	33	4	11.9	17	22	3,000	94/74	92/74	90/73
Baltimore, MD	39	2	7	14	17	4,600	94/75	91/75	89/74
Birmingham, AL	33	3	13	17	21	2,600	96/74	94/75	92/74
Bismarck, ND	46	5	-32	-23	-19	8,800	95/68	91/68	88/67
Boise, ID	43	3	1	3	10	5,800	96/65	94/64	91/64
Boston, MA	42	2	-1	6	9	5,600	91/73	88/71	85/70
Burlington, VT	44	3	-17	-12	-7	8,200	88/72	85/70	82/69
Charleston, WV	38	2	3	7	11	4,400	92/74	90/73	87/72
Charlotte, NC	35	1	13	18	22	3,200	95/74	93/74	91/74
Casper, WY	42	5	-21	-11	-5	7,400	92/58	90/57	87/57
Chicago, IL	41	5	-8	-3	2	6,600	94/75	91/74	88/73
Cincinnati, OH	39	1	0	1	6	4,400	92/73	90/72	88/72
Cleveland, OH	41	2	-3	1	5	6,400	91/73	88/72	86/71
Columbia, SC	34	0	16	20	24	2,400	97/76	95/75	93/75
Dallas, TX	32	5	14	18	22	2,400	102/75	100/75	97/75
Denver, CO	39	4	-10	-5	1	6,200	93/59	91/59	89/59
Des Moines, IA	41	3	-14	-10	-5	6,600	94/75	91/74	88/73
Detroit, MI	42	2	-3	3	6	6,200	91/73	88/72	86/71
Great Falls, MT	47	3	-25	-21	-15	7,800	91/60	88/60	85/59
Hartford, CT	41	5	-4	3	7	6,200	91/74	88/73	85/72
Houston, TX	29	5	24	28	33	1,400	97/77	95/77	93/77
Indianapolis, IN	39	4	-7	-2	2	5,600	92/74	90/74	87/73
Jackson, MS	32	2	16	21	25	2,200	97/76	95/76	93/76
Kansas City, MO	39	1	-4	2	6	4,800	99/75	96/74	93/74
Las Vegas, NV	36	1	18	25	28	2,800	108/66	106/65	104/65
Lexington, KY	38	0	-1	3	8	4,600	93/73	91/73	88/72
Little Rock, AR	34	4	11	15	20	3,200	99/76	96/77	94/77
Los Angeles, CA	34	0	36	41	43	2,000	93/70	89/70	86/69
Memphis, TN	35	0	10	13	18	3,200	98/77	95/76	93/76
Miami, FL	25	5	39	44	47	200	91/77	90/77	89/77
Milwaukee, WI	43	0	-11	-8	-4	7,600	90/74	87/73	84/71
Minneapolis, MN	44	5	-22	-16	-12	8,400	92/75	89/73	86/71
New Orleans, LA	30	0	28	29	33	1,400	93/78	92/77	90/77
New York, NY	40	5	6	11	15	5,000	92/74	89/73	87/72
Norfolk, VA	36	5	15	20	22	3,400	93/77	91/76	89/76
Oklahoma City, OK	35	2	4	9	13	3,200	100/74	97/74	95/73
Omaha, NE	41	2	-13	-8	-3	6,600	94/76	91/75	88/74
Philadelphia, PA	39	5	6	10	14	4,400	93/75	90/74	87/72
Phoenix, AZ	33	3	27	31	34	1,800	109/71	107/71	105/71
Pittsburgh, PA	40	3	-1	3	7	6,000	91/72	88/71	86/70
Portland, ME	43	4	-10	-6	-1	7,600	87/72	84/71	81/69
Portland, OR	45	4	18	17	23	4,600	89/68	85/67	81/65
Portsmouth, NH	43	1	-8	-2	2	7,200	89/73	85/71	83/70
Providence, RI	41	4	-1	5	9	6,000	89/73	86/72	83/70
Rochester, NY	43	1	-5	1	5	6,800	91/73	88/71	85/70
Salt Lake City, UT	40	5	0	3	8	6,000	97/62	95/62	92/61
San Francisco, CA	37	5	36	38	40	3,000	74/63	71/62	69/61
Seattle, WA	47	4	22	22	27	5,200	85/68	82/66	78/65
Sioux Falls, SD	43	4	-21	-15	-11	7,800	94/73	91/72	88/71
St. Louis, MO	38	4	-3	3	8	5,000	98/75	94/75	91/75
Tampa, FL	28	0	32	36	40	680	92/77	91/77	90/76
Trenton, NJ	40	1	4	11	14	5,000	91/75	88/74	85/73
Washington, DC	38	5	7	14	17	4,200	93/75	91/74	89/74
Wichita, KS	37	4	-3	3	7	4,600	101/72	98/73	96/73
Wilmington, DE	39	4	5	10	14	5,000	92/74	89/74	87/73
ALASKA									
Anchorage	61	1	-29	-23	-18	10,800	71/59	68/58	66/56
Fairbanks	64	5	-59	-51	-47	14,280	82/62	78/60	75/59
CANADA									
Edmonton, Alta.	53	3	-30	-29	-25	11,000	85/66	82/65	79/63
Halifax, N.S.	44	4	-4	1	5	8,000	79/66	76/65	74/64
Montreal, Que.	45	3	-20	-16	-10	9,000	88/73	85/72	83/71
Saskatoon, Sask.	52	1	-35	-35	-31	11,000	89/68	86/66	83/65
St. John, Nwf.	47	4	1	3	7	8,600	77/66	75/65	73/64
Saint John, N.B.	45	2	-15	-12	-8	8,200	80/67	77/65	75/64
Toronto, Ont.	43	4	-10	-5	-1	7,000	90/73	87/72	85/71
Vancouver, B.C.	49	1	13	15	19	6,000	79/67	77/66	74/65
Winnipeg, Man.	49	5	-31	-30	-27	10,800	89/73	86/71	84/70

(1) Handbook of Fundamentals, ASHRAE, Inc., NY 1989
(2) Local Climatological Annual Survey, USDC Env. Science Services Administration, Asheville, NC

Crews

Crew No.	Bare Costs Hr.	Daily	Incl. Sub O & P Hr.	Daily	Cost Per Labor-Hour Bare Costs	Incl. O&P
Crew A-13	Hr.	Daily	Hr.	Daily	Bare Costs	Incl. O&P
1 Equip. Oper. (light)	$31.10	$248.80	$47.10	$376.80	$31.10	$47.10
1 Large Prod. Vac. Loader		490.25		539.30	61.28	67.41
8 L.H., Daily Totals		$739.05		$916.10	$92.38	$114.51
Crew B-1	Hr.	Daily	Hr.	Daily	Bare Costs	Incl. O&P
1 Labor Foreman (outside)	$26.65	$213.20	$41.65	$333.20	$25.32	$39.55
2 Laborers	24.65	394.40	38.50	616.00		
24 L.H., Daily Totals		$607.60		$949.20	$25.32	$39.55
Crew B-2	Hr.	Daily	Hr.	Daily	Bare Costs	Incl. O&P
1 Labor Foreman (outside)	$26.65	$213.20	$41.65	$333.20	$25.05	$39.13
4 Laborers	24.65	788.80	38.50	1232.00		
40 L.H., Daily Totals		$1002.00		$1565.20	$25.05	$39.13
Crew B-3	Hr.	Daily	Hr.	Daily	Bare Costs	Incl. O&P
1 Labor Foreman (outside)	$26.65	$213.20	$41.65	$333.20	$26.64	$41.05
2 Laborers	24.65	394.40	38.50	616.00		
1 Equip. Oper. (med.)	32.60	260.80	49.35	394.80		
2 Truck Drivers (heavy)	25.65	410.40	39.15	626.40		
1 F.E. Loader, T.M., 2.5 C.Y.		778.40		856.25		
2 Dump Trucks, 16 Ton		899.20		989.10	34.95	38.45
48 L.H., Daily Totals		$2956.40		$3815.75	$61.59	$79.50
Crew B-3A	Hr.	Daily	Hr.	Daily	Bare Costs	Incl. O&P
4 Laborers	$24.65	$788.80	$38.50	$1232.00	$26.24	$40.67
1 Equip. Oper. (med.)	32.60	260.80	49.35	394.80		
1 Hyd. Excavator, 1.5 C.Y.		728.80		801.70	18.22	20.04
40 L.H., Daily Totals		$1778.40		$2428.50	$44.46	$60.71
Crew B-4	Hr.	Daily	Hr.	Daily	Bare Costs	Incl. O&P
1 Labor Foreman (outside)	$26.65	$213.20	$41.65	$333.20	$25.15	$39.13
4 Laborers	24.65	788.80	38.50	1232.00		
1 Truck Driver (heavy)	25.65	205.20	39.15	313.20		
1 Tractor, 4 x 2, 195 H.P.		240.60		264.65		
1 Platform Trailer		143.00		157.30	7.99	8.79
48 L.H., Daily Totals		$1590.80		$2300.35	$33.14	$47.92
Crew B-6	Hr.	Daily	Hr.	Daily	Bare Costs	Incl. O&P
2 Laborers	$24.65	$394.40	$38.50	$616.00	$26.80	$41.37
1 Equip. Oper. (light)	31.10	248.80	47.10	376.80		
1 Backhoe Loader, 48 H.P.		218.80		240.70	9.12	10.03
24 L.H., Daily Totals		$862.00		$1233.50	$35.92	$51.40
Crew B-11B	Hr.	Daily	Hr.	Daily	Bare Costs	Incl. O&P
1 Equipment Oper. (med.)	$32.60	$260.80	$49.35	$394.80	$28.63	$43.92
1 Laborer	24.65	197.20	38.50	308.00		
1 Dozer, 200 H.P.		880.80		968.90		
1 Air Powered Tamper		21.10		23.20		
1 Air Compr. 365 C.F.M.		147.60		162.35		
2-50 Ft. Air Hoses, 1.5" Dia.		10.00		11.00	66.22	72.84
16 L.H., Daily Totals		$1517.50		$1868.25	$94.85	$116.76
Crew B-11C	Hr.	Daily	Hr.	Daily	Bare Costs	Incl. O&P
1 Equipment Oper. (med.)	$32.60	$260.80	$49.35	$394.80	$28.63	$43.92
1 Laborer	24.65	197.20	38.50	308.00		
1 Backhoe Loader, 48 H.P.		218.80		240.70	13.68	15.04
16 L.H., Daily Totals		$676.80		$943.50	$42.31	$58.96

Crew No.	Bare Costs Hr.	Daily	Incl. Sub O & P Hr.	Daily	Cost Per Labor-Hour Bare Costs	Incl. O&P
Crew B-11M	Hr.	Daily	Hr.	Daily	Bare Costs	Incl. O&P
1 Equipment Oper. (med.)	$32.60	$260.80	$49.35	$394.80	$28.63	$43.92
1 Laborer	24.65	197.20	38.50	308.00		
1 Backhoe Loader, 80 H.P.		244.20		268.60	15.26	16.79
16 L.H., Daily Totals		$702.20		$971.40	$43.89	$60.71
Crew B-12C	Hr.	Daily	Hr.	Daily	Bare Costs	Incl. O&P
1 Equip. Oper. (crane)	$33.70	$269.60	$51.00	$408.00	$31.00	$46.92
1 Equip. Oper. Oiler	28.30	226.40	42.85	342.80		
1 Hyd. Excavator, 2 C.Y.		951.20		1046.30	59.45	65.40
16 L.H., Daily Totals		$1447.20		$1797.10	$90.45	$112.32
Crew B-14	Hr.	Daily	Hr.	Daily	Bare Costs	Incl. O&P
1 Labor Foreman (outside)	$26.65	$213.20	$41.65	$333.20	$26.06	$40.46
4 Laborers	24.65	788.80	38.50	1232.00		
1 Equip. Oper. (light)	31.10	248.80	47.10	376.80		
1 Backhoe Loader, 48 H.P.		218.80		240.70	4.56	5.01
48 L.H., Daily Totals		$1469.60		$2182.70	$30.62	$45.47
Crew B-17	Hr.	Daily	Hr.	Daily	Bare Costs	Incl. O&P
2 Laborers	$24.65	$394.40	$38.50	$616.00	$26.51	$40.81
1 Equip. Oper. (light)	31.10	248.80	47.10	376.80		
1 Truck Driver (heavy)	25.65	205.20	39.15	313.20		
1 Backhoe Loader, 48 H.P.		218.80		240.70		
1 Dump Truck, 12 Ton		306.00		336.60	16.40	18.04
32 L.H., Daily Totals		$1373.20		$1883.30	$42.91	$58.85
Crew B-19	Hr.	Daily	Hr.	Daily	Bare Costs	Incl. O&P
1 Pile Driver Foreman	$32.90	$263.20	$55.20	$441.60	$31.52	$50.93
4 Pile Drivers	30.90	988.80	51.85	1659.20		
2 Equip. Oper. (crane)	33.70	539.20	51.00	816.00		
1 Equip. Oper. Oiler	28.30	226.40	42.85	342.80		
1 Crane, 40 Ton & Access.		935.60		1029.15		
60 L.F. Leads, 15K Ft. Lbs.		105.00		115.50		
1 Hammer, 15K Ft. Lbs.		367.20		403.90		
1 Air Compr., 600 C.F.M.		249.20		274.10		
2-50 Ft. Air Hoses, 3" Dia.		35.40		38.95	26.44	29.09
64 L.H., Daily Totals		$3710.00		$5121.20	$57.96	$80.02
Crew B-25	Hr.	Daily	Hr.	Daily	Bare Costs	Incl. O&P
1 Labor Foreman	$26.65	$213.20	$41.65	$333.20	$27.00	$41.75
7 Laborers	24.65	1380.40	38.50	2156.00		
3 Equip. Oper. (med.)	32.60	782.40	49.35	1184.40		
1 Asphalt Paver, 130 H.P		1465.00		1611.50		
1 Tandem Roller, 10 Ton		183.40		201.75		
1 Roller, Pneumatic Wheel		247.00		271.70	21.54	23.69
88 L.H., Daily Totals		$4271.40		$5758.55	$48.54	$65.44
Crew B-34K	Hr.	Daily	Hr.	Daily	Bare Costs	Incl. O&P
1 Truck Driver (heavy)	$25.65	$205.20	$39.15	$313.20	$25.65	$39.15
1 Truck Tractor, 240 H.P.		376.00		413.60		
1 Low Bed Trailer		221.60		243.75	74.70	82.17
8 L.H., Daily Totals		$802.80		$970.55	$100.35	$121.32
Crew B-34L	Hr.	Daily	Hr.	Daily	Bare Costs	Incl. O&P
1 Equip. Oper. (light)	$31.10	$248.80	$47.10	$376.80	$31.10	$47.10
1 Truck, Stake Body, 1.5 ton		120.20		132.20	15.03	16.53
8 L.H., Daily Totals		$369.00		$509.00	$46.13	$63.63

Crews

Crew No.	Bare Costs		Incl. Sub O & P		Cost Per Labor-Hour	
Crew B-34M	Hr.	Daily	Hr.	Daily	Bare Costs	Incl. O&P
1 Equip. Oper. (light)	$31.10	$248.80	$47.10	$376.80	$31.10	$47.10
1 Truck, Stake Body, 3		138.00		151.80	17.25	18.98
8 L.H., Daily Totals		$386.80		$528.60	$48.35	$66.08
Crew B-53	Hr.	Daily	Hr.	Daily	Bare Costs	Incl. O&P
1 Equip. Oper. (light)	$31.10	$248.80	$47.10	$376.80	$31.10	$47.10
1 Trencher, Chain, 12 H.P.		79.20		87.10	9.90	10.89
8 L.H., Daily Totals		$328.00		$463.90	$41.00	$57.99
Crew B-72	Hr.	Daily	Hr.	Daily	Bare Costs	Incl. O&P
1 Labor Foreman (outside)	$26.65	$213.20	$41.65	$333.20	$28.87	$44.32
3 Laborers	24.65	591.60	38.50	924.00		
4 Equip. Oper. (med.)	32.60	1043.20	49.35	1579.20		
1 Pvmt. Profiler, 750 H.P.		4368.00		4804.80		
1 Hammermill, 250 H.P.		1291.00		1420.10		
1 Windrow Loader		799.40		879.35		
1 Mix Paver 165 H.P.		1670.00		1837.00		
1 Roller, Pneu. Tire, 12 T.		247.00		271.70	130.87	143.95
64 L.H., Daily Totals		$10223.40		$12049.35	$159.74	$188.27
Crew B-80A	Hr.	Daily	Hr.	Daily	Bare Costs	Incl. O&P
3 Laborers	$24.65	$591.60	$38.50	$924.00	$24.65	$38.50
1 Flatbed Truck, 3 Ton		138.00		151.80	5.75	6.33
24 L.H., Daily Totals		$729.60		$1075.80	$30.40	$44.83
Crew C-1	Hr.	Daily	Hr.	Daily	Bare Costs	Incl. O&P
3 Carpenters	$31.55	$757.20	$49.30	$1183.20	$29.83	$46.60
1 Laborer	24.65	197.20	38.50	308.00		
32 L.H., Daily Totals		$954.40		$1491.20	$29.83	$46.60
Crew C-11	Hr.	Daily	Hr.	Daily	Bare Costs	Incl. O&P
1 Struc. Steel Foreman	$37.65	$301.20	$68.35	$546.80	$34.84	$61.19
6 Struc. Steel Workers	35.65	1711.20	64.75	3108.00		
1 Equip. Oper. (crane)	33.70	269.60	51.00	408.00		
1 Equip. Oper. Oiler	28.30	226.40	42.85	342.80		
1 Truck Crane, 150 Ton		1538.00		1691.80	21.36	23.50
72 L.H., Daily Totals		$4046.40		$6097.40	$56.20	$84.69
Crew D-1	Hr.	Daily	Hr.	Daily	Bare Costs	Incl. O&P
1 Bricklayer	$32.40	$259.20	$49.80	$398.40	$28.50	$43.80
1 Bricklayer Helper	24.60	196.80	37.80	302.40		
16 L.H., Daily Totals		$456.00		$700.80	$28.50	$43.80
Crew D-7	Hr.	Daily	Hr.	Daily	Bare Costs	Incl. O&P
1 Tile Layer	$30.40	$243.20	$44.85	$358.80	$27.15	$40.05
1 Tile Layer Helper	23.90	191.20	35.25	282.00		
16 L.H., Daily Totals		$434.40		$640.80	$27.15	$40.05
Crew D-8	Hr.	Daily	Hr.	Daily	Bare Costs	Incl. O&P
3 Bricklayers	$32.40	$777.60	$49.80	$1195.20	$29.28	$45.00
2 Bricklayer Helpers	24.60	393.60	37.80	604.80		
40 L.H., Daily Totals		$1171.20		$1800.00	$29.28	$45.00
Crew D-10	Hr.	Daily	Hr.	Daily	Bare Costs	Incl. O&P
1 Bricklayer Foreman	$34.40	$275.20	$52.85	$422.80	$29.94	$45.85
1 Bricklayer	32.40	259.20	49.80	398.40		
2 Bricklayer Helpers	24.60	393.60	37.80	604.80		
1 Equip. Oper. (crane)	33.70	269.60	51.00	408.00		
1 Truck Crane, 12.5 Ton		493.40		542.75	12.34	13.57
40 L.H., Daily Totals		$1691.00		$2376.75	$42.28	$59.42

Crew No.	Bare Costs		Incl. Sub O & P		Cost Per Labor-Hour	
Crew D-11	Hr.	Daily	Hr.	Daily	Bare Costs	Incl. O&P
1 Bricklayer Foreman	$34.40	$275.20	$52.85	$422.80	$30.47	$46.82
1 Bricklayer	32.40	259.20	49.80	398.40		
1 Bricklayer Helper	24.60	196.80	37.80	302.40		
24 L.H., Daily Totals		$731.20		$1123.60	$30.47	$46.82
Crew D-12	Hr.	Daily	Hr.	Daily	Bare Costs	Incl. O&P
1 Bricklayer Foreman	$34.40	$275.20	$52.85	$422.80	$29.00	$44.56
1 Bricklayer	32.40	259.20	49.80	398.40		
2 Bricklayer Helpers	24.60	393.60	37.80	604.80		
32 L.H., Daily Totals		$928.00		$1426.00	$29.00	$44.56
Crew F-3	Hr.	Daily	Hr.	Daily	Bare Costs	Incl. O&P
4 Carpenters	$31.55	$1009.60	$49.30	$1577.60	$31.98	$49.64
1 Equip. Oper. (crane)	33.70	269.60	51.00	408.00		
1 Hyd. Crane, 12 Ton		636.00		699.60	15.90	17.49
40 L.H., Daily Totals		$1915.20		$2685.20	$47.88	$67.13
Crew F-4	Hr.	Daily	Hr.	Daily	Bare Costs	Incl. O&P
4 Carpenters	$31.55	$1009.60	$49.30	$1577.60	$31.37	$48.51
1 Equip. Oper. (crane)	33.70	269.60	51.00	408.00		
1 Equip. Oper. Oiler	28.30	226.40	42.85	342.80		
1 Hyd. Crane, 55 Ton		1156.00		1271.60	24.08	26.49
48 L.H., Daily Totals		$2661.60		$3600.00	$55.45	$75.00
Crew F-5	Hr.	Daily	Hr.	Daily	Bare Costs	Incl. O&P
1 Carpenter Foreman	$33.55	$268.40	$52.40	$419.20	$32.05	$50.08
3 Carpenters	31.55	757.20	49.30	1183.20		
32 L.H., Daily Totals		$1025.60		$1602.40	$32.05	$50.08
Crew G-3	Hr.	Daily	Hr.	Daily	Bare Costs	Incl. O&P
2 Sheet Metal Workers	$37.00	$592.00	$57.15	$914.40	$30.83	$47.83
2 Building Laborers	24.65	394.40	38.50	616.00		
32 L.H., Daily Totals		$986.40		$1530.40	$30.83	$47.83
Crew G-4	Hr.	Daily	Hr.	Daily	Bare Costs	Incl. O&P
1 Labor Foreman (outside)	$26.65	$213.20	$41.65	$333.20	$25.32	$39.55
2 Building Laborers	24.65	394.40	38.50	616.00		
1 Light Truck, 1.5 Ton		120.00		132.00		
1 Air Compr., 160 C.F.M.		86.40		95.05	8.61	9.47
24 L.H., Daily Totals		$814.20		$1176.45	$33.93	$49.02
Crew L-1	Hr.	Daily	Hr.	Daily	Bare Costs	Incl. O&P
1 Electrician	$37.60	$300.80	$56.15	$449.20	$37.47	$56.28
1 Plumber	37.35	298.80	56.40	451.20		
16 L.H., Daily Totals		$599.60		$900.40	$37.47	$56.28
Crew L-2	Hr.	Daily	Hr.	Daily	Bare Costs	Incl. O&P
1 Carpenter	$31.55	$252.40	$49.30	$394.40	$27.63	$43.17
1 Carpenter Helper	23.70	189.60	37.05	296.40		
16 L.H., Daily Totals		$442.00		$690.80	$27.63	$43.17
Crew L-4	Hr.	Daily	Hr.	Daily	Bare Costs	Incl. O&P
2 Skilled Workers	$32.25	$516.00	$50.50	$808.00	$29.40	$46.02
1 Helper	23.70	189.60	37.05	296.40		
24 L.H., Daily Totals		$705.60		$1104.40	$29.40	$46.02

Crew No.	Bare Costs		Incl. Sub O & P		Cost Per Labor-Hour	
	Hr.	Daily	Hr.	Daily	Bare Costs	Incl. O&P
Crew L-6	Hr.	Daily	Hr.	Daily	Bare Costs	Incl. O&P
1 Plumber	$37.35	$298.80	$56.40	$451.20	$37.43	$56.32
.5 Electrician	37.60	150.40	56.15	224.60		
12 L.H., Daily Totals		$449.20		$675.80	$37.43	$56.32
Crew Q-1	Hr.	Daily	Hr.	Daily	Bare Costs	Incl. O&P
1 Plumber	$37.35	$298.80	$56.40	$451.20	$33.63	$50.78
1 Plumber Apprentice	29.90	239.20	45.15	361.20		
16 L.H., Daily Totals		$538.00		$812.40	$33.63	$50.78
Crew Q-2	Hr.	Daily	Hr.	Daily	Bare Costs	Incl. O&P
2 Plumbers	$37.35	$597.60	$56.40	$902.40	$34.87	$52.65
1 Plumber Apprentice	29.90	239.20	45.15	361.20		
24 L.H., Daily Totals		$836.80		$1263.60	$34.87	$52.65
Crew Q-5	Hr.	Daily	Hr.	Daily	Bare Costs	Incl. O&P
1 Steamfitter	$37.60	$300.80	$56.80	$454.40	$33.85	$51.13
1 Steamfitter Apprentice	30.10	240.80	45.45	363.60		
16 L.H., Daily Totals		$541.60		$818.00	$33.85	$51.13
Crew Q-6	Hr.	Daily	Hr.	Daily	Bare Costs	Incl. O&P
2 Steamfitters	$37.60	$601.60	$56.80	$908.80	$35.10	$53.02
1 Steamfitter Apprentice	30.10	240.80	45.45	363.60		
24 L.H., Daily Totals		$842.40		$1272.40	$35.10	$53.02
Crew Q-9	Hr.	Daily	Hr.	Daily	Bare Costs	Incl. O&P
1 Sheet Metal Worker	$37.00	$296.00	$57.15	$457.20	$33.30	$51.43
1 Sheet Metal Apprentice	29.60	236.80	45.70	365.60		
16 L.H., Daily Totals		$532.80		$822.80	$33.30	$51.43
Crew Q-10	Hr.	Daily	Hr.	Daily	Bare Costs	Incl. O&P
2 Sheet Metal Workers	$37.00	$592.00	$57.15	$914.40	$34.53	$53.33
1 Sheet Metal Apprentice	29.60	236.80	45.70	365.60		
24 L.H., Daily Totals		$828.80		$1280.00	$34.53	$53.33
Crew Q-11	Hr.	Daily	Hr.	Daily	Bare Costs	Incl. O&P
1 Sheet Metal Foreman (inside)	$37.50	$300.00	$57.90	$463.20	$35.28	$54.48
2 Sheet Metal Workers	37.00	592.00	57.15	914.40		
1 Sheet Metal Apprentice	29.60	236.80	45.70	365.60		
32 L.H., Daily Totals		$1128.80		$1743.20	$35.28	$54.48
Crew Q-19	Hr.	Daily	Hr.	Daily	Bare Costs	Incl. O&P
1 Steamfitter	$37.60	$300.80	$56.80	$454.40	$35.10	$52.80
1 Steamfitter Apprentice	30.10	240.80	45.45	363.60		
1 Electrician	37.60	300.80	56.15	449.20		
24 L.H., Daily Totals		$842.40		$1267.20	$35.10	$52.80
Crew R-3	Hr.	Daily	Hr.	Daily	Bare Costs	Incl. O&P
1 Electrician Foreman	$38.10	$304.80	$56.90	$455.20	$37.02	$55.42
1 Electrician	37.60	300.80	56.15	449.20		
.5 Equip. Oper. (crane)	33.70	134.80	51.00	204.00		
.5 S.P. Crane, 5 Ton		163.20		179.50	8.16	8.98
20 L.H., Daily Totals		$903.60		$1287.90	$45.18	$64.40

Location Factors

Costs shown in *Means cost data publications* are based on National Averages for materials and installation. To adjust these costs to a specific location, simply multiply the base cost by the factor for that city. The data is arranged alphabetically by state and postal zip code numbers. For a city not listed, use the factor for a nearby city with similar economic characteristics.

STATE/ZIP	CITY	Residential	Commercial
ALABAMA			
350-352	Birmingham	.87	.88
354	Tuscaloosa	.80	.78
355	Jasper	.76	.77
356	Decatur	.78	.79
357-358	Huntsville	.85	.86
359	Gadsden	.79	.80
360-361	Montgomery	.82	.80
362	Anniston	.72	.73
363	Dothan	.77	.76
364	Evergreen	.78	.76
365-366	Mobile	.80	.81
367	Selma	.78	.76
368	Phenix City	.81	.79
369	Butler	.77	.75
ALASKA			
995-996	Anchorage	1.27	1.26
997	Fairbanks	1.26	1.25
998	Juneau	1.26	1.25
999	Ketchikan	1.33	1.32
ARIZONA			
850,853	Phoenix	.91	.88
852	Mesa/Tempe	.89	.86
855	Globe	.87	.84
856-857	Tucson	.89	.86
859	Show Low	.88	.84
860	Flagstaff	.91	.87
863	Prescott	.88	.84
864	Kingman	.88	.84
865	Chambers	.86	.83
ARKANSAS			
716	Pine Bluff	.80	.80
717	Camden	.69	.69
718	Texarkana	.73	.72
719	Hot Springs	.68	.68
720-722	Little Rock	.82	.82
723	West Memphis	.77	.77
724	Jonesboro	.77	.77
725	Batesville	.74	.74
726	Harrison	.75	.75
727	Fayetteville	.68	.65
728	Russellville	.76	.73
729	Fort Smith	.82	.79
CALIFORNIA			
900-902	Los Angeles	1.07	1.07
903-905	Inglewood	1.04	1.04
906-908	Long Beach	1.05	1.05
910-912	Pasadena	1.05	1.05
913-916	Van Nuys	1.07	1.07
917-918	Alhambra	1.07	1.07
919-921	San Diego	1.09	1.05
922	Palm Springs	1.08	1.04
923-924	San Bernardino	1.07	1.03
925	Riverside	1.11	1.07
926-927	Santa Ana	1.08	1.05
928	Anaheim	1.10	1.08
930	Oxnard	1.12	1.07
931	Santa Barbara	1.10	1.07
932-933	Bakersfield	1.11	1.06
934	San Luis Obispo	1.12	1.07
935	Mojave	1.08	1.04
936-938	Fresno	1.12	1.08
939	Salinas	1.11	1.11
940-941	San Francisco	1.21	1.24
942,956-958	Sacramento	1.12	1.11
943	Palo Alto	1.14	1.17
944	San Mateo	1.15	1.18
945	Vallejo	1.10	1.13
946	Oakland	1.15	1.18
947	Berkeley	1.15	1.18
948	Richmond	1.14	1.17
949	San Rafael	1.25	1.19
950	Santa Cruz	1.15	1.13
951	San Jose	1.22	1.20
952	Stockton	1.12	1.08
953	Modesto	1.12	1.08

STATE/ZIP	CITY	Residential	Commercial
CALIFORNIA (CONT'D)			
954	Santa Rosa	1.13	1.16
955	Eureka	1.08	1.07
959	Marysville	1.09	1.08
960	Redding	1.11	1.10
961	Susanville	1.11	1.10
COLORADO			
800-802	Denver	1.00	.96
803	Boulder	.88	.85
804	Golden	.99	.95
805	Fort Collins	.97	.91
806	Greeley	.90	.85
807	Fort Morgan	.97	.91
808-809	Colorado Springs	.95	.93
810	Pueblo	.94	.92
811	Alamosa	.89	.87
812	Salida	.89	.87
813	Durango	.89	.87
814	Montrose	.86	.85
815	Grand Junction	.89	.85
816	Glenwood Springs	.98	.93
CONNECTICUT			
060	New Britain	1.05	1.06
061	Hartford	1.04	1.05
062	Willimantic	1.04	1.05
063	New London	1.05	1.04
064	Meriden	1.05	1.06
065	New Haven	1.06	1.07
066	Bridgeport	1.03	1.06
067	Waterbury	1.06	1.06
068	Norwalk	1.03	1.07
069	Stamford	1.05	1.09
D.C.			
200-205	Washington	.94	.96
DELAWARE			
197	Newark	1.01	1.02
198	Wilmington	1.01	1.02
199	Dover	1.01	1.02
FLORIDA			
320,322	Jacksonville	.83	.82
321	Daytona Beach	.86	.85
323	Tallahassee	.74	.76
324	Panama City	.69	.71
325	Pensacola	.83	.81
326,344	Gainesville	.83	.80
327-328,347	Orlando	.85	.83
329	Melbourne	.89	.88
330-332,340	Miami	.83	.85
333	Fort Lauderdale	.82	.84
334,349	West Palm Beach	.85	.82
335-336,346	Tampa	.78	.80
337	St. Petersburg	.79	.81
338	Lakeland	.78	.80
339,341	Fort Myers	.78	.78
342	Sarasota	.77	.79
GEORGIA			
300-303,399	Atlanta	.85	.90
304	Statesboro	.71	.73
305	Gainesville	.74	.79
306	Athens	.76	.81
307	Dalton	.67	.66
308-309	Augusta	.75	.76
310-312	Macon	.80	.80
313-314	Savannah	.79	.80
315	Waycross	.73	.73
316	Valdosta	.75	.75
317	Albany	.76	.78
318-319	Columbus	.77	.77
HAWAII			
967	Hilo	1.26	1.22
968	Honolulu	1.27	1.23

Location Factors

STATE/ZIP	CITY	Residential	Commercial
STATES & POSS.			
969	Guam	1.34	1.30
IDAHO			
832	Pocatello	.93	.92
833	Twin Falls	.78	.77
834	Idaho Falls	.82	.81
835	Lewiston	1.08	1.00
836-837	Boise	.94	.93
838	Coeur d'Alene	.94	.87
ILLINOIS			
600-603	North Suburban	1.11	1.10
604	Joliet	1.11	1.10
605	South Suburban	1.11	1.10
606	Chicago	1.15	1.14
609	Kankakee	1.03	1.03
610-611	Rockford	1.06	1.05
612	Rock Island	1.07	.98
613	La Salle	1.08	1.01
614	Galesburg	1.08	1.01
615-616	Peoria	1.09	1.02
617	Bloomington	1.05	1.01
618-619	Champaign	1.05	1.02
620-622	East St. Louis	1.00	1.00
623	Quincy	1.00	.98
624	Effingham	1.02	.99
625	Decatur	1.01	.98
626-627	Springfield	1.03	.99
628	Centralia	.98	.98
629	Carbondale	.97	.97
INDIANA			
460	Anderson	.94	.92
461-462	Indianapolis	.97	.95
463-464	Gary	1.04	1.02
465-466	South Bend	.94	.92
467-468	Fort Wayne	.91	.92
469	Kokomo	.92	.91
470	Lawrenceburg	.92	.89
471	New Albany	.92	.88
472	Columbus	.94	.91
473	Muncie	.92	.91
474	Bloomington	.95	.93
475	Washington	.92	.92
476-477	Evansville	.93	.93
478	Terre Haute	.95	.94
479	Lafayette	.91	.91
IOWA			
500-503,509	Des Moines	.96	.92
504	Mason City	.88	.82
505	Fort Dodge	.86	.80
506-507	Waterloo	.87	.82
508	Creston	.88	.83
510-511	Sioux City	.94	.88
512	Sibley	.79	.77
513	Spencer	.79	.77
514	Carroll	.83	.78
515	Council Bluffs	.95	.89
516	Shenandoah	.81	.76
520	Dubuque	1.00	.89
521	Decorah	.87	.78
522-524	Cedar Rapids	1.00	.92
525	Ottumwa	.94	.86
526	Burlington	.92	.86
527-528	Davenport	.99	.97
KANSAS			
660-662	Kansas City	.99	.97
664-666	Topeka	.85	.84
667	Fort Scott	.86	.84
668	Emporia	.82	.81
669	Belleville	.85	.79
670-672	Wichita	.89	.86
673	Independence	.81	.78
674	Salina	.84	.80
675	Hutchinson	.78	.75
676	Hays	.83	.79
677	Colby	.83	.79
678	Dodge City	.83	.80
679	Liberal	.77	.74
KENTUCKY			
400-402	Louisville	.94	.91
403-405	Lexington	.86	.83

STATE/ZIP	CITY	Residential	Commercial
KENTUCKY (CONT'D)			
406	Frankfort	.90	.84
407-409	Corbin	.76	.71
410	Covington	.98	.95
411-412	Ashland	.96	.97
413-414	Campton	.75	.72
415-416	Pikeville	.81	.82
417-418	Hazard	.75	.72
420	Paducah	.96	.92
421-422	Bowling Green	.94	.90
423	Owensboro	.89	.87
424	Henderson	.94	.92
425-426	Somerset	.75	.71
427	Elizabethtown	.93	.89
LOUISIANA			
700-701	New Orleans	.88	.87
703	Thibodaux	.85	.85
704	Hammond	.83	.82
705	Lafayette	.83	.80
706	Lake Charles	.82	.82
707-708	Baton Rouge	.81	.80
710-711	Shreveport	.80	.80
712	Monroe	.78	.78
713-714	Alexandria	.77	.77
MAINE			
039	Kittery	.84	.86
040-041	Portland	.89	.91
042	Lewiston	.90	.91
043	Augusta	.86	.86
044	Bangor	.91	.91
045	Bath	.87	.87
046	Machias	.85	.85
047	Houlton	.87	.87
048	Rockland	.84	.84
049	Waterville	.84	.83
MARYLAND			
206	Waldorf	.87	.87
207-208	College Park	.90	.90
209	Silver Spring	.89	.89
210-212	Baltimore	.91	.91
214	Annapolis	.88	.89
215	Cumberland	.86	.87
216	Easton	.72	.72
217	Hagerstown	.89	.88
218	Salisbury	.75	.76
219	Elkton	.81	.82
MASSACHUSETTS			
010-011	Springfield	1.02	1.01
012	Pittsfield	.98	.98
013	Greenfield	1.00	.98
014	Fitchburg	1.06	1.02
015-016	Worcester	1.10	1.06
017	Framingham	1.04	1.05
018	Lowell	1.07	1.07
019	Lawrence	1.07	1.07
020-022, 024	Boston	1.14	1.15
023	Brockton	1.04	1.06
025	Buzzards Bay	1.01	1.03
026	Hyannis	1.03	1.04
027	New Bedford	1.05	1.06
MICHIGAN			
480,483	Royal Oak	1.03	1.02
481	Ann Arbor	1.04	1.03
482	Detroit	1.09	1.08
484-485	Flint	.98	.99
486	Saginaw	.96	.97
487	Bay City	.96	.97
488-489	Lansing	1.02	.99
490	Battle Creek	1.01	.95
491	Kalamazoo	1.00	.93
492	Jackson	.99	.96
493,495	Grand Rapids	.89	.86
494	Muskegon	.95	.92
496	Traverse City	.90	.86
497	Gaylord	.88	.89
498-499	Iron Mountain	.98	.95
MINNESOTA			
550-551	Saint Paul	1.14	1.12
553-555	Minneapolis	1.17	1.13

Location Factors

STATE/ZIP	CITY	Residential	Commercial
556-558	Duluth	1.02	1.03
559	Rochester	1.05	1.02
560	Mankato	1.00	.99
561	Windom	.91	.90
562	Willmar	.94	.93
563	St. Cloud	1.13	1.05
564	Brainerd	1.07	.99
565	Detroit Lakes	.91	.98
566	Bemidji	.92	.99
567	Thief River Falls	.87	.94
MISSISSIPPI			
386	Clarksdale	.68	.65
387	Greenville	.79	.75
388	Tupelo	.69	.70
389	Greenwood	.70	.67
390-392	Jackson	.79	.75
393	Meridian	.75	.74
394	Laurel	.71	.67
395	Biloxi	.83	.79
396	McComb	.79	.77
397	Columbus	.69	.70
MISSOURI			
630-631	St. Louis	.99	1.02
633	Bowling Green	.92	.94
634	Hannibal	.98	.92
635	Kirksville	.85	.89
636	Flat River	.94	.96
637	Cape Girardeau	.92	.95
638	Sikeston	.90	.92
639	Poplar Bluff	.90	.92
640-641	Kansas City	1.05	1.02
644-645	St. Joseph	.92	.96
646	Chillicothe	.81	.85
647	Harrisonville	1.01	.99
648	Joplin	.83	.85
650-651	Jefferson City	.97	.91
652	Columbia	.99	.93
653	Sedalia	.99	.92
654-655	Rolla	.94	.88
656-658	Springfield	.86	.88
MONTANA			
590-591	Billings	.92	.90
592	Wolf Point	.90	.88
593	Miles City	.90	.88
594	Great Falls	.91	.90
595	Havre	.89	.88
596	Helena	.90	.89
597	Butte	.90	.89
598	Missoula	.88	.87
599	Kalispell	.87	.86
NEBRASKA			
680-681	Omaha	.92	.91
683-685	Lincoln	.90	.85
686	Columbus	.77	.76
687	Norfolk	.84	.83
688	Grand Island	.88	.84
689	Hastings	.84	.80
690	Mccook	.78	.74
691	North Platte	.85	.81
692	Valentine	.76	.72
693	Alliance	.73	.70
NEVADA			
889-891	Las Vegas	1.05	1.04
893	Ely	.93	.94
894-895	Reno	.94	.99
897	Carson City	.96	.99
898	Elko	.91	.93
NEW HAMPSHIRE			
030	Nashua	.92	.93
031	Manchester	.92	.93
032-033	Concord	.91	.92
034	Keene	.76	.77
035	Littleton	.80	.81
036	Charleston	.75	.75
037	Claremont	.74	.75
038	Portsmouth	.90	.89

STATE/ZIP	CITY	Residential	Commercial
NEW JERSEY			
070-071	Newark	1.11	1.10
072	Elizabeth	1.08	1.06
073	Jersey City	1.10	1.09
074-075	Paterson	1.09	1.09
076	Hackensack	1.08	1.08
077	Long Branch	1.08	1.06
078	Dover	1.10	1.08
079	Summit	1.07	1.05
080,083	Vineland	1.09	1.06
081	Camden	1.09	1.06
082,084	Atlantic City	1.09	1.06
085-086	Trenton	1.09	1.08
087	Point Pleasant	1.08	1.06
088-089	New Brunswick	1.10	1.08
NEW MEXICO			
870-872	Albuquerque	.88	.90
873	Gallup	.88	.90
874	Farmington	.88	.90
875	Santa Fe	.87	.89
877	Las Vegas	.87	.89
878	Socorro	.87	.89
879	Truth/Consequences	.86	.86
880	Las Cruces	.84	.84
881	Clovis	.89	.89
882	Roswell	.90	.90
883	Carrizozo	.90	.90
884	Tucumcari	.89	.89
NEW YORK			
100-102	New York	1.33	1.33
103	Staten Island	1.30	1.30
104	Bronx	1.28	1.28
105	Mount Vernon	1.19	1.19
106	White Plains	1.19	1.19
107	Yonkers	1.21	1.21
108	New Rochelle	1.19	1.19
109	Suffern	1.14	1.14
110	Queens	1.29	1.29
111	Long Island City	1.30	1.30
112	Brooklyn	1.30	1.30
113	Flushing	1.31	1.31
114	Jamaica	1.29	1.29
115,117,118	Hicksville	1.24	1.24
116	Far Rockaway	1.31	1.31
119	Riverhead	1.26	1.26
120-122	Albany	.96	.96
123	Schenectady	.96	.96
124	Kingston	1.11	1.09
125-126	Poughkeepsie	1.13	1.11
127	Monticello	1.10	1.08
128	Glens Falls	.93	.91
129	Plattsburgh	.94	.92
130-132	Syracuse	.97	.95
133-135	Utica	.89	.92
136	Watertown	.90	.93
137-139	Binghamton	.93	.93
140-142	Buffalo	1.06	1.02
143	Niagara Falls	1.06	1.02
144-146	Rochester	.98	.99
147	Jamestown	.97	.93
148-149	Elmira	.94	.92
NORTH CAROLINA			
270,272-274	Greensboro	.75	.76
271	Winston-Salem	.74	.75
275-276	Raleigh	.76	.76
277	Durham	.75	.76
278	Rocky Mount	.68	.68
279	Elizabeth City	.69	.69
280	Gastonia	.73	.74
281-282	Charlotte	.73	.74
283	Fayetteville	.75	.75
284	Wilmington	.73	.74
285	Kinston	.67	.67
286	Hickory	.65	.66
287-288	Asheville	.72	.74
289	Murphy	.66	.67
NORTH DAKOTA			
580-581	Fargo	.80	.85
582	Grand Forks	.76	.81
583	Devils Lake	.78	.83
584	Jamestown	.75	.80
585	Bismarck	.81	.85

Location Factors

STATE/ZIP	CITY	Residential	Commercial
NORTH DAKOTA (CONT'D)			
586	Dickinson	.81	.84
587	Minot	.83	.87
588	Williston	.79	.83
OHIO			
430-432	Columbus	.98	.96
433	Marion	.93	.94
434-436	Toledo	1.02	1.01
437-438	Zanesville	.93	.92
439	Steubenville	.97	.97
440	Lorain	1.03	.97
441	Cleveland	1.09	1.03
442-443	Akron	1.00	.99
444-445	Youngstown	1.00	.97
446-447	Canton	.96	.95
448-449	Mansfield	.96	.94
450	Hamilton	1.00	.94
451-452	Cincinnati	1.00	.94
453-454	Dayton	.93	.92
455	Springfield	.95	.93
456	Chillicothe	1.02	.96
457	Athens	.91	.90
458	Lima	.95	.94
OKLAHOMA			
730-731	Oklahoma City	.81	.83
734	Ardmore	.82	.81
735	Lawton	.84	.83
736	Clinton	.79	.81
737	Enid	.82	.81
738	Woodward	.81	.81
739	Guymon	.68	.67
740-741	Tulsa	.84	.81
743	Miami	.85	.82
744	Muskogee	.74	.72
745	Mcalester	.75	.76
746	Ponca City	.81	.80
747	Durant	.78	.80
748	Shawnee	.78	.80
749	Poteau	.84	.80
OREGON			
970-972	Portland	1.07	1.05
973	Salem	1.05	1.04
974	Eugene	1.05	1.04
975	Medford	1.05	1.04
976	Klamath Falls	1.05	1.04
977	Bend	1.05	1.04
978	Pendleton	1.02	1.00
979	Vale	.98	.96
PENNSYLVANIA			
150-152	Pittsburgh	1.02	1.00
153	Washington	1.00	.98
154	Uniontown	.99	.97
155	Bedford	1.01	.94
156	Greensburg	1.00	.98
157	Indiana	1.03	.96
158	Dubois	1.02	.95
159	Johnstown	1.03	.96
160	Butler	1.00	.97
161	New Castle	1.00	.97
162	Kittanning	1.01	.98
163	Oil City	.89	.94
164-165	Erie	.97	.96
166	Altoona	1.03	.95
167	Bradford	.97	.96
168	State College	.95	.95
169	Wellsboro	.92	.93
170-171	Harrisburg	.96	.95
172	Chambersburg	.94	.93
173-174	York	.96	.94
175-176	Lancaster	.94	.92
177	Williamsport	.89	.88
178	Sunbury	.94	.93
179	Pottsville	.93	.92
180	Lehigh Valley	1.02	1.01
181	Allentown	1.02	1.01
182	Hazleton	.96	.96
183	Stroudsburg	.99	.98
184-185	Scranton	.94	.97
186-187	Wilkes-Barre	.92	.95
188	Montrose	.92	.95
189	Doylestown	.94	1.05

STATE/ZIP	CITY	Residential	Commercial
PENNSYLVANIA (CONT'D)			
190-191	Philadelphia	1.13	1.11
193	Westchester	1.07	1.06
194	Norristown	1.09	1.07
195-196	Reading	.95	.96
PUERTO RICO			
009	San Juan	.85	.85
RHODE ISLAND			
028	Newport	1.00	1.02
029	Providence	1.00	1.02
SOUTH CAROLINA			
290-292	Columbia	.71	.74
293	Spartanburg	.70	.72
294	Charleston	.72	.74
295	Florence	.70	.72
296	Greenville	.69	.72
297	Rock Hill	.63	.66
298	Aiken	.81	.85
299	Beaufort	.67	.69
SOUTH DAKOTA			
570-571	Sioux Falls	.87	.81
572	Watertown	.83	.78
573	Mitchell	.83	.77
574	Aberdeen	.86	.80
575	Pierre	.85	.79
576	Mobridge	.84	.77
577	Rapid City	.84	.78
TENNESSEE			
370-372	Nashville	.86	.86
373-374	Chattanooga	.81	.80
375,380-381	Memphis	.86	.86
376	Johnson City	.81	.80
377-379	Knoxville	.79	.79
382	Mckenzie	.76	.76
383	Jackson	.71	.78
384	Columbia	.78	.78
385	Cookeville	.76	.76
TEXAS			
750	Mckinney	.87	.80
751	Waxahackie	.81	.81
752-753	Dallas	.89	.85
754	Greenville	.77	.72
755	Texarkana	.86	.76
756	Longview	.83	.73
757	Tyler	.90	.79
758	Palestine	.71	.71
759	Lufkin	.74	.74
760-761	Fort Worth	.83	.82
762	Denton	.86	.77
763	Wichita Falls	.79	.79
764	Eastland	.72	.71
765	Temple	.76	.75
766-767	Waco	.80	.79
768	Brownwood	.71	.70
769	San Angelo	.78	.74
770-772	Houston	.87	.88
773	Huntsville	.72	.72
774	Wharton	.74	.75
775	Galveston	.85	.86
776-777	Beaumont	.80	.82
778	Bryan	.80	.81
779	Victoria	.76	.76
780	Laredo	.75	.76
781-782	San Antonio	.80	.81
783-784	Corpus Christi	.78	.77
785	Mc Allen	.76	.74
786-787	Austin	.77	.80
788	Del Rio	.66	.66
789	Giddings	.71	.70
790-791	Amarillo	.80	.80
792	Childress	.74	.77
793-794	Lubbock	.77	.78
795-796	Abilene	.78	.78
797	Midland	.76	.77
798-799,885	El Paso	.78	.77
UTAH			
840-841	Salt Lake City	.91	.90
842,844	Ogden	.90	.88

Location Factors

STATE/ZIP	CITY	Residential	Commercial
UTAH (CONT'D)			
843	Logan	.91	.89
845	Price	.80	.79
846-847	Provo	.90	.89
VERMONT			
050	White River Jct.	.77	.76
051	Bellows Falls	.77	.76
052	Bennington	.77	.76
053	Brattleboro	.77	.77
054	Burlington	.85	.86
056	Montpelier	.83	.84
057	Rutland	.86	.85
058	St. Johnsbury	.74	.75
059	Guildhall	.73	.74
VIRGINIA			
220-221	Fairfax	.89	.90
222	Arlington	.89	.90
223	Alexandria	.91	.92
224-225	Fredericksburg	.83	.83
226	Winchester	.77	.78
227	Culpeper	.78	.79
228	Harrisonburg	.74	.75
229	Charlottesville	.83	.81
230-232	Richmond	.86	.84
233-235	Norfolk	.82	.82
236	Newport News	.82	.81
237	Portsmouth	.81	.81
238	Petersburg	.86	.84
239	Farmville	.73	.72
240-241	Roanoke	.76	.75
242	Bristol	.79	.74
243	Pulaski	.72	.71
244	Staunton	.75	.74
245	Lynchburg	.80	.76
246	Grundy	.71	.71
WASHINGTON			
980-981,987	Seattle	.98	1.03
982	Everett	.95	1.01
983-984	Tacoma	1.04	1.02
985	Olympia	1.04	1.02
986	Vancouver	1.09	1.03
988	Wenatchee	.92	.96
989	Yakima	1.00	.98
990-992	Spokane	.98	.97
993	Richland	.99	.98
994	Clarkston	.97	.96
WEST VIRGINIA			
247-248	Bluefield	.89	.89
249	Lewisburg	.91	.91
250-253	Charleston	.95	.95
254	Martinsburg	.83	.83
255-257	Huntington	.93	.95
258-259	Beckley	.93	.93
260	Wheeling	.93	.95
261	Parkersburg	.92	.94
262	Buckhannon	.97	.94
263-264	Clarksburg	.97	.94
265	Morgantown	.97	.94
266	Gassaway	.94	.94
267	Romney	.91	.91
268	Petersburg	.94	.92
WISCONSIN			
530,532	Milwaukee	1.02	1.01
531	Kenosha	1.01	1.00
534	Racine	1.05	1.00
535	Beloit	1.01	.98
537	Madison	1.00	.98
538	Lancaster	.96	.94
539	Portage	.98	.96
540	New Richmond	1.04	.96
541-543	Green Bay	1.00	.97
544	Wausau	.99	.94
545	Rhinelander	1.00	.96
546	La Crosse	.98	.95
547	Eau Claire	1.04	.96
548	Superior	1.04	.98
549	Oshkosh	.98	.95

STATE/ZIP	CITY	Residential	Commercial
WYOMING			
820	Cheyenne	.84	.80
821	Yellowstone Nat. Pk.	.79	.76
822	Wheatland	.81	.77
823	Rawlins	.80	.76
824	Worland	.77	.75
825	Riverton	.80	.77
826	Casper	.85	.81
827	Newcastle	.78	.74
828	Sheridan	.82	.79
829-831	Rock Springs	.82	.77
CANADIAN FACTORS (reflect Canadian currency)			
ALBERTA			
	Calgary	1.00	.97
	Edmonton	1.00	.97
	Fort McMurray	.99	.96
	Lethbridge	.99	.96
	Lloydminster	.99	.96
	Medicine Hat	.99	.96
	Red Deer	.99	.96
BRITISH COLUMBIA			
	Kamloops	1.02	1.03
	Prince George	1.03	1.04
	Vancouver	1.05	1.06
	Victoria	1.04	1.05
MANITOBA			
	Brandon	.97	.96
	Portage la Prairie	.96	.96
	Winnipeg	.97	.96
NEW BRUNSWICK			
	Bathurst	.93	.91
	Dalhousie	.93	.91
	Fredericton	.96	.94
	Moncton	.93	.91
	Newcastle	.93	.91
	Saint John	.96	.94
NEWFOUNDLAND			
	Corner Brook	.95	.94
	St. John's	.95	.94
NORTHWEST TERRITORIES			
	Yellowknife	.92	.91
NOVA SCOTIA			
	Dartmouth	.96	.95
	Halifax	.96	.95
	New Glasgow	.96	.95
	Sydney	.94	.93
	Yarmouth	.96	.95
ONTARIO			
	Barrie	1.08	1.06
	Brantford	1.09	1.07
	Cornwall	1.07	1.05
	Hamilton	1.11	1.07
	Kingston	1.08	1.06
	Kitchener	1.04	1.03
	London	1.08	1.06
	North Bay	1.07	1.05
	Oshawa	1.08	1.06
	Ottawa	1.08	1.06
	Owen Sound	1.08	1.06
	Peterborough	1.07	1.05
	Sarnia	1.10	1.08
	St. Catharines	1.04	1.02
	Sudbury	1.04	1.02
	Thunder Bay	1.04	1.03
	Toronto	1.11	1.10
	Windsor	1.05	1.03
PRINCE EDWARD ISLAND			
	Charlottetown	.92	.90
	Summerside	.92	.90

Location Factors

STATE/ZIP	CITY	Residential	Commercial
QUEBEC			
	Cap-de-la-Madeleine	1.02	1.01
	Charlesbourg	1.02	1.01
	Chicoutimi	1.01	1.00
	Gatineau	1.01	1.00
	Laval	1.02	1.01
	Montreal	1.07	1.01
	Quebec	1.09	1.02
	Sherbrooke	1.02	1.01
	Trois Rivieres	1.02	1.01
SASKATCHEWAN			
	Moose Jaw	.91	.91
	Prince Albert	.91	.91
	Regina	.92	.92
	Saskatoon	.91	.91
YUKON			
	Whitehorse	.92	.91

Glossary

Adobe
Earthen, sun-cured brick. A relatively labor-intensive, but low-embodied energy material, adobe provides a large thermal heat sink that soaks up excess heat during hot days and re-releases it during cool nights, thereby moderating a building's internal temperature.

Active walls
Building walls that act as a generator or collector of energy. An example is a double glass wall that collects solar energy and is designed to reflect excess heat when desired interior envelope temperatures have been reached. This combination reduces the net heating and cooling load of a facility.

Air doors
Sometimes called *air walls*, typically used for garage-type or larger doors to reduce infiltration and ex-filtration. An air door creates an invisible barrier of high-velocity air that separates different environments.

Airflow retarders
Continuous materials that resist differences in air pressure caused by mechanical systems, the stack effect, and wind. Effective materials for retarding airflow include gypsum board, sheathing materials, rigid insulation, and sprayed foam insulation.

Annual fuel utilization efficiency (AFUE)
A seasonal efficiency rating that is an accurate estimation of fuel used for furnaces and direct-fired forced hot air systems. It measures the system efficiency and accounts for startup, cool-down, and other operating losses.

Audio masking system
A device to reduce distracting sounds and increase speech privacy. Some systems provide protection from laser beams and other high-tech sound detection devices.

Backcasting
A creative thinking process in which the desired result of a project is first envisioned, and only then are different means of achieving it proposed. Solutions tend to be less constrained by preconceived ideas and notions.

Battery charge controller
A device that modulates the charge current into a battery to protect against overcharging and the associated loss of electrolytes. A low-voltage disconnect protects the battery from becoming

excessively discharged by disconnecting the load.

BEES
Building for Environmental and Economic Sustainability, a methodology that considers multiple environmental and economic impacts over the building product's entire life cycle to develop a rational decision-making scoring system. BEES software contains the pertinent data for 65 building products, and the computational engine that generates the BEES scores.

Biodegradable
A biodegradable product returns to the earth naturally under exposure to the elements. For example, an abandoned barn will eventually collapse and disappear.

Biomimetic
A technology used for carbon monoxide detectors. Drawbacks include false alarms and slow reset capabilities.

Blast furnace slag
A waste product of steel production. It can be used to replace aggregate in concrete mix to reduce energy consumption and solid waste.

BLCC 5.1-02
A National Institute of Standards and Technology (NIST) software program that performs life-cycle analysis of buildings and components, useful for comparing alternate designs that have higher initial costs, but lower operating costs over the life of the building.

Brownfield sites
Abandoned industrial sites that often require remediation prior to new construction.

Building integrated photovoltaics (BIPV)
Substituting a conventional part of building construction with photovoltaic material. One-for-one replacements of shingles, standing seam metal roofing, spandrel glass, and overhead skylight glass are currently on the market.

Certified wood
Wood from well-managed forests that replenishes, rather than depletes, old growth timber. In green building, certified wood should be used for any wood application for which it is available.

Chilled water system
A cooling system in which the refrigerant expands through the thermal expansion valve. In order for the system to operate, the refrigerant must be compressed from a low temperature gas to a high temperature.

Chromated copper arsenate (CCA)
A highly-toxic chemical used to pressure-treat wood. Treated wood cannot be disposed of without potential issues of toxic runoff or smoke (if the wood is burned).

Cob
Earth and straw molded by hand into sculptural walls that work well in hot, dry climates along the same principle as adobe. Cob can be used in other climates, but the building may require supplemental insulation or additional heating or cooling.

Combustion efficiency
A measurement typically used to define the efficiency of boilers and hot water heaters while they are running.

Commissioning
The process of ensuring that building systems are designed, installed, functionally tested, and capable of being operated and maintained to conform to the design intent.

Commissioning plan
A document or group of documents prepared by the commissioning agent that defines the commissioning process in the various phases of the project.

Commissioning report
The primary record document for commissioning for each specific system, as well as the building as a whole. The report should include a description of installed systems and commissioning tasks, the commissioning plan, completed pre-functional test checklists and functional performance tests, and findings and recommendations.

Conduction
The transfer of heat across a solid substance. Every material has a specific conductivity (U-value) and resistance (the inverse of the U-value, called the R-value). Metal is a particularly good conductor.

Convection
The transfer of heat in a fluid or gas, such as in air, experienced as a cold draft next to a leaky window or an open door. Methods of preventing convective heat transfer include sealing gaps around windows, doors, electrical outlets, and other openings in the building envelope.

Daylighting
Admitting natural light into a space, including distributing light at uniform levels, avoiding glare and reflections, and controlling artificial light to achieve energy and cost savings.

Daylight transmittance
The percentage of visible light that a glazing transmits.

Dead band widening system

A control system for boilers and furnaces that allows for a wide system dead band, or time delay, from set point. Burners can be shut off longer and stay on longer, with fewer cycles. Avoiding short boiler cycling increases the net system efficiency.

Deconstruction

A green building strategy that involves re-use of construction materials salvaged from buildings that are being demolished or remodeled. New building designs may include plans for deconstruction and later re-use of materials.

Design charette

An intense effort to complete a design in a short period of time by addressing the project's goals, needs, and limitations to find creative, but realistic solutions.

Direct expansion system (DX)

A cooling system where the refrigerant expands through the thermal expansion valve. The heat is then removed from the air stream by way of the air stream DX coil. For a DX system to operate, the refrigerant must be compressed from a low-to a high-temperature gas.

Direct solar gain

Solar heating achieved when sunlight enters a room directly, and heats the room or is stored in massive walls or floor.

Discounting

Adjusting cash flows to a common point in time (often the present) when an analysis is performed, or a decision has to be made in the green building process. The conversion of all costs and savings to time-equivalent "present values" allows them to be added and compared in a meaningful way. To make future costs and savings time-equivalent, they must be adjusted for both inflation and the real earning power of money.

DOE-2

A sophisticated U.S. Department of Energy software program designed to predict hourly energy use and energy cost of a building, given weather data, a description of the building and its HVAC equipment, and the utility rates structure.

Down-cycling

Using one product's materials to make other products, such as turning plastic soda containers into park benches (rather than reused or remade into soda containers). This approach is preferable to disposing of materials directly into landfills, but less favored than recycling.

Earth coupling

The practice of building into the ground to take advantage of the vast thermal mass of the ground, which remains a constant temperature at a certain depth below grade (depending on the climate).

Earth sheltering

The practice of building into the ground or earth-berming to protect the building from inclement weather, such as strong wind. Takes advantage of the vast thermal mass of the ground, which remains at a constant temperature at a certain depth below grade (depending on the climate).

Electric screw compressor

An electric-powered rotary compressor that uses less electricity than traditional reciprocating refrigeration compressors (typically .7-.95 kWh / ton Hr).

Electric scroll compressor

An electric-powered rotary compressors that uses less electricity than traditional reciprocating refrigeration compressors (typically .9-1.4 kWh / ton Hr).

Embodied energy

The energy needed to produce a building product, not accounting for transportation, durability, reuse, and recycling.

Emissivity

A product's ability to emit thermal radiation, expressed as a fraction between zero and one. Most non-metallic solids have a high emissivity, while shiny metals have the lowest. Fenestrations that reflect radiant rays have a low emissivity. *(See also "Low-emissivity [low-E] coatings.")*

Energy-10

A whole-building energy analysis software program that performs hourly energy simulations in order to quantify, analyze, assess, and illustrate the effects of changes in building insulation, windows, lighting systems, and mechanical systems, as well as daylighting, passive solar, and natural ventilation.

Energy efficiency ratio (EER)

A measure of energy efficiency in the cooling mode that represents the ratio of total cooling capacity to electrical energy input.

EnergyPlus

Energy analysis software that includes simulation time steps of less than an hour, including solar thermal, multi-zone airflow, photovoltaic, and fuel cell simulations. The modular structure is designed to facilitate future third party development.

Energy recovery ventilator (ERV)

Mechanical equipment that is added to the ventilation system, which features a heat exchanger to provide controlled ventilation into a building, while increasing energy efficiency.

Energy Star®
A voluntary U.S. Environmental Protection Agency and Department of Energy whole building standard for rating the energy efficiency of appliances, homes, and commercial buildings.

Enthalpy wheels
Also referred to as *heat wheels*, a heat recovery system that removes moisture from the ambient air while also cooling the ventilated air by passing all incoming air over a desiccant-coated wheel. This process removes up to 85% of heat/moisture.

Environmental building consultant
A specialist in sustainable building design. This member of the green project team makes recommendations regarding the impact of building materials as they are produced and the waste generated in the construction process and over the product life cycle.

Evaporative cooling
The drawing of heat from the air to vaporize water, making the resultant air cooler but more humid.

Filtering faucet
A faucet that incorporates separate channels for filtered and unfiltered water.

Fly ash
A waste product from coal-fired power plants. Up to 70% of the aggregate used in traditional concrete mixes can be replaced with fly ash to reduce energy consumption and solid waste, while strengthening the concrete.

Formaldehyde
A toxic, colorless, pungent-smelling chemical used to manufacture building materials and products, such as glue in fiberboard. Sources of formaldehyde include building materials; smoking; household products; and the use of un-vented, fuel-burning appliances, such as fork lifts, gas stoves, and kerosene space heaters.

Green process
Manufacturing products with consideration for the source of materials, energy-efficient production methods, use of recycled materials in packaging, reclaiming manufacturing waste, and prudent use of energy.

Green products
Sustainable products that maintain or improve the human environment while diminishing the impact on the natural environment.

Green roof
Also called a *living roof*, a roof with a layer of soil and plantings that dissipates solar heat, absorbs water run-off, generates oxygen, and gives the roof space a garden-like appearance. The roofing becomes its own ecosystem with plantings and grass contained within the membrane.

GreenSpec Directory™
A compilation of over 1,500 energy-efficient, environmentally-friendly building products selected by the editors of *Environmental Building News*. It also contains guideline specification language.

Glare
The difference in luminance ratio between a window and its adjoining space. Also light hitting a person's eyes directly from a fixture, causing discomfort and reducing visual acuity.

Gray water
Wastewater recycled from showers, baths, and laundry, which can be used for watering plants, cooling HVAC equipment, and other purposes, conserving water, especially in warm months.

Heat mirror technology
A type of window design that uses a low-emissivity coated film product suspended inside or between the panes of an insulating glass unit. This is a lower-cost alternative to low-E glass double-pane units.

Heat recovery ventilators
Ventilators that capture heat from the exhausted air (or pre-cool the incoming air, depending on the climate).

Heat sink system
An energy recovery system that uses the exhaust over a thermal heat sink, then switches the incoming air to travel over the heat sink that was heated by the exhaust air.

HOT2000™
Simulation software designed primarily for low-rise residential buildings; it evaluates the effectiveness of cooling and heating, including passive solar systems. This program generates detailed monthly and annual tables on heat loss HVAC loads and the cost of energy use.

Hybrid photovoltaic generator system
A power system that combines solar photovoltaics with a conventional generator system to minimize life cycle costs. The system takes advantage of the low operating cost of a photovoltaic array and the on-demand capability of a generator. To optimize cost, a PV system can incorporate a generator to run infrequently during periods when there is no sun. The PV array typically provides 70-90% of the annual energy, and the generator provides the remainder.

Indirect gain
Solar heating of a space without allowing the sun's rays to enter the space, achieved by installing glazing a

few inches in front of a south-facing high-mass wall.

Indoor air quality (IAQ)

The measure of a building's air in terms of health content, proper humidification, and odor. Indoor air quality is affected by airborne particles generated within or brought into a building or from construction or other materials installed in the building, which can cause physical discomfort, illness, and damage to furnishings and equipment as they are re-circulated.

Infill

Building on a vacant site within an established urban area (rather than on the outskirts).

Infiltration

The entering and/or escaping of air from one space to another or from the outdoors, usually due to pressure or temperature differential. Infiltration occurs in routes established during construction, or over time as buildings settle or move slightly, and cracks are established.

Internal rate of return measures (IRR)

The interest rate that will equate the stream of costs and savings. The calculated interest rate is compared against a specified minimum acceptable rate of return, usually equal to the discount rate. The calculation of the traditional IRR assumes that any proceeds from a project can be reinvested at the calculated rate of return over the study period.

Inverter

Power conditioning equipment for photovoltaic systems used to convert DC power from the photovoltaic arrays, wind turbines, water turbines, fuel cells, or batteries to AC power for the appliances. A rotary inverter is a DC motor driving an AC generator. More common are static inverters, which use power transistors to achieve the conversion electronically.

Isolated gain

Solar heating achieved using an attached sunspace, such as a greenhouse.

LEED

Leadership in Energy and Environmental Design, a U.S. Green Building Council rating system for commercial, institutional, and high-rise residential buildings. Used to evaluate environmental performance from a "whole building" perspective over a building's life cycle.

Life-cycle assessment (LCA)

An evolving, multi-disciplinary approach to measuring environmental performance that analyzes all stages in the life of a product: raw material acquisition, manufacture, transportation, installation, use, recycling, and waste management.

Light pipes

Pipes lined with highly reflective film used to reflect light from a roof aperture to a space that may not be directly beneath the roof and which cannot therefore accommodate a standard skylight. They are best suited for small spaces like bathrooms or hallways.

Light shelves

A daylighting system that uses sun path geometry to bounce light off a ceiling, to project light deeper into a space, distribute light from above, and diffuse it to produce a uniform light level below.

Low-emissivity (low-E) coatings

Coatings applied to glass that allow the transmission of short-wave energy (visible light) but have a low emissivity to long-wave infrared radiation (heat). The result is a reduction in the facility's net heating and cooling requirements. The lower the emissivity, the lower the resultant U-value of the window.

Metal oxide semiconductor (MOS)

A technology used for carbon monoxide detectors. Potential drawbacks include cross-sensitivity and resulting false alarms, and inability to read below 100 PPM.

Mold

Small organisms found almost everywhere, including on plants, foods, and leaves. Mold is the most common medium for growth and development of airborne bacteria. *(See also "stachybotrys.")*

Native landscape

Landscape that is adapted to thrive in the local environment, where it needs no irrigation or fertilizer, is ecologically diverse enough to resist pests, and provides free stormwater management. *(See also "xeriscaping.")*

Net metering

Allowing electric meters of generating facilities to turn backwards when the generators produce more energy than customers demand. Net metering allows customers to use the energy their own system generates (e.g., solar) to offset their consumption over an entire billing period, not just at the time the electricity is produced.

Net savings (NS)

A measure of long-run profitability of an alternative relative to a base case. The NS can be calculated as an extension of the life-cycle costing (LCC) method as the difference between the LCC of a base case and the LCC of an alternative.

Non-potable substitution system
A system that uses by-product water to replace potable water for systems that do not require fresh water.

Passive solar heating
Design strategies that contribute to the requirements of the heating load without requiring an energy input to operate (no pumps or fans). Architectural elements, such as windows, insulation, and mass, operate as a system without the need for power input to mechanical equipment. Passive solar designs are categorized as direct gain, sunspaces, or Trombe walls.

Payback period (PB)
Measures the length of time until accumulated savings are sufficient to pay back the initial cost. Discounted payback (DPB) takes into account the time value of money by using time-adjusted cash flows. If the discount rate is assumed to be zero, the method is called simple payback (SPB).

Performance-based fee
A fee structure that rewards the consultant's effort of minimizing the project's life-cycle cost. The designer's fee is based on a measurement such as energy use or operating cost of the completed design.

Photovoltaics (PV)
Devices that convert sunlight directly into electricity. PVs generate power without noise, pollution, or fuel consumption, and are useful where utility power is not available, reliable, or convenient.

Plastic curtains
Curtains or strip doors that reduce infiltration and ex-filtration within a building consisting of several strips of heavy plastic (can be clear) that form a fairly tight seal yet allow easy passage through them. They are an economical solution for protecting employees and goods from adverse environmental conditions.

Polymer, perfluorooctane suphonate (PFOS)
A potentially toxic organic compound used to treat carpeting, leather, paper, and other materials.

Pressure reset system
A control system for boilers and furnaces that allows wide fluctuations in pressure. As a result, the burners can be shut off longer and stay on longer, with fewer cycles. Avoiding short cycles increases the net system efficiency.

Radiation
The transfer of heat from a warmer body to a cooler one. One way to stop radiation heat transfer is by using reflective surfaces, such as a reflective roof.

Rammed earth
Earth formed into thick, durable monolithic walls. Used in hot, dry climates along the same principles as adobe. Can be used in other climates, but may require supplemental insulation or additional heating or cooling.

Recycling
Reusing, reprocessing, or refabricating products after their initial use. Recycled products include soda cans, bottles, asphalt paving, masonry, metal framing, insulation, toilet compartments, and carpet.

Recycled content
Products fabricated with post-consumer materials or post-industrial by-products, such as steel, plastic lumber, and carpet cushion.

Reset controls
Controls for hot water systems that inversely monitor the hot water loop set point as compared to the outdoor temperature. For example, the system may be set for 180° F when the outdoor temperature is 0° F, and, inversely, the loop temperature could be 120° F when the outdoor air temp is 45° F.

Roof washer
A system for diverting the first rainfall, which contains impurities washed from the roof, so that only cleaner water that follows can be collected.

R-value
The measurement of the insulation effectiveness of the window (R = 1/U). The higher the R-value, the better the insulating performance.

Savings-to-investment ratio (SIR)
A dimensionless measure of performance that expresses the ratio of savings to costs, recommended for setting priority among projects when the budget is insufficient to fund all cost-effective projects. The numerator of the ratio contains the operation-related savings; the denominator contains the increase in investment-related costs.

Seasonal energy efficiency ratio (SEER)
A measure of energy efficiency that represents the total cooling of a central air-conditioner or heat pump in BTUs during the normal cooling season, as compared to the total electric energy input (in watt-hours) consumed during the same period.

Selective glazing
Glazing that screens out the infrared and ultraviolet portions of the solar spectrum, but allows visible light to pass. Selective glazing is recommended if a clear appearance is desired, or if a high visible transmittance is required to meet daylighting goals.

Selective surface

A blackened metal foil that has a high absorbtivity in the short wavelength solar spectrum, but a low emissivity in the long wavelength infrared spectrum, thus reducing radiant heat loss off the surface. Used in Trombe walls for passive solar heating or in solar collectors to heat water.

Sick building syndrome (SBS)

Health problems experienced by building occupants that can be attributed to building problems, such as poor air quality caused by off-gassing of volatile organic compounds (VOCs) from modern finish materials, poorly vented combustion appliances, equipment and chemicals, or molds and microbial organisms.

Solar collectors, high-temperature

Large solar collector systems that surround an absorber tube with an evacuated borosilicate glass tube to minimize heat loss, and often utilize mirrors to concentrate sunlight on the tube. High-temperature systems are required for absorption cooling or electricity generation, but are used for mid-temperature applications such as commercial or institutional water heating as well.

Solar collectors, low-temperature

Unglazed and uninsulated solar thermal collectors that operate at up to 18° F (10° C) above ambient temperature, and are most often used to heat swimming pools.

Solar collectors, mid-temperature

Flat plate solar thermal collectors with cover glass and insulation that produce water 18-129 F° (10-50 C°) above the outside temperature, and are most often used for heating domestic hot water.

Solar heat gain coefficient (SHGC)

The percentage of solar energy either directly transmitted or absorbed and re-radiated into the building, ranging from 0.0-1.0 (the lower the number, the lower the solar heat gain). SHGC has replaced the older term *shading coefficient* (SC); SHGC=0.87*SC.

Solar heating

Methods of heating using the sun, which include passive solar (direct, indirect, and isolated gain), solar water heating, and solar ventilation air preheating.

SPARK

Simulation Problem Analysis Research Kernel, a sophisticated software program that can model complex building envelopes and mechanical systems, running up to 10-20 times faster than other simulation programs.

Stachybotrys

A greenish-black mold found on cellulose products (such as wood or paper) that have remained wet for several days or longer. Stachybotrys does not grow on concrete, linoleum, or tile.

Stack effect

Warmer air rising, causing high pressure at the top of a building and low pressure at the bottom. At points of greater pressure differential, such as the attic and basement, it is especially crucial to seal air leaks and use airflow retarders.

Statement of work

A written statement describing the procurement of architectural and engineering services, including preliminary or schematic design, design development, and construction document preparation.

Sun-tempered buildings

Buildings designed using standard construction methods but deliberately oriented on the site and featuring carefully designed windows to reduce the heating load significantly.

Sustainable design

Design that considers environmental and human health and well-being and resource efficiency, in addition to the traditional criteria of function, cost, and aesthetics.

Sustainability

Refers to renewable products whose selection takes into consideration the use of available resources. Sustainability considers the whole instead of specifics, emphasizing relationships rather than pieces in isolation. Use of wood from well-managed forests for building framing is an example of renewable and sustainable product selection.

Temperature differential

The difference in temperature between two spaces within the building, or between the indoor and outdoor temperature. Temperature differential causes natural convection currents and air to migrate through cracks and open doors, windows, or other means of egress.

Thermal chimney

A chimney using solar energy to heat air, which rises and is exhausted out of the top, causing a natural convection loop as cooler air is drawn into the building (sometimes through a cool underground duct) to replace the exhausted hot air.

Thermal mass cooling

In a climate with a wide diurnal temperature swing, thermal mass cooling works by running cool nighttime air across a large indoor building mass, such as a slab. The cool thermal mass then absorbs heat during the day.

Third-party commissioning

Independent assessment of systems to

ensure that their installation and operation meets design specifications and are as efficient as possible. When the building is completed, third-party building commissioning can save as much as 40% of a building's utility bills for heating, cooling, and ventilation. *(See also "commissioning.")*

Transpired solar collector
A low-cost, high-performing solar collector made of a painted metal plate perforated with small holes. Outdoor air for ventilation is heated as is it drawn in through the perforated collector.

Urban heat islands
Asphalt-laden cities, which are several degrees hotter than surrounding areas.

Urea-formaldehyde foam insulation (UFFI)
Insulation used in wall cavities as an energy conservation measure during the 1970s that was found to have relatively high indoor concentrations of formaldehyde.

U-value
The measurement of heat loss or gain due to the differences between indoor and outdoor air temperatures (BTUs/hr/S.F.). $U = 1/R$. The lower the U-value, the better the insulating performance.

Vapor barriers
Material used to prevent the passage of vapor or moisture into a structure or another material, thus preventing condensation and reducing latent loads on air conditioning systems. Polyethylene, the foil facing on insulation, and asphalt-impregnated building paper can serve as vapor barriers.

Ventilation
The movement of air in and out of a building, accomplished by mechanical ventilation or infiltration. Under current standards (usually ASHRAE guidelines), ventilation requirements for the building depend on usage, type, and or the projected occupancy for the space.

Vestibule
A passageway or anteroom serving as an air lock at a building's entrance. Vestibules minimize the infiltration and ex-filtration of exterior conditions into the space within the building envelope.

Volatile organic compounds (VOCs)
Organic chemicals used in products that are harmful when released (off-gassed) during use. Most paints, coatings, and adhesives for finishes such as flooring and wall coverings off-gas VOCs that can cause headaches, nausea, and throat and eye irritation. Low- or zero-VOC products are readily available today.

Wind electric system
A single turbine, smaller than the utility-scale models, but much more efficient than the old-fashioned windmill, producing clean, affordable electricity for a rural home, farm, or business.

Window tinting
Film applied to windows to reduce the amount of solar heat transmission through the glass by increasing the solar reflection (not necessarily visible reflection) and solar absorption of the glass.

Xeriscaping
Using native, drought-tolerant, or well-adapted plant species in dry climates to avoid the need for irrigation.

Appendix: Solar Resources

Andy Walker, Ph.D, PE

Solar Radiation

It is useful to first consider sunlight in space before the atmosphere affects it. In space, the sun shines with an intensity that averages 1,366 W/m² over the year—up to 3.3 % higher in winter and up to 3.3% lower in summer. This fluctuation is due to the fact that the path of the earth around the sun is not exactly circular, and the earth is closer to the sun in winter. Solar flares, sunspots, and other phenomena also cause measurable fluctuations.

About 6% of sunlight is ultraviolet light, while 48% is visible light, and 46% is infrared light. Figure 1 shows a standard spectral distribution of sunlight in space and on earth. It is no coincidence that the solar spectrum peaks in the visible light range (0.38 to 0.70 micrometers wavelength). This is because our eyes evolved in sunlight. Artificial light can only approximate this spectrum; and it does so often quite poorly. For typical atmospheric conditions, the direct (shadow-casting) solar radiation perpendicular to a surface on earth is 779 W/m². This value is enhanced by diffuse solar radiation reflected from clouds, dust, or other objects. Values that exceed 1,000 W/m² are often measured on Earth, especially under bright conditions and when sunlight is reflected from snow cover on the ground.

The Effect of Latitude

The axis around which the earth rotates every day is tilted at an angle of 23.45° relative to the axis around which the earth revolves around the sun every year. In summer, the northern hemisphere is tilted toward the sun. By winter, the earth has revolved around to the other side of the sun, and the northern hemisphere is tilted away from the sun.

The angle at which the earth's axis is tilted is known as the declination. The declination (d) varies *sinusoidally* from a minimum of -23.45° on the winter solstice (December 22) to a maximum of 23.45° on the summer solstice (June 21). The declination is zero on the spring equinox (March 21) and the fall equinox (September 23). For areas between the Tropic of Capricorn (23.45° South) and the Tropic of Cancer (23.45° North) the sun is directly overhead at noon at least one day a year. At latitudes north of the Tropics, the sun is lower in the sky. North of the Arctic Circle, the sun does not shine for at least one day a year in winter and shines (albeit in a low position in the sky) for 24 hours for at least one day in summer.

The hour angle (h) is the angle at which the earth has rotated around its own axis, measured from the noon hour at the rate of 15° per hour (corresponding to 24 hours/day). At 10 a.m., the hour angle would be h = –30; at 11 a.m. h = –15; at 12 noon h = 0; at 1 p.m. h = 15; and at 2 p.m. h = 30. The angle measured from the horizon up to the sun is called the *altitude angle* (a) and may be calculated from:

$$\text{Sin } a = \cos (L) \times \cos (d) \times \cos (h) + \sin (L) \times \sin (d)$$

The angle measured on the horizontal from a line due south to the azimuth of the sun, the azimuth angle (z) may be calculated from:

$$\text{Sin } z = \sin (h) \times \cos (d)/\cos (a)$$

These two angles, as illustrated in Figure 2, allow us to predict precisely the location of the sun in the sky as a function of local latitude, time of day, and day of year. These simplified equations are not valid early in the morning or late evening in summer months, when the sun is north of due east and also due west.

Since the sun is higher in the sky in summer and lower in winter, it is possible to describe an overhang length that provides shade in summer but allows solar heating in winter. An overhang which provides

Figure 1

The solar spectrum in space and after the effects of the atmosphere. Sunlight is absorbed by ozone, carbon dioxide, and water vapor and scattered by dust and clouds in the atmosphere.

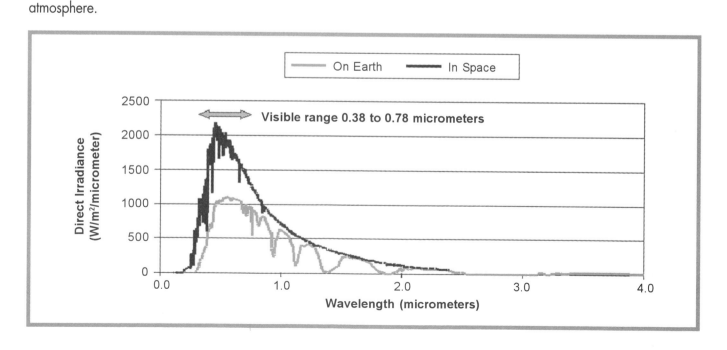

complete sun at noon on the winter solstice is determined by the conditions h = 0 and d = -23.45°. An overhang dimension which provides complete shade at noon on the summer solstice is defined by the conditions h = 0 and d = 23.45°. This shading geometry, illustrated in Figure 3, is very useful in window design, but is seldom optimal because of spring heating and fall cooling requirements in buildings.

Orientation of Solar Collectors

Solar collectors are positioned to correspond to the position of the sun in the sky. In order to maximize winter gains, the collector should be tilted up from the horizontal at a tilt angle equal to latitude +15°. To maximize summer gains, it should be tilted at latitude -15°. A tilt angle equal to the local latitude maximizes year-round average solar gain. South-facing vertical surface is an acceptable orientation if solar gain is needed only in the winter at high latitudes and is often used in solar ventilation air preheating systems. Racks of solar collectors must be spaced apart to avoid shading. This requires more roof or land area. One supplier of photovoltaic systems prefers to mount the collectors flat on the horizontal roof, requiring more collectors for a given amount of power, but avoiding the need for rack hardware and avoiding shading considerations. Such a flat, horizontal mount has good summertime performance, since the sun is almost directly overhead in summer.

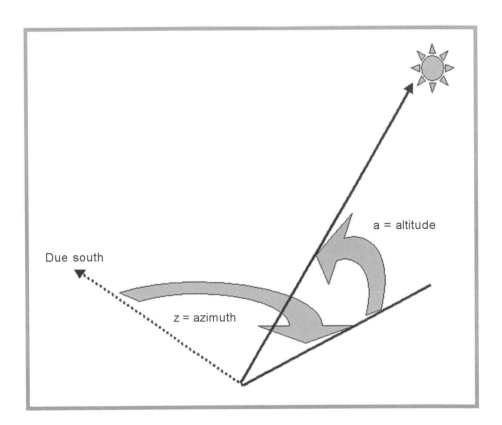

Figure 2

The altitude angle of the sun above the horizon and the azimuth angle, measured from due south, precisely locate the sun in the sky.

Moving racks are available to track the azimuth of the sun from east to west as it moves across the sky, or to track the altitude of the sun as it rises and sets. This is an example of "one-axis" tracking. "Two-axis" tracking would track both the azimuth and the altitude to keep the solar collectors facing directly toward the sun at all times. One-axis tracking is common for photovoltaics systems, and has maximum benefit during summer and at low latitudes. About 40% more energy can be collected by tracking the sun in the summer. Two-axis tracking would be required for focusing collectors that need to directly face the sun for proper alignment of the optics. Tracking is rare for solar thermal collectors, since plumbing connections are not as flexible as electrical connections.

Photovoltaic Devices and Systems

Photovoltaics are made from semi-conductor materials such as silicon. Each silicon atom has four electrons bound to it in a valence band. The atoms of a silicon crystal arrange themselves in a tetrahedron (three-sided pyramid) structure such that one silicon atom shares its four valence electrons with the four surrounding silicon atoms. When the photovoltaic material is exposed to light of sufficiently short wavelength, the light energy is absorbed and raises an electron from the valence band to a conduction band. Ordinarily, this electron would just fall back down to the valence band and release the captured energy as heat. However, in a photovoltaic device, an electric field is established

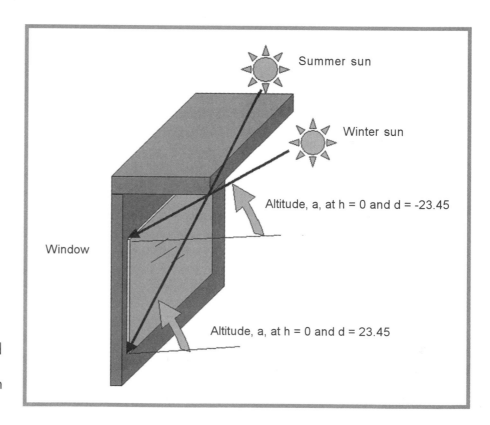

Figure 3
Window overhang dimensions to provide complete shade at noon on the summer solstice (d = 23.45°) and complete sun on the winter solstice (d = -23.45°) can be calculated from the altitude angle.

to send this free electron through an external circuit where it can do useful work. The electric field is set up by replacing some of the silicon atoms with phosphorus (which has an extra electron) on one side of a silicon wafer, and some with boron (which has one less electron) on the other side of the wafer. The junction between these n-type (negative) and p-type (positive) semiconductors is called the p-n junction. No material is consumed in the process of generating electricity, and it continues indefinitely, as long as the junction is exposed to light.

Cells are manufactured by first growing a single crystal from a vat of molten silicon, slicing it into thin wafers, and diffusing boron into one side and phosphorus into the other. The integrity of the crystalline structure is key to the high efficiency (10-13%) of these devices, called *single crystal cells*. In 1998, 30,758 kW of single crystal cells were sold for $108 million, an average of $3.51/Watt.

Variations on this process include pouring the molten silicon into an ingot and cooling it at a rate that maximizes the size of the crystals. Cells manufactured in this way are called poly-crystalline or *multi-crystalline cells*. The grain boundaries visible in these cells cause a resistance to electron migration; thus they have an efficiency slightly lower than that of single crystal cells, at 10-12%. In 1997, 16,428 kW of multicrystalline cells sold for $56 million, an average of $3.40/Watt.

Thin film, or *amorphous PV* cells don't grow crystals at all, but rather, deposit a thin film of the material onto a glass or stainless steel substrate. Without the crystalline structure, amorphous cells are less efficient than crystalline cells—with efficiencies of 4-8%. In 1997, 2,000 kW of amorphous PV cells sold for $11 million; an average of

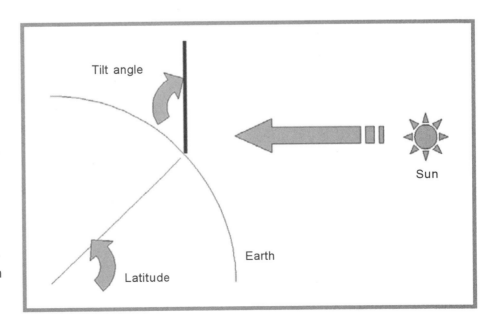

Figure 4
On an annual average, a tilt up from the horizontal equal to the local latitude maximizes solar gains.

5.83/Watt. The ability to remove the growing and slicing of crystals from the manufacturing process, as well as using less material in the cell fabrication, promises to lower the cost of thin film PV technologies. Thin film PV can also be made flexible, making it a popular application on curved surfaces like sailboat roofs.

PV manufacturing is a rapidly evolving science. Many research efforts are under way with advanced materials and manufacturing techniques, including multi-layer cells with different materials able to utilize different parts of the solar spectrum. The results of this research will be PV that costs less and works better, making this new technology even more competitive in the energy marketplace.

Power is lost as it passes through each component in a system. For example, perhaps 20% may be lost in the round-trip efficiency of the batteries, and another 10% lost as the DC (direct current) power is converted to AC (alternating current) power in the inverter. While the PV module may be 10% efficient at converting sunlight to electric power, the whole system may be only 5 or 6% efficient after considering these losses.

A simple *Direct Drive PV System* connects the PV array directly to a DC load without the use of batteries or an inverter. Controls are often used to match the characteristics of the load to the output of the PV array, and to turn the load off when solar power is insufficient. Direct drive systems are used for water pumping, since it is easier and less expensive to store water than it is to store electric charge in a battery.

For applications that require DC electricity on demand (such as at night), a *DC PV System with Battery Storage* can be utilized. This type of system is widely used for lighting, but is also common for emergency

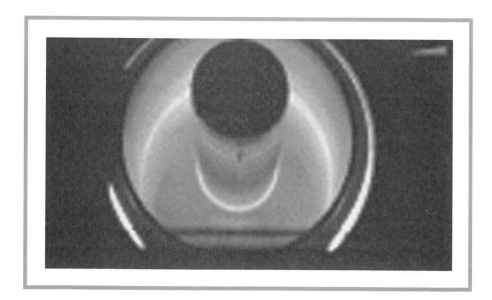

Figure 5
Growing a single crystal of silicon.
(Photo courtesy of NREL.)

call boxes, communications, and other small loads that do not require higher-voltage AC power.

Several battery types are available, each with their own cost, performance, and maintenance issues. The *deep cycle* batteries used in PV systems are physically different from batteries designed to cycle quickly, such as those used in automobiles.

The configuration of the battery bank is an important design task. Each cell of a lead-acid battery is about 2 volts, and cells are wired in series to provide the system designed voltage. It is preferable to connect larger cells in series than it is to add another series string in parallel. This is because if a cell begins to fail, the current will go through the parallel string and the weak cell will get weaker. There is a trade-off to consider in that if a battery in the series string fails, the battery bank as a whole may fail unless there are other strings in parallel to provide service. Two or three parallel strings are recommended for reliability.

If a site is served by an electric utility, batteries (and associated controls) are not required, since the utility can provide power when solar energy were not available. Solar energy systems can even be designed to feed power back into the grid when it exceeds the load on site. The economics of utility-connected or *grid-connected PV systems* depend on the cost of power at a site and what the utility will credit a PV system owner for power supplied to the grid. These factors are heavily influenced by the policy of the utility board and of the regulators who implement state law and federal policy. Utility policies regarding customer-owned PV that are connected to the grid vary from the encouraging to the downright punitive. Your utility is the best source of information (consider contacting them directly), and many utilities have PV connection policies posted on their Web sites with other tariffs.

Figure 6
Direct drive PV System. (Graphic by Jim Leyshon.)

Standardization in both the business practices and in the electrical engineering of utility connections will do much to promote solar power by streamlining transactions and improving safety and reliability.

Power produced by PV modules is DC, and use of common 120 V AC appliances requires a piece of power conditioning equipment called an "inverter." Inverters vary in cost and performance. True sine wave inverters are perhaps the most expensive, but deliver high-quality power. "Modified" sine wave inverters have other waveforms (step-shaped), which may cause problems in the operation of sensitive electronic equipment. Inverters are sophisticated solid state devices which can serve several useful control and safety functions as well. For example, standards UL1741 and IEEE 1929 require inverters to automatically disconnect from the utility system if the utility power is interrupted—to protect utility workers who may be working on the disconnected line.

It is rarely cost effective to meet 100% of a load using solar energy, since a battery and PV array would have to be very large to provide power during extended cloudy periods. The life-cycle cost economics are usually optimized by including a generator (fueled by propane or diesel fuel), to provide power under worst-case solar conditions.

Simple hand calculations can help inform an early evaluation of photovoltaics.

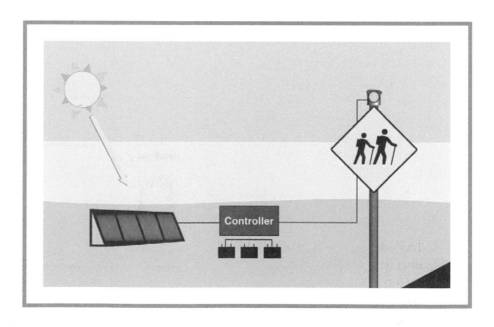

Figure 7
DC PV system with battery storage and charge controller. (Graphic by Jim Leyshon.)

As an example, let's consider photovoltaics to displace use of a propane-fueled generator in Bettles, Alaska. First estimate the daily electric load:

Lights	120 Watts × 4 hours/day =	480 Wh/day
Television	250 Watts × 2 hours/day =	500 Wh/day
Clock	20 Watts × 24 hours/day =	480 Wh/day

Total Daily Load = 1.460 kWh/day

Dividing by 0.8 for an 80% battery round trip efficiency, and dividing by 0.9 for a 90% inverter efficiency produces a total load of 2,028 kWh which must be provided by the PV. For Bettles, from the NREL Solar Data Summary, with 2 Axis Tracking, the maximum and average daily solar radiation are: I max = 9.5, I ave = 4.8, and I min = 0.1 (kWh/m²/day = sunhours/day)

I min is low because there is no winter sun near the arctic circle. As a result, we need a hybrid PV system used in conjunction with a propane generator. One common sizing strategy is to size the PV system to meet the load on the sunniest day of the year and use some generator power on days with less sun. This ensures that the PV capacity is fully utilized (another strategy would be to size the PV to meet the load on the cloudiest day of the year, and this would be required if no generator, utility, or other source of power were available). To find the rated power of the PV system, after losses in the battery and inverter, we divide the load by the maximum daily solar radiation:

$P_{rated} = L / I_{max}$ = 2.028 kWh/day / 9.5 sunhours/day = 213 Watts.

The annual fuel savings due to use of the PV would be the rated PV capacity times the annual average solar resource divided by generator efficiency: $E_s = P_{rated} I_{ave} 365 / \eta_{generator}$ = 213 Watts × 4.8 sunhours/day × 365 days/year/6 kWh/gallon of propane = 62 gallons propane/year.

Hourly computer simulation programs available to model PV system performance include TRNSYS, WATSUN-PV, and Energy-10. For building-integrated applications, Energy-10 is unique in its capability to

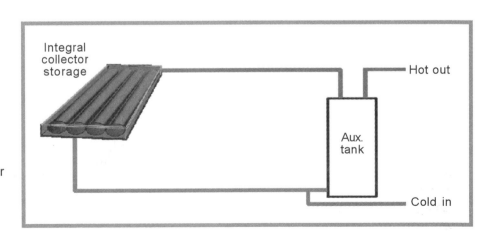

Figure 8
Integrated collector storage (ICS) solar water heating system preheats water for auxiliary (backup) heater. (Graphic by Jim Leyshon.)

model both the building electrical requirements and the concurrent output of the PV system, both as a function of weather and other factors, such as building occupancy schedules. FRESA and RETScreen are two programs useful for conducting cursory screening analysis early in project development.

Solar Water Heating System Configurations

In addition to solar collectors, all solar hot water systems have thermal storage, system controls, and a conventional backup system. Storage is required to couple the timing of the intermittent solar resource with the timing of the hot water load. As a rule of thumb, one to two gallons of storage water per square foot of collector area is adequate. Storage can either be potable water or non-potable water if a load side heat exchanger is used. For small systems, storage is most often in the form of glass-lined steel tanks. Active systems have a "delta T" (temperature difference) controller to start and stop the pumps. If the temperature in the solar collector outlet exceeds the temperature in the bottom of the storage tank by a set amount (say 6° C), the controller will start the pumps. When this temperature difference falls below another set value (say 2° C), the controller will stop the pumps. The controller will also have a high-limit function to turn off the pumps if the temperature in the storage tank exceeds a third setting, say, 90° C. It is not economical to design a solar water heating system to meet 100% of the load, so a backup, conventional heater is still needed to meet hot water demand on cloudy days or when the solar system is down for service.

This discussion describes only the basic configuration. It is important to acknowledge that other components like pressure relief valves, temperature-control valves, check valves, and shut-off valves are also required, not only for proper operation, but also for safety. Perhaps the most important of these is the tempering valve. The solar preheat high-limit temperature may be set high (perhaps 90° C) to store more heat in the preheat tank. To avoid scalding, this high temperature water must not be delivered to the taps. The tempering valves serve the function of mixing with cold water to achieve the desired delivery temperature. Bypass piping and valves allow the conventional system to provide hot water if the solar heating system is down for any reason.

Passive Systems include *Integral Collector Storage* (ICS) and *Thermosyphon* systems. ICS systems expose a volume of potable water to solar heat. While ICS manufacturers warranty their collectors against freezing, the pipes running to and from the ICS system on the roof would be at risk for freezing. Since it would be difficult to remove mineral scale built up in the tank, ICS systems offer minimal hard water tolerance. An advantage of ICS systems is that they have no moving parts and very low maintenance requirements. Because the cover glass has more heat loss than a well-insulated tank, ICS systems are used mainly for low temperature applications or to meet a lesser fraction of the load than systems with an insulated tank.

Thermosyphon systems mount a storage tank above the collector and rely on the buoyancy of the heated fluid to circulate heat between the collector and the storage tank. A backup electric heating element can also be placed in the tank above the collector, eliminating the backup heater altogether. One manufacturer fills the collector with a freeze-proof fluid, and transfers the heat to potable water by a heat exchanger in the tank. As with the ICS system, freeze protection is not provided for the water pipes that must attach to the tank on the roof. These systems have minimal hard water tolerance, but also low maintenance requirements because they have no moving parts.

Below are terms related to Active Solar Water Heating Systems:
- **Open Loop:** Potable water enters and leaves the system.
- **Closed Loop:** Fluid circulates but never leaves the system.
- **Direct:** Potable water is heated by the sun directly in the solar collector.
- **Indirect:** The solar collector heats a non-freezing fluid, and the heat is transferred to the potable water by a heat exchanger.

An active, open-loop system offers no freeze protection, minimal hard water tolerance, and consequently high maintenance requirements. This type of system is more efficient than other active types since it only uses one pump and there is no temperature drop across a heat exchanger.

A closed loop, indirect, active solar water heating system circulates a non-toxic, non-corrosive, non-freezing fluid such as propylene glycol between the solar collector and a heat exchanger which is located inside a heated space. This arrangement offers excellent freeze protection. Since the heat transfer surfaces in the collector are not exposed to

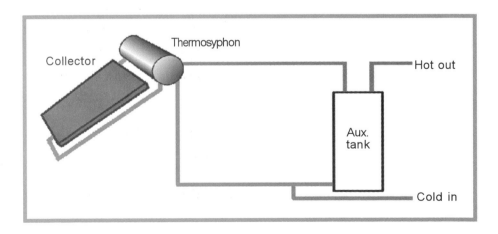

Figure 9

Thermosyphon solar water heating system. (Graphic by Jim Leyshon.)

potable water, and since those in the heat exchanger can be cleaned, this system also offers good tolerance to minerals in the water. There are, however, several moving parts and electronic controls that can fail, leading to higher maintenance requirements for this type of system.

Another way to avoid freezing in the collector would be to allow the water to drain out of the collector and back into a small drain-back tank whenever the system is not collecting solar heat. Also, in buildings where hot water might not be used for days or weeks at a time, draining the heat transfer fluid out of the collector avoids degradation of the fluid or other damage that may be caused by excessive temperature. Drain-back systems offer good freeze protection, good overheating protection, and good hard water tolerance. In this configuration, it is important to ensure that all pipes are installed with sufficient slope to cause the fluid to drain back. Failure of the fluid to drain back, and corrosion allowed by the air in the system lead to higher maintenance requirements for these types of systems.

Supplementary Information on Solar Ventilation Preheating

Solar ventilation preheating takes advantage of a concept common in fluid mechanics and heat transfer known as *boundary layer theory*. In airflow, heat transfer is dominated by convection and flow is dominated by momentum. However, in a very thin boundary next to a solid object (the *boundary layer*) heat transfer is dominated by conduction and flow is dominated by viscosity. As illustrated in Figure 13, the key to the perforated collector lies in the heated boundary layer being drawn in through small holes before it has a chance to mix with the outdoor air.

Figure 14 shows how the temperature of the ventilation air increases as it is drawn through the plate for various air flow rates and various levels of solar radiation. Typically, an increase of 30° F (15° C) in the temperature of the ventilation air can be expected on winter days.

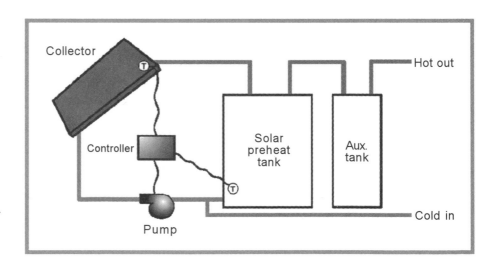

Figure 10
Active, direct, open loop solar water heating system. (Graphic by Jim Leyshon.)

A simple hand calculation can be used to inform early decisions about the use of solar ventilation preheating on a building. First calculate the area of wall required, $A_c = V_{bldg} / v_{wall}$, where: A_c = solar collector area (m²); V_{bldg} = building outside air flow rate (CFM or l/min), and v_{wall} = per-unit-area airflow through wall (CFM/ft² or l/min/m², typically 4 to 8CFM/ft²—if wall area is sufficient, use the lower value of 4 CFM/ft²).

Annual useful energy from the collector is given by q_{useful} (kWh/m²/year) read from the map of Figure 4.31 in Chapter 4.

Annual Heat Energy Savings is then $Q_{solar} = A_c \times q_{useful} \times$ (days per week/7). Heat recovery off the south wall is estimated by $Q_{htrec} = A_c U_{wall}$ HDD × number of hours/day/24 × days/week/7 and $Q_{saved} = (Q_{solar} + Q_{htrec})/n_{heating}$, where Q_{solar} = annual heat delivery of solar system (kWh/yr); Q_{htrec} = heat recovery off south wall (kWh/year); U_{wall} = heat loss coefficient of building wall (W/Cm²); HDD = heating degree days for the site (Cdays); and $n_{heating}$ is the building heating system efficiency.

Parasitic Fan Power is subtracted from these savings and is estimated by: $Q_{fan} = A_c q_{fan} \times$ hours/day × number of days/week × number of weeks/year, where: q_{fan} = fan energy required to pull air through collector (typically 1 W/ft²).

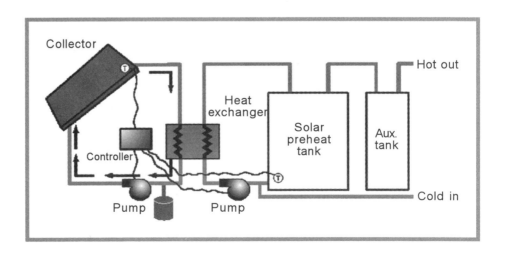

Figure 11
Active, closed loop, indirect solar water heating system. (Graphic by Jim Leyshon.)

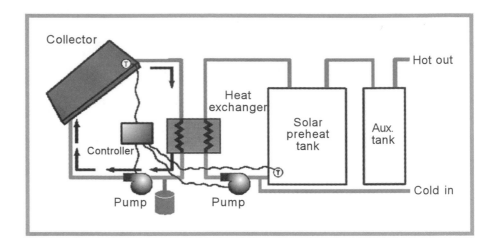

Figure 11

Active, closed loop, indirect solar water heating system. (Graphic by Jim Leyshon.)

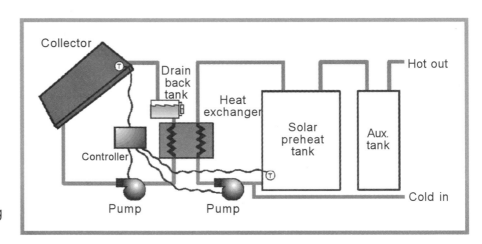

Figure 12

Drain-back active solar water heating system. (Graphic by Jim Leyshon.)

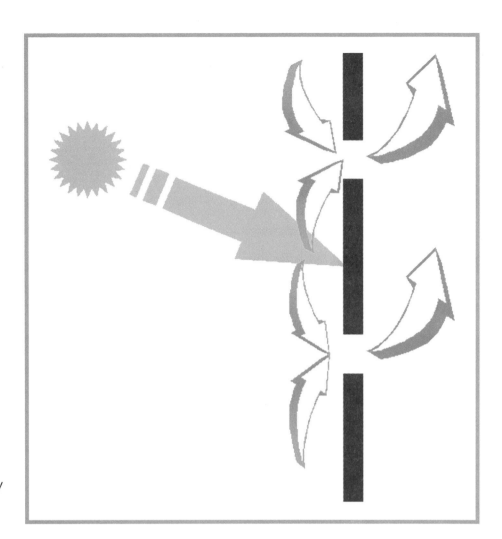

Figure 13
Heat loss off the front of the perforated plate solar collector is re-captured as the thermal boundary layer is drawn in through the holes. (Graphic by Jim Leyshon.)

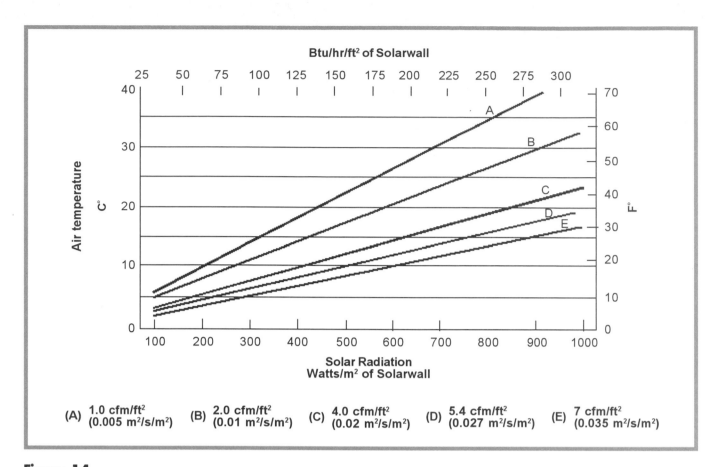

Figure 14
Air temperature increase as a function
of air flow rate and solar radiation.
(Courtesy of Craig Christensen,
NREL.)

Resources

The following resources can also be accessed directly through the book's dedicated Web site: **http://www.rsmeans.com/supplement/green.html**

Green Building/Sustainability

American Institute of Architects Committee on the Environment (AIA COTE)
1735 New York Avenue, N.W.
Washington, DC 20006-5292
202-626-7300
http://www.e-architect.com

Architects, Designers, & Planners for Social Responsibility
Northern California Chapter
P.O. Box 9126
Berkeley, CA 94709-0126
510-845-1000
http://www.adpsr-norcal.org

Argus Clearinghouse: Sustainable Development
http://www.clearinghouse.net/cgi-bin/
chadmin/viewcat/Environment/
sustainable_development?kywd++

Built Environment Center
http://sustainable.state.fl.us/fdi/edesign/
resource/index.html

Center for Maximum Potential Building Systems, Inc.
8604 FM 969
Austin, TX 78724
512-928-4786
http://www.cmpbs.org

Center for Neighborhood Technology
2125 W. North Avenue
Chicago, IL 60647
773-486-7600
http://www.cnt.org

Center for New Urbanism
5 Third Street
Suite 725
San Francisco, CA 94103
415-495-2255
http://www.cnu.org

Center for Resourceful Building Technology
P.O. Box 100
Missoula, MT 59806
406-549-7678
http://www.crbt.org

Center for Sustainable Systems
430 East University Avenue
Ann Arbor, MI 48109-1115
734-936-2637
http://css.snre.umich.edu

Center of Excellence for Sustainable
Development
U.S. Department of Energy
Part of the Energy Efficiency and
Renewable Energy Network
http://www.sustainable.doe.gov/
buildings/affhousing.shtml

Coop America - Green Pages Online
1612 K Street, N.W.
Suite 600
Washington, DC 20006
800-58-GREEN
http://www.coopamerica.org/gp

Development Center for Appropriate
Technology
P.O. Box 27513
Tucson, AZ 85726-7513
520-624-6628
http://www.dcat.net

Environmental Health Watch
4115 Bridge Avenue, #104
Cleveland, OH 44113
216-961-4646
http://www.ehw.org

Environmental Home Center
1724 Fourth Avenue South
Seattle, WA 98134
800-281-9785
http://www.built-e.com

Environmental Organization Web
Directory
http://www.webdirectory.com

Global Environmental Options (GEO)
http://www.geonetwork.org —
Homepage

http://www.greendesign.net —
Database of green building
information

http://www.green-power.com/links/
index.html — Information on green
power and electricity restructuring

http://www.greenliving.org — Tips for
greening homes and offices

Global Green USA Headquarters
227 Broadway Street
Suite 302
Santa Monica, CA 90401
310-394-7700
http://www.globalgreen.org

Green Building Council
1015 18th Street, N.W.
Suite 805
Washington, DC 20036
202-82-USGBC
http://www.usgbc.org

Green Building Program, National
Association of Home Builders
400 Prince George's Boulevard
Upper Marlboro, MD 20774
301-249-4000
http://www.nahbrc.org/green1.asp?
TrackID=&CategoryID=1599&Type=

Green Clips
Archives on the latest in sustainable
design for buildings, green
architecture, and related government
and business topics with summaries of
recent articles in the media.
http://www.greendesign.net/greenclips/
index.html

The Green Guide Institute
P.O. Box 567
Prince Street Station
New York, NY 10012
212-598-4910
http://www.thegreenguide.com

Green Meeting/Conference
A multimedia tool to assist planners
and service providers (e.g., hotels,
printers, and caterers) to recognize and
practice green opportunities.
http://www.epa.gov/opptintr/epp/
conference.htm

Green Roundtable
201 Winchester Street
Brookline, MA 02446
617-374-3740
http://www.greenroundtable.org

GreenSeal
1001 Connecticut Avenue, N.W.
Suite 827
Washington, DC 20036-5525
202-872-6400
http://www.greenseal.org

A Guide to Internet Resources in
Sustainable Development
http://www.caf.wvu.edu/gdsouzawww/
guide.html

Guide to Sustainable Design,
Development, & Policy Resources on
the Web
http://www.lib.virginia.edu/fine-arts/
sustain.html

New Green Products On-line
http://home.earthlink.net/~dlombard/
product.htm

Oikos Product Directory
(formerly REDI database of products/
materials)
Iris Communications, Inc.
P.O. Box 20
Lorane, OR 97451
541-767-0355
http://www.oikos.com

Smart Growth
Sustainable Communities Network
C/O CONCERN
1794 Columbia Road, N.W.
Washington, DC 20009
202-962-3582
http://www.smartgrowth.org

Solstice/Center for Renewable Energy
and Sustainable Technology
http://www.solstice.crest.org/
sustainable/index.shtml

Sustainable Building Industry Council
1331 H Street, N.W.
Suitc 1000
Washington, DC 20005
202-628-7400
http://www.sbicouncil.org/home/
index.html

Sustainable Building Sources
http://www.greenbuilder.com/general/
BuildingSources.html

Sustainable Development International
Henley Publishing Ltd
Trans-World House
100 City Road
Old Street
London
http://www.sustdev.org

Sustainable Product Purchasers Coalition
ZGF Partnership
320 S.W. Oak Street,
Suite 500
Portland, OR 97204
http://www.sppcoalition.org

Urban Ecology, Inc.
405 14th Street
Suite 900
Oakland, CA 94612
510-251-6330
http://www.urbanecology.org

U.S. National Park Service
1849 C Street, N.W.
Washington, DC 20240
202-208-6843
http://www.nps.gov/sustain

WorldBuild, Inc.
2269 Chestnut Street, #981
San Francisco, CA 94123
415-352-5200
http://www.worldbuild.com

Indoor Air Quality (IAQ)

Air Infiltration & Ventilation Centre
INIVE eeig
Boulevard Poincaré 79
B-1060 Brussels
Belgium
http://www.aivc.org

American Indoor Air Quality Council
P.O. Box 11599
Glendale, AZ 85318-1599
800-942-0832
http://www.iaqcouncil.org

American Society of Heating, Refrigerating, & Air-Conditioning Engineers (ASHRAE)
1791 Tullie Circle, N.E.
Atlanta, GA 30329
404-636-8400
http://www.ashrae.org

Association of Specialists in Cleaning & Restoration (ASCR)
8229 Cloverleaf Drive
Suite 460
Millersville, MD 21108
800-272-7012
http://www.ascr.org

Building Science Corporation
70 Main Street
Westford, MA 01886
978-589-5100
http://www.buildingscience.com

California Indoor Air Quality Program
2151 Berkeley Way
Berkeley, CA 94704
510-540-2476
http://www.cal-iaq.org

EPA Healthy Indoor Painting Practices
http://www.epa.gov/opptintr/exposure/
docs/publication.htm

EPA Indoor Air Quality
http://www.epa.gov/iaq

Healthy Homes Partnership USDA & HUD
http://www.uwex.edu/healthyhome

Healthy House Institute
430 N. Sewell Road
Bloomington, IN 47408
812-332-5073
http://www.hhinst.com/index.html

Healthy Indoor Air for America's Homes
Montana State University Extension Service
Taylor Hall
Bozeman, MT 59717
406-994-3451
http://www.montana.edu/wwwcxair

Indoor Environment Notebook
IAQ questions answered by Thad Godish,
Ph.D., Ball State University
http://web.bsu.edu/ien

Institute of Inspection Cleaning & Restoration
2715 E. Mill Plain Blvd.
Vancouver, WA 98661
360-693-5675
http://www.iicrc.org

International Society of Indoor Air Quality & Climate
c/o Finnish Society of Indoor Air
Quality and Climate
P.O. Box 25
FIN-02131, Finland
http://www.isiaq.org

MidAtlantic Environmental Hygiene Resource Center
Mold remediation and IAQ training
3624 Market Street
First Floor East
Philadelphia, PA 19104
215-387-4096
http://www.mehrc.org

National Institute of Building Sciences (NIBS)
1090 Vermont Avenue, N.W.
Washington, DC 20005
202-289-7800
http://www.nibs.org/projects.html

Soap & Detergent Association
1500 K Street, N.W.
Suite 300
Washington, DC 20005
202-347-2900
http://www.sdahq.org/health

World Health Organization - Air Quality Guidelines
Avenue Appia 20
1211 Geneva 27
Switzerland
http://www.who.int/peh/air/Airqualitygd.htm

Energy Efficiency & Renewable Energy

Alliance to Save Energy
1200 18th Street N.W.
Suite 900
Washington, DC 20036
202-857-0666
http://www.ase.org

American Council for an Energy-Efficient Economy (ACEEE)
1001 Connecticut Avenue, N.W.
Suite 801
Washington, DC 20036
202-429-8873
http://www.aceee.org/index.htm

American Refrigeration Institute (ARI)
4100 N. Fairfax Drive
Suite 200
Arlington, VA 22203
703-524-8800
http://www.ari.org

American Solar Energy Society, Inc. (ASES)
2400 Central Avenue
Suite G-1
Boulder, CO 80301
303-443-3130
http://www.ases.org/solar

American Wind Energy Association
122 C Street, N.W.
Suite 380
Washington, DC 20001
202-383-2500
http://www.awea.org

Building Environment & Thermal Envelope Council (BETEC)
National Institute of Building Sciences
1090 Vermont Avenue, N.W.
Suite 700
Washington, DC 20005-4905
202-289-7800
http://www.nibs.org/betechm.html

Center for Renewable Energy & Sustainable Technology
REPP-CREST
1612 K Street, N.W.
Suite 202
Washington, DC 20006
202-293-2898
http://solstice.crest.org/index.shtml

Center of Excellence for Sustainable Development
U.S. Department of Energy
Office of Energy Efficiency and Renewable Energy
Denver Regional Support Office
1617 Cole Boulevard
Golden, CO 80401
800-363-3732
http://www.sustainable.doe.gov

Department of Energy
1000 Independence Avenue, S.W.
Washington, DC 20585
1-800-dial-DOE
http://www.energy.gov/house/index.html

Efficient Windows Collaborative
Alliance to Save Energy
1200 18th Street, N.W.
Suite 900
Washington, DC 20036
202-530-2231
http://www.efficientwindows.org

Energy Central Electric Power Information Resource
303-782-5510
http://www.energycentral.com

Energy Efficiency & Renewable Energy Network (EREN)
Office of Building Technology
U.S. Department of Energy
1000 Independence Avenue, S.W.
Washington, DC 20585
202-586-9220
http://www.eren.doe.gov/buildings

Energy Efficient Building Association, Inc.
10740 Lyndale Avenue South
Suite 10W
Bloomington, MN 55420-5615
952-881-1098
http://www.eeba.org

The Energy Ideas Clearinghouse
WSU Energy Program
P.O. Box 43165
Olympia, WA 98504-3165
1-800-872-3568
http://www.energyideas.org

Energy Star
Hotline: 1-888-STAR-YES
http://www.energystar.gov

Illuminating Engineering Society of North America
120 Wall Street
Floor 17
New York, NY 10025-4001
212-248-5000
http://www.iesna.org

International Energy Agency, Energy Conservation in Buildings & Community Systems
Department of Energy
Building Systems & Materials Division
Mail Stop EE-421
1000 Independence Avenue, S.W.
Washington DC 20585
202-586-9445
http://www.ecbcs.org

National Database of State Incentives for Renewable Energy
Lists, by state, renewable energy incentives for homeowners and businesses.
http://www.dcs.ncsu.edu/solar/dsire/dsire.cfm

National Wind Technology Center
http://www.nrel.gov/wind

Northeast Sustainable Energy Association
50 Miles Street
Greenfield, MA 01301
413-774-6051
http://www.nesea.org

Online Fuel Cell Information Center
Fuel Cells 2000
1625 K Street, N.W.
Suite 725
Washington, DC 20006
202-785-4222
http://www.fuelcells.org

Portland Energy Conservation Incorporated
1400 S.W. 5th Avenue
Suite 700
Portland, OR 97201
503-248-4636
http://www.PECI.org

Pure Wind
Pacific Gas and Electric Company
Contributions Department
P.O. Box 770000, B32
San Francisco, CA 94177
415-973-7000
http://www.purewind.net

Renewable Energy Policy Project & Center for Renewable Energy & Sustainable Technology
1612 K Street, N.W.
Suite 202
Washington, DC 20006
http://www.crest.org

Southface Energy Institute
241 Pine Street
Atlanta, GA 30308
404-872-3549
http://www.southface.org

Building Rating Systems, Codes, Standards, & Guidelines

American Lung Association
Health House® Program
490 Concordia Avenue
St. Paul, MN 55103-2441
877-521-1791
http://www.healthhouse.org

American National Standards Institute (ANSI)
1819 L Street, N.W.
Washington, DC 20036
202-293-8020
http://www.ansi.org

American Society for Testing & Materials (ASTM)
100 Barr Harbor Drive
P.O. Box C700
West Conshohocken, PA 19428-2959
1-800-262-1373
http://www.astm.org

American Society of Heating, Refrigerating, & Air-Conditioning Engineers, Inc. (ASHRAE)
1791 Tullie Circle, N.E.
Atlanta, GA 30329
404-636-8400
http://www.ashrae.org

Building Codes Assistance Project
1612 K Street, N.W.
Suite 202
Washington, DC 20006
202-293-2898
http://solstice.crest.org/efficiency/bcap

Building Officials & Code Administrators International (BOCA)
4051 West Flossmoor Road
Country Club Hills, IL 60478
708-799-2300
http://www.bocai.org

Building Research Establishment Environmental Assessment Method (BREEAM)
ECD Energy and Environment Canada Ltd.
165 Kenilworth Avenue
Toronto, ON M4L 3S7
416-699-6671
http://www.breeamcanada.ca

Climate Cool
Climate Neutral Network
610 Middlecrest Road
Lake Oswego, OR 97034
503-697-2798
http://www.climateneutral.com

Construction Specifications Institute (CSI)
99 Canal Center Plaza
Suite 300
Alexandria, VA 22314
800-689-2900
http://www.csinet.org

EarthCraft
EarthCraft House
Greater Atlanta Home Builders Association
P.O. Box 450749
Atlanta, GA 31145
770-938-9900
http://www.southface.org/home/ech/echintro.htm

Energy Efficient Building Association
Criteria for Energy & Resource Efficient Buildings
10740 Lyndale Avenue South
Suite 10W
Bloomington, MN 55420-5615
952-881-1098
http://www.eeba.org/infocentral/criteria.htm

Energy Star
http://www.energystar.gov

Forest Stewardship Council
1155 30th Street, N.W.
Suite 300
Washington, DC 20007
202-342-0413
http://www.fscoax.org

Global Ecolabeling Network
http://www.gen.gr.jp

Green Building Guidelines
Sustainable Buildings Industry Council
1331 H Street, N.W.
Suite 1000
Washington, DC 20005
202-628-7400
http://www.sbicouncil.org

Green Seal
1001 Connecticut Avenue, N.W.
Suite 827
Washington, DC 20036-5525
202-872-6400
http://www.greenseal.org

GreenSpec
Building Green
122 Birge Street
Suite 30
Brattleboro, VT 05301
http://www.greenspec.com

High Performance Building Guidelines
New York City Department of Design
and Construction
30-30 Thomson Avenue
Long Island City, NY 11101
718-391-1000
http://www.ci.nyc.ny.us/html/ddc/
html/highperf.html

International Code Council (ICC)
5203 Leesburg Pike
Suite 600
Falls Church, VA 22041
703-931-4533
http://www.intlcode.org

International Conference of Building Officials (ICBO)
5360 Workman Mill Road
Whittier, CA 90601-2298
800-284-4406
http://www.icbo.org

International Organization for Standards (ISO)
1 rue de Varembe
Case postale 56
CH-1211 Geneva 20
Switzerland
http://www.iso.org

International Performance Measurement & Verification Protocol (IPMVP)
For commercial and industrial facility operators, offers standards for measurement and verification of energy and water efficiency projects.
http://www.ipmvp.org

National Conference of States on Building Codes & Standards, Inc.
505 Huntmar Park Drive
Suite 210
Herndon, VA 20170
http://www.ncsbcs.org

National Fire Protection Association International (NFPA)
1 Batterymarch Park
Quincy, MA 02269-9101
617-770-3000
http://www.nfpa.org

The Natural Step
116 New Montgomery Street
Suite 800
San Francisco, CA 94105
415-318-8170
http://www.naturalstep.org

Southern Building Code Congress International (SBCCI)
900 Montclair Road
Birmingham, AL 35213-1206
205-591-1853
http://www.sbcci.org

U.S. Green Building Council's Leadership in Energy & Environmental Design (LEED)
1015 18th Street, N.W.
Suite 805
Washington, DC 20036
202-82-USGBC
http://www.usgbc.org

Government Organizations
Energy Star
Hotline: 1-888-STAR-YES
http://www.energystar.gov

Fannie Mae
3900 Wisconsin Avenue, N.W.
Washington, DC 20016-2892
202-752-7000
http://www.fanniemae.com

Intergovernmental Panel on Climate Change
IPCC Secretariat
C/O World Meteorological Organization
7bis Avenue de la Paix
C.P. 2300, CH- 1211
Geneva 2, Switzerland
http://www.ipcc.ch

Natural Resources Canada
613-995-0947
http://www.nrcan.gc.ca

New York State Research & Development Authority (NYSERDA)
17 Columbia Circle
Albany, NY 12203-6399
1-866-697-3732
http://www.nyserda.org

Partnership for Advancing Technology in Housing (PATH)
451 7th Street, S.W.
Room 8134
Washington, DC 20410-0001
202-708-4277
http://www.pathnet.org

U.S. Department of Energy (DOE)
1000 Independence Avenue, S.W.
Washington, DC 20585
800-dial-DOE
http://www.energy.gov/
Also part of DOE:

Energy Efficiency & Renewable Energy Network
http://www.eren.doe.gov

Energy Information Administration
http://www.eia.doe.gov

Federal Energy Management Program
http://www.eren.doe.gov/femp

Office of Building Technology, State, & Community Programs
http://www.eren.doe.gov/buildings

Software & Case Studies
http://www.eren.doe.gov/buildings

U.S. Environmental Protection Agency (EPA)
The EPA has ten regions throughout the United States; consult the Web site for specific information. The contact information for the Mid-Atlantic region is:

U.S. EPA Region 3
1650 Arch Street (3CG00)
Philadelphia, PA 19103-2029
215-814-5000
http://www.epa.gov

U.S. Housing & Urban Development Department (HUD)
451 7th Street, S.W.
Washington, DC 20410
202-708-1112
http://www.hud.gov

U.S. Census Bureau
Washington, DC 20233
301-763-INFO
http://www.census.gov

Professional Associations

Affordable Comfort Incorporated
32 Church Street
Suite 204
Waynesburg, PA 15370
724-627-5200
http://www.affordablecomfort.org

Air Conditioning Contractors of America
2800 Shirlington Road
Suite 300
Arlington, VA 22206
703-575-4477
http://www.acca.org

Air Conditioning & Refrigeration Institute (ARI)
4100 N. Fairfax Drive
Suite 200
Arlington, VA 22203
703-524-8800
http://www.ari.org

Alternative Fluorocarbons Environmental Acceptability Study
AFEAS Program Office
RAND Environmental Science & Policy Center
1200 South Hayes Street
Arlington, VA 22202-5050
http://www.afeas.org

American Architectural Manufacturers Association
1827 Walden Office Square
Suite 104
Schaumburg, IL 60173-4268
847-303-5664
http://www.aamanet.org

American Council for an Energy-Efficient Economy
1001 Connecticut Avenue, N.W.
Suite 801
Washington, DC 20036
202-429-8873
http://www.aceee.org

American Gas Association
400 N. Capitol Street, N.W.
Washington, DC 20001
202-824-7000
http://www.aga.org

American Institute of Architects
1735 New York Avenue, N.W.
Washington, DC 20006
800-AIA-3837
http://www.aia.org

American Society of Heating, Refrigerating, & Air-Conditioning Engineers, Inc. (ASHRAE)
1791 Tullie Circle, N.E.
Atlanta, GA 30329
404-636-8400
http://www.ashrae.org

American Society of Mechanical Engineers
22 Law Drive
Fairfield, NJ 07007-2900
1-800-THE-ASME
http://www.asme.org

American Solar Energy Society
2400 Central Avenue
Suite G-1
Boulder, CO 80301
303-443-3130
http://www.ases.org

American Wind Energy Association
122 C Street, N.W.
Suite 380
Washington, DC 20001
202-383-2500
http://www.awea.org

The Association of Energy Engineers
4025 Pleasantdale Road
Suite 420
Atlanta, GA 30340
770-447-5083
http://www.aeecenter.org

Association of Higher Education
Facilities Officers (APPA)
1643 Prince Street
Alexandria, VA 22314
703-684-1446
http://www.appa.org

**Building Owners & Managers
Association (BOMA)**
1201 New York Avenue, N.W.
Suite 300
Washington, DC 20005
202-408-2662
http://www.boma.org

Edison Electric Institute
701 Pennsylvania Avenue, N.W.
Washington, DC 20004-2696
202-508-5000
http://www.eei.org

**Energy & Environmental Building
Association**
10740 Lyndale Avenue South
Suite 10W
Bloomington, MN 55420-5615
952-881-1098
http://www.eeba.org

**Gas Appliance Manufacturers
Association (GAMA)**
2107 Wilson Boulevard
Suite 600
Arlington, VA 22201
http://www.gamanet.org

**International Facility Management
Association (IFMA)**
1 E. Greenway Plaza
Suite 1100
Houston, TX 77046-0194
713-623-4362
http://www.ifma.org

Manufactured Housing Institute
2101 Wilson Boulevard
Suite 610
Arlington, VA 22201-3062
703-558-0400
http://www.mfghome.org

**National Association of Demolition
Contractors**
16 N. Franklin Street
Suite 203
Doylestown, PA 18901-3536
215-348-4949
http://www.demolitionassociation.com

**National Association of Energy
Service Companies**
1615 M Street, N.W.
Suite 800
Washington, DC 20036
202-822-0950
http://www.naesco.org

**National Association of Home
Builders (NAHB)**
1201 15th Street, N.W.
Washington, DC 20005
800-368-5242
http://www.nahb.com

**National Association of Housing &
Redevelopment Officials**
630 Eye Street, N.W.
Washington, DC 20001
877-866-2476
http://www.nahro.org

**National Association of State Energy
Officials (NASEO)**
1414 Prince Street
Suite 200
Alexandria, VA 22314
703-299-8800
http://www.naseo.org

**National Center for Appropriate
Technology (NCAT)**
P.O. Box 3838
Butte, MT 59702
406-494-4572
http://www.ncat.org

**Natural Resources Defense Council
(NRDC)**
40 West 20th Street
New York, NY 10011
212-727-2700
http://www.nrdc.org

Residential Energy Service Network
P.O. Box 4561
Oceanside, CA 92052-4561
760-806-3448
http://www.natresnet.org

Solar Energy Industries Association
1616 H. Street, N.W.
8th Floor
Washington, DC 20006
202-628-7745
http://www.seia.org

U.S. Green Building Council
1015 18th Street, N.W.
Suite 805
Washington, DC 20036
202-82-USGBC
http://www.usgbc.org

**Weatherization Assistance Program
Technical Assistance Center**
400 North Capitol Street, N.W.
Suite 395
Washington, DC 20001
202-624-5867
http://www.waptac.org

Other Organizations

**Economic Input-Output Life Cycle
Assessment**
Green Design Initiative, Carnegie
Mellon
http://www.eiolca.net

**Environmental Building Association of
N.Y. State, Inc.**
126 State Street, 3rd Floor
Albany, NY 12207-1637
518-432-6400 ext. 227
http://www.eba-nys.org

Habitat for Humanity International
Partner Service Center
Habitat for Humanity International
121 Habitat St.
Americus, GA 31709
229-924-6935
http://www.habitat.org

Research Organizations

Brookhaven National Laboratory
P.O. Box 5000
Building 725B
Upton, NY 11973-5000
http://www.bnl.gov

Building & Fire Research Laboratory
(National Institute of Standards and Technology)
100 Bureau Drive
Stop 8600
Gaithersburg, MD 20899-8600
301-975-5900
http://www.bfrl.nist.gov

Buildings Technology Center
(Oak Ridge National Laboratory)
P.O. Box 2008
One Bethel Valley Road
Oak Ridge, TN 37831
http://www.ornl.gov/btc

Electric Power Research Institute
3412 Hillview Avenue
Palo Alto, CA 94304
http://www.epri.com

Florida Solar Energy Center
1679 Clearlake Road
Cocoa, FL 32922
321-638-1000
http://www.fsec.ucf.edu

Lighting Research Center
Rensselaer Polytechnic Institute
21 Union Street
Troy, NY 12180
518-687-7100
http://www.lrc.rpi.edu

National Association of Home Builders Research Center
400 Prince George's Boulevard
Upper Marlboro, MD 20774
301-249-4000
http://www.nahbrc.org

National Renewable Energy Laboratory (NREL)
1617 Cole Boulevard
Golden, CO 80401-3393
303-275-3000
http://www.nrel.gov

Pacific Northwest National Laboratory Buildings Program
P.O. Box 999
Richland, WA 99352
1-888-375-PNNL (7665)
http://www.pnl.gov/buildings

Rocky Mountain Institute
1739 Snowmass Creek Road
Snowmass, CO 81654-9199
970-927-3851
http://www.rmi.org

U.S. EPA Environmentally Preferable Purchasing Program (EPP)
1200 Pennsylvania Avenue, N.W.
Mail Code 7409-M
Washington, DC 20460
http://www.epa.gov/opptintr/epp

U.S. EPA New Building Design Guidance & Target Finder
1-888-STAR-YES
http://www.energystar.gov

U.S. GSA Planet GSA
1800 F Street, N.W.
Washington, DC 20405
http://www.gsa.gov/planetgsa

Building-Related Software

Building Energy Software Tools
Over 160 energy-related software tools for buildings, with an emphasis on renewable energy and achieving energy efficiency and sustainability in buildings.
Office of Building Technology
U.S. Department of Energy
1000 Independence Avenue, S.W.
Washington, DC 20585
202-586-9220
http://www.eren.doe.gov/buildings/tools_directory

Building Life-Cycle Cost Program
BLCC5.1-02, 2002
National Institute of Standards and Technology
Gaithersburg, MD 20899
http://www.eren.doe.gov/femp

Building for Environmental & Economic Sustainability (BEES) System
Evaluates the relative environmental and economic impacts of building materials.
BEES2.0
National Institute of Standards and Technology
Gaithersburg, MD 20899
http://www.bfrl.nist.gov/oae/software/bees.html

Green Building Advisor
A software program directed at developing healthy indoor spaces, while reducing environmental impacts of building projects.
Renewable Energy Policy Project & Center for Renewable Energy and Sustainable Technology
1612 K Street, N.W.
Suite 202
Washington, DC 20006
http://solstice.crest.org/software-central/gba

State & Municipal Initiatives

Arizona

Scottsdale's Green Building Program — City of Scottsdale, Arizona
The program monitors and scores construction projects for 150 green measures.
Green Building Office
Community Design Studio
7506 E. Indian School Road
Scottsdale, AZ 85251
480-312-7990
http://www.ci.scottsdale.az.us/greenbuilding

California

Los Angeles Sustainable Building Initiative

All new city projects that are over 7,500 square feet must meet the U.S. Green Building Council's LEED rating system.
http://www.ci.la.ca.us/SAN/lasp/sbi-draft-nov2001.htm

Santa Monica Green Building Design & Construction Guidelines

Required and recommended guidelines for builders and developers for commercial and municipal developments and remodeling projects. The program's goal is to reduce life-cycle environmental impacts.
http://greenbuildings.santa-monica.org

Colorado

Built Green — Denver, Colorado

Funded by the State of Colorado, this program supports the Denver Metro Homebuilder Association's "Green Built" Program, providing substantial public relations, builder training, and a home rating system.
Home Builders Association of Metro Denver
1400 S. Emerson
Denver, CO 80210
303-778-1400
http://www.builtgreen.org

Green Points Building Program — City of Boulder

Promotes sustainable construction for projects not eligible for the Denver Metro Home Builder Association's "Built Green" program. This program is the only regulated (e.g., non-voluntary) green building program and has a component for remodeling (including small projects), as well as new construction.

Public Works and/or Planning Departments
P.O. Box 791
Boulder, CO 80306
303-441-3200
http://www.ci.boulder.co.us/buildingservices/codes/greenpoints/greenpoints.htm

Florida

Process Guidelines for High-Performance Buildings

An interactive database of guidelines for high-performance building design, construction, and operation — developed for the State of Florida, but usable by anyone.
http://sustainable.state.fl.us/fdi/edesign/resource/index.html

Georgia

Georgia Tech's Sustainable Facilities & Infrastructure Program

Contains selected publications, information about courses and training opportunities, databases, and links to the best green building sites.
http://maven.gtri.gatech.edu/sfi

Nebraska

State of Nebraska Executive Orders 98-1 (Renewables) and 98-6 (Efficiency)

(For State Agencies)
Encourages the use of renewable energy and greater energy efficiency, particularly for state facilities.
402-471-1999

New Mexico

EEBA Building America Partner Program

Home Builders Association of Central New Mexico
NASFA, the State of New Mexico, PNM, Fannie Mae, and Owens Corning are program partners in this first environmental building rating system in the state for energy-efficient residences.
P.O. Box 1881
Los Lunas, NM 87031
505-866-6479
http://www.bapartner.org

Ohio

Cleveland Green Building Coalition

A non-profit organization that supports green building projects in Cleveland and Northeast Ohio. Provides education, information, and consultation.
http://www.clevelandgbc.org

Oregon

Green Building Initiative — City of Portland, Oregon

Their "Integrated Building Design" provides actions and opportunities from pre-design through operations and maintenance. Their "Green Building Guidelines" provide specific opportunities in building design and construction practices.
The Jean Vollum Natural Capital Center
721 NW 9th Avenue
Room 350
Portland, OR 97209
503-823-7725
http://www.sustainableportland.org/FSgrated.html

Pennsylvania

Commonwealth of Pennsylvania/Build Green

The Governor's Green Government Council (GGGC)
Created in l998 to ensure state adoption of sustainable, environmentally friendly operation policies.
http://www.gggc.state.pa.us

Texas

Green Building Ordinance—Frisco, Texas

This program provides standards for energy efficiency, water conservation, indoor air quality, and recycling for residential buildings.
http://www.ci.frisco.tx.us/planning/greenbuilding_index.htm

Green Building Program – City of Austin

The City of Austin has promoted green building through a city resolution adopted in 1994. The program has a residential and a commercial component, which rates the following dwelling features for sustainability: water, energy, materials, and solid waste.
P.O. Box 1088
Austin, TX 78767
512-974-2000
http://www.ci.austin.tx.us/greenbuilder

Washington

Build a Better Kitsap

(For homes in Kitsap County, Washington)
A network of architects, builders, subcontractors, suppliers, and real estate agents working to provide cost-effective quality homes that help preserve the Northwest environment.

Home Builders Association of Kitsap County
5251 Auto Center Way
Bremerton, WA 98312
360-479-5778
http://www.kitsaphba.com/bbk.html

BUILT GREEN™

An environmental building program to help Puget Sound homebuyers find quality, affordable homes to protect their health and the environment. The program provides a rating system for remodeling and new home construction.
Master Builders Association of King and Snohomish Counties
2155 112th Avenue, N.E.
Bellevue, WA 98004
425-451-7920
http://www.builtgreen.net

Energy Program Building Standards

Washington State has progressive energy and ventilation construction standards, which include building codes that apply to all new and remodeled residential and commercial construction in the state, and voluntary construction standards for manufactured housing.
WSU Cooperative Extension Energy Program
925 Plum Street, S.E.
Building #4
P.O. Box 43165
Olympia, WA 98504-3165
http://www.energy.wsu.edu/buildings

Evergreen Building Guide — City of Issaquah, Washington

Guide outlines a four-star rating system for creating a regional definition for green homes and neighborhoods.
425-837-3400

Seattle Sustainable Building Action Plan & Built Smart

(For Multi-Family Projects in the City of Seattle)
The program operates a voluntary rating and green certification system for multi-family projects. One rebate example is that $0.55-0.65 per square foot is paid for meeting insulation requirements.
206-684-4286

Seattle Sustainable Building Policy

Established in 2000, the program rates city projects according to the U.S. Green Building Council's LEED™ system. Projects that are city-funded and over 5,000 square feet must meet the LEED Silver rating.
http://www.cityofseattle.net/sustainablebuilding/SBpolicy.htm

Publications: Magazines & Newsletters

The Air Conditioning, Heating & Refrigeration News

755 W. Big Beaver Rd., Suite 1000
Troy, MI 48084
1-800-837-8337
http://www.achrnews.com

Appliance Magazine

Dana Chase Publications, Inc.
1110 Jorie Boulevard, CS9019
Oak Brook, IL 60522-9019
http://www.appliance.com

Appliance Manufacturer Magazine

5900 Harper Road
Suite 105
Solon, OH 44139-1835
http://www.ammagazine.com

Architectural Record

http://www.archrecord.com

The Architectural Review

http://www.arplus.com
A European source and magazine on architecture, contains extensive information on designs.

Builder Magazine
One Thomas Circle, N.W.
Suite 600
Washington, DC 20005
202-452-0800
http://www.builderonline.com

Building Design & Construction
http://www.bdcmag.com

Building Operating Management
Trade Press Publishing Corporation
2100 W. Florist Avenue
Milwaukee, WI 53209
414-228-7701
http://www.facilitiesnet.com/bom

Buildings Magazine
Stamats Communications, Inc.
Stamats Buildings Group
615 5th Street, S.E.
P.O. Box 1888
Cedar Rapids, IA 52406-1888
http://www.buildings.com/
Buildingsmag/default.asp

Design Cost Data
http://www.dcd.com

Energy User News
Business News Publishing Company
755 W. Big Beaver Road
Suite 1000
Troy, MI 48084
847-291-5224
http://www.energyusernews.com

Engineered Systems
Business News Publishing Company
755 W. Big Beaver Road
Suite 1000
Troy, MI 48084
http://www.esmagazine.com

Environmental Building News
Building Green
122 Birge Street
Suite 30
Brattleboro, VT 05301
802-257-7300
http://www.BuildingGreen.com
A monthly newsletter with information
on environmental design and
construction.

Environmental Design & Construction
755 W. Big Beaver Road
Suite 1000
Troy, MI 48084
http://www.edcmag.com
A bi-monthly publication covering
environmentally sound building design
and construction.

Facilities Design & Management
http://www.fdm.com

Green @ Work
www.greenatworkmag.com
A monthly publication that covers
aspects of businesses, their leaders,and
products.

*Heating/Piping/Air Conditioning
(HPAC Engineering)*
1300 E. 9th Street
Cleveland, OH 44114
216-696-7000
http://www.hpac.com

Home Furnishings News
http://www.hfnmag.com

Home Energy Magazine
2124 Kittredge Street, #95
Berkeley, CA 94704
510-524-5405
http://www.homeenergy.org/tocs.html

Home Power Magazine
P.O. Box 520
Ashland, OR 97520
800-707-6585
http://www.homepower.com

Indoor Air Bulletin
Information Service, Inc.
P.O. Box 8446
Santa Cruz, CA 95061-8446
408-426-6522
This monthly publication focuses on
indoor air quality, and considers all
aspects of indoor environment
important to occupant health, comfort,
and productivity.

IS, Interiors & Sources Magazine
http://www.isdesignet.com
Deals extensively with interior design,
materials, and indoor air quality
issues.

The Journal of Light Construction
186 Allen Brook Lane
Williston, VT 05495
802-879-3335
http://www.jlconline.com

Natural Home
P.O. Box 553
Mount Morris, IL 61054-7470
800-340-5846
http://
www.naturalhomemagazine.com

New Urban News
P.O. Box 6515
Ithaca, NY 14850
607-275-3087
This bi-monthly newsletter provides
current information on traditional
neighborhood development and
planning projects around the country.

New Village
2000 Center Street
Suite 120
Berkeley, CA 94704
510-845-0685
http://www.newvillage.net
A semi-annual journal published by
the national organization Architects/
Designers/Planners for Social
Responsibility (ADPSR).

504

Remodeling Online
One Thomas Circle, N.W.
Suite 600
Washington, DC 20005
202-452-0800
http://www.remodeling.hw.net

Residential Architect
One Thomas Circle, N.W.
Suite 600
Washington, DC 20005
202-452-0800
http://ra.hw.net

Solar Today Magazine
American Solar Energy Society
2400 Central Avenue
Suite G-1
Boulder, CO 80301
303-443-3130
http://www.solartoday.org
A bi-monthly magazine covering innovative passive and active solar house designs, solar technologies, building performance, cost-effective designs, and case studies.

The Urban Ecologist
Urban Ecology
405 14th Street
Suite 900
Oakland, CA 94612
510-251-6330
http://www.urbanecology.org

Publications: Books

A Better Place to Live: New Designs for Tomorrow's Communities.
Michael Corbett. Published by Rodale Press, 1981. A guide to building and planning considerations for more sustainable development and living.

Architecture and the Environment: Bioclimatic Building Design. David Lloyd Jones. Published by The Overlook Press, 1998. Fifty examples of architecture throughout the world built according to bioclimatic—or "green"—guidelines. Past, present, and future examples are accompanied by charts of building energy features, energy performance, and environmental health features.

Biomimicry: Innovation Inspired by Nature. Janine M. Benyus. Published by Quill, an imprint of William Morrow & Company, 1997. Biomimicry shows how nature offers countless examples of how to design our products, our processes, and our lives. Benyus, a noted science writer, explains how this new science is transforming everything from harnessing energy to feeding the world. www.biomimicry.net

Building Air Quality, A Guide for Building Owners and Facility Managers. Published by EPA and NIOSH. http://www.cdc.gov/niosh/baqtoc.html

Building Economics: Theory and Practice. T.R. Ruegg and H.E. Marshall. Published by Van Nostrand Reinhold, New York, 1990.

Climatic Building Design: Energy-Efficient Building Principles and Practices. Donald Watson and Kenneth Labs. Published by McGraw-Hill Book Company, 1983. An introduction and reference guide to climatic design, the art and science of using the beneficial elements of nature to create environmentally-sensitive buildings. Sections include a background in the scientific principles underlying climatic design; a designer's guide and catalog of the practices of climatic design and construction; and ways of analyzing local climatic data.

Climatic Considerations in Building and Urban Design. Baruch Givoni. Published by Van Nostrand Reinhold, 1998. Written in clear and concise language, this book is the most comprehensive, up-to date reference available on building and urban climatology.

Commissioning to Meet Green Expectations. Available at www.PECI.org

Contractor's Guide to Value Engineering. Published by the U.S. Department of Defense, Army Materiel Command, 2001. http://www.iea.ria.army.mil/ve/html/Contractor'sGuide.htm

The Death and Life of Great American Cities. Jane Jacobs. Published by Random House, 1961. Offers valuable lessons not yet learned about building healthy, safe, and habitable cities.

Design with Nature. Ian L. McHarg. Published by John Wiley & Sons, 1992. Presents a thorough analysis of the relationship between the built environment and nature. This was one of the first books to bring forward planning concepts in environmental sensitivity, and has since served as the guide for a number of developments including Civano in Tucson, Arizona.

EBN Archives CD-ROM. Edited by Alex Wilson and Nadav Malin. This CD-ROM includes all back issues of *Environmental Building News*, with a cumulative index, a comprehensive green building products directory, and detailed bibliography of green building resources. http://www.buildinggreen.com

Ecological Design. Sim Van der Ryn and Stuart Cowan. Published by Island Press, 1995. This book discusses how the living world and humanity can be reunited by making ecology the basis for design. Ecological design, the marriage of nature and technology, can be applied at all levels of scale to create revolutionary forms of buildings, landscapes, cities, and technologies. Design principles are presented that can help build a more efficient, less toxic, healthier, and more sustainable world.

The Ecology of Building Materials. Bjorn Berge, translated by Filip Henley. Published by Architectural Press, 2001. An in-depth review of building materials' composition and properties from an ecological perspective. Includes recommendations of environmentally friendly construction methods, as well as materials and a wide offering of alternative, and often historic methods. Helpful illustrations, tables and charts.

Energy Price Indices and Discount Factors – April 2002, Annual Supplement to Handbook 135, NISTIR 85-3273-17. S.K. Fuller and A.S. Rushing. Published by the National Institute of Standards and Technology, 2002.

The Energy Source Directory. Published by Iris Communications. Provides access to over 500 products that help make homes energy-efficient. Information about air barriers, heat recovery ventilators, sealants, heating and cooling equipment, solar water heaters, and insulation materials, etc. The directory is indexed by manufacturer, product name, and product category.

Energy Wi$e Construction Funding for Green Buildings. Jan McAdams.

Environmental Design Charrette Workbook. Donald Watson. Published by the American Institute of Architects, 1996. Highlights design workshops dealing with energy efficiency, building technology, environmental approaches to landscaping, waste prevention and resource reclamation, and planning and cultural issues.

Environmental Remediation Estimating Methods. Richard R. Rast. Published by R.S. Means Co., Inc., 1997. Estimating guidance for over 50 types of remediation technologies—from air sparging and air stripping to drum removal, excavation and extraction, landfill disposal, piping, UST closure, transportation and more.

Environmental Resource Guide. The American Institute of Architects. Published by John Wiley & Sons, Inc., 1998. Provides a comprehensive guide to resources for environmental building, updated three times a year. Project reports present case studies that incorporate environmental concepts and technologies. Material reports detail the environmental aspects and life-cycle of building materials.

E SOURCE Atlas Series. Published by E SOURCE. http://www.shop.oikos.com/catalog

Facilities Maintenance & Repair Cost Data. Published by R.S. Means Co., Inc., 2002. Provides costs for all aspects of facilities maintenance, including maintenance and repair, preventive maintenance, and general maintenance, with complete details about repair frequencies of thousands of work items.

Green Architecture. James Wines. Published by Benedikt Tascen Verlag GmbH, 2000. A discussion about what makes a building green, complete with a wide range of images and case studies.

Green Architecture: Design for an Energy-Conscious Future. Brenda and Robert Vale. Published by Bulfinch Press, 1991. Provides an overview of resource-conscious building and an exploration of the relationship between the built environment and such critical

problems as power supply, waste and recycling, food production, and transportation.

Green Building Advisor CD ROM. Building Green, Inc., 1999. An interactive CD-ROM featuring specific design strategies that can improve the environmental performance, cost-effectiveness, and healthiness of a building and its site, from pre-design through occupancy. http://www.crest.org/software-central/gba

Green Building: A Primer for Builders, Consumers, and Realtors. Bion D. Howard. Published by Building Environmental Science and Technology. http://www.nrg-builder.com/greenbld.htm

Green Building Materials: A Guide to Product Selection and Specification. Ross Spiegel and Dru Meadows. Published by John Wiley & Sons, 1999. A hands-on guide to today's wide range of green building materials including what they are, where to find them, and how to use them effectively.

Green Building Resource Guide. John Hermannsson, AIA. Published by Taunton Press, 1997.

Green Development: Integrating Ecology and Real Estate. Rocky Mountain Institute: Alex Wilson, Jenifer L. Uncapher, Lisa McManigal, L. Hunter Lovins, Maureen Cureton, William D. Browning. Published by John Wiley & Sons, Inc, 1998. Every stage of the development process is examined in detail: market research, site planning, design, approvals, financing, construction, marketing, and occupancy.

Green Developments CD-ROM. Rocky Mountain Institute, 2001. Enables viewers to explore 200 individual green real-estate development case studies. It features photographs, plans, and drawings along with video and audio clips of projects, resources, Web-links, financing, marketing, and approvals highlights, and an introduction to the green development approach and sustainable building.

Greening the Government Through Efficient Energy Management. Executive Office of the President, Executive Order 13123, June 1999.

The Green Pages. A 350-page interior specifier's guide to environmental products. Cross-references interior design products (linking energy-efficient lighting fixtures, for example, with energy-efficient lamps), as well as directing designers to special environmental consultants, contractors, advocacy groups, books, and related services. Compares sustainable interior products to conventional counterparts and quantifies their impact on the environment.

GreenSpec Directory: Product Directory with Guideline Specifications. From the editors of *Environmental Building News.* Published by BuildingGreen, Inc., 1999-2001. A cohesive product directory with manufacturers' literature, and guideline specification, for building professionals.

Growing Greener: Putting Conservation into Local Plans and Ordinances. Randall Arendt. Published by Island Press, 1999. An illustrated workbook that presents a new look at designing subdivisions while preserving green space and creating open space networks. Explains how to design residential developments that maximize land conservation without reducing overall building density.

A Guide to Intentional Community and Cooperative Living. Published by the Fellowship for Intentional Community. Information on more than 700 intentional communities from around the world.

The Harris Directory. The Harris Reports. A Web data base of more than 5,000 recycled and pollution-preventing materials for home, office, and garden; including products that contain less toxic ingredients and offer safer cleaning options. http://www.harrisdirectory.com

Healthy House books. John Bower. Published by the Healthy House Institute. A number of books on how to design, build, and create a healthy house can be found at http://www.hhinst.com/booksvideos.html

Historic Preservation: Project Planning & Estimating. Swanke Hayden Connell Architects. Published by R.S. Means Co., Inc., 2000. Expert guidance on managing historic restoration, rehabilitation, and preservation—and determining and controlling the cost. Includes restoration techniques for over 75 materials.

The HOK Guidebook to Sustainable Design. Sandra F. Mendler, AIA and William Odell, AIA. Published by John Wiley & Sons, 2000. A comprehensive, practical guide for architects, engineers, planners, interior designers, and landscape architects to integrate sustainable architecture in their work.

Homemade Money. Richard Heede and the Staff of Rocky Mountain Institute. Published by Brick House Publishing Company, 1995. Describes practical ways to save energy and

dollars in an existing or new residence. http://www.rmi.org.

How Buildings Learn. Stewart Brand. Published by Viking Penguin, 1994. Discusses how buildings adapt over time. Photos of case studies are used throughout to show before/after states of buildings. Design principles are described for creating an adaptable/flexible building.

LEED (Leadership in Energy and Environmental Design) Green Building Rating System: Version 2.0. U.S. Green Building Council (USGBC), 2000. LEED is a self-assessing system designed for rating new and existing commercial, institutional, and high-rise residential buildings. http://www.usgbc.org

Life-Cycle Costing Manual for the Federal Energy Management Program, NIST Handbook 135. S.K. Fuller and S.R. Peterson. Published by the National Institute of Standards and Technology, 1995. http://www.bfrl.nist.gov/oae/publications/handbooks/135.html

Life-Cycle Cost Methodology and Procedures. Code of Federal Regulations, 10 CFR 436, Subpart A, Federal Energy Management and Planning Programs. December 1990.

Natural Capitalism: Creating the Next Industrial Revolution. Paul Hawken, Amory Lovins, & L. Hunter Lovins. Published by Little, Brown and Company, 1999. This groundbreaking book describes a future in which business and environmental interests increasingly overlap, and in which companies can improve their bottom lines and help solve environmental problems. http://www.rmi.org

The Natural House Book: Creating a Healthy, Harmonious, and Ecologically-Sound Home Environment. David Pearson. Published by Simon & Schuster/Fireside, 1989. A handbook for a healthy, environmentally benign, natural home; including principles, elements, and spaces.

Natural Ventilation in Buildings: A Design Handbook. Edited by Francis Allard. Published by James & James, 1998. This book describes the real potential of natural ventilation, its appropriate use, design and dimensioning, and how to overcome barriers.

The Next American Metropolis: Ecology, Community, and the American Dream. Peter Calthorpe. Published by Princeton Academic Press, 1993. Places the "American Dream" of a suburban home for the nuclear family in its historical and ecological context. It suggests mechanisms of transit-oriented development including mixed-use, pedestrian-friendly pockets. Features case studies from across the U.S.

The Not So Big House: A Blueprint for the Way We Really Live. Sarah Susanka, 1998. Explores the modern home and how to create intimate, livable spaces without owning massive homes.

The Once and Future Forest: A Guide to Forest Restoration Strategies. Leslie Jones Sauer. Published by Island Press, 1998. Developed by landscape design firm Andropogon Associates, this is a guidebook for restoring and managing natural landscapes. Focusing on remnant forest systems, it describes methods of restoring and linking forest fragments to re-create a whole landscape fabric.

The Passive Solar Energy Book. Edward Mazria. Published by Rodale, 1979. A complete guide to the passive solar home, greenhouse and building design.

A Pattern Language. Christopher Alexander, et al. Published by Oxford University Press, 1977. Volume 2 of the Centre for Environmental Structure series. Illustrates a new architecture and planning theory that reflects the traditional ways in which people created their living environment. It explains the language of "the Timeless Way of Building" from discussion of community to individual building elements.

A Practical Guide for Commissioning Existing Buildings. Available at http://www.PECI.org

A Primer on Sustainable Building. Dianna Lopez Barnett and William D. Browning. Published by Rocky Mountain Institute, 1995. Provides an overview for architects, builders, developers, students, and others interested in environmentally responsive home building and small commercial development. Topics include: site and habitat restoration, transportation integration, food producing landscapes, energy efficient design, materials selection, indoor air quality, cost implications, and more.

Rebuilding Community in America: Housing for Ecological Living, Personal Empowerment, and the New Extended Family. Ken Norwood, AICP and Kathleen Smith. Published by the Shared Living Resource Center, 1995. Explores co-housing as well as other forms of community-oriented living.

The Regional City: Planning for the End of Sprawl. Peter Calthorpe, 2001. Addresses how to redesign our current growth into livable and workable communities. Also explores the problems with sprawl and what to do next.

R.S. Means Environmental Remediation Cost Data. Published by R.S. Means Co., Inc., 2002. Provides a systematic menu of costs for each type of remediation technology. Features detailed line items, component costs, forms, instructions, and guidelines to prepare and verify cost estimates for any type of remediation project.

R.S. Means Site Work & Landscape Cost Data. Published by R.S. Means Co., Inc., 2002. Provides costs to plan, budget, and estimate sitework construction with accuracy.

Rural by Design. Randall Arendt, et al. Published by APA Planners Press, 1994. Advocates creative, practical land-use planning techniques to preserve open space and community character. Case studies demonstrate how rural and suburban communities have preserved open space, established land trusts, and designed affordable housing appropriate for their size and character.

Standards on Building Economics, Fourth Edition. American Society for Testing and Materials (ASTM), 1999.

Sustainable Building Technical Manual. Co-sponsored by Public Technology Incorporated, U.S. Green Building Council, and U.S. Department of Energy. Published by Public Technology, Inc., 1996. Addresses green building practice from pre-design issues and site planning through operations and maintenance.

Sustainable Communities: A New Design Synthesis for Cities, Suburbs, and Towns. Sim Van der Ryn and Peter Calthorpe. Published by Sierra Club Books, 1986. Covers a range of issues dealing with sustainability for urban and suburban renovation through an in-depth look at several case studies and essays on community sensitivity, transportation, and economics.

Techniques for Treating Uncertainty and Risk, NIST SP 757. H.E. Marshall. Published by the National Institute of Standards and Technology, 1988.

Value Engineering: Practical Applications. Alphonse J. Dell'Isola. Published by R.S. Means Co., Inc., 1997. Provides techniques to control costs and maximize quality in facilities design, construction, and operations.

The Value Engineering Process. Published by the U.S. Department of Transportation, Federal Highway Administration, 2002. http://www.fhwa.dot.gov/ve/verev.htm

Visions for a New American Dream. Anton Nelessen. Published by APA Planners Press, 1994. Provides practical information to help planners and designers create small communities that combine the best design principles of the past with the technological advances of the present to combat suburban sprawl.

Whitestone Maintenance & Repair Cost Reference, Sixth Edition. Expert coverage of maintenance and repair budgeting and financial benchmarking. Building maintenance 50-year cost profiles are provided for 50 building types and identify the most costly repair tasks and costs by building system.

Index

Assemblies, for cost data, 417-432
Atria, 18
Atrium, 96, 256
Audio masking, 167
Australian sword fern, 150
Award of bid, 235
Awnings, 95

B

Backcasting, 225-226
Bacteria growth, 163
Bamboo, 145, 169
Batteries, for PV systems, 106
    charge controller, 107-108
Berkeley Solar Group, 309
Bidding, 178, 191, 236
Biodegradable products, 234
Biological sewage treatment
    systems, 16
Biomass energy, 10, 14
Biophilia, 18
Blast, 183
Blast furnace slag, 29
Boilers, 258, 308
    hot water, 69
    steam, 69
Bonneville Power Administration, 249
Boric acid, 28
Boston sword fern, 150
BREEAM, 221
Brownfield, 14, 177, 200-201
Building Automation Systems (BAS),
    257
Building component standards, 210
Building Control System (BCS), energy
    saving strategies, 76-77
    CO_2 control, 76
    discharge reset, 76
    energy monitoring and trending, 76
    enthalpy-based economizer
      controls, 76
    occupancy control, 77
    static pressure reset, 76
    VFD, 77
Building Design & Materials, 16
Building economics, 285
Building envelope, 57-61

Building Environmental Performance
    Assessment Criteria (BEPAC), 179
Building for Environmental and
    Economic Sustainability (BEES),
    267-281, 286, 311-312
Building geometry, 307
Building Life-Cycle Cost Program
    (BLCC), 286, 299, 300, 311
Building orientation, 4, 307
Building permits, for wind systems,
    136-137
Building plan, 185
Building Research Establishment
    Environmental Assessment Method
    (BREEAM), 178-179
Building-integrated photovoltaics, 110
Buy-down funds, wind, 134, 135

C

Cabinetry, 33, 145
Cadmium telluride, 48
Cahners Residential Group, 203
Capacity for removing particulates,
    148
Capital investment, 290
Capital replacement costs, 293, 297
Carbon absorption, 163
Carbon dioxide, 272, 273
Carbon dioxide monitors, 16
Carbon monoxide, 145, 149-150
Carpet cushion, 230
Carpet, 16, 24, 44, 145, 169, 220,
    230, 234, 236, 254, 256
Case studies, of green building
    projects, 317-347
Casein, 169
Cash flows, 295
Caulking, 254
CDC, 143
CE, 68
Ceiling tiles, 145, 256
Cellulose, 145, 223
Cement, 25
Ceramic tile, 44, 169
Certified value specialist, 285
Certified wood, 168, 231
Channeling, 163

Charge controller, for PV system, 107-
    108
Chauffage, 206
Checklist, of green products, 230
Chemical recontamination, 163
Chilled water systems, 75
Chillers, 254, 258, 308
Chlordane, 28
Chlorine, 27, 171
Chromated copper arsenate (CCA), 32
Cistern, 15, 27, 61
Civil engineer, role of, 176
Clay, 29
Cleanup, of mold, 144
Clerestory windows, 94
CLF, 78
Climate Cool™, 216
Climate Neutral™, 216
CO_2 control, 76
Coatings, 43-44
Cob, 53, 54
Cogeneration, 50, 81
Collectors, transpired, 119
Colorado Built Green Mortgage, 205
Combustion Efficiency (CE), 68, 69
COMcheck-Plus, 312
Commissioning, of green buildings,
    193, 249-264
    acceptance phase, 260-263
    checklist, 251-253
    commissioning plan, 254-255
    construction documents review,
      256-257
    construction phase, 257-260
    design phase, 253-257
    post-acceptance phase, 263-264
    programming phase, 251-253
    specifications, 255
Commissioning agent, 249, 250, 254,
    257, 258, 259, 260, 261, 262, 264
    hiring of, 251
    role of, 177
Commissioning authority, 193
Commissioning plan, 167, 250, 254-
    255
Commissioning report, 250, 262-263
Compact fluorescent lamps, 51, 78
Compliance, 305-314